Cause Lawyering

OXFORD SOCIO-LEGAL STUDIES

General Editor: Keith Hawkins, Reader in Law and Society, and Fellow and Tutor in Law of Oriel College, Oxford.

Editorial Board: John Baldwin, Director of the Institute of Judicial Administration, University of Birmingham; William L. F. Felstiner, Professor of Sociology, University of California–Santa Barbara; Denis Galligan, Professor of Socio-Legal Studies and Director of the Centre for Socio-Legal Studies, Oxford; Sally Lloyd-Bostock, Senior Research Fellow, Centre for Socio-Legal Studies, Oxford; Doreen McBarnet, Senior Research Fellow, Centre for Socio-Legal Studies, Oxford; Simon Roberts, Professor of Law, London School of Economics.

International Advisory Board: John Braithwaite, Australian National University; Robert Cooter, University of California–Berkeley; Bryant Garth, American Bar Foundation; Volkmar Gessner, University of Bremen; Vittorio Olgiati, University of Milan; Martin Partington, University of Bristol.

Oxford Socio-Legal Studies is a series of books exploring the role of law in society for both an academic and a wider readership. The series publishes theoretical and empirically informed work by social scientists and lawyers, from the United Kingdom and elsewhere, that advances understanding of the social reality of law and legal processes.

CAUSE LAWYERING

Political Commitments and
Professional Responsibilities

Edited by

AUSTIN SARAT & STUART SCHEINGOLD

New York   Oxford   •   Oxford University Press   1998

Oxford University Press

Oxford   New York
Athens   Auckland   Bangkok   Bogota   Bombay   Buenos Aires
Calcutta   Cape Town   Dar es Salaam   Delhi   Florence   Hong Kong
Istanbul   Karachi   Kuala Lumpur   Madras   Madrid   Melbourne
Mexico City   Nairobi   Paris   Singapore   Taipei   Tokyo   Toronto   Warsaw

and associated companies in
Berlin   Ibadan

Copyright © 1998 Oxford University Press, Inc.

Published by Oxford University Press, Inc.
198 Madison Avenue, New York, NY 10016

Oxford is a registered trademark of Oxford University Press

Cause lawyering : political commitments and professional
responsibilities / edited by Austin Sarat and Stuart Scheingold.
p. cm.—(Oxford socio-legal studies)
Includes bibliographical references and index.
ISBN 0-19-511319-5; ISBN 0-19-511320-9 (pbk.)
1. Law and politics.   2. Sociological jurisprudence.   3. Public
interest law.   4. Practice of law.   I. Sarat, Austin.
II. Scheingold, Stuart A.   III. Series.
K487.P65Z92   1997
340'.115—dc21   96-40934

9 8 7 6 5 4 3 2 1
Printed in the United States of America
on acid-free paper

Acknowledgments

This project has been, from its inception, a genuine collaboration, first between the two editors, and then among all of the participants. We are grateful to the extraordinary group of scholars who pooled their efforts to understand cause lawyering for their energy, interest, and insight. We would like to thank Terrence Halliday, formerly chair of the Working Group on the Comparative Study of the Legal Profession, for his encouragement. Finally, we are grateful for the hospitality of Amherst College, which generously hosted a conference of our collaborators. Support for this project was provided by a grant from the Program on Law and Social Science of the National Science Foundation.

Contents

Contributors, ix

1. *Cause Lawyering and the Reproduction of Professional Authority:* An Introduction, 3
   AUSTIN SARAT & STUART SCHEINGOLD

I. Contexts and Conditions of Cause Lawyering

2. *The Causes of Cause Lawyering:* Toward an Understanding of the Motivation and Commitment of Social Justice Lawyers, 31
   CARRIE MENKEL-MEADOW

3. *Speaking Law to Power:* Occasions for Cause Lawyering, 69
   RICHARD ABEL

4. *The Struggle to Politicize Legal Practice:* A Case Study of Left-Activist Lawyering in Seattle, 118
   STUART SCHEINGOLD

II. Cause Lawyering and the Organization of Practice

5. *Norris, Schmidt, Green, Harris, Higginbotham & Associates:* The Sociolegal Import of Philadelphia Cause Lawyers, 151
   AARON PORTER

6. *Still Trying:* Cause Lawyering for the Poor and Disadvantaged in Pittsburgh, Pennsylvania, 181
   JOHN KILWEIN

7. *Critical Lawyers:* Social Justice and the Structures of Private Practice, 201
   LOUISE TRUBEK & M. ELIZABETH KRANSBERGER

8. *Destruction of Houses and Construction of a Cause:* Lawyers and Bedouins in the Israeli Courts, 227
   RONEN SHAMIR & SARA CHINSKI

III. Strategies of Cause Lawyering under Liberal Legalism

  9. *Rethinking Law's "Allurements":* A Relational Analysis of Social Movement
      Lawyers in the United States, 261
      MICHAEL MCCANN & HELENA SILVERSTEIN

 10. *Caring about Individual Cases:* Immigration Lawyering in Britain, 293
      SUSAN STERETT

 11. *Between (the Presence of) Violence and (the Possibility of) Justice:* Lawyering
      against Capital Punishment, 317
      AUSTIN SARAT

IV. The Possibilities of Cause Lawyering beyond Liberal Legalism

 12. *Cause Lawyering in the Third World,* 349
      STEPHEN ELLMANN

 13. *Lawyers' Causes in Indonesia and Malaysia,* 431
      DANIEL LEV

 14. *Attorneys for the People, Attorneys for the Land:* The Emergence of Cause
      Lawyering in the Israeli-Occupied Territories, 453
      GEORGE BISHARAT

 15. *Cause Lawyers and Social Movements:* A Comparative Perspective on
      Democratic Change in Argentina and Brazil, 487
      STEPHEN MEILI

 16. *All or Nothing:* An Inquiry into the (Im)Possibility of Cause Lawyering under
      Cuban Socialism, 523
      RAYMOND MICHALOWSKI

Select Bibliography, 547

Index, 552

Contributors

RICHARD ABEL is Professor of Law at University of California–Los Angeles.

GEORGE BISHARAT is Professor of Law at Hastings College of Law.

SARA CHINSKI is affiliated with the Department of Sociology at Tel-Aviv University.

STEPHEN ELLMANN is Professor of Law at New York Law School.

JOHN KILWEIN is Associate Professor of Political Science at the University of West Virginia.

M. ELIZABETH KRANSBERGER works at the New College of California.

DANIEL LEV is Professor of Political Science at the University of Washington.

MICHAEL MCCANN is Professor of Political Science at the University of Washington.

STEPHEN MEILI is affiliated with the Center for Public Representation and is Clinical Associate Professor of Law at the University of Wisconsin.

CARRIE MENKEL-MEADOW is Professor of Law at Georgetown University.

RAYMOND MICHALOWSKI is Professor in the Department of Criminal Justice at Northern Arizona University.

AARON PORTER is Assistant Professor of Sociology at the University of Illinois.

AUSTIN SARAT is William Nelson Cromwell Professor of Jurisprudence and Political Science at Amherst College.

STUART SCHEINGOLD is Professor of Political Science at the University of Washington.

RONEN SHAMIR is Professor of Sociology at Tel-Aviv University.

HELENA SILVERSTEIN is F. M. Kirby Assistant Professor of Government and Law at Lafayette College.

SUSAN STERETT is Associate Professor of Political Science at the University of Denver.

LOUISE TRUBEK is Clinical Professor of Law at the University of Wisconsin.

Cause Lawyering

CHAPTER 1

Cause Lawyering and the Reproduction of Professional Authority

An Introduction

AUSTIN SARAT & STUART SCHEINGOLD

Legal professions everywhere both need and at the same time are threatened by cause lawyering. They need lawyers who commit themselves and their legal skills to furthering a vision of the good society because this "moral activism"[1] puts a humane face on lawyering and provides an appealing alternative to the value-neutral, "hired-gun" imagery that often dogs the legal profession.[2] Yet cause lawyering is everywhere a deviant strain within the legal profession.[3] What distinguishes the morally activist lawyer is that she "shares and aims to share with her client responsibility for the ends she is promoting in her representation."[4] In so doing she elevates the moral posture of the legal profession beyond a crude instrumentalism in which lawyers sell their services without regard to the ends to which those services are put. Cause lawyers thus reconnect law and morality[5] and make tangible the idea that lawyering is a "public profession," one whose contribution to society goes beyond the aggregation, assembling, and deployment of technical skills.[6] In this way lawyers committed to using their professional work as a vehicle to build the good society help legitimate the legal profession as a whole.[7]

But they also threaten the profession by destabilizing the dominant understanding of lawyering as properly wedded to moral neutrality and technical competence. In many countries lawyers are, to varying degrees, pledged to principles of "partisanship" and "nonaccountability," which require that they "advocate their clients' causes regardless of their own personal beliefs."[8] By rejecting nonaccountability, if not partisanship, cause lawyers establish a point from which to criticize the dominant understanding from inside the profession itself. They denaturalize and politicize that understanding.[9] Cause lawyering exposes the fact that it is contingent and constructed and, in so doing, raises the political question of whose interests the dominant understanding serves.[10] The result is a threat to ongoing professional projects and the political immunity of the legal profession and the legal process.

In many nations the profession regularly represents itself as serving equally and concurrently the public interest and the interests of individual clients without adequately acknowledging the tension between these two conceptions of professional responsibility.[11] Thus lawyers are encouraged by the organized profession to undertake a variety of pro bono activities and to support legal aid and legal services programs. But this work is seen as ancillary to the central activity of the legal profession, which is to provide fee-for-service lawyering to individual and institutional clients. Moreover, conventional public service efforts of this sort have been for the most part confined to responding to unmet legal needs[12] and to allying the profession with consensual civic activism.

Cause lawyering, in contrast, is frequently directed at altering some aspect of the social, economic, and political status quo.[13] Because it gives priority to political ideology, public policy, and moral commitment, cause lawyering often attenuates, or transforms, the lawyer-client relationship—a cornerstone of the established conception of professional responsibility.[14] Serving the client is but one component of serving the cause.[15] "The politically motivated lawyer," Luban argues, "acts ethically not by evading the essentially political character of relationships but by responsibly representing the political aims of her entire client constituency even at the price of wronging individual clients. The key point is that a responsible representative must keep one eye on the interests of future generations."[16] Because it shifts cause and moral commitment from the margins to the core of legal practice, cause lawyering works at cross-purposes to market-driven conceptions of professionalism.[17] Finally, the political edge of cause lawyering tends to embroil the profession in conflicts with the state and with a wide variety of vested interests. It is in this way that cause lawyering both tests the limits of accepted modes of legal practice and exposes discontinuities in the profession's pledge to promote both public and private interests—to do good while doing well.

What is cause lawyering, and how does it differ from other styles/kinds of lawyering? Who are cause lawyers, and what are the social, political, and professional conditions that make it possible for lawyers to devote their professional lives to "moral activism"? What motivates them to work outside of, and against, the professional mainstream, to sacrifice income, prestige, and, in some countries, to risk their lives? What are their law practices like? How do they fund the representation of marginalized interests and impecunious clients? Do they organize their work settings in ways that are consonant with the political values they are pursue? And how do they go about advancing the causes for which they work? To what extent do they limit themselves to conventional legal strategies, and to what extent do they ally themselves with social movements in pushing the boundaries of law and politics? These are the questions that the essays in this book address. As such they help illuminate the politics of professionalism and the way law and politics are both mutually constitutive and yet necessarily somewhat autonomous.

The Parameters of Cause Lawyering

While cause lawyering is significant in the way it both serves and challenges legal professionalism, providing a single, cross-culturally valid definition of the concept is impossible. How is one to mark the boundary suggested above between conventional pro bono activities and cause lawyering? If, for example, redressing unmet legal needs does not in itself qualify as lawyering for a cause, what are we to make of postmodern approaches that identify the personal as political and that thus would see the empowerment of individual clients as a crucial form of struggle against the status quo?[18] Must lawyers be *self-consciously* committed to a cause in order to be included, or is it sufficient that cause lawyers undertake a variety of pro bono activities in response to a sense of professional responsibility? Is cause lawyering an intrinsically "altruistic" activity, or can it be driven by ordinary career objectives? Must cause lawyering be somehow unremunerative? And what are we to make of the disparate modes of cause lawyering that have been identified in the relevant literature: human rights lawyering, critical lawyering, feminist lawyering, radical lawyering, civil rights and civil liberties lawyering, environmental lawyering, poverty lawyering, and the like? In what sense do these activities relate to, and differ from, one another?

The objective of this introductory essay is not to provide answers to these questions. We wish instead to acknowledge that cause lawyering is a contested concept and to identify the terrain on which this contest takes place. It is for this reason that we talk about the parameters rather than the definition of cause lawyering. Indeed, we have chosen the term "cause lawyering" precisely because it conveys a core of meaning in many historical and cultural contexts while being sufficiently inclusive to accommodate a range of forms. It is, in other words, important to think of cause lawyering as a protean and heterogeneous enterprise that continues to reinvent itself in confrontations with a vast array of challenges.

To maximize our understandings of the forms of cause lawyering and the challenges it confronts, we have chosen a cross-cultural and comparative perspective. The comparative analysis of cause lawyering reveals variation and commonality across political and legal boundaries. Liberal regimes with well-entrenched rule-of-law systems can be expected to provide more and different opportunities for cause lawyering than authoritarian regimes that do not afford their citizens even the most minimal of human rights.[19] In authoritarian settings, cause lawyering is cast in a largely defensive role—struggling to afford a modicum of protection against arbitrary arrest and imprisonment, torture, and other acts of political repression.[20] Liberal regimes enable lawyers to adopt more affirmative strategies. Such strategies include efforts to extend the reach and meaning of established rights as well as more ambitious efforts to reconceive the liberal conception of rights to promote more egalitarian distributions of power and material wealth.[21] Of course, even when liberal regimes are secure, cause lawyers are not relieved of their defensive burdens. Established rights are always in some jeopardy. By the same token the human rights work of cause lawyers in authoritarian states makes them perforce the carriers of liberal values with transformative potential.

The scope of cause lawyering is also influenced, however, by the prevailing legal tradition.[22] In common law countries, the boundaries between law and politics tend to be readily permeable. There are many lawyers; they are trained to think of themselves as generalists; and they regularly move back and forth between private practice and public service as judges, prosecutors, bureaucrats, and politicians. Moreover, the relative autonomy of courts allows cause lawyers, like lawyers in general, to fashion litigation into an assertive political weapon. This is particularly the case in the United States, which has tended to lead the way in developing techniques and strategies for moving beyond a defensive conception of cause lawyering.

In contrast, law and lawyers tend to play a more confined and technical role in civil law systems.[23] There are fewer lawyers; they are trained as specialists; and their career tracks are established earlier, with little if any movement among the different tracks. Courts are less independent and more reluctant to protect and extend rights or to impinge on state policies and prerogatives. As a result the boundary between law and politics is more clearly etched in civil law systems than in the common law, where it tends to lose much of its meaning. Interestingly, however, the timidity of courts in civil law systems and the frustration of cause lawyers with litigation can lead them to adopt more overtly political strategies.[24]

Generalizations based on legal tradition and regime type are, however, confounded both by variations within traditions and types and by forces that cut across them. The role of lawyers and the scope for legal activity is, for example, considerably broader in the American than in the British common law system.[25] Similarly, in times of crisis, liberal regimes may undertake repressive measures that undermine the rule of law and drive cause lawyers into defensive postures.[26] Conversely, authoritarian regimes that engage in widespread human rights violations are sometimes responsive to cause lawyering—albeit episodically and unpredictably.[27] This responsiveness can be attributed at least in part to exogenous forces. Authoritarian regimes in former colonies may, for example, be residually influenced by the rule-of-law tradition, processes and institutions that were imparted by the colonial power and are still transmitted by indigenous lawyers who seek training abroad. Indeed, these days cause lawyering is emerging as something of a transnational force in its own right. Certainly, the influence of the American cause-lawyering experience is readily observable in the practices and aspirations of cause lawyers in both civil and common law countries. More broadly, international human rights organizations lend sustenance and direction to cause lawyering around the world.[28]

While cause lawyering is a concept meant to accommodate great diversity, it must also enable us to identify the boundary that separates it from conventional lawyering. This necessarily fluid and permeable boundary is particularly difficult to draw at one end of the cause-lawyering continuum. Here cause lawyering involves working within accepted professional understandings of skilled and zealous client representation. The mission is both to make the profession live up to its own avowed ideals and to somehow stretch those ideals from the representation of individual litigants to causes. Because cause lawyering is sometimes wedded to established rights, the rule of law, and technical excellence, it is not always easy to distinguish it from the practices of mainstream lawyers who take seriously the profession's responsibility to serve the public interest as well as the interests of their clients. Moreover, involvement in pro bono activities may take lawyers back and forth between cause and conventional public service lawyering. At this end of the continuum, cause lawyers tend to be distinguished primarily by a willingness to undertake controversial and politically charged activities and/or by a sense of commitment to particular ideals.

At the other end of the continuum are more radically disposed cause lawyers who challenge established conceptions of professionalism with efforts to decommodify, politicize, and socialize legal practice.[29] While they may be forced by necessity to defend established rights, their real goal is to contribute to the kind of transformative politics that will redistribute political power and material benefits in a more egalitarian fashion.[30] Their primary loyalty is not to clients, to constitutional rights, nor to legal process but to a vision of the good society and to political allies who share that vision. Moreover, they may also want to incorporate into their practices these broader social values. For them the professional project is very much about the decommodification of legal services and about closing the gap that divides lawyers from clients, from staff, and most significantly from communities, organizations, and interests that they choose to serve.[31] These aspirations are sufficiently at odds with established political, professional, and career structures to entangle radical cause lawyers in a variety of destabilizing conflicts and contradictions.

This determination to politicize legal practice foreshadows the boundary problems at this end of the cause-lawyering continuum. The problems emerge more explicitly when frustrations with the halting tempo and uncertain consequences of litigative strategies lead to adoption of political strategies and to close association with social movements.[32] Of course, insofar as cause lawyers make themselves available to counsel and defend movement activists, they are working well within even fairly restrictive definitions of professional responsibility. Involvement in organizing activities and political mobilization moves lawyers closer to, and in some settings, beyond generally accepted understandings of the appropriate role of legal professionals.[33] And how are we to think of situations in which cause lawyers become so intensively engaged in the movement that they participate in legally proscribed activities?[34] Do they at some point test, and perhaps cross, the nethermost boundaries of the professional project? Whether these boundaries are drawn by the profession or constructed in each lawyers' own consciousness, cause lawyering may so merge with political activism as to be indistinguishable from it.

Cause Lawyering and the Democratic Project

The democratic aspirations associated with cause lawyering are both dependent on and inhibited by the relative autonomy of the law. Whether cause lawyers are struggling for basic liberal rights or working on behalf of broader democratic values, they are usually swimming against the prevailing political tide. Law must somehow and to some extent trump politics if cause lawyering is to be success-ful.[35] But in order to accomplish anything substantial, cause lawyers must neces-sarily become embroiled in controversial issues of politics and public policy. In so doing they put the legitimacy of an independent law at risk and thus subject their project to backlash and to the *force majeur* that is at the disposal of the state.

The threshold problem is whether and to what extent law can ever effectively trump politics, and this is clearly a contested issue.[36] Law is surely a derivative institution—ultimately dependent on and defined by the state and the broader culture. This realization has led some to discount the potential of cause lawyering. Even with respect to a certifiably liberal goal like equality before the law, there is evidence that ostensibly liberal regimes can and do deploy the law in exclusionary ways. Thus, formal equality has been deemed compatible with disqualification on the basis of race, gender, religion, and the like. For cause lawyers with transforma-tive aspirations the obstacles are still more formidable, because the law in liberal states tends to be more concerned with the abuse of state power than with "em-powering people with participatory rights and substantive entitlements."[37] And the close connection between law and liberal capitalism has tended to exclude economic interpretations of equality before the law—leaving outcomes to the market.[38]

From this perspective, law reflects, and is sustained by, a disembodied concep-tion of politics, democracy, and rights.[39] If so, lawyers can at best play an amelio-rative role, restricted to individual client service and without systemic conse-quences.[40] At worst, these ameliorative activities are seen as cooptive and individualizing—confirming the established order and diverting energies from challenges to it.[41]

There are, however, more positive views of the opportunities available to cause lawyers. E. P. Thompson suggests that, at least in rule-of-law states, the law be understood as an "arena of struggle"—a complex, contradictory, and open-textured setting that provides opportunities to challenge the status quo.[42] In part, this is based on a recognition that legally enforceable, well-entrenched constitutional rights provide an important bulwark for protection against arbitrary practices.[43] But it can also be argued that cause lawyers can use rights claims to construct culturally based discourses of affirmative resistance.[44] These discourses expose the "illusion of equality"[45] that obscures power differentials endemic to social cleavages, whether defined by gender, race, class, caste, religion, language, ethnicity, or sexual preference.

There is some preliminary evidence suggesting that cause lawyers can overcome the defenses of formal equality.[46] But this evidence is spotty, largely confined to the United States, and, in any case, indicates that cause lawyers must both utilize and transcend law and litigation.[47] Insofar as they confine themselves to legal processes, they remain bound to liberal institutions, values, and practices. And even if they are upon occasion able somehow to defeat the defenses of the legal process, their gains remain vulnerable in the face of a hostile political climate.

It is for this reason that cause lawyers who wish to go beyond defensive strategies choose to ally themselves with, or become part of, social movements. These days, with left-wing movements in so many nations in such disarray,[48] cause lawyers with transformative aspirations tend to find themselves facing two equally unattractive options. They can, on the one hand, learn to live with reduced—that is, largely defensive—expectations. On the other hand, they can continue to pursue transformative strategies that are likely to be futile or even to backfire.

A poststructural rethinking of the democratic project does, however, afford some respite from this double bind.[49] Poststructural theories locate domination in cross-cutting social cleavages (race, gender, sexual orientation, age, etc.) and at microsites of power (the family, the workplace, schools, social service agencies, and the like). These microsites present less daunting targets for cause lawyers, who in effect turn away from high-impact, class action litigation and/or frontal assault on the institutions of the state. They focus instead on the empowerment of individual, or perhaps small groups of, clients.[50] With less at stake politically and more at stake legally, legal institutions may well come closer to living up to their professed ideals.

This poststructural notion of client empowerment at microsites of power is associated with a so-called critical conception of cause lawyering.[51] Among other things, critical cause lawyering implies a different understanding of the lawyer-client relationship. Attorneys are admonished to relate to clients as listeners and learners rather than as translators. "Because that process [of translation] is distorting, certain meanings will be lost."[52] It is, of course, client meanings that are distorted and lost, with the result that the client is disempowered, mystified, and alienated. The alternative is for the lawyers and clients to become part of a "network of problem-solving practitioners" in which people learn from one another and "conspire together"[53] on behalf of remedies that serve the client's "needs and aspirations."[54] After all, it is the clients, rather than the lawyers who know and experience the microsites of power that are the essential focus of poststructural conceptions of the democratic project.

Cause Lawyering and the Professional Project

Just as cause lawyering sometimes breaches the boundary separating law and politics, so too does it breach the boundary between the political and the professional. Policing this boundary is one of the principal tasks of the organized profession, but it can never be completely successful in doing so. This is because cause lawyers defend their work from within the ideology of professionalism. From Brandeis[55] to Kronman,[56] there have been cohorts within the profession arguing that public service and political commitment are central to what it means to be a lawyer. Expelling the political from the professional is thus an insurmountable task.

In its effort to lend coherence to professionalism and to identify common ground and unity among lawyers, in many nations the organized bar offers professionalism as a set of essential attributes. These attributes are supposed to distinguish occupations from professions and professions from one another. In this way a coherent notion of professionalism lays the groundwork for claims of particular privileges that are accorded to lawyers.[57] Only insofar as lawyers share among themselves agreed-upon standards of technical competence and ethical probity are they entitled to monopolize the provision of legal services.

The experienced world of legal professionalism is, of course, much more complex than any organized profession would have us believe. There is usually as much division as unity and as much conflict as consensus over the meaning of professionalism.[58] Accordingly, it is not surprising that critics of professionalism present it, not as a set of essential attributes but instead as a way of describing the constructs and institutions through which occupations seek control of the market for their services.[59] Moreover, while the bar emphasizes the underlying unity of lawyers, critics highlight stratification and conflict.[60] They argue that professionalism is a tool used by particular segments of the bar to assert and protect their own privileged positions against the challenges of outside groups.[61] Professionalism is, in this view, an excuse for excluding those groups and for marginalizing new entrants to the bar. Instead of building consensus, enhancing ethical standards, and raising levels of competence, professionalism is seen as part of a top-down project of social control.[62]

But professionalism should not be regarded merely as a rhetorical device that disguises the pursuit of self-interest as public-spiritedness.[63] It can also be thought of as providing a linguistic passageway from the expression of particular preferences and interests to the taken-for-granted realm of seemingly eternal verities and uncontested, essential truths. Use of that passageway is particularly salient in periods when lawyers' practices are, or are perceived to be, unsettled. Professionalism becomes, at those times, a means through which lawyers respond to changes in their community and their practices. It is, moreover, a way of marking differences, of translating those differences into issues of right and wrong and of staking out a claim to the high moral ground.

This elasticity makes professionalism available as symbolic capital in the clash of cultures among lawyers. It provides practicing lawyers with "maps of problematic social reality,"[64] which help to constitute and to express their particular interests. Thus it operates as ideology by giving meaning to social relations, histories, and activities of lawyers and by connecting their ideas and values with their interests and positions. As ideology, professionalism takes on meaning in the localities and conditions in which lawyers practice. Place and time shape the fragments and configurations used to construct a variety of maps of social reality, each claiming the label of professionalism.[65]

Yet despite their local origins, ideologies of professionalism, like other ideologies, are proclaimed in global terms.[66] They deny the connection between the ideas they express and the particular associations and arguments in which they are grounded.[67] Each asserts its singularity while defining contingent practices as universal and necessary.[68] Each involves "conventionalized invocations of norms that simultaneously suggest and (seek to) eliminate competing ideologies."[69] Because it is robust in these credible meanings, professionalism provides conceptual terrain for plausible claims by different segments of the bar to respectability and legitimacy.

The elasticity of professionalism means that it can be appropriated and deployed by lawyers representing a wide range of interests and approaches to practice, including cause lawyers. Ideologies of professionalism, like other ideologies, become meaningful by creating distinctions and turning them into oppositions— for example, the opposition between lawyering for clients and lawyering for causes. Moreover, those ideologies favor particular views of legal practice by asserting their claim to general respect and allegiance. Each of those ideologies seeks to provide an exclusive, normatively coherent, and authoritative portrait of lawyering; yet in juxtaposition they suggest instability and indeterminacy in the very heart of the legal profession's idea of itself.

Viewed in this way professionalism is as meaningful, important, and accessible to cause lawyers as it is to dominant practitioners. It matters at least as much to lawyers struggling to gain acceptance as to those defending a position of privilege. In this context professionalism is neither a set of essential attributes nor a singular tool produced and used by the powerful in a struggle to suppress the powerless. It is far too vague, complex, and contradictory to serve either purpose.[70] Even the American Bar Association's Commission on Professionalism acknowledges, although it does not make much of it, that professionalism "is an elastic concept the meaning and application of which are hard to pin down."[71]

The essays in this volume chronicle the efforts of cause lawyers in disparate settings to stake out their own terrain and in the process to find a tenable position within the profession. In some instances this may entail explicit appropriation of the global claims of the professionalism. Cause lawyers may, in other words, counterpoise their own professional vision of lawyering for a cause against the conventional commitment to client service. They may do so either to defend and legitimate their enterprise in the face of external opposition or to articulate and reinforce coherence and *esprit* of the cause-lawyering cohort. More often, cause lawyers are too taken up with the day-to-day struggle of maintaining their practices and pursuing their political objectives to devote much energy to staking out professional terrain. But their struggles enable us to explore the ways in which the plight of cause lawyers is caught up in, and influences, the circumstances, the conditions, and the legitimacy of the broader profession. Cause and conventional lawyers draw reluctant sustenance from one another. They are wary competitors whose fates are inextricably, interdependently, and often irksomely linked in a common enterprise.

The essays that follow illustrate the complex and varied relationship between cause lawyering and the nature and meaning of professionalism in the practice of law as well as the way cause lawyering illuminates instabilities in the boundaries between law and politics. They examine the challenges of making a living while advocating for a cause. They highlight the strategies used, and those rejected, as lawyers work to advance their vision of the good society. And throughout they stress the local and contextual quality of cause lawyering. Thus they show the great diversity of styles, strategies, and substance that is described by the term "cause lawyering."

In the first section of this book—"Contexts and Conditions of Cause Lawyering"—we explore the circumstances and contingencies that shape cause lawyering. We inquire about the political and professional contexts in which cause lawyering occurs. We ask what personal and professional factors explain why particular lawyers devote themselves to serving political causes.

The first essay, by Carrie Menkel-Meadow, addresses the question of what kind of people are willing and able to use their professional skills in the service of moral and political ends. It describes the personal motivations and commitments that underlie cause lawyering, or what Menkel-Meadow calls "lawyering for the good." Menkel-Meadow argues that we can understand those motivations and commitments by asking the more general question of "what makes people want to do 'good.' " To answer that question her essay provides a comprehensive overview of the literature on altruism and a more particular look at the experience of "rescuers," namely people who tried to save the lives of Jews threatened by the Nazis.

Menkel-Meadow argues that the sources of the personal commitment that sustains cause lawyering are located in what she calls "universalistic" and "inclusive" orientations toward the world. These orientations challenge prevailing conceptions of professionalism, which stress neutrality, distance, and the segregation of personal and role morality. "Universalistic orientation" refers to the fact that cause lawyers see themselves and their welfare as inseparable from the welfare of humanity as a whole; "inclusive orientation" suggests that they regard others and their fate as part of the self and its fate. The self-conceptions of cause lawyers, Menkel-Meadow suggests, are "tied to moral saving behavior, [and] rescuing . . . [is] an act of moral 'self-affirmation.'" This is not to say that all cause lawyers are alike or that their motivations are solely other-regarding. Surely that is not the case. But, in Menkel-Meadow's view, altruism and other-regardingness are at the core of what cause lawyers do, whether their lawyering is oriented toward systemic change or simply saving particular individuals from repressive acts by their government.

Richard Abel's "Speaking Law to Power: Occasions for Cause Lawyering" moves from an analysis of the personal motivations underlying cause lawyering to an examination of the political situations and opportunities that give rise to it. Abel sees cause lawyering as occupying an indeterminate position at the intersection of law and politics. The job of the cause lawyer is, in Abel's words, to "speak law to power," that is, to use law to defend individuals and groups against state repression or to use law, in a more positive way, to advance the goals of particular political and social movements. Following up on E. P. Thompson's (1975) understanding of law, Abel contends that cause lawyering exposes the contradictions and instabilities built into liberal legalism. Law in liberal regimes, he suggests, is "simultaneously rule and politics, ideal and reality, neutral and partisan. . . . Here . . . I want to attend to the possibilities as well as the limitations of liberal legalism, the moments when law offers leverage to the relatively powerless as well as those when it is wielded, or trumped, by power. These," Abel argues, "are the occasions for cause lawyering."

Abel examines institutions of liberal legalism—what he calls the "spatial organization of power," the electoral process, legislatures, executives, judiciaries, and the legal profession—around which cause lawyering activity is organized. He also discusses the way cause lawyering is implicated in, and the way cause lawyers react to, regime changes. Abel provides a comparative and cross-cultural overview of the opportunities those institutions and situations provide for cause lawyers. He notes how lawyers in parliamentary democracies seek to structure legislative processes to increase the power of hitherto powerless groups, and how in authoritarian regimes they try to enhance legislative autonomy in the face of threats by the executive or the military. In addition, everywhere, Abel argues, cause lawyers seek to maximize the independence of the judiciary. And, he claims, cause lawyers in many countries seek change in the legal profession itself. While they rely on the organized profession to help safeguard them from political attack, they also seek to make the profession as a whole more socially responsible.

Abel draws several general lessons about the conditions and contingencies that shape cause lawyering. He concludes that cause lawyering will be most successful "when a confident government is engaged in social change." It will be least successful "when a frightened government is desperately scrambling to retain power." Moreover, almost everywhere cause lawyering is "more powerful as a shield against abuse than as a sword to achieve substantive goals." In the end, Abel provides a vivid picture of the way cause lawyering destabilizes the distinction between law and politics as well as the personal and professional risks that cause lawyers run in attempting to use law as a limit on power.

The third essay, by Stuart Scheingold, addresses the effects of political conditions and factors on cause lawyering in a single place. Scheingold is interested in the fate of what he calls "left-activist lawyers" in the hostile political environment of the mid-1990s United States. He sees left-activist lawyers as a particular subset of cause lawyers. The former go "beyond the notion of lawyers simply doing good. . . . The two things that distinguish the left-activist project are its fundamental challenges to the society and to the profession." These lawyers have had to cope with the triumph of the ideology of the free market, a growing malaise on the political Left, radical reductions in publicly supported legal services, and an increasingly insecure and competitive legal market.

In the face of the challenges of the nineties, however, it is precisely the commitment to politicization that seems to be fading. Left-activists in Seattle see themselves less and less as part of a unified political movement; they are now more fragmented and more likely to be focusing on discrete short-term goals. They face a constriction of professional opportunities in both public and private practice settings and a hostile legal and political climate. In response, they are scaling back their expectations and shifting emphasis from efforts to transform the legal, political, and social systems to providing meaningful assistance to those who are oppressed or victimized. In so doing they are becoming less distinctive and more like other kinds of cause lawyers for whom success in defensive action is about all the success that can be attained. Scheingold suggests that the crucial question for the future of left-activist lawyering in Seattle is whether there will be a new generation, whether a new cohort of politically committed progressives will be interested in or able to find a niche in the legal profession.

In part 2 of this book—"Cause Lawyering and the Organization of Practice"— we move away from these large questions about personal motivation and the impact of political, social, and legal conditions on cause lawyers and ask whether particular kinds of practice and particular organizations of practice are more conducive to cause lawyering than are others. The essays in this section describe in detail how particular kinds of cause lawyers organize their practices. Each attends to the complex intersections of moral and political commitment and the organization of work.

Aaron Porter's "Norris, Schmidt, Green, Harris, Higginbotham & Associates: The Sociolegal Impact of Philadelphia Cause Lawyers" is a case study of one firm whose lawyers were, for a long time, particularly well known for their activities in promoting the cause of racial justice in the United States. The Norris firm had a long history of training distinguished black lawyers, many of whom have held prominent positions in the legal establishment. But Porter is particularly interested in the firm as an embodiment of what he calls "Hamiltonian jurisprudence." That view, developed by Charles Hamilton Houston, encouraged black professionals to focus on building their own communities as a strategy for empowering African Americans to participate meaningfully in American society. It also emphasized the need to train and use black lawyers rather than rely on whites to provide skill and political commitment. Finally, Hamiltonian jurisprudence saw law as a key tool for social engineering and social change.

The Norris firm, in Porter's view, grew out of the experience of racial segregation, which severely limited opportunities for black professionals. In this sense it shows how exclusion and discrimination produce resistance and how lawyers play a role in that effort. The firm responded to the reality of segregation by emphasizing its distinctiveness as a servant of, and spokesman for, the interests of the black community. Indeed, Porter emphasizes the closeness of the ties that developed between the firm and the community; he suggests that the Norris firm provides one model for cause lawyering in which lawyers work hand in hand with members of the community they serve to build and develop that community.

Moreover, the Norris firm served as a training ground for cause lawyering. It self-consciously and explicitly transmitted the lessons of Hamiltonian jurisprudence to the lawyers it hired. As Porter puts it, ". . . [T]he firm continued its familiar course, including the involvement of its members in the black community and in city politics . . . [While] trying to eradicate racial inequality through the sociolegal process."

While cause lawyering may occur in publicly funded settings like legal aid centers or legal services offices, as Scheingold and Porter suggest, it is found in private settings as well. John Kilwein's "Still Trying: Cause Lawyering for the Poor and Disadvantaged in Pittsburgh, Pennsylvania" is a study of the dispersion of cause lawyering throughout a community in a network of individual, private lawyers, each of whom displays a shared commitment to a social or political cause. It identifies a discrete, though loosely organized, network of lawyers in that community who devote some proportion of their work to lawyering against poverty.

According to Kilwein there is, however, a significant divide among poverty lawyers in Pittsburgh, between those who focus solely on individual client lawyering and those who combine that approach with either what Kilwein calls "impact lawyering" (e.g., the use of class actions to remedy barriers that affect the poor as a group) or "mobilization lawyering" (e.g., working on community organization and empowerment issues outside traditional legal settings). The former orient their practices toward meeting the unmet legal needs of the poor, while the latter seek to use law or political action to produce structural changes. This divide is one that many of the essays in this volume explore. Lawyers who emphasize serving individual clients see lawyering for the poor as a "professional responsibility" and do not challenge prevailing ideologies of professionalism, while impact or mobilization lawyers tend to have liberal political attitudes and to have organized their professional life to express those beliefs. They provide classic instances of Luban's (1988) "moral activism" and reject the separation of personal morality and professional identity.

For lawyers of all types, however, lawyering for the poor in a private practice setting is demanding and difficult. Professional responsibility or political commitment must be balanced with the need to make a living; commitment to a cause must be balanced with the need to do well enough to keep a practice going. In the end, these tasks are so demanding that Kilwein suggests that cause lawyers in private practice may be an endangered species.

The next essay in part 2 also focuses on cause lawyers in private practice, again in the United States. But unlike Scheingold and Kilwein its authors suggest that many cause lawyers have successfully adopted new styles and new strategies to cope with the difficulties of doing cause-lawyering work in the United States in the 1990s. Whereas in the sixties and seventies cause lawyers tended to gravitate to publicly funded practice settings, today, Trubek and Kransberger argue, significant and growing numbers of socially conscious lawyers are engaged in fee-for-service activities. The public interest/fee-for-service divide that for many years characterized the organization of cause lawyering in the United States is, as a result, no longer as analytically useful as it once was. In both these settings, cause lawyers attempt to realize and express their political values.

Trubek and Kransberger direct our attention to a new kind of cause lawyering, what Trubek and Kransberger call "critical lawyering." Critical lawyering is responsive to changed economic realities (e.g., the defunding of publicly supported public interest law) and to the emergence of new theoretical perspectives, in particular feminism and critical race theory. Those cause lawyers who embrace critical practice select practice areas such as family law and the representation of minority businesses, based on perceived community needs and the ability of these lawyers to pursue their social justice concerns. In addition, they seek to transform lawyer-client relations, engage in broad social justice activities, and structure an egalitarian workplace.

Among critical lawyers, lawyer-client relations are more cooperative and less hierarchical. Lawyers seek to empower clients even in the course of what looks like providing traditional legal services. But the attorneys that Trubek and Kransberger studied went beyond client-oriented practice to engage in community organizing, legislative lobbying, and other "political" activities designed to advance their own conception of social justice. In so doing, they help to destabilize traditional conceptions of lawyering. Finally, they have turned their attention to the development of workplace conditions that accord with their own social justice values. Combining these new conceptions of lawyer-client relations, broad political activism, and a more humane work environment, Trubek and Kransberger argue, they "offer a desirable model for the use of law for social change."

Ronen Shamir and Sara Chinski's essay describes a split in the organization of cause lawyering similar to the public interest/fee-for-service split that Trubek and Kransberger portray. Their essay is based on an empirical study of lawyers who represent Bedouins in cases involving allegations of illegal housing construction in Israeli courts. These cases are used by Israeli authorities to control and harass the Bedouins, who were deported from their traditional lands and then forbidden to develop the lands on which they currently reside.

The Bedouins are represented by two types of lawyers: local, private practitioners, on a fee-for-service basis, and lawyers affiliated with the Association for the Support and Defense of Bedouin Rights. These two different kinds of lawyers come to this work for very different reasons. The former are motivated by a sense of injustice, but not a particular or deep commitment to the Bedouin cause. They are, however, marginal practitioners for whom representing Bedouins is part of a strategy for economic survival. The latter are more recognizable as the kind of lawyer that Menkel-Meadow described. They have a clear ideological commitment to lawyering as a moral vocation, and they see the treatment of the Bedouins as an issue of civil rights. Somewhat surprisingly, however, the private practitioners survive longer in the field and continue representing Bedouins long after the affiliated lawyers have burned out or moved on to another cause. Lawyers who take on causes as part of their ongoing private, fee-for-service practice, Shamir and Chinski contend, come closer to "realizing lawyering for a cause"—in terms of their "endurance, experience, commitment, and proximity to any client"—than do lawyers in a recognizable public interest setting.

By attending to these two different types of lawyers Shamir and Chinski insist that we can see that causes are constructed in the process of legal representation rather than found as existing social facts. We can also see the internal stratification that marks any field of cause lawyering. Finally, we can see the power of rules of legitimate professional practice, codes of appropriate behavior, and the symbolic capital available to the legal profession. Cause lawyering, they contend, is "an unstable professional type that is constituted . . . not only by . . . [individual] practices but also by the professional field."

Essays in the third part of this volume—"Strategies of Cause Lawyering under Liberal Legalism"—ask how cause lawyers go about defending victims of state oppression like the Bedouins in Israel or how they use law as a tool of progressive social change. They examine the way cause lawyers both appeal to, and transcend, a "myth of rights." They show how they use "conservative" legal institutions to foster progressive social change, and they analyze the relationship between cause lawyers and social movements whose causes they seek to advance.

Michael McCann and Helena Silverstein's "Rethinking Law's 'Allurements': A Relational Analysis of Social Movement Lawyers in the United States" lays out and then challenges what they see as a common critique of cause lawyering. According to that critique cause lawyers are generally unable to transcend the myth of rights or to successfully use legal institutions to promote change. Instead they end up reinforcing rather than destabilizing the boundary between law and politics. Critics assume, first, that "cause lawyers are heavily inclined toward litigation as the preferred means to achieve reform goals" and that this preference for litigation leads to distortion in the strategy and tactics of the social movements to which they are connected. In addition, the legalistic propensities of cause lawyers, so the critics allege, inhibit the development of alternative movement strategies. "Lawyers, it is suggested, push movements in narrow directions that are, at best, ineffective and, at worst, harmful."

Based on their own research on the pay equity and animal rights movements in the United States, McCann and Silverstein argue that the critique of cause lawyering is overdrawn. Lawyers can and do serve movements in a variety of ways. They contribute important strategic resources to the advancement of movement goals and are typically well aware of the limits of legalism. Cause lawyers tend to be cautious, critical, and sophisticated about the use of law, especially litigation. As a result, they are usually committed to encouraging movements to develop a wide range of strategies in which litigation can sometimes play a part.

The extent to which cause lawyers emphasize a legalistic strategy is, McCann and Silverstein suggest, highly variable. It is a function of the formal roles that lawyers occupy in movement organizations, the general structure of those organizations, the particular opportunities and constraints facing a social movement, and the experience of movements in using legal tactics. Moreover, cause lawyers typically do not dominate the movements they serve, but rather are responsive, in their advocacy of particular strategies, to the goals and needs of those movements. This, McCann and Silverstein believe, means that the standard critique of cause lawyers is far too simple, and that those lawyers can and do play an important role in politicizing the legal process.

Litigation, however, may be an attractive strategy for cause lawyers in situations where other alternatives are unavailable or ineffective, even if it is not generally transformative. It is a strategy that cannot be discarded where other forms of lawyer activism are underdeveloped. This, Susan Sterett argues, is the case with regard to immigration issues in Great Britain. Immigration is today a very salient factor in British politics. Both major political parties advocate restricting immigration, and, unlike the United States, there is no bill of rights to which cause lawyers can appeal. In those circumstances lawyers are limited to relying on creative interpretations of existing legal rules.

Sterett suggests that litigation based on statutory interpretation is an act of "resistance" when carried out on behalf of powerless groups. However, litigation on behalf of those groups is likely to be most effective when the claims raised are procedural rather than substantive and when they are narrowly framed. Thus, in the immigration context, cause lawyers generally seek to show that rules have been inappropriately applied and/or that they should be interpreted in light of some other generally agreed-upon principle. In the British context, then, cause lawyers individuate their claims and assure judges of the limited consequences of a ruling adverse to the government.

In these circumstances litigation has been useful for individual clients. It has, however, also been useful as a way of raising public consciousness about immigration issues. Its very individualized character means that litigation dramatizes individual injustices and forces issues that would not otherwise penetrate public consciousness onto the political agenda. What looks from the perspective of major impact litigation quite modest is, in Sterett's view, an important resource in the struggle to protect immigrants against arbitrary, capricious, and oppressive government action.

The next essay in part 3 asks the question of what cause lawyers can do when they are engaged in a "losing cause." The context for this examination is the death penalty in the United States. The essay, "Between (the Presence of) Violence and (the Possibility of) Justice: Lawyering against Capital Punishment," by Austin Sarat is based on a study of those lawyers who specialize in representing persons on death row. Whereas twenty-five or thirty years ago such lawyers looked to law to achieve the abolition of capital punishment, today that is no longer a realistic prospect. Since the mid-1970s the political and legal climate for abolition of the death penalty has become more and more hostile. And in this climate death penalty lawyers have themselves not escaped condemnation as ideological rogues who regularly violate the canons of their profession to carry on a guerilla war against capital punishment. Indeed, to oppose the death penalty through the legal process in the United States in the 1990s is, Sarat contends, not unlike fighting against apartheid in South African courts, or litigating on behalf of Palestinians in the Occupied Territories.

What strategies do lawyers in a losing cause pursue? What counts as success in their work? Death penalty lawyers in the United States litigate not to abolish capital punishment, but to keep their clients alive for as long as possible. "Keeping your client alive 'for an additional thirty days' becomes the measure of political and personal accomplishment when the prospect of a frontal assault on the death penalty seems so remote." In addition, death penalty lawyers believe that they have succeeded when they invest with dignity the lives of those they cannot save. Here, as in several of the other essays in this volume (see, e.g., Porter, Trubek and Kransberger, Shamir and Chinski), we again see a blurring of the distinction between cause lawyering and client lawyering that fuels so much of the mainstream criticism of cause lawyers.

Death penalty lawyers often take a principled stance in favor of "pushing the ethical limits" as they try to save the lives of their clients. In the face of what they believe to be the oppression represented in and by capital punishment they engage in what they regard as a form of civil disobedience and seek to "throw sand in the machine." But strategically there is more to being a lawyer in a losing cause than throwing sand in the machine. The lawyers Sarat studied self-consciously orient themselves to the future. They see themselves as bearing witness to the injustices of the present, and they use litigation as a way of memorializing those injustices. They seek to "make a record" as a way of appealing to the future. Litigation for them thus has two audiences, the audience of the present and an audience of the future, an audience whose attention to the cause of abolition will be galvanized, these lawyers believe, by the cumulation of individual stories of injustice. Thus "what seems 'fruitless' now takes on meaning when viewed in the long term. A society now unwilling to see linkages among poverty, neglect, and the death penalty, may, 'a hundred years from now' be more receptive."

Writing about the conditions and contexts conductive to cause lawyering Abel noted the singular significance of liberal legalism with its insistence on the autonomy (semiautonomy) of law and the state. Yet several of the other essays collected in this volume show that liberal legalism in and of itself is not enough to guarantee the success of cause lawyering. Now, in the final part of this volume, we inquire into the possibilities of cause lawyering beyond the boundaries of liberal legalism. We ask what it means to be a politically committed lawyer where liberal traditions are highly contested, suspended, or simply nonexistent.

The first essay in part 4, by Stephen Ellmann, provides a broad overview of cause lawyering in the Third World. It is based on a survey of twenty-two public interest law groups in eighteen countries. In each of those countries cause lawyering has emerged as a reformist response to conditions of social, political, or economic injustice. Despite the absence of liberal legalism, Ellmann argues that cause lawyering is made possible in Third World countries by "traditions of legal independence and professional commitment."

Ellmann suggests that to understand the development and practices of cause lawyers in those countries we must not only take account of factors indigenous to each national setting but also pay attention to both the rise of what he calls "an international human rights culture" and the attractiveness of legal tools as levers for change. The human rights culture, he claims, is recognizable in the large number of cause-lawyering projects now under way in the Third World and in the active efforts of institutions in the West to support human rights and cause lawyering throughout the world. Those projects are dependent on financial assistance from the West, but Western influence is not only financial. Western cause-lawyering styles, Ellmann argues, "have considerable appeal" throughout the Third World. Yet he warns that we should not overestimate the extent to which cause lawyering in the Third World is simply a Western product. In many different countries cause lawyers have developed distinctive practices and approaches that are today being borrowed or imitated in the West.

Cause lawyering in the Third World is primarily defensive and oriented to the traditional virtues of legality. Thus cause lawyers also are able to mobilize and draw on the symbolic capital of the organized legal profession. The price of doing so is that they must avoid being seen as political. They must use their lawyering skills to achieve political ends without being seen as openly partisan. Professionalism is sufficiently indeterminate in its meaning that it is available as a legitimating cover for the work that cause lawyers do. However, allying themselves with the mainstream bar means that cause lawyers may not be representative of their client groups and, indeed, that they may not be in an effective position to challenge prevailing social hierarchies and to speak for the people or to enable the people to speak for themselves. While cause lawyering in the Third World, Ellmann contends, "is as subject to the dangers of paternalism or insensitivity as lawyering anywhere else," those lawyers are today using a variety of devices in what Ellmann sees as a valuable attempt to cross "the barriers of class, culture, and privilege" separating them from their clients.

The next essay in part 4, by Daniel Lev, explores similarities and differences between cause lawyers in two Asian nations, Indonesia and Malaysia. Lev argues that, despite deep, important differences in these two cultural contexts, the causes to which activist lawyers are devoted are similar—namely establishment or protection of the rule of law. On Lev's account the rule of law may be the desired result of, rather than a necessary predicate to, the activities of cause lawyers. Thus in Indonesia cause lawyers have been fighting to *establish* a regime of legality in which the government respects and protects judicial integrity and judicial independence. In Malaysia activist lawyers have played a key role in trying to *defend* the rule of law against increasing governmental interference. In both countries lawyers have had to defend their own professional independence against government efforts to curb it.

Unable to rely on a judiciary under attack to defend its independence or theirs, cause lawyers in Indonesia and Malaysia have been successful in using the media to mobilize sentiment supportive of the rule of law. They have turned traditional values of the legal profession itself into a political lever against state-sponsored repression. And they have done so at great personal and professional risk.

Lev concludes his essay by speculating on the reasons why these cause lawyers take such risks. He discounts the kind of motivational analysis provided by Menkel-Meadow and the professional self-interest argument of the kind made by Shamir and Chinski. Instead he suggests that we need to pay attention to ideology, to the shared values that lawyers hold as lawyers. Activist lawyers in Indonesia and Malaysia are almost all litigators who, Lev tells us, "take seriously the importance of strong and reasonably autonomous courts." Moreover, they share an urge to "surround society with a defensive shield of transcendent values against state power." In the end Lev's paper reminds us that cause lawyering is context-specific; where the liberal legalism is secure, lawyer activists are among its major critics; where it is either nonexistent or in jeopardy, they are among its major defenders.

George Bisharat's study of Palestinian lawyers in the Occupied Territories also draws our attention to the context-specificity of cause lawyering. Like Abel, he suggests that legal institutions independent enough to constrain state power are essential to the full development of politically committed lawyering. Like Lev, he sees Palestinian lawyers as committed to the realization of the rule of law in the Occupied Territories. Yet Palestinian cause lawyering has had what Bisharat sees as a stunted development.

Bisharat identifies four factors that, in his view, explain why Palestinian cause lawyering has been so slow to develop. The first is the peculiar combination of legalism and repression practiced by the Israeli military authorities. This means that there is little that lawyers can do as lawyers to advance the central goals of the Palestinian movement, namely, self-determination and national independence. This is not a situation where there are persuasive and available legal arguments of the kind noted by Ellmann. And, even if there were more legality and less repression, the nature of the cause itself is one the pursuit of which does not require, or perhaps even benefit from, the distinctive skills of lawyers. Third, like the Bedouin lawyers described by Shamir and Chinski, those Palestinian lawyers who have become cause lawyers have done so as much out of economic necessity, in a market with large numbers of lawyers and few opportunities, as out of ideological commitment. And finally, cause lawyering is based on a conception of legality and lawyering that is foreign to Palestinian society.

Yet in spite of these factors Palestinians have become involved in cause-lawyering activities. They have been drawn into it as a form of defensive service to the nationalist cause, seeking at most to ameliorate the damage done by the occupying forces. They seek to advance classic notions of the rule of law. And, especially since the Intifada, they have been aided by the development of some organizations designed to advance Palestinian rights through law. But Bisharat, like Scheingold, Kilwein, Trubek and Kransberger, and Shamir and Chinski, notes the continued importance of individual, private practitioners. Some of those lawyers come from local professional elites; many turn to military court practice as a strategy of economic survival. Yet whatever their social background, Palestinian cause lawyers have focused almost exclusively on the nationalist struggle rather than on inequities internal to the Palestinian community. Indeed, Bisharat argues, unlike the lawyers studied by Trubek and Kransberger, these lawyers enact in their professional practices and day-to-day activities the hierarchical practices that typify Palestinian society.

Finally, Bisharat argues that Palestinian lawyers have clearly played a secondary role in the nationalist struggle. Indeed, there has been little coordination between lawyers and political activists about how to gain political advantage from the repressive actions of the Israeli occupiers. Yet Bisharat thinks it would be a mistake to dismiss Palestinian cause lawyering as entirely inconsequential. While they do not "conform to the model . . . of the cause lawyer who consciously selects law as a profession . . . to advance a social or political agenda," a model developed in Menkel-Meadow's paper, they have been "sensitized to the political movement" by indignities heaped on them as professionals pursuing a rather traditional professional mission. Their politicization has, in fact, made them reasonably effective actors in the struggle to galvanize public opinion in the occupied territories, in Israel, and beyond even as they have been relatively unsuccessful in their more strictly legal activities.

Unlike Palestinian cause lawyers who reenforce traditional social hierarchies even as they participate in the national struggles, cause lawyers in Brazil and Argentina, countries that have recently undergone transitions to democracy after long periods of repressive military rule, have openly and actively allied themselves with grassroots, community-based social movements. They have helped to develop an "alternative law movement" that seeks to break with the traditional conservatism of the legal profession in both countries and to develop new strategies designed to bring about progressive social change. This is true, Stephen Meili suggests, in part because in neither country is there an independent judiciary that might be hospitable to legal claims on behalf of the socially disadvantaged. As a result, cause lawyers have had to find roles in social movements other than being litigators.

Meili's paper examines how Brazilian and Argentinian lawyers have, in fact, served those movements. He describes them as being consultants who provide information and advice about the ramifications of actions or strategies that a community group has adopted or is considering. Meili notes that cause lawyers typically do not play important leadership roles. Instead, they assist the movements by providing legal training in such a way as to decrease their members' dependence on professional expertise.

The activities of these movement-oriented cause lawyers have been criticized by more traditional human rights lawyers in both countries. Unlike the latter for whom opposition to state repression is the cause, lawyers who work with grassroots movements are interested in social transformation. They seek to lend whatever expertise they have as lawyers to the cause of egalitarian social change. In so doing they destabilize the boundary between law and politics and find new uses for legal knowledge.

Meili suggests that cause lawyering is further developed in Brazil than in Argentina because of the more violent and repressive activities of the Argentinian military dictatorship, which made war on progressive lawyers and destroyed the infrastructure of community groups. In Brazil, under the military regime, community groups were given more room to operate. Moreover, there is somewhat greater support for cause lawyering in the Brazilian bar, and a slightly more receptive climate in the Brazilian judiciary. In the end, Meili concludes that the prevalence and effectiveness of social-movement cause lawyering depends most heavily on such external factors rather than the kinds of personal and professional proclivities emphasized by Menkel-Meadow.

We conclude this volume by inquiring about the possibilities for cause lawyering under state socialism. The last essay, a study of cause lawyering in Cuba by Raymond Michalowski, argues that cause lawyering can and does occur even where the legal regime does not embrace conceptions of procedural justice and individual rights. Cuba, Michalowski asserts, does not provide the conditions necessary for the typical image of cause lawyering, namely lawyers working with or for independent, progressive social movements struggling against a more conservative political regime. All lawyers in Cuba work in law collectives organized under a central national organization. And they are all formally obligated to use their professional skills to advance the cause of socialism. In this sense, Cuban lawyers are all politicized in a way that goes against the grain of the ideal of neutrality that is characteristic of the legal profession in the United States.

Michalowski argues, however, that there are significant differences among Cuban lawyers in their orientations toward practice, with only a small percentage being what he calls "socialist activists," namely lawyers who chose legal practice as an opportunity to serve the cause of socialism. Such lawyers and their less-politicized counterparts can operate through the national organization of law collectives to push for changes in social policy as well as in the policies governing legal practice. Those organizations, while they limit the political independence of Cuban lawyers, provide effective avenues for influencing government action. They have enabled lawyers to bring about significant reforms, reforms that better enable them to serve their clients and provide some limited opportunities to provide effective representation even where the interests of the government are at stake. Thus the Cuban case shows that in socialist societies activist lawyers can shape social change like their counterparts in liberal legal regimes. It alerts us, Michalowski argues, to the need for greater attention to "the multiplicity of ways in which lawyers can serve as proactive agents of social change, other than as antigovernment litigators."

The essays collected in this volume illustrate the great diversity of cause lawyering in the United States and other liberal legal regimes, as well as in societies without liberal legality. Both here and abroad cause lawyering is sometimes defensive, that is, oriented toward preventing or stopping violations of individual or group rights, and sometimes active in seeking social transformation. It is sometimes embedded in, and sometimes independent of, social movements working for a shared political goal. Moreover, sometimes cause lawyering draws on mainstream professional values, while sometimes it frontally challenges those values. But everywhere it occurs cause lawyering forces us to reconsider and reexamine the meaning of those values as well as the legitimacy and stability of the boundary between law and politics.

Notes

1. David Luban, *Lawyers and Justice: An Ethical Study* (Princeton, N.J.: Princeton University Press, 1988), xvii.

2. For a vigorous defense of the hired-gun theory see Monroe Freedman, *Lawyers' Ethics in an Adversary System* (Indianapolis, Ind.: Bobbs-Merrill, 1975).

3. Madelaine Petrara,"Dangerous Identifications: Confusing Lawyers with Their Clients," *Journal of the Legal Profession* 19 (1994), 179.

4. Luban, *Lawyers and Justice*, xxii. See also Nancy Polikoff, "Am I My Client?: The Role Confusion of a Lawyer Activist," *Harvard Civil Rights–Civil Liberties Law Review* 31 (1996), 458.

5. Anthony Alifieri, "Mitigation, Mercy, and Delay: The Moral Politics of Death Penalty Abolitionists," *Harvard Civil Rights–Civil Liberties Law Review* 31 (1996), 326. Alfieri argues that "[p]rogress in law and politics, however slow and inconsistent, turns on moral vision. . . . Professing moral theory in practice is our professional responsibility" (352).

6. Louis Brandeis, "The Opportunity in Law," in *Business—A Profession* (Boston: Hale, Cushman and Flint, 1933). Also Robert Gordon, "The Ideal and the Actual," in *The New High Priests: Lawyers in Post–Civil War America,* ed. G. Gawalt (Westport, Conn.: Greenwood Press, 1984); Robert Gordon,"Lawyers As the American Aristocracy," unpublished essay, Yale Law School, 1986; Robert Gordon, "The Independence of Lawyers," *Boston University Law Review* 68 (1988), 1.

7. For an interesting discussion of the question of legitimation in regard to the legal system itself see Stephen Ellmann, "Struggle and Legitimation," *Law and Social Inquiry* 20 (1995), 339.

8. Luban, *Lawyers and Justice,* 16.

9. William Simon, "Visions of Practice in Legal Thought," *Stanford Law Review* 36 (1984), 469.

10. Richard Abel, "Why Does the American Bar Association Promulgate Ethical Rules?" *Texas Law Review* 59 (1981), 639.

11. Simon William, "The Ideology of Advocacy," *Wisconsin Law Review* 1978 (1978), 30.

12. Barbara Curran, "American Lawyers in the 1980s: A Profession in Transition," *Law and Society Review* 20 (1986), 19.

13. In this volume we are excluding "right-wing" lawyers from our consideration of cause lawyering. We do so because, at least until very recently in the United States, moral activism was almost entirely associated with lawyering for progressive causes. It is too soon in the development of conservative cause lawyering to provide a reliable assessment; however, the increasing prominence of right-wing cause lawyering suggests that it is now an important focus for research.

14. Derrick Bell, "Serving Two Masters: Integration Ideals and Client Interests in School Desegregation Litigation," *Yale Law Journal* 85 (1976), 470.

15. Deborah Rhode,"Class Conflicts in Class Actions," *Stanford Law Review* 34 (1982), 589.

16. Luban, *Lawyers and Justice,* xxv. Also Gary Bellow, "Steady Work: A Practitioner's Reflections on Political Lawyering," *Harvard Civil Rights–Civil Liberties Law Review* 31 (1996), 300. For a different point of view see Petrara, "Dangerous Identifications."

17. Richard Abel, "Lawyers," in *Law and the Social Sciences,* ed. Leon Lipson and Stanton Wheeler (New York: Russell Sage, 1987).

18. Anthony Alfieri, "Reconciling Poverty Law Practice: Learning Lessons of Client Narrative," *Yale Law Journal* 100 (1991), 2107. Also Lucie E. White, "Subordination, Rhetorical Survival Skills, and Sunday Shoes: Notes on the Hearing of Mrs. G.," *Buffalo Law Review* 38 (1990), 1.

19. Stephen Ellmann, "Law and Legitimacy in South Africa," *Law and Social Inquiry* 20 (1995), 407.

20. George Bisharat, "Courting Justice? Legitimation in Lawyering under Israeli Occupation," *Law and Social Inquiry* 20 (1995), 349. Jane Kaufman Winn and Tang-Chi Yeh, "Advocating Democracy: The Role of Lawyers in Taiwan's Political Transformation," *Law and Social Inquiry* 20 (1995), 561.

21. Peter Gabel and Paul Harris, "Building Power and Breaking Images: Critical Legal Theory and the Practice of Law," *New York University Review of Law and Social Change* 11 (1982–83), 369.

22. For an important survey of the connection between legal traditions and lawyering see Richard Abel and P. S. Lewis, *Lawyers in Society,* 3 vols. (Berkeley: University of California Press, 1989).

23. John Merryman, "On the Convergence (and Divergence) of the Civil and Common Law," *Stanford Journal of International Law* 17 (1981), 357.

24. Stuart Scheingold, "Notes on Reinscribing Rights with Culture," paper presented at the annual meeting of the Law and Society Association, Toronto, Canada, June 1–4, 1995.

25. P. S. Atiyah and R. S. Summers, *Form and Substance in Anglo-American Law: A Comparative Study of Legal Reasoning, Legal Theory and Legal Institutions* (Oxford: Clarendon Press, 1987).

26. Isaac Balbus, *The Dialectics of Legal Repression: Black Rebels before American Courts* (New York: Russell Sage, 1973).

27. Richard Abel, *Politics by Other Means: Law in the Struggle against Apartheid* (New York: Routledge, 1995). Also Ellmann, "Law and Legitimacy"; Francis Snyder, "State of Siege and the Rule of Law in Argentina," *Lawyer of the Americas* 15 (1984), 503.

28. This is not meant to suggest that cause lawyering in former colonies is simply a Western import or that its prospects and properties are driven solely by cosmopolitan rather than local forces.

29. Stuart Scheingold, "Radical Lawyers and Socialist Ideals," *Journal of Law and Society* 15 (1988), 122, and Stuart Scheingold, "The Contradictions of Radical Legal Practice" in M. Cain and C. Harrington, eds., *Lawyering and Its Limits* (Milton Keynes, United Kingdom: Open University Press, 1994).

30. "[P]olitical lawyering," Martha Minow claims, "involves deliberate efforts to use law to change society or alter allocations of power." See Martha Minow, "Political Lawyering: An Introduction," *Harvard Civil Rights–Civil Liberties Law Review* 31 (1996), 289.

31. See Louise Trubek, "Embedded Practices: Lawyers, Clients, and Social Change," *Harvard Civil Rights–Civil Liberties Law Review* 31 (1996), 432.

32. Joel Handler, Ellen Jane Hollingsworth, and Howard Erlanger, *Lawyers and the Pursuit of Legal Rights* (New York: Academic Press, 1978).

33. This problem is explicitly addressed in Polikoff, "Am I My Client?"

34. Martha Minow,"Breaking the Law: Lawyers and Clients in Struggles for Social

Change," *University of Pittsburgh Law Review* 52 (1991), 723. See also Kathryn Abrams, "Lawyers and Social Change Lawbreaking: Confronting a Plural Bar," *University of Pittsburgh Law Review* 52 (1991), 753.

35. Abel, *Politics by Other Means.*

36. Stuart Scheingold, *The Politics of Rights: Lawyers, Public Policy, and Political Change* (New Haven: Yale University Press, 1974).

37. Rajiv Dhavan, "Whose Law? Whose Interest?" in *Public Interest Law,* ed. Jeremy Cooper and Rajiv Dhavan (Oxford: Blackwell, 1986).

38. Michael McCann, "Equal Protection for Social Inequality," in *Judging the Constitution,* ed. Michael McCann and Gerald Houseman (Boston: Little, Brown, 1989).

39. D. Held, "Power and Legitimacy in Contemporary Britain," in *State and Society in Contemporary Britain,* ed. G. McLennan et al. (Cambridge: Polity Press, 1984). Also Judith Shklar, *Legalism* (Cambridge, Mass.: Harvard Press, 1964), and Paul Hirst, *Law, Socialism and Democracy* (London: Allen & Unwin, 1986).

40. See Richard Abel, "Lawyers and the Power to Change," *Law and Policy* 7 (1985) (special issue); Richard Abel, "Law without Politics," *UCLA Law Review* 32 (1985), 474; Richard Abel, "Lawyers and the Decline of Professionalism," *Modern Law Review* 49 (1986), 1; Richard Abel, "The Transformation of the American Legal Profession," *Law and Society Review* 20 (1986), 7; Nikolas Rose, "Unreasonable Rights: Mental Illness and the Limits of the Law," *Journal of Law and Society* 20 (1985) 199; and Jack Katz, *Poor People's Lawyers in Transition* (New Brunswick, N.J.: Rutgers University Press, 1982).

41. R. Lefcourt, *Law against the People* (New York: Vintage, 1971). See also Karl Klare, "Judicial Deradicalization of the Wagner Act and the Origins of Modern Legal Consciousness, 1937–1941," *Minnesota Law Review* 62 (1978), 265; Linda Medcalf, *Law and Identity* (Beverly Hills: Sage, 1978); R. Bruun, "The Boldt Decision," *Law and Policy* 4 (1978), 271.

42. E. P. Thompson, *Whigs and Hunters* (New York: Pantheon, 1975).

43. Thompson, *Whigs and Hunters*; Ronald Dworkin, *Taking Rights Seriously* (Cambridge, Mass.: Harvard University Press, 1977) and *A Bill of Rights for Britain* (London: Chatto & Windus, 1990); Roberto Unger, *Politics,* vol. I, *False Necessity* (New York: Cambridge University Press, 1987); J. Keane, *Socialism and Civil Society* (London: Verso, 1987).

44. Sally Merry, "Resistance and the Cultural Power of Law," *Law and Society Review* 29 (1995), 11.

45. Martha Fineman, *The Illusion of Equality: The Rhetoric and Reality of Divorce Reform* (Chicago: University of Chicago Press, 1991).

46. Elizabeth Schneider, "The Dialectic of Rights and Politics: Perspectives from the Women's Movement," *New York University Law Review* 61 (1986), 589. Also Michael McCann, *Rights at Work* (Chicago: University of Chicago Press, 1994); Lisa Bowers, "Queer Acts and the Politics of 'Direct Address': Rethinking Law, Culture and Community," *Law and Society Review* 28 (1995), 1009.

47. Aryeh Neier, *Only Judgment: The Limits of Litigation in Social Change* (Middletown, Conn.: Wesleyan University Press, 1982).

48. As Minow puts it, "The present moment is a tough one for political lawyers." Minow, "Political Lawyering," 290.

49. E. Laclau and C. Mouffe, *Hegemony and Socialist Strategy: Towards a Radical Democratic Politics* (London: Verso, 1985).

50. Alfieri, "Reconciling Poverty Law Practice"; White, "Subordination, Rhetorical Survival Skills."

51. Peter Fitzpatrick, "Law as Resistance," in *The Critical Lawyers' Handbook,* ed. Ian Grigg-Spall and Paddy Ireland (London: Pluto Press, 1992).

52. Alfieri, "Reconstructing Poverty Law Practice," 1234.

53. Gerald Lopez, *Rebellious Lawyering: One Chicano's Vision of Progressive Law Practice* (Boulder: Westview Press, 1992), 52–54.

54. Lopez, *Rebellious Lawyering*, 60–61.

55. Brandeis, "The Opportunity in Law."

56. Anthony Kronman, *The Lost Lawyer: Failing Ideals of the Legal Profession* (Cambridge, Mass.: Harvard University Press, 1993).

57. Anthony Abbott, *The System of the Professions* (Chicago: University of Chicago Press, 1989).

58. Rayman Solomon, "Five Crises or One: The Concept of Legal Professionalism, 1925–1960," in *Lawyers' Ideals/Lawyers' Practices: Transformations in the American Legal Profession*, ed. Robert Nelson et al. (Ithaca: Cornell University Press, 1992).

59. See, for example, Margali Larson, *The Rise of Professionalism* (Berkeley: University of California Press, 1997); Terrence Johnson, *Professions and Power* (London: Macmillan, 1972).

60. Abel, "Why Does the American Bar Association Promulgate," and "Lawyers and the Decline of Professionalism."

61. Jerold Auerbach, *Unequal Justice: Lawyers and Social Change* (New York: Oxford, 1976).

62. Abel, "Why Does the American Bar Association Promulgate."

63. Elliot Friedson, *The Profession of Medicine* (New York: Dodd, Mead, 1972); Auerbach, *Unequal Justice*; Ivan Illich, *Disabling Professions* (London: Marion Boyers, 1977).

64. Clifford Geertz, *The Interpretation of Cultures* (New York: Basic Books, 1973), 220.

65. Robert Nelson and David Trubek, "Introduction: New Problems and New Paradigms in Studies of the Legal Profession," in *Lawyers' Ideals/Lawyers' Practices: Transformations in the American Legal Profession*, ed. Robert Nelson et al. (Ithaca: Cornell University Press, 1992).

66. Jorge Larrain, *The Concept of Ideology* (Athens: University of Georgia Press, 1979).

67. Peter Gabel, "Reification in Legal Reasoning," *Research in Law and Sociology* 3 (1980), 125, and Robert Gordon, "Legal Thought and Legal Practice in the Age of the American Enterprise, 1870–1920," in *Professions and Professional Ideologies in America*, ed. G. Geison (Chapel Hill: University of North Carolina Press, 1983), 70–110.

68. See Unger, *Politics*.

69. Carol Greenhouse, "Courting Difference: Issues of Interpretation and Comparison in the Study of Legal Ideologies," *Law and Society Review* 22 (1988), 687.

70. See Simon, "Visions of Practice."

71. American Bar Association Commission on Professionalism, *'In the Spirit of Public Service': A Blueprint for the Rekindling of Lawyer Professionalism* (Chicago: American Bar Association, 1986), 10.

PART I

Contexts and Conditions of Cause Lawyering

The Causes of Cause Lawyering

Toward an Understanding of the
Motivation and Commitment of
Social Justice Lawyers

CARRIE MENKEL-MEADOW

> Whoever saves a single soul, it is as if he had saved the whole world.
> —From the Talmud, medal inscription for those Righteous
> among the Nations of the World, Yad Vashem,
> honored rescuers of the Jews

What Makes a Cause Lawyer?

What makes some people want to do "good" with the professional and human tools they are given or develop, rather than use them exclusively for self-interest or the facilitation of evil, oppression, or preservation of the status quo? What is "good" and "evil" in the practice of law? These are questions that have consumed me since long before I went to law school. Indeed, they are part of a deeper human inquiry: why do people choose to do good, do nothing or cause harm?

As the child of Holocaust survivors (not camp survivors, just refugee survivors), I have been concerned with questions of good and evil, morality, the rule of law, and human motivation. Others have shared this concern and the study of Holocaust rescuers has become a subfield of social psychology—the study of pro-social or altruistic behavior.[1] Recently, those who have focused on the study of rational action have recognized that human motivations are more complex than a simple bipolar conception of self-interest (a Hobbesian world of contractually suppressed self-concern) versus a romanticized notion of "other-regarding" behavior (the utopian communitarian visions of many political philosophers) and there is growing recognition of the study of "mixed-motive" behavior.[2] It is against this backdrop of trying to understand why human beings do what they do that I want to explore, at the risk of plowing through already well-tilled soil, why some lawyers do what they do—when they turn to working for a "cause," including the "simple" cause of service to individuals in need. Like others who are concerned about these issues, I ask, "Can moral courage be taught? Could children [would-be lawyers] learn not only to distinguish right from wrong but also to develop moral integrity to act on that distinction?"[3] In the context of delivering legal services, why do some legal professionals understand and act on "the morality of service"[4] while others choose to serve themselves, often in the guise of serving existing institutions?

In many ways the study of the Holocaust, though horrific in the deeds upon which it focuses, presents an easier question for a scholar[5]—the deeds of good and evil are clearer, even if motivation remains somewhat more opaque. Yet for the student of altruistic (or empathic) lawyering, as I have called it,[6] problems of definition abound. What is "lawyering for the good?"[7] What are the causes, "social justice" issues, and goals that qualify as "good?" How should the means used to achieve ends be judged in assessing "good" lawyering?[8] How can we assess the motivations of lawyers—by their self-proclaimed objectives, by their actions, by the effects of their actions?[9] Is it possible to alter the motivations, attitudes, and behaviors of lawyers or law students? How do individual psychological factors interact with social, institutional, and environmental constraints and opportunities?[10]

In this essay I seek to explore the questions we should ask to understand the motivations of lawyers who seek to "do good." For obvious reasons, given the vagueness of this or any other phrase we might use, I will begin with some discussion of definitions and boundaries. Next I will review some of the theoretical and empirical literature on human motivation for prosocial behavior and speculate on how such work might be applied to the study of why cause lawyers do what they do, thus broadening, contextualizing, and situating the discussion of what it means to be a "cause" lawyer in the more timeless concerns of what it means to be a moral human being. It should not be surprising that motivations and behaviors are varied, if sometimes patterned, and I will explore some of those patterns to trace the ebbs and flows of political, emotional, and social commitments. Third, I will draw on my own primary investigations (currently focused on feminist cause lawyers, but drawing also on my past work with legal services attorneys)[11] and the work of other researchers to illuminate what we already know about the motivations of cause lawyers. Finally, I will examine some of the issues involved in maintaining commitment—what "causes" cause lawyers to keep going when their causes are losing[12] or social or personal environments change.

Like many stories of human motivation, a study of the "causes" of cause lawyering necessarily involves interactions of individual, personal, and emotional commitments to collective, political, and social goals. For most cause lawyers there is often a tension between service to particular individuals and efforts to achieve structural or institutional change. For some lawyers these conflicts are easily reconciled; for others they provide a source of constant challenge. And, lest we think lives are orderly or social science can explain all variables, for many cause lawyers, commitments, careers, and case and job choices may be the result of chance, serendipity, or circumstance. What is interesting is what people do with the opportunities or experiences they are given.

Problems of Definition: Goals, Practices, and Forms of Cause Lawyering

The central questions implicated in the definition of cause lawyering ask (1) what cause lawyering is (what goals/objectives it seeks to advance), (2) what activities and practices are constitutive of it,[13] (3) what motivates it, and (4) what sustains and supports it. (See the appendix to this chapter, Inventory of Questions Defining Cause Lawyering.)

A review of the relevant literature and the papers collected in this volume reveals a wide array of general definitions of cause lawyering. Such lawyering as I have called "lawyering for the good" others have called "social justice" lawyering, "public interest" lawyering,[14] "rebellious" lawyering,[15] "activist" lawyering, progressive lawyering, "transformative" lawyering, equal justice lawyering, "radical" lawyering,[16] lawyering for social change,[17] "critical" lawyering,[18] socially conscious lawyering, lawyering for the underrepresented, lawyering for the subordinated, "alternative" lawyering, political lawyering, and "visionary" lawyering,[19] to name but a few of the variations.[20] And these are only generic definitions, as distinguished from the "cause-specific" labels of civil rights, poverty, legal aid, environmental, labor, death penalty, feminist, disability, and defense lawyering.

Descriptions of cause lawyering raise a host of boundary questions. What kinds of political goals or ends must be served to qualify? What kinds of activities or practices count? What sites of practice are included and are any disqualifying? How much must traditional conceptions of lawyering be involved? How much commitment must a cause lawyer have to the "rule of law" or tradition?[21] At what point does legal dissidence disqualify one from being a cause lawyer? Putting these more abstract concerns into concrete situations we might further ask whether all government lawyers, working for "the public interest," qualify, or whether we make individualized judgments about what ends particular lawyers are seeking to achieve. Is the environmental defense lawyer in the U.S. Department of Justice politically and morally equivalent to the environmental prosecutor in the same agency, much less lawyers representing the Sierra Club? Does the lawyer who writes welfare regulations to increase work requirements in federal or state agencies qualify? In addition, questions of "political correctness" and moral judgment have been with us since we began defining an alternative to private, fee-for-service lawyering. Do private personal-injury lawyers who bring mass tort actions against corporations who produce toxic products count?[22] When these lawyers make vast sums with contingency fees? Does the location of work in a profit-making setting affect how we view the work? Do private, large law firm lawyers doing pro bono work count as cause lawyers if they work specifically on one cause, like capital punishment, or if they work on any case involving underrepresented people?

What does it mean to have a cause, and must that cause be located on the left to liberal side of the political spectrum? How, for example, do we define the cause lawyering of the Right to Work Foundation,[23] the Mountain States Defense Fund,[24] the Pacific Foundation, Right to Life, and others committed to causes that we who "founded" the public interest movement find abhorrent?[25]

At a theoretical level, conceptions of cause lawyering depend on the point of view of the definer. Yet, what and whose goals are to be determinative of what a cause is? Is it enough to seek redress on behalf of an individual who is "subordinated" to another?[26] Or must cause lawyering seek broad reformation of an unjust law or practice?[27] Recapitulating old debates, authors of the papers in this volume assume certain stances or definitions of the cause lawyer. They ask if a cause lawyer is a representative of a "person" or an "idea"[28]—in old terms, a direct-service-of-individual-client lawyer or a "law reform" (class action or rule change) lawyer. Ronen Shamir and Sara Chinski explore a particularly problematic aspect of this old dichotomy. They find that in the representation of Bedouins being displaced for criminal violation of Israeli construction rules, claims of individual and particularistic need are more likely to win than arguments based on collective appeals to group or racial justice. Thus, the cause lawyer must represent a person in the context of satisfying important individual housing needs by renouncing claims for more generalized "equal" justice treatment. The tension in individual representation by claiming "this client, this story, this case is different and thus requires special court relief" resonates to those who have demanded equitable relief from courts in a wide variety of matters—landlord-tenant, criminal liability and sentencing, child custody, employment, and consumer collections. The Bedouin housing struggle thus concretely illustrates a very important general point: the law acts on individuals in individual cases. Cause lawyers who, alternatively, seek to attack the injustice of whole regimes generically may have to compromise individual claims and potentially fail (at least in the short run, where judges are reluctant to strike down whole legal regimes).[29]

From the other end of the legal spectrum, Raymond Michalowski suggests that cause lawyering, as conventionally defined with a Western capitalist legal regime at the definitional core, assumes a dissident role toward the state, thus excluding the cause lawyering of Cuban socialist lawyers, who, working *within* a regime-sponsored, decentralized system of law collectives, or (*bufetes colectivos*) and a centralized organization (National Organization of Bufetes Colectivos [ONBC]) work toward the accomplishment of both individual and group ends that many would find compatible with left conceptions of cause lawyering. Thus, definitions of cause lawyering must be culturally located as well.

The organization of the state and of legal regimes also affects how cause law-yering can be expressed. For example, civil law systems allow fewer litigated challenges to rules; common law systems without constitutions or procedures and rules for class actions are less amenable to American-style group relief or rule challenge. The relation of an independent judiciary and constitutionalism to the legislative body and administrative state will affect what cause lawyers can do—see the role of lawyers, both indigenous and as external consultants, in the creation of new legal regimes in the former Communist bloc nations. At the same time, political challenges to the efficacy of a "rights"-based strategy have caused some analysts to question whether attempts at legal reform can ever be effective in the larger political and social struggles for equality and justice.[30]

Cause lawyering must also be personally defined—does the focus, goal, and objective of cause lawyering look the same to the lawyer who does it, the client who experiences it, the judge who listens to it, and the academic who analyzes it? Do political refugees want their own repatriation individually legalized or are they willing to attempt a more general, but likely losing, challenge to systemic exclusion based on racism?[31] If cause lawyering is primarily "political,"[32] what moral obligation does the cause lawyer have to the individuals or groups who represent the cause?[33] In this sense, David Luban's phrase "the good lawyer" takes on at least a double meaning—is the lawyer's "good" measured by what she or he does for the larger cause or by the moral value of the relationship between lawyer and client?[34] Who decides how the cause-lawyering work will be carried out—lawyer, client, group, social movement, or organization?[35] Recent literature in the United States has challenged both the professional dominance model and the counterproposals that decisions about a case should be left to the client for client empowerment. A more complex model of "moral dialogue"[36] between lawyer and client with ends and means mutually determined and dynamically altered as conditions change is currently the preferred choice, at least among those who write about client decision making in the context of political lawyering.[37]

More problematic in defining the scope of cause lawyering is the effort to describe the practices that constitute it. Practitioners, as well as scholars, have too often bought into an "imperialism" of cause lawyering determined by American legal practices. Thus, litigation is often privileged over other forms of legal action, and law reform, class action, and group litigation are often privileged over individual cases. Critiques of the litigation model of cause lawyering have come from a number of sources. First, after the historical flowering of victories in process,[38] civil rights,[39] and reproductive rights,[40] a more problematic era of defeats in the U.S. Supreme Court in the more difficult areas of income distribution, poverty rights, and civil rights for gays[41] has raised questions about the efficacy of test case litigation. While cause lawyering was always recognized as "political," early victories also led lawyers to assume their politics would prevail if the advocacy was "good" (i.e., persuasive) enough and that lawsuits would be effective educational and organizing devices. With the political climate changing in the 1970s and 1980s, cause advocates had to recognize that litigation strategies must contend with the politics of the judiciary and conventional party politics. Although never totally abandoned, cause advocates returned (where they could)[42] to legislative advocacy and lobbying, particularly in states (and the Congress) that maintained Democratic majorities, even if Republican executives chose the judiciary more conservatively. Although too complex a story to recount here, the once popular class action fell into disuse, except where attorneys fees guaranteed an economic interest for lawyers independent of the minuscule financial gain to clients.[43] Second, litigation itself was criticized as a way of accomplishing client goals, both from a political perspective and from a more general critique of the American adversarial legal system.[44] More radical political critics did not necessarily advocate alternative dispute resolution or legislative advocacy but urged cause lawyers to dramatically present their causes in a variety of different sites, such as the streets, to challenge conventional legal strategies and to give a more direct voice to clients who chose to politicize the legal process, including both literal and figurative street "theater."[45] Critical scholars, feminists, and some race critics began to critique conventional modes of legal action, the dependence on "legal rights" and the role of the courts in providing lasting and substantive legal victories.[46]

More recently, analysts of cause lawyering have identified a number of different strategies to be employed in using law for social change and have argued that these strategies must be contextually appropriate. For example, Susan Sturm identifies four kinds of public interest legal strategies: individual service, impact litigation, institutional change, and political empowerment models.[47] She then offers a framework for assessing what kinds of strategies might be appropriate for different causes and constituencies: (1) What are the legal needs of the clients? (2) What is the political/institutional environment in which clients live/work/act, and what is the institutional/political environment of those who will decide matters pertaining to the client's interests (i.e., courts, workplaces, legislatures, hospitals, prisons, government agencies, corporations)? (3) What remedies are possible (both from formal court proceedings and other possible ways of "resolving" or dealing with the legal issues identified)? And finally, (4) what advocacy method is most likely to be effective in the context specific environment for the remedies sought? Thus, in her own area of corrections reform, Sturm suggests that institutional reform is most appropriate because national law reform is politically unlikely and would be insufficiently sensitive to local issues, and individuals have few resources with which to pursue legal actions. Thus, strategies that attempt to ensure some form of institutional accountability are most likely to be effective in developing prison reform and corrections conditions improvement.

Similarly, those who have attempted to apply innovative collaborations with client groups, following the "critical-lawyering" critique of conventional practices have changed the sites of law practice (to local community centers) or moved to less legalistic, more client-centered definitions of goals that include more broadly defined (and less legalistic) kinds of activities.[48] Does accompanying a woman to an abortion clinic ringed with right-to-life protesters count as cause lawyering? Is a city attorney who refuses to prosecute homeless people for vagrancy a cause lawyer when his refusal to act is based on his commitment to a cause and results in his firing?[49] Does the lawyer who conducts community education programs at a church participate in cause lawyering? What about the lawyer who acts as a mediator in a neighborhood dispute center who doesn't call upon her legal skills to resolve a neighbor-to-neighbor conflict? Thus, the parameters of behaviors, practices, and activities that constitute cause lawyering may themselves be changing—merging the legal with the nonlegal and problematizing the definitions and boundaries of cause lawyering developed by those who "constructed" public interest lawyering in the more glorious days of easier conventional legal victories.

In a negative sense, the descriptions of what constitutes cause-lawyering activities can be culled from the efforts to prohibit such activities in disciplinary proceedings (e.g., client solicitation by public interest agencies), regulations (the Legal Services Corporation's prohibitions on activities such as lobbying, particular causes such as abortion and school desegregation, and clients such as undocumented workers) and political efforts to limit such work (as in the Heritage Foundation's attempts to promote legislation against certain kinds of lawyers or to severely limit certain kinds of practices or choices of clients).[50]

Cause lawyering, then, is constructed out of a myriad of sources—legal regulations,[51] practitioner descriptions, the actual practices of lawyers and other legal workers,[52] clients, judges, legislators, law teachers and students, and lastly, analysts, scholars, and social critics such as ourselves who seek to develop boundaries so we can understand this work.

From my own perspective of seeking to understand what motivates a lawyer to undertake work that is less well compensated than traditional private legal work and that may involve some personal, physical, economic, and social status risks, cause lawyering is *any activity that seeks to use law-related means or seeks to change laws or regulations*[53] *to achieve greater social justice—both for particular individuals (drawing on individualistic "helping" orientations) and for disadvantaged groups.* Whether the means and strategies used are legally based "rights" strategies[54] or more broadly based "needs" strategies,[55] the goals and purposes of the legal actor are to *"do good"—to seek a more just world—to do "lawyering for the good."* Whether such work requires self-sacrifice or particular kinds of altruistic motivations to be sustained is the question to which I now turn.

What Motivates the Cause Lawyer: Of Altruism, Empathy, Self-Interest, and Mixed Motives

In seeking to understand what motivates people to become cause lawyers we are between several levels of analysis. At the most general level are questions of human motivation—why does anyone do anything? At a more specific level—why do some people seek to "do good" and engage in some self-sacrificing behaviors for the "betterment"[56] of others?[57] And at its most concrete level, we seek to understand why a particular group of professionals, with high investments in training and expertise, seek to employ these particular acquired skills in service to particular ends—in short, why the use of law for social change and why the sacrifice of some forms of personal gain to attempt to achieve social justice.

In the era before organized social science, political philosophers often posited particular human motivations—such as the self-interest of Hobbes's *Leviathan* or Machiavelli's *The Prince* or the well-intentioned, if exclusionary, participatory citizen of Plato's *Republic*. More recently, those who assume self-interest (the economist's self-maximizing rational man) have had to contend with empirical inquiries into what actually motivates people and how counterintuitive acts of "other-regarding" behavior can be explained. Extreme cases of failure to act (the Kitty Genovese murder in New York in 1964)[58] and heroic activity (the rescue of Potomac river plane crash victims by Leonard Scutnik[59] and rescuers of the Jews in World War II)[60] have spawned a new field of study in social psychology—the determinants of prosocial behavior—as biologists, game theorists, and even rational-choice theorists have begun to explore explanations for both human and animal behavior that cannot be explained solely by self-interest.[61] I have reviewed this literature in some depth elsewhere[62] in an effort to ask whether empathic and altruistic motivations are possible in a profession that is structured on the basis of adversarial conceptions of "beating" the other side.

Surprisingly little of the writing on cause or public interest lawyers focuses expressly and systematically on the roots of commitment, whether psychological, political, or experiential. Here I suggest that study of prosocial behavior might usefully be applied to cause lawyering. Can we differentiate those who work for causes from those who work for money or "intellectual challenge"? Can we identify patterns of motivation and commitment?

For purposes of examining the relevance of the prosocial (principally the study of altruism) literature to an understanding of cause lawyers' motivations, several points are significant: first, at the individual level of motivation, humans seldom act from a unidimensional, single-purpose motivation. Thus, more interesting studies of human behavior are currently focused on the "mixed motives" that are more accurate explanations of our behavior.[63] Second, at both the individual and group level, efforts (particularly in the studies of gentile rescuers of Jews from the Nazis) to elaborate clear patterns of demographic or other characteristics of "helpers" have largely failed, though some patterns are more common than others.[64] Third, whatever the personality, political, or other "dispositional" factors that may be present in "helpers" or "activists," environments, situations, and circumstances are crucial and interact strongly with whatever individual motivations may be present. As an illustration, Eve Fogelman, in seeking to understand gender differences in rescuer behavior, found that capacity or willingness to engage in certain kinds of rescue behavior were related to both skill levels and opportunities. Thus, where physical strength or a particular skill was called for (e.g., swimming), the different genders were differentially equipped to engage in particular helping acts, and where children had to be rescued, stereotypic assumptions about female nurturance of children enabled women to rescue where men would or could not.[65] Fourth, and most difficult to assess in relation to cause lawyering, it is not clear whether dispositions to help, to serve people or causes, are the product of experiences (including socialization and learning) or psychological dispositions.[66] Must a cause lawyer have an experience of injustice or pain[67] to be strongly motivated to initiate and sustain such work or is it possible to be committed to cause lawyering with virtually no experiential connection to the human and social justice issues?[68] What implications are there here for the recruitment and retention of cause lawyers?

Scholars of "helping" behavior themselves differ on what psychological or emotional state is necessary to actualize an orientation to do "good" at the level of action and behavior. Some suggest, for example, that it is necessary for an actor to empathize with the plight of the person being helped—to understand and "feel with"[69] their situation, while others suggest that some prosocial acts are often taken without "thought" or "emotion" at all. Many rescuers of the Jews, for example, acted spontaneously and without conscious reflection of what they were doing—when asked to help, they simply did.[70] Thus, some response to a request for help may motivate prosocial behavior and may explain how some private lawyers can become responsive to requests for their participation in particular causes.

Yet it is instructive to examine the patterns revealed by studies of the extreme acts of helping behavior engaged in by rescuers. Most robust of the findings, by a number of researchers, was an identification of rescuers with a generalized humanity—"Every other person is basically you."[71] "You help people because you are human and you see a need."[72] In the words of Samuel and Pearl Oliner, rescuers had both a universalistic orientation, seeing themselves as part of humanity, and an inclusiveness orientation, experiencing the rescued as part of themselves.[73] Implicit in the study of these orientations of rescuers is a belief in the equality and reciprocity of the human condition. Rescuers acted both because they saw the reality of the person in pain as "other" and because they could imagine themselves requiring such aid. (Thus, we recognize that we are potentially equal in our needs and rights to be, and we act both from a concern for the other and a concern that we too might require aid at some point.)[74] It would be interesting to know whether cause lawyers are more likely than those who pursue more conventional careers to exhibit this "fellow feeling" and whether this fellow feeling is the result of experiences of injustice or inequalities or generalized personality orientations.[75]

In seeking to understand both the personality and situational factors that influence people to become helpers or rescuers, researchers have been able to identify some patterns that characterize and distinguish helpers from nonhelpers, but it is not clear how these characteristics operate in connection with situational instances of need and opportunity to help.[76] Rescuers of Jews were likely to come from families where discipline was explained and rationalized (a focus on explained "justice"?), where they had been responsible for some caring function (usually of siblings),[77] where they had experienced some personal suffering or loss (illness, death of a loved one) and had recovered, and most significantly, had a strong sense of self (a "centered" self)[78] and personal efficacy.[79] Eva Fogelman found that rescuers were likely to have experienced love and to seek to return it. The Oliners found that rescuers, as compared to a control group, matched for social and demographic characteristics, were more empathic and more easily moved by pain than nonrescuers. Thirty-seven percent of their rescuers were moved to their first helping act by an empathic reaction. Thus, emotional depth and ability to "take the part of the other" may be one important component of helping behavior.[80] Whether moral conscience should be based on religious, ideological, or emotional grounds, those who acted from "moral" grounds felt some reciprocity with their fellow human beings.

Researchers focused on understanding "helping" or "altruistic" behavior have been divided by those who have tried to analyze the demographic or *predisposi*-tional factors or qualities that can help identify those who are more likely to act (most have concluded there are very few such factors)[81] and those who seek to understand the individual reasons for acting *following* the behavior. Eve Fogelman demonstrates the complexity of such analysis. She characterized her rescuers as forming five basic motivational patterns—those with strong moral codes (religiously, ideologically, or emotionally based conceptions of morality); those with strong affinity to Jews (either through love, relationship, or identification with "the other"); concerned professionals, who found helping and rescuing a part of their professional responsibilities;[82] network rescuers who became bound to others in the struggle against an abhorrent regime and engaged in interactive group support; and child rescuers, who became actively engaged in rescue behavior by following in the footsteps of powerful parental role models.[83] That there are so many varieties of characteristics and motivational patterns for rescue should not surprise us. The failure of human beings to submit to a neat taxonomy is both a tribute to the human spirit and a frustration to social science.

Exploring the motivations of rescuers from a different angle, philosophers and rational-choice theorists have sought to explain how these individuals, who rescued at great personal risk to themselves, were able to "conquer" the self-interest of self-preservation and act from a place of great personal danger. As several commentators have noted, we have trouble believing that people would act so unselfishly; thus many analysts seek to explain how the acts of rescue were both self-interested and altruistic at the same time, contributing to the focus on "mixed-motive" behavior in the recent literature. It is hard to see, however, the self-interest in cases of World War II rescuers since most acted without any visibility or any hope of reward and recognition. Indeed, severe punishment or death was the most likely result if acts of rescue were discovered.

Several philosophers, however, have explicated theories that expand our conception of such altruistic behavior with obvious relevance to the study of motivations of cause lawyers. Neera Kapur Badhwar has argued that these rescuers acted from the self-interest of "true expression of their selves."[84] Since their self-conceptions were tied to moral saving behavior, rescuing was an act of moral "self-affirmation." Since altruistic motivations were how such rescuers defined themselves, their actions were sincere expressions of their own "self"-interest.[85] Badhwar further argues that this mutuality of altruism and self-interest should cause us to consider more carefully the moral valences to be attached to both self-interest and altruism. If altruism is the "mere" expression of the self than it may or may not be a "moral" good—unless one separately analyzes consequences of such acts. Conversely, if "altruism" is the expression of self-interest in the form of self-affirmation, then the expression of self through the good acts of altruism, in this sense, may be a moral good. Should cause lawyers be considered any more "moral" than noncause lawyers (whatever that might be)[86] if the only reason they became lawyers was to seek social change and thereby "express themselves"[87] in that way?

On another level, William Galston has identified varieties of altruistic behaviors that also demonstrate the different ways of expressing "good" behavior. For example, "cosmopolitan" altruism, of the sort expressed by the rescuers, focuses on the assistance of needy strangers— action directed toward "the human race as a whole."[88] Such recognition of a variety of types of altruism (cosmopolitan altruism, as distinguished from personal or communal or kin[89] altruism) demonstrates that altruism and self-interest exist on a behavioral continuum, not as polarized opposites. Those who saved Jews often did so at great risk to and over the objections of their families, in what Galston calls the "negation of particularistic obligations and the attenuation of special emotional ties" for attachment to the greater community.[90] Ironically, in order to do what they did, rescuers often had to ignore or refuse what others told them to do—so the decision to act on behalf of some necessarily conflicted with the needs and interests of others, often those closest to the actors.

Other forms of mixed-motive altruism include acts of care or helping at some cost to the actor, but with some benefit as well. Is the student who tutors in the inner city to be considered less "good" because he also knows that an entry on his resumé about his activities is likely to help him in the job market or in getting into graduate school?[91] Do cause lawyers who achieve fame and psychic reward "gain" by their activity and lose their claim to be altruistically motivated? If they are "coopted" by increased prestige or fame, have they lost their claims to "moral superiority"?

We also know from these studies and other contexts that helping or altruistic behavior is often situational—thus, some situations may produce helping responses in some actors and not in others.[92] Helping motivations may change over time as well. Any viewer of *Schindler's List* can observe what many rescuers describe as a growing commitment to a cause once engaged in it, irrespective of its success.[93]

As such, the complex factors that interact to produce those who are motivated to work for or help others include a mix of biological[94] and familial predispositions, social characteristics and personal traits, life experiences,[95] personality attributes, social statuses, moral, religious, or ideological value systems, and situational opportunities or settings for expression of such values or attributes.[96] This more complete, yet complex, understanding of altruistic motivations, then, should aid investigation of how cause lawyers are inspired to work for the "good."

The Motivations of Cause Lawyers

While cause lawyers would seem to provide as fertile a ground for study of prosocial behavior as rescuers (and indeed, are a less extreme sample), little work has actually focused directly on the question of motivation to engage in cause lawyering. Most vivid are personal stories told through the memoirs or biographies of noted legal activists[97] or the more fictional treatments in the novels of inspirational lawyers, like Harper Lee's *To Kill a Mockingbird*. This section analyzes altruistic motivations as applied to the cause lawyer, from the little data we have available.

Some would date the origins of cause lawyering to legal activism in the abolitionist movement, in efforts to redefine slave law;[98] others to the work of lawyers in the Progressive era who sought legal regulation and increased court involvement in a host of social issues, such as child welfare, labor, work and health safety standards, trade, and education.[99]

Reginald Heber Smith's study of the inadequate representation of some segments of the population[100] at the turn of the century led the American Bar Association to begin to support local legal aid efforts supported by charitable contributions and time donated by private attorneys. Eventually some legal aid programs became sufficiently supported to maintain small, but regular, staffs (often consisting of women or minority attorneys who could not find employment in more conventional private practices).[101] Reginald Heber Smith's name was eventually chosen to serve as an inspirational source of status and some financial support for a committed group of legal services activists in the 1960s and 1970s.[102]

To some, the "New Dealers" were cause lawyers, committed to the legal-realist-inspired beliefs in rationalized and social scientific reform of the state by administrative regulation and substantive expertise.[103] These lawyers were clearly committed to a cause—did they engage in altruistic or empathic lawyering? Must a cause lawyer give something up to be so classified? Was the permanent or temporary removal from a lucrative private law practice to serve in government the work of a cause lawyer? Note that Louis Brandeis, for example, combined a commitment to regulation as a cause with a lucrative practice, the only risk of which was a challenge to his ethics that almost cost him a seat on the U.S. Supreme Court.[104]

Still other sources of cause lawyers date from government efforts to silence radical members of the Communist Party or other dissident or unpopular groups, starting with labor in the nineteenth century[105] to the Yippies of the 1960s.[106] The American Civil Liberties Union was founded to raise First Amendment defenses for social protestors and pacifists during World War I and was among the first legal organizations to employ "nonlegal" means in the form of grassroots organizing and demonstrations to raise public consciousness about issues and to create "test" cases for litigation purposes.[107] As Robert Coles[108] and others have chronicled,[109] hundreds of law students and lawyers were motivated by the civil rights movement to move to the South in the early 1960s to engage in a range of legal battles including desegregation of public facilities, schools, and voter registration drives in one of the first concerted "mass" movements of altruistic professionals.

The social and political activism of the 1960s, fueled by the civil rights movement, the antiwar (Vietnam) movement, the antipoverty movement,[110] and the feminist movement, produced a variety of legal strategies and law reform organizations designed to challenge existing laws and practices and to urge the development of new rules and principles through legal action. The success of many of the new "public interest" law firms led to the founding of a variety of new organizations, some associated with particular *issues*[111] like environmentalism (e.g., Natural Resources Defense Council), free speech and consumer rights, and others with the growing development of *"identity" politics* (e.g., Mexican American Legal Defense Fund, Women's Legal Defense Fund, and Lamda Defense Fund), most often patterned on the highly successful National Association for the Advancement of Colored People Legal Defense Fund (now the LDF).

Although the glory days of law reform seem at the moment to be over (as defined by victories in the Supreme Court), in fact, new causes and interest groups spawned by highly committed and motivated students continue to be founded and increasingly explore strategies beyond traditional litigation.[112] Many organizations have banded together in either loose consortiums (e.g., the Alliance for Justice in Washington and Women's Way in Philadelphia) for fund-raising, lobbying, and legal strategy development or more formal consortiums of multi-issue public interest work (e.g., the former Center for Law and Social Policy and the Institute for Public Representation at Georgetown). Thus, while legal victories and financial support may be ebbing, law students and committed lawyers continue to develop desires and strategies to form new organizations and new outlets for the expression of their social justice goals.

The limited research that exists on the motivations of public interest lawyers has been narrowly focused on demographic and social factors, believed by some to be strong indicators of commitment. Not surprisingly, like the effort to isolate patterns of social and demographic indicators of rescuers, this research has largely been unproductive, or at least unable to predict with any degree of reliability who will become a cause lawyer and who will remain one. Researchers such as Er-langer,[113] Ladinsky,[114] and Handler[115] have all found that lawyers entering legal services, for example, were as heterogeneous as all lawyers entering practice.

In her study of women lawyers, Cynthia Fuchs Epstein found that women law students, in the 1960s, like their male counterparts, were likely to come from professional homes and were slightly more likely to come from homes where both mothers and fathers worked.[116] In attempting to assess whether motivations to study law or enter particular forms of practice were gendered, Epstein concludes that there is much stereotyping of claimed motivations and little empirical support for actual differences in motivation. She argues that often law schools thought that women had more of a "social reformer" or "do-gooder" approach to law study, which served to exclude women from law study where admissions officers thought women were too fragile to survive in the competitive law school and business law world. Yet in her own interviews of women lawyers, Epstein found that women expressed similar reasons and similar "motivating factors" to engage in public interest law (such as having read a biography of Clarence Darrow)[117] as did men. She does, however, acknowledge that while there may have been some channeling of women to what they were thought to be good at (social work and family law), women did have "an underdog's sympathy for humanitarian causes."[118] Whether women (and other "subordinated") groups are more or less likely to identify with or develop empathic reactions to other subordinated people remains a highly contestable issue.[119] More recent studies are divided on the issue of whether women articulate different motives for attending law school and are more likely to express commitments to social justice than men.[120]

In my own research on feminist cause lawyers one finds a mixed pattern. Some interviewed speak of early commitments to women's causes and see them-selves as continuing the tradition of activist lawyers of the nineteenth century who fought for suffrage and women's rights.[121] Women who were disproportionately represented in early representation of the poor and many modern feminist law-yers, like Sylvia Law, continued this path, while radicalizing and professionalizing it.[122] Other modern feminist lawyers describe their commitments to cause lawyer-ing as being effected by their inability to get jobs in more conventional law firms. Both Ruth Bader Ginsburg and Sandra Day O'Connor tell similar stories of their being directed to secretarial positions after graduating from law school. Justice Ginsburg became one of the leading feminist advocates of test cases before the Supreme Court before becoming an academic, and Justice O'Connor served as a legislator as well as a state court judge, seeking the approval of the electorate, where approval of male peers may have been initially difficult. A founder of one of the leading feminist cause-lawyering programs, the National Women's Law Center, reports that after serving briefly in a law firm, she took up her life's work for women's causes at the suggestion of others because there were inadequate outlets for other public interest work. Like many other activists she was initially affected by identification with other nonprofessional women in the workplace.[123] Women cause lawyers who work on other "public interest" causes (than women's rights) often report they began their public interest career in part because they were not permitted to rise in law firms or other government service,[124] suggesting that career paths can often have external, negative influences, as well as positive attractions. Still, these women did not lose their motivation to pursue legal work, and public interest legal work at that, rather than give up and go home.

Studies that have explicitly focused on the motivations of cause lawyers, however, are surprisingly rare. Though there is a spirited debate about what is included in cause lawyering—whether work from within the state counts, whether individual client representation matters as much as cause representation[125]—few have inquired directly to ask cause lawyers why they do what they do and what they consider to be the goals of their work. In assessing how law school socialization coopts public interest orientations, Robert Stover found that one-third of the entering first-year class at the University of Denver Law School initially expressed altruistic goals (defined as a desire to use one's position as an attorney to help others and to work for social and political change) with respect to what they wanted to do with their legal careers, but this figure was decreased by half by the end of law school.[126] Stover's public-interest-minded lawyers expressed such motivations as: "I wanted to use what I know in a constructive way for the greater good";[127] have a career serving "human/humane interests";[128] "help persons or groups with whom you identify or sympathize";[129] and, "use my skills for the advancement of women."[130] Stover found that these altruistic expressions were eroded during law school (through lack of reinforcement, he suggests) and replaced by craft interests in "doing legally challenging and complex work" as students gained a more "realistic" assessment of what job opportunities were available in the competing private practice spheres. Interestingly, Stover suggests that those who were successful in maintaining their public interest commitment were able to do so by forming support groups and immersing themselves in a public interest "subculture" in response to the dominant culture of law school, perhaps demonstrating the importance of the "network" in maintaining altruistic actions and motivations.[131]

In my own empirical research on legal services attorneys in the late 1970s and early 1980s, we asked lawyers explicitly what motivated them to work in the poverty law area, with low salaries, crushing caseloads, an increasingly hostile political environment, and an increasing bureaucratization of practice organization. The cohort of lawyers we studied (in two separate programs, one urban, one rural, in

California) came of legal age in the 1960s and 1970s and were expressly political in their motivations for joining such a practice. For example, many of these lawyers, particularly those who came from the rural program with its emphasis on farm-worker organizing, were themselves former members of client constituencies. Several attorneys had parents who had worked in the fields and were mistreated by growers. Thus, as one lawyer put it, they were moved from an experiential base to "do something for my people. I suffered discrimination myself. People who were poor have been the basis of my life experience. . . . Now I know that nobody can communicate better with my people than I can, than other Raza lawyers can. I want to educate my people, show them how the system works, to show them how they can change the system, to show them what power really is and how to exercise the wise use of power." [132]

Yet motivations to do poverty lawyering are as varied as rescuer motivations. While in the legal context some lawyers stress causes and system change, just as many focus on individual human helping acts: "I have a real strong desire to see a person not get stepped on—I guess based on my religion." Or from another legal services lawyer: "I don't know whether you could call me a progressive. . . . My concerns are people-oriented. . . . My concern is that the political environment in which we live take into consideration poor people, and people in general. . . . Humanism and those kinds of things . . . I don't think that capitalism is bad per se, I just think there are some bad parts to it."

Criminal defense lawyer Charles Ogletree reports a strong identification with a high school classmate, who though talented in school and athletics, wound up on death row, and a sister in law enforcement who was murdered while she slept. He continues to see his job as service to the indigent criminal defendant, as he seeks to inspire others to do the same. [133] Thus, personal connections to those who need "legal help" and "remembering where I came from" often motivate those who struggle at both the individual and institutional level of legal change and representation.

Not unlike rescuers, some cause lawyers feel that they *have* to do what they do—it is both an expression of their self and a moral imperative. As one lawyer expressed it: "If there was no poverty I would not be here, because I would rather be out of doors and you know . . . outside, doing things. . . . I kind of feel like I *have* to do this . . . maybe it is a guilt thing. I have been lucky in life and I felt like you know I owed [it] to people, to pay it back to them. This drives me a lot."

People who choose law to actualize "helping" behavior have made other choices as well. Among the more politically or ideologically committed, legal advocacy is still work within the system. As one lawyer said: "I chose law, not bombings and going underground." At the same time, cause lawyering remains within the legal arena and is "help" removed from the most direct and intimate forms of human helping, such as social work, education, nursing, or medicine. Legal help is more often commitment to abstract principles or symbols, as well as people, and thus may constitute yet another form of altruism, beyond cosmopolitan altruism—perhaps we could call it "principled altruism."

The modern cause lawyer, then, is not unlike the lawyer of the "mediating" class described by Tocqueville in the nineteenth century. In addition to translating between classes, the cause lawyer seeks to work within the system, to use the law, either to change it or to hold it to its promises,[134] but retaining a more abstract commitment to symbols, regimes, and rules beyond the relief of individual pain. (Law, after all, mostly "compensates" by giving money for real pain.) In the 1980s I concluded that well-intentioned legal services lawyers, motivated from both political and humanitarian concerns, were constrained in the context in which their altruism was expressed—the institutionalization and funding problems of legal services tamed politically radical lawyers and frustrated individual-case service lawyers. Thus, altruistic motives are not enough—the situational and social structural aspects of lawyering work do influence who will be able to express their impulses to make the world a better place and how they will be able to do so.

In my interviews of feminist cause lawyers a slightly different motivational pattern emerges. While most founders of feminist legal organizations are committed to feminist causes and have indeed experienced the harms of the groups they are trying to help (illegal abortions, employment discrimination, family law problems, domestic violence), for most of the "founding" generation, women's advocacy began when these women were excluded from the core legal work of civil rights lawyering (i.e., important "trials") or when they were asked to help a client who saw their civil rights expertise as relevant. For example, one founder began her work because the secretaries at a noted public interest law firm asked her to take on women's issues, suggesting the "push-pull" effects of occupational choice for women.[135] For many advocates of women's legal issues there was little law to match the cause. Thus, like the first generation of civil rights lawyers and poverty lawyers, feminist advocates had to match their cause to the existing categories of law in order to both change the law and alleviate individual pain.[136] Women's rights advocates attempted to change rape law, create new legally cognizable categories in sexual harassment and pornography,[137] obtain legal recognition and punishment of domestic abuse, and alter decades of regulations on reproduction. This was not always easy, and women advocates, like other cause lawyers, are now exploring the sacrifice of individual lives to "greater" causes.[138] Yet while the social research fails to conclusively establish gender differences in empathy[139] and altruistic motives, the women cause lawyers I interviewed virtually always told a story of a particular individual they helped or how the "quality of women's lives" was improved by some legal strategy—thus women did seem more likely to "personalize, and humanize" their tales of commitment to cause lawyering.[140]

Thus, we know remarkably little about what actually makes lawyers commit themselves to particular causes, particular people, or particular issues and what makes some altruistic-minded people choose law[141] as their preferred occupation for expressing such interests. The little we know should offer some inspiration to others to study these issues more systematically. As in other fields of work, it might be useful to chart the generational goals and differences in motivations of those who have come to cause lawyering.[142] Other factors to consider include historical events (e.g., what galvanized the civil rights and antiwar movements or AIDS activism) and the more "negative" motivational factors (e.g., righteous indignation or anger at evildoers or victimizers).

Commitment to Cause Lawyering: Issues in the Creation and Sustenance of Motivation

As individuals who have chosen legal careers from which to express their commitment to social change and helping, cause lawyers currently suffer from a variety of discouraging forces. While not overcome by the total judicial hostility of the pre-*Brown* years, nor by the total absence of resources with which NAACP lawyers had to do their work,[143] for many cause lawyers these are not easy times. What do such lawyers do to keep the commitment fires burning, particularly as they age and need both more income to support children and parents and less stressful lives to preserve their own health? Here I identify some tensions or impediments for maintaining commitment and motivation and report on adaptations that committed cause lawyers have made.

First, the legal context has clearly changed for most causes. A decade of Republican appointments to courts have caused most public interest lawyers to revamp their legal strategies. For those who sought reward and satisfaction in high court victories, the 1980s were a decade of trying to avoid the Supreme Court. Many issues are now more complex and less obviously framed to benefit all disadvantaged people. For example, has the Due Process revolution helped poor people gain greater access to courts and substantive entitlements like welfare and health benefits or have new lines of legality, regulation, and the bureaucratic state impeded access to real goods and services? Recently, in commenting on her own long career of public service as a public interest lawyer and a judge, Patricia Wald spoke of the importance of being a realistic "causist" lawyer.[144] Judge Wald has focused on the importance of recognizing that disadvantaged groups often compete for limited resources in the lawsuits that they bring, especially against the state. She has suggested that lawyers more realistically assess the costs and likely consequences of litigation as the most efficacious means of effecting change. She also suggests that a career of public interest work must be considered over the long haul and not simply for quick short-term victories. Two of her own major test cases continue to be litigated ten and twenty years after initial filing, in the very courts in which she now sits as a judge.

The complexities of competing "needy" populations is demonstrated in the more recent mass tort litigation. As plaintiffs' personal injury lawyers (many of them former legal services attorneys) attempt to gain compensation for asbestos-injured workers, they are often pitted against the strategic use of bankruptcy, which also hurts present workers. Thus, deserving people are pitted against each other while corporate America continues to demonstrate how the "rich get richer."

Second, and a related aspect of the more complex legal environment for cause lawyering, is the increasing dissension or difference within disadvantaged groups seeking cause representation—women battle with women over abortion and pregnancy treatment rights, residents of public housing do legal battle with each other over drug-related evictions and police searches for weapons, and gays face an electorate that thinks they don't deserve "special" rights. Each of these tensions draws sharp cleavages in the civil rights community. While "rainbow coalitions" make good campaign- and community-organizing rhetoric, the reality is that often "have-not" groups compete with one another over limited social services, jobs, tax revenues, and human relations.[145]

Third, causes seem highly susceptible to manipulation by those outside of the legal community. While most feminist activists applauded the increased recognition of sexual harassment after the Clarence Thomas hearings and domestic violence after the Nicole Simpson murder, the media has constructed the salience of these issues with public figures and often distort the reality and more difficult legal issues implicated in dealing with these causes. Though sexual harassment claims appear to have increased after Anita Hill courageously went public, it is not clear that public hearings are the best way to deal with these issues.[146]

Fourth, in dramatic ways the work environment has changed with increased bureaucratization and less autonomy, even in the most change-oriented public interest practices. The first generation may have struggled with few resources, but they were easily gathered for strategy meetings and direct involvement with clients. The increased hierarchy of some successful public interest organizations has resulted in the same job dissatisfaction and frustration that exists in many conventional legal organizations. Although there is evidence that some highly motivated, committed workers seek satisfaction in the intrinsic value of what they do[147] and not money or prestige, others seek more autonomy, authority, salary, or freedom in their jobs. The need to structure "careers" in law does not leave cause lawyers immune from their own forms of "climbing the ladder."

Most ironic is the natural cooptation of working as a social change agent within legal institutions. In creating legal arguments, lawyers legitimize at least some aspects of the system, and the kinds of legal arguments and reasoning that they employ often cut them off from more imaginative ways of solving problems. By its method of reliance on principle and precedent, the legal system demands that cause lawyers assimilate their claims to already existing frameworks, only occasionally ruptured by the creation of new causes of action or legal theories. In part due to their success, many causes are now represented by relatively well-funded private and public donations and have graduated to established lobbying and interest groups. (Is it a good thing for social change that the NAACP, the

Children's Legal Defense Fund, the Women's Legal Defense Fund, and the Sierra Club are now included in legislative hearings and administrative regulatory proceedings?)[148]

Sadly, cause lawyering may have sown the seeds of some of its own difficulties—with interest and litigation groups drawn on "identity" politics lines, it becomes increasingly difficult to develop the sort of "cross-class collaborations" intended by some of the early architects of economic cause lawyering.[149]

Some cause lawyers doubt their own efficacy. Are there variations in the successes, both in terms of legal change and social impact, of different cause lawyers and the different causes for which they work?[150]

So—how do cause lawyers sustain their commitment? Despite the troubles outlined above, there are more absolute numbers of cause lawyers than ever before. Year after year law students complain that they cannot find jobs in the public interest sector.[151] The best news is that one of the most robust findings of the limited motivational literature is that lawyers, once committed to public interest concerns are often committed for life. In my study of legal services lawyers, I found that even when demoralized attorneys leave legal services practice, they are less likely than law students to move to private corporate practices. Often they seek to develop small or solo practices that develop a mix of cause and personal injury or domestic relations fee-generating cases.[152] Some seek to continue to do personal service work in new practice areas—such as prepaid insurance plans or legal clinics.

Most interestingly, many have reconstructed what we consider to be cause lawyering. As former legal services lawyers take on claims of injured workers or consumers and challenge toxic dumps or defective products, they have styled themselves as "policers of the corporate state." Thus, from both the individual and class action cases that they bring, these lawyers view themselves as monitoring the harms that corporate America produces, seeking through their legal work individual compensation, public exposure, and restructured regulatory and remedial schemes to police what the formal state will not. In one sense this is a creative and more direct attack on the causes of inequality and "evil" than exists in many forms of cause lawyering. Hampered by regulations and resource problems, earlier legal services lawyers, for example, were more likely to bring lawsuits against a set of limited government agencies than private corporations. The "new" cause lawyers have taken on private corporate interests more directly and can, where they are very successful, finance their own work with attorneys' fees that liberate them from the limitations of prescribed and regulated advocacy.[153] Increasingly, public interest lawyers have moved into other spheres—legislative advocacy, local government, traditional electoral politics—all while preserving many of the same commitments to social change and human caring that motivated them in the first place. While I am not entirely convinced, some like Robert Gordon and Anthony Kronman argue that even corporate lawyers are subject to their calling as "civic republicans" to do good and contribute to public accountability.[154] Thus, we are returned to the questions of boundaries—what is a cause, and what legal work qualifies to be considered cause lawyering?

If those who are motivated to help others or to "do good" are to be formed, encouraged, and sustained, we must uncover both the attributes and experiences that reinforce whatever those predispositions might be. We know that some stood by as Jews were carried off and murdered, as Kitty Genovese was killed, and as thousands have been killed in recent years in Eastern Europe and Africa. Most lawyers go off to seek personal gain in their salaries, relatively high social status, and intellectually interesting work. But we also know that some people saved Jews and several jumped into freezing water to pull out airplane crash victims, just as some lawyers choose to make less money to work for the "greater good," however they define it. Samuel Oliner began the rescuer study with his wife, Pearl Oliner, in part, in order to rehabilitate his belief in human goodness after his own Holocaust experience had caused him to witness the most horrific human atrocities. I undertook this project to help further our understanding of what motivates us to do good with what we have and how can we make more "fellow feeling" in the world.

Social psychologists, legal scholars, lawyers, and educators have offered us some useful prescriptions for building and preserving social commitments. Rational, not physical, discipline, lots of love, role modeling and demonstrations of altruistic acts, reward for doing good, empathy training, and "turn-taking,"[155] as well as responsibility for others and some experience of loss survived are all themes in the literature, both of what motivates "other"-directed behavior and what sustains it. As at least one writer has argued, one of the values of mandatory pro bono requirements in law school is to explicitly teach a "morality of professional service" that includes unpaid legal work and provides the experiential base from which such lawyering work will be seen as the norm rather than the exception.[156] We also know that lawyers need to think they are efficacious, whether in the winning of lawsuits, drafting of legislation, or "writing the record of future history."[157] It is on this level that cause lawyers get into trouble, for if it is "people we represent, not ideas,"[158] then we will have to measure effectiveness by saving single souls, as well as ideas, and we will have to understand what we can do to make lawyers, and all people, care enough about their fellow human beings to want to "lawyer for the good."

Appendix

Inventory of Questions Defining Cause Lawyering

1. What is the cause? (Goals/objectives of the legal activity)

2. Who has determined the goals?
   lawyers
   individual clients

    client groups
    social movements
    external forces
    the state
    other causes (e.g., abortion, environment)

3. How is the cause-lawyering work conducted? What activities/practices constitute it?
    litigation
    legislation
    social movement advocacy/demonstrations
    political action
    formal bar association activity
    community organizing

4. Who is the (is there a) client? Are conventional professional norms and models employed? Nonclient causes?

5. How is the work financially supported?
    fees-private, statutory
    governmental/public support
    private (nonclient support)—foundations, charitable contributions

6. What is the relationship of the legal cause work to social movement/social
   justice issues?
    political struggles—challenges to the state or a social organization
    relation to mainstream political power (e.g., voting rights)

7. In what political/legal regime is the cause work located?
    organization and structure of the state:
       democratic-capitalist
       socialist
       authoritarian-military, fascist
    legal system:
       civil
       common
       constitutional/process orientation rules
    divided or unitary bar
         (barrister/solicitor split)
       role of notaries and other legal functionaries
       judicial structure
          career, special training, class
          elected, relation to political sphere

8. How "law-infused" is the work?

"legal rights" strategies

social protest movement/community organizing

social work—individual "helping" orientation (therapeutic, "needs"-based)

problem-solving (legal and social, mediative)

locus of work in legal or nonlegal locales

9. How efficacious is the cause lawyering—what has it accomplished?

rule changes

political organizing

redistribution of wealth/power

dignity/equality

social practices changes (i.e., custody to gays, singles)

reorganizations (of workplaces, governmental entities, private organizations)

removal of harms (toxic substances, medical practices)

education/consciousness raising—particular social action groups/general public

10. What institutionalization of the cause and lawyering has occurred/is possible?

individual level vs. organizational or cause level

recruitment

retention

motivation

Notes

1. See, e.g., Eva Fogelman, *Conscience and Courage: Rescuers of the Jews during the Holocaust* (New York: Anchor Books, 1994); Kristen R. Monroe, Michael C. Barton, and Ute Klingeman, "Altruism and the Theory of Rational Action: Rescuers of Jews in Nazi Europe," *Ethics* 101 (1990), 103–122; and Samuel P. Oliner and Pearl Oliner, *The Altruistic Personality: Rescuers of Jews in Nazi Europe* (New York: Free Press, 1988).

2. See, e.g., Jane J. Mansbridge, ed., *Beyond Self Interest* (Chicago: University of Chicago Press, 1990).

3. Fogelman, *Conscience and Courage*, xv.

4. Howard Lesnick, "Why Pro Bono in Law Schools," *Law and Inequality* 13 (1994), 25–38.

5. Actually, as befits the scholarly tradition of the Talmud, the criteria for being honored at Yad Vashem are far from simple and have led to spirited debates and definitional disputes. See Fogelman, *Conscience and Courage*, 11–16.

6. Carrie Menkel-Meadow, "Is Altruism Possible in Lawyering?," *Georgia State University Law Review* 8 (1992), 385–419; and Carrie J. Menkel-Meadow, "The Power of Narrative in Empathetic Learning: Post-Modernism and the Stories of Law," *UCLA Women's Law Journal* 2 (1992), 287–307 (reviewing Patricia J. Williams, *The Alchemy of Race* [1990]).

7. I began by calling this "good lawyering" in the philosophical sense intended by David Luban and others. See David Luban, ed., *The Good Lawyer: Lawyers' Roles and Lawyers' Ethics* (Totawa, N.J.: Rowman & Allanheld, 1983); and David Luban, *Lawyers and Justice: An Ethical Study* (Princeton: Princeton University Press, 1988), exploring both the ends and means of lawyering in service of "justice." But this phrase is too often confused with "good" lawyering in the quality sense of craft—"good" lawyering acquits a guilty defendant, or strategic maneuvers enable a corporate wrong-doer to accomplish its ends. Thus, with all of the difficulties of definition of "cause lawyering" or social justice lawyering explored more fully in the text, I prefer to use the phrase "lawyering for the good"—this remains problematic in its seeming focus on ends only (however contested those might be). I intend to include means in "lawyering for the good" too.

8. Am I right to think that process has always been a woman reformer's concern— that Emma Goldman, among others, reminded us, that we had to think about *how* we made the revolution.

9. The study of public interest lawyers has long circled around this question of empirical assessment of the effects of public interest lawyering. See Burton A. Weisbrod, Joel F. Handler, and Neil Komesar, *Public Interest Law: An Economic and Institutional Analysis* (Berkeley: University of California Press, 1978); Joel F. Handler, *Social Movements and the Legal System: A Theory of Law Reform and Social Change* (New York: Academic Press, 1978); and Anita P. Arriola and Sidney M. Wolinsky, "Public Interest Practice in Practice: The Law and Reality," *Hastings Law Journal* 34 (1983), 1207–1229.

10. This question is often framed in the literature as whether law school socialization "changes" do-gooders into greedy cogs in the legal corporate machine. See, e.g., Robert V. Stover, *Making It and Breaking It: The Fate of Public Interest Commitment during Law School,* ed. Howard S. Erlanger (Urbana: University of Illinois Press, 1989). Do market and economic (supply-and-demand) forces affect the prosocial activity of lawyers—were the 1980s different for would-be social justice lawyers than the 1960s and 1970s?

11. Carrie Menkel-Meadow and Robert Meadow, "Resource Allocation in Legal Services: Attorney Decisions in Work Priorities," *Law and Policy Quarterly* 5 (1983), 237–256; Robert Meadow and Carrie Menkel-Meadow, "Personalized or Bureaucratized Justice in Legal Services: Resolving Sociological Ambivalence in the Delivery of Legal Aid for the Poor," *Law and Human Behavior* 9 (1985), 397–413; Robert Meadow and Carrie Menkel-Meadow, "The Origins of Political Commitment: Social Background and Ideology Among Legal Services Attorneys," paper presented at the annual meeting of the Law and Society Association, Toronto, Canada, June 1982.

12. See Austin Sarat, "Between (the Presence of) Violence and (the Possibility of) Justice: Lawyering against Capital Punishment," Chap. 11 of this volume.

13. One advantage of revisiting this now old question in the postmodernist era is the explicit recognition that cause lawyering is socially constructed, thus changeable, with respect to the times, the actors, the issues. I find this stance compatible with my own view that causes do change and that lawyering for "the good" changes as social forces construct both new opportunities for change and new "evils" to combat. See Joel F. Handler, "Postmodernism, Protest and the New Social Movements," *Law and Society Review* 26 (1992), 697–830; and Pauline Marie Rosenau, *Post-Modernism and the Social Sciences* (Princeton, N.J.: Princeton University Press, 1992). Concretely put, the question of whether prosecution constitutes public interest lawyering has long been debated by funding sources, pro bono programs, and radical lawyers and law students. Given many of the "new" social movements, such as feminism, green politics, and environmentalism, this question is now more readily answered yes. Prosecution of rape, pollution, corporate corruption, and political

corruption are clearly considered lawyering for the good, even if individual prosecution of minor drug offenses remains more problematic. See for example, Judge Jack Weinstein's refusal to apply the sentencing guidelines to minor drug offenders as an act of judicial civil disobedience, in Gary Panter, "Benchmark," *New Yorker* (May 3, 1993), 34–36.

14. Nan Aron, *Liberty and Justice for All: Public Interest Law in the 1980s and Beyond* (Boulder, Colo.: Westview Press, 1989); and Council for Public Interest Law, *Balancing the Scales of Justice: Financing Public Interest Law in America* (Washington, D.C.: Council for Public Interest Law, 1976).

15. Gerald P. Lopez, *Rebellious Lawyering: One Chicano's Vision of Progressive Law Practice* (Boulder, Colo.: Westview Press, 1992).

16. Marlise James, *The People's Lawyers* (New York: Holt, Rinehart & Winston, 1973).

17. Robert L. Rabin, "Lawyers for Social Change: Perspectives on Public Interest Law," *Stanford Law Review* 28 (1976), 207–261.

18. Louise G. Trubek, "Critical Lawyering: Toward a New Public Interest Practice," *Boston University Public Interest Law Journal* 1 (1991), 49–56; and Ruth Buchanan and Louise G. Trubek, "Resistances and Possibilities: A Critical and Practical Look at Public Interest Lawyering," *New York University Review of Law and Social Change* 19 (1992), 687–719.

19. William H. Simon, "Visions of Practice in Legal Thought," *Stanford Law Review* 36 (1984), 469–507.

20. For a partial, not exhaustive, list of efforts to define and describe cause or public interest lawyering see, among those sources already cited here, Lois H. Johnson, "The New Public Interest Law: From Old Theories to a New Agenda," *Boston University Public Interest Law Journal* 1 (1991), 169–191; Gordon Harrison and Sanford M. Jaffe, *The Public Interest Law Firm: New Voices for New Constituencies* (New York: Ford Foundation, 1973); Jack Katz, *Poor People's Lawyers in Transition* (New Brunswick, N.J.: Rutgers University Press, 1982); Karen O'Conner and Lee Epstein, "Rebalancing the Scales of Justice: An Assessment of Public Interest Law," *Harvard Journal of Law and Public Policy* 7 (1984), 483–505; Philip G. Schrag, *Counsel for the Deceived* (New York: Pantheon Books, 1972); Stuart A. Scheingold, *The Politics of Rights: Lawyers, Public Policy and Political Change* (New Haven: Yale University Press, 1974); Elizabeth M. Schneider, "The Dialectic of Rights and Politics: Perspectives from the Women's Movement," *New York University Law Review* 61 (1986), 589–652; Gerald A. Rosenberg, *The Hollow Hope: Can Courts Bring about Social Change?* (Chicago: University of Chicago Press, 1991); Mark Kessler, *Legal Services for the Poor* (New York: Greenwood Press, 1987); Richard Kluger, *Simple Justice* (New York: Knopf, 1975); Jonathan D. Casper, *Lawyers before the Warren Court: Civil Liberties and Civil Rights* (Urbana: University of Illinois Press, 1972); and Patricia M. Wald, "Whose Public Interest Is It Anyway? Advice for Altruistic Young Lawyers," *Maine Law Review* 47 (1995), 3–33. For the broadest possible definition see recent law school definitions of public interest lawyering as consisting of any work for nonprofit organizations or government in Lesnick, "Why Pro Bono in Law Schools," or nonlaw firm and noncorporate "public service work" as defined by the Public Interest Law Scholars Program (PILS), Georgetown University Law Center. This does not include the rich literature of biographies of public interest, civil rights, and radical lawyers, such as Arthur Kinoy and Thurgood Marshall.

21. For an interesting taxonomy of progressive lawyers as dedicated to traditional, redemptive, or civic humanitarian values, see Peter Margulies, "Progressive Lawyering and Lost Traditions," *Texas Law Review* 73 (1995), 1139–1183.

22. Especially when they define themselves as "policers of the harms caused by the rapacious entrepreneurial activity of the modern industrial age," as one such firm defined itself in its brochure.

23. A cause organization devoted to the defeat of unionization and labor-protective legislation.

24. An organization mobilized to defeat environmental regulation and litigation that limit development of land and mineral resources, funded by real estate developers and the oil and gas industry.

25. This is both a philosophical and political issue and a practical one. As both law firms and the organized bar increasingly impose pro bono requirements on their members, what qualifies as a "pro bono" ("for the good" cause) activity must be defined and is often the source of contested debate. "Symposium on Mandatory Pro Bono," *Hofstra Law Review* 19 (1991), 739–1270; and "Minnesota Symposium: Legal Education and Pro Bono," *Law and Inequality* 13 (1995), 1–98.

26. In a recent profile, criminal defender and Harvard law professor Charles Ogletree noted that winning as a public defender was becoming harder to justify as he increasingly recognizes "that the victims and the criminals so closely resemble each other. They are both black and poor. . . . When victims become indistinguishable from clients, I become very introspective about what I am doing in the process, very self-critical about the role lawyers play." Sara Lawrence-Lightfoot, *I've Known Rivers: Lives of Loss and Liberation* (Reading, Mass.: Addison-Wesley, 1994), 130.

27. One troubling way to consider these issues is when the cause is raised in other than "typical" ways—claims of sexual harassment by men for example—see Michael Crichton's novel, *Disclosure: A Novel* (New York: Knopf, 1993)—or when causes (in the form of real people) compete with one another, such as when public housing residents demand the summary eviction of drug dealers from public housing. For one of the classic illustrations of the inherent conflicts in reconciling people's conflicting desires with causes, see Derrick A. Bell, "Serving Two Masters: Integration Ideals and Client Interests in School Desegregation Litigation," *Yale Law Journal* 85 (1976), 470–516.

28. Ronen Shamir and Sara Chinski, "Destruction of Houses and Construction of a Cause: Lawyers and Bedouins in the Israeli Courts," chap. 8 in this volume.

29. For an interesting story of how one radical lawyer, William Kunstler, lost a criminal case by appealing to general injustice and failing to "investigate" and argue the particular facts, see Steven Phillips, *No Heroes, No Villains: The Story of a Murder Trial* (New York: Random House, 1977).

30. See, e.g., Peter Gabel, "The Phenomenology of Rights: Consciousness and the Pact of the Withdrawn Selves," *Texas Law Review* 61 (1984), 1563–1599; Mark V. Tushnet, "Truth, Justice and the American Way: An Interpretation of Public Law Scholarship in the Seventies," *Texas Law Review* 57 (1979), 1307–1359; Mark V. Tushnet, "Critical Legal Studies and Constitutional Law: An Essay in Deconstruction," *Stanford Law Review* 36 (1984), 623–647; and Alan David Freeman, "Legitimizing Racial Discrimination through Anti-Discrimination Law: A Critical Review of Supreme Court Doctrine," *Minnesota Law Review* 62 (1978), 1049–1119.

31. Susan Sterett, "Caring about Individual Cases: Immigration Lawyering in Britain," chap. 10 of this volume. On the effects of law reform lawsuits on individual lives see Norma McCorvey, *I Am Roe: My Life, Roe v. Wade and Freedom of Choice* (New York: Harper Collins, 1994); Sarah Ragle Weddington, *A Question of Choice* (New York: Putnam's, 1992); and Peter H. Irons, *The Courage of Their Convictions: Sixteen Americans Who Fought Their Way to the Supreme Court* (New York: Free Press, 1988).

32. Richard Abel, "Speaking Law to Power: Occasions for Cause Lawyering," chap. 3 of this volume.

33. Paul R. Tremblay, "Toward a Community-Based Ethic for Legal Services Practice," *UCLA Law Review* 37 (1990), 1101–1156; Stephen Ellmann, "Client-Centeredness Multiplied:

Individual Autonomy and Collective Mobilization in Public Interest Lawyers' Representation of Groups," *Virginia Law Review* 78 (1992), 1103–1173.

34. Like the individual service–law reform dichotomy in public interest work, the tensions of who determines the goals of representation—lawyer "political or professional judgment" versus client self-determination—remain the unsolved "old chestnuts" of our inquiry. For some other expressions of these tensions, see the attempt to separate means-objectives decisions in the formal rules of ethics for American lawyers, Model Code of Professional Responsibility, Ethical Consideration 7-7 (1969), and Model Rules of Professional Conduct, Rule 1.2 (1983). In one sense this debate has framed much of clinical education in the United States, see, e.g., Gary Bellow, "Turning Solutions into Problems," *NLADA Briefcase* 34 (1977), 106–125; Gary Bellow, "On Teaching the Teachers: Some Preliminary Reflections on Clinical Education as Methodology," in *Clinical Education for the Law Student,* ed., Council for Legal Education for Professional Responsibility (New York: Council for Legal Education for Professional Responsibility, 1973); and David A. Binder and Susan C. Price, *Legal Interviewing and Counseling: A Client-Centered Approach* (St. Paul, Minn.: West Publishing, 1977). These originators of clinical legal education have employed widely disparate approaches to political cause vs. "client-centered" lawyering. In clinical education circles this debate is often framed as the "client service" vs. "educational mission" tension: see James H. Stark, Jon Bauer, and James Papillo, "Directiveness in Clinical Supervision," *Boston University Public Interest Law Journal* 3 (1993), 41–140. For differences in goals about the purposes of clinical education as a political activity see, e.g., Carrie J. Menkel-Meadow, "The Legacy of Clinical Education: Theories about Lawyering," *Cleveland State Law Review* 29 (1980), 555–574.

35. Questions of who should control the legal work and make decisions about it, of course, are not limited to cause lawyering. There is a vast literature on lawyer-client decision making, see, e.g., William H. Simon, "Ethical Discretion in Lawyering," *Harvard Law Review* 101 (1988), 1083–1145; Mark Spiegel, "Lawyering and Client Decisionmaking: Informed Consent and the Legal Profession," *University of Pennsylvania Law Review* 128 (1979), 41–140; Douglas E. Rosenthal, *Lawyer and Client: Who's in Charge* (New York: Russell Sage Foundation, 1974); and William H. Simon, "Lawyer Advice and Client Autonomy: Mrs. Jones's Case," *Maryland Law Review* 50 (1991), 213–226.

36. The phrase is Warren Lehman's, "In Pursuit of a Client's Interest," *Michigan Law Review* 77 (1979), 1078–1098.

37. See, e.g., Lucie E. White, "Subordination, Rhetorical Survival Skills and Sunday Shoes: Notes on the Hearing of Mrs. G.," *Buffalo Law Review* 38 (1990), 1–58; Anthony V. Alfieri, "Reconstructive Poverty Law Practice: Learning the Lessons of Client Narrative," *Yale Law Journal* 100 (1991), 2107–2147; Phyllis Goldfarb, "A Theory-Practice Spiral: The Ethics of Feminism and Clinical Education," *Minnesota Law Review* 75 (1991), 1599–1699; and Stephen Ellman, "Lawyers and Clients," *UCLA Law Review* 34 (1987), 717–779.

38. E.g., *Goldberg v. Kelly,* 397 U.S. 254 (1970); and *Sniadach v. Family Finance Corp.,* 395 U.S. 337 (1968) (procedural due process cases). The "process" revolution came to somewhat of an "end" in *Mathews v. Eldridge,* 424 U.S. 319 (1976).

39. *Brown v. Board of Education,* 347 U.S. 483 (1954); and *Reed v. Reed,* 404 U.S. 71 (1977).

40. *Roe v. Wade,* 410 U.S. 113 (1973).

41. See, e.g., *Jefferson v. Hackney,* 406 U.S. 535 (1972); *Maher v. Roe,* 432 U.S. 464 (1977); *Bowers v. Hardwick,* 478 U.S. 186 (1986); and *Wards Cove Packing Co. v. Atonio,* 490 U.S. 642 (1989).

42. Regulations prohibited federally supported legal services lawyers from expressly lobbying. See the Legal Services Corporation Act and accompanying regulations, 42 U.S.C. §2996 et seq.; and 45 Fed. Reg. §1600 et seq.

43. This occurred principally in consumer and securities class actions that were likely to benefit the middle class.

44. See Warren Burger, "Isn't There a Better Way?," *American Bar Association Journal* 68 (1982), 274–277; Carrie J. Menkel-Meadow, "Toward Another View of Legal Negotiation: The Structure of Problem-Solving," *UCLA Law Review* 31 (1984), 754–842; Carrie J. Menkel-Meadow, "The Trouble with the Adversary System in a Post-Modern, Multi-Cultural World," *William and Mary Law Review* 38 (1996), 5–44; and Frank E. A. Sander, "Varieties of Dispute Processing," *Federal Rules Decisions* 70 (1976), 111–134.

45. See, e.g., Peter Gabel and Paul Harris, "Building Power and Breaking Images: Critical Legal Theory and the Practice of Law," *New York University Review of Law and Social Change* 11 (1983), 369–411; Lucie E. White, "Mobilization on the Margins of the Lawsuit: Making Space for Clients to Speak," *New York University Review of Law and Social Change* 16 (1987), 535–564.

46. Kimberlé Williams Crenshaw, "Race, Reform and Retrenchment: Transformation and Legitimation in Antidiscrimination Law," *Harvard Law Review* 101 (1988), 1331–1387; and Martha Fineman, *The Illusion of Equality: The Rhetoric and Reality of Divorce Reform* (Chicago: University of Chicago Press, 1990). Cf. Patricia J. Williams, *The Alchemy of Race and Rights* (Cambridge, Mass.: Harvard University Press, 1991).

47. Susan P. Sturm, "Lawyers at the Prison Gates: Organizational Structure and Corrections Advocacy," *University of Michigan Journal of Law Reform* 27 (1993), 1–129.

48. See Buchanan and Trubek, "Resistances and Possibilities"; Louise Trubek and M. Elizabeth Kransberger, "Critical Lawyers: Social Justice and the Structure of Private Practice" (chap. 7 of this volume); and Lucie E. White, "Collaborative Lawyering in the Field? On Mapping the Paths from Rhetoric to Practice," *Clinical Law Review* 1 (1994), 157–171. The classic, historical framing of legal action determined by clients is Stephen Wexler's "Practicing Law for Poor People," *Yale Law Journal* 79 (1970), 1049–1067. See also the descriptions of law practice in Lopez, *Rebellious Lawyering*.

49. E.g., the disciplining of Bob Myers as described in *California Lawyer*, the magazine of the California Bar Association.

50. See Marshall J. Breger, "Legal Aid for the Poor: A Conceptual Analysis," *North Carolina Law Review* 60 (1982), 281–363.

51. Current debates about the boundaries of legal practice occupy the bar associations and state regulators who must decide what constitutes legal practice—see debate on Model Rules of Professional Conduct, Rule 5.7 (1983); and current approaches to mediation activity, in the Joint Standards for Mediators, ABA, AAA, and the Society of Professionals in Dispute Resolution (1994).

52. See Milner S. Ball's profile of Henry Schwartzchild in *The Word and the Law* (Chicago: University of Chicago Press, 1993).

53. Note that in the Reagan-Bush years, cause lawyers were most often engaged in arguing to sustain the status quo or prevent "bad" change. Note also that the definitions of cause and public interest lawyering that use change all seem to assume "change" for the better (i.e., for more equality, empowerment, and other "left"-like reforms). There has been plenty of legal change in the last ten years, but most public interest lawyers would hardly call it good.

54. Gabel, "The Phenomenology of Rights"; Mark V. Tushnet, "An Essay on Rights," *Texas Law Review* 62 (1984), 1363–1403; Mark V. Tushnet, "The Critique of Rights," *Southern Methodist University Law Review* 47 (1993), 23–34.

55. For the gendered aspects of defining the source of legal goals as needs see Johanna Brenner, "Towards a Feminist Perspective on Welfare Reform," *Yale Journal of Law and Feminism* 2 (1989), 99–129.

56. Among the first to study acts of human compassion, empathy, and altruism were Adam Smith in *The Theory of Moral Sentiments* (Philadelphia: Anthony Finely, 1817) and Auguste Comte, who first gave altruism its name ("altrui" from the Italian for "the other"), *System of Positive Polity* (1875; New York: B. Franklin, 1968). As the cycles of scholarly interest turn, the most recent systematic study of altruism was Harvard sociologist Pitirim Sorokin's, who in the 1940s and 1950s headed an institute on "altruistic love," which he believed was the only way to reform the world. See Morton M. Hunt, *The Compassionate Beast: What Science Is Discovering about the Humane Side of Humankind* (New York: Morrow, 1990), 27.

57. Not all cause lawyers are self-sacrificing. The literature almost always assumes income and prestige deprivation, but often cause lawyers may make more money in some forms of organized cause lawyering (class actions, plaintiffs' personal injury work) and many gain fame and prestige by what they do. I have often referred to this as the stars, hearts, or dollar sign choices of lawyers playing the game of Careers (the Milton Bradley board game).

58. Hunt, *The Compassionate Beast*, 164.

59. Alfie Kohn, *The Brighter Side of Human Nature: Altruism and Empathy in Everyday Life* (New York: Basic Books, 1990).

60. Fogelman, *Conscience and Courage*.

61. See, e.g., Robert M. Axelrod, *The Evolution of Cooperation* (New York: Basic Books, 1984); Mansbridge, ed., *Beyond Self-Interest;* Herbert A. Simon, "A Mechanism for Social Selection and Successful Altruism," *Science* 250 (1991), 1665–1668; William M. Landes and Richard A. Posner, "Altruism in Law and Economics," *American Economic Review* 68 (1978), 417–421; Robert Wuthnow, *Acts of Compassion, Caring for Others and Helping Ourselves* (Princeton, N.J.: Princeton University Press, 1991); Thomas Nagel, *The Possibility of Altruism* (Oxford: Clarendon Press, 1970); Edward O. Wilson, "The Genetic Evolution of Altruism," in *Altruism, Sympathy and Helping: Psychological and Sociological Principles,* ed. Lauren Wispe (New York: Academic Press, 1978); and James Q. Wilson, *The Moral Sense* (New York: Free Press, 1993).

62. See Menkel-Meadow, "Is Altruism Possible in Lawyering?"

63. See, e.g., Jon Elster, "Selfishness and Altruism," Mansbridge, "On the Relation of Altruism and Self-Interest," and Amartya Sen, "Rational Fools: A Critique of the Behavioral Foundations of Economic Theory," in *Beyond Self-Interest,* ed. Mansbridge; and Neera Kapur Badhwar, "Altruism versus Self-Interest: Sometimes a False Dichotomy," in *Altruism,* ed. Ellen Frankel Paul, Fred Miller Jr., and Jeffrey Paul (New York: Cambridge University Press, 1993).

64. Most interesting are conflicting identifications of patterns. Fogelman, for example, did find evidence of group or "network" rescuing behavior, see *Conscience and Courage,* 203–220, as did Philip Paul Hallie in *Lest Innocent Blood Be Shed: The Story of the Village of Le Chambon and How Goodness Happened There* (New York: Harper & Row, 1979), while other students of rescuer behavior claim that most rescuers acted alone. See Monroe, Barton, and Klingeman, "Altruism and the Theory of Rational Action"; Kristin R. Monroe, "John Donne's People: Explaining Differences between Rational Actors and Altruists through Cognitive Frameworks," *Journal of Politics* 53 (1991), 394–433; and Oliner and Oliner, *The Altruistic Personality.*

65. See Fogelman, *Conscience and Courage,* 237–251, citing and relying on Kay Deaux, *The Behavior of Women and Men* (Monterey, Calif.: Brooks/Cole, 1976). Note that Fogelman comes out on the side of no clear predetermined gender differences in rescuing behavior: "In the end Carol Gilligan's different voice was not so different after all. It was a shared voice of common decency and humanity." Fogelman, *Conscience and Courage,* 251.

66. Thus, in a recent and provocative article Cynthia Ward argues that it is impossible and perhaps dangerous to assume that psychological concepts and approaches to empathy can be translated to the political sphere. She argues that feminists and others who have argued that empathy can be used to enhance both equality and diversity in a liberal state fail to take account of different capacities for empathy in the polity. "A Kinder, Gentler Liberalism? Visions of Empathy in Feminist and Communitarian Literature," *University of Chicago Law Review* 61 (1994), 929–955. See also variations in motivation for service described in Robert Coles, *The Call to Service: A Witness to Idealism* (Boston: Houghton Mifflin, 1993).

67. See the different lawyering experiences produced by similar poverty-stricken backgrounds in the lives of Clarence Thomas and Charles Ogletree. Lawrence-Lightfoot, *I've Known Rivers.*

68. One leading cause lawyer reported to me that she became an activist lawyer because while traveling home by train from graduate school in philosophy, her neighbor in the train asked her, "How can you read Aristotle when the world is a such a mess?" This was the early 1960s and my respondent immediately transferred from graduate study in philosophy at Johns Hopkins to law school at Harvard and later became one of the leading public housing and homelessness lawyers in the country. Interview with Florence Roisman, professor of Law, Widener College of Law, September 30, 1994. Is this an illustration of serendipity in motivation to become a cause lawyer or was the disposition already there, needing to be activated? How many people change their career plans based on one comment from someone else?

69. It is important here to distinguish empathy from sympathy. In sympathy we try to understand the situation or condition of the other but usually remain within our selves and our own value system. In empathy we "feel with" the other person, in terms of their situation—experiencing true "intersubjectivity." Thus, the image that one stands in the other's shoes, but in empathy, *"with the other's feet (values)."* See Carrie Menkel-Meadow, "Measuring Both the Art and Science of Mediation," *Negotiation Journal* 9 (1993), 321–325, esp. 322–323.

70. Fogelman, *Conscience and Courage.*

71. Monroe, Barton, and Klingeman, "Altruism and the Theory of Rational Action," 114.

72. Ibid., 118.

73. Oliner and Oliner, *The Altruistic Personality,* 165–166, 176, 178, 183.

74. Biologists have posited that this "reciprocal altruism" is what motivates altruism to extend beyond kinship groups. See Wilson, *The Moral Sense* and Simon, "A Mechanism for Social Selection and Successful Altruism."

75. To my knowledge, there is no research that explicitly "controls" for motivation by matching cause lawyers with more conventional lawyers in other standard demographic categories such as the rescuer studies attempted to match rescuers with nonrescuers. It might be possible to conduct a study of those lawyers who were Reggies or workers in the Law Students Civil Rights Research Council or Lawyers' Committee for Civil Rights and compare them to lawyers who went to more conventional legal practices.

76. For example, as indicated above, situational factors that influence whether people will help or not include opportunity to help (most rescuers were asked for help), social support for such action (most rescuers had to obtain some support from their families to share food, clothing, and lodging), economic resources and living conditions and the characteristics of those seeking help (Jewish women who looked more like Aryans were more likely to be helped than men with very obvious Jewish characteristics). Fogelman, *Conscience and Courage,* xiv, 61, 237–251.

77. Giving support to the notion that strong senses of "justice" and "equality" are developed in families with sibling rivalry.

78. Fogelman, *Conscience and Courage*; Badhwar, "Altruism versus Self-Interest."

79. Most significantly, when rescuers are compared to nonrescuers or "bystanders," the latter (the more common form of humanity we encounter every day) were likely to say, "What can I, a single person do?" while rescuers were more likely to say, "If I don't act, who will?" Fogelman, *Conscience and Courage*, 58–60, 68–69.

80. Oliner and Oliner, *The Altruistic Personality*; and Hunt, *The Compassionate Beast*, 203. To the extent that empathic reactions are one element of helping behavior, interesting questions are raised about variations in the capacity of individuals to respond empathically to others and whether such empathy can be "learned" and "taught." Most of the rescuer researchers are of the view that role modeling by loving parents and particular curricular reforms in early education can increase the capacity of individuals to be empathic. See Hunt, *The Compassionate Beast*, 209–224. The Oliners also found that rescuers were more likely to be able to "take the part of others" who were different from themselves, what they call "extensivity"—how strongly one felt that justice is not just for oneself and your own kind, but for others beyond your group. *The Altruistic Personality*, 204.

81. See Monroe, Barton, and Klingeman, "Altruism and the Theory of Rational Action."

82. It is interesting to note that there were no lawyers among those with a professional orientation. Helping professionals came from the fields of nursing, medicine, psychology, and social work. Fogelman, *Conscience and Courage*, 193.

83. For further elaboration of these characteristics of rescuers see ibid., 157–235.

84. Badhwar, "Altruism versus Self-Interest."

85. This argument is consistent with Fogelman's finding that many rescuers engaged in altruistic activities both before and after the war. Indeed, because of their strong sense of duty and self-abnegation, many rescuers refused honors following the war. See Fogelman, *Conscience and Courage*, 273–298.

86. Would conventional lawyers define themselves as committed to the cause of maintaining or facilitating capitalism or commerce? See Anthony T. Kronman's recent effort to define lawyering as creating a "transactional community" with lawyer-statesmen facilitating a political community, *The Lost Lawyer: Failing Ideals of the Legal Profession* (Cambridge, Mass.: Belknap Press of Harvard University Press, 1994).

87. Apologies to Madonna—"Express Yourself!"

88. William Galston, "Cosmopolitan Altruism," in *Altruism*, ed. Ellen Frankel Paul, Fred D. Miller Jr., and Jeffrey Paul (New York: Cambridge University Press, 1993).

89. Many studies of prosocial behavior reveal that we all have the capacity for some forms of altruistic behavior, beginning with care for our children, parents, or other close relatives or friends. The question remains as to why some of us seem more likely to extend this care beyond our immediate care groups, see Peter Singer, *The Expanding Circle: Ethics and Sociobiology* (New York: Farrar, Straus & Giroux, 1980); Joan C. Tronto, *Moral Boundaries: A Political Argument for an Ethic of Care* (New York: Routledge, 1994); and Marilyn Friedman, *What Are Friends For?: Feminist Perspectives on Personal Relationships and Moral Theory* (Ithaca, N.Y.: Cornell University Press, 1993).

90. Such "megalopsychia" (greatness of soul), according to Friedman (*What Are Friends For?*, 126, 132–133, characterizes many of the "altruistic" cause fighters of our time. See biographies of Gandhi and Martin Luther King Jr., who worked hard for the greater good of their people and sacrificed, to some degree, not only themselves, but their families. Erik H. Erikson, *Gandhi's Truth on the Origins of Militant Nonviolence* (New York: Norton, 1969); David J. Garrow, *The FBI and Martin Luther King, Jr.: From "Solo" to Memphis*

(New York: Norton, 1981); and Ralph Abernathy, *And the Walls Came Tumbling Down: An Autobiography* (New York: Harper & Row, 1989).

91. See Coles, *The Call of Service,* 90–94.

92. In studying voting patterns, for example, political scientists David Sears and Carolyn Funk have noted that voters do not always vote with their "self-interest" in mind, particularly with respect to tax measures (such as voting increased taxes for items of collective but not individual use) and interest groups (such as women and the elderly) who often don't support those measures that would be of benefit to them. "Self-Interest in American's Political Opinions," in *Beyond Self-Interest,* ed. Mansbridge, 147–170.

93. Indeed, some rescuers became more confirmed in their commitment as things seemed virtually impossible to change. Many rescuers continued their work for four to five years, even when it looked as if the Germans would win. Does this explain the strong commitment of Sarat's death penalty lawyers, even after recent Supreme Court cases make success less and less likely?

94. See Wilson, *The Moral Sense,* and Axelrod, *The Evolution of Cooperation,* for descriptions both of the transmission of altruistic genes in the species gene pool and assumptions that individuals may carry "altruism" genes.

95. The biographies we read are great sources of how life experiences are the material out of which some choose to identify with the powerless (e.g., Erickson, *Gandhi's Truth on the Origins of Militant Nonviolence,* and Garrow, *The FBI and Martin Luther King, Jr.*), and others choose to "transcend" their difficulties and identify with the privileged classes in their lawyering work (e.g., Clarence Thomas). See also David B. Wilkins, "Two Paths to the Mountaintop?: The Role of Legal Education in Shaping the Values of Black Corporate Lawyers," *Stanford Law Review* 45 (1993), 1981–2026.

96. See Hunt, *The Compassionate Beast,* 33–35.

97. See some recent efforts to tell the "practice biographies" of some cause lawyers in Ball, *The Word and the Law*; and Michael J. Kelly, *Lives of Lawyers* (Ann Arbor: University of Michigan Press, 1994), 145–194. It is striking how many of Ball's lawyers themselves were refugees from the Nazis or one generation removed from this experience. It would be interesting to systematically study how many cause lawyers were either themselves the victims of political or racial injustice or members of subsequent generations. Also interesting to pursue is why some victims of injustice become cause lawyers and others become defenders of the system. See Stephen C. Carter, *Reflections of an Affirmative Action Baby* (New York: Basic Books, 1991); and Clarence Thomas, contrasted to such lawyers as Charles Ogletree in Lawrence-Lightfoot, *I've Known Rivers,* 130. See also inspirational stories of public interest lawyers compiled by Frank Askin for the Alliance for Justice (unpublished manuscripts compiled in preparation for *Lawyering for Change,* October 1994).

98. See A. Leon Higginbotham, *In the Matter of Color: Race and the American Legal Process* (New York: University of Oxford Press, 1978).

99. Katherine Kish Sklar, *Florence Kelley and the Nation's Work* (New Haven: Yale University Press, 1995); and Aron, *Liberty and Justice for All,* p. 7. See biographies of Brandeis, e.g., Phillipa Sturm, *Louis D. Brandeis: Justice for the People* (Cambridge, Mass.: Harvard University Press, 1984); and Clyde Spillenger, "Elusive Advocate: Reconsidering Brandeis as the People's Lawyer," in *Yale Law Journal* 105 (1996), 1445–1535.

100. Reginald Heber Smith, *Justice and the Poor* (1919; New York: Arno Press, 1971).

101. See Jerold S. Auerbach, *Unequal Justice: Lawyers and Social Change in Modern America* (New York: Oxford Universtiy Press, 1976); Carrie J. Menkel-Meadow, "Legal Aid in the United States: The Professionalization and Politicization of Legal Services in the 1980s," *Osgoode Hall Law Journal* 29 (1984), 29–67; and Richard L. Abel, "Law without Politics: Legal Aid under Advanced Capitalism," *UCLA Law Review* 32 (1985), 474–621.

102. The Reginald Heber Smith fellowship program in legal services, like the Lawyers' Committee for Civil Rights and the Law Students Civil Rights Research Council fellowships, was designed to attract "the best and the brightest" to social justice lawyering by providing social, financial and political support and networks. See Amy Ruth Tobol, "Cause Lawyering and the Law Students Civil Rights Research Council: It's Not Like Club Med," paper presented to the annual meeting of the Law and Society Association, Phoenix, Ariz., June 1994. These organizations represent the "mixed motives" of progressive lawyers. Virtually all of the participating lawyers were motivated by strong political beliefs or individual helping orientations, but some of them also sought the "self-interest" of social support and comraderie in struggle and the "stars" of prestige and the few "dollars" that these fellowships provided in the game of legal careers.

103. See, e.g., Kronman, *The Lost Lawyer*.

104. John P. Frank, "The Legal Ethics of Louis D. Brandeis," *Stanford Law Review* 17 (1965), 683–709; and Spillenger, "Elusive Advocate."

105. See William E. Forbath, *Law and the Shaping of the American Labor Movement* (Cambridge, Mass.: Harvard University Press, 1989); and Daniel R. Ernst, *Lawyers against Labor: From Individual Rights to Corporate Liberalism* (Urbana: University of Illinois Press, 1995).

106. See David T. Dellinger, *Tales of Hoffman* (New York: Bantam Books, 1970).

107. See Ann Fagan Ginger, *The Relevant Lawyer* (New York: Simon & Schuster, 1972).

108. Coles, *The Call of Service*.

109. See, e.g., Taylor Branch, *Parting the Waters: America in the King Years, 1954–1963* (New York: Simon & Schuster, 1988); and Jack Greenberg, *Crusaders in the Courts: How a Dedicated Band of Lawyers Fought for the Civil Rights Revolution* (New York: Basic Books, 1994).

110. Frances Fox Piven and Richard A. Cloward, *Poor People's Movements: Why They Succeed, How They Fail* (New York: Pantheon Books, 1977).

111. Virtually all of these legal causes were spurred by the development of a social movement following publication of a popular book or exposé. See, e.g., Michael Harrington, *The Other America: Poverty in the United States* (Baltimore: Penguin, 1962); Rachel Carson, *The Silent Spring* (Boston: Houghton Mifflin, 1962); Betty Friedan, *The Feminine Mystique* (New York: Norton, 1963); and Ralph Nader, *Unsafe at Any Speed* (New York: Grossman, 1965).

112. See efforts by law students and their teachers chronicled in Howard S. Erlanger and Gabrielle Lessard, "Mobilizing Law Schools in Response to Poverty: A Report on Experiments in Progress," *Journal of Legal Education* 43 (1993), 199–226; and White, "Collaborative Lawyering in the Field?"

Public interest lawyers of the 1980s often had to use conventional legal strategies and more creative ideas to resist regressive change proposed or imposed by Republican administrations.

113. Howard S. Erlanger, "Lawyers and Neighborhood Legal Services: Social Background and the Impetus for Reform," *Law and Society Review* 12 (1978), 253–274; Howard S. Erlanger, "Social Reform Organizations and Subsequent Careers of Participants: A Follow-Up of Early Participation in the OEO Legal Services Program," *American Sociological Review* 42 (1977), 233–248.

114. Jack Ladinsky, "Careers of Lawyers, Law Practice and Legal Institutions," *American Sociological Review* 28 (1963), 47–54; Jack Ladinsky, "The Impact of Social Backgrounds of Lawyers on Law Practice and the Law," *Journal of Legal Education* 16 (1963), 127–144.

115. Joel F. Handler, Ellen Jane Hollingsworth, and Howard S. Erlanger, *Lawyers and the Pursuit of Legal Rights* (New York: Academic Press, 1978).

116. Cynthia Fuchs Epstein, *Women in Law,* 2nd ed. (Urbana: University of Illinois Press, 1993).

117. See Milner Ball's description of Steve Wizner's reasons for entering law school, *The Word and the Law,* 61.

118. Ibid., pp. 39–40. Epstein has strongly asserted that compassion and working for social causes in the legal profession are inaccurately labeled as "feminine" attributes. *Women in Law,* 40, 385–386. For my own disagreements with this view, see Carrie Menkel-Meadow, "Women in Law," *American Bar Foundation Research Journal* 1983 (1983), 189–202; Carrie Menkel-Meadow, "Portia in a Different Voice: Speculations on a Women's Lawyering Process," *Berkeley Women's Law Journal* 1 (1985), 39–63; Carrie Menkel-Meadow, "The Feminization of the Legal Profession: The Comparative Sociology of Women Lawyers," in *Lawyers in Society: Comparative Theories,* ed. Richard Abel and Philip S. C. Lewis (Berkeley: University of California Press, 1988).

119. Some, myself included, argue that subordinated groups have been forced to develop "empathic" responses or bilingualism in order to survive (women learn mainstream "male" culture; blacks learn mainstream "white" culture) and thus, have a greater capacity (some would say out of necessity) to take the part of the other and to empathize with the other. See Carrie Menkel-Meadow, "What's Gender Got to Do With? The Politics and Morality of an Ethic of Care," *New York University Review of Law and Social Change* 22 (1996), 265–293; Williams, *The Alchemy of Race and Rights;* Mari J. Matsuda, "When the First Quail Calls: Multiple Consciousness as Jurisprudential Method," *Women's Rights Law Reporter* 14 (1992), 297–300; Mari J. Matsuda, "Beside My Sister, Facing the Enemy: Legal Theory Out of Coalition," *Stanford Law Review* 43 (1991), 1183–1196. This is one explanation for why women and minorities are overrepresented among those in public interest practice. Others have argued that it is the dominant groups who most have to engage in empathic response for social justice to occur—they must see the world from the place of the excluded. See Wald, "Whose Public Interest Is It Anyway?" The current analysis of gender differences sparked Eve Fogelman to find out if there were gender differences in rescuing behavior. She concluded that both men and women who rescued expressed similar "humanitarian" reasons and that what was gendered was opportunities to engage in particular rescuing acts. Fogelman, *Conscience and Change,* 247–251.

120. For example, compare Suzanne Homer and Lois Schwartz, "Admitted but Not Accepted: Outsiders Take an Inside Look at Law School," *Berkeley Women's Law Journal* 1 (1990), 1–74; Janet Taber et al., "Gender Legal Education and the Legal Profession: An Empirical Study of Stanford Law Students and Graduates," *Stanford Law Review* 40 (1988), 1209–1297; Rand Jack and Dana C. Jack, *Moral Vision and Professional Decisions: The Changing Values of Women and Men Lawyers* (New York: Cambridge University Press, 1989); and Robert Stover, *Making It and Breaking It* (Urbana: University of Illinois Press, 1989) (finding that women were three times as likely to express an altruistic interest in public interest practice as men law students) (all arguing for some forms of gender difference in motivation and type of law practice engaged in), with David L. Chambers, "Accommodation and Satisfaction: Women and Men Lawyers and the Balance of Work and Family," *Law and Social Inquiry* 14 (1989), 251–287; and Lee Teitelbaum, Antoinette Sedillo Lopez, and Jeffrey Jenkins, "Gender, Legal Education and Legal Careers," *Journal of Legal Education* 41 (1991), 443–481 (both suggesting that whatever differential motivations may once have existed no longer are true, as women are just as likely to express interest in and find success with private law firm practice).

121. See Barbara Allen Babcock, "Western Women Lawyers," *Stanford Law Review* 45 (1993), 2179–2186; Virginia G. Drachman, *Women Lawyers and the Origins of Professional*

Identity in America (Ann Arbor: University of Michigan, 1993); and Karen Berger Morello, *The Invisible Bar: The Woman Lawyer in America, 1638 to the Present* (New York: Random House, 1986).

122. Martha F. Davis, *Brutal Need: Lawyers and the Welfare Rights Movement, 1960–1973* (New Haven: Yale University Press, 1993).

123. Interview with Marcia Greenberger, copresident, National Women's Law Center (October 24, 1994).

124. Florence Roisman, for example, reports she began work with a neighborhood legal assistance program in the District of Columbia after she was denied a position as an appellate lawyer in the antitrust division of the Justice Department. Interview (September 1994).

125. See initial statement of definition of this cause-lawyering project, Austin Sarat and Stuart Scheingold, "cause lawyering entails a self-conscious choice to give priority to causes rather than to client service, as such." Memorandum in preparation for publication of this volume (July 25, 1992). In an Alliance for Justice Survey conducted in 1983–84 of 158 public interest groups, 41 percent classified themselves as "cause-defined" and 59 percent as "client-defined." Aron, *Liberty and Justice for All*, 25.

126. Stover, *Making It and Breaking It*. For earlier studies see, e.g., James C. Foster, "Legal Education and the Production of Lawyers to (Re)Produce Liberal Capitalism," *Legal Studies Forum*, 9 (1985), 179–211; Robert Granfield, "Legal Education as Corporate Ideology," *Sociological Forum* 1 (1986), 514; Howard S. Erlanger, "Young Lawyers and Work in the Public Interest," *American Bar Foundation Research Journal* 1978 (1978), 83–104; Audrey James Schwartz, "The Paper Chase Myth: Law Students in the 1970s," *Social Perspectives* 28 (1985), 87–100; and James M. Hedegard, "Causes of Career Relevant-Interest Changes among First Year Law Students: Some Research Data," *American Bar Foundation Research Journal* 1982 (1982), 789–867.

127. Stover, *Making and Breaking It*, 10.

128. Ibid., 17.

129. Ibid., 20.

130. Ibid.

131. Stover, like others, was interested in suggesting what kinds of activities were likely to preserve or enhance such commitments to public interest practice, and he suggests a variety of ways in which cause and public interest subcultures should be nurtured where law students are forming job choices. See also Jan C. Costello, "Training Lawyers for the Powerless: What Law Schools Should Do to Develop Public Interest Lawyers," *Nova Law Journal* 10 (1986), 431–448. One of the key questions in altruism studies is whether prosocial behavior is discouraged or reinforced by group or joint action or depends on individual motivation. In the "bystander" studies following the Kitty Genovese murder, researchers found that people were less likely to engage in helping behavior if there were others around (what can one person do?). See Bibb Latane and John Darley, "Group Inhibition of Bystander Intervention in Emergencies," *Journal of Personality and Social Psychology* 10 (1968), 215–237. This is in distinct contradiction to the "network rescuers" found by Fogelman and the French town of Le Chambon. See Hallie, *Lest Innocent Blood Be Shed*.

132. Quotations are taken from interviews and field notes and an unpublished paper, Robert Meadow and Carrie Menkel-Meadow, "The Origins of Political Commitment."

133. Lawrence-Lightfoot, *I've Known Rivers*.

134. See Johnson, "The New Public Interest Law," for a description of the "corrective" nature of public interest practice—a desire to facilitate and improve democratic participation on behalf of those excluded, through the use of law. Consider the tension between

using the law for progressive change and using law to prevent change when political and legal change are regressive.

135. See Emily Couric, *Women Lawyers: Perspectives on Success* (New York: Harcourt Brace Jovanovich, 1984), 109.

136. For my arguments that these lawyers crafted new legal theories and claims and thus altered the very categories of law see Carrie J. Menkel-Meadow, "Mainstreaming Feminist Legal Theory," *Pacific Law Journal* 23 (1992), 1493–1542.

137. Catherine A. MacKinnon, *Only Words* (Cambridge, Mass.: Harvard University Press, 1993); Catherine A. MacKinnon, *Sexual Harassment of Working Women* (New Haven: Yale University Press, 1979).

138. See McCorvey, *I Am Roe*; and Weddington, *A Question of Choice*.

139. See sources collected in Kohn, *The Brighter Side of Human Nature*, 123–124; and Alfie Kohn, *No Contest: The Case against Competition* (Boston: Houghton Mifflin, 1986), 168–181.

140. This is a highly speculative and idiosyncratic conclusion. I am mindful of the men who have fostered the narrative tradition in law: Derrick Bell, Richard Delgado, Milner Ball, Charles Lawrence, Clark Cunningham, to name but a few. While women writers have been drawing much attention to the practice of narrative approaches to law, Patricia Williams, Robin West, Toni Massaro, Lynn Henderson, Kathryn Abrams, and Lucie White, to name a few, my field interviews did reveal gender differences in how lawyers talked about their causes and cases and the source of their commitments.

I can't resist a gender-based interpretation here. Austin Sarat's powerful report of the death penalty lawyers he studied draws on an evocative claim that these lawyers keep working, despite the current inhospitable legal environment, because they are "writing a story" or "making a record" or "making history"—a claim to a more just future and to the meaningfulness of what they do. Yet these lawyers also talk about the human connection they often feel to the particular individual they are representing—that they can feel some sympathy, empathy, and concern for their clients in those moments. Would I write a different story from Austin about these lawyers? How do we construct the explanations or "narratives" about their goals, purposes, and motivations?

141. As contrasted to social work, grassroots organizing or other social change traditions, see, e.g., Robert Coles, *Dorothy Day: A Radical Devotion* (Reading, Mass.: Addison-Wesley, 1987).

142. See Helen S. Astin and Carole Leland, *Women of Influence, Women of Vision: A Cross-Generational Study of Leaders and Social Change* (San Francisco: Jossey-Bass, 1991), chronicling three generations of innovators in educational leadership—the instigators, the innovators, and the inheritors. There is room here for both a systematic study of public interest lawyer motivation (as distinguished from conventional lawyer motivation) and a separate study of the history and generational changes in careers of public interest lawyers. Women lawyers, in particular, are underrepresented in the existing literature on cause lawyers. There is still no definitive history of the modern women's rights movement and the role lawyers played in it. Cf. Karen O'Connor, *Women's Organizations' Use of the Courts* (Lexington, Mass.: Lexington Books, 1980). We are just beginning to see important books on the role of women in the early legal progressive movement, see Sklar, *Florence Kelley and the Nation's Work*; Robyn Muncy, *Creating a Female Dominion in American Reform, 1890–1935* (New York: Oxford University Press, 1991); Blanche Wiesen Cook, *Eleanor Roosevelt, 1884–1933* (New York: Viking, 1992); and Guida West and Rhoda L. Blumberg, eds., *Women and Social Protest* (New York: Oxford University Press, 1990). Thanks to Florence Roisman for this observation.

143. See, e.g., Mark V. Tushnet, *Making Civil Rights Law: Thurgood Marshall and the Supreme Court, 1936–1961* (New York: Oxford University Press, 1994).

144. Wald, "Whose Public Interest Is It Anyway?".

145. Lisa Ikemoto, "Traces of the Master Narrative in the Story of African American/ Korean American Conflict: How We Constructed 'Los Angeles,' " *Southern California Law Review* 66 (1993), 1581–1598.

146. For a moving and brave account of the problems of seeking too much punishment in such cases, see Kathleen Daly, "What Would Have Been Justice?" (address to the Law and Society annual meeting Plenary, Philadelphia, Pa., June 1992). See also, Anita Hill and Emma Cole Jordan, *Race, Gender, and Power in America: The Legacy of the Hill-Thomas Hearings* (New York: Oxford University Press, 1995); and Toni Morrison, *Race-ing Justice, En-gendering Power: Essays on Anita Hill, Clarence Thomas, and the Construction of Social Reality* (New York: Pantheon Books, 1992).

147. E.g., Juliet Schor, *The Overworked American: The Unexpected Decline of Leisure* (New York: Basic Books, 1991). See also Jack Katz's description of how legal services lawyers construct "meaning" in their work, *Poor People's Lawyers in Transition*.

148. Some have suggested, for example, that as part of the governing infrastructure, such groups participate too readily in the political process of compromise. Others suggest that this is much better than having causes framed in polarized litigation where one party may lose completely, and these days it is the cause lawyers who lose more often. (*Quaere* whether it is empirically true that cause lawyers are all losing more than before? Are there variations in the success rates of particular causes, e.g., civil rights, environmentalism, consumer rights?)

149. See Ed Sparer's working and nonworking poor coalitions on unemployment compensation and welfare in "Fundamental Human Rights, Legal Entitlements and the Social Struggle: A Friendly Critique of the Critical Legal Studies Movement," *Stanford Law Review* 36 (1984), 509–574. See also Davis, *Brutal Need;* and Piven and Cloward, *Poor People's Movements.* Is American cause lawyering peculiarly troubled by these developments where class analysis has been difficult to sustain both in litigation strategies and in larger social movements?

150. For some attempts to study the "impact" of cause lawyering, at least in traditional litigation, see Jesse H. Choper, "Consequences of Supreme Court Decisions Upholding Individual Constitutional Rights," *Michigan Law Review* 83 (1984), 1–212; Howard Glickstein, "The Impact of Brown vs. Board of Education and Its Progeny," *Howard Law Journal* 23 (1980), 51–55 (impact studies of prison and welfare litigation); Sturm, "Lawyers at the Prison Gates"; Mark V. Tushnet, *The NAACP's Legal Strategy against Segregated Education, 1925–1950* (Chapel Hill: University of North Carolina Press, 1987); and Richard Kluger, *Simple Justice: The History of Brown v. Board of Education and Black America's Struggle for Equality* (New York: Knopf, 1975).

151. This issue of supply and demand in public interest work is currently being explored by scholars, the National Association for Public Interest Law, and the National Association of Law Placement. See also Erlanger, "Young Lawyers and Work in the Public Interest."

152. See Kelly, *Lives of Lawyers;* and Carroll Seron, *The Business of Practicing Law: The Work Lives of Solo and Small-Firm Attorneys* (Philadelphia: Temple University Press, 1996). See also Milner Ball's profile of Margaret Taylor, who uses her cause-lawyering background as a judge, in *The Word and the Law,* 24–38.

153. So, for example, asbestos personal injury lawyers now talk of themselves as cause lawyers and move from one "disaster" to another, championing the rights of the injured.

See Gene Locks's argument that he was like Abe Lincoln in Georgine, in Carrie J. Menkel-Meadow, "Ethics and the Settlement of Mass Torts: When the Rules Meet the Road," *Cornell Law Review* 80 (1995), 1159–1221, esp. 1163.

154. Robert W. Gordon, "The Independence of Lawyers," *Boston University Law Review* 68 (1988), 1–83; Kronman, *The Lost Lawyer;* and Robert W. Gordon and William Simon, "The Redemption of Professionalism," in *Lawyers' Ideal/Lawyers' Practices: Transformations in the American Legal System,* ed. Robert L. Nelson, David M. Trubek, and Raymond L. Solomon (Ithaca, N.Y.: Cornell University Press, 1992).

155. For wonderful, accessible, and useful hints on how to create and sustain empathy and altruistic behavior see Kohn, *The Brighter Side of Human Nature;* Hunt, *The Compassionate Beast;* and Wuthnow, *Acts of Compassion, Caring for Others and Helping Ourselves.*

156. Lesnick, "Why Pro Bono in Law Schools."

157. Sarat, "Between (the Presence of) Violence and (the Possibility of) Justice."

158. Shamir and Chinski, "Destruction of Houses and Construction of Cause."

CHAPTER 3

Speaking Law to Power

Occasions for Cause Lawyering

RICHARD ABEL

Under what circumstances does law check power? That it can do so at all reflects the fundamental contradiction of liberalism. Law is simultaneously rule and politics, ideal and reality, neutral and partisan, above the fray and in the midst of it. Most of the time law reflects, reproduces, and reinforces existing power inequalities. Anatole France's now clichéd observation perfectly captures the paradoxical effect of blind justice in an unjust society. More recently, Marc Galanter's pathbreaking article elaborated the ways in which lawyers and courts routinely amplify the advantages of the "haves."[1] I have expressed similar skepticism in criticizing informal justice and legal aid.[2] Here, however, I want to attend to the possibilities as well as the limitations of liberal legalism, the moments when law offers leverage to the relatively powerless as well as those when it is wielded, or trumped, by power. These are the occasions for cause lawyering.

Power inequality assumes many guises. Some have a material base: control of the means of production in the Marxist formulation, wealth and income disparities in the liberal. Both approaches recently have broadened their conception of resources to include intangibles like knowledge, educational credentials, and cultural capital. A second manifestation of inequality reflects differential ability to participate in and influence the polity: the size and organization of interest groups, their material resources and political sophistication, access to the media, ideological position, and incumbency. A third kind of inequality is located in the social system: status differences associated with nationality, language, gender, race, religion, sexual orientation, and physical or mental disability. Public and private forms of power are inextricably connected, sometimes indistinguishable. In this essay, however, I will concentrate on the confrontation between law and state power. Because law constitutes the state, law can reconfigure state power. Because the state usually acts through law, the state can be constrained by law. State action generally is more visible than private. Private power claims immunity from legal interference; with the shift toward conservatism and the collapse of Communism, such claims have been increasingly vociferous and successful.

There are several conventional approaches to the clash between law and power. Courses, treatises, and articles on constitutional law, civil rights, women and the law, disability, the environment, labor, and sexual orientation deal with the legal structure of the state and enumerate the rights of citizens against it and each other. Advocacy scholarship exposes the atrocities of evil regimes.[3] Historians write narratives of struggle.[4] Members of subordinated groups identify the sources of disadvantage and prescribe responses.[5] There are biographies and autobiographies of cause lawyers and lawyering organizations.[6] I want to draw on all these sources, but for a different purpose. I am interested in how the structure, process, and personnel of legal institutions shape the interaction between law and power. Because the outcome is indeterminate, I will often pose questions rather than offer answers: not *whether* law makes a difference, because it unquestionably does, but rather *when* and *what* difference it makes. As other commentators have remarked, cause lawyering has been unduly focused on litigation.[7] Therefore I will organize my discussion around a broader spectrum of institutions: the spatial configuration of the polity, the electoral process, the three branches (legislature, executive, and judiciary), and the legal profession. I conclude with a brief discussion of the special case of regime changes.

Spatial Organization of Power

All polities allocate power across various levels of the state hierarchy from apex to base. These usually are structured in spatial units of diminishing size, from global to regional, national, and local (although fascist or corporatist polities may also define them functionally). The distribution of power within this hierarchy can have profound consequences for the relatively powerless, but the effect is situationally specific. In recent years, ethnic and ethnoreligious separatist movements have sought greater local autonomy to preserve their culture and language: Basques and Catalans in Spain; Bretons, Occitanians, and Corsicans in France; Walloons in Belgium; Tyrolese in Italy; Québecois in Canada; Puerto Ricans in the United States; native peoples in the United States, Canada, and Australia (among others); the Celtic fringe in Great Britain; Turks in Cyprus; East Timorese in Indonesia; Kashmiri and Punjabi peoples in India; Tamils in Sri Lanka; Kurds in Turkey, Iraq, Iran, and Syria; Moslems in the Philippines; Turks in Bulgaria; Hungarians in Romania; Palestinians in Israel, Polisario rebels in Morocco. Virtually every country created by the European partition of Africa is riven by tribal loyalties— even one as "ethnically" homogeneous as Somalia. The former Soviet Union, Czechoslovakia, and Yugoslavia have fissioned and continue to subdivide. Even stable polities like the United States exhibit constant power struggles between the nation, states, cities, and neighborhoods (witness the controversy generated by New York's experiment with school decentralization).

Localism, however, may augment rather than reduce power inequalities.[8] The claim by antebellum southern states to "nullify" federal law and their subsequent invocation of "states' rights" were transparent excuses for racial oppression. The "sagebrush" rebellion in western states is a smokescreen for large companies to despoil the land for mining, grazing, and logging, seize water resources, and foster suburban sprawl. The Northern League in Italy and Basques and Catalans in Spain seek autonomy partly to protect their wealth against redistribution to poorer regions. The Republicans' "Contract with America" has the same goal, as evidenced by the resistance of many state governors and big-city mayors. Margaret Thatcher was even more shamelessly opportunistic, centralizing some powers to cripple Labour-dominated northern cities, while decentralizing the governance of London to empower Conservative-dominated boroughs and school districts.

Larger political units may be more universalistic, perhaps because it is easier to sympathize with difference and disadvantage at a distance. Northern whites, for example, supported the southern civil rights movement; the antiapartheid movement was generously financed by northern Europe and North America; French intellectuals have embraced the Bosnian cause. Larger polities can also redistribute wealth: farming subsidies in the European Union, federal tax revenues and state rather than local financing of public schools in the United States. Market forces constantly press for freer trade, but though this may harmonize regulatory regimes, it also may encourage a race to the bottom to attract foreign investment. And, of course, the largest polities have been colonial empires, ruthlessly suppressing local resistance, eradicating languages, cultures and religions, imposing racial hierarchies, and exterminating indigenous peoples.

Cause lawyers can exploit the tensions between center and periphery, apex and base. They can invoke treaties and conventions against state signatories, federal constitutions, and laws against local polities. The German Federal Constitutional Court, for instance, has ordered Bavaria to remove crucifixes from classrooms. Cause lawyers also can champion the claims of minorities to local autonomy, bashing remote bureaucrats and extolling the virtues of government close to the people. The choice of strategy in each case will be historically specific: for decades American civil rights lawyers depended on the federal Constitution, statutes, courts, and law enforcement personnel to protect southern blacks; recently some blacks have sought local empowerment in schools, universities, neighborhoods, cultural milieus, electoral districts, and economic enterprises.

Electoral Process

Because elections are quintessentially political, law plays a limited role. Courts hesitate to interfere before balloting and are even more reluctant to question outcomes.[9] In 1994, for example, the California Supreme Court refused to disqualify an initiative to overrule local antismoking ordinances despite evidence that many who signed the petition placing it on the ballot were unaware of Philip Morris's sponsorship and mistakenly believed it tightened the regulations. Nevertheless, law shapes the electoral process wherever it occurs; and only a few countries still reject elections altogether—even Kuwait, Saudi Arabia, and Cuba are contemplating or experimenting with them.

Law determines who is eligible to vote. The fundamental egalitarianism of democracy creates almost irresistible ideological pressures for universal suffrage. Property qualifications, for example, have been eliminated everywhere. African Americans challenged the white primary and literacy tests and secured passage of the Civil Rights Act of 1965, subjecting many southern districts to federal surveillance. South African courts protected the "Cape Coloured" franchise until the National Party packed the bench.[10] P. W. Botha's 1983 constitutional "reform" gave Indians and "Coloureds" their own parliamentary chambers (while preserving a veto for the Nationalist-controlled President's Council). The struggle against apartheid was preeminently a demand for the vote. Women also have fought for and won suffrage almost everywhere. Even in South Africa—at that time the only country in the world practicing de jure racial discrimination—KwaNdebele women persuaded the supreme court to grant them the franchise in their homeland.[11] Eligibility continues to expand elsewhere, too: the voting age has been lowered in many countries; colonies may seek to participate in elections in the metropole; some European nations allow noncitizens to vote, generating arguments that the United States should follow suit.[12] Formal eligibility, however, is not identical to electoral power; other factors influence who uses the right. Democrats have passed "motor voter" laws to increase the proportion of eligibles who are registered, but several states resisted implementation.[13] Oregon's use of mail balloting augmented turnout and helped elect a Democrat to fill Senator Robert Packwood's seat. Republicans have used absentee ballots to increase the turnout among retired voters sympathetic to their goals. Because turnout varies with the offices at stake (which affects media coverage and campaign spending), the scheduling of elections can influence outcome, regardless of who or how many are eligible to vote.

Districting (including at-large elections) affects the weight of votes. Gerrymandering, for example, can confer advantages on political parties, as well as racial and other social categories. Right-wing whites in South Africa continue to urge the creation of their own "volkstaat." The U.S. Supreme Court has required that voting districts be of roughly equal size; recently, however, efforts to increase the representation of racial minorities by manipulating the shape of districts have been successfully attacked on equal protection grounds. Voting algorithms such as first-past-the-post systems, proportional representation, and cumulative and preferential balloting also shape the relative power of majorities and minorities. The furor over Clinton's nomination of Lani Guinier for assistant attorney general and his subsequent withdrawal of her name are evidence of the importance of the choice of algorithm.[14] The number and structure of parties and the way they choose candidates and draft platforms shape the mix of political voices. Governments may seek to reduce party influence by making some elections nonpartisan, though federal judges have found this violative of First Amendment rights of speech and assembly.

Incumbency offers enormous advantages, through habitude, publicity, and material favors. Korean presidents amassed a slush fund of over $600 million; Liberal Democrats ruled Japan for nearly five decades after World War II; Nationalists wielded power in South Africa from 1948 to 1994; the Institutional Revolutionary Party (PRI) has governed Mexico since the revolution. In 1993 President Carlos Salinas de Gortari allegedly gave a dinner party at which the thirty guests were asked to contribute $25 million each. Emilio Azcarraga, whose $2.8 billion fortune (the largest in Latin America) derived largely from ownership of 90 percent of Mexican television, said he would be happy to give three times as much. Another guest had amassed $2.1 billion by buying the state telephone monopoly; a third had bought the state bank.[15] In the United States, questions remain whether Reagan promised arms to Iran in exchange for its delay in releasing American hostages—the so-called October Surprise, which helped him defeat Carter.[16] Such abuses have spawned anti-incumbent sentiment among voters and a proliferation of term limit laws.

Liberalism's profound ambivalence about the ways in which power may shape electoral outcomes creates both opportunities and obstacles for cause lawyering. Laws place some limits on the role of money: capping campaign contributions, disqualifying some contributors, compelling disclosure, and forbidding explicit favors; but those seeking to translate economic power into political influence have launched successful constitutional attacks on some of these restrictions. The law may require the media to grant access and equal time to candidates and parties; but the media resist any interference with their pursuit of profit. The liberal state has been cautious about compromising its claim to neutrality by financing electoral politics, especially given the difficulty of formulating a principle for allocating funds to parties. In response to political machines that rewarded votes with jobs, governments have barred civil servants from political activity, only to relax this prohibition in recognition of public employees' claims to political participation. Courts, too, have wavered over whether those advocating unpopular positions in elections to fill offices or decide on referenda should enjoy the protection of anonymity or whether voters should be entitled to know the identity of political speakers.

The law everywhere proscribes corruption and ballot tampering. "Tangentopoli" continues to unfold in Italy, implicating members of all political parties as *mani pulite* and virtually destroying the Christian Democrats, who had dominated every coalition since World War II. Similar scandals have wracked Japan and Korea. Foreign observers play an increasingly important role in assuring regularity where democratic traditions are weak. Yet votes are sold openly in Thailand and electoral results manufactured in Mexico. There is strong evidence that Lyndon Johnson began his career by fraudulently winning election to the House of Representatives.[17] Governments sometimes ban political parties on the right or left as undemocratic. Just as South Africa banned the Communist Party for over three decades, so Russia's Central Election Commission banned the democratic and economically liberal Yabloko party, only to be overruled by the country's supreme court.[18] Algeria simply disregarded the electoral victory of Islamic fundamentalists.[19] General Efraín Ríos Montt defied Guatemalan courts, which declared him constitutionally ineligible to run for president in 1995 because he had seized that office by coup in 1982.[20]

Although courts rarely intervene in elections, cause lawyers can use law to structure the competition for political power in numerous ways. The hegemony of democratic ideals gives them leverage to demand that autocratic or military regimes defer to the electorate and that suffrage be universal and votes weighted equally. Lawyers can seek to configure districts and voting algorithms to maximize the power of subordinated people and organize the timing and process of elections to increase turnout. They can facilitate participation by new political parties and seek term limits to reduce the advantages of incumbency. Most important, if also most difficult, they can restrain the translation of economic power into political dominance, devising rules limiting campaign contributions, equalizing media access, and prohibiting political activity by government employees. They can expose the more blatant forms of political corruption and sometimes even invalidate fraudulent elections.

Legislature

Some of the questions just posed about the polity as a whole can be reiterated about the legislature. What are the implications of a bicameral legislature? How is the second house chosen, and what does it represent: political units (states, provinces) or traditional rulers (e.g., Indian maharajahs, African chiefs)? Paradoxically, in Great Britain the largely hereditary House of Lords offered greater resistance to Margaret Thatcher's conservative program than did the democratically elected Commons. In addition, although South Africa's 1983 constitution allowed the new "Coloured" and Indian houses to be trumped by the white President's Council, the political costs of doing so empowered those houses to block some of the most vicious apartheid legislation and deeply embarrass the Nationalist government. We take it for granted that legislatures act by simple majority. Yet Lani Guinier has urged consideration of voting algorithms that would increase the weight of persistent minorities, such as races in the United States. It takes a supermajority to propose and adopt constitutional amendments in the United States; some state and local polities require supermajorities for tax increases, and the Republicans have urged Congress to adopt supermajorities, too.

The problem of curbing the influence of economic resources on political power recurs within the legislature. In Britain, legislators must "declare their interests." Laws may require lobbyists to register and clients to report or limit donations. Nonprofit organizations may lose their tax-exempt status by entering the political arena. Yet here, too, there is tension with constitutional protections of speech. Some interests are well organized and powerful, while others are too disorganized to address or influence legislatures. Yet when external power is deployed to organize a constituency by compelling or encouraging membership in voluntary organizations such as professional associations and trade unions (thereby overcoming the free rider problem), the rights of dissidents may prevent those collectivities from speaking.[21] The relatively powerless, effectively excluded from legislatures captured by special interests, may try to circumvent these barriers by resorting to the initiative process. Laws will define the form of the proposition and number of signatures needed to put such initiatives on the ballot; but here, too, money may be decisive—in defeating referenda, if not in passing them.[22] And this mechanism is equally available to the powerful: the religious Right seeking to stigmatize gays and lesbians, xenophobes scapegoating immigrants, the tobacco industry hoping to overturn antismoking ordinances, racial majorities trying to end affirmative action.

The composition and organization of the legislature may affect its receptivity to the powerless. Racial minorities and women no longer face legal barriers; but they remain greatly underrepresented. (Although personal identity, of course, does not determine political orientation.) One reason may be the role of occupations like law as stepping-stones to politics. Another is the unadmitted reluctance of whites to vote for blacks: witness the difference between opinion polls and results in the defeats of Governor Wilder in Virginia and Mayor Dinkins in New York. In an effort to address such underrepresentation, the British Labour Party has resolved that women will constitute half of its parliamentary candidates.

Party strength is vitally important. In some countries, a single party has been hegemonic for decades: the Nationalists in South Africa (for thirteen years Helen Suzman was the sole Progressive), Christian Democrats in Italy, and Liberal Conservatives in Japan. Some parties may be numerically strong but marginalized because they are blacklisted: the Italian Communists were excluded from every one of the dozens of postwar coalitions, despite being the second largest party for most of that period. National cultures differ in the vigor of legislative debate among the various parties and in the breadth of the ideological spectrum—contrast the U.S. Congress with the British Parliament, for example. Most legislatures now permit some live media coverage. Legislatures necessarily delegate much of their work to committees and thus must define their substantive jurisdiction, membership, and process. This may influence which subjects receive attention and how parties and individual legislators acquire power. Committees, in turn, rely on lobbyists for information and often drafting: following their 1994 congressional victory Republicans invited lobbyists to participate in committee drafting sessions.

In countries with long democratic traditions legislatures take their autonomy for granted. Even within the British Commonwealth, however, the governor general long enjoyed the power as the Crown's representative to dissolve national legislatures and call new elections. Autocratic executives may suspend the legislature. And the military may threaten or carry out a coup—often claiming to defend democracy against dictatorship or corruption.

Legislative power is never unlimited. It is distributed between local and national levels in federal polities. Even nations are beginning to surrender some sovereignty to regional groupings, although they may reserve the right to derogate from such agreements.[23] Even where a parliament is supreme, it may feel constrained by an unwritten constitution of past practices or by natural law. Thus, it may aspire to enact laws that are general, prospective, precise, nondiscriminatory, and minimally invasive of individual freedom. A professional drafting office may be more strongly imbued with these values than a legislature.

Although the South African Parliament was supreme and unconstrained by a bill of rights until 1994, it sometimes displayed reluctance to overrule judicial "misinterpretations" of its laws. When the Appellate Division construed the Defence Act as imposing a *maximum* prison sentence for refusal to serve in the military, although the statute clearly intended the specified term to be *mandatory*, Parliament refrained from rewriting the law.[24] When the Appellate Division held that the state president had acted from improper motives in incorporating the district of Moutse into the KwaNdebele homeland, Parliament did not reaffirm its delegation of power. However, it had already passed another law allowing the state president to alter homeland boundaries unconstrained by any criteria, and courts refused to review his subsequent use of that power in other cases.[25] Furthermore, South African legislators sometimes extrapolated the American conservative critique of judicial review as countermajoritarian by claiming that Parliament had a *duty* to correct a court's misinterpretation of legislative intent.

Unfortunately, legislatures sometimes disregard both tradition and natural law by conferring broad discretion on the executive: retroactive punishment in Nazi Germany, the notorious "sus" law in the United Kingdom and its counterparts in the United States—vagrancy and disorderly conduct laws.[26] Unstable or fearful regimes demand extraordinary powers, especially during wartime.[27] The Northern Ireland (Emergency Provisions) Act 1991 criminalizes "directing, at any level, the activities of an organisation which is concerned in the commission of acts of terrorism" or possessing something "in circumstances giving rise to a reasonable suspicion that the item is . . . for a purpose connected with the commission, preparation or institution of acts of terrorism."[28] Legislatures may use their investigative powers to abridge individual liberty, as the Senate Internal Security Sub-committee and House Committee on Un-American Activities did during the anti-Communist witch-hunts of the 1950s. The prospect of judicial review may discourage a legislature from exercising its own judgment about the constitutionality of a law—discrimination against aliens, for instance. All three houses of the South African Parliament refused to hear the Moutse district's petition seeking recision of its incorporation into KwaNdebele because suit had just been filed to block Moutse's excision from Lebowa, another homeland, rendering the matter sub judice.[29] Neither constitution nor natural law greatly limits the legislation with the greatest impact, such as taxation and spending (although equal protection may constrain it). The relatively powerless can sometimes persuade legislatures to refrain from exercising power, but they find it more difficult to move legislatures to enact laws curbing private power in the market, the workplace, housing, public accommodations, the environment, and so forth. And the powerful have successfully advanced constitutional and natural law arguments against such state intervention: witness the social statics of Herbert Spencer earlier in this century and the market idolatry of Milton Friedman more recently.

Cause lawyers can seek to structure legislatures to redress power imbalances by altering the composition of and relations between chambers, defining voting algorithms to ensure that persistent minorities are heard, and requiring supermajorities or consensus for fundamental decisions. They can attempt to limit the influence of money on legislation and equalize the organizational strength of extraparliamentary groups. They can challenge hegemonic parties by exposing corruption and abuses of power and curbing the advantages of seniority. The political weakness of outsiders may paradoxically free them to speak truth to power—as Helen Suzman did for decades in South Africa. Cause lawyers can defend legislative autonomy against threats from the executive or military and persuade the legislature to delegate only limited power to the executive. By appealing to the constitution (written or unwritten) and natural law principles they can urge the legislature to curb its own power. They can resist legislative witch-hunts while persuading the legislature to investigate abuses of private power. Most important, but most difficult in an era when the Right has defined government as the enemy, they can encourage the legislature to counterpose state power to private oppression and exploitation.

Executive

The executive is more constrained by law than the legislature is. In parliamentary regimes the prime minister and cabinet stand or fall with their party's legislative majority and can be removed by the crown or president. If coalitions are necessary to form a government, power is unstable and constantly renegotiated. Because of the salience of high executive office, personal identity assumes heightened political significance, as shown by the attention to Kennedy's Catholicism, Geraldine Ferraro's gender, or Jesse Jackson's race. In deeply divided societies, president and prime minister may alternate between factions, as used to occur between Muslims and Christians in Lebanon. Because the executive symbolizes national unity it must appear to remain above the fray despite being the focal point of intense partisan contest. Some polities locate the unifying functions in a crown (Britain, Belgium, Norway, the Netherlands, Spain) or ceremonial president (France, Germany, Italy, Israel). Many countries constrain the participation of executive officials in electoral politics, for instance, the Hatch Act and its state counterparts. Merit-based career civil services may increase fidelity to law (as well as technical expertise), though they may become bureaucratic obstructions when a new regime seeks to change fundamental policies, as happened, for instance, in the transition from Communism in Eastern Europe or in postapartheid South Africa.

The executive is limited not only by natural law and constitutions but also by the legislature. Executive actions can be challenged as ultra vires, or for failure to give reasons, or because the authorizing legislation is too broad or vague. Lacking a constitution, South African courts elaborated administrative law in the 1980s to constrain an oppressive and overweening executive. In two landmark decisions the Appellate Division granted permanent urban residence to men who had met the statutory requirement of working for a single employer for ten years (overturning an administrative ruling that the necessary continuity was broken by annual vacations) and recognized the right of their wives and children to live with them.[30] It also invalidated the state president's forced removal of the Magopa people from land they had owned for seventy-five years because the executive order had failed to specify their destination, denying Parliament a meaningful opportunity for review.[31] The Supreme Court ordered the white superintendent of a black township to allocate building sites and houses to residents, finding that he lacked legislative authority for his attempt to disestablish the community. It rejected the government's invocation of a law on homelessness to justify imposing harsh regulations on people it sought to force out of their homes.[32] The Appellate Division ruled that the statutory objective of ethnically homogeneous homelands prevented the government from incorporating the district of Moutse into the KwaNdebele homeland, with which it differed significantly in language and culture.[33]

Yet a regime that monopolized formal power, like South Africa until 1994, could easily circumvent such obstacles by changing the rules. Frustrated in its effort to incorporate Moutse into KwaNdebele, the government used a different law, which imposed *no* criteria, to incorporate Braklaagte and Leeuwfontein into Bophuthatswana.[34] The *New Nation,* the leading black opposition weekly, could not enjoin a three-month suspension because the law authorized the home affairs minister to act on purely subjective grounds.[35] And though the courts invalidated several Emergency regulations, the government ultimately devised a statutory formula that convinced the Appellate Division to give it free rein.[36]

Insecure regimes generally arrogate greater powers to themselves, proscribing hostile groups and actions prospectively rather than punishing individuals for crimes retrospectively.[37] The day after the Reichstag fire (probably set by the Nazis to justify their repression) Hitler issued a "Decree for the Protection of the People and the State," banning opposition parties, suspending the right of assembly, controlling the press, and assuming the power to detain without trial.[38] Under German occupation the French legislature granted Maréchal Pétain absolute powers, over the opposition of only eighty of the six hundred members.[39] Britain banned the Irish Republican Army and the Irish National Liberation Army and made it a crime to arrange or address a meeting of three people known to support those organizations, wear clothing indicating support, or broadcast speakers representing them. The Public Order Act 1936 allowed a chief police officer to impose any conditions that "appeared necessary" on public speeches or marches and seek a generic ban from the Home Office or local authority. The 1986 act extended this to public assemblies, already subject to control as a public nuisance. Magistrates have broad discretion in proscribing threatening, abusive, or insulting words and behavior likely to provoke a breach of the peace. Government has used these powers against trade unions, antinuclear and peace campaigns, and even the annual druidic gathering at Stonehenge.[40] The British government has wielded extraordinary powers in Northern Ireland for more than two decades.[41] And both Gorbachev and Yeltsin claimed broad authority during the uncertain transition from Communism.

The powerful, like the powerless, also can mobilize administrative law arguments (just as they can challenge legislation on constitutional grounds). The requirement of environmental impact statements, imposed to prevent private depradations, can be turned against government regulations. The conservative assault on government increasingly demands that regulations survive cost-benefit analyses and evaluations of their impact on the deficit and that property owners be compensated for any adverse impact from regulations, treated as a form of taking.

Because conventional separation-of-powers doctrine charges the executive with the task of administering laws, the criminal enforcement apparatus of prosecutors, police, and prisons properly receives close scrutiny. The organization of the prosecutorial function may influence its fidelity to law and resistance to political pressure. For a long time Britain entrusted the task to privately practicing barristers, who might appear for the Crown in one case and the defense in the next. Indeed, the "cab rank" rule obligates barristers to accept any client able to pay the fee. At the other extreme, the British police once prosecuted minor crimes, even though they were personally invested in securing a conviction. Both have now been replaced by the Crown Prosecution Service, which closely resembles a district attorney's office (though it still briefs privately practicing barristers in serious cases). When the executive itself is suspected of crime, the law may provide for a special prosecutor, untarnished by political affiliation with the accused, as in the Watergate, Iran Contra, and Whitewater affairs. The United States is unusual in electing chief state and local prosecutors, thereby making them more responsive to popular sentiment. This may encourage their offices to devote greater resources to crimes against women or quality-of-life offenses (graffiti, homelessness); it also makes them vigorous advocates of severe penalties. There has been little effort to ensure that prosecutorial staffs reflect the demographic composition of the population (or even the legal profession). But when the defendant chooses a lawyer whose identity may appeal to the jury, the prosecution usually responds in kind: women in the Menendez case and Christopher Darden against Johnnie Cochrane (both African American) in the O. J. Simpson criminal trial.

Prosecutors may select crimes and individuals who have been accused in order to design trial strategies for political objectives: increasing support for the regime, stigmatizing and discrediting opponents (both individuals and groups), and advancing their own careers. The trials of Socrates and Jesus are famous historical examples. Modern instances include the French prosecution of Dreyfus to feed anti-Semitism and Nazi attempts to blame the Reichstag fire on Communists and the assassination of vom Rath on the Jews (the Jewish accused claimed his motive was homosexual jealousy).[42] Communist regimes made extensive use of political prosecutions: examples include the 1930s Moscow show trials and the trials of Romanian justice minister Lucretiu Patrascanu, Hungarian foreign minister Laszlo Rajk and others, Albanian interior minister Koci Xoxe, Bulgarian party official Traicho Kostov, and Polish prime minister Wladyslaw Gomulka. Yugoslavia charged Cardinal Aloysius Stepinac with forced conversions of Eastern Orthodox Serbs under the Croat Ustaschi regime of Ante Pavelic, which was backed by Nazis and Italian fascists. Stalin anticipated his fabrication of the "doctors' plot" by masterminding the prosecution of Rudolf Slansky and ten other Czechs.[43] American prosecutors sought to connect the 1887 Haymarket bombing with anarchism, to convict the anarchists Sacco and Vanzetti of murder, and connect Eugene Victor Debs's 1918 anticonscription trial with subversion; the state fed anti-Communist hysteria through the prosecutions of Alger Hiss, the Rosenbergs, and members of the Communist Party.[44] West Germany prosecuted Heinrich Agartz for treason because his biweekly *Economic and Social Correspondence,* unable to survive on the four hundred copies it sold in the West, was sustained by the East German government's purchase of two thousand copies.[45] Although prosecutors are supposed to be politically neutral, they tend to favor the powerful: capital against labor, the state against civil rights and antiwar protesters.[46] In South Africa they favored Inkatha over the African National Congress.[47]

The prosecutorial role breeds passionate hostility to crime and criminals. Prosecutors wage moral crusades against prostitution, alcohol, drugs, gambling, pornography, homosexuals, the homeless, aliens, gangs, and mugging.[48] They publicize and devote extraordinary resources to high-profile crimes: sensational murders, sexual abuse of children, offenses with a racial dimension, crimes by or against police. They display excessive credulity toward police witnesses, to the point of complicity in police perjury. They suppress exculpatory evidence: in order to convict Michael McMahon and Patrick Murphy of the murder of Reginald Stevens, the British prosecutor concealed witness misidentifications and police payments to witnesses.[49] During the 1992 trial of a white policeman from Teaneck, New Jersey, for killing a black teenager, sheriff's deputies arrested a prosecution witness in front of television cameras inside the courthouse, using a two-year-old warrant, and a New York policeman paralyzed by a youth's bullet was wheeled into the courtroom during the proceedings, in direct contravention of the judge's orders.[50]

Once prosecutors publicly embrace a theory of the case they are extremely reluctant to confess error.[51] The British Home Office refused to postpone the 1953 execution of John Christie in order to allow a full investigation of his belated confession to murdering the wife of Timothy Evans (for which Evans had been executed). A 1966 Home Office inquiry reiterated its confidence in Evans's guilt. Only the intervention of a new home secretary later that year secured a posthumous pardon from the queen.[52] The British government persistently maintained the guilt of James Hanratty, hanged for what were known as the A6 murders, despite repeated confessions by Peter Alphon, the original police suspect.[53] After the Court of Appeal twice denied a full rehearing to Michael McMahon and Patrick Murphy, convicted of murdering Reginald Stevens, the home secretary finally asked the queen to remit the remaining sentence but not to grant a full pardon.[54] The British government has repeatedly refused a posthumous pardon to Derek Bentley, a nineteen–year-old epileptic with an IQ of sixty-six, who was hanged in 1952 for allegedly shouting "Let him have it" to a sixteen–year-old companion who shot a police officer to death. Several hundred Members of Parliament twice sought a reinvestigation. A police eye-witness who denied hearing Bentley shout was not called to testify. Linguistic analysis of Bentley's "confession" revealed that it was written by someone of at least average intelligence.[55]

If prosecutors sometimes display excessive zeal, they can also ignore crimes and victims. Women and racial minorities have complained about being ignored or trivialized. Organized crime and drug traffickers often seem immune from prosecution. Following the 1918–19 uprising in Bavaria, 2,209 Communists were imprisoned; after the 1920 right-wing Kapp putsch a single fascist was sentenced to "honorable arrest."[56] South African prosecutors conducted superficial investigations and inquests into notorious security force murders of antiapartheid activists: Griffiths and Victoria Mxenge, the Pebco Three, Matthew Goniwe and his three companions, David Webster, and Anton Lubowski.[57] Even motivated prosecutors may lack adequate resources or legal authority, as Italian magistrates complained during their investigation of Tangentopoli. Prosecutors generally tend to protect security forces. In Northern Ireland security force suspects cannot be compelled to testify. Although police killed 233 civilians there between 1969 and 1984, there were only twenty trials, and the sole policeman convicted of murder was released after serving three and a half years.[58] The Salvadoran army murdered nearly 1,000 civilians at El Mozote in 1981, but the crime was only exposed by a U.N.-sponsored truth commission in 1992.[59] In the United States prosecutions have been suspended for fear the accused will reveal state secrets.[60] When the South-West African attorney general prosecuted soldiers for murdering civilians in Namibia, South African state president Botha simply terminated the trial.[61]

If the executive objects to convictions, it can use its unlimited power to pardon or grant clemency, as Ford did for Nixon and Reagan for Weinberger. The eighteenth-century British Crown systematically used such powers to create an image of mercy and inspire a sense of dependence.[62]

Although prosecutors make the crucial decisions in the criminal justice system, cause lawyering tends to focus on the police, who are both more visible and more vulnerable because lower in status and more tightly constrained by rules.[63] There are urgent demands that the police mirror the demographics of the population they serve, especially with respect to race; they may even have to live in the community. This does not assure legality—black South African police were no less oppressive than their white counterparts; indeed, their insecurities may have made them more brutal.[64] States must choose between national police forces (which can threaten the civilian regime and oppress local communities) and local ones (more tempted by corruption, susceptible to political pressure, and insensitive to minorities). Liberal reformers have hoped that requiring a college education and improving training will increase respect for legality. Career structure may be relevant: in what other occupation do experienced practitioners retire at forty—often to take more lucrative positions in private security? (The latter, which outnumbers public policing, is subject to far less scrutiny.) Police do sometimes refrain from abusing their powers, even under pressure from above. In the United Kingdom, the chief constable of Cornwall, John Anderson, refused to clear antinuclear protesters from Central Electricity Generating Board property in Luxulyan in 1981. An assistant chief constable, Wyn Jones, declined to arrest women blocking the entrances to Greenham Common in 1982.[65]

Internal disciplinary procedures have been as ineffective in controlling the police as they have in other closed occupations, like law and medicine. The officers who beat false confessions out of the Birmingham Six (accused of IRA bombings) were exonerated by police investigation. Although some prison wardens were disciplined, they were acquitted of all criminal charges. Civil actions against the police were dismissed on grounds of estoppel. Of the more than 5,000 cases heard by the British Police Complaints Authority in 1987, fewer than 800 resulted in any discipline and fewer than 150 in more than advice and admonishment.[66] The police have been just as successful as the older professions in preventing external regulation, in the form of civilian review boards.

As in other hermetic settings, the conspiracy of silence is almost perfect: intense social and economic sanctions and widespread personal complicity strongly discourage whistle-blowing. For the same reason, however, the rare breach can have a profound effect, as when Lt. Gregory Rockman testified to police violence against "coloured" youths on the Cape Flats, or Butana Almond Nofemela and Dirk Coetzee exposed the South African police hit squads.[67] Such betrayals usually occur because one branch of the security apparatus seeks to protect itself by implicating another: the South African Prisons Department preserved the evidence showing that torture of Port Elizabeth detainees occurred not on their watch but in police headquarters; English prison wardens and doctors eventually revealed the force used by police to coerce confessions from the Birmingham Six.[68]

Yet individual offenders rarely suffer serious punishment. South African security forces enjoyed immunity for actions performed "in good faith." And fearing that this was insufficient protection, F. W. de Klerk conferred indemnity on 3,500 police just before losing office in April 1994.[69] The state is quite prepared to pay the high cost of continuing police illegality. South Africa annually paid millions of rands to those tortured, assaulted or killed by police; American municipalities pay far more. By 1991, the south Yorkshire police had paid more than £500,000 to thirty-nine men mistreated during the 1984 miners' strike and the Derbyshire police another £50,000.[70] The few police charged and convicted often receive clemency or pardon. This is most likely after a regime change. Hitler granted the SA and SS an amnesty from prosecution for detaining and torturing opponents during the first months of his rule.[71]

Apathy toward police misconduct periodically is punctuated by moral panics: purges, replacement of the police chief, and sporadic special commissions and prosecutorial investigations. The media may be a more effective scourge: exposure is the greatest deterrent to police abuses. Dr. Wendy Orr's documentation of systematic torture by the Port Elizabeth police during the 1985 Emergency in South Africa quickly stopped the abuses—if only temporarily.[72] In the American South, as well, police atrocities attracted the media spotlight: who can forget Birmingham police chief "Bull" Connor turning his dogs and fire hoses on peaceful demonstrators?[73]

All these remedial mechanisms fail to discourage police illegality because they leave intact the incentives that encourage it. Police are attracted to the career by the desire to fight crime and rewarded for their success in solving serious crimes and convicting prominent criminals.[74] Poorly paid but constantly exposed to the fabulous wealth of organized crime, they are sorely tempted by corruption. Police kidnap suspects in foreign countries: the Israelis seized Eichmann, the French Klaus Barbie, the United States the murderers of Klinghoffer, as well as Panamanian president Manuel Noriega and other Latin American drug dealers, and South Africa seized Ebrahim Ismail Ebrahim. They arrest without cause, using excessive force, often to harass without expecting to prosecute or convict. Vague offenses like vagrancy, loitering, trespass, breach of the peace, unlawful assembly, or disorderly conduct offer ready pretexts, as do traffic violations. Police excesses can provoke resistance, creating further justification for arrest. They conduct searches and seizures without reasonable cause and plant incriminating evidence, such as drugs and weapons. In 1980 the United Kingdom had about four hundred warrants outstanding for tapping phones and fifty for opening mail. It used these powers against striking trade unions (e.g., at Grunwick) and separatists (e.g., Welsh nationalists).[75] It also intercepted communications with the Canadian High Commission, Greenpeace, the El Salvador Human Rights Campaign, the Campaign for Nuclear Disarmament, and trade unions. Although the government appointed a tribunal of lawyers to hear complaints against snooping, none of the sixty-eight was upheld; and courts lacked power to review.[76] The FBI's Cointelpro similarly violated the privacy of the Socialist Workers Party and other organizations in the United States. Police entrap people into committing crimes (especially drug deals) and use informers and provocateurs (especially against political opponents).[77] They detain without trial. The 1974 British Prevention of Terrorism Act (passed within forty-two hours of the Irish Republican Army bombing in Birmingham and renewed annually thereafter) allowed the police to detain without charges or access to a solicitor for up to five days; more than 4,000 were detained between 1977 and 1990; only 6 of the 169 detained in 1990 were ever prosecuted under the act.[78]

Police coach and coerce witnesses, use force to extract confessions, and suppress exculpatory evidence. They conduct line-ups in ways that are known to produce mistaken eyewitness identifications.[79] In the United Kingdom, they fabricated confessions by the "Tottenham Three" for the murder of Police Constable Keith Blakelock; the Court of Appeal later overturned their convictions when electrostatic deposition analysis revealed the falsification.[80] They used verbal abuse, violence, sleep deprivation, denial of tobacco, clothes, blankets and food, lengthy questioning, psychotropic drugs, and finally threats to family and lovers to extract "confessions" from the "Guildford Four" and five of the Birmingham Six. Police bullied a defense witness into altering evidence that would have corroborated the (true) alibi of one of the Guildford Four and concealed his original statement from the defense. Another alibi witness and her mother were treated so badly they did not testify. Police concealed an interview with a witness who offered an alibi for Gerald Conlon; *In the Name of the Father* (the film version of Conlon's autobiography) dramatized the discovery of this evidence in a scene where Gareth Peirce (played by Emma Thompson) finds the police file labeled "Not to be disclosed to the defence." Police instructed forensic scientists to alter evidence connecting the Balcombe Street gang (the IRA's Active Service Unit in London) to the Guildford and Woolwich bombings. Police discredited the gang's confessions to those bombings; when forced to admit their accuracy, the police insisted (without any evidence) that the Guildford Four must have been the gang's accomplices. A police superintendent concocted a false schedule so that his officers could coordinate their lies about the length of the interrogation of the Birmingham Six. The police counseled the crucial forensic scientist while he was testifying.[81]

Police are, if anything, even more invested than prosecutors in maintaining their theory of the case and less willing to confess error. British police discredited the confession of David Ware to the murder of Olive Balchin and may have persuaded him to repudiate it, thereby securing the conviction of Walter Rowland. Ware later confessed to attempting the murder of yet another woman, for which he was convicted.[82] In 1974 Judith Ward was convicted, on the basis of a confession and forensic tests for nitroglycerine, of killing twelve people by bombing a British army bus. When the judgment was overturned in 1991 because the confession was shown to be coerced and false and the forensic test worthless, the assistant chief constable who had secured the conviction expressed nothing more than "regret" for Ward's seventeen years of wrongful imprisonment.[83] British police used all their power to suppress an investigation into security force killings of civilians in Northern Ireland.[84] They sought to cover up the use of excessive force to repress racial disturbances in Southall.[85] Police rightly fear that any such finding of error will undermine all their efforts. After the West Midlands Serious Crime Squad was disbanded for misconduct in 1989, the Court of Appeal overturned all eight of the squad's convictions it reviewed.[86]

Sometimes police largely bypass the legal system. They may restrict freedom of movement, by force or threat of arrest, as in the summer solstice gatherings at Stonehenge, the 1984–85 British miners' strike, and the strike against Rupert Murdoch's News International printing plant in Wapping.[87] Los Angeles declared extensive curfews in response to civil unrest following the acquittal of four police for beating Rodney King. Localities often impose permanent curfews on youths, exclude gang members from parks, and criminalize homelessness. Latin American police murder street children. South African security forces engaged in "dirty tricks" against opponents: harassing phone calls, burglaries, tampering with automobiles, defamatory posters, dead animals and excrement left at houses, arson, and bombing.[88] They attempted and committed assassinations both inside South Africa (Steve Biko, Griffiths and Victoria Mxenge, Matthew Goniwe and his three companions, the "Pebco Three," and David Webster among others) and outside (Ruth First, Dulcie September, and Albie Sachs). They killed hundreds of civilians in massacres at Sharpeville, Soweto, Uitenhage, Sebokeng, Bisho, and many less notorious incidents. And, like prosecutors, they also fail to protect the weak from private power: spousal and child abuse, crime in poor neighborhoods, white-collar crime, and private vigilantism (against racial minorities, gays and lesbians, the poor).

If the generalized executive—prosecutors and police—face temptations to over- and sometimes underenforce the law, so do all the specialized agencies. Welfare officials arbitrarily deny benefits, subject clients to discourtesy and delay, and violate their privacy through interrogations and searches.[89] The U.S. Immigration and Naturalization Service raids residences and workplaces, sweeps up people on the streets, detains them in harsh conditions without access to lawyers, and deports them after perfunctory hearings.[90] The Internal Revenue Service harasses taxpayers through audits and unjustified claims (sometimes at the behest of the executive—as happened with Nixon's "enemies" list).[91] The military excludes the eager and conscripts the unwilling; it imposes harsh discipline and discharge without due process. Regulatory agencies conduct inspections and enforce rules to the letter. All of these agencies also wink at illegality, either through favoritism or corruption.

Cause lawyers have many more opportunities to check executive power than they do to challenge legislation or elections. Some checks on executive power come from outside the system: prime ministers can be brought down by scandal. Others are governmental. Titular rulers (presidents, representatives of the crown or metropole) may intervene in the name of legality. Law can keep civil servants out of politics, though politics may be necessary to keep bureaucrats from obstructing change. Cause lawyers can use administrative law to discipline executive action because, while the administrative state cannot function without extensive delegation of state power, legislatures are determined to control bureaucratic discretion. Cause lawyers may also invoke the due process protections of criminal law on behalf of those charged with opposing the state; yet only a constitution prevents the legislature from endowing the executive with plenary emergency powers and abrogating civil liberties.

Cause lawyers may be able to exploit the basic contradiction that the executive is motivated to implement substantive policies (and rewarded for doing so) but simultaneously constrained to observe legality. Cause lawyers may insist on the independence of prosecutors and challenge the subordination of the criminal process to partisan political ends (as in show trials). Similarly they may protest lenience toward abuses of power—failure to investigate or prosecute, nominal sentences, indemnity, pardon and clemency. While police are more susceptible to engaging in misconduct they are also very susceptible to legal correction. Cause lawyers can press the state to discipline and prosecute; they themselves can initiate and control civil actions, making illegality intolerably costly (in both economic and political terms). By pitting officers and agencies against each other they can puncture the conspiracy of silence. They can try to change the composition, culture, and incentive structure of police forces. They can elaborate and insist upon compliance with due process protections against oppressive behavior: searches, seizures, interrogations, infiltration. The armory of legal weapons devised to control the police can be applied to the numerous other executive agencies that exercise power over individuals.

Judiciary

The preceding discussion of the legislature and executive has repeatedly looked to litigation as a check on political power. Indeed, cause lawyering always has seen the judiciary as offering the greatest opportunities to the powerless. Courts purport to be less overtly political, to apply law rather than make it in response to electoral or interest group pressures, to listen to argument rather than money. Courts are always open and cannot ignore petitioners (although they can give them short shrift). It is less costly to obtain a hearing in a court than to get the attention—much less the votes—of a majority of legislators (although full-scale litigation can be phenomenally expensive). And legal expertise confers a monopoly over courtroom advocacy, whereas in political arenas cause lawyers must compete with other representatives and advisers.[92]

Institutional variables may influence judicial independence. Courts with general jurisdiction are thought to be more independent than those with specialized subject matters, such as patents, tax, claims against the government, labor, or administrative law.[93] States sometimes create special courts in order to repress opponents. After 1935 the Nazis tried Communists, Socialists, and Social Democrats before *Sondsgerichte* (special judges). Their jurisdiction was expanded in 1938 to include vaguely defined offenses, often related to mass mobilization, which carried harsh penalties. By 1943 the *Sondsgerichte* handled two-thirds of all criminal cases in Hamburg. The Nazis also created the *Volksgerichthof* (People's Court), which sentenced more than five thousand to death for offenses against dignitas or "public attempts to paralyze or undermine the will of the Germans or an allied nation to defend itself."[94] At the recommendation of Lord Diplock, Britain passed the 1973 Northern Ireland (Emergency Provisions) Act creating the so-called Diplock Courts, which sat without juries and permitted convictions based on uncorroborated confessions. By the end of the decade, 80 percent of convictions in Britain for sectarian or antigovernment acts rested on confessions.[95] Military courts are even more closely identified with the state; under the Nazis they sentenced an estimated thirty-three thousand to death.[96] Accusatorial and inquisitorial systems offer different opportunities for cause lawyering, although it would oversimplify to call either one more hospitable than the other.[97] Some courts exclude lawyers, ostensibly to make judicial procedures more accessible and comprehensible to lay litigants; but the American experience with small claims courts has not inspired great confidence in the potential of lay litigation to level the playing field. The separation of powers is an axiom of liberal political theory, yet many states charge the lowest level of magistrates with administrative duties that may compromise their independence.

Appeals conventionally are seen as a means of correcting error; and appellate courts are portrayed as more independent as well as technically more proficient.[98] States sometimes curtail the right of appeal, as in collateral attacks on the death penalty in America and sentences of religious fundamentalists in Algeria.[99] Governments may make review contingent on the executive: after a cursory reading the British Home Office decides which of the thousands of petitions by convicted criminals will be heard by the Court of Appeal. Appeal also may be a means of disciplining overly independent lower courts. In Nazi Germany, an appeal to the Führer could lead to a new trial before a special panel of the German Supreme Court; an appellate court that accepted a plea of nullity could then instruct the trial court how to proceed.[100]

Although both laypeople and legal scholars persist in describing courts in the idiom of mechanical jurisprudence—a slot-machine theory of justice in which uncontested facts logically compel decisions—everyone knows that the identity of judges makes a difference.[101] How else to explain the American obsession with the selection of Supreme Court Justices: the Senate's rejection of Nixon's nominations of Carswell and Haynsworth, Reagan's of Bork and Ginsberg, and the furor over Bush's successful nomination of Thomas?[102] Why do we talk of the "Warren" and "Rehnquist" Courts? Why do lawyers shop among forums and strategize to appear before particular judges through creative scheduling and recusal motions? Why have cause lawyers shifted their energies from federal to state courts in recent years? Why the concern that the judiciary reflect the race and gender composition of the population?[103]

The selection process may affect judicial independence. The United States is unique in electing judges. In some American jurisdictions parties nominate, often in exchange for contributions of time or money, and nomination may effectively determine the outcome. In others, races are ostensibly nonpartisan. Not surprisingly, voters seem even less well informed about judicial candidates than about those running for executive or legislative office. Washington chief justice Keith Callow was defeated for reelection by Charles W. Johnson, an unknown solo practitioner who had never held office, did not campaign, and ran only because he thought the election should be contested. Observers attributed Johnson's victory to his common surname, which voters confused with either a Tacoma television anchor, a former state senate sergeant at arms, or a superior court judge.[104] Bar associations often pass on the fitness of both electoral candidates and executive nominees, although they make only crude distinctions between the most and the least qualified. The United States is also unusual in holding public hearings (the new South African Judicial Service Commission adopted that practice in making recommendations to President Mandela for the Constitutional Court, although it declined to admit radio or television).

When the judiciary frustrates the objectives of the political branches, they may respond by packing the court. Roosevelt threatened to do so when the Supreme Court kept invalidating New Deal legislation. In South Africa the National Party expanded and packed the Appellate Division after it nullified efforts to strip Cape Coloured of the franchise.[105] Argentine president Carlos Saul Menem used busboys and clerks to constitute a quorum during a night-time session of Congress, which elevated to the Supreme Court a vice minister of public works, who promptly blocked a corruption investigation into his former department.[106] Ferdinand Marcos filled the Philippine Supreme Court with judges who upheld his authoritarian rule.[107]

Polities also differ in their mechanisms for removing judges. Impeachment is extraordinarily rare, usually restricted to corruption. In California, judges are appointed to the state supreme court but then must stand for reelection. Although incumbency traditionally has assured victory, conservatives defeated chief justice Rose Bird and associate justices Cruz Reynoso and Joseph Grodin because of their opposition to the death penalty.[108]

Polities differ greatly in the career paths of judges. Almost all judges are legally trained (although this is not a prerequisite for the U.S. Supreme Court). Some polities retain lay judges at the bottom of the hierarchy: lay magistrates in England, justices of the peace in the United States. Nazi Germany appointed laymen to the Volksgerichthof.[109] It may matter whether lawyers qualify via apprenticeship or the university and whether judges are apprenticed, receive formal training, or are just thrown in at the deep end. The complicity of German judges with Nazism provoked debate about whether jurisprudential traditions of natural law or positivism are more supportive of judicial independence.[110] In civilian jurisdictions, law students with the best academic qualifications join the magistracy after graduation and ascend a civil service ladder via meritocratic promotion (often based on further examinations). Younger judges in some civil law countries—notably France and Italy—have formed professional associations, often critical of the state. This may help explain the vigor of Italian magistrates in uncovering *mani pulite* in the Tangentopoli scandal. In common law countries lawyers become judges after many years of practice; where the profession is divided, they must be barristers and, where the bar is stratified, senior counsel. Some American jurisdictions have begun to educate the bench about racism and sexism in the courtroom.

Common law jurisdictions (and a few civil law) use juries in criminal matters. (Juries also hear civil disputes in the United States and defamation cases in Britain.) For a long time juries excluded those without property, women, and racial minorities; some still exclude those with disabilities. The source of the venire (e.g., registered voters, driver's licenses), the failure of those summoned to appear (half in California), excuses (from, e.g., mothers of small children, lawyers, sole entrepreneurs), and voir dire challenges (whether for cause or peremptory) further distort the composition of juries. The state may influence selection overtly in "blue ribbon juries" (through educational or occupational qualifications) or covertly (through jury vetting in politically sensitive cases in Britain). The parties may jockey for a more favorable jury by selecting a venue—compare Simi Valley in the first unsuccessful (state) prosecution of the police who beat Rodney King with downtown Los Angeles in the second successful (federal) prosecution.

Juries have the capacity (if not the right) to nullify the law, sometimes acquitting protesters against the Vietnam War,[111] but more often acquitting whites of crimes against blacks. Two juries hung in the prosecution of white racist Byron de la Beckwith for murdering black civil rights activist Medgar Evers in Mississippi in 1962, although Beckwith acknowledged owning the murder weapon. In the first trial the governor walked into the courtroom and warmly shook the accused's hand before the all-white jury. In the second, the Sovereignty Commission (established by the state to resist integration) screened the jurors, and two police supported the accused's alibi. Beckwith was retried thirty years later and finally convicted and sentenced to life imprisonment. But the murderers of Emmett Till in 1955 and the three civil rights workers killed in Philadelphia, Mississippi, in 1964 were never convicted of any state crime.[112] Ironically, the refusal of white South African juries to convict whites of crimes against blacks was the reason they were replaced with two assessors picked by the judge. Northern Ireland eliminated juries in the "Diplock Courts" in order to secure convictions of IRA members.

States attempt to insulate courts from outside influence while they are deliberating. Laws forbid the bribing of judges and tampering with juries, whose members are denied contact with the media and sometimes sequestered; their identities may be concealed, and they may be prohibited from talking about the case afterward. Witnesses may be allowed to testify in camera or with concealed identities or may be hidden by witness protection programs after the trial. Similarly, sub judice rules and exclusion of the media from the courtroom limit public discussion of ongoing trials and protest demonstrations. Some jurisdictions, like Singapore, criminalize any criticism of the judicial system.[113] At the opposite extreme, judges may be threatened or killed for their decisions—by Colombian drug lords, the Sicilian mafia, or the Peruvian Sendero Luminoso. Or the executive may remove them, as Malaysia did its chief justice.[114]

The influence of these characteristics of structure, process, and personnel on judicial independence and efficacy are tested when the law confronts power in two archetypal situations: reactively in the political trial and proactively in the law reform or test case. Law can be a durable shield even when the state mobilizes all its considerable forces of repression.[115] Eighteenth-century English courts sometimes mitigated the harshness of the criminal law.[116] Antebellum American courts sometimes saved fugitive slaves and their protectors from southern laws.[117] A South African court dismissed the charges against all 156 accused (including Nelson Mandela) in their 1956–60 treason trial. A quarter-century later Justice Milne threw out evidence of allegedly subversive statements because of errors in transcription and translation, dismissing treason charges against 22 antiapartheid activists and trade unionists. In 1989 Justice van der Walt not only acquitted 5 Alexandra township organizers but also reprimanded the state for having charged them with treason in the first place. Although Justice van Dijkhorst convicted 11 United Democratic Front members of treason, sentencing 5 to long prison terms, the

Appellate Division overturned the judgment for procedural errors.[118] Disregarding both explicit legislative history and the statute's plain meaning, the Appellate Division interpreted mandatory prison terms for conscientious objectors as maxima, making clear its resentment of legislative constraints on judicial discretion.[119] U.S. district judges have expressed strong hostility to the federal sentencing guidelines, stretching or manipulating them and sometimes simply ignoring them.

The legal shield can be strengthened or weakened in many ways. Courts become production lines for conviction during times of civil unrest, such as the late 1960s in the United States.[120] The right against self-incrimination can be diluted if judge or jury may draw inferences from the accused's refusal to testify. Northern Ireland authorized convictions based on uncorroborated confessions (often tainted by coercion); courts relied heavily on informers.[121] Judges can deny bail or set it high and delay trials, forcing resistance movements to deplete their treasuries to free members.[122] South African attorneys general had unreviewable discretion to prohibit bail. The South African subversion statute allowed a court to infer the requisite mens rea from the mere commission of the act.[123] Eager to move their dockets, judges may reward accused who plead guilty and punish those who insist on trials. Judges and juries may be unduly credulous toward police witnesses and skeptical of the defense. The South African judge and assessors who convicted the "Sharpeville Six" of murder and sentenced them to death disregarded overwhelming evidence that a confession had been coerced.[124] British courts convicted innocent men and women of murders and IRA bombings on the basis of coerced confessions.[125] Also in Britain, the conviction of Michael Luvaglio and Dennis Stafford for murdering Angus Sibbet was overturned because of the judge's obvious partisanship toward the prosecution.[126] Both trial and appellate courts placed excessive faith in the chemical tests for nitroglycerine administered to the Birmingham Six and "Maguire Seven" (convicted as accomplices of the Guildford Four), despite such basic errors as the failure to confirm the results by other methods or retain samples for retesting. The tests were later shown to produce false positives with many ordinary household substances. Courts may reproduce inequalities by awarding lenient sentences to the powerful: whites in the American South, aristocrats in England, wealthy Americans like de Lorean and Milken, military figures like Oliver North.[127]

If police and prosecutors are reluctant to admit their own mistakes, judges resist finding error anywhere in the legal system.[128] The judge who presided over the trial that convicted six innocent men for the Birmingham IRA bombings told the jury that the state had presented "the clearest and most overwhelming evidence I have ever heard in a case of murder."[129] When the Court of Appeal upheld the convictions of four innocent people for the IRA Guildford bombing, Lord Roskill declared that there were "no lurking doubts whatever in our minds."[130] Home secretary Douglas Hurd opposed a reinvestigation of the forensic evidence for fear it would have "awkward" and "disruptive" consequences. The onus was properly on the defense to attack the convictions.[131] A magistrate refused to charge the three Surrey police officers who had coerced the Guildford Four into making false confessions because too much time had passed and the investigator had failed to read the police their rights before interviewing them![132] Lord Denning offered the most egregious illustration of hostility to truth when he dismissed civil actions against the west Midlands police who had beaten confessions out of the Birmingham Six.

> If [the accused] won, it would mean that the police were guilty of perjury; that they were guilty of violence and threats; that the confessions were involuntary and improperly admitted in evidence; and that the confessions were erroneous. That would mean that the Home Secretary would have either to recommend that they be pardoned or to remit the case to the Court of Appeal. That was such an appalling vista that every sensible person would say, 'It cannot be right that these actions should go any further.'[133]

If courts sometimes acquiesce or become complicit in state repression in liberal polities, they are even less independent in authoritarian regimes. In Nazi Germany courts not only failed to acquit but even perverted the law for political ends. Regular courts convicted of sabotage those who stole candy allegedly intended for the army; they convicted a German Jew of violating German race laws by becoming engaged to a German woman in Vienna, holding that Germans carried their personal law with them.[134] Vichy courts aggravated rather than mitigated the severity of race laws, construing the Statut des Juives to compel individuals to *disprove* their Jewishness and abdicating decision-making power in such cases to an administrative agency.[135] Communist regimes made extensive use of show trials— most recently Cuba to justify the execution of General Ochoa Sanchez and China to repress dissidents after Tiananmen Square.[136] South African courts failed to protect the opposition press from censorship, accepting that the executive had untrammeled discretion to suspend newspapers.[137]

Protesters sometimes invite prosecution in order to raise the legal shield and use the court as a platform: suffragists, conscientious objectors (to both World Wars, the Vietnam War, and conscription in South Africa), Gandhi and his followers (first in South Africa and then in India), the Defiance Campaign in South Africa (against pass laws and segregation of public facilities), American civil rights activists, antinuclear and antiwar campaigns, environmentalists, animal rights advocates (against laboratory experimentation, factory farming, and blood sports), religious groups offering sanctuary to Central American immigrants, feminists against pornography, AIDS activists, and antiabortion campaigns.[138] Resistance can extend into the trial itself. Although defiance by the "Chicago Eight" may have contributed to their convictions, it also provoked blatant misconduct by Judge Julius Hoffman, exposing him to media ridicule and appellate reversal.[139] In South Africa, the people of Mogopa returned to clean the cemetery of the village from which they had been forcibly removed and dared the government to repeat that atrocity. Their successful reoccupation inspired similar efforts at Goedgevonden and elsewhere, as grand apartheid collapsed at the end of the 1980s.[140] The Latin American poor long have used similar strategies to obtain both agricultural land and urban housing plots. Defendants commonly seek to broaden the scope of the trial by offering evidence that their actions are justified and the state's illegitimate, when measured by ethical values or political objectives; the state naturally seeks to prosecute the case as an ordinary crime.

Dissidents may expose state action to public scrutiny and critique by disseminating classified information and challenging the state to prosecute. The *New York Times* successfully resisted a government injunction against publishing the Pentagon Papers; and the subsequent prosecution of Daniel Ellsberg for releasing them was aborted after the FBI broke into his psychiatrist's office. But such tactics are less successful in Britain (which also lacks a freedom of information act). For decades the media complied with government "D-notices" telling them what not to publish. Sarah Tisdall was imprisoned for giving the *Guardian* information about Cruise missile deliveries to Greenham Common. Clive Ponting was prosecuted for giving M.P. Tom Dalyell documents from Defence Secretariat 5 about the sinking of the *General Belgrano* during the Falklands War. But Ponting was acquitted even though the government vetted the jury, held part of the trial in camera, and prohibited Dalyell and Channel 4 TV from discussing it. When the British Broadcasting Corporation produced "The Secret Society" about the Zircon affair—a £500 million electronic surveillance project pursued without parliamentary approval—and the *New Statesman* published the contents, both institutions were searched and the BBC enjoined, although the program was ultimately broadcast. One of the most notorious cases was Peter Wright's *Spycatcher*, the autobiography of a former MI5 member about burglaries and bugging of political parties and trade unions, an attempt to assassinate Egyptian president Nasser, and efforts to discredit Harold Wilson's Labour government. Australia enjoined publication. When the *Guardian* and the *Observer* published summaries, they also were enjoined. After the Australian injunction was dissolved, the *Independent, Evening Standard,* and *Daily News* published further material and were held in contempt, even though not covered by the original injunction. When the *Sunday Times* started to serialize the American edition, it also was held in contempt.[141]

The relatively powerless find it far more difficult to use law effectively as a sword.[142] In some polities parliamentary supremacy and the absence of a bill of rights leave petitioners dependent on natural law arguments. Yet even in the hostile terrain of South Africa, plaintiffs persuaded courts to invalidate the incorporation of Moutse into the homeland of KwaNdebele (because the government's goal was administrative efficiency rather than political development) and compel that homeland to enfranchise women (even though South Africa disenfranchised blacks).[143] The long American tradition of judicial review fostered the emergence of public interest lawyering by the American Civil Liberties Union and the National Association for the Advancement of Colored People in the 1920s. The American labor movement made a momentous decision to use law to counterbalance the power of capital.[144] The civil rights movement is the preeminent success story (notwithstanding recent revisionism).[145] During the last three decades law has played an increasingly pivotal role in social movements on behalf of those oppressed because of race, ethnicity, religion, gender, poverty, incarceration, sexual orientation, or disability, as well as movements to protect the environment.[146]

As a sword, however, law may be ornamental or two-edged. Judges are adept at devising reasons for not exercising power, anxious about being attacked as political or exposed as impotent. They invoke doctrines of ripeness, standing, case and controversy, political question, exhaustion of administrative remedies, and abstention. They grant and elaborate defenses of sovereign immunity, act of state, and political question. Their antimajoritarian anxiety is reinforced by respected legal scholars: for example, Herbert Wechsler's critique of the *Brown* decision for offending "neutral principles," Alexander Bickel's praise of the Supreme Court's "passive virtues," contemporary conservative mystifications of "original intent" and "strict construction."[147] Governments fearful of judicial obstruction may enact ouster clauses—as South Africa successfully immunized its Emergency Regulations from judicial scrutiny.[148] Many victories, legislative or judicial, are largely symbolic, difficult or impossible to implement.[149] South African administrators dragged their feet for five years before fully complying with decisions affirming the right of black workers to live in cities with their dependents.[150] And judicial victories can be reversed: by legislatures where parliament is supreme, by constitutional amendment where it is not—as exemplified by American conservatives seeking to restore school prayer and outlaw abortion.

Furthermore, the powerful may be more adept at wielding the legal sword to entrench their power. Capital used injunctions against labor; southern segregationists used them against civil rights demonstrators.[151] Constitutional arguments frustrate the exercise of state power on behalf of the powerless. Opponents invoked the Due Process Clause against New Deal legislation, the Equal Protection Clause against affirmative action, the Fourth Amendment prohibition of unreasonable search and seizure against health and safety regulation in the workplace, the Fifth Amendment limit on takings against environmental measures, the First Amendment protection of free speech against the regulation of tobacco advertising, campaign contributions, pornography or hate speech, and the Second Amendment against gun control. The judiciary obstructed Allende in Chile; the new Canadian Charter of Rights was promptly and effectively used by vested interests.[152]

Dominant groups have sought to portray themselves as oppressed by Big Government: tobacco companies have identified themselves with civil rights, environmental despoilers with unemployed workers. Conservatives have funded "nonprofit" law firms. They have used "strategic lawsuits against public participation" (SLAPPs) to suppress opponents.[153] Yet the latter have turned that weapon against the dominant (SLAPPbacks). When the California agribusiness giant J. B. Boswell sued Kern County farmers for defamation for an $8,000 ad they published concerning the Peripheral Canal, the latter sued Boswell for malicious prosecution, winning $3.5 million compensatory and $10 million punitive damages. When Shell Oil sued a Sacramento lawyer for alleging that their plastic pipe posed health hazards, he won $175,000 compensatory and $5 million punitive damages.[154]

Cause lawyers may concentrate on litigation in part because their skills are essential; but the judicial forum is particularly attractive to the powerless as well because courts *must* hear every claim and give reasons for their decisions. Cause lawyers may try to render courts more hospitable by campaigning for judicial independence, general rather than specialized jurisdiction, full appellate review as of right, and a bench whose demographics mirror the larger society. They may use the procedures for appointment, discipline, and removal to exclude the most implacably hostile and seek to educate sitting judges about racism and sexism. They can insist on representative juries and exclude those with potential biases. They can mobilize favorable public opinion while seeking to insulate the court when opinion is hostile. When the state stages show trials, cause lawyers can indict the government before the court of public opinion, exposing gross procedural irregularity and substantive inequality. Indeed, activists sometimes invite the government's resort to legal and illegal coercion in order to expose its inability to offer a convincing justification. Cause lawyers seek to broaden the factual inquiry, invoke extralegal norms, and locate the controversy in its broader social and political context. One of the most effective defenses may be the threat to reveal state secrets. Even tragic defeats can strengthen a cause, as in the execution of Ken Saro Wiwa and the other Ogboni political activists in Nigeria. Because legal systems are deeply invested in the integrity of their procedures, the demonstration of egregious error in one instance casts doubt on all other decisions. Although it is potentially more rewarding to use law as a sword in the judicial arena, cause lawyers encounter jurisdictional limitations, excessive judicial caution, obstacles in implementation, and the real possibility of legislative reversal. Yet even paper victories have value because of the substantial political cost to the state of disregarding or nullifying them.

Legal Profession

Although laypeople occasionally mobilize the law themselves, legal assistance usually is indispensable. The demographic representativeness of the profession may affect both the accessibility of lawyers and their sympathy and commitment. Most countries excluded women until the late nineteenth or early twentieth centuries and racially oppressed groups even longer. In 1933 the Nazis forced out all women and most Jews (who constituted 20 percent of the bar—60 percent in Berlin, perhaps 80 percent in Vienna). The remaining Jews could not belong to firms with Aryans, represent Aryans, or publish books or articles. In 1938 they were demoted to "Jewish legal advisers."[155] Women and especially racially oppressed categories remain underrepresented in most legal professions and concentrated in the lower strata. Virtually all southern white lawyers refused to take civil rights cases.[156] Complaints of spousal abuse have risen as the number of women lawyers increased—evidence that women clients find them more accessible and sympathetic. Even after ascriptive barriers fall, political tests may remain. The Nazis expelled Communists and other political opponents; during the 1950s American states refused to admit them; the postwar German *Berufsverbot* excluded Communists from government jobs. Nazis disciplined lawyers for criticizing judges, making disparaging remarks about the law, being overly friendly with government opponents, failing to shout "Heil Hitler," and not participating in Nazi fundraising activities.[157] Authoritarian regimes imprison or harass opposition lawyers.[158] If local lawyers cannot or will not represent unpopular clients, foreign lawyers may seek admission pro hac vice: northerners in the American South, English barristers in the former colonies.

The willingness and capacity of lawyers to represent controversial clients or causes may vary with their training. An academic education in law may foster greater independence than an apprenticeship. Entry barriers also affect the number and backgrounds of those who qualify and consequently the cost of legal services. English barristers claim that their greater distance from clients (who are mediated by solicitors) and the requirement of solo practice keep them more independent than either solicitors or lawyers where the professions are fused. They also point to the "cab rank" rule, which obligates them to accept any client (although barristers and their clerks can manipulate fees and schedules to avoid unpopular clients). If private practitioners are more independent than corporate counsel and especially government employees, do the greater numbers and prestige of the former in the common law world help to explain the greater visibility of cause lawyering in the United States and United Kingdom compared with Germany or Japan? Lawyers in the Communist world were few, low in status, and usually dependent on the government; it is hardly surprising they rarely opposed the regime.[159] Among private practitioners, what is the influence of firm size and degree and content of specialization by subject and client? Large-firm lawyers have far greater resources, but they also may be more dependent on corporate clients, whom they fear to alienate.[160]

Cultural variables may influence willingness to champion causes. Inquisitorial systems may dilute loyalty to client, but adversarial systems continue to debate competing obligations to the legal system and society—to disclose evidence, for instance, or prevent perjury by clients and witnesses.[161] The Nazi regime elevated the defense lawyer's duty to the state above that to the client, praising a lawyer as an "Organ der Rechtspflege" for denouncing his own clients in the People's Court.[162] During the trial of those accused of murdering German Communist Party leaders Karl Liebknecht and Rosa Luxemburg, a member of the federal prosecutor's staff, Mr. Jorns, advised the *defense*. When this was exposed, he sued for defamation. After two lower courts found for the defendants on the ground of truth, the German Supreme Court instructed them to whitewash Jorns, who then was appointed first president of the People's Court.[163] When the Nazis prosecuted Hershel Grynszpan for assassinating Ernst vom Rath, Hitler assigned the case to George Thierack, president of the People's Court, who himself instructed the defense lawyer.[164] Between the wars Japan strongly encouraged mediation in place of trials.[165] The defense lawyers for those charged in the Tiananmen Square demonstration, appointed only three days before trial, simply pleaded for mercy rather than offering any defense.[166] Even when governments do not intervene, lawyers for unpopular causes often share the stigma of their clients: Americans accused of Communism during the McCarthy era, members of the IRA in the United Kingdom, Palestinians in Israel, the Red Army Faction in Germany, former Nazis and Arab terrorists in France, gays and lesbians in many countries. Yet advocates representing the antiapartheid movement in South Africa were not reviled as supporters of the African National Congress, perhaps because many continued to have an active apolitical practice.[167]

Paradoxically, unrepresented defendants may have advantages: greater autonomy and scope to address political issues, judicial solicitude, and jury sympathy. Anarchists Alexander Berkman and Emma Goldman insisted on appearing pro se, he in his 1892 assassination defense, both in their 1917 anticonscription campaign. Samuel Lovejoy testified for a day and a half about toppling a nuclear power plant weather tower in western Massachusetts in 1977.[168] Colin Ferguson, who defended himself against charges of killing six people on the Long Island Railroad in 1993, challenged Nassau County's jury selection process as racially biased and sought to subpoena President Clinton and former governor Cuomo.[169]

The single most important variable may be financial support for needy clients. Lawyers with profitable private practices may be able to defray the cost of political cases.[170] Rules about legal costs and contingent fees may influence self-funded cause lawyering. National legal cultures differ greatly in their sense of obligation to provide free legal advice or representation. Large American firms sometimes compete in conspicuous displays of altruism: encouraging their lawyers to work pro bono, establishing legal clinics, and sponsoring public interest fellowships. Professional associations may reinforce such activity by publishing the names of participating firms; a few law schools have required students to perform pro bono services. But though American governments and bar associations have flirted with mandatory pro bono, they ultimately backed away. There may be an inverse relationship between state support for legal services and voluntary contributions by private practitioners.

Private philanthropy may contribute to institutions (public interest law firms) or causes (legal defense funds). The growth of human rights lawyering in South Africa in the 1980s reflected the generous support of West European and North American public and private donors: approximately £100 million to the International Defence and Aid Fund during its twenty-five years, millions more to the Legal Resources Centres, the Centre for Applied Legal Studies, Lawyers for Human Rights, and the Black Lawyers Association. The more distant the source of funds, the less constraint on how they are used. American philanthropies risk losing their tax-exempt status if beneficiaries engage in "political" activities. Even without such restrictions, public interest law firms may tailor their activities to maximize the likelihood of refunding. Conservative causes have established their own nonprofit law firms, generously funded by corporations, churches, wealthy individuals, and foundations.

Government legal aid programs usually are the largest source of support, but they frequently limit the clients served, subject matter of cases, and legal strategies.[171] Caseload pressures produce routinization, replacing vigorous advocacy with reasonable accommodation. A constitutional right to counsel is a recent innovation, protected by just a few countries: the South African Appellate Division rejected such a claim in 1992, although the new constitution may change this. Studies have compared the expertise and energy of public defenders, court-appointed counsel, and private defense lawyers.[172] Judges may assign cases to compliant lawyers and discipline vigorous advocates, using either contempt powers or Rule 11 proceedings.[173] British judges may express their hostility to political lawyers and causes in awarding costs.[174] Even a sympathetic government cannot equalize legal resources, however, especially for facilitative functions, in societies riven by structural inequalities; compare prosecution and defense, tort plaintiffs and defendants (as in the tobacco litigation), or labor and management.[175] One of the Guildford Four (who faced life imprisonment for an alleged IRA bombing) was represented by a solicitor with no experience defending serious crimes; his solo practice consisted of property and matrimonial matters. Prior to trial, the other three saw only articled clerks! Counsel for at least one accused was instructed the night before the trial began.[176] The prison duty solicitor who initially interviewed the Birmingham Six ignored evidence of torture.[177]

Professional associations can play a crucial role in encouraging cause lawyering. They can seek the power to discipline, thereby protecting lawyers from state "discipline" or repression. To discourage the emergence of an independent legal profession in the Occupied Territories, Israel assumed disciplinary powers over Palestinian lawyers in 1967.[178] Professional associations may help to deliver legal services: two former American Bar Association presidents founded the Lawyers Committee for Civil Rights under Law in 1964 to provide representation in the South; the ABA has been a strong supporter of federal legal services programs since their inception. Lawyers (like everyone) sometimes seem better able to perceive injustice at a distance than at home. Most professional associations champion "neutral" process values, but a few are openly partisan: compare the American Civil Liberties Union with the National Lawyers Guild, the Lawyers Committee for Civil Rights under Law with the Lawyers Constitutional Defense Committee (all in the United States), Justice with the Haldane Society (in the United Kingdoom), Lawyers for Human Rights with the National Association of Democratic Lawyers and the Black Lawyers Association (in South Africa), the International Commission of Jurists with La Ligue des Droits de l'Homme, the International Juridical Association, and the International Association of Democratic Lawyers (in the world arena).[179] Professional associations have a spotty record of resisting threats to the rule of law. Bar associations did not stand up to McCarthyism in the United States, the German occupation in France, or fascism in Italy or Brazil.[180] Nevertheless, professional bodies in Ghana, Malaysia, and the Occupied Territories of Israel have threatened to strike in support of the judiciary, and Egyptian lawyers have resisted the state attack on lawyers who represent religious fundamentalists.[181]

Although criminal defendants can sometimes derive political advantages from representing themselves, cause lawyers usually are indispensable when the powerless seek to interpose law against power. A number of variables shape the quantity and quality of cause lawyering: the backgrounds of lawyers, the mode of training, the size and structure of the privately practicing bar, the professional culture's support for altruism, ethical norms balancing the lawyer's obligation to client and to the larger society, and public identification of lawyers with unpopular clients. Professional associations can confer legitimacy on cause lawyers as defenders of the rule of law; and, as already noted, the profession's insistence on self-regulation can protect cause lawyers from state repression. Beyond these social, political, and cultural influences, material resources are critical. Although private philanthropy has played an invaluable role in launching cause lawyering efforts and supporting them during particularly visible struggles, public funds are the principal source for routine representation. Both constrain the content and quality of cause lawyering.

Regime Changes

The encounter between law and politics emerges in sharp relief before, during, and after a change of regime.[182] Sometimes the rupture is sudden—imperial conquest, violent revolution, military defeat; sometimes it takes years or decades for old wrongs to be righted. Legal systems have struggled with the aftermath of rebellion and revolution (the Glorious Revolution in England, the French Revolution), internal colonialism (aborigines in the United States, Canada, and Australia), racism (slavery in the United States, apartheid in South Africa), civil war (the trials of Justice Chase and President Johnson during the Confederacy), fascism (the Nuremberg and Tokyo war crimes trials, fascism in Italy, collaboration in France and Belgium, claims for restitution in Korea and China), the Holocaust (Israel's prosecution of Eichmann and Demjanjuk), dictatorship in Latin America (Chile, Argentina, El Salvador), and now the crimes of Communism (imprisonment, execution, expropriation) and war crimes in Serbia.[183]

The legal system seems powerless to judge incumbent regimes, as we see from the cases of Rhodesia after the Unilateral Declaration of Independence, South Africa's occupation of Namibia, and the mining of Nicaraguan harbors by the United States. When the outcome of a power struggle is still in doubt, legal processes are similarly unpredictable. Undefeated on the battlefield, Bosnian Serbs refused to deliver war criminals to the U.N. tribunal in The Hague in compliance with the accord they signed in Dayton.[184] Russia remains embattled with the former constituents of the Soviet Union, as the bloody battle over Chechnya painfully illustrated. Russian courts have had to consider charges that the Communist Party is illegal, as well as judge the August 1991 attempted coup.[185] Gorbachev and Yeltsin clashed over the Gorbachev Foundation, Gorbachev's obligation to heed subpoenas, and even his right to a passport.[186]

All the conventions of legal process are questioned in such circumstances. What substantive rules can be applied to conduct lawful at the time it occurred? Defending himself to a parliamentary committee, General Wojciech Jaruzelski has claimed that the Polish constitution permitted imposition of martial law, which was necessary to forestall a Soviet invasion.[187] What is the difference between war and crime? An Israeli retired general's 1995 admission that he and another officer had executed forty-nine Egyptian prisoners of war in the Sinai Peninsula in 1956 led to fierce debates over the military justifications for the atrocity.[188] Who should be judged: the leaders (who may claim ignorance of the acts charged and still enjoy public support) or their underlings (who will claim to have been following orders)? The unified Germany has failed to prosecute or seriously punish most East German leaders—notably Premier Erich Honnecker and spy chiefs Markus Wolf and Erich Mielke—while trying border guards for killing those who sought to escape to the West and purging low-level Stasi (secret police) informers.[189] When Hungary jailed two seventy–year-old militiamen for shooting into a crowd during the Soviet invasion thirty-nine years earlier the country's anti-Communist president questioned the verdicts, "especially when we don't know who gave the orders to shoot."[190] When charges are brought, they often are incidental to the real evil. Todor Zhivkov, who ruled Bulgaria for thirty-five years, was convicted not for imprisoning, torturing, or killing his opponents but for embezzling $1 million and allowing Communist Party members access to cheap cars, apartments, and villas.[191] (Similarly, leaders of organized crime in the United States tend to be prosecuted for income tax evasion, perjury, and jury tampering rather than murder, drug dealing, prostitution, gambling, or extortion.)

The choice of court is often contested. When René Bousquet was indicted in 1989 for crimes during the Vichy regime, the government argued that he could be tried only by a special high court of justice, which had been abolished shortly after World War II.[192] After Argentine president Alfonsín acknowledged the jurisdiction of the military court to try those implicated in the "dirty war," the court simply failed to act. Eventually he transferred the case to the federal court.[193] Honduran military officers, supported by the country's military commander, have refused to appear before civilian courts to stand trial on murder charges.[194] After initial defiance, two former Chilean generals convicted of the assassination of Orlando Letelier and Ronni Moffitt in Washington twenty years earlier, finally surrendered to begin serving six- and seven-year sentences.[195] Sandinista general Humberto Ortega Saavedra remained army commander under President Violeta Barrios de Chamorro. Eight of his bodyguards have been prosecuted for murdering Jean Paul Genie, the son of a wealthy Nicaraguan family. The deputy police commander investigating the Genie killing was shot to death by another policeman. The civil judge in that case bowed to a Sandinista law giving the military courts exclusive jurisdiction. Frustrated, the National Assembly sought assistance in the investigation from the Venezuelan police.[196] Sometimes the new regime contents itself with investigation and exposure without punishment. Truth commissions have been established or contemplated in Argentina, Chile, El Salvador, Guatemala, Honduras, Haiti, and South Africa.[197]

Investigations often are delayed by politics. France is still dealing with the German occupation more than half a century after liberation: Jean Leguay died ten years after being indicted without ever having been tried; Maurice Papon, indicted in 1980, still had not been tried by 1992; Paul Touvier, chief of the pro-Nazi militia in Lyons, was sentenced to death in absentia in 1946—the statute of limitations for ordinary crimes ran out in 1967, and Georges Pompidou pardoned him in 1971. When Touvier was flushed out of hiding in 1989 (having been protected by the Catholic Church for decades), he was charged with crimes against humanity (for which there was no statute of limitations), but the trial court found no evidence of such crimes.[198] President François Mitterand expressed such outrage that the case was reopened, and Touvier was finally convicted and sentenced to life imprisonment in April 1994.

In most instances, however, punishment is light. René Bousquet, the highest police official of Vichy, was sentenced to only five years denial of the right to vote or hold public office, and even this was suspended.[199] Although Argentina initially filed 1,700 cases against seven hundred officers, only nine were tried and five convicted; two received life sentences and the others four and a half to seventeen years' imprisonment. The more people implicated, the fewer are likely to be punished. The allies originally identified 3,669,230 former Nazis. But after a pretense of de-Nazification, most were reemployed by government (in contradistinction to the Berufsverbot, which denied employment to Communists). Although the highest Nazi judges were sentenced to life imprisonment, none served more than ten years and most less than five.[200] In contrast, Germany still has not rehabilitated notable opponents of the Nazi regime, like the Nobel Prize–winning editor Carl von Ossietzky and the theologian Dietrich Bonhoeffer.[201] Governments often pardon former leaders and grant blanket amnesties to followers. El Salvador's president Cristiani pushed an amnesty through the legislature within days after a truth commission implicated the military in numerous murders. In his last moments in office, South African president de Klerk amnestied former law and order minister Adriaan Vlok and 3,500 police officers.[202] Peru amnestied the military for all offenses committed against guerrillas and civilians in the previous fifteen years.[203]

Regime changes offer cause lawyers a rare opportunity to put on trial those who have abused their power. The procedural obstacles and often unsatisfactory outcome, however, reveal the inescapably political base of law. Adversaries contest jurisdiction, composition of the court, and substantive law. Superiors and inferiors seek to blame one another. It is difficult to pin the label of crime on acts that were legal at the time committed or are hard to distinguish from warfare. Tribunals indulge in endless delay, tend to focus on the marginalia of ordinary crimes, and ultimately impose inadequate penalties. Law may speak truth to power, but it is often truth without consequences.

Conclusion

This chapter begins to explore the paradox that law, which necessarily reflects power, sometimes can be a source of what Galbraith called countervailing power. That potential derives from several sources. The state is not monolithic: power is divided among branches and within them; institutions and officials differ in incentive and culture. The state also is somewhat autonomous; Marxism long ceased trying to read off superstructure from base. Unlike market behavior and realpolitik, law inherently embodies and expresses ideals. Few polities today openly oppose democracy and equality.

I attempted to draw a first, crude, map of the loci of cause lawyering, the instances where law confronts and thus may constrain politics. Only after that is greatly refined will we be able take the next step of assessing outcomes. These are indeterminate: every legal tactic devised by the powerless can be appropriated by the powerful, often with greater effect. But further study may allow us to discern patterns in the differences across societies and times, among subject matters, and between adversaries. The strength of law varies directly with the vigor of the social movements using it. Absent any internal opposition, law is supine in the face of state power, as in Nazi Germany. The strength of law also varies directly with the support it receives in the media and from outside the society—two phenomena that often are closely related. The press, both domestic and foreign, were jubilant when South African courts confronted apartheid; foreign governments extolled the rule of law; and foreign donors generously supported human rights lawyers. Northerners, the national media, and the federal government played a similar role in the civil rights struggle in the American South. Cause lawyering is most successful when a confident government is engaged in social change and most often frustrated when a frightened government is desperately scrambling to retain power. It may be more effective in attacking the peripheries of power than the core—forced removals in South Africa, for instance, rather than the Emergency. Since it depends on divisions within the state, it is stymied when the executive assumes absolute power (the extreme being military rule). Law, like any remedial mechanism, is more likely to be employed at a distance: courts correcting police rather than internal police disciplinary procedures, war crimes punished years or decades later. Law prefers to articulate procedural rules rather than dictate outcomes. It expresses universal values in the language of rights but abdicates distributive questions to politics and market. It is more powerful as a shield against abuses than as a sword to achieve substantive goals, as the protector of negative liberties rather than the guarantor of positive ones.

For all its limitations, however, law is indispensable, a source of hope and leverage to those who lack any other. One price of liberation is eternal cause lawyering.

Notes

1. Marc Galanter, "Why the 'Haves' Come Out Ahead: Speculations on the Limits of Legal Change," *Law and Society Review* 9 (1974), 95.

2. Richard L. Abel, "Socializing the Legal Profession: Can Redistributing Lawyers' Services Achieve Social Justice?" *Law and Policy Quarterly* 1 (1979), 5; Richard L. Abel, "The Contradictions of Informal Justice," in *The Politics of Informal Justice*, vol. 1: *The American Experience*, ed. Richard L. Abel (New York: Academic Press, 1982), 267; Richard L. Abel, "Law without Politics: Legal Aid under Advanced Capitalism," *UCLA Law Review* 32 (1985), 474.

3. See, e.g., the reports of Amnesty, Human Rights Watch, the International Commission of Jurists, and the Lawyers Committee for Human Rights.

4. E.g., David J. Garrow, *Liberty and Sexuality: The Right to Privacy and the Making of Roe v. Wade* (New York: Macmillan, 1994) (abortion); Mark Tushnet and Katya Lezin, "What Really Happened in *Brown v. Board of Education?*," *Columbia Law Review* 91 (1991), 1867 (school desegregation); Susan E. Lawrence, *The Poor in Court: The Legal Services Program and Supreme Court Decision Making* (Princeton, N.J.: Princeton University Press, 1990); Martha F. Davis, *Brutal Need: Lawyers and the Welfare Rights Movement, 1960–1973* (New Haven, Conn.: Yale University Press, 1993); Sidney L. Harring, *Policing a Class Society: The Experience of American Cities, 1876–1915* (New Brunswick, N.J.: Rutgers University Press, 1994) (Indian sovereignty).

5. E.g., Derrick A. Bell Jr., *Race, Racism, and American Law* (Boston: Little Brown, 1973); Derrick A. Bell Jr., *And We Are Not Saved* (New York: Basic Books, 1987); Derrick A. Bell Jr., *Faces at the Bottom of the Well: The Permanence of Racism* (New York: Basic Books, 1992); Richard Delgado and Jean Stefancic, *Failed Revolutions: Social Reform and the Limits of Legal Imagination* (Boulder, Colo.: Westview Press, 1994).

6. E.g., Mark Tushnet, *The NAACP's Legal Strategy against Segregated Education, 1925–1950* (Chapel Hill: University of North Carolina Press, 1987); Mark Tushnet, *Making Civil*

Rights Law: Thurgood Marshall and the Supreme Court, 1936–1961 (New York: Oxford University Press, 1994); Jack Greenberg, *Crusaders in the Courts* (New York: Basic Books, 1994); John J. Abt with Michael Myerson, *Advocate and Activist: Memoirs of an American Communist Lawyer* (Urbana: University of Illinois Press, 1993); Arthur Kinoy, *Rights on Trial: The Odyssey of a People's Lawyer* (Cambridge, Mass.: Harvard University Press, 1983); J. L. Chestnut and Julia Cass, *Black in Selma: The Uncommon Life of J. L. Chestnut, Jr.* (New York: Anchor Books, 1990).

7. Burton A. Weisbrod, Joel F. Handler, and Neil K. Komesar, eds., *Public Interest Law: An Economic and Institutional Analysis* (Berkeley: University of California Press, 1978).

8. On the political contingency of decentralization, see Joel F. Handler, *Down from Bureaucracy: The Ambiguity of Privatization and Empowerment* (Princeton, N.J.: Princeton University Press, 1996).

9. Otto Kirchheimer, *Political Justice: The Use of Legal Procedure for Political Ends* (Princeton, N.J.: Princeton University Press, 1961), 55–56.

10. T. R. H. Davenport, *South Africa: A Modern History* (Cape Town: Macmillan, 1986), 363–366, 377–379.

11. Richard L. Abel, *Politics by Other Means: Law in the Struggle against Apartheid, 1980–1994* (New York: Routledge, 1995), chap. 11.

12. Jamin B. Raskin, "Legal Aliens, Local Citizens: The Historical, Constitutional and Theoretical Meanings of Alien Suffrage," *University of Pennsylvania Law Review* 141 (1993), 1391.

13. California, Illinois, Pennsylvania, South Carolina, and Michigan. *Los Angeles Times,* January 24, 1995, A3.

14. Lani Guinier, *The Tyranny of the Majority: Fundamental Fairness in Representative Democracy* (New York: Free Press, 1994).

15. *New York Times,* March 9, 1993, A1. The PRI responded by setting a $333,000 limit on donations to the party trust fund, while exempting all other contributions. *Los Angeles Times,* March 10, 1993, A12.

16. *New York Times,* April 15, 1991, A15.

17. Robert A. Caro, *The Years of Lyndon Johnson,* vol. 1 (New York: Knopf, 1982); Robert Dallek, *Lone Star Rising: Lyndon Johnson and His Times, 1908–1960* (New York: Oxford University Press, 1991).

18. Michael Specter, "Russian Court Puts Key Party Back on Ballot," *New York Times,* November 5, 1995, §1 p. 1.

19. The Islamic Salvation Front, the Front for National Liberation, and the Front of Socialist Forces together won 85 percent of the vote in 1991—the only free parliamentary election in Algerian history. *New York Times,* January 14, 1995, 5.

20. Larry Rohter, "Guatemalan Ex-Dictator Is Trying to Make a Comeback at the Polls," *New York Times,* May 28, 1995, §1 p. 4. He narrowly lost the election.

21. Theodore J. Schneyer, "The Incoherence of the Unified Bar Concept: Generalizing from the Wisconsin Case," *American Bar Foundation Research Journal* [1983], 1 (bar associations).

22. Daniel H. Lowenstein, "Campaign Spending and Ballot Propositions: Recent Experience, Public Choice Theory and the First Amendment," *UCLA Law Review* 29 (1982), 506.

23. When the European Court of Human Rights invalidated Britain's seven-day detention law, the government simply derogated from the European Convention on Human Rights and Fundamental Freedoms on the ground of a "public emergency threatening the life of the nation." That was subsequently challenged before the court. *Fox, Campbell and Hartley v. U.K.* (1990) 13 EHHR 157. See generally Conor Gearty, "Freedom of Assembly

and Public Order," in *Individual Rights and the Law in Britain,* ed. Christopher McCrudden and Gerald Chambers (Oxford: Clarendon Press, 1994).

24. Abel, *Politics by Other Means,* chap. 4.

25. Ibid., chap. 11.

26. Ingo Müller, *Hitler's Justice: The Courts of the Third Reich* (Cambridge, Mass.: Harvard University Press, 1991), chap. 4; Peter Hain, *Political Trials in Britain* (London: Quartet, 1984), 270.

27. E.g., A. B. Brian Simpson, *In the Highest Degree Odious: Detention without Trial in Wartime Britain* (New York: Oxford University Press, 1993) (Britain).

28. Gearty, "Freedom of Assembly and Public Order."

29. Abel, *Politics by Other Means,* chap. 11.

30. Ibid., chap. 3.

31. Ibid., chap. 10.

32. Ibid., chap. 12.

33. Ibid., chap. 11.

34. Ibid.

35. Ibid., chap. 8.

36. Stephen Ellmann, *In a Time of Trouble: Law and Liberty in South Africa's State of Emergency* (Oxford: Clarendon Press, 1992).

37. See David Bonner, *Emergency Powers in Peacetime* (London: Sweet & Maxwell, 1985); Richard Vogler, *Reading the Riot Act: The Magistracy, the Police and the Army in Civil Disorder* (Milton Keynes, United Kingdom: Open University Press, 1991); E. Fraenkel, *The Dual State* (New York: Octagon, 1969) (Nazi Germany); Franz Neumann, *Behemoth: The Structure and Practice of National Socialism, 1933–1944* (New York: Octagon, 1972) (Nazi Germany); Phil Scraton, ed., *Law, Order and the Authoritarian State* (Milton Keynes, United Kingdom: Open University Press, 1987) (Britain); Stuart Hall, *Drifting into a Law and Order Society* (London: Cobden Trust, 1980) (Britain); A. Jamieson, *The Heart Attacked: Terrorism and Conflict in the Italian State* (London: Marion Boyars, 1989) (Italy); Michael Keren, "Law, Security and Politics: An Israeli Case Study," *International Journal of the Sociology of Law* 21 (1993), 105 (Israel); Paula R. Newberg, *Judging the State: Courts and Constitutional Politics in Pakistan* (New York: Cambridge University Press, 1995) (Pakistan).

38. Müller, *Hitler's Justice,* 27–29.

39. Richard Weisberg, "Legal Rhetoric under Stress: The Example of Vichy," *Cardozo Law Review* 12 (1991), 1371.

40. K. D. Ewing and C. A. Gearty, *Freedom under Thatcher: Civil Liberties in Modern Britain* (Oxford: Clarendon Press, 1990), 137–169, 192–208, 241–248.

41. See Kevin Boyle, Tom Hadden, and Paddy Hillyard, *Law and State: The Case of Northern Ireland* (London: Martin Robertson, 1975); Kevin Boyle, Tom Hadden, and Paddy Hillyard, *Ten Years On in Northern Ireland* (London: Cobden Trust, 1980); Michael Farrell, *Emergency Legislation: The Apparatus of Repression* (Derry: Field Day Theater , 1986); Emma Mulloy, *Emergency Legislation: Dynasties of Coercion* (Derry: Field Day Theater, 1986); Paddy Hillyard, *Suspect Community: People's Experience of the Prevention of Terrorism Acts in Britain* (London: Pluto Press, 1993); Lawyers Committee for Human Rights, *Human Rights and Legal Defense in Northern Ireland: The Intimidation of Defense Lawyers; the Murder of Patrick Finucane* (New York: LCHR, 1993); cf. Gerard Hogan and Clive Walker, *Political Violence and the Law in Ireland* (Manchester: Manchester University Press, 1989) (Ireland).

42. Kirchheimer, *Political Justice,* 101–105; Müller, *Hitler's Justice,* chap. 4.

43. Kirchheimer, *Political Justice,* 99–100; George Pattee, *The Case of Cardinal Aloysius Stepinac* (Milwaukee: Bruce Publishers, 1953); Karel Kaplan, *Report on the Murder of the*

General Secretary (Columbus: Ohio State University Press, 1990), reviewed by Josef Skvorecky in "The Theater of Cruelty," *New York Review of Books,* August 16, 1990, 41.

44. Walter Schneir and Miriam Schneir, *Invitation to an Inquest: A New Look at the Rosenberg-Sobell Case* (New York: Doubleday, 1965); Michael R. Belknap, *Cold War Political Justice: The Smith Act, the CIA, and American Civil Liberties* (New York: Greenwood Press, 1978).

45. Kirchheimer, *Political Justice,* 92–95. Agartz was acquitted.

46. Steven E. Barkan, *Protesters on Trial: Criminal Justice in the Southern Civil Rights and Vietnam Antiwar Movements* (New Brunswick, N.J.: Rutgers University Press, 1985).

47. See Abel, *Politics by Other Means,* chap. 6.

48. Stanley Cohen, *Folk Devils and Moral Panics: The Creation of the Mods and Rockers* (London: Macgibbon & Kee, 1972); Stuart Hall, Chas Chritcher, Tony Jefferson, John Clarke, and Brian Roberts, *Policing the Crisis: Mugging, the State, and Law and Order* (London: Macmillan, 1978) (mugging); Sidney L. Harring, *Policing a Class Society: The Experience of American Cities, 1876–1915* (New Brunswick, N.J.: Rutgers University Press, 1983) (vagrants).

49. Bob Woffinden, *Miscarriages of Justice* (London: Hodder & Stoughton, 1988), chaps. 6–7.

50. The jury acquitted. *New York Times,* October 13, 1992, A15.

51. Ludovic Kennedy, *Ten Rillington Place* (London: Gollancz, 1961); Ludovic Kennedy, Lord Devlin, Tom Sargant, Bryan Magee, Oonagh McDonald, Wendy Mantle, and Gareth Pierce, *Wicked beyond Belief* (London: Granada, 1980); Woffinden, *Miscarriages of Justice. The Thin Blue Line,* a documentary movie about the wrongful conviction of Randall Dale Adams for killing a police officer, is an American example.

52. Woffinden, *Miscarriages of Justice,* chap. 1.

53. Ibid., chaps. 3–4; Jean Justice, *Murder versus Murder* (Paris: Olympia Press, 1964); Lord Russell of Liverpool, *Deadman's Hill: Was Hanratty Guilty?* (London: Secker & Warburg, 1965); Paul Foot, *Who Killed Hanratty?* (London: Jonathan Cape, 1971). Louis Blom-Cooper, Q.C., who initially expressed confidence in the convictions in his book *The A6 Murder: Regina v. James Hanratty: The Semblance of Truth* (Harmondsworth, United Kingdom: Penguin, 1963), later called his earlier conclusion "rash." Foot, *Who Killed Hanratty?*

54. Woffinden, *Miscarriages of Justice,* chap. 7; Kennedy et al., *Wicked beyond Belief.*

55. *New York Times,* January 24, 1992, B9, and October 2, 1992, B9. Interest in the case was renewed by the feature film *Let Him Have It.*

56. Müller, *Hitler's Justice,* chap. 1.

57. See Abel, *Politics by Other Means,* chap. 7.

58. Gearty, "Freedom of Assembly and Public Order."

59. *New York Times,* October 22, 1992, A1.

60. Richard L. Abel, "From the Editor," *Law and Society Review* 11 (1977), 747; Joe Trento, "Inside the Helms File," *National Law Journal* 1 (December 22, 1980), cited in David Luban, "The Adversary System Excuse," in *The Good Lawyer: Lawyers' Roles and Lawyers' Ethics* (Totowa, N.J.: Rowman & Allenheld, 1984), 85 n. 10.

61. Abel, *Politics by Other Means,* chap. 7.

62. Douglas Hay, "Property, Authority and the Criminal Law," in Douglas Hay, Peter Linebaugh, John G. Rule, E. P. Thompson, and Cal Winslow, *Albion's Fatal Tree: Crime and Society in Eighteenth-Century England* (New York: Pantheon, 1975).

63. See Paul Chevigny, *Edge of the Knife: Police Violence in the Americas* (New York: New Press, 1995) (Latin America); Lawyers Committee for Human Rights, *The Nigerian Police Force: A Culture of Impunity* (New York: LCHR, 1992).

64. In Port Elizabeth during the 1985 Emergency, black police tortured hundreds of detainees under the supervision of white superiors. Abel, *Politics by Other Means*, chap. 7.

65. Hain, *Political Trials in Britain*, 250–253.

66. Ewing and Gearty, *Freedom under Thatcher*, 47; Grant McKee and Ros Franey, *Time Bomb* (London: Bloomsbury, 1988).

67. Gregory Rockman, *Rockman: One Man's Crusade against Apartheid Police* (Melville: Senior Publications, 1989); Abel, *Politics by Other Means*, chap. 7.

68. Abel, *Politics by Other Means*, chap. 7; Chris Mullin, *Error of Judgement: The Truth about the Birmingham Bombings*, rev. ed. (Swords, Ireland: Poolbeg, 1990), chaps. 20–23.

69. Anthony Lewis, "Truth and Healing," *New York Times*, January 16, 1995, A11.

70. *Guardian*, October 23, 1991, 3; see also Bernard Jackson with Tony Wardle, *The Battle for Orgreave* (Brighton, United Kingdom: Vanson Wardle Productions, 1986).

71. Müller, *Hitler's Justice*, chap. 7.

72. Abel, *Politics by Other Means*, chap. 7.

73. Barkan, *Protesters on Trial*, 60–86, contrasts the strategies of southern segregationists in Birmingham and Selma, Alabama, with those in Albany, Georgia, and Danville, Virginia.

74. Jerome Skolnick, *Justice without Trial: Law Enforcement in Democratic Society* (New York: John Wiley, 1966).

75. Hain, *Political Trials*, 44, 47; Jack Dromey and Graham Taylor, *Grunwick: The Workers' Story* (London: Lawrence and Wishart, 1978); Geoff Bell et al., *The Battle of Grunwick* (n.p. 1977).

76. Ewing and Gearty, *Freedom under Thatcher*, 52–54, 72–79.

77. Tony Gifford, *Supergrasses: The Use of Accomplice Evidence in Northern Ireland* (London: Cobden Trust, 1984).

78. Gearty, "Freedom of Assembly and Public Order."

79. C. A. Elizabeth Loftus and Gary L. Wells, "The Malleability of Eyewitness Confidence: Co-Witness and Perseverance Effects," *Journal of Applied Psychology* 79 (1994) 714. Confronted with these findings, a spokesman for the New York City Police Department refused to discuss lineup procedure. "Our policy is to protect the integrity of the procedures we use. We don't comment on our procedures for lineups or photo arrays because it would contaminate the process." *New York Times*, January 17, 1995, B7.

80. *Guardian*, September 27, 1991, 1; Paul Okojie, "Black People and the Miscarriage of Justice: A Review of the Campaign to Free the Tottenham Three," *Sage Race Relations Abstracts* 16 (no. 3) (August 1991), 21; David Rose, *A Climate of Fear: The Murder of PC Blakelock and the Case of the Tottenham Three* (London: Bloomsbury, 1992).

81. Woffinden, *Miscarriages of Justice*, chaps. 6–7, 13–14; Gerry Conlon, *Proved Innocent: The Story of Gerry Conlon* (London: Hamish Hamilton, 1990), 66–95, 210–215; McKee and Franey, *Time Bomb*, chaps. 10–12, 31, 34, 41; Mullin, *Error of Judgement*, chap. 42 and "Aftermath."

82. Woffinden, *Miscarriages of Justice*, chap. 2.

83. *New York Times*, May 12, 1992, A4.

84. John Stalker, *Stalker: Ireland, 'Shoot to Kill' and the 'Affair'* (Harmondsworth, United Kingdom: Penguin, 1988); Peter Taylor, *Stalker: The Search for the Truth* (London: Faber & Faber, 1987).

85. National Council for Civil Liberties, *Southall, 23 April 1979: The Report of the Unofficial Committee of Enquiry* (London: NCCL, 1980); National Council for Civil Liberties, *The Death of Blair Peach: Supplementary Report of the Unofficial Committee of Enquiry* (London: NCCL, 1980); Robin Lewis, *Real Trouble: A Study of Aspects of the Southall Trials*

(London: Runnymede Trust, 1980); Martin Kettle and Lucy Hodges, *Uprising! The Police, the People and the Riots in Britain's Cities* (London: Pan, 1982) (racial unrest generally).

86. *Guardian,* October 22, 1991, 2.

87. National Conference for Civil Liberties, *Civil Liberties and the Miners' Dispute: First Report of the Independent Inquiry* (London: NCCL, 1984); National Conference for Civil Liberties, *Stonehenge: A Report into the Civil Liberties Implications of the Events Relating to the Convoys of Summer* (London: NCCL, 1986); National Conference for Civil Liberties, *No Way in Wapping: The Effect of Policing of the News International Dispute on Wapping Residents* (London: NCCL, 1986); Geoffrey Goodman, *The Miners' Strike* (London: Pluto Press, 1985); Jim Coulter, Susan Miller, and Martin Walker, *A State of Siege: Politics and Policing of the Coalfields: Miners' Strike 1984* (London: Canary Press, 1984); Bob Fine and R. Millar, eds., *Policing the Miners' Strike* (London: Lawrence & Wishart for Cobden Trust, 1985); Roger Geary, *Policing Industrial Disputes: 1893 to 1985* (Cambridge: Cambridge University Press, 1985); Penny Green, *The Enemy Without: Policing and Class Consciousness in the Miners' Strike* (Milton Keynes, United Kingdom: Open University Press, 1990); Phil Scraton and Phil Thomas, eds., "The State v. The People: Lessons from the Coal Dispute," *Journal of Law and Society* 12, no. 3 (Winter 1985).

88. Abel, *Politics by Other Means,* chaps. 4, 7.

89. Chris Jones and Tony Novak, "Welfare against the Workers: Benefits as a Political Weapon," in *Digging Deeper: Issues in the Miners' Strike,* ed. Huw Beynon (London: Verso, 1985) (denial of benefits to striking coal miners); Ros Franey, *Poor Law: The Mass Arrest of Homeless Claimants in Oxford* (London: Campaign for Single Homeless People, 1983) (mass arrest of homeless claimants).

90. A federal judge ruled that the INS could not rely on secret evidence of alleged national security dangers to deport two Arab men accused of membership in the Popular Front for the Liberation of Palestine. *Los Angeles Times,* January 25, 1995, B3.

91. David Burnham, *A Law unto Itself: Power, Politics and the IRS* (New York: Random House, 1989).

92. John Heinz, Edward O. Laumann, Robert L. Nelson, and Robert H. Salisbury, *The Hollow Core: Private Interest in National Policymaking* (Cambridge, Mass.: Harvard University Press, 1993).

93. Lawrence Baum, "Judicial Specialization, Litigant Influence and Substantive Policy: The Court of Customs and Patent Appeals," *Law and Society Review* 11 (1977), 823.

94. Udo Reifner, "The Bar in the Third Reich: Anti-Semitism and the Decline of Liberal Advocacy," *McGill Law Journal* 32 (1986), 111; Müller, *Hitler's Justice,* chaps. 7, 17–20.

95. Hain, *Political Trials,* 224.

96. Müller, *Hitler's Justice,* chap. 20.

97. For an argument that Taiwan's choice of the German Civil Code made it less receptive to cause lawyering, see Jane Kaufman Winn and Tang-chi Yeh, "Advocating Democracy: The Role of Lawyers in Taiwan's Political Transformation," *Law and Social Inquiry* 20 (1995), 561.

98. Martin Shapiro, "Appeal," *Law and Society Review* 14 (1980), 629.

99. *New York Times,* October 15, 1992, A6.

100. Müller, *Hitler's Justice,* 129–131.

101. See, e.g., Shimon Shetreet, *Judges on Trial: A Study of the Appointment and Accountability of the English Judiciary* (Amsterdam: North-Holland Publishing, 1976); J. A. G. Griffith, *The Politics of the Judiciary* (Manchester: Manchester University Press, 1977).

102. Ethan Bronner, *Battle for Justice: How the Bork Nomination Shook America* (New York: Norton, 1989); Paul Simon, *Advice and Consent: Clarence Thomas, Robert Bork and the Intriguing History of the Supreme Court's Nomination Battles* (Bethesda, Md.: National

Press Books, 1992); A. Leon Higginbotham, "An Open Letter to Justice Clarence Thomas from a Federal Judicial Colleague," *University of Pennsylvania Law Review* 140 (1992), 1005; Robert Chrisman and Robert C. Allen, *Court of Appeal: The Black Community Speaks Out on the Social and Sexual Politics of Clarence Thomas v. Anita Hill* (New York: Ballantine Books, 1992); David Brock, *The Real Anita Hill* (New York: Free Press, 1993); Jane Mayer and Jill Abramson, *Strange Justice: The Selling of Clarence Thomas* (Boston: Houghton Mifflin, 1994); Joseph L. Rauh Jr., "Nomination and Confirmation of Supreme Court Justices: Some Personal Observations," *Maine Law Review* 45 (1993), 7; Stephen L. Carter, *The Confirmation Mess* (New York: Basic Books, 1994).

Two Clinton nominees for U.S. District Judge withdrew their names in response to the November 1994 Republican sweep of Congress and the accession of Orrin Hatch to the Senate Judiciary Committee chair. The Police Officers Research Association of California called Samuel Paz, former president of the ACLU of southern California, an enemy of law enforcement. Judith McConnell, a California Superior Court judge for fourteen years, had awarded custody of a sixteen–year-old boy to the lover of his deceased father rather than the boy's mother. Another judge had earlier granted custody to the gay father, and the boy wished to continue living with the father's lover. *Los Angeles Times,* January 21, 1995, B3.

103. The Alliance for Justice, an umbrella organization for cause lawyering groups, closely monitors these statistics. Presidential ideology dramatically affects the composition of the judiciary. Women were 17 percent of Carter's appointments but only 12 percent of Reagan's and Bush's; blacks were 14 and 3 percent respectively. *New York Times,* March 8, 1993, A1.

104. *New York Times,* September 28, 1990, B10.

105. Davenport, *South Africa,* 363–366, 377–379.

106. *New York Times,* October 3, 1992, 15.

107. C. Neal Tate and Stacia L. Haynie, "Authoritarianism and the Functions of Courts: A Time Series Analysis of the Philippine Supreme Court, 1961–1987," *Law and Society Review* 27 (1993), 707.

108. Joseph R. Grodin, *In Pursuit of Justice* (Berkeley: University of California Press, 1989).

109. Müller, *Hitler's Justice,* chap. 17.

110. Compare H. L. A. Hart, "Positivism and the Separation of Law and Morals," *Harvard Law Review* 71 (1958), 593, with Lon Fuller, "Fidelity to Law," *Harvard Law Review* 71 (1958), 630. A test using the resistance of judges in Argentina and Brazil found no correlation with jurisprudential perspective, see Marc Osiel, "Dialogue with Dictators: Judicial Resistance in Argentina and Brazil," *Law and Social Inquiry* 20 (1995), 481.

111. Barkan, *Protesters on Trial.*

112. *New York Times,* October 15, 1992, A8; *Los Angeles Times* October 22, 1992, A1. Between 1881 and 1966 nearly five thousand blacks were known to have been lynched in the South, five hundred in Mississippi alone; whites were rarely convicted of such crimes.

113. Christopher Lingle and the *International Herald Tribune* were held in contempt of court for an article criticizing unnamed "intolerant regimes" in Asia that use "a compliant judiciary" to bankrupt opposition politicians. *New York Times,* January 18, 1995, A5.

114. Tun Mohammed Salleh bin Abas and K. Das, *May Day for Justice* (Kuala Lumpur: Magnus Books, 1989); H. P. Lee, "A Fragile Bastion under Siege—The 1988 Convulsion in the Malaysian Judiciary," *Melbourne University Law Review* 17 (1990), 386.

115. There is a large literature on political trials, e.g., Charles L. Abel and Frank H. Marsh, *In Defense of Political Trials* (New York: Greenwood Press, 1993); Cathi Albertyn and Dennis Davis, "The Censure of 'Communism' and the Political Trial in South Africa," in *Censure, Politics and Criminal Justice,* ed. Colin Sumner (Milton Keynes, United Kingdom:

Open University Press, 1990); Francis A. Allen, *The Crime of Politics: Political Dimensions of Criminal Justice* (Cambridge, Mass.: Harvard University Press, 1974); Theodore L. Becker, ed., *Political Trials* (New York: Bobbs-Merrill, 1971); Michael R. Belknap, ed., *American Political Trials* (Westport, Conn.: Greenwood Press, 1981); Michael R. Belknap, ed., *American Political Trials*, rev. ed. (Westport, Conn.: Greenwood Press, 1994); Ron Christenson, *Political Trials: Gordian Knots in the Law* (New Brunswick, N.J.: Transaction Books, 1986); Dennis Davis, "Political Trials in South Africa," in *Crime and Power in South Africa: Critical Studies in Criminology*, ed. Dennis Davis and Mana Slabbert (Cape Town: David Philip, 1985); Dennis Davis, "Violence and the Law: The Use of the Censure in Political Trials in South Africa," in *Political Violence and the Struggle in South Africa*, ed. N. Chabani Manganyi and André du Toit (London: Macmillan, 1990); Leon Friedman, ed., *Southern Justice* (New York: Pantheon, 1965); Leon Friedman, "Political Power and Legal Legitimacy: A Short History of Political Trials," *Antioch Review* 30 (1970), 157; Kirchheimer, *Political Justice*; Barkan, *Protesters on Trial*; Hain, *Political Trials in Britain*; Robert Hariman, ed., *Popular Trials: Rhetoric, Mass Media, and the Law* (Tuscaloosa: University of Alabama Press, 1990); J. Willard Hurst, "Treason in the United States," *Harvard Law Review* 58 (1945), 226–272, 395–555, 806–857; Barton Ingraham, *Political Crime in Europe: A Comparative Study of France, Germany and England* (Berkeley,: University of California Press, 1979); Reginald Major, *Justice in the Round: The Trial of Angela Davis* (New York: Third Press, 1973); W. H. McConnell, "Political Trials East and West," *Saskatchewan Law Review* [1974], 131; Richard H. Mitchell, *Janus-Faced Justice: Political Criminals in Imperial Japan* (Honolulu: University of Hawaii Press, 1992); Jessica Mitford, *The Trial of Dr. Spock* (New York: Knopf, 1969); New York Review of Books, *Trials of the Resistance* (New York: NYRB, 1970); William Preston, *Aliens and Dissenters: Federal Suppression of Radicals, 1903–1933* (Cambridge, Mass.: Harvard University Press, 1963); Julian C. Roebuck and Stanley C. Weaber, *Political Crime in the United States: Analyzing Crime by and against Government* (New York: Praeger, 1978); Arthur J. Sabin, *Red Scare in Court: New York versus the International Workers Order* (Philadelphia: University of Pennsylvania Press, 1993); Stephen Schafer, *The Political Criminal* (New York: Free Press, 1974); Schneir and Schneir, *Invitation to an Inquest*; Colin Sumner, "Rethinking Deviance: Towards a Sociology of Censures," *Research in Law, Deviance and Social Control* 5 (1983), 187; Colin Sumner, ed., *Censure, Politics and Criminal Justice* (Milton Keynes, United Kingdom: Open University Press, 1990); Austin T. Turk, *Political Criminality: The Defiance and Defense of Authority* (Newbury Park, Calif.: Sage Publications, 1982).

116. Douglas Hay et al., *Albion's Fatal Tree*; E. P. Thompson, *Whigs and Hunters: The Origin of the Black Act* (New York: Pantheon, 1975).

117. Robert M. Cover, *Justice Accused: Antislavery and the Judicial Process* (New Haven, Conn.: Yale University Press, 1975).

118. Abel, *Politics by Other Means*, chap. 9.

119. Ibid., chap. 4.

120. Isaac Balbus, *The Dialectics of Legal Repression: Black Rebels before the American Courts* (New York: Russell Sage, 1973).

121. Hain, *Political Trials in Britain*, 224; Gifford, *Supergrasses*.

122. Barkan, *Protesters on Trial*; Chestnut and Cass, *Black in Selma*.

123. But Justice van der Walt still required proof of mens rea beyond a reasonable doubt and found that the state had not met its burden. Abel, *Politics by Other Means*, chap. 9.

124. Prakash Diar, *The Sharpeville Six* (Toronto: McClelland & Stewart, 1990).

125. McKee and Franey, *Time Bomb*; Woffinden, *Miscarriages of Justice*; Conlon, *Proved Innocent*; Mullin, *Error of Judgement*.

126. Woffinden, *Miscarriages of Justice,* chap. 5; David Lewis and Peter Hughman, *Most Unnatural: An Inquiry into the Stafford Case* (Harmondsworth, United Kingdom: Penguin, 1971); Sir David Napley, *Not without Prejudice* (London: Harrap, 1982).

127. John Z. de Lorean and Ted Schwarz, *Delorean* (Grand Rapids, Mich.: Zondervan, 1985); Fenton Bailey, *Fall from Grace: The Untold Story of Michael Milken* (Secaucus, N.J.: Carol Publishing, 1992).

128. On English miscarriages of justice, see R. T. Paget and S. S. Silverman, *Hanged– An Innocent?* (London: Gollancz, 1953); Michael Eddowes, *The Man on Your Conscience* (London: Cassell, 1955); F. Tennyson Jesse, *The Trials of Evans and Christie* (London: William Hodge, 1957); Robert Kee, *Trial and Error* (London: Hamish Hamilton, 1986); Peter Hain, *Mistaken Identity: The Wrong Face of the Law* (London: Quartet, 1976); Leslie Hale, *Hanged in Error* (Harmondsworth, United Kingdom: Penguin, 1961); Ian Gilmour and John Griff, *The Case of Timothy Evans: An Appeal to Reason* (London: Spectator, 1956).

129. Woffinden, *Miscarriages of Justice,* 405.

130. McKee and Franey, *Time Bomb,* 393.

131. *Guardian,* September 24, 1991, 6 and October 3, 1991, 2.

132. *Guardian,* October 24, 1991, 2. They were subsequently charged. *New York Times,* January 25, 1993, 2.

133. Woffinden, *Miscarriages of Justice,* 412.

134. Udo Reifner, "The Bar in the Third Reich: Anti-Semitism and the Decline of Liberal Advocacy," *McGill Law Journal* 32 (1986), 101.

135. Weisberg, "Legal Rhetoric under Stress."

136. Kirchheimer, *Political Justice,* 99–105; Kaplan, *Report on the Murder of the General Secretary;* Müller, *Hitler's Justice,* chap. 4; Pattee, *The Case of Cardinal Aloysius Stepinac;* Leopold Labedz and Max Hayward, eds., *On Trial: The Case of Sinyavsky (Tertz) and Daniel (Arzak)* (London: Collins & Harvill, 1967); Debra Evenson, *Revolution in the Balance: Law and Society in Contemporary Cuba* (Boulder, Colo.: Westview Press, 1994).

137. Abel, *Politics by Other Means,* chap. 8.

138. Horace C. Peterson and Gilbert C. Fite, *Opponents of War, 1917–1918* (Madison: University of Wisconsin Press, 1957); Lawrence M. Baskir and William A. Strauss, *Chance and Circumstance: The Draft, the War, and the Vietnam Generation* (New York: Vintage, 1978); Steven E. Barkan, "Political Trials and the *Pro Se* Defendant in the Adversary System," *Social Problems* 24 (1977), 324; Barkan, *Protesters on Trial;* John F. Bannan and Rosemary S. Bannan, *Law, Morality and Vietnam: The Peace Militants and the Courts* (Bloomington: Indiana University Press, 1974); Mortimer R. Kadish and Sanford H. Kadish, *Discretion to Disobey: A Study of Lawful Departures from Legal Ethics* (Stanford, Calif.: Stanford University Press, 1973); Michael Useem, *Conscription, Protest and Social Conflict* (New York: John Wiley, 1973); Norman Dorsen and Leon Friedman, *Disorder in the Courts* (New York: Pantheon, 1973).

139. David Danelski, "The Chicago Conspiracy Trial," in *Political Trials,* ed. Theodore L. Becker (Indianapolis: Bobbs-Merrill, 1971); J. Anthony Lukas, *The Barnyard Epithet and Other Obscenities: Notes on the Chicago Conspiracy Trial* (New York: Harper & Row, 1975); Jason Epstein, *The Great Conspiracy Trial* (New York: Vintage Books, 1970); Tom Hayden, *Trial* (New York: Holt, Rinehart & Winston, 1980); Dorsen and Friedman, *Disorder in the Courts;* John Schultz, *The Chicago Conspiracy Trial,* rev. ed. (New York: Da Capo Press, 1993); R. J. Antonio, "The Processual Dimension of Degradation Ceremonies: The Chicago Conspiracy Trial: Success or Failure?," *British Journal of Sociology* 23 (1972), 287.

140. Abel, *Politics by Other Means,* chap. 10.

141. Peter Thornton, *The Civil Liberties of the Zircon Affair* (London: National Council

for Civil Liberties, 1987); Malcolm Turnbull, *The Spy Catcher Trial* (London: Heinemann, 1988).

142. See, e.g., Weisbrod et al., *Public Interest Law*; Nan Aron, *Liberty and Justice for All: Public Interest Law in the 1980s and Beyond* (Boulder, Colo.: Westview Press, 1989); Jeremy Cooper and Rajeev Dhavan, eds., *Public Interest Law* (Oxford: Basil Blackwell, 1986); Mark Kessler, *Legal Services for the Poor* (Westport, Conn.: Greenwood Press, 1987); Carol Harlow and Richard Rawlings, *Pressure through Law* (London: Routledge, 1992); Gerald P. López, *Rebellious Lawyering: One Chicano's Vision of Progressive Law Practice* (Boulder, Colo.: Westview Press, 1992); Richard F. Klawiter, "¡La Tierra Es Nuestra! The Campesino Struggle in El Salvador and a Vision of Community-Based Lawyering," *Stanford Law Review* 42 (1990), 1625; William A. Bogart, *Courts and Country: The Limits of Litigation and Social and Political Life of Canada* (New York: Oxford University Press, 1994).

143. Abel, *Politics by Other Means,* chap. 11.

144. Karl Klare, "Judicial Deradicalization of the Wagner Act and the Origins of Modern Legal Consciousness, 1934–1941," *Minnesota Law Review* 62 (1978), 265.

145. Compare Clement Vose, *Caucasians Only: The Supreme Court, the NAACP, and the Restrictive Covenant Case* (Berkeley: University of California Press, 1959); Jonathan D. Casper, *Lawyers before the Warren Court: Civil Liberties and Civil Rights, 1957–1966* (Urbana: University of Illinois Press, 1972); Richard Kluger, *Simple Justice: The History of* Brown v. Board of Education *and Black America's Struggle for Equality* (New York: Vintage, 1975); Tushnet, *The NAACP's Legal Strategy against Segregated Education*; Tushnet, *Making Civil Rights Law*; Tushnet and Lezin, "What Really Happened"; Bell, *And We Are Not Saved*; Kimberlé Williams Crenshaw, "Race, Reform and Retrenchment: Transformation and Legitimation in Antidiscrimination Law," *Harvard Law Review* 101 (1988), 1331; Taylor Branch, *Parting the Waters: America in the King Years, 1954–1963* (New York: Simon & Schuster, 1988); Harrell Rodgers and Charles Bullock, *Law and Social Change: Civil Rights Laws and Their Consequences* (New York: McGraw Hill, 1992); Michael Klarman, "*Brown,* Racial Change and the Civil Rights Movement," *Virginia Law Review* 80 (1994), 10; Richard Couto, *Ain't Gonna Let Nobody Turn Me Round: The Pursuit of Racial Justice in the Rural South* (Philadelphia: Temple University Press, 1991); Stephen Wasby, *Race Relations Litigation in an Age of Complexity* (Charlottesville: University of Virginia Press, 1994); Jack Bass, *Taming the Storm: The Life and Times of Judge Frank M. Johnson Jr. and the South's Fight over Civil Rights* (New York: Doubleday, 1993); and Greenberg, *Crusaders in the Courts;* with Alan Freeman, "Legitimizing Racial Discrimination through Antidiscrimination Law: A Critical Review of Supreme Court Doctrine," *Minnesota Law Review* 62 (1978), 1049; Stephen C. Halpern, *On the Limits of the Law: The Ironic Legacy of Title VI of the 1964 Civil Rights Act* (Baltimore, Md.: Johns Hopkins University Press, 1995); and Gerald N. Rosenberg, *The Hollow Hope: Can Courts Bring about Social Change?* (Chicago: University of Chicago Press, 1991).

146. E.g., Frances Fox Piven and Richard A. Cloward, *Poor People's Movements: Why They Succeed, How They Fail* (New York: Pantheon, 1977); John Gaventa, *Power and Powerlessness: Quiescence and Rebellion in an Appalachian Valley* (Oxford: Clarendon Press, 1988); Paul D. Wellstone, *How the Rural Poor Got Power: Narratives of a Grass-Roots Organizer* (Amherst: University of Massachusetts Press, 1978); Adeline Gordon Levine, *Love Canal: Science, Politics, and People* (Lexington, Mass.: Lexington Books, 1982); Kristin Bumiller, *The Civil Rights Society: The Social Construction of Victims* (Baltimore, Md.: Johns Hopkins University Press, 1988); Frank Upham, *Law and Social Change in Postwar Japan* (Cambridge, Mass.: Harvard University Press, 1987); Philip G. Schrag, *Counsel for the Deceived: Case Studies in Consumer Fraud* (New York: Pantheon, 1972); Lawrence, *The Poor in Court*; Davis, *Brutal Need*; Garrow, *Liberty and Sexuality.*

147. Herbert Wechsler, "Toward Neutral Principles of Constitutional Law," *Harvard Law Review* 73 (1959), 1; Alexander Bickel, *The Least Dangerous Branch: The Supreme Court at the Bar of Politics,* 2nd ed. (New Haven: Yale University Press, 1986).

148. Ellmann, *In a Time of Trouble.*

149. Thurman Arnold, *The Symbols of Government* (New Haven: Yale University Press, 1935); Thurman Arnold, *The Folklore of Capitalism* (New Haven: Yale University Press, 1937); Murray Edelman, *The Symbolic Uses of Politics* (Urbana: University of Illinois Press, 1964); Murray Edelman, *Politics as Symbolic Action* (Chicago: Markham, 1971); Murray Edelman, *Political Language: Words That Succeed and Policies That Fail* (New York: Academic Press, 1977); Murray Edelman, *Constructing the Political Spectacle* (Chicago: University of Chicago Press, 1988); Joseph R. Gusfield, *Symbolic Crusade: Status Politics and the American Temperance Movement* (Urbana: University of Illinois Press, 1963); Joseph R. Gusfield, *The Culture of Public Problems: Drinking-Driving and the Symbolic Order* (Chicago: University of Chicago Press, 1981); Stuart A. Scheingold, *The Politics of Rights: Lawyers, Public Policy and Political Change* (New Haven: Yale University Press, 1974); Joel F. Handler, *Social Movements and the Legal System: A Theory of Law Reform and Social Change* (New York: Academic Press, 1978).

150. Abel, *Politics by Other Means,* chap. 3.

151. Felix Frankfurter and Nathan Greene, *The Labor Injunction* (New York: Macmillan, 1930); William Forbath, *Law and the Shaping of the American Labor Movement* (Cambridge, Mass.: Harvard University Press, 1989); Chestnut and Cass, *Black in Selma*; Barkan, *Protesters on Trial,* 60–86 (civil rights).

152. On Chile, see Heleen F. P. Ietswaart, "The Allende Regime and the Chilean Judiciary," in *The Political Economy of Law: A Third World Reader,* ed. Yash Ghai, Robin Lukcham, and Francis Snyder (Delhi: Oxford University Press, 1987). On Canada, see Allan Hutchinson and Patrick Monahan, *The Rule of Law: Ideal or Ideology* (Toronto: Carswell, 1987); Judy Fudge and Harry Glasbeek, "The Politics of Rights: A Politics with Little Class," *Social and Legal Studies* 1 (1992), 45.

153. Penelope Canan and George W. Pring, "Studying Strategic Lawsuits against Public Participation: Mixing Quantitative and Qualitative Approaches," *Law and Society Review* 22 (1988), 385; Penelope Canan, Gloria Satterfield, Laurie Larson, and Martin Kretzmann, "Political Claims, Legal Derailment, and the Context of Disputes," *Law and Society Review* 24 (1990), 923; George W. Pring and Penelope Canan, *SLAPPs: Getting Sued for Speaking Out* (Philadelphia: Temple University Press, 1996).

154. *Los Angeles Times,* May 3, 1991, A3; Edmond Costantini and Mary Paul Nash, "SLAPP/SLAPPback: The Misuse of Libel Law for Political Purposes and a Countersuit Response," *Journal of Law and Politics* 7 (1991), 417.

155. Müller, *Hitler's Justice,* chap. 8; Kirchheimer, *Political Justice*; Reifner, "The Bar in the Third Reich," 115–18; Martin Bennhold, "Lawyers in Exile," *International Journal of the Sociology of Law* 17 (1989), 63; L. D. Fernandez, "The Law, Lawyers and the Courts in Nazi Germany," *South African Journal on Human Rights* 1 (1985), 124.

156. In the 1960s fewer than 3 percent of southern white lawyers had ever taken a civil rights case; there were only three black lawyers in Mississippi, one in Alabama, and eighty in the entire South. Barkan, *Protesters on Trial,* 39–46; see also Chestnut and Cass, *Black in Selma.*

157. Reifner, "The Bar in the Third Reich," 112–13.

158. See the case studies by the Lawyers Committee for Human Rights.

159. E.g., Kirchheimer, *Political Justice,* 275–276 (only about seven hundred lawyers in East Germany in 1961); Louise I. Shelley, *Lawyers in Soviet Work Life* (New Brunswick, N.J.: Rutgers University Press, 1984).

160. The eminent Baltimore firm of Piper & Marbury set up a pro bono clinic in a poor neighborhood but then prevented its lawyer from taking a case that might have created precedent adverse to its paying clients. Alan Ashman, *The New Private Practice: A Study of Piper & Marbury's Neighborhood Law Office* (Chicago: National Legal Aid and Defender Association, 1972). Although large firms rarely derive more than 5 percent of their income from any one client, individual lawyers generate 30–40 percent of their incomes from a single client. Robert L. Nelson, *Partners with Power: The Social Transformation of the Large Law Firm* (Berkeley: University of California Press, 1988).

161. E.g., Luban, "The Adversary System Excuse"; David Luban, *Lawyers and Justice: An Ethical Study* (Princeton, N.J.: Princeton University Press, 1988); David Luban, "Are Criminal Defenders Different?" *Michigan Law Review* 91 (1993), 1729; William Simon, "Reply: Further Reflections on Libertarian Criminal Defense," *Michigan Law Review* 91 (1993), 1767.

162. Müller, *Hitler's Justice,* chap. 8; Udo Reifner, "Individualistic and Collective Legalization: The Theory and Practice of Legal Advice for Workers in Prefascist Germany," in *The Politics of Informal Justice,* vol. 2: *Comparative Studies,* ed. Richard L. Abel (New York: Academic Press, 1982); Reifner, "The Bar in the Third Reich," 102, 109, 111; Matthew Lippman, "They Shoot Lawyers, Don't They?: Law in the Third Reich and the Global Threat to the Independence of the Judiciary," *California Western International Law Journal* 23 (1993), 257.

163. Kirchheimer, *Political Justice,* 214.

164. Ibid., 101–105; Müller, *Hitler's Justice,* chap. 4.

165. John Owen Haley, "The Politics of Informal Justice: The Japanese Experience, 1922–1942," in *The Politics of Informal Justice,* vol. 2: *Comparative Studies,* ed. Richard L. Abel (New York: Academic Press, 1982).

166. *New York Times,* February 11, 1991, A5.

167. Ellmann, *In a Time of Trouble,* attributes this, and the willingness of some of the best lawyers to take political cases, to the divided profession. Some lawyers, of course, were closely identified with the ANC, notably Bram Fischer and Albie Sachs.

168. Barkan, *Protesters on Trial,* 20, 23, 105–118.

169. *New York Times,* January 18, 1995, A13.

170. See Richard L. Abel, ed., "Lawyers and the Power to Change," *Law and Policy* 7(1) (1985).

171. See Abel, "Law without Politics."

172. E.g., Michael McConville and Chester L. Mirsky, "Criminal Defense of the Poor in New York City," *New York University Review of Law and Social Change* 15 (1986–87), 581–964.

173. Barkan, *Protesters on Trial,* 46–50; cf. Kirchheimer, *Political Justice,* 252–253 (French cases, especially concerning Algeria).

174. Hain, *Political Trials in Britain,* 99, 217.

175. Abel, "Socializing the Legal Profession."

176. McKee and Franey, *Time Bomb,* pp. 175–177, 233. This is not uncommon in Britain. See John Baldwin and Michael McConville, *Negotiated Justice: Pressures on Defendants to Plead Guilty* (London: Martin Robertson, 1977); Michael McConville, Jacqueline Hodgson, Lee Bridges, and Anita Pavlovic, *Standing Accused: The Organization and Practice of Criminal Defence Lawyers in Britain* (Oxford: Clarendon Press, 1994).

177. Mullin, *Error of Judgement,* chap. 19.

178. George Emile Bisharat, *Palestinian Lawyers and Israeli Rule: Law and Disorder in the West Bank* (Austin: University of Texas Press, 1989), 152.

179. Kirchheimer, *Political Justice*, 257; Barkan, *Protesters on Trial*, 39–46.

180. Jerold S. Auerbach, *Unequal Justice: Lawyers and Social Change in Modern America* (New York: Oxford University Press, 1976), chaps. 8–9; Terence C. Halliday, *Beyond Monopoly: Lawyers, State Crises, and Professional Empowerment* (Chicago: University of Chicago Press, 1987), chap. 9 (United States); Ronen Shamir, "The Bar Association Hasn't Got the Guts to Speak: The Untold Story of the American Bar Association's Committee on the New Deal," Working Paper 92–02 (Chicago: American Bar Foundation, 1992); Richard Weisberg, *The Failure of the Word: The Protagonist as Lawyer in Modern Fiction* (New Haven: Yale University Press, 1984); Weisberg, "Legal Rhetoric under Stress" (France); Vittorio Olgiati, "The Law 'In Motion' and the Role of Lawyers during the Fascist Dictatorship in Italy," paper presented at the annual meeting of the ISA Research Committee on Sociology of Law, Caracas, July 3–8, 1989.

181. Robin Luckham, "Imperialism, Law and Structural Dependence: The Ghana Legal Profession," in *Lawyers in the Third World: Comparative and Developmental Perspectives*, ed. C. J. Dias, R. Luckham, D. O. Lynch, and J. C. N. Paul (Uppsala: Scandinavian Institute of African Studies and New York: International Center for Law in Development, 1981); Lee, "A Fragile Bastion under Siege" (Malaysia); Mohammed Salleh bin Abas and Das, *May Day for Justice* (Malaysia); *Los Angeles Times*, May 17, 1994, A8, May 18, 1994 A14, June 24, 1994, A11 (Egypt); Bisharat, *Palestinian Lawyers and Israeli Rule* (occupied territories).

182. See *Law and Social Inquiry*, "Symposium: Law and Lustration: Righting the Wrongs of the Past," *Law and Social Inquiry* 20, no. 1 (1995); Amnesty International, "Sri Lanka: Time for Truth and Justice," *Law and Society Trust Fortnightly Review* 5, no. 91 (April 1, 16, 1995), 7.

183. On the English and French revolutions, see Kirchheimer, *Political Justice*, 304–305; Barry M. Shapiro, *Revolutionary Justice in Paris, 1789–1790* (New York: Cambridge University Press, 1993). On Germany, see Karl Lowenstein, "Reconstruction of the Administration of Justice in American Occupied Germany," *Harvard Law Review* 61 (1948), 419; Kirchheimer, *Political Justice*, 8; Eugene Davidson, *The Trial of the Germans* (New York: Collier Books, 1966); Bradley F. Smith, *Reading Judgment at Nuremberg* (New York: Basic Books, 1977); Müller, *Hitler's Justice*, chaps. 22–23, 26–30; Telford Taylor, *The Anatomy of the Nuremberg Trials: A Personal Memoir* (New York: Knopf, 1993). On Italy, see Roy Palmer Domenico, *Italian Fascists on Trial, 1943–1948* (Chapel Hill: University of North Carolina Press, 1991); Celestine Bohlen, "Italy Opens Trial in Wartime Massacre in Rome," *New York Times*, December 8, 1995, A4 (SS Capt. Erich Priebke, extradicted from Argentina for Ardeatine Caves massacre). On Japan, see John L. Ginn, *Sugamo Prison, Tokyo* (Jefferson, N.C.: McFarland, 1992). On France, see Alain Finkielkraut, *Remembering in Vain: The Klaus Barbie Trial and Crimes against Humanity* (New York: Columbia University Press, 1992); Richard Bernstein, "French Collaborators: The New Debate," *New York Review of Books* 39, no. 12 (1992), 37. On Belgium, see Luc Huyse and Steven Dhondt, *La Répression des collaborateurs, 1942–1952: un passé toujours présent* (Brussels: CRISP, 1993). On Latin America, see Mark Osiel, "The Making of Human Rights Policy in Argentina," *Journal of Latin American Studies* 18 (1986), 135; Amnesty International, *Argentina: The Military Juntas and Human Rights: Report of the Trial of the Former Junta Members, 1985* (London: Amnesty International Publications, 1987); Peter Snow, "Judges and Generals: The Role of the Argentine Supreme Court during Periods of Military Government," *Jahrbuch des Öffentlichen Rechts der Gegenwart* 24 (1975), 609; Ariel Dorfman, "Death and the Maiden," *Index on Censorship* 20, no. 6 (June 1991), 5. On the Communist regime in Ethiopia, see *New York Times*, November 11, 1994, A4; *Los Angeles Times*, December 14, 1994, A8. For fictional treatments

of post-Communism, see Ivan Klíma, *Judge on Trial* (New York: Knopf, 1993); Julian Barnes, *The Porcupine* (New York: Vintage, 1993); for nonfictional, see Tina Rosenberg, *The Haunted Land: Facing Europe's Ghosts after Communism* (New York: Random House, 1995). On Serbia, see United Nations, *Report of the International Tribunal for the Prosecution of Persons Responsible for Serious Violations of International Humanitarian Law Committee in the Territory of the Former Yugoslavia since 1991* (New York: United Nations, 1994).

184. Jane Perlez, "Problems Hamper the Crime Inquiry in Bosnia Conflict," *New York Times*, January 28, 1996, A1.

185. All the accused were acquitted. *New York Times*, August 11, 1994, A7; *Los Angeles Times*, August 12, 1994, A10.

186. *New York Times*, October 3, 1992, A3, October 4, 1992, A8, October 8, 1992, A8, October 9, 1992, A3; *Los Angeles Times*, September 30, 1992, A4, October 2, 1992, A4, October 3, 1992, A1.

187. Stephen Engelberg, "Jaruzelski Facing Accusers, or Is It Other Way Around?," *New York Times*, December 13, 1992, A12.

188. Serge Schmemann, "After a General Tells of Killing P.O.W.'s in 1956, Israelis Argue over Ethics of War," *New York Times*, August 21, 1995, A5.

189. Five years after reunification, Germany finally filed charges against former premier Egon Krenz and six other Politburo members. *Los Angeles Times*, January 10, 1995, A4; Mary Williams Walsh, "Tempered Justice in Germany," *Los Angeles Times*, March 2, 1995, A1; Alan Cowell, "German Ruling Absolves Spies of Former East," *New York Times*, May 24, 1995, A1; "East Germany's Old Spymaster Talks: He Has Regrets, but Is Uncontrite," *New York Times*, June 2, 1995, A1; Tina Rosenberg, "Where's the Crime?" *New York Times*, June 2, 1995, A29; Mary Williams Walsh, "Ex-Chief of E. German Secret Police Freed," *Los Angeles Times*, August 2, 1995, A5; Stephen Kinzer, "Germany Suffers New Setabck in Trials of East's Leaders," *New York Times*, October 19, 1995, A3; "Ex-East German Spymaster Finds Polishing His Image Is Hard," *New York Times*, December 8, 1995, A4.

190. Jane Perlez, "Hungarian President Questions Prosecution of '56 Militiamen," *New York Times*, February 16, 1995, A7.

191. *Los Angeles Times*, September 5, 1992, A4.

192. Bernstein, "French Collaborators."

193. Osiel, "The Making of Human Rights Policy in Argentina"; Amnesty International, *Argentina*.

194. Larry Rohter, "Honduras Faces Up to 80's 'Dirty War,' " *New York Times*, December 21, 1995, A6.

195. Calvin Sims, "Case of '76 U.S. Assassination Reaching Final Stage in Chile," *New York Times*, May 15, 1995, A5; "Growls from Military Echo in Peru and Chile," *New York Times*, June 20, 1995, A5; "Chile's Armed Forces Allow Arrest of Convicted General," *New York Times*, June 21, 1995, A7.

196. *New York Times*, July 4, 1992, A2.

197. Chile (1993); *New York Times*, June 24, 1994, A2 (Guatemala); Noga Tarnopolsky, "Murdering Memory in Argentina," *New York Times*, December 12, 1994, A19 (op ed); Anthony Lewis, "Truth and Healing," *New York Times*, January 16, 1995, A11 (South Africa); Bob Drogin, "Seeking the Truth, Not Vengeance, in S. Africa," *Los Angeles Times*, February 4, 1995, A1; Rohter, "Honduras Faces Up to 80's 'Dirty War.' "

198. Bernstein, "French Collaborators."

199. Although the case was reopened in the 1990s, he was murdered by an insane gunman.

200. Kirchheimer, *Political Justice,* 8; Lowenstein, "Reconstruction of the Administration of Justice"; Müller, *Hitler's Justice,* chaps. 22–23, 26–30.

201. Stephen Kinzer, "A Few Bits of Nazi Past Still Linger," *New York Times,* May 28, 1995, A5; "Exoneration Still Eludes an Anti-Nazi Crusader," January 13, 1996, A2.

202. *New York Times,* January 16, 1995, A11.

203. Calvin Sims, "Growls from Military Echo in Peru and Chile," *New York Times,* June 20, 1995, A5.

CHAPTER 4

The Struggle to Politicize Legal Practice

A Case Study of Left-Activist Lawyering in Seattle

STUART SCHEINGOLD

Cause lawyering cuts against the grain of a widely accepted belief that law and lawyers are supposed to be apolitical agents for resolving society's conflicts while somehow remaining unsullied by them. This commitment to autonomy is institutionalized in a variety of practices and understandings relating to the rule system, to courts and judges, and to the legal profession. With respect to the profession, for example Simon notes that, according to a core component of the "ideology of advocacy," lawyers are supposed to be both partisan and neutral.[1] They are expected to defend their clients in a vigorous and partisan manner while remaining neutral to their clients' objectives, activities, and identities.

Cause lawyering, in contrast, is not about neutrality but about choosing sides. Put another way, cause lawyers are focused on the broader stakes of litigation rather than on the justiciable conflict as such or on the narrow interests of the parties to that conflict. Cases have significance to cause lawyers not as ends in themselves but as means to advance causes to which the lawyers are committed. Cause lawyers choose cases, clients, and careers according to what they stand for. The essential question is whether there is something at stake in which the cause lawyer believes and is, thus, worth fighting for.

Left-Legal Activism

While all cause lawyering entails a rejection of neutrality, the left-activist cause lawyers who are the focus of this chapter raise that struggle to another level. They do not simply choose sides; they aspire to politicize legal practice. That is to say, they are committed both to a transformative politics and to a fusion of their political lives and their legal practices. Put another way, these conceptions go beyond the notion of lawyers simply doing good—working, that is, to alleviate poverty or homelessness, to protect the environment, to expand human rights, and the like. The two things that distinguish the left-activist project are its fundamental challenges to the society and to the profession.[2]

The National Lawyers Guild (NLG) has traditionally been the organizational stronghold of left-activist cause lawyering in the United States.[3] Consider the current preamble to the NLG constitution:

> The National Lawyers Guild is an association dedicated to the need for basic change in the structure of our political and economic system. We seek to unite the lawyers, law students, legal workers, and jail house lawyers of America in an organization which shall function as an effective political and social force in the service of the people, to the ends that human rights shall be regarded as more sacred than property interests.[4]

This stance has led to the Guild's association with left-wing causes and an avowedly political approach to lawyering. It thus provides a kind of natural home for what I am calling left-activist lawyers.

Accordingly, this paper focuses on the subset of Seattle cause lawyers who identify with the National Lawyers Guild. The mostly qualitative data that will be presented are derived from interviews during 1993 and 1994 with a snowball sample of twenty-five Seattle area lawyers who identify with the Guild (see Table 1). The semistructured interviews were taped and transcribed; each one lasted about one and a half hours.

This essay does not, however, take it for granted that identification with the Guild leads to a coherent and cohesive left-activist cohort—much less to distinctively left-activist forms of legal practice.[5] Despite a commitment to left-wing causes, Seattle's left-activists are ideologically divided. Most of them tend to identify with Marxism or with socialism more generally. Others have resisted that identification—thinking of the themselves as progressives, left-wing democrats, or some eclectic leftist mix. They are also distributed through a variety of practice sites including small-firm and solo private practice as well as salaried positions in the legal services, public defender, and other social action programs. Finally, and irrespective of their ideological aspirations or where they practice, left-activists must somehow accommodate to the political and professional contradictions that are intrinsic to left-activist legal practice.

While all of these matters will be pursued in this chapter, they are not particularly problematic. Left-activists seem to live with, and to shrug off, their ideological differences. Similarly, they tend to distribute themselves among practice sites according to their own preferences and proclivities. And when conditions are otherwise propitious, the contradictions and accommodations of left-activist lawyering are relatively easy to live with even if the result is something less than the fusion of transformative political goals with legal practice. These days, however, left-legal activism is under political and professional pressures that threaten its vitality, its distinctive character, its unity, and, indeed, its future.

Left-Activism under Siege

The period of the 1960s and early 1970s was both politically and professionally supportive of left-activist cause lawyering. The civil rights, antiwar and antipoverty movements were gaining ground in the courts and in the political process more generally. Moreover a prosperous and stable economy provided public and private sector opportunities in a legal market not yet saturated by lawyers. For Seattle's left-activists, these opportunities were found principally in a legal collective and in the legal services program. The National Lawyers Guild provided the social and ideological glue that held the cohort together and gave broader meaning to their activities.

The 1980s were more of a mixed bag. Politics took a sharp right turn and the legal services program, in particular, was put under ever-increasing budgetary and policy pressure. On the other hand, the practices of the Reagan administration tended to galvanize the Left and provided the impetus for a host of campaigns into which left-activists could pitch themselves with considerable enthusiasm. Looking back, a respondent now in salaried practice and then contemplating a career in the law, remembers the 1980s as a lively time. "I did a lot of more general political work. Political organizing around issues of Central American solidarity. That was in the years of the big show-downs with Congress and Contra aid in Nicaragua and aid to El Salvador. I was real active. . . . I was real active in the Pledge of Resistance. I was active in CISPES and people like that. I worked in a steel fabricating shop as a grunt hauling steel around."[6] The legal profession was, however, already changing in ways that have proven inimical to cause lawyering. Still, an active Lawyers Guild tended to give a sense of vitality to left-activists already in practice and encouragement to law students preparing for legal careers.

More recently, the political and professional tides have turned more unequivocally against left-activist lawyering. The collapse of socialism has resulted in an ideological malaise accompanied by some centrifugal forces that have tended to distance left-activists from one another and from the Lawyers Guild as well. Practice sites have become less hospitable to left-activism and to cause lawyering in general. In private practice, the heart of the problem is a more commercial ethos that squeezes resources and deflects attention from cause lawyering. For those in salaried practice, program funding tends to be inadequate and uncertain. And the political opponents of the embattled legal services program have specifically targeted left-activists as well as social reform policies in general.

Generational Variation

The burdens of adversity are not, however, being borne equally within Seattle's left-activists cohort but are apportioned along generational lines. As Table 1 indicates, three generations of left-activist lawyers are represented in this Seattle case study. Very little will be said about the first generation, who began to practice in 1930s, because only two of these lawyers were available to be interviewed, and they are in partial retirement. Attention will instead be focused on the second, generation who began to practice in the late 1960s and early 1970s, and the third generation, who began to practice in the 1980s and 1990s.[7]

The first generation was the most sorely tested. They had to face the hard times of the Depression as well as the McCarthyite repression of the late 1940s and early 1950s. For them, the issue was really one of professional survival.

The second generation had the advantages of a favorable market for legal services, a profession that was less hostile to them than to their predecessors, and a political climate that was genuinely supportive. Understandably these young lawyers saw themselves as the cutting edge of progressive professional and political change. The most pressing problem currently facing second-generation left-activists is how to make their peace with reduced expectations. As one second-generation left-activist ruefully put it to a venerated first-generation colleague: "At least you guys got to believe in something for your whole life before it fell apart."[8]

Given the third generation's relatively recent entry into the profession, they are of course, less settled. Although a few seem to have established secure and satisfying positions, these third-generation left-activists are more likely to be searching to determine where and how to combine their political aspirations with a career in the legal profession. They seem to take as a given, however, what has required difficult adjustments by second-generation left-activists—namely, that small and infrequent victories are about all that can be expected from lawyering, per se. It is, therefore, these third-generation left-activists who, by force of circumstance, are taking the lead in trying to reshape left-activist lawyering so that it will be more consonant with the current political and professional ethos and, indeed, with their own sensibilities.

At its core, then, this chapter is primarily about the efforts of Seattle's left-activist cause lawyers to meet the challenges of the 1990s. It is also about the toll that these difficult times are taking on individual lawyers and on the left-activist cause lawyering enterprise itself. While a core of left-activist lawyers remain dedicated practitioners of cause lawyering, the future and the character of left-activist cause lawyering in Seattle are less clear. The commitment to politicization seems to be fading or is being transformed in ways that blur the distinction between left-activists and other cause lawyers. Nurturing what remains of the distinctive mis-

Table 1. Seattle Cause Lawyers Who Identify with the National Lawyers Guild, by Year of Law School Graduation

Interviewee No.	Sex	Age	Race	Religion	Law School	Year of Graduation	Law Review	Firm Type
Group 1 (graduated 1930s and 1940s)								
028	M	85	W	Methodist	Harvard	1935	No	Solo
033	M	76	W	Methodist	U Wash	1943	No	Solo
Group 2 (graduated 1960s and 1970s)								
023	M	50	W	Catholic	U Wash	1969		Small gen. practice
024	F	42	W	Quaker	U Penn	1974	No	Small gen. practice
025	M	44	W	Protestant	Stanford	1974	No	Small gen. practice
037	M	41	W	Jewish	U Wash	1976	No	Solo
041	M	48	W	Baptist	U Wash	1970	No	Salaried
043	F	44	W	Catholic	Wayne St.	1974	Yes	Small gen. practice
048	M	45	W	Mormon	U Michigan	1975	No	Salaried
049	F	46	W	Presbyterian	U Wash	1975	No	Solo
053	F	46	W	None	Boston U	1973	No	Salaried
058	F	43	W	Catholic	U Wash	1977	No	Solo
069	M	49	W	Jewish	U Wash	1974		Salaried
077	F	?	W	Jewish	Boston U.	1975		Salaried
084	M	47	W	Catholic	UCalSF	1971	Yes	Small gen. practice

Group 3 (graduated 1980s and 1990s)

052	F	38	W	Catholic	Antioch	1986	No	Salaried
055	F	28	W	None	Harvard	1992	Yes	Small gen. practice
057	F	45	W	None	U Puget Sound	1987	Yes	Small gen. practice
062	M	37	B	Catholic	Harvard	1981	No	Small gen. practice
067	F	43	W	Episcopalian	Lewis & Clark U	1982	No	Solo
070	M	35	W	Jewish	U Illinois	1985	Yes	Salaried
071	F	43	W	Catholic	U Wash	1987	No	Salaried
074	F	50	W	Protestant	none/clerk	1986	n/a	Small gen. practice
075	M	32	W	Jewish	U Michigan	1986	Yes	Salaried
091	M	40	W	Presbyterian	U Wash	1988	Yes	Salaried

sion of left-activist cause lawyering is, moreover, inhibited by the problems that third-generation left-activists are having securing positions as lawyers.

Even under the best of circumstances, left-activist lawyering is an enterprise dogged by contradictions and more or less satisfactory accommodations to them. The next section of this essay will explore these optimal circumstances of left-activist lawyering. The obstacles confronting left-activism have, of course, been mounting in recent years. These obstacles and their disproportionate impact on third generation left-activists will be the focus of section 3. The concluding section will consider the problems and prospects of left-activism in the years ahead.

Optimal Left-Activism

It has long been argued that left-activist (or "radical") lawyering is a contradiction in terms and thus an inherently problematic enterprise.[9] There are both political and professional dimensions to these contradictory circumstances. Left-activist lawyers are both aware of their predicament and resistant to its implications. The result is that at best left-activism is fraught with compromise.

Political Contradictions and Accommodations

The central political contradiction of left-activist cause lawyering is that it seeks transformative goals while working within legal processes that are wedded to the established order. As Alan Thomson has put it, left-activist lawyers (or "critical" lawyers, to use his term) are trying to use "the law to fight the system which (theory tells us) law maintains."[10] Rights strategies and litigative tactics seem, therefore, bound to fail in confrontations that left-activist lawyers seek with what Peter Fitzpatrick refers to as the "surpassing" dimension of law—that is with "some unifying 'sovereign' location such as the state."[11] The high stakes of such confrontations lead established authorities to bend the rules to protect the status quo whenever really important issues are litigated. Making things still worse, according to some critics of left-activist cause lawyering, legal challenges to the foundations of established authority are counterproductive as well as ineffectual. The materially inconsequential victories erratically available by way of the legal process may well enhance the legitimacy of the prevailing order and, thus, inhibit the mobilization of political opposition.[12]

Seattle's left-activists are not unmindful of these problems and have adjusted to them in two different ways. On the one hand, they seek connections with social movements to lend political weight to what they can accomplish as lawyers. On the other, they have scaled down their expectations for what can be achieved with conventional cause-lawyering techniques. Accordingly, the buoyancy of the left-activist enterprise is directly linked to the vitality of like-minded social movements. Implicit in this analysis is a distinction that left-activists tend to make between their legal and their political work. This distinction is in itself an acknowledgment that the struggle to politicize legal practice can never be entirely successful. But if the political and legal lives of left-activist cause lawyers can never be entirely fused, there are sharp variations in how close they can come to their ideal.

Given their underlying skepticism about the transformative potential of law and litigation, it stands to reason that left-activist cause lawyers would value association with grassroots movements engaged in direct action on behalf of issues of broad import. This work has principally been in defense of movement activists engaged in direct action. Defense of activists may or may not end up in court, but when it does, left-activists prefer to use the courtroom as a public forum rather than to establish a precedent or gain an acquittal. As a long-time legal services attorney put it: "The legal stuff is secondary. . . . [I]t's probably not even secondary. It's relatively unimportant." [13] Occasional opportunities for impact litigation have also arisen in connection with movement activity, but they are few and far between.

In the 1960s and early 1970s, left-activists lawyers thought of themselves as members of *the* movement—an amorphous construct comprising the civil rights, antiwar, and antipoverty movements. All of these were seen as synergistically contributing to a more just, egalitarian, and democratic society. Thus, criminal defense work on behalf of antiwar protesters was seen as part of, and a direct contribution to, the broader political struggle. Although legal services attorneys had a more restricted mandate, they perceived their efforts on behalf of welfare recipients, migrant workers, prisoners, and other dispossessed Americans as contributing to a politically vibrant battle against poverty and racism in the United States. One attorney, now in personal injury practice, recalled with considerable satisfaction the notoriety and the conflict generated by her suits against the jail in a small town in eastern Washington. [14]

While the social movement scene in Seattle remained lively through the 1970s and into the 1980s, the contribution of left-activist lawyering evolved in revealing ways. The most overtly political work tended to take place outside, or at the margins of, legal practice and to become the province of salaried lawyers. Consider, for example, the work of a second-generation legal services attorney:

> I did a fair amount of work regarding southern Africa, support work. . . . [W]e did some Kruegerrand demonstrations, that must have been in the late '70s. There was this activist group here, the American Friends Service Committee, who were doing a lot. We had a study group and we did a campaign against SeaFirst [Bank] at the time, who had some investments in South Africa. Eventually I got into some antinuclear work. I ended up for a long time doing criminal defense of people doing civil disobedience, particularly against the Trident base but also against Central America issues in the early 80s. [15]

A third-generation attorney for a small social action organization made much the same point about her work with the Tenants Union, the Displacement Coalition, and Operation Homestead—grassroots groups dedicated to affordable housing.[16]

Similarly, labor movement–related litigation against the Marcos government in the Philippines proved incompatible with private practice. Thought of by the attorneys in distinctly political terms, this suit was on behalf of the widows and children of two murdered, anti-Marcos, Filipino American labor officials. The lead attorney saw the underlying political principles at stake as follows: "And that I think would be a universally recognized good principle, that foreign dictators not be able to operate in intelligence operations in the United States using their agents in order to harass and intimidate and, in this case, to execute people who oppose their regime."[17] A slightly different spin was offered by one of the other participating attorneys: "That was a pretty interesting experience. It's probably more like the classic image of the radical lawyer, working on this very dramatic case, suing Marcos. It was a successful case and so that was very nice to have something as exciting as getting awards and actually collecting money for these kids. The legal work itself was often very political. That was that very dramatic intersection [between politics and law]."[18]

But this litigation was, however, conducted at the margins of private and salaried practice. The lead attorney stuck with the case for about ten years including three years during which he withdrew from private practice to devote himself to the case.[19] Those who assisted him were also working on their own time as, for example, the legal services attorney quoted above: "Because of my time limitations working with Legal Services I could only work on this stuff at night and on weekends. I did more briefing—legal research, summary judgment-type stuff and less of the discovery-related or depositions and the day-to-day motions."[20] The underlying point is, to repeat, that political lawyering occurs primarily outside the boundaries of practice. For that reason salaried practice, with clearer demarcations between personal and professional time, is more amenable to social movement work.

As for what can be accomplished within the realms of private and salaried practice, the tendency is to think more in terms of being on the right side than in terms of transformative objectives. The following comment by a veteran legal services attorney is typical: "But if the question is, do I think I am making a big impact on the system or moving the society toward change by using the legal system, I have some serious doubts about whether I am doing that or not. Some days I feel like there's no use dealing with the system and other times there's some give and you get something for somebody."[21] Note the shift from system change to providing meaningful assistance to those who are victims of that system. Thus a kind of least-common-denominator commitment to victims became, even in this more propitious period, the ideological principle driving left-activist lawyering in Seattle. Even for the avowedly socialist contingent, socialism has been more about taking sides in the ongoing struggle between domination and resistance—representing the "powerless"[22]—than about a blueprint for a better world or even a strategy for reforming what we already have.

Taking sides in this way lowers the stakes of cause lawyering but raises further questions about what lawyers can do to defend victims and reduce victimization. Generally speaking, Seattle's left-activists think in terms of impact litigation, empowerment of individual litigants, and supporting social movements. While preferences vary among lawyers and shift according to circumstance, there is a tendency rooted in both instrumental and expressive reasons for litigation to become the preferred tactic.

Despite their professed skepticism about the law, Seattle's left-activists do seem to believe that litigation can work. A surprisingly conventional understanding of the process was put to me by one of the more politically enterprising second-generation left-activists: "All law is premised upon the doctrine of stare decisis. All law is premised upon precedent. And therefore really the whole nature of law is to look at cases that have been resolved either by jury or by courts, either on the trial level or in the appellate level for guidance about how conduct, including corporate conduct or individual conduct, should be regulated."[23] While others might take issue with this formulation, they would probably accept to a significant extent the dual assumptions driving this kind of thinking. Litigation puts direct pressure on the losing litigant and indirect pressure on those engaged in similar activities. Accordingly, the more noteworthy the target, the heavier the direct and indirect effects of litigation.

Even those who are more skeptical about litigation are attracted to it: Consider the mix of skepticism and engagement of a second-generation solo practitioner: "I think it's also very important . . . to empower people in their daily lives because I really believe that the way things change is not so much by impact litigation but by people feeling more sense of power in their daily lives, and being able to take more control and not being so downtrodden and powerless. I think our society does a lot to make people feel very powerless."[24] Nonetheless, she also said, "I think if I got a Genius grant and didn't have to do anything else I would definitely try to do impact litigation. I love doing litigation."[25] Similarly, a second-generation attorney who does not often go to court recalled her appearance on behalf of some demonstrators as "very dramatic": "After we won and the demonstration happened I remember thinking: 'This day is why I went to law school. This is a demonstration that wouldn't have happened.' "[26] Litigation can, in other words, be seen as part strategy and part vocation.

Professional Contradictions and Accommodations

In a number of ways, the aspiration to politicize legal practice, even in a watered-down form, puts left-activists at odds with generally accepted professional understandings of representation.[27] Unlike the traditional civil liberties lawyer, who will defend legal and constitutional principles—free speech for Nazis, fair trials for right-wing terrorists, and so forth—left-activists narrow their conception of representation to political allies. A politicized left-wing conception of legal practice precludes defense of political opponents irrespective of the legal and constitutional issues that are at stake. Similarly, in their willingness to help make the courtroom into a political forum for their clients, Seattle's left-activists have found themselves in conflict with more conventional lawyers for whom "the lawsuit is the main event" and "victory in the court" room the essential objective.[28] The aspiration of some left-activists to develop relationships with clients and staff that are purged of hierarchical tendencies[29] has also been professionally problematic.

These significant *tensions* with conventional understandings of legal practice aside, the truly *contradictory* element of left-legal activism is the deeply felt commitment to decommodify delivery of legal services.[30] To serve their normally impecunious clients, left-activists must somehow transcend the constraints of the market. Lawyers in private practice are, however, necessarily a part of the market. They are small-business persons who must somehow pay the bills and are not, therefore, immune from market pressures. For some left-activists, it is the aversion to commodification that leads them to salaried practice where they can escape the market and achieve a measure of decommodification. Salaried practice does not, however, confer immunity from the financial pressures associated with the commodified delivery of legal services. The budgetary and policy constraints associated with salaried practice are to a significant degree indistinguishable from the comparable constraints of a commodified market for legal services.

The closest approximation to the ideal of left-activist private practice in Seattle was a legal collective that functioned for more than a decade. Despite some variation in membership, the collective was a stable presence and the major private practice site of left-activist cause lawyering in Seattle.[31] The personal, the political, and the professional all came together in the collective. The sense of commitment to, and involvement in, "the movement" has already been discussed. The activism associated with the civil rights, antiwar, and antipoverty movements were all seen as synergistically interrelated and leading inevitably to social justice. Within the collective, a concerted effort was also made to model the just, egalitarian, and democratic political vision that drives left-legal activism: "We maintained the principles that everybody got paid equally whether they were lawyers or not and everybody had equal decision-making power and so everybody being equal partners. Even though the Bar Association said that's unethical, nobody ever complained."[32] It was also a time when decommodification seemed easily within reach. The market for legal services was favorable, and the material needs of these dedicated, young, and unencumbered lawyers were modest.

The collective was no panacea. It proved inefficient to have attorneys handling both lay and professional responsibilities: "We started out taking turns trying to provide work help—take turns answering phones and people doing their own typing, and we fairly quickly were convinced that a simple division of labor was something we needed to do just to survive."[33] Clients resisted efforts to alter conventional power relationships with attorneys.[34] Similarly, the initial salary plan of complete parity gave way to a more qualified scheme, and in the long run even that proved unworkable. Problems arose over how to compensate those with heavier family responsibilities and over whether people were pulling their weight. These problems seem to have contributed to the collapse of the collective.[35]

Nonetheless, the collective provided a setting that nurtured the radical aversion to hierarchy. Serious efforts were also made to reshape relationships among lawyers, staff, and clients. Traditional salary differentials were sharply curtailed and a participatory decision-making process established. The collective did, albeit not without controversy, take meaningful steps to put its antihierarchy principles into practice.

The principal salaried counterpart to the collective was initially the federally funded legal services program. Like the lawyers in the collective, the Guild-oriented legal services attorneys were also an eclectic mix of socialists and left-liberals who saw themselves as part of an increasingly successful movement against poverty and racism. These lawyers enjoyed notable successes on behalf of prisoners, migrant workers, victims of police abuse, and others similarly victimized. In later years when it became more difficult to secure jobs in a constantly shrinking legal services program, the public defender program became a more prominent home for left-activist lawyers.

Both programs provided a much appreciated refuge from the market. In part, this is simply a matter of personal taste. As a third-generation left-activist in the public defender program put it:

> Why am I not doing private practice? Probably the biggest reason is, if I want to run a small business I could have stayed in Chicago and been a wedding photographer like my father, my grandfather, my brother. I'm serious about that. I grew up in a family of small businessmen. I've chosen something else in part because I'm not very good at the business sense, and I have absolutely no desire to run my own office, to build clients, to pay support staff. I prefer to have a regular income and not have to worry about business details.[36]

But the aversion to the market cuts a good deal more deeply for left-activists. This response captures only one aspect of what is deemed objectionable about private practice.

Of course, for the socialists, an aversion to the market is also directly linked to ideological principle. But irrespective of ideology, fee-for-service lawyering can take a pervasive moral and emotional toll on left-activists. A legal services attorney who had a stint in private practice with the collective put it this way: "[T]he worst thing about private practice was that I thought about money every single day.

. . . [T]here's an interesting tension when you get into thinking about what people are paying you, you also inevitably think about how much work you should
do on their case. . . . So I was constantly dealing with that tension. And I found
that I didn't like the sort of ways I was thinking about things where 'how much
more should I do' was always on my mind." [37] Some cause lawyers, in other words,
simply find it very difficult to feel good about themselves in the commodified
setting that is necessarily part and parcel of private practice. And of course salaried
practice has its more positive appeals as has already be discussed. One way or
another salaried practice makes it possible to devote oneself more or less full-
time to cause work—whether representing society's victims in their regular jobs
or working with social movements during their free time. [38]

It bears repeating, however, that salaried practice, while insulating Left-
activists from the market, as such, does not free them of the contradictions of
commodification. In *salaried practice,* the constraints are imposed from above by
the funding source. These constraints can take the form of rules that explicitly
prohibit certain kinds of activities and/or tight budgets that keep the emphasis on
run-of-the-mill client service. In the good times of the 1960s and 1970s these constraints did not bear very heavily on left-activists in salaried practice. That is no
longer the case, as will be discussed in the next section.

A last thing to keep in mind about the good old days of left-legal activism is how
important the Guild was. The political, the professional, the social, and even the
inspirational converged within the Guild:

> [T]he Lawyers Guild, locally it's been important because it's been a source of—
> just being around people with similar values is comforting somehow. Nationally,
> I'd been involved with the national board of the Guild for a couple years. Nation-
> ally, the Guild has been a large source of inspiration for me because you see all
> these people doing all these things across the country. I also have a lot of respect
> for the Guild because it was one of the very few organizations that didn't knuckle
> under during the McCarthy era. [39]

Left-activist attorneys tended to organize much of their social lives around the
Guild and that, of course, meant spending a good deal of time with one another.
Since they were working in different places, the Guild was, therefore, a source of
cohesion.

Within the Guild political priorities were developed, contacts were made with
grassroots organizations, support activities were coordinated. Thus, when the
house of the South African consul in Seattle, Joseph Swing, was picketed:

> I had a couple of different hats. One was that I was partly coordinating the legal
> defense. Every week somebody would get arrested, and so you'd kind of arrange
> in advance who was going to get arrested and you'd brief them and give them a
> whole statement of rights and explain to them that they shouldn't bring any

pocket knives. . . . Then the police would give them a ticket and send them home, basically, and they'd show up at their arraignment. And we'd assign them to private attorneys, and there were occasional times when there were mass arrests. . . . This was not legal work, this was political work—coordinating, as a Lawyers Guild person, coordinating the legal representation because we know all the lawyers. We had collected people who were going to be the defense lawyers.[40]

The Guild was, in short, a powerful presence in the lives of left-activists particularly with respect to their sense of political efficacy. This too has changed as will shortly become clear.

The Burdens of the 1990s

As has already been suggested, the political and professional conditions facing left-activist cause lawyers have become increasingly adverse. The impact of adversity has, however, been borne most heavily by third-generation left-activists—particularly those in private practice. Since these third-generation attorneys are by definition the future of the left-activist project, the drying-up of congenial career opportunities when combined with the overall political malaise casts a dark shadow over the enterprise.

Political Disarray

Among the heaviest burdens being borne by Seattle's left-activist cohort is the ideological malaise that has enveloped the American Left. Although by no means doctrinaire socialists, Seattle's left-activist lawyers find themselves cast adrift by the apparent collapse of socialism as a unifying ideal, however vaguely defined.[41] Put in somewhat different terms, the sense of belonging to something bigger—"the movement" that sustained left-activists in the early days—has been lost. As one of the founding members of the collective put it: "[W]e didn't have the illusion that we personally as lawyers were going to be the leadership of some social change, but we did have the illusion that there were going to be other movements that were going to keep growing and getting stronger."[42] But just what is there to give meaning and direction to "the long haul" in the face of an increasingly mean-spirited, inegalitarian, and ascendant capitalism?

Certainly, there is no shortage of causes for left-activists to support. Feminism, gay and lesbian rights, immigrant rights; opposition to the death penalty; support of the working class, the homeless, the poor, racial minorities, and other causes all beckon to left-activist lawyers. But these causes no longer seem synergistically linked to one another. As a second-generation salaried attorney put it: "One of the reasons I think that you don't see a lot of good political lawsuits—you know, there's no movements, there's no nothing."[43] Put another way, there are, according to a third-generation salaried attorney centrifugal forces within the left-activist cohort.

> We are so atomized these days, and in fact in this office, because there's twelve of us and we're atomized within our office because we're so buried with work and we're a little bit touchy these days with each other. I think capitalism is more cunning these days. Ronald Reagan was a great organizing tool for the Left, because he was so blatantly inhumane and dishonest and cruel. I think those of us who have believed in socialism and have always criticized capitalism, there's not a clear institutional foe. It's like the whole institution is the foe, and it always has been but it was simpler to think of the Vietnam war as a symbol of everything else that's wrong, and to radicalize people and to get a movement going based upon this very important thing.[44]

A second-generation attorney in solo practice made much the same point in talking about the weakening influence of the Guild as an umbrella organization—a point that will be taken up further at the conclusion of this section: "When I was in law school all the activists were collected in the Lawyers Guild. We fragmented into women's groups or minority groups. It sort of takes away from some of the people who would have been together in the Lawyers Guild."[45] There are really two points to be made here. On the one hand, while left-activists are not in conflict, they are increasingly at arm's length from one another and from the sustaining force of movement politics. On the other hand, at least in Seattle, few of the many causes that beckon to left-activists have spawned active social movements.

There is also, of course, a sense among left-activists that the political and legal tide is running against them. The opportunities that once were so promisingly and so abundantly available seem to be steadily shrinking. The legal services program has been embattled and on the defensive for many years. "When I first came into legal services: 'We're going to do impact work addressing the underlying causes of poverty.' Well, we're not, and it's not possible in my opinion to do that through legal services or legal work, and I'm not sure that it's very likely that that's going to be done in any good way in any other arena. If I thought there was something I could do that was a more effective way to work on these issues I would do it."[46] Left-activists, as well as other cause lawyers, are also discouraged about the conservative drift of the courts. And the tort and regulatory systems, which over the years have been the primary vehicles available for cause lawyering on behalf of consumers, employees, and environmental activists, seem vulnerable to the conservative tide. The second-generation left-activist who was the lead attorney in the Marcos suit charged that the Reagan administration had "put the regulatory agencies . . . on Quaaludes."[47] He went on to complain that the Manhattan Institute in combination with the insurance industry had orchestrated a legislative and public relations campaign against the civil justice system. The results, as he saw them at the time of our interview in early 1994, were a variety of restrictions that state legislatures were putting on tort litigation and juries that increasingly "view the civil justice system with a very jaundiced eye as a result of this campaign."[48] Since the time of that interview, the Republican Party's Contract with America has made still clearer the conservative hostility to the civil justice system (Item 9) and to the anti–death penalty bar (Item 2).

Coping with Political Adversity

By and large, the dominant response to the unfavorable trends of the 1990s has been sharply curtailed expectations—a tacit abandonment of transformative objectives. Of course, as was discussed above, these altered expectations have been developing for some years. "So I think it was a significant adjustment as the 70s wore on to see those movements fall apart or tear each other apart and go off in all different directions and learn that history wasn't just going in one direction. There are ups and downs . . . and [we need] to adjust to the idea of not living for the short-term crisis but for the long haul."[49] Still, into the 1980s, the movement scene remained active if more and more diffuse.

Of course, litigation continues to be seen by some left-activists in political terms. They believe that it will occasionally serve as a "catalyst"—promoting changes, for example, in abusive police[50] or corporate behavior: "I've done toxic tort cases here and some civil rights law, some employment discrimination cases. And toxic torts you can get into generally—this idea of a sort of corporate America exposing people heedlessly to toxic substances and people dying from it and everything. So I can get into it on a political level."[51] Those sentiments lead to a search for ways of maximizing opportunities for impact litigation. To this end, Seattle's left-activists regularly work with and for litigation-minded organizations like the American Civil Liberties Union (ACLU), the Northwest Women's Law Center (NWLC), and the Northwest Immigrants Rights Project (NWIRP). Similarly, legal services attorneys enlist pro bono support from corporate firms and the public defender program has an appeals program that serves roughly the same purpose.

Others turn away from impact litigation or are inclined, in this time of judicial resistance, to subordinate it to other strategies. An NWLC litigation project underwent a conversion with respect to "nonenforcement of protective orders" in Idaho: "Here there was a case, facts that were possibly relevant, and therefore we pursued it as a litigation strategy, and in effect we established that maybe there are other ways to do this: by training the judges, by training the police officers on enforcement, and things like that. We ended up with an alternative strategy. . . . That was one where we got into it because there was a possible litigation and we found alternatives to that as we went on."[52] This turning away from litigation tends to be associated with a related tendency to focus on discrete short-term goals like saving families from deportation orders, keeping prisoners alive as long as possible, or protecting welfare benefits.

For at least some left-activists this reduction in scale is not so much a tactical retreat as a reinterpretation of what it means to politicize legal practice. Thus, a second-generation left-activist, formerly a public defender and now in private practice: "My basic political beliefs are a kind of 'anti-ism' stance."[53] This attorney who is in solo practice focuses on gays and juveniles and sees her role as empowering individual litigants. In part, this means serving as a role model: "If you're gay it doesn't mean you have to commit suicide when you're twenty-one. There is a way to survive in society and you might be able to find one. A lot of these kids don't have any adult that they've been able to talk to about it."[54] It also means combining representation in juvenile court with efforts to help these kids turn their lives around.

> I feel very strongly that teenagers in this society are really disenfranchised and get a very bad deal. They get very bad deals from the courts. There's limited things that you can actually do often, but it's another one of those situations where I really try in my dealings as a lawyer to empower them as best I can in terms of taking what charge they can over their own lives. Setting up some other options sometimes for them. I have kids that sort of connect with me for years. A lot of these kids really don't have anybody, or who they have has been such a problem for them that it's really a mess.[55]

A similar point was made by a third-generation public defender who argued that her successful representation of a juvenile regularly harassed by the police had given the young man a measure of self-respect and the sense that he had choices in life.[56] Empowerment was also prominent in the activities of a salaried third-generation immigrants rights attorney. He devoted a good deal of time to educating immigrants about their right to remain silent on the premise that the power of Immigration and Naturalization Service agents could frequently be neutralized in this way.[57]

About the only remaining repository of large-scale transformative visions seems to be the civil justice system and more specifically the Trial Lawyers for Public Justice (TLPJ). One of the founding member of the collective, whose work on the Marcos case has already been mentioned, envisions the possibility of a comprehensive public interest movement organized under the auspices of the TLPJ:

> What I'm trying to get at in terms of the legal public interest movement as a whole is the interrelationship. It's not enough for the NAACP Legal Defense Fund and Evergreen Legal Services and MALDEF—the Mexican American Legal Defense [and Education] Fund—to go off and do their own work. That's fine. They're doing excellent work. All of 'em are. But where is . . . the connection? Where is the understanding of seeing these important legal efforts as parts of a whole? That's what this [TLPJ] conference was all about.[58]

TLPJ activists, thus, envisage litigation in combination with other strategies spearheading a broadly based consumer movement.

[P]ublic justice is not limited to trial lawyering. In fact it's predominantly a consumer movement. It's predominantly the environmental movement, the women's movement, the civil rights movement, all the various movements that we brought together. So it's not going to be the TLPJ that to me is the movement. It's going to be the TLPJ as part of a public interest movement of activists and lawyers. That's where I see the shape of things to come in the 1990s and the next century. And we're taking steps to build that alliance.[59]

Faith in the power of civil litigation is bolstered for this attorney by his own litigative successes—first against Marcos and later against the Exxon and Boeing corporations, for example. Even more tellingly, albeit perversely, he is encouraged by the tort reform movement, led by the Manhattan Institute and the insurance industry. From his perspective, tort reform becomes not simply an effort to protect profits but an ideologically engaged right-wing struggle and thus a tribute to the substantial political threat posed by civil litigation. .

For many in the left-activist cohort, however, neither a reduction in scale nor a reliance on the civil justice system is satisfactory. Those who continue to think of themselves as Marxists or socialists tend to see this as a disheartening retreat but differ in their reactions to it. Some are neither surprised nor inclined to give up:

I think I never thought that the law is a lever that's gonna make fundamental changes in society, and I think that it's primarily a reflection of other social forces rather than itself being a social force. But, on the other hand, I do think that the law is the mechanism and the forum in which our society ostensibly vindicates its claims to justice and democracy and fairness and other fundamental values. . . . I think that it's possible to make reality better by vigorously demanding that the system live up to its claims. . . . [I]nstitutions are guilty of either active injustice or negligence and [if] no one makes them do what they're supposed to be doing they're going to be off the hook.[60]

Others seem more demoralized—bereft of a political vision that is relevant to their practice and/or discouraged by the entirely defensive and largely futile battles they must wage against the powerful forces of domination.

It is at this point that we encounter the first hint of the divisions between second- and third-generation left-activists.[61] Especially among third-generation left-activists in salaried practice there is a constant search for instances of direct action that they can support as lawyers and/or participate in as demonstrators. Consider the following interplay between two third-generation public defenders:

One demonstration that [a colleague] and I were legal observers at we were getting very frustrated because the cops were making up all of these stupid rules and in this age of civil disobedience it was like the people doing the demonstration could only think of either totally disobeying or totally obeying. We ended up with me being the legal observer and [my colleague] going and leading, showing ways to keep moving and not doing what they say but also not doing what they would be able to arrest you for. I don't think anybody in the ACLU would do that.[62]

Moreover, at least one of these public defenders seems fairly optimistic about the social movement scene. "Act Up has been more active than most other groups in the last several years, and Earth First! has been active. And I've spent increasing amounts of time with Earth First! people; Act Up because there's a lot of members very active, Earth First! in some ways because they still get singled out for government persecution so readily whenever they try to do anything.[63] Nor is it beyond this enterprising young attorney to organize his own movement when the situation seems to demand it. "I strongly felt that we don't need a new jail and I organized Citizens Against Another Jail of which I was not the only member but I was easily the most active member. I worked very hard. Spoke wherever I could speak. Interviewed over radio and talk-shows and things like that. Ultimately, as with ever other battle I've ever fought, it was unsuccessful. That was my first real taste of anything that looks like normal electoral politics."[64] Recall, in contrast, the complaint of a dedicated and prominent second-generation salaried left-activist, "[T]here's no movements, there's no nothing.[65] There is, however, reason to be cautious about making this particular matter into a generational divide insofar as most second- *and* third-generation left-activists are pessimistic about the social movement scene.

Professional Adversity and Generational Divergence

In the professional realm the generational divide is much clearer, and it poses a substantial threat to the left-activist cohort. At the same time that the forces of ascendant capitalism have impinged on the political opportunities available to left-activists, professional opportunities have been restricted by the increasingly competitive market faced by law firms and by a contraction of positions available in salaried practice. Adding to these career burdens is the increasing expense of litigation. Taken together, these harsh realities have made decommodification much more difficult than was the case in the heady days of the 1960s and early 1970s. In the final analysis, left-activist lawyers are forced into cost benefit decisions about cases that, while still emphasizing social justice and political change, cannot escape the kind of unwelcome bottom-line calculations that are inherent in conventional private practice and in the business world more generally.

This professional adversity is not, however, shared evenly within the left-activist cohort. It is experienced much more in some practice sites than in others, and third-generation left-activists are to be found disproportionately in more problematic sites. Conversely, second-generation left-activists are more likely to have secure and responsible positions in financially stable settings where their values are respected, their work is appreciated, and their priorities honored. Of course, there are exceptions to these generalizations, but they are sufficiently valid to explain a significant cleavage that has developed between second- and third-generation left-activists. The character and consequences of that cleavage are, in effect, the theme of this section of the paper.

With the legal services program shrinking and other salaried practice jobs few and far between, the major dependable site of left-activist salaried practice has become the public defender program. A veteran legal services attorney summed up the shifting fortunes of the legal services and the public defender programs as follows:

> So when you shrink in size from maybe forty-five attorneys to fifteen and seven of them haven't left, you know you're siphoning people through a few spots—and fewer every year whenever someone stays. Public defender, on the other hand . . . used to be about [the same size with the same politics]. Now public defender is probably eighty or a hundred. That tells you something about the society too, with various funding for fifteen people to do civil legal services and the criminal representation, which is driven by constitutional rights to representation, when there's that amount of criminal prosecutions going on. Where are we putting our justice resources?[66]

This shift in the center of gravity of left-activism is not in and of itself a bad thing. Indeed, with legal services under seemingly endless and ever more serious political assault, the shift, as such, could be seen as a step in the right direction and as a way of stabilizing the left-activist cohort.

There are, however, a number of problematic and divisive features to what is taking place. Most obviously, insofar as a job with legal services is no longer a realistic prospect, career options for new attorneys, the lifeblood of the left-activist movement, are narrowed. As for those already practicing, connections are attenuated between second-generation attorneys in legal services and third-generation attorneys in the public defender's office and elsewhere. Consider the following comment of second-generation legal services attorney: "Once you've been there for a while you're part of that permanent community. That is a community I think who regards themselves as legal services folks or ex–legal services folks."[67] And as will become clear below, these centrifugal forces tend to undermine the vitality of the Guild, which has in the past provided much of the glue that held the left-activist cohort together.

Moreover, while the work of the legal services program, especially these days, is not necessarily more satisfying than work in other sites of salaried practice, the second-generation legal services attorneys interviewed for this project do escape some of the burdens that third-generation attorneys working elsewhere find so taxing. The main problem has to do with what third-generation attorneys see as a backbreaking workload: "I love the work but the pace is impossible. I have had one weekend off since January and regularly work into the night. And that is true of virtually everyone in my division. It's now 5:30 p.m. on Friday night and this office looks like mid-day."[68] It is not only that the workload makes it more difficult to do the job but that it cuts into the time that is available for the outside political activity. It is, of course, this outside activity that left-activists tend to see as the most politically meaningful aspect of their political lives. Along similar lines, a third-generation left-activist working for a social action organization also felt some need to curtail her outside political activities, particularly insofar as it involved civil disobedience: "Yeah. And there are many times . . . I'm not sure how often I've gotten involved with civil disobedience, it's really an insignificant number of times, but when I do that, I always keep in mind that I'm taking a big risk here. . . .I can't get [my agency] drawn into a big controversy."[69] Of course, legal services attorneys are also under close scrutiny, not, I gathered, in a way that limits what they do with their free time but rather in order to make certain that none of their office time is given to politically proscribed activities. With respect to workload, my impression is that this is less of an issue at legal services. It also seems that the second-generation attorneys are, perhaps for life cycle reasons, more resigned to an unpromising social movement scene and thus to confining their cause lawyering activities pretty much to their jobs.

In private practice, there are parallel cleavages between second- and third-generation left-activists. The divergence seems, however, less pronounced for solo practitioners than those in small firms. It was surprising to discover that, with one revealing exception, all of the respondents have been able to decommodify substantial portions of their practices. This ordinarily means that the paying elements of their practices—personal injury work, family law, criminal defense, or certain kinds of immigration representation—finance pro bono or reduced-fee cause lawyering. But it is also true that some cause lawyering actually does bring in money. Tort litigation is the obvious example, but compensation is available for death penalty work, and the courts are authorized by statute to award reasonable fees in certain kinds of civil rights cases. As for the other paying portions of their practices, these attorneys take pains not to be on the wrong side: defendant insurance companies in personal injury cases, abusive or homophobic spouses in family law, and so on. Typical, therefore, were the comments of a second-generation solo practitioner who considered herself "lucky" to be able to "make a living . . . in a field where I can choose to do things that are, if not major political cases, at least consistent with the political beliefs that I have, working for people in the situations that they're in. And so I've been able to choose areas that I find interesting and enjoy my work. It's not necessarily synonymous with my political work, but it's the kind of work that I can determine my own time on."[70] The chances of getting involved in "major political cases" are greater for a partner in one of three small firms that have sufficient capital to finance impact litigation. On the other hand, those in solo practice do not have to worry about contributing their fair share to firm overhead or responding to the occasional partner who— even in these politically committed firms may wish to alter the way the balance is struck between causes and money.

As to generational cleavage, the third-generation respondents in small-firm practice are all partners in one of the three professionally and politically congenial firms mentioned above. These are choice positions, and while two third-generation left-activists are members of these firms—one a partner[71]—it may not be irrelevant that both have Harvard law degrees. Probably more typical is the case of a woman who has a job that enables her to do the kind of police misconduct work that interests her but who has "been working three and a half years in a small firm . . . where I kind of have to be careful about my political . . . my outside activities. I'm just kind of scared about it, let's just put it that way. My direct supervising partner knows about what I do, and he is supportive of it, but there are other senior partners, and I just have to be careful."[72] In other words, there seem to be only three firms in Seattle that are welcoming to left-activists, and in these hard times other jobs, insofar as they are available, are likely to be less satisfactory and partnership perhaps out of reach. For those who are sufficiently enterprising, solo practice is, of course, an option that has been workable and satisfying.[73]

The partial eclipse of the Guild in recent years is both evidence of and a contributor to the troubled circumstances of left-legal activism in Seattle. In better times the Guild was at the core of the left-activist enterprise and served a variety of purposes. It provided ideological direction and a social network. It mobilized and coordinated legal resources and also supported the University of Washington student chapter that recruited law students for the left-activist enterprise. However, at the time of my interviewing in 1993 and 1994 there was widespread agreement among left-activists that the Seattle chapter of the Guild had fallen on hard times. The second generation, which had been the chapter's sustaining force had drifted away, and the third generation was slow and rather ineffectual in taking on the burdens of leadership.

To a substantial degree the withdrawal of the second generation can be attributed to life cycle and political factors over which the Guild really has little, if any, control: "It's in a fallow period for me, but I've had a question about whether that's me or the Guild. I think I'm at a period where, because of family obligations, I don't just have the time. But I think there is a fallow period, and I think it does have to do with the Left or whatever—the social movements getting kind of moribund. I think there's not much to hook up with now. . . . I don't know whether it's a political thing or if it's the aging of the 60s generation—I'm 45— and is it that it's somehow not as relevant now."[74] Second-generation left-activists tend to have heavy family and firm responsibilities that eat into the time that they once made available for Guild activities and political work more generally. Of course, family ties also mean less need for the socializing that once made the Guild so central to their lives. Moreover, second-generation left-activists have to some extent, as was suggested above, simply made their peace with discrete causes and limited goals—immigration, gay and lesbian rights, death penalty work, and so on. Given the malaise and centrifugal forces within the Left the Guild is, thus, less able to provide, and the second generation are less inclined to seek, the overarching ideological perspective that would give a shared transformative meaning to their work.

There are those who are inclined to believe that it is less a matter of them drifting away from the Guild than of the Guild failing to maintain its relevance in an admittedly difficult period. According to a legal services attorney and longtime Guild activist:

> The Guild has played a very limited role in economic justice work. There is a period in the mid-1980s after they disbanded the Legal Services Corporation, it was kind of a network for legal services lawyers, but most of that has been recreated outside of the Guild. There is an economic rights task force that periodically has gone through revival periods. I participated in it for ten years or so but very ad hoc, on the national level . . . [I]t's kind of floundered in terms of "What is its role and what can it contribute?" [75]

Another-third generation attorney in solo practice suggests that the Guild with its "vaguely left" values and "vast array of people" is stretched "too thin" and unable to come up with a unifying agenda.[76] One of the founding members goes so far as to believe that because "the movement as it existed in the 1960s and 1970s doesn't exist anymore—and the Guild was part of that—I think it's probably going to be a political anachronism. I don't think it's going to survive seventy years. I don't think it's going to be around in another ten or fifteen years."[77] According to these views, the Guild is, at least in part, responsible for some its problems.

The third generation is generally speaking in closer touch with and more dependent upon the Guild, but their stories tend to reinforce the sense of a chapter in trouble. The then president of the chapter—chosen, she said "because there wasn't anybody else"—noted that a shrinking membership is both a sign, and a cause, of trouble. She noted how much easier it was to attract members to the ACLU committee on which she served:

> [The Guild] has a much smaller membership, a lot of members dropped out, and their financial base is much smaller, minuscule. . . . As a result of that we don't really have a staff person. . . . The people on the ACLU Police Practices Committees are still dues-paying Lawyer's Guild members. . . . But I think probably at some point in their careers . . . if you're going to be in an organization really actively, that you want an organization where there's a staff person there who can do the work for you.[78]

But this point begs the question about why the organization is shrinking and that takes us to familiar terrain.

The intense job pressures experienced by those in the public defender office and the pull of family responsibilities have already been mentioned. A single mother in salaried practice is inactive in the Guild, because of "my daughter, frankly,"[79] and another salaried attorney talked about his young son "who's twenty months old," so he goes "home to my family and I don't do much outside political work anymore because I feel like I'm making a real political contribution doing what I do now."[80] With respect to Guild, per se, he says, "I mean, they're my comrades and colleagues. . . . In a sense it's kind of unfair of me not to go to the meetings. . . . I'm in contact with Guild people all the time so I feel like I'm doing Guild work during the day. That's a problem with the Guild, because [public defenders and others who could contribute] are so exhausted. Those are some of the people that really are on the cutting edge of realizing the creeping police state that is going on."[81] Indeed, one of the most committed Guild members decided that the only way he could assume an effective leadership role was to became a part-time public defender.[82]

Most fundamentally, however, there is reason to believe that the Guild is simply out of touch with the most immediate concerns of its members. On the one hand, they have less need for an umbrella organization and on the other hand the issues that preoccupy the Guild seem rather distant. Thus, according a public defender, "[I]t's really fallen down in terms of domestic issues."[83] As if to illustrate this point one of the local leaders mentioned that the Guild nationally had made asylum for Haitian boat people a priority matter.[84] The underlying problem, as she went on to point out, is that in the absence of the "unified political vision" of the 1970s, the organization is having trouble defining itself in ways which are relevant to its diverse membership: "We're finding that a very large contingent of our membership are gays and lesbians. And, they, many in that contingent are wanting to define the struggle slightly differently, not in class terms. And then there are those who want to continue to frame the issues in class terms. So this is why I'm having a little difficulty getting at the legal significance. We're working on it. Check with us in a year."[85] The upshot seems to be that while they still feel a general kinship with the Guild, many second- as well as third-generation people do not see it as relevant to their cause lawyering practice or to their increasingly diverse priorities.

The Prospects for Left-Activist Lawyering

Convergent political and professional forces are both weakening and altering left-activist cause lawyering in Seattle. Left-legal activists are unable to transcend the ideological vacuum and political malaise that burden the Left these days. And the weakness and disarray on the Left stands in sharp and demoralizing contrast to the strength and confidence of an ascendant Right that is, moreover, increasingly targeting the legal arena. With the tools of their trade threatened, the sights of budget cutters and political opponents trained on the legal services program, the job market tight, and private practitioners under increased financial pressure, left-activists and cause lawyers in general have good reason to feel themselves under siege.

Under the circumstances, it would be easy to exaggerate and indeed to mis-construe the current threat to left-activist lawyering. While times are tough for left-activists, things are not as professionally difficult as they were during the De-pression nor as politically hazardous as they were in the McCarthy period. To some extent, then, the present situation looks bleak or even hopeless only when measured against the unusual conditions and unrealistic expectations of the 1960s and early 1970s. Moreover, with a plethora of unresolved and unaddressed prob-lems festering in this society and the conservative agenda likely to add to these difficulties, the political scene could change dramatically in ways that revivify the Left and left-legal activism along with it. Nor should the dedication of left-activist lawyers be discounted in assessing the future.

If, however, left-activist cause lawyers may be counted on to persevere, the left-activist project in Seattle does seem to be undergoing a significant change—a change that is blurring the distinction between left-activist cause lawyering and other forms of cause lawyering. In the first place, left-activists seem increasingly skeptical about the likelihood of politicizing their practices. Most would probably agree with the sentiments of a third-generation attorney who compared his work as a public defender to

> being a social worker, like trying to run a shelter. I don't consider it part of a real attempt at forming political change, structural change, the kind that we eventually need. It is however on a psychological level [that] it meets a lot of my needs. The work is that I'm fighting the state; I'm representing the oppressed, to put it crudely, on a one-to-one, one-at-a-time basis. Ultimately it's a way of paying the bills while doing work that I think is socially useful. I think of being a P.D. as being socially useful. I'm distinguishing between "socially useful" and "politically radical."[86]

In other words, with the possible exception of the two attorneys associated with the Trial Lawyers for Public Justice,[87] left-activists are increasingly inclined to dis-tinguish between doing effectual work in their practices on behalf of society's victims and promoting significant change outside their legal practices in social movement work.

To survive in these disheartening circumstances, left-activists have adopted a variety of strategies and rationales. One response is to put whatever energy is available into organizations that show a taste for direct action politics like Act Up or into causes like homelessness that seem to have a potential for movement building. Another is to distinguish between a transformative politics that is not really within reach of lawyers acting on their own and more modest and discrete "political" contributions that litigation can sometimes make. Thus, a salaried attorney acknowledged that "lawyers are the buffers between poor people and the system. I don't believe in large-scale political change occurring through legal action and lawyers."[88] Yet speaking of his work with the Northwest Immigrants Rights Project, he asserted, "I feel like I'm making a real political contribution doing what I do now."[89] Still others, simply make their peace with what they can do with various forms of legal representation—conventional client service, empowerment strategies, or impact litigation. This kind of work may be part and parcel of their "day jobs" in private and salaried practice or done on a pro bono basis—working with such reform-minded organizations as the ACLU or the Northwest Women's Law Center.

Finally, those who adopt an "anti-ism" position and choose to define politics in personal terms seem to be moving in a poststructuralist direction. This approach locates domination at microsites of power and in cross-cutting social cleavages. It, therefore, becomes appropriate to organize resistance around any of these cleavages—race, gender, sexual orientation, age, and so on. Similarly any of the multiple sites of domination are appropriate as targets: the family, the workplace, schools, social service agencies, and the like. In contrast, structural theory locates domination in class conflict as well as state and corporate power, which become the necessary and sufficient targets of effective resistance.[90]

In practice, what all of these strategies have in common is a tendency to make more hazy the line separating left-activist cause lawyers from other cause lawyers. At the beginning of this paper, I identified left-activism as going "beyond the notion of lawyers simply doing good—working, that is, to alleviate poverty or homelessness, to protect the environment, to expand human rights, and the like." Clearly many left-activists are resigning themselves to this more conventional terrain. And as the interviews suggest, the declining fortunes of the Guild reflect this kind of hollowing out from above and below of left-legal activism. Whether the willingness of left-activists to put aside their search for ideological unity reflects a principled "anti-ism" stance or an acceptance of the inevitable, the result is that the principal purposes served by Guild no longer seem meaningful. At the same time, as Guild members lower their sights and focus on more immediate objectives, they find themselves more in tune with the practical day-to-day efforts of other organizations.

The troubling question posed by all of this does not really have to do with the staying power of second- and third-generation attorneys now practicing or even with whether they play a distinctive role. Second-generation left-activists are well situated to weather the political and professional adversity of the 1990s. Third-generation left-activists are in a more tenuous situation but seem to be sufficiently resourceful and dedicated to meet the challenge. Some members of the left-activist cohort continue to engage in political action and to seek out and support social movements. Even the left-activists who drift away to more main-stream organizations attempt to introduce more politicized conceptions of organizational missions.[91]

The real issue is whether Seattle left-activism as an enterprise has, in the altered circumstances of the 1990s, sufficient vitality to reproduce itself in the years ahead—to nurture, in other words, a fourth generation. Recall that the roots of the second generation can be traced to the antiwar, antipoverty, and civil rights movements of the 1960s, and that the third generation cut its teeth on the threats posed by the Reagan administration. Moreover, both generations were able to call upon the Lawyers Guild, which provided a congenial and supportive student subculture in law school and a focal point for social activity and consciousness-raising in the professional world. For the time being, at least, the next generation cannot draw much inspiration from the political setting. They also seem likely to face an even tighter job market burdened by heavy debts incurred while in law school. And, of course, the survival strategies undertaken by the second and third generations are marginalizing the Guild. Under the circumstances, the reproductive capacity of left-legal activism remains much in doubt.

Notes

The research for this study was conducted under a grant from the Law and Social Science Program of the National Science Foundation (SES-9213147 A001). I am especially grateful to its then director, Michael Musheno, for his encouragement. I am also indebted to Lisa Miller and David Vega for thoughtful and enthusiastic research assistance. Helpful comments on an earlier version of this paper were provided by Michael McCann, Austin Sarat, David Sugarman, and other participants in the conference on cause lawyering at Amherst College in August 1994.

1. William Simon, "The Ideology of Advocacy," *Wisconsin Law Review* 1978 (1978), 36.

2. Those who write about what I am calling left-activist lawyering have characterized roughly the same enterprise in a variety of ways, such as activist lawyering, cause lawyering, critical lawyering, progressive lawyering, radical lawyering, rebellious lawyering, and socialist lawyering. It would, of course, have been possible to recycle any of the other terms but only by altering their intrinsic meanings. All these conceptions share a focus on the inclination and capacity of lawyers, as lawyers, to promote progressive social change. It is with considerable reluctance that I add "left-activist lawyering" to this profusion of terms. I do so to provide an umbrella concept with which to collect and to synthesize the full range of principles and practices found in the existing literature. Taken together these analyses alert us to a wide range of basic dissatisfactions with conventional legal practice while at the same time suggesting alternatives to it. The multiplicity of terms, however, encourages differentiation among, rather than aggregation of, the dissatisfactions with, and the alternatives to, conventional practice. Each term is in some measure exclusive, championing different values and establishing different priorities. This is, in short, contested terrain and to choose one of these terms is to exclude some aspects of others. "Left-activist lawyering" comes without this intellectual baggage and is offered in a spirit of inclusion.

3. There are both liberal and radical strands woven into the Guild's history, but the organization and its lawyers have consistently been at the cutting edge of professional and political change. Jerold S. Auerbach, *Unequal Justice: Lawyers and Social Change* (New York: Oxford University Press, 1976), 198–210 and 234–37.

4. Victor Rabinowitz and Tim Ledwith, eds., *A History of the National Lawyers Guild, 1937–1987* (New York: National Lawyers Guild, 1987), back cover. A comparison of this 1971 version of the preamble with the original suggests how much more assertive the Guild became in the years after its founding in 1937. There was no mention in the original preamble of the need for "basic change in the structure of our political and economic system" or for lawyers as "an effective political and social force." The tone was more liberal and reformist with an emphasis on extending rights and a more flexible approach to precedent. Ann Fagan Ginger and Eugene M. Tobin, eds., *The National Lawyers Guild: From Roosevelt through Reagan* (Philadelphia: Temple University Press), 11.

5. This is part of a broader study of cause lawyering in Seattle. In order to establish whether these Guild lawyers form a distinctive left-activist cohort it will, of course, be necessary to compare them to the other cause lawyers who were interviewed for this project. Stuart Scheingold, Lisa Miller, and David Vega, "The Social Organization of Cause Lawyering," paper presented at the annual meeting of the Law and Society Association, Chicago, Illinois, May 27–30, 1993 and Stuart Scheingold, "Sites of Cause Lawyering: Explaining the Variation," paper presented at the annual meeting of the Law and Society Association, Toronto, Canada, June 1–4, 1995.

6. 091, 12. The first number in the interview citations refers to the respondent and the second number to the relevant page number in the transcript.

7. It could be argued that it would have been better to draw these generational boundaries according to age. The result would have been to include in the second generation those (mostly women) who took time out from school after completing their undergraduate education. These older, third-generation left-activists were, unlike the others in their cohort, influenced by the spirit of the sixties. The interviews suggested, however, that their expectations, opportunities, choices, and prospects as lawyers have been influenced more by when they went to law school and when they began to practice than by their ages.

8. 077, 18.

9. Stuart A. Scheingold, *The Politics of Rights: Lawyers, Public Policy and Political Change* (New Haven: Yale University Press, 1974), 177–81 and Stuart A. Scheingold, "The Contradictions of Radical Law Practice," in *Lawyers in a Postmodern World: Translation and Transgression*, ed. Maureen Cain and Christine B. Harrington (Buckingham, United Kingdom: Open University Press, 1994), 265–285.

10. Alan Thomson, "Foreword: Critical Approaches to Law: Who Needs Legal Theory?," in *The Critical Lawyers' Handbook*, ed. Ian Grigg-Spall and Paddy Ireland (London: Pluto Press, 1992), 6.

11. Peter Fitzpatrick, "Law as Resistance," in ibid., 46.

12. Robert W. Gordon, "New Developments in Legal Theory," in *The Politics of Law: A Progressive Critique*, ed. David Kairys (New York: Pantheon, 1990). But see Richard Abel, "Law without Politics: Legal Aid under Advanced Capitalism," *UCLA Law Review* 32 (1985), 604–606.

13. 048, 10.

14. 024, 10. Despite this notoriety, and much to her surprise, the local bar voted her a "lawyer of the year award" (ibid.).

15. 048, 2.

16. 052, 7.

17. 084, 1.
18. 077, 10.
19. 084, 1.
20. 077, 10.
21. 048, 8.
22. 048, 9.
23. 084, 1.
24. 058, 5.
25. 058, 5.
26. 077, 16.

27. William Simon, "Visions of Legal Practice in Legal Thought," *Stanford Law Review* 36 (1984), 469–507.

28. 048, 10–11.

29. Anthony Alfieri, "Stances," *Cornell Law Review* 77 (1992), 1233–1257, and Gerald P. Lopez, *Rebellious Lawyering: One Chicano's Vision of Progressive Law Practice* (Boulder, Colo: Westview Press, 1992).

30. Scheingold, "The Contradictions of Radical Law Practice," in *Lawyers in a Postmodern World,* ed. Cain and Harrington.

31. Among the twenty-five left-activists included in this study, seven were in the collective at one time or another—all drawn from the thirteen-member second-generation contingent. Another of Seattle's second-generation left-activists (077) worked in an East Coast collective before moving to Seattle, where she became a legal services attorney. Only two members of the collective stayed on throughout the entire period, but others were involved for extended periods and were deeply influenced, even inspired, by their experience in the collective. It should be pointed out that at least two members of the collective did not identify with Guild and tended to think of themselves as liberals (032, 039).

32. 023, 4.
33. 023, 4.
34. 023, 18.
35. 048, 5.
36. 070, 1. See also 075, 13–14.
37. 048, 4–5.

38. Public defenders were also attracted by the autonomy that they had in handling their cases and objected to the supervision that they felt they would be subjected to in private practice. "I don't actually have a great desire to work for someone else. . . . I've been working for myself for years now. . . . [There I would] have people above me . . . [here] I get my clients. I do what I want." (075, 13. Also 070, 14).

39. 048, 13.
40. 077, 12.

41. See, for example, Norman Rush, "What Was Socialism . . . and Why We Will All Miss It So Much," *Nation* 268 (1994): 90–94.

42. 023, 9.
43. 048, 10.
44. 091, 19.
45. 058, 12.
46. 077, 14.
47. 084, 7.
48. 084, 8.
49. 023, 9.

50. 025, 24; 037, 10.

51. 024, 15–16.

52. 055, 9–10.

53. 058, 13.

54. 058, 7. It is worth noting, however, that she still sees it important in these encounters to think of herself as an attorney and not as a social worker.

55. 058, 6. Another third-generation left-activist public defender is a good deal more ambivalent about the consequences of empowerment. "There are times that we can help people to become empowered or to empower themselves. I have mixed feelings even about that because sometimes from doing that you're giving a false message, which is that the system works" (071, 11).

56. 071, 11.

57. 091, 14.

58. 084, 4.

59. 084, 29–30.

60. 023, 11.

61. These divisions will figure much more prominently in the analysis of professional adversity—the next order of business.

62. 071, 14.

63. 075, 7.

64. 075, 10–11.

65. 048, 10.

66. 077, 16.

67. 077, 16.

68. 071, See also 075, 15.

69. 052, 8.

70. 049, 7.

71. 062.

72. 057, 2.

73. 067.

74. 048, 14.

75. 077, 15.

76. 058, 11.

77. 084, 20.

78. 057, 6.

79. 052, 7.

80. 091, 12.

81. 091, 19–20.

82. 075.

83. 071, 13.

84. 067, 12.

85. 067, 10.

86. 075, 14.

87. 084 and 043.

88. 091, 8–9.

89. 091, 12.

90. A more eclectic structuralism accommodates legal action that is not in itself transformative but can be seen as a contribution to transformation. "Since the social relations between the classes are fragmented, the central antagonism takes the form of many specific

conflicts, for example, over housing, the environment, racial and gender oppression." Robert Fine and Sol Picciotto, "On Marxist Critiques of Law," in *The Critical Lawyers' Handbook*, ed. Grigg-Spall and Ireland, 18. While at first glance this version of structuralism may seem indistinguishable from poststructuralism, it actually is closer to the liberal reform mode, because the objective of legal action is to get social rights incorporated into bourgeois law: "[T]he right to work is recognized not as a right for the millions of unemployed, but as the right of the strike-breaker or non-union member. There is no right to decent housing, but only a right to be undisturbed in the possession of one's own home whether it is a hovel or a palace. Other social rights, such as health, are not recognized as legal entitlements" (ibid., 19).

91. Left-activists do not blend seamlessly into their new organizations precisely because they continue to think about themselves as politically engaged lawyers. Theirs is a vision that is marked by an impatient opposition to the forces of domination and a determined commitment to resistance. The result is that they tend to be attracted to somewhat different causes than other cause lawyers and that they are not really motivated by, or committed to, legal and constitutional rights, as such. These rights are means to a political ends. Left-activists are, therefore, more likely to be pushing themselves and their organizations into terrain that is politically and professionally controversial and, indeed, risky. Thus, the practice and even more so the ethos of left-legal activism continues to be distinctive, if not as distinctive as it once may have been or as distinctive as its ideals would imply.

PART II

Cause Lawyering and the Organization of Practice

Norris, Schmidt, Green, Harris, Higginbotham & Associates

The Sociolegal Import of Philadelphia Cause Lawyers

AARON PORTER

A Social Fabric, Civil Causes, and African American Lawyers

This chapter provides an account of how and why the law firm of Norris, Schmidt, Green, Harris, Higginbotham & Associates sought to transform the professional and social fabric in Philadelphia and went on to bring about changes at the federal level, through the legal and political process. This account of the law firm, its practices, and the effect its members had on the larger social milieu of the city supplies an important framework for assessing how "cause lawyers" emerge and impact racial or social inequality with policy implications for the contemporary United States.

The Norris firm was founded by Harvey N. Schmidt in the early 1950s, when African Americans were virtually excluded from white law firms, state and federal clerkships, and professional opportunities in the corporate mainstream. It became the nurturing ground of legal giants who acted as agents for social change. Compared to major law firms in Philadelphia, the Norris firm produced a disproportionate number of state and federal judges and officials. Firm members who received Third Circuit appointments include A. Leon Higginbotham Jr., the second African American to be appointed U.S. district judge, and former chief judge of the appeals court; Clifford Scott Green, the third African American to be appointed U.S. district judge; Herbert Hutton, the fifth African American to be appointed U.S. district judge; and William F. Hall Jr., the first African American appointed U.S. magistrate judge. The firm also produced Doris Mae Harris, the second African American woman appointed to the Philadelphia common pleas court; Schmidt, the first African American to serve as a member of the Registration Commission in Philadelphia, who later became a common pleas judge; and many others, including William H. Brown III, of Schnader, Harrison, Segal & Lewis, who became chair of the U.S. Equal Employment Opportunity Commission (EEOC).

This group of lawyers gradually moved into distinguished positions of power and influence. Their entrance into the profession, however, exemplifies the effects of segregation, including the effects of white professional organizations as they operated in our society and impacted the cause lawyering, as I will demonstrate. There are very few comprehensive studies on African American lawyers. Those that have been published include the works of Fitzhugh Lee Styles, Genna Rae McNeil, John Hope Franklin, Geraldine Segal, J. Clay Smith, Linn Washington, and Gilbert Ware, all of which address what African American lawyers were doing in times of segregation and the gradual increase in their professional opportunities over time.[1] Most of these works are biographical in nature and provide important background for learning "who's who" in the law among African American lawyers. Sociologists, however, would want to know how these life histories of African American lawyers speak to larger organizational and societal issues, a point that I discuss in this chapter. The story of the Norris firm and the lawyers associated with it does speak to such larger issues and fills a gap in the historical record. For, while there are many studies of white lawyers, white law firms, white legal careers, there are very few of black lawyers, their professional practices in the context of their law firms, and their place in the legal profession as such.

William Hale, a student of Everette Hughes, wrote one of the earlier (1949) comparative studies. His article makes clear the utility, strictly for sociological theoretical purposes, of such work, by emphasizing the kind of legal work available to lawyers of different races, especially in a severe, restrictive societal setting, and how that experience shapes their careers and professional conduct.[2] The work available to lawyers of the Norris firm is a key variable that I document here. The many studies of white lawyers and white law firms, such as those by Erwin Smigel, Jerome E. Carlin and Robert Nelson,[3] acquire new dimensions when compared with this study of how a black law firm could be successful under racially segregated or confining conditions, and how its competitive position was enhanced by changes in federal law, which gave it a new kind of work to exploit.

The second main area that I explore is the development of political and social power in the black community and its role in cause lawyering. I show how professional development intersects with the development of black urban political organization, for example, in the mobilization of black votes by Austin Norris, who combined journalism, law, Garveyism, and other interests to develop a power base that made him important to white politicians in the city. Norris parlayed that power base into a position on a regulatory board, which made him someone white business people had to pay attention to and deal with. In other words, white business and political leaders alike had to deal with Norris not only because of his street savvy in influencing the black vote throughout the city and across the state but also because he was a smart "Yale-ee" who became a national expert and policy maker in the law of eminent domain, especially in Philadelphia.

The actions of the Norris firm's lawyers can be seen through the development and activities of their professional institution. A study of this particular institution also provides insights into the social structure of the United States and its racial relations and why cause lawyering as a professional practice was planted in the midst of this law firm like seed taking root and growing over time. I discuss this process below, but first I will provide a theoretical discussion of institutions so that the relevance of cause lawyering among these law firm members can take shape in context.

Customs, Practices, and Professional Behaviors

Robert Park and Ernest Burgess (1967) note that studying institutions helps eluci-date the continuity and organization of society since institutions are part of and emerge from our social structure.[4] This perspective serves as a basis for analyzing how the rise and fall of the Norris law firm contributes to our understanding of racial change and progress inasmuch as it relates to professional mobility among African American attorneys and the community at large. A definition of what is meant by the term "institution," however, is needed in order to provide a clearer understanding of this chapter's focus on its subject.

Institutions may be classified in at least three ways. This is evident when we look at what is meant by the term "institution." The popular definition of the term is "a custom, practice, relationship, or behavioral pattern of importance in the life of a community or society."[5] It is also an established organization housed in a building or physical structure and an organization that is dedicated to a public service or a culture. This basic three-part definition is generally accepted by sociologists, who use it to shape and advance our notions of how institutions develop and operate. First, as the dictionary definition states, an institution is an established practice at the heart of the social and political life of a people. Second, as sociologists define them, institutions provide an orderly way to arrange and regulate human actions in a confined location for the purpose of a larger good. Third, as the work of Walter Powell and Paul Dimaggio indicates,[6] institutions can become linked with other organizations in cultural relationships. These linkages can become complex in their makeup and impact the public sphere or social fabric in a number of ways, depending on how specialization in a particular field or profession is used within the context of other organizations or on the net effect or movement from one institution to another.

Sociologists then enlarge these definitions by providing contexts and concepts for the usage of the term. Early sociologists, classical theorists like Herbert Spencer, saw institutions as established practices. Spencer perceived society as a social organism that consisted of various parts that sustained, distributed, and regulated functions in societies.[7] He identified various types of institutions, including domestic, industrial, political, and professional ones. John Sirjamaki remarked of Spencer that "[h]is assumptions about societies and institutions rested on postulates of social evolution, and led him to believe that, as societies progressed toward higher levels of cultural development, their institutions became increasingly specialized in form and activities, but continued nevertheless integrated and interdependent."[8] William Sumner developed a similar organic definition of institutions, arguing, however, that institutions consisted of doctrines and the structures by which one employed them. Thus, he says, institutions arose from societal or group mores as "were made more definite and specific as regards the rules, the prescribed acts, and the apparatus to be employed."[9] Stuart Chapin added to Sumner's account of institutions by noting that institutions arose as groups strove to satisfy basic individual and group needs while establishing stable patterns to meet those needs.[10] L. Hobhouse perceived institutions in terms of the principles that govern the relations of individuals; he saw institutions as systems of adjustments to one's conditions of life rather than as apparatuses devised to meet just individual needs.[11]

The sociological definition of institutions reflects how a group sets standards of behavior by which to conduct its activities. This arrangement has both a macro and micro aspect to it. On the one hand, M. MacIver and C. H. Page, for instance, note that institutions are "established forms or conditions of procedure" established by larger organizations.[12] On the other hand, as Talcott Parsons and Edward Shills indicate, institutions set standards of social behavior that become organized into stable patterns of activity regulated by norms in *local* contexts.[13] From the work of these earlier sociologists to the contemporary sociological work of Powell and Dimaggio, institutions are seen in terms of the theories by which they operate. These characterizations of institutions for the most part hold true for the law firm of Norris and his colleagues. In one case, lawyers of the firm had to follow the rules by which their conduct as lawyers was prescribed by the larger legal profession. In another case, they also had to set principles by which they operated in terms of their professional activities.

Institutions like law firms in the black community, especially during times of racial segregation, were dependent on the various social organisms in the community. Black lawyers and their professional practices were like fibers that became part of the social fabric of the black community. In this case, the interests of black lawyers and the black community as a whole were mutually dependent on each other, especially in terms of clients or civil rights cases, as Hale made clear in his 1949 paper.[14] In the case of the Norris firm, the institution (as Hobhouse would describe it) represented an adjustment to conditions of life. This can be seen through an analysis of how law firms emerge in "mainstream" white society and how the Norris firm in particular became an important institution in which the social, professional, and political life of its lawyers was based.

Moving beyond Racial Exclusion

Richard Abel's seminal work, *American Lawyers,* situates for us a structural analysis of the legal profession. Abel discusses the legal profession from the latter part of the nineteenth century to the contemporary period but concentrates on the professional opportunities for elite organizations of white lawyers. Building on Magali Larson's description of an elite business sector that emerged during the industrialization period,[15] Abel reworked Larson's paradigm through a Weberian and Parsonian analysis to show how the large law firm pioneered its way in the United States at the beginning of the twentieth century in close conjunction with the elite white business community.[16]

Abel's analysis shows how law firms developed and how homogeneous white establishment class interests were reflected in the makeup of these firms, as they worked in unison with the business sector. He demonstrates for us how law firms became part of the professional opportunity structure for related white elite organizations, created by explicit ethnoreligious, racial, and sexual discrimination by law schools, state bar examiner organizations, bar associations, and employers who kept those doors of opportunity to mainstream society closed both to people of color and to women. During the period in which the United States had a caste system, defined by race and even in more recent times, the effects of this exclusion were more pronounced for people of color. Nevertheless, even with the almost total exclusion of African Americans along with women and "ethnic" white immigrants from the large law firm and its support structure such as regulatory boards, and legal institutions of prestige and power, these excluded social groups created their own organizations and professional law practices and developed strategies toward social change.[17]

As black lawyers became preoccupied with the racial caste system, they too created their own professional institutions such as bar associations and law firms. J. Clay Smith's work in particular[18] complements the earlier work of such scholars as Jerold Auerbach[19] by opening a window into the organization-building experiences of black lawyers. Moreover, professional organization and institution building, as Smith demonstrates, became a crucial component in black lawyers' campaigns to eradicate racial inequality through the legal and sociopolitical process. In this, they were organically and institutionally linked to the black community and had a systematic connection with black intellectual and social activist thought while preparing the ground foundation for the battle against inequality through legal and political strategies.

This blueprint of what occurred in the U.S. social structure with respect to the legal profession, the industrialization of the nation, and the system of racial caste that operated until recently provides a foundation for exploring how African American attorneys reacted to their exclusion from white law firms and the larger society as a whole. The assumption is that black lawyers were simply solo practioners who shared office space and swam upstream in an effort to make a living. Some scholars believe that segregation afforded black lawyers an opportunity to cash in on a segregated class structure. Smith argues, however, that the adaptation of black lawyers in "the free market was not free." He adds, "Since the white community hardly ever used the services of black lawyers, the black lawyers never developed wealth or influence in the commercial community. In commercial law, during the first one-hundred years of the black legal community, black business was largely restricted to small retail stores and the service type of establishments . . . such as barbershops, beauty parlors, and the mortuary establishments, where whites did not care to compete. Black lawyers survived by necessity, serving a restricted market within the black community which itself often used white lawyers at higher legal fees because they thought justice could be obtained only in this way." [20] Much more than that was occurring in terms of the professional careers of black lawyers. The role of black lawyers and the development of black law firms became an alternative way in which black lawyers confronted and reacted to racial oppression and rejection from a wider social system.

In his last scholarly writings before his death, Supreme Court Justice Thurgood Marshall writes, "[Black lawyers] have used their legal training not only to become masterful technicians but to force the legal system to live up to its creed: the promise of equal justice under law. . . . Negro lawyers had identified the inequities in the legal order and begun to lay the foundation for social change." [21] This effort began in 1844 when Macon B. Allen became the first African American to enter into law, a white man's profession, at a time when blacks were constitutionally enslaved. Allen became a lawyer after the initial debates on nationhood and individual protections against the national government had been determined. [22]

The social structure at that time and prior to Allen's entry into the profession reflects what Alexis de Tocqueville so astutely described in his book *Democracy in America*. [23] If the United States were to undergo a great revolution, Tocqueville noted, African American rage would be at the heart of that change. Tocqueville wrote about his trip around the United States in the 1830s after the French Revolution, and his perspective on the future of the United States was rooted in his understanding of that revolution and of the sharp inequality between black and white Americans. The revolution to which Tocqueville referred did come. It took shape as a righteous rage and as activism against social inequalities. In the case of black lawyers, the movement began in a calm, professional, strategic, and organized manner in the mid-1800s and continued in this manner right up into the 1960s. During this time, there was a division of labor in the civil movements for social change from Reconstruction and the era of industrialization to the 1960s, especially with respect to legal segregation. African American lawyers played a crucial underlying role in the gradual advance toward black civil rights in the U.S. military, education, and the public sphere, including employment, housing, and the like—however much the civil rights movement as a whole played a pivotal role in forcing change in the racial status quo and the creation of overseeing federal and governmental agencies of the 1960s. J. Clay Smith, Genna Rae McNeil, and Richard Kluger demonstrate how African American lawyers began to challenge racial inequities in the legal and social order long before the watershed of the civil rights movement.[24] As a consequence of racial and social inequities in our social structure, the practices of black lawyers, including the creation of their professional institutions and bar associations and their involvement in larger social movements against an oppressive white social system, fall within the category of fighting for equality under the law and share that ethos. Black lawyers were in effect always involved in cause lawyering.

Austin Sarat and Stuart Scheingold suggest that cause lawyers are personally, socially, and politically committed and engaged. Cause lawyers work on behalf of a wide variety of rights claims and policy goals.[25] Menkel-Meadow adds that cause lawyering is an "activity that seeks to use law-related means or seeks to change laws or regulations to achieve greater social justice—both for particular individuals (drawing on individualistic 'helping' orientations) and for disadvantaged groups. Whether the means and strategies used must be legally based 'rights' strategies or more broadly based 'needs' strategies, the goals and purposes of the legal actor are to 'do good.' "[26] Central to her argument is the question why "people seek to do good and engage in some self-sacrificing behaviors for the 'betterment' of others." Noting that there is more behind human motivations than a "bipolar conception of self-interest . . . versus a romanticized notion of 'other-regarding' behavior," Menkel Meadow discusses where cause lawyering begins or ends, who qualifies as a cause lawyer and who does not, and how such a social action differs from what it means to be a moral human being. Implicit in her analysis of cause lawyers is that they are engaged in strategies and tactics in the legal arena and political process in working toward their goals.

These goals can reflect economic, professional and social interests as well as self-interest. Cause lawyers do not simply jump on board in their attempts to "transform some aspect of the social, economic, and political status quo by affiliating with or serving a social movement."[27] Their professional commitment to a cause may satisfy their self-interest because they derive personal satisfaction from it, but this does not mean that they are solely self-motivated creatures of habit in their steps toward equality or social change. Their personal experiences heighten their insights, intensify their efforts, and energize their moral, social, and intellectual involvement. In this sense, cause lawyers become more effective because of their vested interest in social justice. In other words, exclusion, discrimination, or inequities that work in support of the dominant group and against a subordinate group can affect the latter positively. In this, the sting of racial discrimination and its consequent socialization play a major factor in individuals' insights, understandings, and reasons why they work toward sociolegal or political fairness. At the same time, the self-interest of cause lawyers can speak to larger issues in racial or ethnic communities or other socioeconomic circumstances. Where the personal needs and the social needs of communities converge with the interests of the cause lawyers, the mutual needs of both can be addressed, as we see in the civil rights movement's efforts against white domination of other racial groups. The work of Charles Hamilton Houston, the chief engineer behind the legal strategy of the civil rights movement, serves as the clearest example of black cause lawyering.[28] Houston developed a new paradigm in his work on behalf of African American civil rights. As the chief trial lawyer for and then consultant to the National Association for the Advancement of Colored People, Houston and his talented cadre of lawyers from Howard Law School, including Thurgood Marshall, were involved in several court battles. They challenged the constitutionality of segregation and the subordinate role of African Americans in American society. Their collective exclusion from the larger resources of American society was the basis of Houston's philosophy and of his belief in the social cause of change through a sociolegal movement. Houston believed that the popular perception of African American life was a white one, since African Americans did not have access to the wider media. He thought that African Americans in general, and talented African Americans in particular, economically, politically, and professionally deserved the opportunity to participate in American public life while informing others of their plight through their own insights and at various levels. Simultaneously, Houston believed that African Americans should use newspapers to inform and update each other on civil rights issues, using the media for political consciousness-raising. Therefore African American participation in the economic and political life of the country was in the best interests of Houston, his lawyers, and the black community in general. Equal opportunity then was seen to be a basic civil right. Houston recognized that the legal process was a tool for social engineering, that it could be "conceptually applied to free human beings from a status of legal nonbeing to pure legal existence," and bring them from a state of social and professional exclusion to one of inclusion. The Houstonian school of thought used law "as one method to restore and to reclassify the legal metaphysics of black Americans, and others similarly situated . . . [a tool that] in the field of politics, religion, education, law and economics aimed at securing liberty and equality."[29]

Houston, like other black Americans during the days before *Brown*, lived and functioned under the *Plessy* era.[30] He was a "race leader." It was in his self-interest to have a personal commitment toward the idea of fairness in equality of opportunity, although all educated black masses would benefit from such equality. However, Houston also asserted that the African American leadership should not "sell out" other African Americans for personal profit or personal gain but should help advance the black community in areas of social and legal injustice by resorting to the courts. The maintenance of equality under either a conservative or a liberal system of jurisprudence, however, requires both political and economic alertness. Pooling economic resources in the African American community toward that cause meant that economics tied black professional interests with that of the community in building and expanding their civil rights. Economics was not the only self-gratifying reward for black lawyers in the movement. Nor was economics the only influential resource for changing a discriminatory social order. Houston advocated too the use of symbolic power in the form of social capital (gained by a pooling of community resources, i.e., groups, agencies, and institutions in the black community) and applying it in what theorist Pierre Bourdieu calls a political field.[31] It became part of Houston's strategy for social change, on the one hand, while providing status to his group of lawyers through their involvement with various segments of the community, on the other. Bourdieu defines the political field as "both as a field of forces and as a field of struggles aimed at transforming the relation of forces which confers on this field its structure at any given moment." As part of his arsenal, Houston used social capital as a buffer against outside forces that worked toward maintaining a system of inequality, and he used the internal, community field structure to raise African American consciousness and promote actions toward equality.

Houston's approach predates the civil rights legislation of the 1960s in the steps it takes toward black participation in the body politic. His jurisprudence called for lawyers to be social engineers in a democratic society in which individuals are guaranteed the right of life, liberty, and the pursuit of happiness while participating in society.[32]

The social and political steps taken to remedy the racist practices of our past and our present have, for the most part, been modest and slow, and in key periods like the present even backtracking and retrogressive. In no period has the white leadership of the United States moved to carry out a long-term strategy to dismantle the social, economic, and political structures of racism. Cause lawyers are needed in our society. However, cause lawyering can become problematic in many ways. The Norris firm provides a view not only into how "cause lawyers" emerge within our social structure but also into how their work impacts society by undergirding and making sense of racial relations today.

The importance of this law firm can be analyzed in three parts. First, I chronicle its social history as the main African American law firm in the city of Philadelphia between 1952 and 1976, with historical antecedents in earlier periods. Second, because the firm's senior partner was so well connected politically, I focus on Austin Norris, to enlarge our understanding of how an African American lawyer builds a successful professional institution in a segregated social environment, consolidates power, and collective influence for the public good in dealing with cases of racial and social inequality. By understanding the social and economic structural conditions for black lawyers, one gains a better appreciation not only of Norris, but also of cause lawyering in general and the professional and political strategies that made this law firm flourish over time, and allowed its major partners to achieve substantial professional mobility and collective influence. Third, I provide an analysis of why the firm eventually dissolved, what the impact of the dissolution was on the social fabric of Philadelphia, and why its place has not been taken by another comparable firm in the city. I follow this with an analysis of racial change and progress, although contemporary social science research poignantly contends that racial and social inequality persists in the United States. This section of the essay will address the limitations of cause lawyering and ask whether it is needed in contemporary U.S. society.

The Growth of a Professional Institution

The living members of the Norris firm provided a glimpse of their personal and professional experiences in group interviews conducted in April and December of 1990 and 1991 with individual interviews up to 1996.

Harvey Schmidt played a crucial role in the development of the law firm. Educated in the segregated public school system of Philadelphia during the 1920s and early 1930s, he graduated from Cheyney State College, a historically black institution, with a degree in education in 1936, before entering the evening school at Temple University Law School. Schmidt, like other African American law school students, paid for law school by working during the daytime at the post office. At work, he met men with whom he would later practice law. After graduating from Temple in 1943, he followed the traditional pattern among African American lawyers and clerked with his preceptor, E. Washington Rhodes, at the *Philadelphia Tribune* (a historic black newspaper) on 16th Street in the city's seventh ward before becoming one of only two African Americans to pass and be admitted to the state bar in 1944.

Between 1933 and the early part of 1943, no African American was admitted to the practice of law in Pennsylvania. Schmidt went into private practice with two fellow Temple graduates and postal workers, Thomas Reed and Eugene Clarke. They were partners in Clarke, Reed & Schmidt, at 12th and Spruce Streets in the seventh ward as well, during segregationist days when black attorneys could not rent office space in the center of Philadelphia because of informal racial discrimination. "We would [see] vacancies listed in the paper, and we'd go," Schmidt remembers. "They [whites] would say, 'Oh, we just rented that this morning, you are just too late.' You would see the same ad in the paper the next day and the next week. That happened several times, and we were forced to rent at 12th and Spruce from the Odd Fellows, a black fraternal organization."

They occupied this space from 1944 to 1947. Schmidt heard that Dr. Howard Taylor, an African American physician, wanted to sell his building at 410 South

15th Street in the business district of the seventh ward. Taylor's building was sold through the leading African American insurance realtor, Henry Brogden. Other law offices of notable African American lawyers were located in the area—those of Robert N. C. Nix Sr. and Louis Tanner Moore, who was formerly associated with Raymond Pace Alexander. Poor, working, and middle-class blacks lived in the ward, and black churches and other black organizations were stationed there, as W. E. B. Du Bois noted in the *Philadelphia Negro.*[33] Edward Nichols, a former law firm associate of Schmidt's in the late 1950s, recalls the professional environment in the early 1950s: "If they [black lawyers] came in Center City and decided that they wanted a cup of coffee and went into one of the local restaurants down in the center of this town, where the movies were segregated, you were going to get it in a bag to take out because they [whites] knew that no sooner than you asked for it that you meant to say, to go!" Nichols remembers a sign at Broad and Market Streets in the city that read, "We solicit white patronage only." Nichols adds, "The courts were entirely different. There were no black judges at all in the state courts and, of course, on the federal [bench] there was one [William Henry Hastie]. There was one magistrate in the entire city and that was Ed Henry. There was one [black] common pleas court judge in the entire state, and he was in Pittsburgh, Homer Brown." Schmidt recalls that the courts were "very political and that judges were kings." There was no African American representation on many of the state courts. "I can remember one black committeeman who used to say, 'I can do as much for you at the magistrate court as any black lawyer in town,'" Schmidt says. "He was a Republican committeeman connected with a powerful [white] Republican ward leader. Even judges had to be concerned about the influence of a ward leader because he [the judge] ran for election." Schmidt believes that the problems he encountered were connected to the lack of political power among black lawyers. He attempted to overcome the influence of white ward leaders in communities where African Americans were in the majority through the court and political process.

In 1950, Schmidt began to expand his criminal defense law practice. He developed a business clientele with the Hispanic community, usually handling assault and battery cases. He also joined many African American fraternal organizations such as the Elks and Masons, hoping to develop sources of business. In 1952, Schmidt was joined by Clifford Scott Green, who like Schmidt had been excluded from the wider legal community after graduating from Temple Law School. They had a substantial criminal defense practice together in the years before *Gideon v. Wainright,*[34] before poor people were guaranteed a right to counsel. Two years later, Doris Mae Harris and Leon Higginbotham joined the firm. They, too, had endured the sting of racial discrimination in the wider legal community. In essence, then, this narrative reveals what larger social forces, both legal and structural, were at play that affected African American lawyers at the time. First, there were issues of political influence within the legal process; second, there was the issue of racial caste, which best accounts for the social climate at the time. African American lawyers were forced to confront and to react to racial oppression and rejection from the wider system.[35] Moreover, as they became preoccupied with the racial caste system, part of their survival depended on their ability to create their own professional institution, especially because of their limited professional options.

Houstonian Jurisprudence at the Norris Firm

In a segregated society, the firm, like Houston's group of lawyers, worked hard at forging links with the community during the civil rights activism of their times. Their involvement included active participation in the local Young Men's and Young Women's Christian Associations, civic organizations, and the NAACP. "We were the twentieth-century miracle," Higginbotham says. "There was just no firm in the country that had moved the way we had. We had the advantages of a segregated society to the extent that the firm presented for each of us, in the 1950s, the best option in town. You had to almost be like Booker T. Washington who said, 'Cast your bucket down where you are and pull up the resources which are there.' That is what the firm did. There were so many barriers outside that we had to think in terms of building strength from within rather then choosing something which may or may not be slightly more advantageous on a temporary basis."

Building the firm was a gradual process. At first, the firm practiced criminal law, which was the bread-and-butter practice for most African American lawyers. By 1955, members made a conscious decision to become a full-service law firm. Economic circumstances and civil rights activities in the larger society accelerated the process. The firm started to develop a strong political footing given the ethos of the courts. In 1955, Austin Norris, at age sixty-three, was asked to become the firm's senior partner. "He used to come around and visit and talk with us," Schmidt says of Norris. "He was an interesting person and a newspaper man at the time. We sought him out to an extent. There were certain situations that might have had political overtones and sometimes we might talk to him about them and about the people involved, and finally we decided to invite him to join and become senior member of the firm."

Norris had acquired political and social capital in addition to institutional power throughout the 1930s and 1940s when the African American community continued to serve as a haven against racial oppression. He was very active with committee people and most black organizations and institutions in the ward. He brought economic and political stature to the law firm. Born in 1893, Norris was older and more experienced than the other law partners. He was a 1917 Yale law graduate who had served in the army during World War I, where he was involved in social protest activities and would gather letters from fellow African American soldiers describing the racism they encountered. He would mail the letters to influential African American newspaper editors like Robert Vann of the *Pittsburgh*

Courier. The law firm began to reflect Norris's broad experience in the legal, political, and black communities as his fellow law partners began to move from the
community level to a wider base of power.

Norris started his public career as a Republican in the 1920s. Excluded from
white law firms, he was forced to operate within the racial-caste social structure.
After his discharge from the army, he moved in 1919 to Philadelphia, where he
started an African American newspaper, the *Philadelphia American* and wrote
abrasive pieces about the absence of blacks in politics. In the early 1920s, Norris
served as chief counsel for the black nationalist leader Marcus Garvey, through the
local branch of Garvey's United Negro Improvement Association. He cultivated
business relationships with black churches in Garvey's movement and in the seventh ward, like the national African Methodist Episcopal (AME) Church. Garveyism affected Norris profoundly, as his philosophical and strategic view for race
advancement was closely connected to black intellectual thought during the 1920s.
He began to shape his own strategy for race equality, however. By the early 1930s,
Norris, like other African Americans across the country, switched to the Democratic Party, claiming that the Republican Party was not responsive to the needs
of African Americans. His newspaper influenced the African American vote and
penetrated the local political machine at the community level. In 1932, he became
the city's first black ward leader, in the seventh ward, a position that gave him a
community power base. He used his skills as a lawyer to help develop the community and believed that politics was the means to effect change. He encouraged one
of his clients to purchase the noted *Philadelphia Independent,* and its editor, Norris
used the paper to influence the black vote in major local elections. That led to his
patronage appointment on the powerful Republican-controlled Board of Revision
of Taxes in 1937, where the city's political leadership was stationed. Norris became
the first African American to hold such a powerful board position in the city.

"Let me stress one thing, whether you're black or white, power respects
power," says Higginbotham about Norris. "Aus was on the Board of Revision of
Taxes, secretary, and was considered to be the craftsman in that he understood the
law of eminent domain, everything which came before the board. So what it really
meant was that Albert M. Greenfield, who was the leading financier in town, who
had hotels like the Ben Franklin, Bellevue, Carlton, Bankers Security . . . [w]hen
[the leading business and professional leaders in the city] wanted to get their taxes
reassessed, they had to go before the board, and Aus Norris was there." Implicit
in Higginbotham's recollections is that Norris's political and professional position
of power in the city also served as a buffer zone against blatant racial discrimination that he and the law firm received: "Aus had a power base and people who
would normally be racist to someone else would not be racist to him because they
never knew when the day would come when they may have to come before that
board. And I think that was a very significant factor in terms of the sort of immunity the firm got from some of the most rabid aspects of racism."

Norris's understanding of politics rubbed off on his law partners in many ways. First, Norris attempted to get the firm to fight for the interests of African Americans through both political parties. "That's the reason why he insisted that we be divided politically within the firm; half of us were Republican and half were Democrats," says Brown, a Republican member of the law firm between 1955 and 1968. Norris's unyielding views created an intense, hard-working, and supportive law firm environment. His single focus and stubbornness regarding his vision for the law practice and the proper method for establishing black civil rights did not, however, always coincide with the views of the other partners. "One time, Aus and I had a confrontation," Higginbotham says. "I just kept my hands in my pockets because I didn't want to become violent." After *Brown v. Board of Education* in 1954, in which the U.S. Supreme Court struck down the separate-but-equal doctrine of *Plessy v. Ferguson,* Norris and the law firm embarked on an aggressive strategy of winning African American civil rights through litigation. The law firm helped the local branch of the NAACP with discrimination cases in the public school system. In fact, Higginbotham filed the first school desegregation case against the Lower Gwynedd Township School Board for operating an all-black school in Penllyn in Montgomery County. Cecil B. Moore and several other black attorneys inherited the case after Higginbotham left the law firm in 1962.

Throughout the 1950s to the early 1970s, the law firm also helped build African American service organizations and institutions. For instance, in the late 1950s, it helped in the building of a health care facility so that black doctors could practice medicine. "I can recall a group of doctors [who] wanted to get their practice going in West Philly, [and through the work of the law firm] they purchased a building where they put in six offices," Higginbotham says. He adds: "That was a significant matter. We were establishing that a black lawyer could put together these types of commercial enterprises and do them well. We were building up a practice, and I believe that we were charging 30 or 40 percent less than what white law firms still were charging, but you needed that kind of base."

Green, the firm specialist in commercial law, worked on developing and incorporating black businesses. His practice attempted to redress inequalities such as the ban on African Americans owning bars. Most bars were owned by whites, especially in black neighborhoods. His work helped to establish not only a business entrepreneurial class, but also created a financial base for the law firm. By 1958, the firm's church law practice began to materialize. Churches were corporate clients in need of legal assistance with major real estate transactions. They also needed help dealing with schisms within their organizations. The firm used church resources to create health care institutions, job training programs, and commercial enterprises like the Father Divine Tracy Hotel in Philadelphia. By the 1960s, the Norris firm had one of the largest black church practices in the country. "In addition to general business, corporate, tort and probate matters, our firm specialized in church law," says Green, who was charged with handling all church cases; others assisted in complex litigation affairs. "We represented the AME Church, the Trustees of the General Assembly of the Church of the Lord Jesus Christ of the Apostolic Faith and Father Divine. All of these clients have churches throughout the nation and in foreign countries, and our firm was concerned with their legal matters in all jurisdictions." The National Baptist Convention case became one of the most noted cases in the law firm's history. Green and Higginbotham represented the church organization that was threatened by a group of young black ministers who wanted to take over a convention hoping to make the conservative organization more progressive.

In 1960, the law firm split from Schmidt, and became known as Norris, Green, Harris, Higginbotham, & Associates. It moved to the fifteenth floor of the Commercial Trust Building, the first major African American partnership to open shop in Philadelphia's Center City. The new office was located twelve floors above the tax revision board office and across from City Hall, in the hub of the political and business operations of the mainstream. Throughout the 1960s, the law firm represented black radio stations, the National Leader Publishing Company, African American trade unions, and a host of other African American organizations besides its church practice. Often, the law firm helped organizations involved in civil rights activities. In *Scott v. J.P. Campbell College,*[36] the law firm represented the AME church that had incorporated the college, located in racially tense Mississippi. Green says that "a few disgruntled church members" filed a civil suit claiming that the incorporation of the school violated the church's charter. Had they been successful, the college could have been shut down. The state attorney general had intervened as a complainant.

Norris and Green contended that the charges were invalid and that the case involved the college's rights under the U.S. Constitution rather than the state's. They settled the case. "I went to Mississippi with Aus to Campbell College in Jackson," Green says. "We went down very indignant because we thought that the white power structure was trying to close Campbell College because they [the college] were giving support to the Freedom Riders." He adds:

> It was a time of great strife and we went down very indignant. We were going to have this big court battle. We got there and we started talking to people. We found out that the evidence was not as we had supposed, and that legally, we were in a relatively weak position. But Aus walked around that campus talking to kids for a couple days. Then we had a conference with one of the fairest judges I've ever met in my life, in Mississippi. And when Aus finished the judge practically had tears in his eyes as Aus told him what that campus meant to the kids. Not to the bishop who [was] running it, and not to the hierarchy, but to the kids. [We] came out with a result better than anything we had ever hoped for and changed our legal strategy from one where we were just going down there hellbent on fighting to convincing the judge of the right of our cause.

With a changing societal milieu, the law firm started to lose partners as early as 1962 as many of them began to move into the larger professional community and society. Nichols became a minister. President Kennedy appointed Higginbotham the first African American to head the Federal Trade Commission. Two years later, he was given a federal judgeship. Harris left to advise the Small Business Administration before she took a state court judgeship in 1971. Green was appointed to the common pleas bench in 1964 and received a federal judgeship in 1971. In the 1960s, Brown had replaced Higginbotham as the firm's chief trial lawyer, one of the most active trial lawyers in the city, and the law firm was renamed Norris, Brown, & Hall.

Norris sought to fill the gaps in the institution by adding young black lawyers to the firm. The major specialties of the law practice continued as a new group of social engineers, mostly male, became associates and clerks at the law firm from 1962 onward. Between 1962 and 1967, Ronald Davenport, Herbert Hutton, Mansfield Neal, Ira J. K. Wells Jr., Robert W. Williams, Hardy Williams, and Arthur F. Earley became associates at the law firm. Between 1968 and 1970, Prather Randall, Richard Thomas Richards, and Frank Williams joined. University of Pennsylvania Law School graduates Germain Ingram and Robert Paskins, together with Yale Law School graduate Timothy Jenkins, also worked with the law practice in the 1970s. In the late 1960s, when urban renewal was occurring in major cities, many African Americans were not receiving fair market value for their homes in Philadelphia. Norris, who had become a national expert in eminent domain law, moved the firm into the practice of eminent domain. At the same time the firm continued its familiar course, including the involvement of its members in the black community in city politics while helping to build and use underdeveloped institutions in black neighborhoods and trying to eradicate racial inequality through the sociolegal process.

During this period, Norris continued to serve as a buffer for the law firm as his political influence was strong throughout the city. Until his death in 1976, he insisted that the role of African American lawyers was to secure civil rights and to help build and advance the community in light of difficult circumstances. Many of the firm's lawyers continued to carry out this role while adding to it in several ways, as the following section briefly describes.

Seeds Taking Root through Houstonian Jurisprudence

Whites were accustomed to seeing white judges in state and federal courts and may have been concerned when Higginbotham presided over the case of *Commonwealth vs. Local 542* (of the International Union of Operating Engineers).[37] However, his handling of the case clearly established that a black judge, active within the black community, could be objective in cases in which whites were involved. Moreover, through his appointment by Supreme Court Chief Justice Earl Warren to a federal commission to study how minorities and women could be better represented in jury selection, Higginbotham played a key role in developing a national methodology for the selection of pluralistic juries. As a commissioner and a judge, Higginbotham played an important role in correcting major inequalities—utilizing to good effect his insight into how discrimination occurs and how it impacts people in general and African Americans in particular. Congresswoman Eleanor Holmes Norton, former chair of EEOC and Higginbotham's first full-time law clerk, writes:

> Higginbotham's career on the bench began in 1964 at the zenith of the civil rights movement. I was fresh out of law school, but I had no intention of graduating from the civil rights movement. The judge seemed a counterpoint to the times, a black man sanctioned by the establishment with a federal judgeship. His precocious journey to the federal bench at 36 seemed only to reinforce the point. . . . By occupation and experience, Higginbotham was not of the movement generation. Nor did it seem likely that a man who had chosen to become a federal judge sitting in the North would find a place in the work of the civil rights movement. Unlike the lawyers, the demonstrators, the lobbyists, and the legislators of the period, judges lacked the power of initiative. . . . Yet, Higginbotham has left a body of decisions that have had a significant effect on race law. . . . Title VII of the 1964 Civil Rights Act, in particular, proved a probing detector of race and sex discrimination. Higginbotham and other judges sitting in jurisdictions throughout the country were offered thousands of cases that called forth remedies and resulted in important doctrines that affect not only blacks but other unempowered people.[38]

Judge Green presided over the racial discrimination case of *Bolden v. Pennsylvania State Police*,[39] the net effect of which was to increase employment opportunities for poor, working, and middle-class blacks.[39] The case not only ended the racial exclusion of African Americans in state police employment but also increased their opportunities generally within a pluralistic society. Throughout the 1950s and 1960s, Norris along with a host of other African American attorneys had suspected state bar examiner officials of racism because so few blacks were passing the bar exam, especially in Philadelphia. In 1970, Judge Green served as a key member of the investigating committee that found unusual practices against people of color. Because of the report of the Philadelphia Bar Association Special Committee on Pennsylvania Bar Admission Procedures, which became known as the *Liacouras Committee Report*, changes were made in the Pennsylvania bar exam, leading to considerable increases in talented African Americans and other people of color passing the state bar.[40] Norris pushed for African American representation on the regulatory commission to reflect diversity in its membership, and Ira Wells, a former law partner, became the first African American bar examiner for Pennsylvania. He was expected to help keep the organization honest in its activities regarding racial equality and opportunity. William Brown played a vital role in the early 1970s in his position with the EEOC in securing upper-level management opportunities for talented African Americans with AT&T and major oil corporations throughout the nation. As chair of EEOC, Brown and his new cadre of lawyers exposed the hidden discriminatory policies that corporate companies were practicing against African Americans. Other partners and associate lawyers from the firm impacted the social fabric in the city in a number of ways as they assumed new public positions. Harris, for example, assisted African Americans with small business loans. Former law firm members serving in key positions brought about social change by overseeing federal cases as judges and by serving on regulatory boards and commissions from which African Americans had been excluded. They also laid a legal foundation against racial barriers to the entry of blacks into the legal profession and against inequalities in the general employment of poor, working, and middle-income blacks through the cases noted above.

The point here is that the personal and professional socialization of these lawyers and their insight into racial discrimination enabled them to address inequality in the local context and in larger professional institutions. There is an assumption that when middle- and upper-class African Americans have "made it" into the corporate mainstream, they somehow forget past forms of discrimination and work within the milieu of the larger society. Members of the Norris firm, however, had the "advantage" of experiencing racial segregation and discrimination before the process of being assimilated into a wider society. The "cumulative impact" of racism, according to Feagin and Sikes,[41] affects how individual African Americans understand contemporary society. In the case of the law firm, the experiences of its members added to their ability to spot and to alter discriminatory practices, irrespective of race. In this sense, "Norris recognized the concept that the assimilation of blacks into wider professional practices also meant a diminution in the level of control that whites had over blacks to the extent that you have a black power base," Higginbotham says. "You could be able to have leverage because everybody else has a power base."

Contemporary Race Relations and the Work of African American Lawyers

As Higginbotham notes, Norris clearly understood the connections between assimilation and power and influence, especially in terms of racial and ethnic social equality. The very mission of the law firm to fight for racial and ethnic equality of opportunity locally and in the larger society led to its decline, on the one hand, and its reformation, on the other, into an institution that could effect change in the wider social milieu from positions of power. In this way, the firm's partners and associates benefited from social changes of the day, especially the legal movements and civil rights movement of the 1960s. Since society in the 1990s operates on a different basis, it is difficult now to recreate the way in which the firm functioned in that era.

Many whites have come to believe that because of the many changes in racial relations (including the substantial changes in racial relations since the 1960s, especially with regard to legal segregation) African Americans and other people of color already have equal opportunity and are treated fairly in our society. Whites point to major legal changes from the 1954 *Brown* decision to the 1960s civil rights acts regarding the right to vote, public accommodations, and fair housing. They also emphasize the establishment of the U.S. Commission on Civil Rights and the Equal Employment Opportunity Commission. The civil rights movement played a crucial role in the establishment of these acts and commissions. The assumption by whites, therefore, is that our society now operates in a race-neutral way. Cause lawyering has therefore slowed down, especially in dealing with racial and ethnic discrimination. Richard Abel notes, "During the last three decades law has played an increasingly pivotal role in movements for the rights those oppressed because of race, ethnicity, religion, gender, poverty, incarceration, sexual orientation, or disability, as well as the environment." But although there have been many legislative victories, the law is hard to enforce or implement in practice.[42]

I will briefly assess some analyses of racial change and progress in the United States, which reveal a decline in blatant forms of discrimination but suggest a persisting color-line nonetheless. In doing so, I show that cause lawyers are still needed in the African American community because implementation of the law remains a problem, partly because of contemporary relations between the races and partly because of changes in the traditional African American community.[43]

Early theories of assimilation focused on blacks fitting into the white mainstream and were based on egalitarian ideas. In the decades after Gunnar Myrdal's effort to analyze the "American dilemma," many social scientists held optimistic views that integration would succeed and African Americans and other people of color would be progressively included in United States society. Milton M. Gordon, for instance, developed the idea of stages of assimilation and integration for non-Anglo-Protestant groups into a core culture and society that is fundamentally Anglo-Protestant.[44] In his later work Gordon underscores the progressive cultural and structural assimilation of white immigrant Americans and African Americans into U.S. society over many decades, taking a position similar to that of the late Harvard sociologist Talcott Parsons, who in a famous article, "Full Citizenship for the Negro American? A Sociological Problem," argued that full membership in U.S. society for black Americans was part of a broad egalitarian trend and the likely solution for U.S. racial tensions.[45]

Social analysts describe an assimilation process in which most immigrant groups at some point suffer discrimination. However, antiblack discrimination is viewed as different only in degree from the discrimination suffered by white immigrant groups. For people of color, the importance of racial stratification is expected to decline as powerful economic and social forces wipe out vestiges of earlier systems of discrimination. By the 1970s, many scholars and social commentators alike began to believe that class inequality would eventually become more significant than race inequality. William J. Wilson, in one of the most widely discussed books of the decade, *The Declining Significance of Race,* asserted that the dramatic growth of a new African American middle class resulted from a significant decrease in discrimination and from governmental affirmative action.[46] He concluded that the plight of *poor* African Americans should be the new focus of governmental policy. Another reason for much recent scholarly optimism for racial relations is the apparent decline in racist attitudes among white Americans.[47]

Recent studies, however, have questioned these studies. In the 1980s, for example, voices continued to raise questions about white racism in U.S. society. For instance, a group of scholars came together for a conference at the University of Wisconsin (Milwaukee) to revisit racism and discuss how it affects people of color. Papers like "The Political Economy of Racism and the Current Scene" and "Multicultural Education: Fallacies and Alternatives" probed racism in the contemporary United States. The objective of the conference was to take stock of the economic oppression of people of color in a capitalist system, of their resistance to that oppression, and of recent work in social science that supported the status quo in racial relations.[48] By the early 1990s, attention was being paid to actual patterns of racial discrimination and oppression, although much of the reinvigorated research was still coming from scholars of color. This growing research suggests that the optimistic view of a declining significance of race is in error and that most African Americans, including middle-income and upper-income African Americans, face racial discrimination in most areas of their daily lives. It ranges from blatant discrimination like that of the legal segregation period to new, often subtle and covert forms that have flourished under conditions of ostensible desegregation and integration.[49] Scholars show that in many of these cases discrimination continues to affect people of color in areas like environment, employment, public accommodations, and so forth. The problem therefore is that assimilation means more than the adoption of egalitarian principles. In reality, assimilation has meant an attempt to obliterate difference by incorporating others who have been in a subordinate position into a white hegemonic world (a hopeless endeavor, but an ideologically important one) while continuing basic forms of discrimination in new kinds of ways.

Today, the pessimistic view that there is little possibility of significant changes in racism is common among some of the most insightful analysts of U.S. racial relations. Constitutional scholar Derrick Bell argues that racism against people of color is so ingrained in the United States that white Americans will never entertain giving up their privileges; this essentially means that African Americans will *never* gain equality.[50] According to Joe Feagin and Aaron Porter, "[W]hites have written a few freedom checks, such as passing largely unenforced civil rights laws, but these are insufficient for real racial integration and racial equality."[51] Other observers, however, are nonetheless committed to the need for aggressive civil rights action for egalitarian change. Legal scholar Lani Guinier has spelled out her ideas for significantly increasing the political power of black citizens.[52] While the enforcement of the 1965 Voting Rights Act has increased the number of African American–majority voting districts, it has not yet reshaped legislative bodies so that African American officials have real influence on everyday decisions that matter to black and white communities. In a popular book, *Race Matters,* Cornel West notes that the conditions of life of poor African Americans are related more to problems of racial inequality than to "underclass" problems and claims that there is a serious decay of societal leadership as a whole.[53]

Still, the black community's present condition is more than a race matter. The expansion of the black middle class is part of the problem, since many members of that class have not taken leadership roles in building up the black community. Without moving beyond this class difference, failure is imminent in the development of the community. Future change in race relations and conditions in the black community will not come from traditional politics alone but will also require creative, calm, strategic, and organized action. In some cases, other modes of action need to take place including social disruption and a high level of indigenous leadership and organizations connected to institutions in the community, especially through individuals who understand community needs, who know how to move from old causes to new causes, from old paradigms of social thought to new and improved paradigms, which build upon older ones. In this, there is a crucial role for professionals, and for cause lawyers in particular, as in our historic past. The challenge is to find new theories of jurisprudence that reflect the new ways in which racial and ethnic inequality have been manifested. Part of that challenge is to figure out how to build on and strengthen Houston's approach to racial and ethnic inequality by using an approach like that of the Norris firm.

Conclusion

This chapter provides a context for understanding how African American lawyers dealt with the "righteous rage" that they felt as they came up against a social structure that limited their professional career goals and daily lives. Langston Hughes, in his poem "What Happens to a Dream Deferred," points out how underutilized energy can be channeled in many ways, including disruptiveness or a major outburst of passion. The energies of those who experience racial or ethnic inequality can be channeled in productive as well as disruptive ways. In the case of the Norris firm, such energies were directed into cause lawyering, and through an effective and strategic use of social and political power and the legal process the firm's lawyers corrected inequalities.[54] We also see the larger picture (what

Sumner calls the mores of society) in this account of the creation of the law firm, given the racist white legal profession of the time and how black lawyers responded to a social system built on racial caste.

The Norris firm was a product of a racist legal and societal environment at first; it changed as our society changed.[55] At first, the firm's partners and associates were considered the "other" because of their race and were consequently prevented from the full range of professional opportunities in the mainstream or white professional community.[56] They felt the full sting of racial discrimination. Gordon Allport notes, "Discrimination comes about only when we deny to individuals or groups of people equality of treatment which they may wish. It occurs when we take steps to exclude members of an out-group from our neighborhood, school, occupation, or country. Restrictive covenants, boycotts, neighborhood pressure, legal segregation in certain states, 'gentlemen's agreements,' are all devices for discrimination."[57] Because of differential treatments based on race, the law firm's members were forced to operate behind the veil of American society, confined to group life within the traditional African American community. It was within this segregated milieu that the law firm emerged, during a time when the civil rights movement was at its height. In order for the institution and its members to survive as a business, they had to tie their interests to that of the black community to alter their subordinate position. Consider for instance how black lawyers had to generate a client base for their services within a racial caste system. One could argue that black lawyers used the white lawyers' relationship to business as a model and developed relationships with black businesses. However that would be a naive view. The organization-building and client-base services of black lawyers were a self-serving model, since the black cause lawyer was bound to his/her community by racial segregation. The linkage of the black cause lawyer to his/her community in fact led to the development of the black community as an independent entity. Here, Norris's relationship to the Garvey movement figures prominently, especially his idea of working with black organizations and institution building for the betterment of the community. Also we see here in one instance how one cause lawyer served as the legal arm of the black nationalist movement.

Race and economics was the crucial factor in linking the institution to the needs of the community. Members of the Norris firm involved themselves with black fraternal and community organizations, serving as officers of the Philadelphia branch of the NAACP and handling civil rights and racial discrimination cases in education, employment, community development, and other areas of inequality. The notion of white domination of African Americans was at the core of the law firm model, as was the involvement of professional-class African Americans in altering this imbalance of power through collective institutional, legal, and sociopolitical activities. Aldon Morris and Carol Mueller's analysis of collective human behavior serves as a case in point in understanding how this law firm and its members were part of a social movement to end racial domination.[58] They note that any attempt to understand human action attention has to center on the intersection between culture and structure, where culture and structure may function as both constraints and promoters of social change. The system of human domination gives rise to political consciousness: working-class consciousness is the workers' response to class domination while racial consciousness among African Americans is their response to racial domination. In the latter case, this can lead toward the maintenance, overthrow, or altering of systems of human domination. The Norris firm members attempted to do the latter.

By chronicling the social history of this African American law firm, we see how cause lawyers emerge and operate during a critical instance in the life of the country, in Philadelphia in particular. The case study speaks to the institutionalization process, to racial relations, and to the dedication of its members first to public service in the community and then to the regional context, as firm lawyers moved on to larger institutions and organizations of power and influence. We also learn that the law firm of the 1950s and 1960s constituted an established practice that met the basic needs of its members, as Spencer and Chapin would have recognized. In particular, we realize through Spencer's conceptualization how the law firm became more specialized by virtue of its division of labor as changes in society and the profession progressed.

This case study suggests a number of reasons why cause lawyers are made and not born—that is, born with a specific role to play as they participate in movements against social injustices. Cause lawyering is something that you learn how to do; it works in unison with something that you experience, envision, and practice, acting through various strategies and with integrity. Cause lawyers develop and strengthen their skills and legal and political techniques over time, which enable them to engage in social causes, and in some cases, with specific objectives as a consequence of their indigenous experience, concerns, and being. Successful cause lawyering within an institutional context takes time to develop and to implement. The creativity, intensity, and experience of individual lawyers and their collective insight and wisdom at attempts made to resolve issues of concern affects the professional and political strategies that cause lawyers might use. Thus, although larger social and structural conditions may affect why and how lawyers become involved with social movements for change, their socialization process, experience, and vision play a vital role while specific reasons might influence their involvement in a social cause.

This process is readily seen in the case in Philadelphia. In addition to the influences noted above, it also should be pointed out that the philosophical intent of cause lawyers is a very focused one, but the avenues taken to reach those larger goals of concern can be very diverse. The emphasis of this chapter on the career of Norris, the senior partner and chief political organizer in the firm, and the formation, activity, or institutionalization process of the firm serves as a case in point. The overall objective, philosophy, or doctrine (as Sumner calls it) of Norris and the firm was social justice and equality of opportunity. To achieve such an objective takes one to position oneself effectively, and that is a lengthy process. Norris, who was a very influential but largely forgotten figure in the history of Philadelphia, had to develop a philosophical approach to the practice of law. He graduated from Yale Law School before World War I, was involved with the Garveyite movement in the city in the 1920s, and became a major power broker in Philadelphia politics by the late 1930s, before the onslaught of civil rights legislation.

Norris's story tells us about the relationship between African American lawyers and the social fabric of Philadelphia, and what a person had to do in order to survive as an African American attorney. We also learn about the formation and growth of the law firm as an institution and the vision and importance of individuals like Norris, along with Schmidt, Green, and Higginbotham, in setting the standards and social behavior that younger members of the firm would follow. This includes the focus on community involvement, diverse political party affiliation, the workload, and mentoring environment among lawyers associated with the firm.

The Norris case study shows how African American middle-class professionals relate to the community at large. It shows how characteristic kinds of capital formation in the black community (e.g., black doctors, black fraternal organizations, churches and their real estate transactions) create an economic base for a black law firm and how the simultaneous development of civil rights law with its potential for serious litigation provided just the right opportunities for a group of young, smart, and ambitious black lawyers who could join Norris to make the firm work. We see how Norris and the law firm was deeply connected to the infrastructure of a poor, black community as they developed and expanded their law practice. In other words, this study explains how political organization and the collective influence of the firm's lawyers were used to work within the black community while building a base to impact the social fabric and legal community in the city. We also see through Norris and his law firm how a vision of racial and social equality crystallized.

Studying cause lawyering through institutional analysis is useful: it tells us whether or not cause lawyers are needed in our society, since the practices of our society rests on institutions. Cause lawyering can change because institutions can change, as can the ways in which they operate and impact the lives of individuals. Cause lawyering as a concept and a basis for social action can go well beyond its initial goal and make many changes in the process because there are changes in societal conditions. Cause lawyers are more than "legal actors," a role that in many cases merely reflects how white lawyers perceive themselves and their roles. Cause lawyers impact social systems because they differentiate themselves from their legal actions and sees themselves as participants, agents, in social change. In the case of the Norris firm, the cause lawyers had to make this distinction because in a racial caste society, they were victimized in the same way as their clients.

Today, our society and the African American community has changed. In the case of the African American community, the argument goes that because of increased opportunities for talented middle-class African Americans, our society is now a "raceless" one. This argument is flawed not only from the point of view of recent social science research, as I noted above, but also because scholars have focused too exclusively on the growing black middle class. This group has grown, but the lower class has also grown, and at a more rapid rate. This is in part due to structural and racial factors but also in part to the self-interest of the middle class, who, unlike members of the law firm, have individualized their success. The racial caste system forced the Norris firm to identify with the group interests of African Americans. Ironically, the privileges won by this and other law firms opened up opportunities for blacks to succeed and become strong individuals. It follows that in the process the large black community has been robbed of its best and brightest, and left with those, who for one reason or another, could or would not take flight from it. In any case, blacks, whether from the lower or middle or upper class, still experience discrimination at various levels. They may be nonconfrontational in dealing with it because of their lifestyles or because they are trying to make ends meet. Cause lawyers are needed to support the interests of these groups insofar as they still face inequality. At the same time, cause lawyers are needed to shape public policy in dealing with the problems of the inner-city poor, including joblessness. William Julius Wilson writes that the social environment helps shape the life experiences of inner-city residents, adding that "the disappearance of work and the consequences of that disappearance for both social and cultural life are the central problems in the inner-city ghetto. . . . [A] majority of adults in many inner-city neighborhoods are jobless at any given point in time." [59] Yet few lawyers may be interested in dealing with this problem. Because individuals are jobless in the inner city does not mean that discrimination does not occur in the way these communities are treated environmentally, or that jobless individuals do not experience structural and informal discrimination because of their status and plight.

There are limitations to what individuals can do. Racism, sexism and classism, and the problems of the inner-city poor continue, however, to affect our social fabric, and cause lawyers or lawyering for social justice are needed in local, grassroots organizations as well as in larger institutions to help deal with contemporary forms of inequality, like discrimination in housing, education, employment, health care, urban renewal, and other public issues. Support in the form of legal and social movements is needed to resolve the backlog of one hundred thousand discrimination cases filed under the EEOC and in other areas where cause lawyers can operate. Cause lawyers can work toward overcoming new forms of dominance and exploitation with advanced strategies. Some individuals, however, are caught in the world of the urban poor or are preoccupied in maintaining comfortable positions within the mainstream of our "integrated society" and are unable to see, react to, or rally around forms of inequality that persist today. Others may lack the vision or ability, or are caught up in old causes and so cannot move on to new ones. It would be tragic, however, if movements for social justice fade away because the warmth of understanding lights no fire for individuals to see the right causes while their faces are wet with tears.[60] The cause lawyers of tomorrow will come because they are moved by passions of the heart; maybe their voices will sound like drum majors for justice; in their actions, however, they must march against the flow, through uncertain circumstances, in the spirit of what is fair and honorable, like the members of the law firm of Norris, Schmidt, Green, Harris, Higginbotham, and associates.

Notes

1. See Fitzhugh Lee Styles, *The Negro Lawyers' Contributions to Seventy-One Years of Our Progress: 71*[st] *Anniversary Celebrations of Negro Progress, Philadelphia, 1863–1934* (Philadelphia: Summer Press, 1934); also see Styles's *Negroes and the Law: In the Race's Battle for Liberty, Equality, and Justice under the Constitution of the United States: With Causes Célèbres: A Manual of the Rights of the Race under the Law* (Boston: Christopher Publishing House, 1937); Genna Rae McNeil, *Groundwork: Charles Hamilton Houston and the Struggle for Civil Rights* (Philadelphia: University of Pennsylvania Press, 1983); John Hope Franklin and Genna Rae McNeil, eds., *African Americans and the Living Constitution* (Washington, D.C.: Smithsonian Institute Press, 1995); Geraldine Segal, *Blacks in the Law: Philadelphia and the Nation* (Philadelphia: University of Pennsylvania Press, 1983); J. Clay Smith, *Emancipation: The Making of the Black Lawyer, 1844–1944* (Philadelphia: University of Pennsylvania Press, 1993); Linn Washington, *Black Judges on Justice: Perspectives from the Bench* (New York: New Press, 1995); Gilbert Ware, *William Hastie: Grace under Pressure* (New York: Oxford University Press, 1984).

2. William Henri Hale, "The Career Development of the Negro Lawyer in Chicago," Ph.D. dissertation, University of Chicago, 1949.

3. See generally Erwin Smigel, *The Wall Street Lawyer, Professional Organization Man* (Bloomington: Indiana University Press, 1969); Jerome Carlin, *Lawyers on Their Own: A Study of Individual Practitioners in Chicago* (New Brunswick, N.J.: Rutgers University Press, 1962). Also see Jerome Carlin, Jan Howard, and Sheldon L. Messinger eds., *Civil Justice and the Poor: Issues for Sociological Research* (New York: Russell Sage Foundation, 1967); Robert Nelson, *Bureaucracy, Professionalism, and Commitment: Authority Relationships in Large Law Firms* (Chicago: American Bar Foundation, 1987).

4. Robert Park, Ernest W. Burgess, et al., *The City* (Chicago: University of Chicago Press, 1967).

5. *American Heritage Dictionary,* 2nd ed. (Boston: Houghton Mifflin, 1982).

6. See Walter Powell and Paul Dimaggio, *The New Institutionalism in Organizational Analysis* (Chicago: University of Chicago Press, 1991).

7. See Herbert Spencer, *First Principles of a New System of Philosophy* (New York: DeWitt Revolving Fund, 1958).

8. John Sirjamaki, "Education as a Social Institution," in *On Education—Sociological Perspectives*, ed. D. H. Hansen and J. E. Gerstle (New York: Wiley, 1967), 37.

9. William Graham Sumner, *Folkways* (Boston: Ginn, 1907), pp. 53–54.

10. Frances Stuart Chapin, *Contemporary American Institutions: A Sociological Analysis* (New York: Harper and Row, 1935), 14.

11. See Leonard Trelawney Hobhouse, *Social Development* (London: Allen and Allen, 1966).

12. Robert Morrison MacIver and C. H. Page, *Society* (New York: Holt, Rinehart, and Winston, 1949), 15.

13. Talcott Parsons and Edward A. Shills, eds., *Toward a General Theory of Action* (Cambridge, Mass.: Harvard University Press, 1959), 40.

14. See William Henri Hale, "The Career Development of the Negro Lawyer in Chicago."

15. See generally Magali Larson, *The Rise of Professionalism: A Sociological Analysis* (Berkeley: University of California Press, 1977).

16. See Richard Abel, *American Lawyers* (New York: Oxford University Press, 1989).

17. See generally Jerold Auerbach, *Unequal Justice: Lawyers and Social Change in Modern America* (New York: Oxford University Press, 1976); Jerome Carlin, *Lawyers on Their Own*; Michael J. Powell, *From Patrician to Professional Elite: The Transformation of the New York City Bar Association* (New York: Russell Sage Foundation, 1988).

18. Smith, *Emancipation*.

19. See Jerold Auerbach, *Unequal Justice*. Also see endnotes for J. Clay Smith, *Emancipation*, and Genna Rae McNeil, *Groundwork*.

20. Smith, *Emancipation*, 11.

21. Ibid., p. x.

22. Ibid., p. 2.

23. See Alexis de Tocqueville, *Democracy in America*, vol. 2 (New York: Vintage Books, 1990).

24. See Smith, *Emancipation*; McNeil, *Groundwork*; Richard Kluger, *Simple Justice: The History of Brown v. Board of Education and Black America's Struggle for Equality* (New York: Vintage Books, 1975).

25. See Austin Sarat and Stuart Scheingold's "Cause Lawyers and the Reproduction of Professional Authority," introduction to this volume.

26. Carrie Menkel-Meadow, "The Causes of Cause Lawyering: Toward an Understanding of the Motivation and Commitment of Social Justice Lawyers," chap. 2 of this volume.

27. Ibid.

28. Louise G. Trubek and Elizabeth Kransberger, "Critical Lawyers: Social Values and the Structures of Private Practice," chap. 7 of this volume. This essay discusses public interest and private practice services through the activities of cause lawyers. However, the structure upon which a lot of cause lawyering—including pro bono work—is based today, I think, is rooted in the kinds of things that black lawyers like Houston did because of what was occurring in the larger society at that time.

29. J. Clay Smith, "Principles Supplementing the Houstonian School of Jurisprudence: Occasional Paper No. 1," *Howard Law Journal* 32, no. 3 (1989), 500.

30. See Brown v. Board of Education, 347 U.S. 483 (1954) and Plessy v. Ferguson, 163 U.S. 537 (1896).

31. Pierre Bourdieu, *Language and Symbolic Power* (Cambridge, Mass.: Harvard University Press, 1984), 171.

32. For a detailed analysis of Houston's social engineering philosophy, see J. Clay Smith, "Principles Supplementing the Houstonian School of Jurisprudence," 493–504. Smith's analysis is based on Charles Hamilton's "Don't Shout Too Soon," *Crisis* (1936), 79. For an understanding of lawyering see McNeil, *Groundwork*, 216–217.

33. W. E. B. DuBois, *The Philadelphia Negro: A Social Study* (Philadelphia: University of Pennsylvania Press, 1967). In this work, the first urban and sociological study in the United States, DuBois examines the social organization of the community, its stratification, and the plight of the African American community through an analysis of the seventh ward.

34. 372 U.S. 335, 83 S.Ct. 792 9 L.ED. 2D 799 (1963).

35. For an in-depth analysis of racial caste, see the work of Oliver C. Cox, *Caste, Class, and Race: A Study in Social Dynamics* (Garden City, N.Y.: 1948). In short, Cox examines the role of the white economic elite in racial enslavement and the forced migration of blacks from Africa. Cox contends that the worldwide search for cheap labor by a new, profit-oriented capitalist class led to the U.S. system of racial subordination. In his view, fully developed racial ideologies and prejudices developed later to rationalize the economics of enslavement. During the segregation era, blacks experienced racial discrimination in part because of the racial ideologies and prejudices that whites developed about them and because of their exclusion from the wider economic markets.

36. Chancery Court, First Judicial District, Hinds County, Mississippi, No. 60,826 (1962).

37. 388 F. Supp. 155 (E.D. Pa. 1974).

38. Eleanor Holmes Norton, "A. Leon Higginbotham: Master of All Trades," in *Tribute to Judge A. Leon Higginbotham, Jr., Law and Inequality: A Journal of Theory and Practice,* 9, no. 3 (1991), 391–392, 394. See this journal as well for an in-depth analysis of Higginbotham's civil rights cases, the importance of his scholarly writings in race law, and critical commentary on his speeches regarding social equality.

39. 491 F. Supp. 958; 30 Fair Empl. Prac. Cas. [BNA] 694; 23 Empl. Prac. Dec., April 14 (1980).

40. For details, see "Report of the Philadelphia Bar Association Special Committee on Pennsylvania Bar Admission Procedures—Racial Discrimination in Administration of the Pennsylvania Bar Examination," *Temple Law Quarterly*, 44, no. 2 (1971), 159–243.

41. See Joe Feagin and Melvin Sikes, *Living with Racism: The Black Middle-Class Experience* (New York: Beacon Press, 1994).

42. For examples of this point, see Richard Abel, "Speaking Law to Power," chap. 3 of this volume.

43. Portions of this next section are drawn from Joe Feagin and Aaron Porter, "White Racism," *Choice*, February 1996, 906–908 and 911–912.

44. See Milton M. Gordon's *Assimilation in American Life: The Role of Race, Religion, and National Origins* (New York: Oxford University Press, 1964) and *Human Nature, Class, and Ethnicity* (New York: Oxford University Press, 1978).

45. Talcott Parsons and Kenneth B. Clark, *Daedalus: The Negro American* (Boston: Beacon Press, 1969).

46. William J. Wilson, *The Declining Significance of Race* (Chicago: Chicago University Press, 1978). This theme was given more attention in *The Truly Disadvantaged: The Inner City, the Underclass, and Public Policy* (Chicago: University of Chicago Press, 1987). Numerous white, and some black neoconservative, analysts have made much use of this declining-significance-of-race argument. Shelby Steele's *The Content of Our Character: A New Vision of Race in America* (New York: St. Martin's, 1990) deemphasizes the significance of discrimi-

nation as a factor for African Americans, arguing that the memories of past discrimination pull too many African Americans into unnecessary defensiveness. Also drawing on Wilson's ideas is law professor Stephen L. Carter's *Reflections of an Affirmative Action Baby* (New York: Basic Books, 1991), which maintains that racism is significantly declining and no longer holds all African Americans in desperate circumstances. Several major research reports on the socioeconomic situation of African Americans have emphasized racial progress. Works such as J. P. Smith and F. R. Welch, *Closing the Gap: Forty Years of Economic Progress for Blacks* (Rand Corporation Report, 1986) and Gerald D. Jayes and Robin M. Williams, eds., *A Common Destiny: Blacks and American Society* (Washington, D.C.: National Academy Press, 1989), which focuses on black Americans in the late 1980s, provide a major analysis of poor black Americans, but only a brief and generally positive evaluation of the racial situations faced by the black middle class.

47. See Howard Schuman, Charlotte Steeh, and Lawrence Bobo, *Racial Attitudes in America: Trends and Interpretations* (Cambridge, Mass.: Harvard University Press, 1985). This work explores an array of survey data from the 1950s to the 1980s, suggesting that a majority of whites have moved away from old-fashioned racist stereotypes and increased their acceptance of civil rights laws and equality of opportunity. Many U.S. journalists have articulated this common view of the declining significance of race and racism for African Americans and other people of color. For instance, Thomas B. Edsall and Mary D. Edsall, *Chain Reaction: The Impact of Race, Rights, and Taxes on American Politics* (New York: Norton, 1991), link the omnipresent political problems of the Democratic Party to a growing white hostility toward internal problems of black communities such as the maligned black underclass. They go so far as to argue that among white Americans there has been a public repudiation of racism and a stigmatization of overt racist expression over the last few decades.

48. The conference papers were published under the title *Racism and the Denial of Human Rights*, ed. Marvin Berlowitz and Ronald S. Edari (Marxist Educational Press, 1984). They were delivered at the sixth annual conference of Midwest Marxist Scholars, held at the University of Wisconsin–Milwaukee, April 10–12, 1981.

49. See the following works: Lois Benjamin, *The Black Elite: Facing the Color-Line in the Twilight of the Twentieth Century* (Chicago: Nelson-Hall, 1991); Philomena Essed, *Everyday Racism: Reports from Women of Two Cultures* (Claremont, Calif.: Hunter House Press, 1990). Joe Feagin and Melvin Sikes, *Living with Racism: The Black Middle Class Experience* (New York: Beacon Press, 1994); Ellis Cose, *The Rage of the Privileged Class* (New York: Harper Collins, 1995). Cose provides a close look at the rage and anger of the most successful African Americans in regard to the discrimination even in their otherwise privileged lives. Also see, Douglas S. Massey and Nancy A. Denton, *American Apartheid: Segregation and the Making of the Underclass* (Cambridge, Mass.: Harvard University Press, 1993). Their demographic analysis shows how housing markets in U.S. cities are still extremely segregated along racial fault lines. Even middle-class African Americans mostly live in segregated housing areas in suburbs or in neighborhoods adjacent to poorer black communities.

50. Derrick A. Bell, Jr., *Faces at the Bottom of the Well: The Permanence of Racism* (New York: Basic Books, 1992).

51. See Feagin and Porter, "*White Racism*," 911.

52. See Lani Guinier, *The Tyranny of the Majority: Fundamental Fairness in Representative Democracy* (New York: Free Press, 1994).

53. West's book was published in New York by Beacon Press in 1993.

54. Norris and other firm members participated in a number of civic associations, many of which were connected to the African American community. On the one hand,

their activities with community organizations were for business purposes. On the other hand, their involvement with such organizations were also attempts to forge a political base of power and influence in dealing with inequality in the civil arena. This became the basis for using their social capital or power for sociolegal and political purposes. This kind of involvement is perceived as decreasing in American society today with implications for the African American community. For details, see Robert D. Putnam, "Bowling Alone: America's Declining Social Capital," *Journal of Democracy* 6 (1995), 65–78.

55. Something similar happens with race relations today, which are the product of historical changes in relations between African Americans and whites, which are in turn related to broader transformations in the economic and social organization of American society. Apart from Wilson's work (1978 and 1987), also see Gerald David Jaynes and Robin M. Williams Jr., eds., *A Common Destiny: Blacks and American Society* (Washington, D.C.: National Academy Press, 1989). For a historical perspective, see Harold Cruse, *Plural but Equal: Blacks and Minorities in America's Plural Society* (New York: William Morrow, 1987). This work provides a historical understanding of racial progress through a critical analysis of gains and shortcomings in African American civil rights as the United States moved from being a society based on racial caste to become a more pluralistic one.

56. Joe Feagin and Hernan Vera, *White Racism: The Basics* (New York: Routledge, 1995), 7, view white racism as "the socially organized set of attitudes, ideas, and practices that deny African American and other people of color the dignity, opportunities, freedoms, and rewards that this nation offers white Americans," especially attitudes that motivate negative actions against blacks. In this context, negative actions evinced in the attitudes and behaviors of whites deeply rooted in our social structure led to not only black exclusion from large law firms but also the professional practices or organizations of women and white ethnic groups. In addition, the idea of a racial stratified system of professional relations also marked blacks as second-class citizens, as implied throughout this chapter.

57. Gordon Allport, *The Nature of Prejudice* (New York: Doubleday, 1958), 50.

58. Aldon Morris and Carol McClurg Mueller, *Frontiers of Social Movement Theory* (New Haven: Yale University Press, 1992).

59. Wilson, *When Work Disappears: The World of the New Urban Poor* (New York: Alfred A. Knopf, 1996), xix.

60. b. f. maiz, "The Rambling Confession of an Emotional Coward," unpublished manuscript.

CHAPTER 6

Still Trying

*Cause Lawyering for the
Poor and Disadvantaged
in Pittsburgh, Pennsylvania*

JOHN KILWEIN

> I've been around a long time, and it's getting harder and harder to do this work. Judges, juries, really society in general, are getting more conservative. They don't like my clients. They think [the clients] are morally wrong. It's as though their very existence is an ugly intrusion into good, wholesome middle-class America. Then there's the business of it. I have to pay the bills, meet the payroll, and think about my kids' tuition. But I'm *still trying*. Because if I didn't, I just don't know if I'd like being a lawyer or even a member of this society.
>
> (Respondent #09)

This chapter introduces twenty-nine lawyers who practice in Pittsburgh, Pennsylvania. They are all men and women in private practice. They focus on a range of substantive issues, including family law, tort litigation, labor law, discrimination and employment law, civil rights law, and criminal law. Some have specialized practices, others do not. They work in from one-person to twenty-five-person offices. Some are struggling to survive in an increasingly competitive marketplace for legal services where moving beyond "paying the bills" is becoming more difficult. Others have strong, profitable practices with steady streams of clients and fees.

Although these characteristics fill in the background for the group portrait presented here, they are not its focus. What makes these lawyers unique is that they are all cause lawyers: lawyers who have decided to make time in their busy schedules for activities, legal and nonlegal, that improve the lives of disadvantaged Pittsburghers. They serve different disadvantaged groups in different ways, and they present many reasons for doing their cause work. What they share is the desire to use their skills for, as Menkel-Meadow succinctly put it, "lawyering for the good."[1] They work to benefit those in society who are marginalized because they have been labeled as "different" for being poor, women, gay, aliens, African Americans, HIV-positive, or incarcerated.

The composite portrait presented here is a case study designed to develop a better understanding of what cause lawyering for the disadvantaged looks like in one setting. After developing a basic working definition of a cause lawyer and introducing the respondents who participated in this study, I juxtapose the theory and practice of cause lawyering for the disadvantaged. Next, the motivations behind the respondents' cause lawyering are considered. Third, I place the practice of cause lawyering within its context, by asking how these attorneys are connected to their causes, their clients, and ultimately to each other. Finally, I explore the professional and economic implications of doing cause work. Throughout this essay, I examine the political dimensions of cause lawyering, both internal and external to the cause lawyer.

For this project a cause lawyer is defined as an attorney, in private practice, who focuses on the cause of improving the condition of some identifiable portion of the low-income community and other disadvantaged citizens of Pittsburgh. Added to this definition is Menkel-Meadow's notion that by engaging in this kind of work, the cause lawyer incurs personal, physical, economic, or social status risks.[2] I excluded attorneys who work for Neighborhood Legal Services, the local Legal Services Corporation (LSC) grantee. In a very real sense these legal services attorneys are cause lawyers for the disadvantaged, but they were not included in this group portrait since they are not in private practice. However, because many of the issues that surround legal services lawyering are relevant to the focus of this chapter, I drew on their experiences to inform the discussion of cause lawyering for the disadvantaged.

Using contacts in the Pittsburgh legal community and snowball sampling, I was able to identify and interview twenty-nine lawyers who met the definition of a cause lawyer presented above. Lawyers who participated in the study agreed to be interviewed face to face. To avoid creating suspicion or limiting respondent candor, I chose not to use a tape recorder and instead relied on note taking and follow-up phone calls to secure an accurate record of the interviews. With two exceptions, all interviews were conducted in the respondent's office. The length of the interviews ranged from forty minutes to two hours and averaged just over an hour.

The average age for the group was forty-seven, and the respondents' ages were distributed as follows: thirty-nine or younger (two), forty to forty-four (ten), forty-five to forty-nine (ten), fifty to fifty-four (five), and over sixty (two). The great majority of the respondents (twenty-six) had attended law school and developed their professional skills during the late 1960s and 1970s. Six of the twenty-nine respondents are women. Most respondents graduated from one of Pittsburgh's two law schools, Duquesne University (six) and the University of Pittsburgh (ten). The other interviewees studied law at Rutgers (three), Villanova (two), Antioch, Arkansas, Boston College, DePaul, George Washington, Golden Gate, Northeastern, and Notre Dame. Five respondents have a solo operation, seventeen work in a small office (two to five lawyers), two in a medium-sized firm (eight to ten lawyers), two more in a larger firm (nineteen or more lawyers), and one respondent is a salaried attorney working for a medical corporation. Two respondents were prominent Pittsburgh cause lawyers who are now involved in higher education. The respondents specialize in the following substantive areas of law: plaintiff representation in employment, discrimination, and civil rights matters (six), a general practice that combines bankruptcy, family law, criminal defense, and personal injury work (five), representing labor unions (four), plaintiff representation in personal injury and medical malpractice cases (three), consumer law (two), corporate and antitrust law (two), immigration law (two), criminal defense (one), in-house counsel (one), and institutional conditions law (one). One of the respondents who no longer practices law had a corporate practice in one of Pittsburgh's largest law firms; the other focused on employment and discrimination law in a solo practice.

Cause Lawyering for the Disadvantaged: Theory and Practice

To understand what cause lawyers do for their clients and their causes, it is useful to begin with the following normative question: How should a lawyer who is concerned with the legal needs of the disadvantaged go about her or his work? Related questions are: Do poverty cause lawyers have a coherent political position on the poor and their position in various societal systems? Do they have an ideology of poverty cause lawyering? If so, where is it developed? The potential sources of such ideological development include age, race, sex, social background, and where one attended college.[3]

This section presents a continuum of lawyering styles. These are styles that exist or have been proposed to advance the needs of the poor and disadvantaged. They entail many important issues, both practical and theoretical, that might affect a poverty cause lawyer, whether in private practice or a legal services context. Next, the section presents and compares the cause lawyering activities of the respondents with these styles. Among the interviewees several political positions or ideologies of cause lawyering appeared, the motivations and origins of which will be examined in the section following.

The Continuum of Styles of Lawyering

Individual Client Lawyering. At the heart of Anglo-American legal practice is the notion that a professional attorney has a basic professional responsibility to focus on the legal needs and interests of her or his individual clients. Given this tradition, it was only natural when the legal community began to take an interest in the legal needs of the disadvantaged that the effort would be based on individual client lawyering. The basic goal of this style of lawyering is to provide service to individual clients who would otherwise go unrepresented. The reason for this is simple. As a result of their financial situation, the poor have little or no independent access to the civil justice system. Anyone seeking to improve the legal status of the poor must, at some level, deal with the individual, microlevel legal problems of poor clients. Thus, client lawyering for the poor is made up of all of the activities associated with lawyering in general, including counseling clients on their legal situation, negotiating with societal actors on behalf of clients, drafting legal documents for clients, and litigating on behalf of clients before judicial and administrative tribunals.

Despite its prominent place in American legal practice, individual client lawyering has given rise to concerns in the legal assistance community. Although client lawyering solves many individual problems, some people view it with suspicion because it is not designed to change those structural elements in society that adversely affect the poor. Others have criticized client lawyering for the way it is practiced. Bellow, for example, argues that lawyers have become too bureaucratized in their delivery of individual client lawyering, by handling clients' needs in an assembly line fashion that often ignores the uniqueness of each individual's problems.[4] These lawyers force the needs of clients into potentially inappropriate legal solution templates. Worse still, to avoid undertaking more innovative client lawyering, attorneys convince their clients that nothing can be done for their problem.

Impact Lawyering. Through the litigation of class action suits or strategically chosen individual cases, impact lawyering seeks to remedy conditions in society that affect the poor as a group. Its proponents argue that impact litigation is a cost-effective method of providing the poor with legal assistance. Victory in a single impact case will solve not only present-day problems but also those of similarly situated persons in the future. According to advocates, successful impact litigation should not be judged strictly in terms of the litigant involved in the case: it should be evaluated in terms of a group impact. Successful impact litigation should change or eliminate some practice, institution, or actor that is negatively affecting poor persons.

Criticism of impact lawyering has come from many different points along the political spectrum. Conservatives have viewed impact lawyering as needless, leftist social engineering.[5] Others have questioned the ability of litigation and judicial decisions to change policy.[6] Some have taken this critique one step further by arguing that impact litigation can be harmful to the needs of the disadvantaged.[7] For example, Alfieri argued that poverty lawyers who rely on impact and client lawyering help to perpetuate the existing political/economic hegemony and as a result aid in the repression of the poor.[8]

Mobilization Lawyering. Notions of the poor as a community in need of political mobilization were important ideological components of the legal services movement.[9] In practice, community mobilization has played a very minor role in American legal services. For some, the absence of mobilizing work was seen as a fatal flaw in the legal services effort.[10] These critics argue that without political mobilization of the poverty community there can be no real change in the hegemonic structure that adversely affects the poor. Those who practiced poverty law were especially targeted for criticism. Poverty lawyers were criticized for wrongly believing "that the law . . . can be marshaled into an effective instrument to alleviate poverty."[11] They were also accused of operating with the assumption that their clients suffer their fate in an isolated and resigned way, that they are essentially incapable of handling their own affairs, and are dependent on the legal services worker or other social services providers to help them out of their morass.[12] These beliefs lead, it is claimed, to a practice that decontextualizes each client of the poverty lawyer from her or his place in a class struggle.

To remedy these problems, Alfieri called for poverty lawyers to take part in dialogic empowerment.[13] The attorney would attempt to give her or his clients greater class consciousness, a recognition that they are part of an oppressed group in society with a history. To accomplish this, the lawyer would establish a new dialogue with her or his client and demythologize the myth of legal efficacy. Lawyers would do what they can for their clients within the existing legal structure, and additionally would let clients know that the efficacy of traditional legal services is severely limited. Lawyers would also overcome their belief that their clients are ineffective and lacking in self-reliance. This client-lawyer dialogue would occur in a state of mutual affirmation, without the lawyer relying on her or his professional knowledge to dominate the dialogue. The lawyer would also work to develop a client-to-client dialogue. Clients would be made aware that they are part of a greater group whose members suffer similar problems as a result of the hegemonic structure of society. Ideally, similarly situated clients would develop a working dialogue that would eventually lead to a unified mobilization of clients. Finally, the lawyer should foster client-community dialogue, thereby aiding the expansion of class mobilization.

As is the case with most provocative ideas, theories that prescribe mobilization, organization, and deprofessionalization have engendered equally provocative responses. Although he saw great value in training lawyers to have better dialogic skills, Tremblay questions whether the problem should be laid at the feet of poverty lawyers and those who train them.

No doubt there are lawyers who are oppressive, paternalistic, mediocre, or unfeeling bureaucrats. This however is not the problem with poverty lawyering. Rather the defects in poverty lawyering are structural, institutional, political, economic, and ethical. Teaching poverty lawyers to change their attitudes may be critically important, but those attitudes and the resulting behavior are largely products of the conditions under which poverty lawyers work. [14]

Tremblay also pointed out that mobilizing forms of poverty advocacy make an important tradeoff between short-term losses in the form of less traditional representation, in favor of potentially illusory long-term gain such as class mobilizations.[15]

Client Voice Lawyering. Related and yet in many ways distinct from mobilization lawyering is what I call "client voice lawyering." It has often been said that lawyers who represent the poor need to be aware of the potential interpretive violence they perpetrate as they transform their clients' stories into what Gilkerson describes as universal legal narratives, that is, accounts that are accepted and acted upon by the legal system.[16] Lucie White and Austin Sarat in particular show that often what the client truly seeks from her or his legal services attorney is overlooked.[17] Clients want more than a translation of their story into a universal legal narrative; they want the ability to express their own, untranslated personal narratives.

There seems to be a split in this literature over what client voice lawyering will yield. Alfieri, Bachmann, and Lopez view client voice as a vital part of any true mobilization of the client community. White offers a somewhat different interpretation of client voice lawyering.[18] She argues that impact lawyering retains a certain level of effectiveness but that the technique could be improved if the clients were given voice. In a parallel space separated from the structured world of litigation, "clients could speak their own stories of suffering, accountability and change."[19] This dialogue would allow clients to learn about themselves and people like them, about the (in)efficacy of litigation, and the use of power, all of which are mobilizing activities, albeit less grand than those presented by Alfieri.

Observed Styles of Lawyer Practice

The daily practice of the respondents indicates that the debate over lawyering styles is more than academic. The cause practice of the twenty-nine participants in this study included individual representation, impact litigation, and mobilization lawyering. But, despite interesting differences in how they chose to cause lawyer, the respondents bifurcated into practices that focused exclusively on individual client representation (eight respondents), and those who combined individual representation with impact and/or mobilization efforts in a combined style practice. These choices of style appear to be affected by personal experiences, political and legal worldviews, and substantive legal skills.

All of the respondents handled individual, *pro bono* cases as a part of their cause-lawyering practice, but they did so in a number of different ways. Respondents get *pro bono* cases from a number of referral systems that operate in the city. The Allegheny County Bar Association has a general referral service that connects private lawyers with clients who are unable to pay for legal representation and who do not qualify for legal services. For the respondents who had a single style of practice, the bar association served as their main source of *pro bono* work. Also operating in the area are lawyer referral services connected to community, political, and issue groups. Cause lawyers who had a combined practice reported representing clients referred to them by Neighborhood Legal Services, the local chapters of the American Civil Liberties Union, the National Lawyers Guild, Greenpeace and other environmental and antinuclear groups, antiapartheid organizations, peace groups, labor groups, and organizations that represent battered women, political refugees, undocumented aliens, handicapped students, lesbians and gay men, and HIV-positive persons.

Lawyers using both styles of practice shared a belief that a major problem with the justice system is the level of unmet legal need among the disadvantaged and that something had to be done about it. Further, there was agreement that they, as lawyers, had both the ability and the responsibility to work to ameliorate this supply problem. Where the two groups diverged was over the completeness of the individual representation cure.

Lawyers who focused exclusively on representing individuals argued consistently that if the supply of legal services to the poor were increased, the critical deficiency of the legal system affecting the disadvantaged would be corrected. They tended to view this supply problem as being one that affected the disadvantaged in a general way, and they believed in the utility of general responses to the problem made by the organized bar. Through a steady supply of legal services, the poor would be able to take advantage of existing societal and governmental benefits that are more easily obtained by their financially secure neighbors. As will be discussed below, these attorneys were less likely to be connected to community and political groups, and therefore they did not participate in the alternative referral networks these groups maintained. Politically, lawyers who focused exclusively on *pro bono* representation generally described themselves as Democrats, liberals, and/or "left of center." They tended to view their work as the fine-tuning needed to make the justice system and society operate more fairly. These attorneys were comfortable with individual client lawyering. For them, their job was to represent an individual client with a legal problem, guiding her or him through the legal system. One other characteristic distinguished these lawyers from the other respondents. They felt that individual client lawyering was their professional forte, as one lawyer's comments highlighted: "It's not that I have anything against being more political, or taking impact cases. I don't think those things are bad. In fact, that kind of work can really help sometimes. I just don't take any cases like that, because if I tried to represent my clients in that way, I would be doing them a disservice" (Respondent 24).

Unmet legal need was a concern for the twenty-one lawyers who had a combined practice, but it was linked to a different worldview. Many of these lawyers felt that individuals who were part of certain identifiable groups were especially unlikely to receive proper legal assistance. In other words, while it is true that the legal system is not serving the needs of the poor in general, there are certain characteristics or conditions that single out some persons for special marginalization. So the combined-practice lawyers tended to work with the specialized referral networks that sought to provide service to targeted groups or persons. For example, these two lawyers explained why they cause-lawyer in conjunction with cause organizations in the community:

> People with AIDS have special problems, legal and otherwise. A person dealing with that really shouldn't have to worry about whether he can afford a lawyer or not. (Respondent 07)

> I work with the shelters because these women have been beaten up, they have kids they have to provide for, they have to find safe housing, and most important, they have to get away from their husband or boyfriend. The system is getting a little better at dealing with their problems, but it has a long, long, long way to go. (Respondent 25)

Lawyers with a combined practice reported that their connection to the specialized referral networks often stemmed first from their connection to a political or cause organization as a citizen member. As a member of the organization, the lawyer then served the group utilizing her or his professional skills. Although these lawyers viewed individual client lawyering as an incomplete response to the legal problems of the marginalized, they did value it, albeit grudgingly. It was work that had to be done or real people would suffer.

One other aspect of individual client lawyering bears mentioning. A sizable portion of the respondents felt that some of the individual cases they undertook had important policy ramifications. This argument was put forth by lawyers using both styles of practice. Attorneys who represented clients in employment discrimination and civil rights matters were especially likely to make this claim. One attorney's recollections of a case that was settled out of court were typical:

> I had a civil rights case where I got a suburban police department to settle with my client. A large sum of money was involved. This case didn't go to court and the department didn't explicitly admit it was wrong, but you can bet that when people read about the agreement in the paper that they thought to themselves: The department was guilty or it wouldn't have paid the money. Better yet, the settlement will probably make some other ya-hoo cop think twice before he roughs somebody up, at least for a month or two. (Respondent 02)

Twenty-one of the respondents reported that impact litigation made up a considerable portion of their cause work. Again this work was linked to the cause organizations that operate the specialized referral networks. The impact work was connected to larger-scale efforts designed to change policy, law, and social systems in such a way that the status of marginalized groups was improved. Examples of impact work conducted by the respondents included litigation done in conjunction with the ACLU, Neighborhood Legal Services Corporation, and other groups that forced state and federal penal institutions in western Pennsylvania to improve institutional conditions; a class action discrimination suit argued with many of the same organizations that eventually forced several segregated suburban school districts to merge into one more diverse district; and a suit undertaken with the Developmental Disabilities Law Project that resulted in changes in the way local schools dealt with students with various physical and mental challenges.

As one might expect, as a group the impact litigators were uniformly convinced in the utility of their work: individuals won specific cases and the system was changed. Although most complained about the hard work, the missed dinners with family, and the lost wages associated with impact litigation, these litigators liked to litigate. They used terms usually associated with artistic creation as they described the satisfaction that they received from orchestrating a successful class action suit:

> You work hard, very hard, researching, finding witnesses, experts. You prepare your case, then comes the trial. At that point you're basically living and breathing the case. When it comes together and you win, it's a beautiful thing. You really can't beat it. I love it. [Laughing] And you help your clients too. (Respondent 21)

> This is a really stupid way to make a living. I do an incredible amount of work for every case I take. They take years. But I do it because I enjoy it. It allows me to be creative. I get to deal with the Constitution; most lawyers don't. For example, I'm representing two Native Americans prisoners who don't want to cut their hair for religious reasons. That's an interesting job! (Respondent 17)

Some litigators were both cognizant and skeptical of the critiques leveled against impact litigation, as this lawyer strongly put it: "I like to keep up-to-date, so I read some of the critical legal studies stuff. I thought they were full of crap. You make yourself irrelevant by arguing for revolutionary change in a country that elects Reagan in a landslide. So I litigate and I think it means something. I could be wrong, but I hope not" (Respondent 22).

For some respondents who litigate often, recent political changes, like those mentioned by Respondent 23 below, have caused them to reconsider in what forums they choose to take their cases:

> The system is changing. When I first started practicing, if you had a controversial case, or a black client, you gravitated to the federal district court. The judges were probably a little more supportive of my kind of client. The Reagan-Bush appointments have changed that. Juries are another problem. Common pleas

court juries are drawn from [Allegheny] County and are usually more racially and politically mixed. Federal juries are drawn from all over western Pennsylvania. They are white, Republican, rural people who either don't like or don't understand my clients and their cases. (Respondent 23)

These comments by respondents reflect the belief within the legal assistance community that the national political changes of the last fifteen years have adversely affected the success of poverty advocacy. Through the appointments of Presidents Reagan and Bush, the U.S. Supreme Court and much of the federal judiciary have become ideologically more conservative and therefore less receptive to the cause of poverty law. Further, as Champagne and Harpham, Dooley and Houseman, and Jost all show, the Legal Services Corporation pressured local programs to move toward individual client lawyering during this period.[20] For these reasons, Houseman and White argue that the days of bringing cases to the federal judiciary for wide impact litigation victories are behind us.[21] The legal advocacy battlefield has shifted to the states as the federal government yielded more discretion over social programs like Aid to Families with Dependent Children, Social Security, and the Women, Infants, and Children Program (WIC) to state administrative agencies.

For some respondents this change in the landscape of poverty advocacy was expected and affected where they chose to practice: "I never worked for legal services. I never felt you could work for anything related to government. It's inevitable you'll be coopted. I am a total independent. I can take a case that will offend the powers that be, and I can reject any case I want, for whatever reason I want" (Respondent 02). For others the changing landscape acted as impetus to leave legal services and establish a private practice with a cause component:

I loved my time at legal services. When you worked there you felt like you were really doing something and that you were part of team. Then things started to change. There were more and more cases you weren't allowed to take. There were big cuts in funding. There was a lot less support for impact work. So I decided to leave for a couple reasons. I wanted to test myself by seeing if I could survive in private practice. And I wanted to be able to do the work I liked without the restrictions I had at legal services. (Respondent 03)

In spite of what some perceived as its diminishing utility, impact litigation remains an important tool in the arsenal of most of the respondents. Most do not expect radical reform of the system in the near future. If change is to come, it will be through the incremental battles of impact litigation they pursue. They felt that recent political and social changes have made their work more difficult, but the abandonment of impact litigation did not appear to be a viable alternative.

Eighteen respondents reported working closely with political and community groups as part of their cause work. These connections usually resulted from a lawyer becoming actively involved in a group because of an interest in the cause it pursued, and then expanding that involvement. This mobilization work did not involve traditional legal activities. Instead, it was directed at increasing the voice of marginalized groups in political and social contexts. For example, the four labor union attorneys were especially involved in mobilization activities that centered on the needs of rank-and-file union members. Several of these attorneys were actively involved in the organization of employees who sought to purchase a business that their employer was closing. Other examples of interviewees' mobilization activities included organizing residents in a low-income neighborhood into an interest group designed to resist zoning changes that would have adversely affected their community, developing a support organization to facilitate the adjustment of newly admitted political refugees and immigrants to their new country, and involvement in the creation of the Alliance for Progressive Action, a coalition of more than fifty progressive organizations in western Pennsylvania that serves as a clearinghouse for its members.

Interestingly, some respondents reported that they were cutting back on the amount of time they spent on mobilization efforts. They complained that groups tended to form in an ad hoc way around an acute problem and died quickly after the problem was resolved. They reported leaving the experience feeling that mobilization was more trouble than it was worth. Others said they had abandoned the mobilization component of their practice because they felt it was not an efficient use of their time: "When I was more involved in organizing I kept getting the feeling that I was wasting my time. There are people who are natural organizers and they like doing that work. They should do it. And I should be a lawyer" (Respondent 14).

There were no respondents whose practice could be classified as client voice lawyering. Respondents did talk about being cognizant and interested in the special needs of their cause clients and the effect that those needs had on the way they did their cause work. But often they felt what they offered their clients were the skills of a lawyer. They were interested in their clients' societal and political situations. They were interested in their causes. And they reported that they worked to establish a good rapport with their cause clients. But these efforts were means toward ends: helping the client and cause, often by providing the lawyerly guidance that Alfieri and others argued is chimerical. The cause lawyer's monopoly of legal knowledge was seen as a fact of life that could be used to help, not as a pernicious tool of control.

The Motivations behind Cause Lawyering

Why do cause lawyers engage in the sorts of activities introduced above? Respondents cited a wide range of reasons. There were several motivational factors that were mentioned by lawyers who used both styles of cause lawyering. Familial influences served as motivating forces for many. Respondents described the effect that a politically or socially active family member had on their practice of law, for example, a female cause lawyer talked about the influence of her mother on her practice: "I grew up in a working-class, Catholic family of do-gooders, especially my mother. She was a feminist before we ever knew what that meant. She was so actively involved in our community, through the church, charity organizations, and the Democratic Party. I guess I patterned myself after her and this work is part of that" (Respondent 20). Some respondents talked about the motivation created by stressful family events, as this attorney's explanation for his cause lawyering for labor groups highlighted: "I do it partly because of my family. When I was a teenager my dad lost his job in the steel mill and I thought it was needless. Corporations and their managers don't have all the answers and they don't make the best decisions for their workers and the community. I went to law school to learn labor law and give workers more of a say in these decisions that affect them and their communities" (Respondent 11).

Other basic personal factors affecting the choice to cause-lawyer included religious beliefs, attachment to a community, and a commitment to some general notion of fair play, which was illustrated in the comments of this employment lawyer: "Sometimes you just can't let [employers] get away with the things they try. Reagan and Bush wrongly convinced them that at-will employment means that they can fire somebody on a whim. That's not what the law says and it's really fun to stick it to a jerk who thinks that it does" (Respondent 01).

A factor that generally seemed to have little motivational force on the respondents' choice to cause lawyer was legal education, which is not surprising, given the evidence that shows that law school does not transform the values of its students.[22] Respondents described law school as an experience to be endured before they could practice law. Most respondents reported having some level of interest in lawyering for the disadvantaged before they entered law school, albeit with varying degrees of clarity. The comments of a combined-style lawyer on his experiences in law school were fairly typical: "Law school isn't debilitating; it's what you make of it. When I went to law school I found fellow progressives and we made it into our own thing. We worked with the Weathermen and draft resisters and started the law collective. Law school was just something you had to get done before you could be a lawyer, not good or bad" (Respondent 02). Contrary to the general pattern, the respondents who attended Antioch and Northeastern, as well the three respondents who graduated from Rutgers, did report that the curriculum at these schools during the late 1960s and early 1970s had a substantial public interest focus that they found strengthened existing interests.

More commonly mentioned by the interviewees as an important formative element in their cause orientation was the time period in which they began their legal careers. Respondents cited the mood of the country in the late 1960s and early 1970s as an important motivation for choosing a poverty law practice. These attorneys graduated from law school at a time when the somewhat revolutionary ideas of poverty law that were being advanced by reformers like the Cahns were being tested in programs such as the Office of Equal Opportunity's Legal Services. Many found these ideas to be both exciting and validating. Personal factors, like a relative losing his job, merged with changing conceptions of progressive lawyering to form basic commitments to the idea of cause lawyering for the disadvantaged.

Beyond these motivational forces there was again a bifurcation that corresponded with the cause-lawyering style choices of the respondents. Lawyers who focus exclusively on representing individuals were most likely to cite professional responsibility as a factor in their commitment to *pro bono* representation. As the discussion of their practice indicated, these attorneys viewed the basic structure of the justice system as being essentially fair. The critical threat to the system's legitimacy was the difficulty that the indigent have in securing legal services. These lawyers felt that an integral part of being a lawyer was to work to meet the needs of the underserved.

The lawyers with a combined-style practice were more likely to cite their political beliefs as a guiding force behind their cause lawyering. All placed themselves well to the left of the political continuum, by using terms like "very left of center," "progressive," "socialist," "leftist," and "very liberal" to describe their political ideology. And again, for many, the combination of personal experiences and the mood of the country in the 1960s helped to develop these political beliefs, as the recollections of these three respondents indicate:

> The [Vietnam] war really changed the way I thought about things. When I was in school I wasn't interested in politics. Then I was drafted, and before I knew it people were shooting over my head. Then and there I realized the system had failed. Not just because I was drafted, but because we were in that illegal war to begin with. I was radicalized by this and when I got out of the army I decided to use my legal skills to fight criminals like Nixon and everything he represented. (Respondent 23)

> I'm really not sure why it happened. My freshman year I was the treasurer of the Young Republicans, just your average middle-class kid. I went to school in the South and saw the effects of segregation. It was also the time of the peace movement and I got caught up in it. By the time I got to law school, I viewed myself as a radical. I got involved with the law collective, protests, the whole nine yards. (Respondent 17)

> Let's get something straight, I'm a leftist. Take the antiwar movement for example. There were people who marched against the war because they didn't like war. They were pacifists. And there were people who march against the war because they wanted North Vietnam to win and further the revolution. I was in the second group. I carried the Vietcong flag on the streets of Pittsburgh. But times have changed. I'm not as far left as I used to be. I mean I'm not waiting for the revolution anymore. I still think we need a major shake-up, I just don't know if we're going to get it. (Respondent 02)

Nine lawyers reported being heavily involved in the radical student movements of the 1960s. These respondents talked often about the personal transformation that resulted from these political experiences in early adulthood. They developed a deep suspicion of the legitimacy of many basic American institutions. And they found pleasure in beating the "system," as the comments of these attorneys who represented criminal defendants and prisoners make clear:

> I don't trust the government and I really don't trust cops. Anytime I beat them in court I'm having a great day. (Respondent 02)

> I don't like the state being an instrument of oppression. Don't get me wrong, a lot of the guys in [state prison] really deserve to be there. But they don't deserve to be abused by the state while they're in there. (Respondent 17)

For many of the lawyers with a combined-style practice, their politics led them to practices with like-minded colleagues. Eleven had worked on a full-time basis early in their careers for a legal services program, the ACLU, the National Association for the Advancement of Colored People, or other public interest law organizations. They reported that these professional experiences combined with their basic political beliefs to develop a clearer ideology of cause lawyering. As discussed in the preceding section, these lawyers viewed the justice system and society as having basic structural flaws. Their goal was to change both. Toward these ends they pursued causes like desegregation, race and gender equality, environmentalism, and economic reform. Their experiences with public interest work steered their eventual private practice toward a cause focus. In addition to strengthening their worldview, they had learned certain substantive legal skills on these first jobs that were ideally suited for a cause practice.

In a study of the career choice of former OEO Legal Services attorneys, Erlanger found similar effects.[23] Former legal services attorneys tended to move in different career paths than their nonlegal services contemporaries, making them unique in several ways. First, they were less likely to be in private practice, and conversely more likely to work in a government agency or a social organization. Those who did work in private practice tended to work in smaller firms and were far more likely to work with minority clients than their nonlegal services counterparts in the general bar. Finally, Erlanger found that legal services alumni reported doing more *pro bono* work. Erlanger argued that several important and related influences may account for these differences. Obviously the *esprit de corps* of the legal services program had some influence on the former worker, but that worker also became trained in what amounts to a legal specialty, serving the legal needs of disadvantaged clients. Relatedly, the type of professional contacts that these legal services alumni made while in the program probably had something to do with their eventual career choice.

Movements and Networks

In discussing progressive lawyers, Abel argues that they can only achieve their goal of affecting the system by uniting into "larger collectivities."[24] This section examines whether there is a collective movement or network in Pittsburgh that connects private cause lawyers to one another, to government-funded legal services agencies, and to social action organizations that operate to improve the conditions of the disadvantaged. These collectivities would allow their members to mobilize support for their cause while at the same time isolating their opposition. Beyond the important instrumental value of joining like-minded lawyers, Abel's progressive lawyer would benefit from these larger collectivities through the emotional, political, and technical support that others who are involved in similar efforts can provide. He cites as examples of collectivities of progressive lawyers the ACLU and the National Legal Aid and Defender Association. In fact, a number of respondents reported valuing the camaraderie they experienced on the job at legal services programs, the ACLU, the NAACP, or other public interest law organizations.

When asked about the existence of a network or movement of cause lawyers in Pittsburgh, *all* twenty-nine participants made a response similar to this: "There is. It isn't anything organized. We don't have a secret handshake, membership cards, or a lodge. But we know who we are and some of us do get together and talk about our work" (Respondent 07). There appear to be several networks operating within the community of Pittsburgh cause lawyers, and they are rather loose: there is no unified movement of cause lawyers. Instead, individual lawyers are connected to different causes or movements. Several organizations serve the function of providing a meeting place for lawyers to come together and talk about the practice of cause lawyering. Cited by nearly every respondent was the Allegheny County Bar Association's Section on Civil Rights. This organization holds a monthly luncheon meeting where both professional and personal matters are discussed. Also serving as networking bases for cause lawyers were the ACLU's Litigation Section and the NAACP. Although what they expect from the organization varied, as the comments below indicate, eight respondents who are members of the local chapter of the National Lawyers Guild reported that this organization also serves to keep them connected to fellow cause lawyers.

> I belong to the National Lawyers Guild. It's important to me because I get to be with people who care about the things I care about. For example, I am very interested in Cuba and the Cuban Revolution and I've been to Cuba on several Guild tours. So the Guild is about more than just the law. (Respondent 08)

> I'm a member of the Guild. It's a good way to stay current with the law or to discuss strategy. I do have to laugh, though, when people who picked sugar cane in Cuba come to a meeting and show pictures from their trip. But that's okay, because there isn't a Guild mindset. (Respondent 15)

As discussed earlier, many of the lawyers with a combined-style practice are actively involved with local cause organizations. They participate as citizen members, as lawyers who represent the groups and their members in court, and as organizers. Despite these varied forms of participation in cause organizations, there was a consensus among the respondents that functioning as a lawyer was the most productive way they could help their respective causes, as this litigator's comments indicate:

> The law is what you make it. I was an activist before I went to law school. I remember seeing William Kunstler represent H. Rap Brown in New Orleans and thinking what a great way to change things. I went to law school for the sole purpose of being a progressive lawyer, and that's what I am. I'm not going to help any cause or anybody by knocking on doors or handcuffing myself to a waste incinerator. But I am a great lawyer. So I help change things by keeping the organizers and demonstrators out of jail. I think that makes me a real part of the movement. (Respondent 02)

One final note on the existence of a cause lawyer network in Pittsburgh. As the result of a suggestion made by a colleague on a preliminary report of this research, I asked ten of my respondents to look over the list of study participants. I then asked them to comment on the list and make suggestions for additions. Although not a scientific test of group membership, there was a surprisingly high level of agreement that the names on the list comprised a substantial portion of the cause-lawyering community. Also remarkably consistent were the additional names that were suggested by the respondents, those of cause lawyers who were not in private practice. Respondent 07 seemed to be correct when she said, "We know who we are."

Professionalism and Poverty Cause Lawyering

How do poverty cause lawyers conceive of their professional role? Among the major components of traditional legal professionalism are professional knowledge and independence, political independence, and economic autonomy.[25] All raise interesting issues and potential conflicts when considered in the context of cause lawyering.

The professional conceptions of the respondents again bifurcated along practice style choices. The lawyers who exclusively represented disadvantaged individuals *pro bono* were more likely to be concerned with traditional Anglo-American conceptions of professional independence. They empathized with their clients' situations and worked hard to resolve their legal problems, but their practice did not revolve around the causes of their *pro bono* clients. Illustrative are the comments of this attorney: "I like the English system. There it's not considered professional to be associated with a cause or a group. You should be an advocate who can argue any client's case. I am comfortable with the credibility that brings. So I do work that might fit into someone's definition of 'progressive,' but I also defend corporations in civil litigation for the practice. The way I view my professional role there's no contradiction or tension there" (Respondent 20).

The lawyers who had a combined-style practice were more likely to allow their political beliefs and attachments to causes to affect the decision of whom they represented. These respondents built their practices with a determined effort to do work that at best furthers the cause or, at worst, does not set it back.

> I don't buy that a lawyer has to be objective and take any client who walks through the door. That's bullshit. I only represent people who I agree with. I'd never represent a Nazi, a skinhead, or Klansman. I'll give you an example that just happened. I got a call from a high-ranking, white police officer who was being sued for civil rights violations. He had heard that I was one of the best civil rights attorneys in the city, and he wanted me to defend him. I told him that I was one of the best, but that I wouldn't take his case. He wanted a reason. I told him that I don't defend cops, I sue them. His case just didn't fit into my system. (Respondent 02)

> I am a union lawyer. I would never represent a corporation. (Respondent 05)

Many respondents made mention of the increasingly competitive legal marketplace in Pittsburgh. They reported that the population of the metropolitan area has been steadily declining while the number of practicing attorneys has rapidly increased. Especially hard pressed were the attorneys who practiced solo or in a small partnership. Respondents mentioned the difficulties of meeting the overhead of a practice, supporting family needs, and pursuing the cause component of their practice. Many were concerned with how little time they were spending with their spouses and children. Lawyers who represented clients in employment discrimination and civil rights matters were exceptions. They reported that their economic position was healthy as a result of fees that had been awarded by the judiciary in successful suits. In general though, the respondents viewed themselves as an especially harried lot. And some spoke in very nonspecific terms about the need to cut back on their general work effort, including their cause activities. When pressed to explain what cutting back might entail, most preferred to avoid a more specific analysis.

A final note on the professional issues surrounding the cause lawyers in this study. Respondents were asked to comment on how their cause activities affected their status in the general legal community. Many felt that most lawyers and judges were unaware that they were involved in cause lawyering. Others argued that over time the legal community has become accepting of their cause practice, as these comments indicate: "We've been around so long that the bar is starting to get used to us. They probably just think we're a bit strange to give up money to take these cases. But generally we're not disliked or viewed as a threat. I'll tell you who they did view as a threat, Edgar Snyder. He's the revolutionary they feared, with his TV ads and 1–800 numbers" (Respondent 08).

Conclusion

Cause lawyering for the disadvantaged is alive and relatively well in Pittsburgh. It is practiced in different ways for the benefit of different groups. But Pittsburgh's cause lawyers in private practice are getting older. They face important family demands, and they are responding to them by cutting back their time at the office. This can only serve to reduce the amount of cause work done in the city. That having been said, the cause lawyers interviewed for this project are *still trying* to lawyer for the good. They have formed very close links with the city's cause organizations and with their cause clients. These do not appear to be ties that will be broken easily. Yet there is reason to be concerned about the future of cause lawyering in Pittsburgh. All of the respondents in this study fit into Scheingold's first or second generation of left-activist lawyers.[26] They were all trained before 1980. Save for two, they are all over forty. Unlike Scheingold in Seattle, I identified no cause lawyer in Pittsburgh who was trained in the last ten years. This apparent dearth stems in large part from the definition of a cause lawyer used for this study. Respondents identified younger progressive lawyers in Pittsburgh, but they were excluded from the project because they were not in private practice. Instead, they worked for Neighborhood Legal Services, the ACLU, the NAACP, and other public interest law outfits. This situation raises several questions that remain to be answered: Will these younger lawyers follow the same path as their predecessors and move to a private practice with a cause component and, thereby, keep cause lawyering alive in Pittsburgh? Or is cause lawyering as described in this chapter atrophying? I will leave the predictions to Respondent 02: "I think it's kind of funny that you'd be interested in people like me. We're not that special. There have always been people around who wanted to use the law to help, instead of to make money. And unless the world has really changed, there always will be."

Notes

1. Carrie Menkel-Meadow, "The Causes of Cause Lawyering: Toward an Understanding of the Motivation and Commitment of Social Justice Lawyers," chap. 2 of this volume.
2. Ibid.
3. Richard E. Dawson, Kenneth Prewitt, and Karen S. Dawson, *Political Socialization,* 2nd ed. (Boston: Little, Brown, 1977), 59–60.
4. Gary Bellow, "Turning Solutions into Problems: The Legal Aid Experience," *NLADA Briefcase* 34 (1977), 103–134. See also Austin Sarat, " ' . . . The Law Is All Over': Power, Resistance and the Legal Consciousness of the Welfare Poor," *Yale Journal of Law and the Humanities* 2 (1990), 343–379.

5. Samuel Jan Brakel, "Legal Services for the Poor in the Reagan Years," *American Bar Association Journal* 68 (1982), 820–822.

6. See Stuart A. Scheingold, *The Politics of Rights: Lawyers, Public Policy, and Political Change* (New Haven: Yale University Press, 1974); Donald L. Horowitz, *The Courts and Social Policy* (Washington, D.C.: Brookings Institution, 1974); and Gerald N. Rosenberg, *The Hollow Hope: Can Courts Bring about Social Change?* (Chicago: University of Chicago Press, 1991).

7. For example, see Anthony Alfieri, "Disabled Clients, Disabling Lawyers," *Hastings Law Journal* 43 (1992), 769–851; Alfieri, "Reconstructive Poverty Law Practice: Learning Lessons of Client Narrative," *Yale Law Journal* 100 (1991), 2107–2147; Alfieri, "The Antinomies of Poverty Law and a Theory of Dialogic Empowerment," *Review of Law and Social Change* 16 (1987–88), 659–712; and Steve Bachmann, "Lawyers, Law, and Social Change," *New York University Review of Law and Social Change* 13 (1984–85), 1–50.

8. Alfieri, "The Antinomies of Poverty Law," 666–678.

9. See Edgar S. Cahn and Jean C. Cahn, "The War on Poverty: A Civilian Perspective," *Yale Law Journal* 73 (1964) 1317–1352.

10. See Alfieri, "The Antinomies of Poverty Law"; Bachmann, "Lawyers, Law, and Social Change"; and Gerald P. Lopez, "Training Lawyers to Work with the Politically and Socially Subordinated: Anti-Generic Legal Education," *West Virginia University Law Review* 305 (1989) 350–386.

11. Alfieri, "The Antinomies of Poverty Law," 671.

12. Ibid., 673–674.

13. Ibid., 695–711.

14. Paul R. Tremblay, "Rebellious Lawyering, Regnant Lawyering, and Street-Level Bureaucracy," *Hastings Law Journal* 43 (1992), 949–950.

15. Ibid., 954–959.

16. Christopher P. Gilkerson, "Poverty Law Narratives: The Critical Practice and Theory of Receiving and Translating Client Stories," *Hastings Law Review* 43 (1992), 861–945; see also Alfieri, "Disabled Clients"; Alfieri, "Reconstructive Poverty Law Practice"; Bachmann, "Lawyers, Law, and Social Change"; Lopez, "Training Lawyers"; Paul R. Tremblay, "Toward a Community-Based Ethic for Legal Services Practice," *UCLA Law Review* 37 (1990), 1101–1156; Lucie White, "Mobilization on the Margins of the Lawsuit: Making Space for the Clients to Speak," *Review of Law and Social Change* 16 (1987–88), 535–564; and Stephen Wizner, "Homelessness: Advocacy and Social Policy," *University of Miami Law Review* 45 (1990–91), 387–405.

17. Lucie White, "Paradox, Piece-Work, and Patience," *Hastings Law Journal* 43 (1992) 853–945; and Sarat, " ' . . . The Law Is All Over."

18. White, "Mobilization on the Margins."

19. Ibid., 546.

20. Anthony Champagne and Edward J. Harpham, *The Attack on the Welfare State* (Prospect Heights, Ill.: Waveland Press, 1984); John A. Dooley and Alan W. Houseman, *Legal Services History* (Washington, D.C.: NLADA Management Project, 1984); and Kenneth Jost, "LSC Returning to Normalcy, But Skirmishes Continue," *Congressional Quarterly*, June 20, 1990, 1728–1730.

21. Alan W. Houseman, "The Vitality of *Goldberg v. Kelly* to Welfare Advocacy in the 1990s," *Brooklyn Law Review* 56 (1990), 831–859; Houseman, *Legal Services to the Poor and Disadvantaged in the 1980s: The Issues for Research* (Washington, D.C.: Center for Law and Social Policy, 1984); and White, "Mobilization on the Margins."

22. Richard L. Abel, *American Lawyers* (New York: Oxford University Press, 1989), 223; see also Robert V. Stover, *Making It and Breaking It: The Fate of Public Interest Commitment*

during Law School (Urbana: University of Illinois Press, 1989); and Howard S. Erlanger and Douglas A. Klegon, "Socialization Effects of Professional School: The Law School Experience and Student Orientations to Public Interest Concerns," *Law and Society Review* 42 (1978), 11–35.

23. Howard S. Erlanger, "Social Reform Organizations and Subsequent Careers of Participants: A Follow-Up Study of Early Participants in the OEO Legal Services Program," *American Sociological Review* 42 (1977), 233–248.

24. Richard L. Abel, "Lawyers and the Power to Change," *Law and Policy* 7, no. 1 (1985), 14.

25. Rayman L. Solomon, "Five Crises or One: The Concept of Legal Professionalism, 1925–1960," in *Lawyers' Ideals/Lawyers' Practices: Transformations in the American Legal Profession,* ed. Robert L. Nelson, David M. Trubek, and Rayman L. Solomon (Ithaca, N.Y.: Cornell University Press, 1992), 144–176.

26. Stuart A. Scheingold, "The Struggle to Politicize Legal Practice: A Case Study of Left-Activist Lawyering in Seattle," chap. 4 of this volume.

CHAPTER 7

Critical Lawyers
Social Justice and the
Structures of Private Practice

LOUISE TRUBEK & M. ELIZABETH KRANSBERGER

The ideological concepts and institutional structures underlying public interest law are in transition. Since the 1960s, when the conceptual framework and institutional forms of public interest law were developed, academics and practitioners have argued that socially oriented lawyering would and should be carried out primarily in special institutional structures (public interest firms, law school clinics, or legal services offices). They assumed that the private practitioner's contribution to public interest or social lawyering would be marginal or nonexistent. However, theoretical developments,[1] practitioner experience, and the economic realities of the 1990s are forcing a reconsideration of this now assumed separation between socially conscious lawyering and private practice.

In recent years, public interest practitioners and law school clinicians have developed new approaches, sometimes dubbed "critical lawyering,"[2] to advocate on behalf of subordinated groups. Closely related to feminist and critical race jurisprudence, critical lawyering has led some to question the previous division between the nonprofit public interest sphere and private practice. At the same time, recent political developments have indicated that the funding for the Legal Services Corporation is in jeopardy and that the financial base for the nonprofit public interest bar is not likely to expand. Moreover, the current political climate indicates that programs and protections for poor people will be dramatically reduced.

If approaches to lawyering for subordinated groups have changed, prospects for expansion of the separate public interest sphere have dimmed, and the protection of disadvantaged clients is declining, then we need to explore alternative sites for transformative lawyering. In this provisional report of a study of five small firms, we explore socially conscious or critical lawyers who work within the structures of private practice. These lawyers have successfully combined critical lawyering with fee-for-service work. In this essay, we describe the operation of these firms and analyze the key transformative elements of their lawyering. We also discuss the factors that influence these firms' ability to develop and survive and conclude with speculations on future developments.

The Historical Division between Public Interest and Private Bar Public Service Practice

The "professionalism project" of the legal services and public interest lawyers and clinicians who founded law school clinics and established law offices staffed by nonprofit full-time attorneys was an important force in the creation and reinforcement of separate spheres between public interest and private bar practices. Currently, there are approximately six thousand nonprofit full-time staff attorneys or clinical teachers employed by legal services offices, public interest law firms, and law school clinical programs. These institutional settings, and the jobs associated with them, emerged out of intense political struggles in the late 1960s and early 1970s. The founders of these offices and clinics believed that effective advocacy on behalf of unrepresented clients and client groups required independent practice settings and could not depend on fee-for-service financing. To develop these new institutions and jobs and obtain the financial support they required, the founders stressed the unique capabilities of the public interest bar: they argued that the nonprofit structure, supported by public and private gifts and grants or law school budgets, was essential for effective lawyering for social change. To gain status in the legal profession and secure jobs, they claimed, only full-time specialists in nonprofit settings could do the job.

As a result of the legal services and public interest professionalism project, the potential contribution of private practitioners to social change lawyering was devalued: in order to argue for separate, publicly supported practice settings, the social mission of the private sphere was downplayed. Thus, the two separate spheres of public interest law and private practice emerged.

The effort to construct a separate sphere for the public interest bar can also be seen in the literature. Prior to the 1970s, the literature on public service practice described a wide range of locations and types of practice. These included charitable pro bono and contingent-fee practices, as well as general law reform efforts by private practitioners following in the footsteps of Louis Brandeis in the early twentieth century. But by the mid-1970s, when the public interest movement was professionalizing, the focus had narrowed.[3] Thus, *Balancing the Scales of Justice,* a publication produced by the Council on Public Interest Law as part of its efforts to institutionalize this movement, described only those practicing in nonprofit law firms as public interest lawyers.[4] Similarly, the legal services lawyers in the 1960s fought against the "Judicare" model, which paid private practitioners to take cases on behalf of low-income people and insisted on the model of the staff attorney who exclusively practiced poverty law.[5] The professionalism project resulted in the division of the previously amorphous public service mission of the bar into two sectors: the part-time and voluntary pro bono sphere and the full-time, professional public interest sphere. The pro bono lawyers were private practitioners who either took "public interest" cases for free, often on referral from the public interest/legal services bar, or pursued issues in which there were statutory attorneys' fees.

The professionalism project was not simply a self-interested effort to create a limited number of new jobs insulated from market pressures. The lawyers genuinely believed this model would best serve subordinated groups and raise the status of socially committed lawyers within the legal profession. In addition, given the domestic and international economic growth of the United States and the concomitant growth and continued activism of the legal profession during the 1960s, the lawyers justifiably believed the public interest sphere could be sustained and expanded significantly over time.[6] They believed their work could be supported indefinitely by government funding, the private bar, and foundations.

The public interest professionalism project did succeed in some ways, and the model of the full-time staff attorney doing good works has become paradigmatic. As a result, however, a clear distinction between public interest and private bar practitioners has been created. This "bright line" has become accepted by both sides: by the practitioners in the nonprofit staff attorney firms and by those in the fee-for-service firms, and they generally define themselves as one or the other type of practitioner. The full-time public interest lawyers do believe the private practitioners have a role in their overall social mission, albeit a secondary and subordinate one: private practitioners can take routinized cases on a pro bono basis, but only as long as the full-time staff attorneys conceptualize and organize the work.[7]

But the model of the full-time public interest practitioner developed by the professionalism project no longer attracts many recent law school graduates with a desire to do social justice work. Many choose to work in alternative private practices rather than in the shrinking public sector.[8] In addition, newer approaches to lawyering for subordinated people interest these young lawyers. Thus, changes in economic realities and new theoretical insights render the private sector an appealing option for socially conscious lawyering.

Critical Lawyering

A new conception of and strategy for socially conscious lawyering has emerged in the past decade. Termed "critical lawyering" (or "transformative" or "rebellious" lawyering), this strategy aims to provide subordinated groups with greater access to legal representation and better promote social change.[9] While providing practical suggestions for reform, critical lawyering also theorizes social change lawyering more broadly. Critical lawyering has been heavily influenced by theoretical work being done in the legal academy, especially in feminist and critical race jurisprudence.[10] Critical lawyering also seeks to combine both client-centered strategies and those aimed at collective action.

Ruth Buchanan and Louise Trubek have noted that critical lawyering addresses two major concerns: improving lawyer/client relationships to more effectively work on behalf of subordinated groups and rethinking the relationship between legal work and political mobilization.[11] Surveying a diverse and multifaceted literature, they summarized the central tenets of critical lawyering as follows:

> *Humanize*: resist reduction of client stories to legal categories and frame issues in human terms;
> *Politicize*: use critical legal theory to provide insight into the contingent nature of client disempowerment and apply feminist, antiracist and antiheterosexist analysis to help resist marginalization of clients' voices;
> *Collaborate*: encourage participation of clients and client groups in practice decisions and attempt to dismantle the lawyer/client hierarchy;
> *Strategize*: seek to access client experiences regarding strategies for struggle and resistance, develop a healthy skepticism regarding traditional advocacy arenas, and continually reevaluate advocacy effectiveness from a client perspective; and
> *Organize*: encourage organization and collective efforts by clients and work with existing social movements and client groups.

Those who represent subordinated people often find a tension between advocating on behalf of individual clients or cases and politically mobilizing client groups. In legal services jargon, this was often referred to as the "service-impact" dichotomy. Critical lawyering softens the distinction and potential tension between the two, as it views client work as transformative in and of itself. Nonetheless, the ability of lawyers to be both client centered and effective in collective action is questionable. One commentator notes that the "structural, institutional, political, economic and ethical" aspects of lawyering for disadvantaged people will continue to favor the client-centered work and make the achievement of effective group action difficult.[12] Since the lawyers we discuss remain committed to both individual empowerment and collective mobilization, we have kept this caution in mind as we study the firms' attempts to combine these ambitious transformative goals with the maintenance of a viable private practice.

Not only does critical lawyering seek to develop nonhierarchical and humane lawyer/client relationships, but it seeks nonhierarchical and humane workplaces as well. Many traditional law firms, including older public interest firms, do not always consider workplace environments arenas for social change. Critical lawyering seeks to transform the workplace into a collegial and equitable site.[13]

We believe that with their attention to client concerns, social justice, and the workplace, the practitioners we have studied bridge the separate spheres. They are thus change agents, representing the reconfiguration of many areas of public interest and private bar practice. We believe these practices promise to benefit those constituencies by creating an alternative model for the delivery of legal services to traditionally subordinated groups.

Researching Critical Lawyers in Private Practice

Methodology

We decided to explore the way these practitioners attempt transformative lawyering within the structures of private practice. We networked in three urban areas and identified private practitioners who, based on their reputations in the communities for providing services to disadvantaged individuals and groups, seemed to have critically oriented practices. We interviewed twenty-seven attorneys in three communities. The pool was deliberately constructed to include women attorneys and attorneys of color;[14] of the twenty-seven attorneys on our list, nineteen were women, nine were people of color, and six were white men. When interviewing the lawyers, we used a questionnaire designed to provoke a description of their professional life histories and the evolution of their current practice settings.[15]

In this essay, we focus on interviews from lawyers in four firms and one solo practitioner. These practitioners were selected because they appear to exhibit the factors we consider central to critical lawyering. The respondents showed the clearest commitment to social justice, collaboration with clients, and creation of an alternative workplace. Their firms also demonstrated either longevity or a clear view of how funding for the firm would be obtained. We believe these firms span a continuum of "critical lawyering," each negotiating the tensions between private practice and politicized representation in various practice structures.

Some lawyers we interviewed are not featured in this paper for several reasons. Some did not perceive their valuable work as assisting subordinated people, but simply as utilizing attorney fee awards or contingent fee arrangements to earn a living. Some of the firms were structured traditionally, despite their nontraditional demographics (all-women, for example). Finally, since our interviews some of the firms have changed their practices and have moved either into the public sector or into more conventional private practice.

Description of the Firms and Solo Practitioner

The four small firms we discuss are Strickland & Caldwell, Urban Legal Advocates, Smith & Associates, and El Centro. The solo practitioner we discuss is Marcelle Roberts.[16] In this section, we describe both the lawyers' professional histories and their current practice.

STRICKLAND AND CALDWELL

Strickland & Caldwell is comprised of two white women partners, one paralegal, a part-time law clerk, and seven support staff. Both lawyers in the firm are equal shareholders. They engage with their staff in collective management and decision making on the firms' administrative and business matters. Both partners and the paralegal left a large, well-established firm to start this practice.

Many of their initial clients followed Strickland and Caldwell from their old firm, giving them a fairly stable client base. Currently, their practice is primarily in family law, which includes divorce actions and child custody, supplemented by estate planning, appellate, and general practice work. They also take court appointments in guardian ad litem cases, third-party visitation, and lesbian custody cases.[17]

URBAN LEGAL ADVOCATES (ULA)

Urban Legal Advocates, a ten-year-old feminist law collective, is comprised of two white women lawyers, both partners. The firm also has one paralegal, an office manager, and two student interns. In addition, during the summer, they employ as many as six college and law student interns. The lawyers and the office manager are equal members of the collective. Amy, one of the founding members of the firm, identifies herself as a lesbian attorney. She recently took a part-time clinical position at a local law school, where she supervises a housing law practice.

ULA's practice is roughly comprised of 40 percent housing law and 30 percent nontraditional and lesbian family law. The remainder consists of police misconduct, civil rights, employment law, personal injury, criminal appeals, wills, and miscellaneous civil law issues. Despite their small size, ULA is considered the preeminent gay rights firm in their large metropolitan area. In addition, they have contracts to provide legal services to a service union and to an office workers' union of the local college system.[18]

SMITH & ASSOCIATES

Smith, an African American man, is the lead partner of the firm Smith & Associates. The firm consists of seven attorneys. The firm was cofounded by Smith, following the dissolution of a very successful corporate firm, known for its socially responsible activity. He joined with well-known civil rights and employment discrimination attorneys to open this firm.

Smith & Associates' practice is comprised of local community economic development clients and civil rights and employment discrimination cases. The firm is currently the lead counsel for a large class action case, which occupies one attorney almost full-time.[19]

EL CENTRO

El Centro has two attorneys, both white men. The firm utilizes law students and volunteers, and there is no support staff. It was formed as a tax-deductible non-profit organization. When still in law school, the founder decided to open a community-based law office. Before founding El Centro, he did human rights work in Central America.

Sixty percent of the firm's work is comprised of divorce and family law cases. The rest of their practice consists of 15 percent landlord/tenant cases, 12 percent civil/municipal issues, 5 percent criminal law, and another 8 percent miscellaneous issues such as guardian ad litem, workers' compensation, Supplemental Security Income, and unemployment compensation. The firm also has a project that provides legal services to refugees in the community and in Texas, and they provide representation in asylum hearings free of charge.[20]

MARCELLE ROBERTS

Ms. Roberts, an African American woman, is a solo practitioner. She shares office space, machines, and clerical support staff with three other private practitioners. She has been in practice sixteen years. Initially, she practiced with her husband; before that, she was a state hearing examiner.

Over the years, Roberts has narrowed her practice to mainly family law, with the bulk of her practice in divorces. The rest of her practice consists of some additional guardian ad litem work, personal injury, and bankruptcy.[21]

The Transformative Aspects of Their Lawyering

In this section we document and analyze transformative aspects of these firms by adapting the critical lawyering tenets to private practice.[22] We have focused on the following tenets: expression of social concerns in their practice, utilization of a collaborative approach to the lawyer/client relationship, and creation of alternative workplace structures. To describe and highlight these critical tenets, we have relied heavily on the lawyers' own words.

Expressing Social Concerns in Their Practice

The lawyers have developed their practices to enable them to both represent clients in a manner consistent with their social values and advocate with groups on broad social issues. According to the practitioners, these goals can be accomplished through their choice of practice and clients, fees structures, office location, and group mobilization.

PRACTICE AREAS, FEES, AND LOCATION

These practitioners selected their practice areas based on community needs and their social justice concerns. Two of their practice areas, family law and minority business development, enable them to express their commitments to women, gays and lesbians, and people of color. Family law, because of the social context of changing family arrangements, the substantive modifications of family law doctrine, and the need for low-cost services, is an active field for alternative practitioners. Both all-women law firms practice largely in both traditional and lesbian/gay family law. Further, El Centro's low-income Latina clients are primarily interested in family law representation.

The practitioners in this study are aware of the opportunity that family law issues have to transform the material conditions of women's lives, either positively or negatively. Marcelle Roberts observed that "in marital actions . . . the financial strain of separation and divorce continues to have social and gender implications." Both Strickland and Caldwell were feminist activists in legislative and court reforms of family law in the 1970s; this expertise was the basis for their successful entrance into private practice.

The Smith firm, where one of the partners is a well-respected business attorney with many years of corporate experience, is creating a practice that mixes minority business representation with a civil rights and employment discrimination practice. The combination has allowed them to develop a socially committed business practice in the community.

In conjunction with their choice of practice area, several of the firms restricted the clients they would take based on their social justice mission. One commented:

> Part of the reason we have more female clients than males is that violence between male and females is rampant in the Hispanic community. And you will find out in almost every case that there is some form of violence, . . . physical and emotional. It is almost always being perpetuated on the female, so we do not take, as a general rule—though it is not written—men who come in for divorce who have recently left the house.[23]

Another practitioner in housing law stated:

> I won't take any case that walks in the door, and I think some of the factors I use about whether to take a case are very different. For instance, we don't represent landlords. And I've had a lot of judges and opposing counsels tell me that I would be a more well-rounded attorney if I did. . . . For me, the power dynamics in landlord/tenant cases are just so obvious that even if I have a tenant who's an asshole, it's still really easy for me to feel like I'm doing a good thing if I'm helping to preserve this person's basic housing necessities.[24]

All of the firms developed fee structures to enable them to sustain a private practice while expressing a social justice mission. Some of the firms set lower than market fees for service; others serve upper-income clients to support their legislative advocacy and pro bono representations.

ULA's clients are mainly middle to low income, and, by their account, are the people who fall through the cracks of legal service. Their fees range from $75 to $185 per hour. They also offer very affordable rates to low-income persons for routine filings within their specialty; for example, they charge $25 for a motion to vacate a default. In addition, 20 percent of their practice is pro bono work.

A practitioner at ULA described how their fee schedule reflects their social justice mission: "We're affordable. We're the only office in the area that has sliding scale fees. . . . It was important to me to make our office accessible . . . to fill a hole between legal aid and the downtown firms. And there are a growing number of people who are not income eligible for legal aid because their income is too high."[25]

El Centro goes one step further and base their fee schedule on the poverty index. The majority of El Centro's clients are low-income Latina women, with issues of divorce and domestic violence. El Centro refuses service to persons with incomes above $25,000 unless they have seven or more dependents. They also have a two-tier fixed-fee schedule, with one set of rates for people making an income below 125 percent of the federal poverty index, and another for those between the poverty index and $25,000. This fee schedule is published in the community. One of the attorneys commented, "We have the idea that everyone can come up with $30.00 per month for a couple of months. And for the most part they do come up with that per month."[26] El Centro does not take contingency fee cases as "there are enough people who will take clients on a contingency fee so that you are really not helping anyone."[27]

Marcelle Roberts adopts a more informal approach than ULA and El Centro. She has a mixed racial clientele, and 60 percent of her clients are women. Ten percent pay flat fees, another 30 to 40 percent pay a reduced rate, and 50 percent pay full hourly rates. When asked about the influence the ability to pay has on her ability to take a client, she replied: "Payment is a consideration; it is not a major consideration; it is not the sole consideration. There have been times when you take someone regardless of the ability to pay . . . because of the client's need and case issues involved. . . . [W]hile such a client may not be able to pay the required fee, some other arrangements such as very modest installments are made."[28]

ULA and El Centro made self-conscious decisions to practice in the communities they were serving. These were the firms most interested in neighborhood practice; thus, their locations were essential to best serve their low-income inner city constituencies. ULA is located in an ethnically diverse, low-income section of town. One lawyer from the firm explained the importance of location this way: "[T]hat location was important to us because we wanted to be in the community we were serving, as opposed to downtown. It's important for . . . ambiance—how you appear when the client gets there. And what kind of services you're providing, in that, are you providing to a community you're a part of or not."[29]

El Centro is located in a store front in a Latino section of a low-income neighborhood, and that neighborhood determined its practice area, since the firm provides legal services predominantly to low-income Hispanic women. As one lawyer explains, "[Although] I didn't choose that, they come in more often for legal help."[30]

Both Smith & Associates and Marcelle Roberts, however, chose downtown locations. Roberts noted that "[t]he choice of downtown location afforded centralized accessibility by clients from various sections of the city, county, and surrounding counties as well."[31]

COMMUNITY AND COLLECTIVE ACTION

The broader social activities of these lawyers include organizing in their community, lobbying in legislative forums on issues related to their clients, working with community-based organizations that meet the social and legal needs of their clients, advocating for their client's interest in traditional bar organizations, and organizing nontraditional bar groups.

Smith chose two arenas for community and collective action. First, he works to improve the economic and social conditions for African Americans in his practice: he has organized local business clients to promote community economic development within African American neighborhoods and has developed a National Association for the Advancement of Colored People free legal advice clinic for the African American community in his city. Second, Smith works both within the traditional bar and for the development of nontraditional legal associations: he has worked with the American Bar Association on a committee on lawyers' public service responsibility and is active in the State Association of Minority Attorneys.

Strickland and Caldwell are significantly involved in several broader feminist activities. They have a long-standing relationship with groups that provide services to battered women and young single women with children. As a board member of the local Young Women's Christian Association, Strickland has assisted the YWCA in becoming identified as the only organization in the community providing services to single mothers. She is also hoping to develop a volunteer legal services program.

Strickland and Caldwell also work as lobbyists at the local, state, and federal level for issues of women. In both state and federal legislatures, Strickland works on several issues, including child support and child custody issues, for those who cannot afford to pay for such representation. She is also the issues chair for the

State Women's Network, a lobbying group, which enables her to organize around women's issues. In addition, she is active in state and national bar associations. Like Smith, Strickland uses local, state, and national bar associations as arenas for advancing the interests of her constituency.

ULA is engaged in political mobilization as well: both lawyers do a great deal of tenant organizing work as a complement to their tenants' rights practice. The two lawyers are also involved in long-standing national lawyer activist groups such as the National Lawyers Guild, and in local lesbian and gay lawyer groups that strategize on community issues and legal problems. They also participate in community actions, overseeing and participating in demonstrations over local housing policy. Both are very active in the volunteer legal services program of the local bar, working in their homeless program and on their AIDS panel.

Lawyer/Client Collaboration

Every firm we interviewed stressed the importance of creating a more collaborative and less traditionally hierarchical relationship with the client, and insisted on the importance of client empowerment, personal agency, and autonomy.[32] These practitioners believe that subordinated people acquire self-respect and a sense of personal agency when they collaborate with their attorney. In addition, by having the client participate in the legal work, a more efficient work and cost allocation can occur.

Amy, a lawyer from ULA, described her collaborative relationships with clients as follows:

> This is [an important issue] because my clients in particular are usually going through some sort of crisis. . . . [T]ake someone who I'm representing in an eviction case. At the end of the case, if they've won or lost, so they keep their house or lose their house. If I've just kind of taken the case over for them and done this great lawyering job and kept their house, at the end of the case they're not going to feel any better or that they've won or that the system has done anything for them, if the whole thing was a completely alienating experience for them, or they weren't talked to, or didn't take part in the decision making. . . . I think a client who takes part in [the process] and makes some decisions, and loses in the classic legal sense, will still sometimes feel better about the whole thing.[33]

When questioned about what principles were most important in guiding her interactions with clients, Caldwell, a practitioner in the family law practice, stated: "The client's autonomy, and my personal and professional integrity. . . . I see my role with the client as being a resource, but not a decision maker. I try very hard not to be paternalistic. . . . A lot of clients come in and want to be told what to do. They're at a crisis point in their lives, they're confused, they're looking for a direction, they're paying me to tell them what to do. I don't do it."[34] Caldwell describes her holistic approach to lawyer/client relationship: she collaborates with her clients, and tries to make the situation that necessitated contact with the legal system a positive one. She sees her role as lawyer to serve as a resource, a facilitator of informed decision, and a counselor, engaging with the client on intimate issues in a professional manner. She further explains: "[My job is] to explain the way the law works, help *them* gather the information that they need and organize it in such a way that is most helpful to them in decision making, point out options to them that they may not be able to see for themselves. . . . I don't see myself as a decision maker."[35] Caldwell believes that her feminist commitment guides her lawyering in several ways. Stating that she will not "tell people what to do," she tries to make the divorce or estate planning process, for example, an empowering experience: "I try to make it a positive growth experience, not something that's negative and a terrible thing that's happened to them. . . . I say to a lot of my women divorce clients, 'This is your last chance for a college scholarship. What have you always wanted to do?' "[36]

She goes on to explain why she facilitates the process of client empowerment in a divorce action: "[T]hat's when people really reveal the most about themselves. . . . I think the connections you make with people when they're going through difficult times are some very honest connections; they're not always nice, and they're not always pretty, but they're very honest, and given the way our world is, we don't have a lot of opportunities for that. In some ways it is a privilege. And so they deserve my respect."[37] Roberts explained, "[T]he practice of law involves more than the strict adherence of legal principles to case facts. . . . [a] demonstrated sense of personal and professional concern for clients must always be manifest in order to maintain attorney-client relationship."[38]

We questioned these lawyers about what they felt was the proper level of engagement with clients and their issues, given the often conflicting mandates of lawyer neutrality and zealous advocacy found in the Lawyer's Code of Professional Responsibility.[39] In response, some practitioners made reference to personal engagement with the legal issues, while others made differentiations mainly with respect to clients. On professional assumptions about neutrality to issues, one ULA practitioner stated, "I understand the importance of teaching that in law school, that you need to be able to anticipate what the other side will argue so that you can respond to it. But the presumption that there is a decent other side you can argue, and that you should feel okay about arguing, it bothers me."[40]

Another practitioner was asked whether she saw conflicts between her notions of client empowerment and counseling and traditional notions of professionalism. She replied:

> [It's an intimate relationship] because of the needs the client has when he or she comes in. . . . Virtually always in a family law situation . . . people come with

a tremendous amount of emotional need and a tremendous amount of ambivalence. They're not going to be able to give you clear direction until they know
where they're going. I think certainly more in family law, but it applies in every
[practice area]. That's one of the reasons I do the practice that I do. . . . I think
I have an approach that's helpful, and that lets them come out of the situation
feeling like a grown-up who's made a good decision, instead of a kid who's been
patted on the head and patronized. [They come out] feeling like a capable adult
who has handled a difficult situation well. I think that's positive.[41]

One practitioner felt a strong responsibility to be neutral when it came to
clients and clients' issues. However, she distinguished her interaction with the client from her interaction with the system. She stated:

When I started in this practice [I] would go to court commissioner hearings
asking for support. I was a good girl scout and read the statute. And I even
argued about the statute. . . . The commissioners would look at me cross-eyed
[and say] I get $100 bucks a kid. Period. They would say 'I don't care what he
makes.' I say, 'But that's not what the statute says.'

Well, I got emotionally involved with the system's response to these issues.
That's what fueled a lot of my appellate practice; I just appealed them all. And
gradually we got support standards because of that behavior. So my personal
emotional engagement is on how the system deals with these issues that affected
people's daily lives and how they either were indifferent or misused the process
to affect people's daily lives. That was my emotional engagement.[42]

The Attention to Workplace

The feminist and critical lawyering literature identifies the workplace environment
as a key aspect of transformative practice.[43] Humanistic and nonhierarchical approaches to social change require a workplace that embodies these goals. All the
practitioners interviewed structured their workplaces to accord with their social
justice values.

HUMANISTIC ENVIRONMENT OF THE OFFICE

The all-women law firms saw the gender makeup of the firm as central to the
creation of a humanistic environment. Urban Legal Advocates notes that the firm
remains all-women by design, a fact they do not publicize and which has never
been challenged. One lawyer from ULA was quite clear about the relationship
between their decision not to hire to men and the creation of a humane environment: "[we're all women, and that's by design. Although we've had male interns,
we would never hire a man on a full-time basis for a couple of reasons. One is
just sort of our internal office atmosphere—I'm not necessarily putting these in
order of priority—sometimes it's very stressful to be a lawyer and you deal with a

lot of assholes, and we strive to create our office environment as sort of the home you come back to, that's a supportive environment. And I think that's much easier to create with all women." [44]

When Strickland and Caldwell were asked whether the gender makeup of their firm was by design or accidental, the lawyers responded that feminism, rather than gender per se, determines their hiring decisions. Caldwell reports:

> Some of my best friends are men. Seriously, my best friend is a man who's not a lawyer. I wouldn't say categorically that there would not be place for a man in this law firm. There is not a place in this law firm for somebody who is not a feminist, in terms of philosophy and working relationships. Somebody who is not a feminist is not going to be comfortable here. It's just going to be problems from day one.
>
> The five of us make decisions from consensus. Somebody who is not happy with a consensus model of working on things, and a desire to find a compromise that everybody is happy with, rather than saying 'No, I say it's going to be done this way, and so it is' . . . that kind of a person is just not going to be comfortable here, and we wouldn't be comfortable having that kind of a person here. I can think of a lot of women I wouldn't want to have here, too. [45]

Urban Legal Advocates also felt their gender makeup makes an important public educational statement: "Another [important reason] is the statement we want to make to world. We promote ourselves as an all-woman law collective, in part because a certain community is attracted to that, and we educate people who see that this entity exists." [46]

Smith & Associates also attempts to create a humane environment. Smith notes: "[O]ne of the goals of the firm was to have a firm where people are treated in a respectful manner. We don't have an office where some people are expected to make coffee and do grunt work." [47]

Closer relationships with paralegal employees contribute to a more humane environment as well. Smith, for example, holds weekly meetings with the paralegal. Strickland and Caldwell also highlighted the position and role of their paralegal: "Susan Carey, the paralegal, not only has her name up top on the letterhead, but has been involved from the beginning in terms of planning all of this. . . . I've worked with Susan since 1978. We have a very close professional relationship and a tremendous amount of respect for one another. She can do things that I can't do. I know it, she knows it. There isn't this concern about status. Or this concern about 'I'm the lawyer, so you have to go to the courthouse and file.' " [48] Strickland and Caldwell indicated a desire to integrate their workplace with their family and personal lives. The lawyers' and paralegal's teenage children, who do messenger and housekeeping type tasks in the firm, are part of the support staff. Caldwell recounts: "We talked about how neat it would be to have our kids be able to work for us. And they all do. That's been nice, a nice bonus. It's been great for my kids to see what I do during the day, and they've gotten another look at me; a different kind of view of me which has been really a lot of fun."[49]

NONTRADITIONAL ORGANIZATIONAL STRUCTURES

Additionally, the firms have created structures that significantly challenge the traditional law firm model. The organizational structures of these firms span the continuum from the collective to women-run business to the combined law firm/ nonprofit.

Since the inception of their firm, Urban Legal Advocates has been organized as a collective. The nonlawyer office manager and paralegal are equal collective members, earning the same wage as the lawyers. As collective members, all receive bonuses based on the same formula of seniority and status. This firm also utilizes a collective decision-making structure for office management. When asked to define their office structure, an ULA lawyer responded: "We call ourselves a feminist collective. That means partially how we do things internally, in terms of how we treat each other and our lack of hierarchical structure between attorneys and nonattorneys."[50]

In contrast to the collective model adopted by ULA, the Strickland & Caldwell firm use a more traditional partner model. However, they believe the success of their all-women firm makes a significant social statement. According to Strickland and Caldwell, the experience of developing the firm has allowed them to demystify managerial abilities and duties. Caldwell states:

> The thing about this that is just such a riot is that I always thought that these guys really knew how to do business and that I didn't. [Rather,] I didn't think that I couldn't, but I thought they know stuff that I don't know, and they're interested in this and they want to do it and I should just be grateful that they're handling the malpractice insurance, and I don't have to mess with that. . . . There just isn't any magic to this. Anybody with common sense and friends can do it. And the thing about Strickland and me, I think, that made it possible for us to do as well as we did as quickly as we did, is that it was very easy for us to say 'I don't know, I'm going to call somebody.' I don't know how easily guys do this, as least the guys that we worked with. Anything that we came up with that we didn't know about, we knew somebody who did, and it was usually a woman.[51]

The firm that most closely connects the private practice with the public interest nonprofit model is El Centro. For the first two years of practice, the office was funded by the local Catholic parish. In the third year of the practice, the firm was restructured to place the management responsibilities in a board of directors. The board of directors consists of Latino community members, attorneys, and law professors and makes decisions on budgets and salaries. El Centro shifted to the board of directors model to increase chances of obtaining foundation and government grants and decrease dependence on attorney's fees. The lawyers believe that compromising some of their decision-making independence with the creation of a board was worthwhile, given the potential outside financial support for low-income representations that the board could bring to the firm.[52]

Factors Affecting the Continued Viability of the Practices

The values these practitioners are committed to—social justice, collaboration with clients and collegial workplaces—must be negotiated within a broader social context. Their ability to create and continue alternative practices is both assisted and constrained by institutions of the legal profession, economics of the market, and relationships with the client groups.

Attitudes of Mainstream Practice

Our evidence shows that attitudes of mainstream practice can have a positive effect, compelling lawyers to found their own, alternative practices. However, mainstream attitudes can also have a negative effect, threatening the economic viability of alternative practices.[53]

In large part, Strickland & Caldwell was formed in reaction to biased attitudes toward women attorneys and family law in traditional firm. The two women partners were initially part of a large firm, comprised of forty lawyers, ten of whom were partners. When this firm merged with another firm to establish a corporate practice and increase its status, the merger brought "a totally different alignment of gender and of practices to the firm." Caldwell explains: "Strickland and I had mixed feelings about this merger for lots of reasons. I understood the need to make a leap to be perceived as something other than a family law firm, generally. I understood that. But a lot of what was going on felt more like an excited male-bonding experience than a business merger."[54]

After the merger, the two women, working in family law, continued to bring in more money than any other partner, and family law remained the economic base of the firm. However, the firm remained focused on building a reputation in corporate practice, and Strickland and Caldwell recognized that the merger was at least partially motivated by a professional devaluation of family law. Strickland noted:

> What never changed, and to this day I know it's true over there, is this sort of mixed feeling of liking the money family law brought in, but feeling that because that was where most of the money came from, there was a loss of status. It was interesting, you know, because there [are] a lot of problems with family law practice, you have more accounts receivable, you have more complaining clients, a lot

of things that lawyers hate, you have a lot of it in family law that you don't have in corporate practice. Because of that messiness of it, people didn't really like it, and because it reflected on their status. They didn't like being thought of as a family law firm.[55]

Caldwell described how the devaluation of her practice area and herself professionally had a concrete effect on her earnings in comparison to her male counterparts. She recounted: "The other thing I heard was 'You don't need to worry about how much money you make, you have a husband who has a good job. I'm the sole support of my family,' or 'My wife doesn't make nearly as much as your husband does. So if we look at total family income, then let's be fair about this.' "[56]

The environment of the corporate firm, then, compelled Strickland and Caldwell to develop an alternative practice. A report in a Legal Careers Survey of Wisconsin Attorneys (1992–93) shows that Strickland and Caldwell's experience in the larger firm, and their decision to develop their own practice, is not unusual. The report indicates that nearly 40 percent of women work in firms where at least half the attorneys are women. The survey also indicates that 29 percent of the women reported that "gender affects" their practice area, as opposed to 2.9 percent for men; 25.7 percent of women stated that "gender affects" their client contact, as opposed to 4.1 percent for men; and 39.9 percent of the women reported that "gender affects" their job satisfaction, as opposed to 4.6 percent of the men.[57]

Not only do the attitudes in mainstream practice shape the development of alternative feminist firms, but they also compel lawyers interested in representing minority businesses to establish alternative practices. The Smith firm has developed a practice that is largely based on their unique position to represent minority businesses. However, over the last several years, large corporate practices have identified this area as a target for growth, and they are now hiring attorneys of color to provide these services. Thus Smith predicts he will soon struggle to maintain a socially committed practice in direct competition with established corporate firms.

We must begin to view the relationship between traditional and critical practice as one of complex interaction and reaction. At times, the bias and discrimination in mainstream practice compels alternative lawyers to develop their own firms; at other times, business interests of mainstream firms threaten to coopt private critical practitioners.

Organized Bar Activities

Organized bar associations are both hostile to and supportive of transformative work. Our study indicates that the critical practitioners use bar associations for professional support as well as to advocate on behalf of their constituent groups.[58]

Marcelle Roberts is involved in the State Bar Committee on the Participation of Women in the Bar, is a member of the National Association of Female Executives, and participates in the Minority Attorneys Group. Discussing why the bar meetings are helpful, she states, "Just as I learned as a law student, your concept of the right answer is . . . not always the case in working with legal matters. I learned when I went into solo practice that you can have a perspective on a case that does not eventually pan out in court. So, it has been important to talk with others, often at the courthouse, so as not to be out of touch on legal issues. I enjoy those opportunities."[59]

Interestingly, all the attorneys we interviewed cited the importance of bar activities in their professional lives. When Smith embarked on his career, he specifically sought to make the bar association more sensitive to racial issues. One lawyer at Urban Legal Advocates considers her work with the local bar on behalf of homeless persons and persons with AIDS an important element of her practice.

However, the attorneys note that the organized bar's official position often can act against the interests of their clients. According to Strickland, the official position of the Association of Matrimonial Lawyers regarding the value of women's work in the house and on custody is detrimental to the interest of women. While she agrees with the usefulness of bar groups for networking and support, she often finds herself battling against their traditional positions.

Funding the Firms

All the firms must grapple with funding, and the diverse funding schemes utilized by these lawyers allow them to maintain financially viable private practices with social justice missions.

The firms have taken several different routes to enable them to maintain critical practices and make a living. For example, El Centro, the community practice based in the Latino neighborhood, imaginatively combines grant funds with client fees. El Centro was started by grant funds and maintains a nonprofit tax-exempt status, although they require all clients to pay some amount. They meet the Internal Revenue guidelines by maintaining a limit on the income of the clients they serve.

In addition to grant funds, some of the lawyers utilize public/court-granted monies to pay for a particular client representation. The monies are connected to a representation that is required by a court, statute, or constitution. Marcelle Roberts uses guardian ad litem appointments in both juvenile and family court as a funding source. While the payments may not be substantial, they do assist in defraying the overhead costs of law practice.

Labor union contracts for worker legal insurance plans provide a third source of funding. Urban Legal Advocates, for example, has contracts with both public and private labor unions,[60] providing the firm with a small but consistent monthly income.

Strickland and Caldwell structure their private practice to sustain a part-time public interest practice: their client base is comprised mainly of upper-income persons, allowing the firm to spend 20 percent of their time on reduced-fee, pro bono, or public interest representations of poor persons, or for long-term clients unable to pay, with whom they have a commitment. Strickland states, "The number of cases is probably small; it's the hours, though, that's the difference. I would imagine though probably 20 percent of my hours a week are in reduced pay or no-pay cases. A part of that, I spend some time getting other lawyers to do pro bono [work] too."[61]

Personal Income

Considering the financial compensation the lawyers receive, the struggle to maintain their practice often seems overwhelming. Many of the practitioners find they must trade personal financial gain to maintain a socially committed practice.

These practitioners earn incomes ranging from the mid $20,000s through $100,000. Their choice to serve different socioeconomic constituencies and utilize different sources of funding often results in low renumeration. One Urban Legal Advocate lawyer discusses the issue of financial compensation: "I think people have different definitions of being kept afloat. I think I make a very low income for a typical attorney, and I'm comfortable with it. Based on our experience with interviewing for a new attorney, most lawyers aren't comfortable with a low wage. I also have a personal life set-up that I can afford it, so I guess I'm privileged in that way also."[62] This same lawyer went on to note, "I think I'm very privileged to be able to make a living at something that feels worth doing, that I enjoy doing and am good at all at the same time. In the past I had to get those things in different places . . . and I'm very lucky to have those all in what I do now."[63]

Smith describes his practice as a struggle to keep the rent and overhead paid while carrying contingency-based employment discrimination and class action cases. Marcelle Roberts also indicates that attorneys in contingency cases must often "carry the case" to conclusion by paying disbursements and expense advances. Both Smith and Roberts feel that contingency fee arrangements contribute to the "constant financial tension" and financial insecurity they experience.

Identities

Critical lawyering presents a model for practicing law while maintaining a dual commitment to subordinated clients and lawyer integrity. In the alternative practices we studied, the attorneys search for a consonance between their professional role and their personal identity.

Many have argued that lawyers with the same racial, sexual, and/or class affiliations as their clients are best able to identify with and be sensitive to those clients' needs.[64] The practitioners we interviewed, however, demonstrate a more complex relationship between personal identity and commitment to subordinated people. Attorneys who share the same origins and orientations as their constituencies, and those who do not, effectively represent their clients.[65]

El Centro's two white male lawyers are clearly committed to the Latina women of the neighborhood, and the lawyers have built over 60 percent of their practice around the needs of their clients. The lawyers' Catholic background and experience working in Latin America gave them the language knowledge and cultural understanding needed to effectively serve this client group.

Marcelle Roberts, an African American woman, represents clients from diverse backgrounds. She stated, "It's people first of all. It's diverse. . . . I don't know, I couldn't even tell you what the racial breakdown [is], period. It's not more minority, it seems to be fairly even among the minorities; not all African Americans, some who are Hispanic, there are some who are Hmong. It's pretty diverse. It really is. I have thought about it, and I have thought, what do I have here?"[66] Although they are known in the community as feminist activists, the Strickland & Caldwell firm represents equal numbers of men and women in their divorce practice. They do not feel representing men conflicts with their feminist principles.

That these practitioners are able to provide client-sensitive services across race and gender lines is interesting in light of the extensive recent literature, which often argues the necessity for separate providers. These practitioners seem to be able to move across these barriers because of their understanding of client concerns and their humanistic approaches. Others, though, exhibit close involvement with communities of which they are a part. The practitioners who evidence a professional congruence between their race, class, or sexual orientation and their practice speak of the symbolic importance of this consistency. Several of the African American lawyers are very involved in bar groups that promote the participation of minorities in the legal profession, and are active in minority community development work. One of the lesbian attorneys devotes 35 percent of her practice to lesbian family law.

Conclusion

Practices for Social Justice

As we learn that the public interest sphere cannot easily be expanded, and worry that even in its current small size it may not be sustained, we must look again to private practice as a site for transformative lawyering. Examining the work of these private firms is one step toward deconstructing the separate spheres of public interest law and private practice.

The innovative practices of the firms discussed above illustrate a hybrid model of lawyering with many advantages: the attorneys provide client-sensitive representation, create a supportive workplace, and evidence community and political commitments while maintaining a successful private practice. Examples of critical lawyering, these practices offer a desirable model for the use of law for social change.

These practices must be understood as a positive reaction to changes in the public interest bar since the 1960s. Not only have the demographics of the bar changed since then, diversifying the lawyer population and the substantive interests of those in the profession, but the existence of the professional public interest bar during the last twenty years has legitimated a lifetime career working on behalf of subordinated persons. The bar has also created additional funding mechanisms, such as private bar support and government and foundation funding for legal services. Hopefully, the new private practitioners can utilize these sources. It will not be easy, though, for these private firms to continue to provide transformative services: the vagaries of funding, the difficulties of providing collective activities while handling individual cases, and the low remuneration threaten their viability.

One might argue that what we are proposing is a valorization of the privatization of public service representation of poor people[67] in light of cuts in state support for the Legal Services Corporation and other forms of legal aid. However, our study of the firms indicates that continued public dollars may be required to sustain these firms. For example, several of the practices we described are dependent on compensated public defender and guardian ad litem appointments. It may be true, however, as it is in some Western European countries, that if the funding and representation is more broadly spread through the bar, increased government dollars for legal services might follow.[68]

Most importantly, we believe that bridging public interest and private bar practices will provide subordinated groups with access to as many resources as possible. The critical lawyers we studied are well aware they are providing service to clients often ineligible for legal services. Urban Legal Advocates, for example, describes their clientele as the working poor who are not eligible for legal services. El Centro represents people who do meet the legal services income guidelines for eligibility, but whose problems fall into an area not addressed by the local legal services office, or whose income is just above the legal service guidelines. The critical lawyers' hybrid linking of public interest full-time staff attorneys and the private bar will improve the funding base for both groups, facilitate attention to diverse client needs, and improve advocacy for reform of law school and bar groups.

Questions for the Future

We speculate that critical lawyers will be located in the field in increasing numbers. Our student researchers are attracted to alternative private practices and are skeptical about the viability of nonprofit full-time staff attorney careers.[69]

If, as we predict, the critical lawyering model will appeal to lawyers and law students concerned with social justice issues, how will the public interest sector of the bar be affected? Will the professionalism project we described earlier have a negative effect on the development of private critical lawyering? We think these new firms should be valorized and recognized and that the two spheres should be further linked.

We think there is a need for more research on critical lawyers in private practice, emphasizing other transformative aspects of their work. Specifically, their links to community-based organizations and workplace emphases should be further researched. In the future, new institutional settings could develop to link the two spheres.[70]

Resistances will remain. Can these critical lawyers do the demanding and intensive legal work that the public interest sector performs, given their position in the legal market? Does the attention of the new practitioners to workplace and lawyer/client interaction distract from their ability to battle against powerful social and economic structures? Will the income from paying clients be sufficient to support the socially conscious lawyering of the firms? We can expect that the institutional and ideological struggles will continue.

Notes

We wish to thank the students in the fall 1992 and 1993 seminars on "Lawyering in the Public Interest," at the University of Wisconsin Law School for their contributions, as well as the lawyers who graciously gave of their time and spoke so candidly with us about their experiences. We would also like to thank William L. F. Felstiner for his support and the Sarat-Scheingold Cause Lawyering Group for their helpful suggestions.

1. Ruth Buchanan and Louise G. Trubek, "Resistances and Possibilities: A Critical and Practical Look at Public Interest Lawyering," *New York University Review of Law and Social Change* 19 (1992), 687–719. Lois Johnson, "The New Public Interest Law: From Old Theories to New Agenda," *Boston University Public Interest Law Journal* 1 (1991), 169–191.

2. This phrase was originally coined by Trubek in Louise G. Trubek, "Critical Lawyering: Towards a New Public Interest Practice," *Boston University Public Interest Law Journal* 1 (1991), 49–56. Interestingly, a recent publication by a group of English academics and practitioners also uses the phrase "critical lawyers." Ian Grigg-Spall and Paddy Ireland, eds., *The Critical Lawyers' Handbook* (London: Pluto Press, 1992).

3. It is interesting to note that at the same time that the nonprofits were being developed, there was a growth in private practices, mostly founded by young lawyers, to serve various emerging social concerns. These "private public interest law firms" hoped to represent unrepresented groups and clients—environmental organizations, consumer cases, and women—and they worked closely with the then new nonprofit public interest law firms. Many of the practices have not survived, and others have changed and modified over the years. The existence of these alternative firms challenges the historical insistence that separate spheres between socially oriented and private practice must and do exist. *See* Marlise James, *The People's Lawyers: The Radicalization of the Legal Profession* (New York: Holt, Rinehart and Winston, 1973). *See also* Council for Public Interest Law, *Balancing the Scales*

of Justice: Financing Public Interest Law in America (Washington, D.C.: Council for Public Interest Law, 1976), 133–146.

4. The book describes the public interest law centers as "nonprofit, tax exempt groups that devote a large share of their programs to providing legal representation to otherwise unrepresented interests in court or administrative agency proceeding involving questions of important public policy." Council for Public Interest Law, *Balancing the Scales of Justice: Financing Public Interest Law in America*, 81.

5. Samuel J. Brakel, *Judicare: Public Funds, Private Lawyers, and Poor People* (Chicago: American Bar Foundation, 1974).

6. Jeremy Cooper, *Keyguide to Information Sources in Public Interest Law* (New York: Mansell, 1991), 38–39.

7. Efforts to link full-time public interest practitioners, law school clinicians, and private bar lawyers have been attempted in recent years. For example, the private bar has rallied to the defense of the embattled Legal Services Corporation. There has been resistance, however, from the full-time public interest and legal services lawyers who still adhere to the traditional 1960s "law reform" model, oriented around bringing about structural change through focused casework and class action litigation. As a result, the private bar pro bono lawyers are seen as assistants to the legitimate public interest (and legal services) lawyers, but not as transformative lawyers in their own right. Similar tensions have occurred in joint projects among legal academics and the legal services lawyers, who believe law school clinics and students (as well as private attorneys) have little value for poor people and take too much time away from the "real" business of the legal service practice.

8. Robert Granfield, *Making Elite Lawyers* (New York: Routledge, Chapman, and Hall, 1992), 90. *See also* Martin Gottlieb, "A Lawyer for the People Plans to Fight on His Own," *New York Times*, January 28, 1996.

9. Gerald Lopez, *Rebellious Lawyering: One Chicano's Vision of Progressive Law Practice* (Boulder, Colo.: Westview Press, 1992). Anthony Alfieri, "Reconstructive Poverty Law Practice: Learning the Lessons of Client Narrative," *Yale Law Journal* 100 (1991), 2107–2147.

10. Louise G. Trubek, "The Worst of Times . . . and the Best of Times? Lawyering for Poor Clients Today," *Fordham Urban Law Journal* 22 (1995), 1123–1140.

11. Buchanan and Trubek, "Resistances and Possibilities." See also Lopez, *Rebellious Lawyering*, 1–10.

12. Paul R. Tremblay, "Rebellious Lawyering, Regnant Lawyering and Street-Level Bureaucracy," *Hastings Law Journal* 43 (1992), 947–970, 950.

13. For a discussion of a 1960s alternative workplace, *see* Robert Lefcourt, "The First Law Commune," in *Law against the People*, ed. Robert Lefcourt (New York: Vintage Books, 1971), 310–326.

14. The earlier literature on cause lawyering was written about lawyers practicing in the 1960s and 1970s. Since that time, there have been significant changes in the demographics of the bar as the number of women and people of color have increased.

15. Our research was initially linked to the course entitled "Lawyering in the Public Interest," which explores the changing institutional and theoretical underpinnings of public interest practice, and focuses on the new literature describing "critical" methods of public interest lawyering. The course, taught by Louise G. Trubek, examines the history, theory, skills, institutional structures, and locations that constitute a new and critical form of public interest lawyering.

In an effort to ground theory in practice, a fieldwork component was added to the course. The fieldwork focused on the gaps, intersections, and tensions that may exist between progressive theories of lawyering and actual practice: students considered theoretical readings on the tensions between theoretics and practice, and then interviewed practitioners who in some way incorporated a political vision into their representational choices and lawyering strategies.

16. The account in this section is based exclusively on extended interviews with the lawyers in these firms. The names of the lawyers have been changed to protect the anonymity of the lawyers.

17. Strickland [pseud.], interview by author Kransberger, May 20, 1993. Caldwell [pseud.], interview by author Kransberger, May 20, 1993.

18. Amy [pseud.], interview by author Kransberger, June 6, 1994.

19. Smith [pseud.], interview by Carol Rose Ashley, December 12, 1992.

20. Founder [pseud.], interview by Tracey E. Conner, December 2, 1993. John [pseud.], interview by Suzanne M. Kopp, October 22, 1993.

21. Marcelle Roberts, [pseud.], interview by Susan M. Cotten, October 26, 1993.

22. The approach we use builds upon the work of Peter Gabel and Paul Harris. See Gabel and Harris, "Building Power and Breaking Images: Critical Legal Theory and the Practice of Law," *New York University Review of Law and Social Change* 11 (1983), 369–411.

23. John, interview.

24. Amy, interview.

25. Ibid.

26. John, interview.

27. Ibid.

28. Roberts, interview.

29. Amy, interview.

30. John, interview.

31. Roberts, interview.

32. Lucie White, "Subordination, Rhetorical Skills, and Sunday Shoes: Notes on the Hearing of Mrs. G.," *Buffalo Law Review* 38 (1990), 1–58. *See also* Alfieri, "Reconstructive Poverty Law Practice." In contrast, the mainstream literature outlines lawyer control and paternalism as characteristic of most traditional lawyer/client relationships. Ann Shalleck, "The Feminist Transformation of Lawyering: A Response to Naomi Cahn," *Hastings Law Journal* 43 (1992), 1071–1079. William L. F. Felstiner and Austin Sarat, "Enactments of Power: Negotiating Reality and Responsibility in Lawyer/Client Interactions," *Cornell Law Review* 77 (1992), 1447–1498.

33. Amy, interview.

34. Caldwell, interview.

35. Ibid.

36. Ibid.

37. Ibid.

38. Roberts, interview.

39. Some of the new public interest lawyering literature discusses the ways in which traditional notions of lawyer neutrality and conduct can be problematic when dealing with traditionally subordinated groups, and thus suggests alternative conceptions of lawyer engagement with clients and their issues. *See* White, "Subordination, Rhetorical Skills and Sunday Shoes"; Alfieri, "Reconstructive Poverty Law Practice."

40. Amy, interview.

41. Caldwell, interview.

42. Strickland, interview.

43. *See* Trubek, "Critical Lawyering, Towards a New Public Interest Practice," 56. Nancy Dowd, "Work and Family: The Gender Paradox and the Limitation of Gender Discrimination Analysis in Restructuring the Workplace," *Harvard Civil Rights–Civil Liberties*

Law Review 24 (1989), 78–172. See also David Chambers, "Accommodation and Satisfaction: Women and Men Lawyers and the Balance of Work and Family," *Law and Social Inquiry* 14 (1989), 251–287.

44. Amy, interview.

45. Caldwell, interview.

46. Amy, interview.

47. Smith, interview.

48. Caldwell, interview.

49. Ibid.

50. Amy, interview.

51. Caldwell, interview.

52. John, interview.

53. John Heinz and Edward O. Laumann, *Chicago Lawyers: The Social Structure of the Bar* (New York: Russell Sage, 1982).

54. Caldwell, interview.

55. Strickland, interview.

56. Caldwell, interview.

57. Virginia Sapiro, "Gender Equity in Wisconsin Legal Careers," *Wisconsin Lawyer* 67 (February 1994), 7–12.

58. Nelson and D. Trubek identify bar associations as important areas for both the development of practice skills and arenas for social change. Nelson and D. Trubek, "Arenas of Professionalism: The Professional Ideologies of Lawyers in Context," in *Lawyers' Ideals/ Lawyers' Practices: Transformations of the American Legal Profession,* ed. Nelson, Trubek and Rayman L. Solomon (Ithaca, N.Y.: Cornell University Press, 1992), 177–214.

59. Roberts, interview.

60. In her writings, Seron has identified legal insurance plans as new sources of funding for provision of legal services for middle class clients. Carroll Seron, "Managing Entrepreneurial Legal Services: The Transformation of Small-Firm Practice," in *Lawyers' Ideals/ Lawyers' Practices* ed. Nelson, Trubek, and Solomon, 63–92.

61. Strickland, interview.

62. Amy, interview.

63. Ibid.

64. For a discussion of this issue see Dan Danielsen and Karen Engle, introduction to *After Identity,* ed. Danielsen and Engle (New York: Routledge, 1995), xiii–xix.

65. *See* Martha Fineman, "Feminist Legal Scholarship and Women's Gendered Lives," in *Lawyers in a Postmodern World,* ed. Maureen Cain and Christine B. Harrington (Birmingham, United Kingdom: Open University Press, 1994), 229–246. A study of teachers of African American children reached a similar conclusion. Gloria Ladson-Billings, *The Dreamkeepers: Successful Teachers of African American Children* (San Francisco: Jossey-Bass, 1994).

66. Roberts, interview.

67. We would like to thank Joel Handler for this insight. For an interesting discussion of privatization see Ted Kolderie, "The Two Different Concepts of Privatization," *Public Administration Review* 46 (1986), 285–291.

68. Western European countries have an alternative legal aid model where the bulk of service to low-income people is provided by private practitioners who are paid directly by state monies for each transaction. This legal aid model assists the "social practitioners." Another important distinction between the United States and Western European countries is the rigid income definition that determines eligibility. In many European countries, the

income limits for eligibility for subsidy for legal representation are higher than in the United States and subject to a sliding scale. A greater percentage of the population is able to receive legal services through a private practitioner, and the practitioner receives some subsidy from the state. For a discussion of Nordic, English, and Dutch legal aid programs see Jeremy Cooper, "English Legal Services: A Tale of Diminishing Returns," *Maryland Journal of Contemporary Legal Issues* 5, no. 2 (1994), 247–269. Jon T. Johnsen, "Nordic Legal Aid," *Maryland Journal of Contemporary Legal Issues* 5, no. 2 (1994), 301–331. Nick Huls, "From *Pro Deo* Practice to a Subsidized Welfare State Provision: Twenty-Five Years of Providing Legal Services to the Poor in the Netherlands," *Maryland Journal of Contemporary Legal Issues* 5, no. 2 (1994), 333–348.

69. Robert Stover, *Making It and Breaking It* (Urbana: University of Illinois Press, 1989). Rebecca Arbogast et al., "Revitalizing Public Interest Lawyering in the 1990's: The Story of One Effort to Address the Problem of Homelessness," *Howard Law Journal* 34 (1991), 93–113.

70. Trubek, "The Worst of Times . . . The Best of Times?," 1123–1140.

CHAPTER 8

Destruction of Houses and Construction of a Cause

Lawyers and Bedouins in the Israeli Courts

RONEN SHAMIR & SARA CHINSKI

The focus of this chapter is on lawyers who represent Bedouins in Israeli courts. Specifically, we are interested in cases involving—from the formal standpoint of the law—the "vast phenomenon of illegal Bedouin construction" in violation of the state's planning and construction laws. We posit that these constructions, illegal for having been built without appropriate construction permits, assume broader significance when evaluated in light of the Bedouin historical and cultural experience under Israeli state control. We want to briefly provide readers with this experience in order to clarify our reasons for looking at legal representation in such matters as a form of "lawyering for a cause."

The Israeli Bedouins are an indigenous population of roughly one hundred thousand desert dwellers who are currently considered one of the most underprivileged sectors in Israeli society.[1] In the early 1950s the Bedouins were uprooted from most of the lands that they inhabited and were concentrated in an area of the Israeli Negev (the southern desert area of the country) that became officially known as the "Enclosure Zone." Until the mid-1960s the Bedouins were subjected to a strict military government rule that confined them to the Enclosure Zone and regulated the minute details of their daily life.

A considerable proportion of the lands from which the Bedouins were evacuated were registered as state property under the provisions of available land laws. In the 1970s, the government initiated a new program of Bedouin transfer. This time, from their scattered forms of dwellings in tents, shacks, and huts into planned townships where they were expected to modernize their way of life. Moshe Dayan, then in charge of the Department of Agriculture, had set the tone already in 1963:

We should transform the Bedouins into an urban proletariat—in industry, services, construction, and agriculture. 88% of the Israeli population are not farmers,
let the Bedouins become the same. Indeed, this will be a radical move which
means that the Bedouin would not live on his land with his herds, but would
become an urbanite who comes home in the afternoon and puts his slippers on.
His children would be accustomed to a father who wears trousers, does not carry
a Shabaria [the traditional Bedouin knife] and does not search for vermin in
public. The children would go to school with their hair properly combed. This
would be a revolution, but it may be fixed within two generations. Without coercion but with governmental direction . . . *the phenomenon of the Bedouins will
disappear.*[2]

The Bedouins—suspecting that by agreeing to move into townships they
waived their ownership rights over lands that they considered as their own—had
been more than reluctant to respond to these resettlement plans. At present, more
than half of the Bedouin population is still scattered across the Negev in more
than a hundred "unrecognized" settlements without running water, electricity, and
other basic utilities.[3]

A whole series of practices were developed by the state in order to make the
lives of recalcitrant Bedouins as unbearable as possible. In 1985, the government
accepted the recommendation of an intergovernmental committee and began to
aggressively rely on the available Law of Planning and Construction as means of
preventing the Bedouins from improving upon their life conditions outside the
townships. The designated areas for the townships were treated as the only lands
upon which Bedouins could legally construct houses. All other areas—not being
regulated under the state's planning programs—became forbidden zones. New
constructions could not be legally built, thousands of already existing dwelling
units became potential targets for demolition, and a massive number of demolition orders have been issued to Bedouins all across the desert.[4] The new policy
is backed by a host of surveillance mechanisms: The Bedouins are periodically
photographed from above and frequently followed on the ground. An impressive
machinery—involving state officials at various levels, supervisors, geographers and
demographers, pilots and drivers, heavy demolition equipment, helicopters and
four-wheel vehicles, and a whole range of communication devices—envelops the
lives of the Bedouins as means of detecting any attempt to improve or expand
existing dwelling units or add new ones.

For the Bedouin, the law is not a source of rights but yet another instrument
of order. The law is not a remote entity but an all-encompassing web of rules that
one must learn to avoid or subvert. Most important, the strict and context-blind
implementation of the Law of Planning and Construction allows the authorities
to avoid having to confront the Bedouins' claims of land ownership. In order to
advance such claims, Bedouins must mobilize resources that are typically beyond
their reach.[5] Further, from the formal standpoint of the law, claims of ownership

or possession of land cannot excuse Bedouins who face criminal charges for violating the Law of Planning and Construction. Thus, from possible claimants in land ownership disputes between them and the government, the Bedouins are transformed into criminal defendants, accused of having built various types of constructions without a permit, or accused of having failed to comply with an administrative demolition order issued against them. In other words, a central characteristic of the Bedouin encounter with the law is that the original collective conflict over land is diffused and fragmented into an endless series of minute and meticulous practices in which the Bedouins are targeted as individual law-breakers.[6]

We wish to trace and analyze this legal deconstruction, and we wish to do so by studying the practices of lawyers who represent them in court. In principle, and given the discretionary powers of courts not to issue demolition orders as a matter of course, lawyers who represent Bedouins may try to convince judges that the formal application of the law to the Bedouins unjustly ignores, and, worse still, perpetuates, historical injustice and cultural oppression. Broad agendas, however, seldom determine the practicalities that lawyers face in their routine representation functions. The prosecution has at its disposal an impressive arsenal of precedents that deny the relevance of the past to the law-breaking activities of the present. Further, such legal tactics typically require greater professional and fiscal resources than the ordinary Bedouin client has at his or her disposal.

Another option open to lawyers is to single out "their" particular case and to plead for some kind of special treatment. In so doing, they increase the likelihood of success. Yet, and this is a dilemma we wish to explore, in so doing they further isolate the case from the general collective context, thus contributing, by their mere position in the legal field, to the reproduction of forces that prevent the Bedouin case from becoming a Bedouin cause. It is around this dilemma, its sources and consequences, that the first part of this study is organized. In its second part, we turn to some broader aspects of legal representation on behalf of Bedouins, tracing the web of representation and its various elements by looking closely at the career of one case that did reach Israel's High Court of Justice.

The Bedouins generate considerable legal work and income for many local lawyers in Beer-Sheba, the regional center whose courts have jurisdiction over the areas in which the Bedouins reside. In fact, there are hardly any lawyers in this town that have not at one time or another represented a Bedouin client. In what follows, we do not try to provide a comprehensive analysis of legal representation on behalf of the Bedouin population. We believe we have identified a core group of lawyers who represent Bedouins in matters of land disputes and demolition orders on a routine and quite intense basis. Our modest purpose here is to provide some insights concerning their patterns of representation, without asserting that these patterns exhaust the terrain.[7]

In general, lawyers come to the task of representing Bedouins in matters concerning housing and property rights by two different tracks. First, a pool of local lawyers with some experience and expertise in handling such cases has developed over the years. These lawyers are directly approached by the Bedouins and provide services for very modest fees. A second option open for Bedouins is to turn to the Association for Support and Defense of Bedouin Rights in Israel (hereafter the Bedouin Association) for free, or almost free legal aid. The Bedouin Association, in turn, pays designated lawyers who assume cases on a retainer basis. At present, the Bedouin Association routinely works with one such lawyer, although it sometimes hires the services of other available lawyers as well. There is little difference in the style of lawyering that is provided through these two tracks. It is mainly the latter form of lawyering, however, that carries an implicit promise of developing more comprehensive legal tactics on behalf of Bedouins. In the first part of this essay we outline the profile of one lawyer who is directly employed by the Bedouins. In the second part, we trace some particular aspects of lawyering on behalf of the Bedouin Association.

As a preliminary comment, however, we wish to emphasize that the lawyers we discuss do not think of themselves as a distinct breed or as sharing a similar professional or ideological trajectory. We identified a rather heterogeneous group: lawyers of different ages, some novices to the profession, others at mid-career, and yet others toward the end of their professional lives. Some are financially secure, others have very modest incomes. Some are public figures, others are not. Some devote considerable time to the representation of Bedouins while others have many other types of clients and cases.

All the lawyers with whom we spoke share a general sympathy for the Bedouins' plight. At the same time, most of them express doubts as to whether a moral commitment to the Bedouins' cause is a necessary condition for effective representation on their behalf. For some of them, although not for all, representation of Bedouins is not perceived as fundamentally different from other types of lawyering. For others, on the other hand, the challenge of representing the Bedouins lies precisely in the fact that it is a task of speaking the voice of the "other" and forcing its experienced sense of marginality on the dominant center. Further, although some of these lawyers occasionally cooperate with one another, and although most of them know about the others, most are also reluctant to think of their activities as part of a network performance. On the contrary, many of these lawyers insist on their being individual professionals who must rely on their own independent judgment and experience when assuming representation tasks on behalf of Bedouin clients.

These basic findings have led us to develop a number of theoretical and methodological guidelines that inform us in this study of "lawyers for a cause." First, we suggest that lawyers for a cause are not necessarily those who consciously and deliberately orient their professional lives toward promoting that cause. It is in the course of engaging in various professional practices that the possibility of becoming or functioning as a lawyer for a cause is realized. In short, one lawyer may "discover" herself as a lawyer for a cause, while another may only be vaguely aware of being so, and yet another, in contrast, may carefully construct a distinct identity and standing in the legal field by using an asserted cause as a professional resource.

Our method of inquiry, accordingly, is informed by a simple principle: we trace *practices* of representation on behalf of Bedouins without assuming that there are some conditions that have to be met in order for these practices to become activities of lawyers who work for a cause. Rather, we treat the cause as an imaginary concept that we abstract from the very act of representation, and we treat lawyers as working for a cause simply because of their objective functions of advocacy on behalf of Bedouins. In this essay, we arbitrarily isolate two episodes of representation through which we discuss, with occasional broader elaboration, some of the patterns, dilemmas, and perceptions that accompany this type of legal practice.

Second, we want to problematize the notion of "cause." Our basic premise is that a "cause" is not an objective fact "out there." A cause, rather, is a socially constructed concept that evolves, if at all, through a process in the course of which experiences, circumstances, memories, and aspirations are framed in a particular way. To speak of lawyers for a cause, therefore, requires caution. The assumed social type of a lawyer for a cause may misleadingly signify an unproblematic acceptance of the cause as a reified fact that one simply promotes through legal means. Yet, inasmuch as the reality of a cause is a constructed and negotiated experience, it is in the very act of legal representation that a cause—abstracted as such by outside observers like us—is asserted or defused, comprehended or dissolved, recognized or silenced. Cause lawyers, in short, are not simply carriers of a cause but are at the same time its producers: those who shape it, name it, and voice it.

Third, we also want to problematize the notion of "representation." We suggest that in the course of representing the client or the "cause," a lawyer always also represents herself in the sense of asserting her position, identity, and trajectory within the professional universe in which she is embedded. We should keep in mind that to be a lawyer for a cause—either objectively performed or subjectively experienced as such—is a function of those who already "belong"; that is, of those whose position within the legal field as certified experts in the rules of the legal game allows them to appear as speakers for the "other" and the "voiceless." We are dealing here with something that cannot be captured by speaking of these lawyers as mere mediators. Lawyers for the Bedouins are at once insiders and outsiders. Their activities may bring about an effective introduction of the other's voice as well as their own enhanced position as distinct type of professional experts. Their activities, however, may lead to the opposite result. The process in the course of which lawyers represent the socially marginalized and the culturally si-lenced may also result in their own professional marginalization and silencing. Lawyers for the Bedouins, in other words, always face the prospects of becoming an "other" in their own professional field. In either case, the representation of Bedouins—regardless of motivations, morality, or ideology—is forever also deter-mined and affected by the subtle understandings of what is and what is not possi-ble within the universe of law, and the objective structural possibilities of action with which one complies in order to play the representation game.

In sum, we assume that a cause lawyer is an unstable professional type that is constituted—and either preserved and celebrated or denied and ignored—not only by her own practices but also by the professional field in which she operates. The representation functions of cause lawyers should immediately sensitize us to the idea that all of their discursive and nondiscursive practices are mediated through the forces that constitute the legal field as a relatively distinct space of activity. Our study of a cause and its carriers, therefore, is for all practical pur-poses a glimpse at the rules of legitimate practice, the explicit and implicit codes of appropriate professional behavior, the tactics of self-assertion, the social net-works of cooperation, the structure of stratification, and the lifestyles and sym-bolic capital that combine to produce the universe within which lawyers and their cause become what they are. The identity of Bedouins in turn, individually and collectively, is thus projected and assumes meaning through the practices of repre-sentatives that are forever constrained in their ability to represent.

Jamia Salah Abu Ayash, a woman from the El-Azazme tribe, stood trial on charges of illegal construction in December 1987.[8] Jamia's defense had been based on pleas for special treatment. She suffered from kidney failure and needed a dialysis treat-ment three times a day. It was the small construction next to her tent, in which the dialysis machine was stored, that had been targeted for demolition. Under the circumstances, the defense asked the court to use its discretionary powers and not issue a demolition order. The prosecution, on the other hand, relied on the strict provisions of the Law of Planning and Construction. This law speaks in a clear universalistic language that does not discriminate among different sections of the population or different areas of the country. When the prosecution asks the court to issue demolition orders to Bedouins, it simply makes the point that it is the court's duty to apply equal treatment for all in its task of preventing the "wide-spread phenomenon of wild unlicensed construction which shows little respect for the law."

The court acknowledged the severe health problem of Jamia and the fact that inappropriate living conditions might have worsened her situation, but nonethe-less went on to argue that however severe a health condition might have been, it still did not permit one to breach the laws of construction in general and the laws of planning and construction in particular. The defendant, the court went on to say, should have sought *residence in a regulated area* and obtained a construction permit like every other citizen in the State of Israel. Consequently, the court fined Jamia and ordered her to demolish the construction.

Ron Lev—a sole practitioner who used to practice in Beer-Sheba and presently runs his modest practice from his apartment near Tel-Aviv—heard about Jamia's case through Nabhan, his Bedouin informant and one of his means of connection to the Bedouin population. Nabhan interested Lev in representing Jamia in an appeal to a district court. As preparations for the appeal were under way, an article in a local Jerusalem newspaper mentioned Jamia's case. The article surveyed the intensive efforts of the state authorities to demolish Bedouin constructions and, among other things, quoted Lev as saying that "this whole matter of house demolition is so terrible that I am certain that it goes on simply because no one is willing to assume responsibility." In his opinion "The Planning and Construction Commission realized that it is possible to demolish houses without trial because the Bedouins are so poor that they cannot afford lawyers." Lev was also specifically cited in reference to Jamia's case, "bitterly saying" that the decision in her case had been reached by "a judge in Israel, not in Sodom."[9]

Lev's comments placed him on a new and unexpected track. A complaint against Lev was filed before the Israeli Bar Association on the grounds that his remarks offended the dignity of the judge who decided the case, thereby violating the bar's code of ethics. Consequently, Lev faced charges in the Bar's District Disciplinary Tribunal. In what Lev described to us as a show of "pure evil," the disciplinary tribunal fined Lev and revoked his license to practice law for a period of six months. Our reading of the protocols of the disciplinary proceedings—both at the District Disciplinary Tribunal and later on appeal to the National Disciplinary Tribunal that upheld the conviction[10]—provides a rare opportunity to examine the self-perception of a lawyer who is compelled to publicly articulate the nature of cause lawyering and to confront it with the prevailing legal culture.

First, it is worth emphasizing that Lev represented himself in these proceedings. We asked him for his reasons not to retain a lawyer:

> I did not think of it before. . . . But now that you ask me I think that it had partly to do with the fact that the very nature of the profession had been on trial. The decision to represent myself expressed the freedom of expression that I asserted in this case. It may sound presumptuous, but I will use the word 'manifesto.' Self-representation represented the very thing for which I struggled. . . . I wanted to represent the freedom of expression because it seems to me as an issue of prime importance for the profession. It is a profession of representation, it is a profession of expression.

Lev, in the name of professional values, attempted to escape the function of the lawyer as a speaker for another. The dialectical tension between representation as a form of objective expertise and representation as a form of silencing in which the voice of the client disappears is manifest here. Lev's position problematizes representation and undermines the distance between personhood and professionalism that the dominant legal ideology tries to maintain. On trial was an issue that had been framed as an illegitimate invasion of the boundaries that protect judges from the law which they make and announce. This fact gives further force and meaning to the tensions that these disciplinary proceedings brought to the surface.

Lev's manifesto contains an explicit articulation of lawyering as a public calling, in an effort to exploit the taken-for-granted assertions of the dominant professional ideology so that the disciplinary tribunal would not take disciplinary measures against him. Not only is the role of lawyers, in general, to "boldly defend the interests of their clients," but they also have a public duty to combine civic and professional responsibilities in a constructive way. Lev warned the tribunal not to take measures that would "intimidate lawyers and deter them from fulfilling their important social role." At this point, his strategy was not to single himself out as one who belongs to a certain professional subculture but to represent himself as an authentic defender of the professional spirit at large: "It seems to me that the harsh examination of the newspaper article by the bar does not correspond to the public role of the bar in protecting the freedom of expression. In examining with a microscope every critical expression of a lawyer concerning legal decisions, we will bring about a situation in which instead of functioning as an active and stimulating factor in our public life, [lawyers] would prefer to remain passive and would avoid from openly voicing opinions. This fact may be very damaging for the state of human rights in Israel."

Lev, in short, did not distance himself from the professional universe. Rather, he tried to place himself within it and at the same time to carefully reframe the professional universe of lawyering as a public vocation. This becomes particularly apparent when Lev framed his position in terms that are considered to match the normative expectations of the profession. On a conceptual level, the whole dispute was framed by Lev as a case of an unacceptable tension between professional work and the freedom of expression. He resolved this tension—and tried to persuade the disciplinary board to adopt this solution—by emphasizing the public duties of the profession. On a personal level, Lev insisted that he was, first and foremost, a cool-headed professional. While in our interview he readily admitted that his style and manners have a somewhat "political," "emotional," and "spontaneous" character, he was not ready to show this profile in the hearing. Answering to implied suggestions that his past record in court singled him out as one who was prone to unprofessional manners, Lev declared, "I am a professional lawyer who does not deal with angers but with laws and facts." In our interview, Lev used his personal professional style as an indication of the commitment that distinguishes him as a lawyer for a cause. In the disciplinary proceedings, this position was replaced with assertions of professionalism.

It is interesting to consider the degree to which this professional norm is also reflected in the self-perceptions of other lawyers who represent Bedouins. Lev, in his appearance before the disciplinary board, played down his own commitment to the cause and preferred to frame the event in terms of the civic duty of a lawyer to exercise free speech. Other lawyers with whom we spoke tended to stress their professionalism and to insist that political or moral commitment to the cause was not an important condition for effective and successful representation. Many acknowledged their principled "sympathy" for the Bedouins—using this specific word—and went on to mention the modest fees they charged. Most, however, denied the relevance of such sympathy to the effective representation of Bedouins at court. None spoke of any connection between sympathy for the Bedouins and a left-oriented political convictions. On the contrary, some think that a lawyer with right-wing political convictions may be equally effective in Bedouin representation and that any lawyer would assume Bedouin representation for the proper fees. As one lawyer put it, "My political convictions have nothing to do with the Bedouin subject." Dov Maller, a lawyer we shall discuss in more detail in the next section of this chapter, was uncompromising on this point: "At court, over-identification with the client may obstruct the case. Judges are not biased and do not silence lawyers. . . . [I]t is legal expertise that matters, at least I would like to believe that. I am not a legal formalist, but I do not buy the idea of legal arbitrariness as well." Another lawyer, when asked about his personal commitments, responded by saying that such a question was totally irrelevant: "You ask personal questions," he said. "This is not an academic interview."

Lev's attempt to situate himself within the legitimate boundaries of the professional universe seems to correspond to the dominant prevailing professional culture of lawyers in Israel. Apart from the Association for Civil Rights in Israel (ACRI)—an established organization that has a large and active legal department—lawyering for a public cause has only recently began to emerge as a legitimate and respectable form of practice. The governing professional norm still emphasizes the idea that a lawyer should not identify with a client's cause. Clear statements to that effect have been voiced in an academic conference on public interest law: "It is a tradition in the legal profession that a lawyer act cautiously and avoid being overidentified with his client and his client's interest. It is advisable that the lawyer retain a certain distance from his client, so that the representation function of his craft is seen and publicly recognized." This norm, according to this approach, preserves the autonomy of the profession and separates law and politics in a way that allows the former "to immunize as many issues as possible from political influence—where things are established on the basis of force—so that these issues may be debated and determined on the basis of shared and neutral principles."[11]

The disciplinary tribunal rejected Lev's attempt to "generalize" his case. The tribunal, in fact, individualized Lev's case in a double sense: it singled out Lev's remark as personally offensive to the judge, and it treated him as an individual deviant who could not defend himself on grounds of professional duties in general. The logic of the disciplinary tribunal in reaching this decision is illuminating. The tribunal distinguished between criticism of the law and its makers in the public arena of the mass media and professional criticism that assumes the form of appeals to a higher judicial instances. Although not explicit, it is clear that the tribunal assumed that legal criticism by jurists should remain within the assumed clearly demarcated boundaries of the legal system. The tribunal's opinion that legal criticism should adhere to "proper style" both insisted on the radical autonomy of law and the necessity of transforming claims of injustice or moral grievances into strict legalistic frameworks. The tribunal thus denied the legitimacy of statements that articulate general narratives of justice in public arenas other than the legal system and at least implicitly encouraged the lawyer to individualize collective grievances.

This tendency toward individualization is of paramount importance for understanding the conditions for promoting a collective grievance, at least as far as communities "other" than Israeli Jews are concerned. Lev himself cannot escape this tendency. While one aspect of Lev's self-representation stresses his commitment to the collective duties of the profession, another aspect operates in a counterdirection. First, the very fact that Lev chose to represent himself seems to have singled him out as a "deviant." Further, Lev did make some comments that suggest that he is at once part of the profession and yet distinct in his particular circumstances. This distinction comes out when he talked of what he perceived as covert discrimination against lawyers who enjoy less power and prestige within the profession. Lev presented the court with a number of public criticisms that other lawyers had voiced about the Israeli system of justice in general and about particular decisions of courts in particular. He compared these statements with his own and asserted that if other lawyers enjoy freedom "to express views on judicial decisions and to describe them as a smear or as corrupted, [he] deserve[d] this freedom as well. There should be no discrimination between a lawyer and a judge, a lawyer and an academic, or between a famous lawyer and an anonymous one."

Here, in a single statement, Lev actually deconstructed the structure of the legal field and placed himself accordingly: "I have a small office," he declared, and "[I earn my] bread with my soul." This sense of being at the bottom of the profession's various scales of professional capital comes out clearly in our interview as well. "This business [of the Bedouins] undoubtedly pushes the lawyer to the margins," he said. Lev spoke in terms of "image": "[L]awyers who work with Arabs have a poor image because Jewish clients prefer to work with lawyers who represent only Jews." Other lawyers for the Bedouins have varied ways of expressing similar sentiments, and there is often this sense of marginality and anonymity that guides their self-perception. "In the case of Bedouins," one lawyer told us, "you get neither financial rewards nor other types of feedback that you may enjoy in civil liberties cases. Here you get no feedback at all and you find yourself lacking in all respects." Another lawyer told us:

> Practically speaking, an ordinary lawyer would not assume a Bedouin case because it is bad business. The representation of raped women is also bad business, here in Israel. In the United States big firms represent pro bono and it serves them well. It is not like that here. . . . [I]f you are a high-class lawyer, not a kid, if you already walk the corridors of power and you have connections here and there and this is already part of your reputation, and then you begin to mess with the fringe of the fringe, and you are not [X] who makes a career of such specific reputation, then you are in trouble—you shelve yourself, you put yourself in a drawer.

This marginality within the field is manifested in other ways as well. We asked one young lawyer about her motivations for representing Bedouins. She described to us how angry she became when she realized the injustice inflicted on the Bedouins. We then asked her whether the small fees involved did not deter her from further activities on behalf of Bedouins: "Well, more cases started to flow in . . . and what happens is that if you have two cases on the same day with the same judge, it is already 600 shekels [$200], and this is already not little money. Well you can get your groceries for this amount, so it is not philanthropy, not at all. I am not a volunteer." Indeed, we watched how Bedouins meet with their lawyers at the outdoor coffee-shop outside the local court in Beer-Sheba. They pay lawyers a few hundred shekels, in cash, no receipts, and buy them coffee and sandwiches. We suspect that this is not exactly the ordinary type of distancing and spatial practices that characterize the upper echelons of the bar.

There are exceptions. Two of the lawyers with whom we spoke are very explicit about their connections with influential political figures, appellate judges, and various policy makers, implicitly suggesting that the position that they enjoy within the legal field is a professional resource that both benefits their clients and secures their own respectable and influential standing. We believe it is not a coincidence that the two lawyers who are particularly explicit about their connections with the high echelons of power belong to an older generation—in age and experience—among the lawyers we interviewed. Both, in fact, talk about their functions on behalf of Bedouins in terms of providing advice and guidance to other lawyers rather than in terms of actual litigation activities.[12] In short, there is an internal hierarchy of prestige and power even within this tiny universe of lawyering. In the next section, we show how this sense of not being sufficiently visible and prestigious dictates litigation strategies.

Lev's assertion of professional marginality somewhat corresponds to the social marginality of his clients. He tried to place the remarks for which he stood trial in context: "I volunteered my services in this case," he said, "because we are dealing here with a poor woman." Lev is, first and foremost, a professional practitioner who works for a living. Yet he also told us that upon encountering his first cases concerning Bedouins—cases with which he became familiar in the course of routine referrals among local lawyers in Beer-Sheba and not because of any premeditated intention to become a "lawyer for the Bedouins"—he immediately experienced "a sense of injustice" and "spontaneous sympathy" for their plight. The representation of the underprivileged in the name of the public duties of the lawyer on the one hand and in the name of a personal sense of injustice on the other hand thus allows Lev to retain a simultaneous proximity and distance vis-à-vis the professional community of which he is part.

But what precisely is this "sense of injustice" and this "spontaneous sentiment of sympathy" of which Lev speaks when he describes his commitment to the cause? It is here that we identify the tension and dilemma that haunt lawyers for the Bedouins. Lev challenged the disciplinary tribunal's assumption that his reference to Sodom was illegitimately offensive. He explained that he was inspired by the Talmudic legend about the people of Sodom: "They [the Sodomites] had a bed in which they put guests down. A tall guest was shortened to fit, a short person was stretched to fit. Then came Eliezer. They told him to lie down. He replied: 'Since my mother died I vowed not to lie down.' " Lev offers an interpretation of this Talmudic episode: "This legend resists the legalistic application of a general norm, that is, "a bed," to any particular defendant, that is, a guest, in a formalistic way [i.e., cutting and stretching] that does not take into account substantive particular circumstances . . . and it [the legend] proves that this may lead to horrific results." Hence Eliezer resistance to the "Law."

The criticism of legal formalism and the reference to normalization (i.e., cutting and stretching that target the body) as a repressive and unjust practice may be exploited at two different and conflicting conceptual levels: an individual level and a collective level. Here, the Talmudic legend is used in order to single out the grievance and suffering of a particular legal subject—a sick and poor woman. The ironic and unintended result, however, is that the particularization of an individual legal subject works against the general claim that the Bedouin community as a whole deserves a substantively different treatment. While the construction of a cause presupposes a collective grievance—however embodied in each particular subject who is constituted through a Bedouin "identity" and a Bedouin "history"—Lev's strategy of defending both himself and his client works toward diffusing it: the collective plight of the Bedouins disappears from sight at the very moment that it is supposed to appear as the general context that explains Lev's professional activities. In the last instance, Lev exploits the Talmudic legend not in order to distinguish the particular history and culture of the Bedouins in general but in order to isolate the case of the Bedouin woman as one who merits particular treatment. In other words, in the same way that Lev's defense of the collective duties of the profession in the disciplinary proceedings is reduced to an individual case of deviance, the legal defense of the Bedouins is constantly pushed away from the general cause toward the particularities of individual cases. The career of a "cause lawyer" and the career of a "cause" constantly interact with one another within the confines and pressures of the legal field.

This problem of having to present courts with cases, rather than causes, significantly complicates the ability of lawyers to advance the general cause of the Bedouins. Indeed, on rare occasions a lawyer may succeed in persuading the court not to apply the general norm that requires builders to obtain construction permits, but this always happens because of some particularities that distinguish and isolate the case as a singular one. The point is, in short, that the ability of any single Bedouin to succeed at court comes at the expense of the court's readiness to acknowledge the collective nature of the issue as a whole.

At work here are systemic pressures—that many lawyers knowingly and unknowingly internalize—to give up generalizations and to maintain a radical distinction between the "law" of the case and the "politics" of the cause. In fact, the more general and abstract a given grievance is, the more political it is perceived to be, something that cannot be resolved by legal means. Thus many of the lawyers for the Bedouins believe that a true and comprehensive solution lies outside the legal field, in the political arena, and they talk about the need to mobilize the Bedouins to exert political pressure, to organize, and "to raid Jerusalem with busloads of demonstrators." Yet all this is not perceived as part of the lawyer's representation duties. Rather, the systemic pressure of the legal field to isolate cases manifests itself in the professional responsibility to one's client; and this responsibility creates a series of dilemmas that are oftentimes resolved in ways that perpetuate the superiority of the single case over the general cause. For example, the daily dilemma of lawyers is whether to advise clients to accept or reject various types of compromises offered to their clients by the state. "I have to take care of practicalities," one lawyer told us. "In fact I do not generally represent people on the principled level. For example, on the issue of lands, the state is currently willing to offer a 20 percent compensation for each claim of land ownership by Bedouins. So I have to consider, because I may have some general ideas, but these ideas may risk the immediate ability of clients to get something that they may not get tomorrow." Lev aptly captured this point: "A lawyer is one who represents another person and not an idea," he admitted. "It would not serve me to tell the judge that the whole Bedouin community has been screwed." [13]

Lev is only one of a number of lawyers who routinely represent Bedouins in an endless and almost Sisyphean attempt to overcome a massive body of precedents that already establish the hopelessness of trying to develop a collective cause as a means of relieving individual Bedouin defendants. A number of lawyers admitted to us that under these circumstances their legal strategy becomes quite simple: gaining more time for their clients. Unofficial norms in the local courts that deal with the Bedouins have already established a grace period that typically lasts from six to twelve months. Lawyers for the Bedouins, on their part, employ various procedural rules in order to extend this period. Of course, gaining time is a routine strategy of lawyers in many areas of the law. Yet it seems to us that the application of such practices as a matter of course in the case of the Bedouins become a subtle and not always intentional way of subverting, or at least challenging, the very integrity of the legal system within which these lawyers and their clients are situated. The explicit tactics of delay and "exhaustion" subvert the prevailing norm that assigns lawyers the dual function of advocating the case of the client and serving as officers of the court; the prosecution in such cases, at least, often bitterly complains to the court about the disregard for "justice" and the abuse of "proper" legal proceedings that such practices represent. Indeed, at least in the case of one lawyer, this is an open challenge to the myth of litigation: "I admit nothing, I concede nothing, and I let them [judges and prosecution] know that dragging my feet is the only option I have."

It is notable that the Bedouin clients are not misguided by their lawyers on this issue. The Bedouins seem to be acutely aware of the fact that the whole legal drama that is being produced on their behalf is geared toward what lawyers describe as an effort to "exhaust the system" and as a drama that is based on the vague expectation that a changing political climate may eventually turn events in favor of the Bedouins. The way this tactic of suspension is framed by one lawyer may be of particular interest:

> When the [Bedouins] approach me, I tell them that I can only offer time. That is, tactics of delays, postponing hearings, making the case bigger than it really is, bringing more witnesses, making longer arguments, when I know there is no chance, and yet I will do my best to frame arguments in the best way I can, and I will summon witnesses and manipulate the case for as long as possible and then I earn time. Yet this time is useless if you do not use it for something. And this is the Bedouins' job. It is their political duty to move things, and I am afraid they do not use it at all.

There is a connection, then, between the delaying tactics of lawyers and the broader issue of turning a case into a cause. Still, as mentioned, it seems that many of the lawyers who are involved consciously restrict themselves to litigation at court and do not want, or cannot, extend their representation further.[14] For some, it is a matter of their own horizon of perception as to what legal representation is. The lawyer quoted above, for example, also suggested that professional ethics prevented her from initiating a case beyond the "focused treatment" that a given case requires. For others, it is first and foremost a matter of a realistic assessment of their ability to devote time and effort to such unrewarding practice: "I would like to be a full-time cause lawyer," one of these lawyers admits, "but I have first to establish my own financial security." In the next section of this paper, we trace forms of lawyering that at least at some point have been geared toward a more comprehensive type of legal representation.

In sum, the type of lawyering we have described is far from being rewarding: the clients are at the bottom of the socioeconomic scale, the fees that can be charged are meager, and the legal expertise and oral skills that are required are rapidly exhausted in the course of this routine litigation. This section sketched the profile—the "standing," so to speak—of one lawyer: R. Lev. Lev is by no means a typical lawyer, simply because we do not think there is one. Lev's story, however, brings to the fore some aspects of the process in the course of which the cause "creates" its legal bearer as much as the reverse is true. Lev's appearance before the disciplinary tribunal formalized and officialized his sense of marginality vis-à-vis the professional hierarchy of power and prestige and vis-à-vis the dominant professional ideology of neutrality. This sense of marginality was shaped in the course of ongoing litigation that confined him to a repetitive chain of individual cases in which the general cause was at once embedded in the proceeding and yet denied and defused. Such experience is not untypical among the lawyers we interviewed. Many of them, especially among the younger ones, describe their "chance" and "coincidental" encounter with the Bedouins, admit to being totally "ignorant" and "naive" with regard to the Bedouin plight prior to this encounter, and discuss their career of Bedouin representation as a process during which they discovered that plight.

In the process, a cause lawyer may be "invented," yet with a perceived sense of marginality and disillusionment about his or her ability to transform the single case into a vehicle for promoting the Bedouin cause and for promoting a legal career into a publicly visible and acknowledged cause activity. The lawyers for Bedouins that we discuss here are acutely sober about their professional standing and about their ability to extract prestige and income from their current careers. It would not be implausible to suggest that at least for some of them, the ability to endure this form of practice reflects nothing more than their own need to survive as practitioners. However, most of the lawyers we interviewed are not entirely dependent on the representation of Bedouins. At least tentatively, therefore, we tend to view them, in spite of their own misgivings about their professional roles, as the "local heroes" of the Beer-Sheba courts and of the Bedouin cause.

In the next section, we want to trace the activities of lawyers for the Bedouins by beginning at the other end of the legal spectrum. We look at the career of a petition to the Supreme Court of Israel that was brought in the name of the collective cause of the Bedouins by lawyers who served the Bedouins in a manner fundamentally different from Lev's.

The Supreme Court of Israel, sitting in its capacity as the High Court of Justice, delivered its quite laconic ruling in the *El-Sanaa* case on June 18, 1992.[15] The *El-Sanaa* case was an attempt to use the particular grievance of some Bedouins as a springboard for developing a general claim on behalf of the Bedouin population as a whole. The petition detailed the history of the Bedouins under Israeli rule since the establishment of the state, and argued that the Bedouins in the Enclosure Zone were at least implicitly promised by the authorities that they would be able to construct their houses in this area in exchange for the lands from which they were originally uprooted. On the basis of these claims, the petition asked the court to order the authorities to suspend attempts to target Bedouin constructions for demolition under the provisions of the planning and construction laws. The four individual petitioners in the case were sponsored by the Bedouin Association, in itself a party to the petition. The petitioners and the Bedouin Association were represented by two lawyers: Saul Snir, a retired Beer-Sheba judge who two years earlier had started a private practice with his daughter, and Amir Yaron, one of the most widely recognized and respected civil rights advocates in Israel.

In principle, the petition could be read as a celebration of a cause-lawyering ideal. Unlike the actions of Lev, who has been accused of transgressing the legitimate boundaries of the legal field by turning to the press, a petition to the Supreme Court is considered as the epitome of a legitimate and an enlightened legal practice. Being a recognized arena for the resolution of cases involving justice (the Supreme Court hears such petitions in its institutional capacity as the high court of justice), the petition provided an opportunity to move from the resolution of any particular case to an overall solution of the Bedouins' collective grievance— an opportunity to effectively realize lawyering for a cause as a practice of articulating a counternarrative of collective suffering and of publicly constructing the relevant community as a cultural "other" whose voice must be heard. At the same time, the petition provided an opportunity for realizing cause lawyering as a visible, strategic, deliberate, resourceful, coordinated, and committed project in the course of which social change could be brought about and its lawyers-carriers could be publicly acknowledged as experts on collective grievances.

The *El-Sanaa* case was not successful. Spread across four and a half pages, the short decision of the court dismissed the petitioners' claims. We are not directly interested, in the present context, in explaining the failure. In what follows, we trace the course that the case took and anchor it in the practices and orientations of its lawyers-carriers. We suggest that underneath the surface of the judicial text lie layers of heterogeneous professional practices of representation. In short, we read the petition as a professional product that, when analyzed, reveals the universe of social and professional networking and the varied professional profiles of the lawyers who became involved with the cause of the Bedouins.

Snir and Yaron—who represented the Bedouins in court and who became the visible public carriers of the cause—entered the picture when advanced drafts of the petition were already more or less in place. In fact, Yaron and Snir were not retained by the Bedouins but were, rather, *selected by other lawyers* for the specific purpose of arguing the case before the Supreme Court. The primary reason for asking these two lawyers to represent the case in court had to do with their presumed public visibility and with their professional reputation. Both qualities, according to the lawyers who selected them, were supposed to affect the attitude of the court and to enhance the media coverage of the petition. "We wanted a 'heavy' lawyer," one of these lawyer observed, and another one added: "We needed a higher caliber [person] than I was. . . . We needed someone with a name because this fact has its independent impact—what can I say—on courts. There is obviously a difference that you can see in the high court when X comes with a case and when Y comes with it. In most cases it is mere politics, especially in the high court."

Snir was approached because in his past role as a judge he had acquired the reputation of being sympathetic to the Bedouins' plight and because, as one lawyer told us, "we thought that his personality and record would attract the attention of the press." One of the qualities Snir brought to the petition was a strong desire to establish himself as a jurist with a commitment to civil rights cases: "Among other things, I do have in my office cases that I consider to be 'ventilators'—that is, world-redeeming cases. . . . I did not volunteer my free services to the Bedouins, yet the work I invested [my time in] was disproportionate to what I could expect in return. . . . [I do wish] to engage in cases of public importance." Doing good, then, as inherent to his perception of himself and as a means to distinguish what he does from ordinary lawyering, are the reasons Snir provides for agreeing to assume the representation of the Bedouin petitioners. At the same time, Snir does not think of such lawyering as a professional duty: "[T]here is no duty to perform good deeds. It is not part of the professional ethics that bind us in a disciplinary sense. Do I see it as a duty? No."

It is interesting to consider the degree to which Snir's sense of professionalism, on the one hand, and his wish to acquire a reputation as a public interest advocate, on the other, may have shaped the particular inputs he had to offer. The raison d'être of the petition—as drafted and prepared by lawyers other than Snir—was grounded in the claim that the Law of Planning and Construction had been illegitimately abused in the case of the Bedouins. In a nutshell, the argument was that the main purpose of the Law of Planning and Construction was to create mechanisms for establishing planning blueprints in direct accordance with the local and regional needs of populations. According to this logic, the penal provisions of the law were only meant to supplement these constructive guidelines for construction. Yet in the Bedouin case, the affirmative provisions of the law did not play any constructive role, whereas the penal provisions were isolated and decontextualized, thus transforming the Law of Construction into a Law of Destruction. Thus the penal provisions of the law served a purpose foreign to the purpose of that same law: The law had been used to force the Bedouins to give up their land ownership claims and to forcefully drive them into townships.

In order to substantiate this claim, the petitioners had to convince the court of the plausibility of a historical narrative that explained and justified the Bedouins' current practices of "illegal" construction. The main argument to that effect was that the Bedouins relied on a governmental promise that they would be allowed to settle on the disputed lands in return for the lands from which they had been deported in the 1950s. Yet it seems that Snir's way of framing the issue may have given a different twist to the cause. In a letter that Snir sent to the state's general attorney on the eve of the petition, he mainly framed the issue as a matter of unfair discrimination of the Bedouins of the Negev in comparison with their brethren who lived in the northern regions of the country and, vaguely, as a matter of illegitimate discrimination of the Bedouins in respect to the Jewish majority. This discrimination, according to Snir, originated in the 1985 report that recommended the demolition of Bedouin constructions in the Negev while decriminalizing vast illegal construction in the northern regions of the country.[16]

The accuracy of this argument notwithstanding, a shift away from the "political," "historical," and "cultural" dimensions of the case toward "equality" issues may be easily detected here. We are not saying, of course, that these dimensions are incompatible. The petition, after all, contained all sorts of arguments. We suggest, however, that particular professional orientations may have given more or less emphasis to certain types of arguments. Snir, accustomed to framing issues in terms of discrimination between two formally "equal" parties, wished to target the mainstream liberal values that were dominant at court. Yet the emphasis on discrimination in this particular case may have obscured the history, the context, and the fundamental conflict over land ownership that were at the heart of the Bedouins' grievance (especially if, as one lawyer who was deeply involved in the petition speculated, "the judges never bothered to read the detailed documents that were appended to the petition.")[17] The discriminatory framing only emphasized the Bedouins' very recent history (1985), and partly substituted an in-depth account for a horizontal view of the Bedouins as yet another community whose conditions must be equalized with others. The transformation of the historical dispossession into a liberal discriminatory framework, in other words, in effect deradicalized the cause.

Snir was not oblivious to the consequences of such reframing. He emphasized discrimination as the essence of the grievance because he believed that "the heart of the problem [was] not legal but political." He added, "I assume heavy responsibility upon myself in this heresy of saying that the entire constitutional law of Israel today amounts to what [the chief justice] wishes it to be. . . . [Y]et I have to provide the court with legalistic rhetoric, to offer it an anchor, but in the end I depend on the answer as to whether the court wishes to help or not." Snir, deeply embedded within the prevailing legalistic culture that treats such "legal realist" expressions as illegitimate and unprofessional, was thus led to develop arguments that the court might easily digest, bypassing painful "political" questions concerning the Zionist project of land acquisition. Further, his attempt to escape the "political" aspect of the case also dictated the specific way in which the discrimination argument was framed. Because emphasizing the discrimination of Bedouins vis-à-vis the Jewish population would have given the case "somewhat political overtones," the Bedouin-South versus the Bedouin-North discrimination framework was preferable: "I did not want to emphasize the question of the ethnic discrimination of Arabs vis-à-vis Jews because that would have pushed the state to embark on a political track. On the other hand, I did not want to give up this argument altogether because that had been the painful element for the group I represented. So I framed it in a vague way. . . . [T]he reader may ask himself what the author means. Does he talk about discrimination of Arabs vis-à-vis Jews or discrimination of Negev Bedouins vis-à-vis the Bedouins of the North? So I gave it this dual expression."

We are not suggesting, of course, that this particular type of argument "explains" the result in court. Rather, our point is that it is through such reframing of arguments that we can identify the heterogeneous materials that various lawyers brought to bear on the cause and on the legal representation of Bedouins in the Israeli legal system.

The selection of Yaron as a lawyer for the petitioners brought yet another professional type, and yet another form of professional capital, into the scene. Young, aspiring lawyers look up to Yaron as a symbol of success: an established, reputable, and financially secure lawyer who, commercial lawyering notwithstanding, invests considerable resources in civil rights–related cases. His standing and reputation are not unfounded. The law offices of Yaron constituted—or at least did for many years—the only well-established private firm in Israel in which one could practice civil rights cases. Yaron's policy—grounded in his own past record as a committed political activist and jurist—is to play host to many apprentices and young lawyers who wish to engage in legal work other than on behalf of commercial clients. Consequently, the Yaron office has produced over the years an impressive dynasty of lawyers oriented toward the liberal and radical political left and trained in representing clients in "problematic" cases that touch upon politically or socially sensitive issues.

Further, Yaron was a natural choice for the petition because of his specific ties with what was referred to by the relevant actors as the "Bedouin File." Originally, the Bedouin File was not much more than the unique relation that developed between Yaron and a Bedouin activist who operates the Bedouin Association almost on his own. At least from 1985 onward this Bedouin activist asked Yaron for help with numerous issues concerning the lives of the Bedouins and, when needed, was provided with free or almost free legal services by several of Yaron's employees. Thus, from 1985 until 1992, the Yaron firm operated as a major clearinghouse for Bedouin cases, mostly involving land disputes and demolition orders. Yaron described this period as one in which the firm had been "flooded with cases. I had mixed feelings about it. Economically, these were losing cases. On the one hand, it was a question of people in distress. On the other hand, it really hurt ongoing office work. I could not devote all my time to this, but somehow we tried to help. So from time to time a few lawyers handled these cases and each time there was someone else in charge." Indeed, a 1991 document of the Yaron firm reveals that Guy Levy, a lawyer in the firm, had been busy at the time coordinating eighty-five Bedouin cases at various stages of litigation among five other lawyers with no formal connections to the Yaron office.[18]

It is noteworthy that although Yaron was a natural candidate for the petition, he was not asked to join the petition at the start: "We thought he was not very interested and that he would not invest in the case," one lawyer told us, perhaps echoing Yaron's own sense of exhaustion after years of providing services to a "lost cause." Yaron was approached, therefore, only after the behind-the-scenes lawyers who orchestrated the case decided that Snir had to be backed by another " 'heavy' lawyer." It was then that Yaron was asked to add his name to the petition; not because he was expected to actually work on it but because of his general standing as an old-time sponsor of the Bedouins and because of his reputation as a lawyer with good professional standing, impressive social connections, and high public visibility. Indeed, Yaron delegated his responsibilities to Levy, by then the coordinator of Bedouin cases, who was aided in the preparations for the petition by one or two other lawyers in the firm.

With Levy we come to recognize the first hidden layer of the petition. Levy was a former South African antiapartheid activist whose commitment to civil rights issues brought him into contact with the Yaron office soon after his arrival to Israel. It seems that Levy's experience also sensitized him to develop the idea that the Bedouins should be treated by the state as a distinct and different cultural community. Levy, for example, was in touch with at least one lawyer from the Minnesota Lawyers International Human Rights Committee. In a letter to Levy, headed "Bedouin Rights Case before High Court of Justice," this lawyer expressed his appreciation for "the humanitarian concerns you [Levy] have for your clients," and advised him on how to pursue the case of the Bedouins in comparative terms. Levy was provided with information on American cases involving treaty rights and was instructed on various possible lines of argument. Among other things, he was advised that "even if the High Court of Justice is unwilling to recognize the validity of the agreements reached between the Bedouins and the Israeli Government, it should recognize that the Bedouins are a dependent people whose rights should be given special protection in light of the ambiguous agreements entered into between them and the Israeli Government."[19]

The petition that Snir and Yaron submitted to the court, accordingly, included an analogy between the Bedouins' asserted land rights and the U.S. Supreme Court's treatment of land disputes involving Native Americans. The Bedouins, the petition stated, were "simple people who struggled for a poor shelter, and not a wealthy corporation. . . . [T]he question of whether they acted upon a governmental promise in this context should be examined not only through the perspective of the government's intentions . . . but mainly through the way these intentions had been interpreted and understood by the Bedouin population. Such an interpretive approach has been applied by the U.S. Supreme Court in connection with treaties between the U.S. government and Indian tribes."[20]

In other words, the interpretive approach that had been nurtured by Levy highlighted the nature of the dispute as a cultural conflict that had to be settled according to unique principles of recognition. This interpretive approach challenged the application of the Planning and Construction Law by emphasizing the perceived understanding of the Bedouins that they would be allowed to settle and build in the Enclosure Zone. Again, although this argument is mentioned in the papers submitted to the court, we do not know the extent to which it had been pressed upon the judges. The formal decision of the court avoided the issue altogether and gave no sign that the matter had registered with the judges at all. Levy, at any rate, seems to have imprinted his own professional orientation on the final product.

As mentioned, however, it was neither Snir nor Yaron and Levy who planned and initiated the petition. Two young lawyers operated behind the scenes and for a time orchestrated the project: Irad Abas and Ilana Ray, both of them "graduates" of the Yaron office. Both lawyers were driven by a distinct professional claim of being legal entrepreneurs on behalf of a cause. They shared an office in Tel-Aviv whose exclusive purpose was to provide legal services to the Bedouin Association. In fact, it was partly due to their own efforts that the Bedouin Association maintained the financial resources that allowed it to fund Ray as a full-time lawyer on its behalf, and to retain Abas as a representative of Shatil—an American-funded organization that trains and educates grassroots groups on how to mobilize for a cause.[21] And it was in this office that entrepreneurial work on a broad basis had begun—mobilizing public support for the Bedouins, planning various legal and political projects, and developing a broad legal agenda.

Abas's former affiliation with Yaron had not been accidental. As an activist in the Association of Civil Rights in Israel (ACRI), he leaned toward civil rights lawyering even as a law student. Yaron's office was an inevitable choice; and it was there that Abas became familiar with the Bedouin File. In 1988 Abas received a grant for a year's study program at the American University in Washington, D.C. The grant came through Shatil, which was in turn supported by the New Israel Fund, a Jewish-American foundation with strong ties to the MacArthur Foundation.

The specific purpose of the grant was to train Israeli lawyers both in substantive relevant areas of the law and, perhaps even more important, in American-style know-how about methods of organizing, mobilizing, and coordinating legal activities for a cause. In return for this investment, Abas committed himself to one year's practice for a cause upon his return to Israel. He fulfilled this obligation by working with Ray for the Bedouin Association, receiving half of his salary from

Shatil and the other half from ACRI, with which he was originally affiliated. Abas, in short, returned to Israel as a "certified" lawyer for a cause. In particular, he assumed upon himself the organizational aspects of legal work: coordinating meetings, writing memos and distributing them, and searching for additional funding: "I was a Shatil person," Abas says, less dominant on strictly legal issues but very instrumental as being "responsible for the social aspects of the work." Apparently, this was a very important function because Shatil was oriented toward what one lawyer described as "American thinking, with internal implicit codes for deciding whom to fund and to what extent funding should be granted."

Ray also began her legal career at Yaron's firm. She recalls herself as a "young and naive girl" with a "youthful psychology" and the idealistic belief that "it was possible to change the world"; and she adds, however, that she also had a "social need" to establish herself in the politically and socially "correct circles" of Tel-Aviv. Yaron's office was, accordingly, "the only option," and it was there that she first heard about the Bedouins: "I had the impression that it was a truly shocking story, you know, all this terrible injustice. That no one knows about. I truly worked on it from the stomach, let's say. . . . I planned to promote this issue." Ray's promotional energies produced one rather immediate result: a 1988 paper entitled "Implementation of the Laws of Planning and Construction to the Negev Bedouins—Discretionary Faults," which Ray wrote as a student at the Tel-Aviv School of Law. This paper would constitute one of the primary foundations of the petition.

In 1989 Ray was asked by the Bedouin Association to leave Yaron's firm and assume a full-time salaried position as its legal representative. We asked Ray whether there was any conflict with Yaron over the idea that she would take the Bedouin File from his office. Ray claimed that she received Yaron's blessing:

> I think there were two reasons for that. First, I felt that to some extent he simply . . . wanted to help. Second, it was me after all that turned [the Bedouin Association] from being a client who did not pay money to one which had all these funds that poured money in. . . . [W]hen I took the file away [Yaron] did not faint because the Association was still a parasite in the office, so whoever was able to help it, let him go. . . . I took the file as an object that everyone wanted to throw to the street, a wounded cat, and he came out of my hands as a prettier cat, financially, and it was only then that everybody jumped in.

Ray's and Abas's claims of professional distinction, then, are based on their promotional capacities and their ability to mobilize legal work for a cause. This claim for distinction, however, has another important dimension. It seems quite obvious that both Ray and Abas were not particularly interested in the routine representation of Bedouins in the local courts but searched, from the outset, for the general and comprehensive project. Ray's remarks to this effect are particularly illuminating. She admitted that she knew very little about the minute proceedings that the Bedouins faced in the local courts: "I did not like to appear there, perhaps I was there once or twice. *One of my conditions* [upon assuming representation of the BA] *was that I would construct the cause but would not appear there.* I did not like it, it is difficult to appear there" (emphasis added).

It is on the basis of such comments that we are also able to identify the distinct asserted professional capital and varied self-perceptions that lawyers bring to the cause (and, vice versa, it is from such comments that we extract our argument that the "cause" shapes and constructs different types of lawyers). Referring to a lawyer who represents Bedouins in the local courts, Ray said: "He is a field lawyer; I appreciate his work. He knows how to plead, he fights, he is a field soldier. I am not like it; it is not my area so to speak. I may appear in a district court [appellate level] with various types of arguments, but I did not like to appear there. . . . Of course, the best are those who are both theoreticians and field-animals." But Ray certainly identifies only with the theoretical or conceptual aspects of legal work.

These comments serve as testimony to the internal stratification and classification that lawyers perceive in the professional grid in which they operate. On the one hand, there are reputed and publicly visible experts who are crowned as the official carriers of the cause (e.g., Yaron). On the other hand, there are field soldiers with few aspirations, whose activities on behalf of Bedouins fuse cause lawyering as a way of life and cause lawyering as a way of making a modest living, obviously a less rewarding form of practice. It is somewhere in between that Ray places herself: not enough of "a high-caliber lawyer" to belong with the acknowledged experts but an entrepreneur and organizer who is able to move from the single case to the general cause. No wonder, therefore, that the idea of the "big case" took shape and emerged in Ray and Abas's office. It was in this office that truly entrepreneurial work began. Lawyers who were known for their work on behalf of Bedouins were approached (e.g., Lev), drafts were circulated, archival work was done, and a series of consultations with reputed legal advisers were launched. One of the lawyers consulted was Meir Maller; it is with Maller—an old-generation lawyer who recently passed away—that we come to identify yet another hidden layer of the final product that was submitted to the court.

The legal ideas on which Ray based the planned petition—most of which were articulated in her 1988 university paper—were not entirely novel. Her work, as well as the various drafts of the evolving petition, was strongly inspired by Maller's early insights. M. Maller was both a reputed and recognized expert on land laws and a politically committed lawyer. He had been a senior member of the Communist Party and, in this capacity, had advocated the plight of the Bedouins in various public forums at a very early stage. Maller, unlike other lawyers we discuss in this article, was thus a unique creature: he enjoyed a considerable reputation as a professional and yet was considered a political and social outcast as are all other Communists in Israel. Maller's self-perception, accordingly, was grounded in his political legacy: "I was the first political lawyer," he described himself to us. But Maller was also a great believer in the integrity of the legal system. Far from present-day realism, if not cynicism, Maller spoke of his motivation to help the Bedouins by using the court as a site of fairness through which the Bedouins could be convinced to become loyal citizens: "The Bedouins were like a tabula rasa upon which one could positively inscribe [fair legal decisions], thereby recruiting them to support the state as such, to make them belong."

Maller was the first lawyer whom the founder of the Bedouin Association ever approached for aid. The connection, once established, was not severed by the association's later ties with Yaron. Further, Maller was frequently consulted by lawyers from Yaron's office on various legal matters concerning the Bedouins. In fact, we find that the principled legal foundation for the Bedouins' petition has been already articulated by Maller in the 1970s. His position came out when he handled a demolition case on behalf of a Bedouin tribal leader who years later would provide the Supreme Court with an affidavit outlining the historical plight of the Bedouins from his own personal point of view. The basic ideas upon which the future petition would rest clearly surfaced in a letter that Maller sent to the planning authorities in January 1977. Maller's answer to the charges against his client—who was required to demolish his house—were based on an uncompromising frontal attack on the legitimacy of using the Planning and Construction Law in the case of the Bedouins:

> The defendant . . . was deported in 1951 from his land and from his stone house that also served as a tribal courthouse . . . under instructions of the military, and under the pretense that this move had only been temporary. . . . After my client's house was demolished by the military—an action that my client considers to be as illegal as the very act of deportation—and after residing with his family for many years in a tent, my client built the targeted construction not later than 1960. . . . My client does not reside in the area of his own free will. This residence was imposed on him by the authorities, and the authorities should bear the responsibility that in the place to which he had been brought he would have humane conditions of residency. . . . The construction—that the authorities should have constructed themselves in 1951—when they transferred my client (as well as the whole tribe)—was constructed by my client with the full knowledge of the authorities . . . and without any objection on their part. . . .
>
> A demolition order for the said construction, if issued, may have one of the following two consequences: (a) a second deportation by the authorities, this time to Bedouin townships that are in fact a kind of a work camp designed to turn him—a sheik and a farmer from generations of farmers—into a hired employee in the construction business or in (Jewish) agriculture and into a dispossessed landowner; or (b) to force him to resume tent residency as was his condition in the 1950s, immediately after the deportation. . . .

The charges, under the circumstances, have nothing to do with the Law of Planning and Construction, as it comes to advance goals that conflict with and are antagonistic to Israel's Declaration of Independence, basic rights of an Israeli citizen . . . and the law as a whole. . . . The purpose of the claim is to use a judicial apparatus as an instrument and a cover to a policy of dispossessing the Bedouins of their lands whose perpetrators are not willing to assume responsibility.[22]

Maller's document, to the best of our knowledge, is the earliest and clearest attempt to introduce the authorities to a counternarrative, one that challenged the popular wisdom about the Bedouins' history, culture, and lives, and one that undermined the pretense of the authorities to simply apply the principles of the rule of law to the Bedouins. The letter cleverly challenged the nomadic and root-less image of the Bedouins by referring to the old stone house and, by referring to the importance of the house as a tribal court, introduced a portrait of the Bedouins as a distinct cultural community with its own legal system that existed prior to Israel's interference. Further, Maller used radical vocabulary. He spoke of deportations, of work camps, of illegal dispossession, of law as a cover, and of irresponsible policy makers. It is this 1977 radical line of defense, to our minds, that served as the basis and inspiration for the arguments brought to the court by Ray, Snir, and other liberal-minded lawyers who handled the case later. The degree to which the original *tone* has been preserved or, alternatively, moderated, soft-ened, and restrained is another matter. Both the attitude of Snir, described above, and the position of other notable players, discussed below, seem to suggest that "something" had been lost in the journey from Maller's early document to the 1992 petition to the court.

With Maller's contribution, we reached the deepest layer of the petition. As we can see, we are dealing here with a network of lawyers who brought to the petition a heterogeneous set of self-perceptions, aspirations, and orientations as to what work for a cause was and what, in fact, a cause meant. Above and beyond these heterogeneous origins, however, there was a general sentiment that seemed to have surrounded the preparations for the petition all along the way. It is note-worthy, in this respect, that Maller, at least in retrospect, thinks that it was a mistake to petition the court: "I am not like Yaron," he told us, "I do not go to court when there is less than 50 percent chances of success, as it may only strengthen the position of the authorities, as has been the case here."

All the lawyers with whom we spoke expressed similar opinions. The petition, they argued, did not rest on solid legal grounds. In fact, various legal experts and advisers, including some of the lawyers who were involved in the matter at Yaron's office, continued to discourage this approach throughout the preparations for the case. A former state attorney with acknowledged experience with petitions to the Supreme Court produced a written opinion on the planned petition (for a consid-

erable sum of money) but refused to assume representation on the grounds that
the case was not strong enough; another lawyer who was approached refused to
assume representation on the grounds that the case was "too political."

The idea that the case was "too political," therefore not ready for judicial
deliberation, was also the formal position of the Association for Civil Rights in
Israel, the well-established and almost official cause-lawyering organization of Israel. The association's senior legal counsel attended a few meetings concerning the
planned petition but declined to offer the association's support. In general, the
case of the Bedouins was not new to the association. Already in 1978, a group of
activists submitted to the association a very well-informed report, which detailed
the legal mechanisms that the State of Israel employed in order to dispossess the
Bedouins of their lands.[23] The inaction of the association and its position in this
matter when asked to add its reputation and clout to further the Bedouins' cause
are illuminating: they imply that issues such as the land rights of the Bedouins
simply fall outside the association's conceptual framework of civil rights.

Abas, in his orchestrating capacity, was acutely aware of the legalistic pru-
dence of ACRI and its tendency to restrict itself to rather narrowly defined civil
rights cases. Accordingly, he tried to put forward a realistic, morally inspired argument in a last effort to persuade the association to lend some form of support to
the petition. His memorandum to the association, a failed attempt to mobilize its
support for the cause, exposes an important aspect of the delicate project that the
lawyers for the Bedouins tried to pursue:

> In the background of the petition is the years-long discrimination toward Arabs
> in this land. I have no doubt in my mind that the story that I outlined above
> could never take place in regard to Jewish citizens. . . . It would not have hap-
> pened to individuals, and certainly not to a population of tens of thousands of
> people. *This argument, which I think we all share, cannot come up in the Supreme
> Court,* mainly because of matters of evidence, but this does not mean that it loses
> its significance as far as our *understanding* of the situation is concerned, and our
> reasons to get involved.[24]

The signals of discouragement apparent in the position of ACRI are part of
a set of pressures—also internalized by sympathetic lawyers and as such even
more constraining—that work toward framing collective grievances in line with
dominant legalistic frameworks. Such framing pressures, in turn, impose limiting
conditions on imaginative and more daring forms of lawyering for a cause. Most
of the lawyers with whom we spoke adopted the liberal-minded legalism that
dominates the legal field. While most of them spoke as "legal realists," insist-
ing that politically sensitive cases such as the Bedouin petition could not be
explained in pure legalistic terms, they nonetheless insisted that the petition of the
Bedouins failed because it was "legally weak." We interpret this seeming contradiction as an indication of the degree to which even lawyers for a cause cannot

escape, in the final instance, the dominant norms that govern their professional universe.

The Supreme Court flatly rejected the petitioners' claims and completely ignored the counternarrative of historic injustice that they tried to construct. Justice Bach, who spoke for the court, outlined a historic and cultural narrative that was fundamentally at odds with the one offered by the Bedouins' lawyers. According to Bach, the Bedouins of the Negev were nomads who resided in temporary units of residence without any appropriate infrastructure. The Bedouins, according to this narrative, had a severe "dwelling problem" that the State of Israel has repeatedly tried to resolve by offering a "permanent solution to . . . the Bedouin section." The current planning programs of the authorities—settling the Bedouins in modern planned towns—now provided adequate housing alternatives for the Bedouins: "The [authorities] employed and employ numerous means in order to ease the plight of the Bedouins and to facilitate their transition from nomadic life to convenient permanent settlements. These means include substantial incentives to every Bedouin over the age of 21 that agrees to move to a permanent settlement and a grant to any Bedouin who destroys the illegal construction in which he resides.[25]

As this judicial text clearly illustrates, the perceived injurious experience of the Bedouins is only one possible way of abstracting a story out of reality. Like every other version of truth, the Bedouins' story of injustice—as told by their lawyers—can be countered with an opposing version. The version that the court articulates sees grace where the former speaks of evil, salvation and good intentions where the former emphasizes oppression, and progress and modernization where the former complains of silencing and denial. The authorities, in the court's account, both sympathize with the Bedouins and seek ways to help them in their times of trouble. The Bedouins are constructed as rootless nomads in search for permanent solutions rather than as a people who wish to cling to lands that they consider their own and to habits that they are reluctant to give up. Their plight, in this account, is not a result of state oppression but of primitive living conditions.

Thus, the judicial version denies the collective cause underlying the practice of illegal construction. From the court's perspective, the demolition of Bedouin houses is no more than a strict application of the rule of law to law-breaking citizens. Illegal construction, in this account, is not a political but a criminal matter. The historical collective origins of the Bedouins' practices of construction—a necessary condition for the social construction of the cause—are dissolved. The general narrative is depoliticized and reappears as a series of individual acts of illegal construction: [W]ith an overall perspective of the historical developments that the Bedouins in this area experience, it is difficult not to sympathize with these people and to feel a desire to help them in their distress. . . . But this sentiment cannot drive us to allow the existence of constructions that were illegally constructed or to order the authorities not to implement the law." [26] This version of the story of the Bedouins, in short, does not give ground to any legal, moral, or political cause.

The legal offices of the Bedouin Association closed even prior to the court's decision (though the association continues to operate on a retainer basis). Ray, like Abas before her, received a grant from the New Israel Fund and moved to Washington, D.C., for a one-year training program in cause lawyering. Still a legal-entrepreneur type in respect to cause lawyering, she nonetheless did not resume her involvement with the Bedouins upon her return to Israel. Ray's reflection on lawyering for the Bedouins, three years after the case and after having been exposed to what she refers to as a "culture of do-gooders" is certainly instructive: "This is not America, where you can live off this [cause-lawyering]," she said. "Nowadays I cannot contribute to organizations. I charge money, I must work for myself, and I cannot provide free services any more." And yet: "I would have liked to deal with women's issues, even discrimination, but not with Bedouins—I do not think it has a chance, it is like grinding water, it is mere politics." Abas, having completed his one-year commitment to Shatil—working for the Bedouins—also admits to us that he "slowly disappeared" from the scene.

The network did not entirely collapse. Rather, the Bedouin File returned to the local courts in Beer-Sheba, where numerous individual Bedouin cases are tirelessly processed on a routine basis. The "field soldiers" remain. Most of the lawyers who worked for the Bedouins through the mediation of the Bedouin Association did not survive in this particular field of practice. From Ray and Abas, the Bedouin File returned to Yaron's office and remained for a while in Levy's hands. Levy, with the approval of the Bedouin Association, wanted to take the Bedouin File with him when he left Yaron to initiate his own private practice. This time, unlike in the case of Ray, Yaron refused, for reasons that are not entirely clear to us. Other lawyers at Yaron's office took on the representation, apparently with little enthusiasm. The file then moved to another lawyer, who assumed representation on a retainer basis for roughly $1,700 a month. Unsatisfied with her performance as well, the Bedouin Association assigned another lawyer, Motti Moren, who once shared office space with Ray and Abas and who currently shares an office with Levy.

It is notable that the potentially more conscientious lawyers who have worked for the Bedouin Association may be marked for their rather rapid turnover as lawyers for a cause. On the other hand, those lawyers who "do good" as an almost incidental part of their practice, those who to a large extent discover themselves as lawyers for a cause and do not practice as entrepreneurs—legal experts on injustice—survive longer in the field. Moren, at any rate, currently represents Bedouins in the Beer-Sheba courts alongside the other "independent" field soldiers.

Representation of Bedouins through the Bedouin Association and representation of Bedouins on a direct lawyer-client basis converge—in terms of practice and, to some degree, in terms of a shared disillusionment. One lawyer said: "I do not believe anymore in talking about the discrimination of the Bedouins. I wouldn't consider it today as a terrible injustice—I have many clients with injustice, everyone claims injustice." And Yaron, the overseer of so much work on behalf of Bedouins admitted: "At present I just want to get rid of people's grievances and not deal with it . . . because I am tired and I am flooded with work and I do not have any time for myself." Yet the most common complaint that lawyers have about their practice concerns their own clients. In one form or another, many of them describe the Bedouins as too passive and too internally divided. They lament the poor organizational skills of the Bedouins and their inability to politically mobilize the cause. Some lawyers think that this issue lies outside their own lawyerly responsibilities: "The legal struggle should have been part of a political struggle. This is the task of the Bedouin Association, but someone else has to tell them that. I cannot talk about it, I cannot even tell them that they do not mobilize their parliamentary weight to solve their problems." Others simply admit that the task is too big for them and that they cannot be expected to do what the Bedouins themselves are not doing.

Yet it also seems to us that there is a difference between representation of Bedouins through the Bedouin Association and representation by the "independent" lawyers. In our field observations we have noticed that, unlike the independent lawyers, the lawyer of the Bedouin Association does not know his clients in person and that this state of affairs sometimes leads to embarrassing situations at court. At least some Bedouin defendants, always accompanied in court by scores of relatives, seem to notice this fact and to express doubts concerning the commitment of cause lawyers who offer services through the Bedouin Association. Common remarks touch upon issues of lawyer-client trust, suggesting that a lawyer who is retained on a strictly commercial basis may be expected to have a higher level of commitment and responsibility toward her or his clients. In other words, independent professional lawyering seems to offer a less alienating and less distant form of lawyer-client relations. One independent lawyer was quite uncompromising on this issue: "This whole issue of free representation is misleading. I try to stay away from all the legal activity organized around the Bedouin Association because it seems to me to be entirely political, and it seems to me that the spirit behind the association simply seeks to ride on the back of the Bedouins to the Parliament. I am different. I do not have a political agenda and I look in practical terms at each case, whether an individual client or groups or tribes."

In sum, we are left with what may be the ultimate paradox of this story. Across various dimensions—endurance, experience, commitment, and proximity to any single client, and even expectations that the Bedouin will "do something political"—it is the independent lawyers and not the officially designated lawyers of the Bedouin Association who seem to be realizing lawyering for a cause. Yet these lawyers, as we tried to show, lack the organizational, financial, and professional orientations and capabilities that may transform cases into causes. These field soldiers, in their representation capacities, more often than not are made as invisible as their clients in the grinding legal machinery they face. It is here that we come back full circle. The cause, as it now stands, is fragmented and dispersed in numerous pieces—cases that are relentlessly processed at the local courts, carried on by a number of disillusioned, somewhat cynical and yet persistent, invisible lawyers who, in the last instance, represent people and not ideas.

Notes

This research was supported by the Israel Foundations Trustees and the Israel Science Foundation administered by The Israel Academy of Sciences and Humanities. We owe many thanks to Nelly Elias, the research assistant of this ongoing project, for her help and dedication. We also wish to thank the participants at the conference on cause lawyering at Amherst College in August 1994 for their insightful comments. The names of lawyers who were interviewed have been changed to protect confidentiality.

1. Adva Center, *A Survey of Bedouin Education in the Negev,* vol. 5 (in Hebrew) (Tel Aviv: Adva Center, 1996); Central Bureau of Statistics, *Population and Housing Survey,* publication no. 6 (in Hebrew) (Jerusalem: Central Bureau of Statistics, 1983). All quotes were translated from the Hebrew by authors.

2. "Moshe Dayan: On the Land Policy and the Bedouin Problem in Israel," *HaAretz,* July 31, 1963 (in Hebrew). Emphasis added.

3. Adva Center, *A Survey of Bedouin Education in the Negev.*

4. Ministry of Interior, *A Report of the Inter-Departmental Committee on Illegal Construction in the Arab Sector* (in Hebrew) (Jerusalem: Ministry of the Interior, 1986). The report, known as the Markovitz Report, suggested the demolition of 6,601 Bedouin constructions in the Negev and stated that "the enforcement of the Law of Planning and Construction in the Bedouin sector is tightly connected to the policy of settlement in the urban existing and planned towns" (p. 59).

5. Gideon Vitkon, Israel land authority commissioner, to member of parliament Haim Oron, May 30, 1989. The letter states that there are roughly 3,200 pending claims of ownership by Bedouins, concerning an area of 1,650,000 dunams. The state has negotiated and settled only 25,000 dunams. Most of the Bedouins refuse to negotiate over the proposed terms.

6. On the resistance of law to arguments that transcend the boundaries of the particular case see R. Shamir, "Suspended in Space: Bedouins under the Law of Israel," *Law and Society Review,* 30, no. 2 (1996), 231–258.

7. This study is based on in-depth, one- to three-hour recorded interviews with fourteen of the lawyers we refer to in this paper. Unless otherwise stated, all the quotes used in this paper are taken from these interviews. Interviews were held from May to October 1994. In addition, the study is based on the archives of the Association for Support and Defense of Bedouin Rights in Israel, field observations at court, analysis of legal documents made available to us by a number of lawyers, court decisions, media reports, and numerous informal conversations with lawyers, clients, observers, and officials.

8. TP 4578/87, *State of Israel v. Jamia Salah Abu Ayash* (in Hebrew) (15.12.87).

9. "Ye'charev Beit'cha" [Your House Shall be Demolished], *Kol Ha'Ir,* September 16, 1988 (in Hebrew).

10. BDM (District Disciplinary Tribunal) 122/91, *The District Committee of the Tel-Aviv Bar v. X;* BDA 7/93, *X v. The District Committee of the Tel-Aviv Bar.* The case finally reached the Supreme Court of Israel, which accepted Lev's appeal on factual grounds, refusing to develop, much to Lev's disappointment, the substantive issues raised by the dispute: ALA 2399/94, *X v. Israel Bar Association,* unpublished, December 31, 1995.

11. A. Ankar, "Public Interest Litigation and the Professional Ethics of Lawyers," *Ha'-Praklit* 34 (1982), 403–412 (in Hebrew).

12. See Andrew Abbott, *The System of Professions* (Chicago: University of Chicago Press, 1988). Distance from clients and the tendency to engage in "theoretical" tasks are sources of internal stratification within a profession: "The professionals who receive the highest status from their peers are those who work in the most purely professional environments" (Abbott, *The Systems of Professions,* 118). Practitioners who move from direct representation to consulting work, advising others on how to litigate, may thus also upgrade their status.

13. For a similar approach see Susan Sterett, "Caring about Individual Cases: Immigration Lawyering in Britain," chap. 10 of this volume.

14. On similar dilemmas of representation, see William H. Simon, "Visions of Practice in Legal Thought," *Stanford Law Review* 36 (1984), 469–507.

15. HCJ 2678/91, *El Sanaa and Others v. The Attorney General and Others,* PD 46:3, 709.

16. S. Snir to the state attorney general, July 23, 1990.

17. The petitioners had no opportunity to make oral arguments in the case. Five minutes after oral arguments began, a bomb threat compelled the evacuation of the court. The court then ordered petitioners to submit their arguments in writing. Snir, like other lawyers whom we addressed, suggest that this fact further diminished the opportunity to draw the attention of the court to the petitioners' plight.

18. G. Levy to U. Mer, August 2, 1991.

19. N. Wiley to G. Levy, May 23, 1991.

20. HCJ 2678/91, *El Sanaa and Others v. The Attorney General and Others,* PD 46:3, 712.

21. Shatil offers training programs and advisory services to grassroots organizations: financial management, seminars, coordination, recruitment, technical support, legal referrals, coalition building, public relations, media projects, etc. It also operates as a clearing house through which financial support is funneled to various groups. In 1989, for example, it had ties to 174 groups, organizations, movements, and action committees, on its support list. The agenda-setting impact of Shatil is an issue that has yet to be studied in depth.

22. M. Maller to the Planning and Construction District Committee, January 23, 1977.

23. A. Brand, R. Mosinzon, D. Amit, G. Eshet, D. Kretzmer, and A. Rinat, "A Report on the Bedouins Claims for Lands in the Negev," (report submitted to the Association for Civil Rights in Israel, Jerusalem, 1978) (in Hebrew).

24. Memorandum addressed to ACRI's Steering Committee, October 1990. Emphasis added. Trans. from Hebrew.

25. HCJ 2678/91, *El Sanaa and Others v. The Attorney General and Others,* PD 46:3, 712. Trans. from Hebrew.

26. Ibid.

PART III

Strategies of Cause Lawyering under Liberal Legalism

Rethinking Law's "Allurements"

A Relational Analysis of Social Movement Lawyers in the United States

MICHAEL MCCANN & HELENA SILVERSTEIN

Many scholars in recent years have examined the relationship between law and the politics of social reform advocacy in the United States. The bulk of this scholarship has been highly circumspect regarding the progressive potential of legal tactics, legal institutions, and cause lawyers for social reform movements. These critical analyses suggest that, at best, cause lawyers and legal activism tend to be ineffective in advancing progressive reform goals. Many scholars go yet further in arguing that lawyers and legal activism often actually divert movement energies away from radical alternatives, thereby unwittingly reinforcing rather than challenging dominant institutional relations and ideologies. As such, critical legal scholars frequently counsel against reliance on litigation, legal discourse, and legal activists in struggles for social change.[1]

We too have been influenced by this critical view of law and lawyers. Indeed, much of our own work has been inspired and informed by skeptical assessments of law in general and the propensities of cause lawyers specifically.[2] However, our recent research has led each of us to reassess this critical stance. Our evidence—gathered from separate studies on the recent movements for gender-based pay equity (or comparable worth) and animal rights in the United States[3]—suggests that many familiar generalizations about cause lawyers are overly broad and inadequately substantiated. Indeed, we have found that lawyers can, under certain circumstances, contribute important strategic resources and skills to the advancement of movement reform goals. In addition, our research has confirmed that many movement lawyers are very aware of the considerable drawbacks associated with using the legal system and, as a result, approach their strategic efforts in a relatively sophisticated, often creative manner.

These findings have not led us to reject outright prevailing critical perspectives. Rather, our aim in this essay is to offer a more nuanced, context-specific, relational understanding of the variable roles and contributions of cause lawyers in different movement settings. These factors include especially (1) the formal roles and relationships of cause lawyers in movement organizations, (2) the general organizational structures of indigenous movement associations, (3) the general context of political opportunities and constraints facing particular social movements, and (4) the historical/political experiences of both movement lawyers and nonlawyers. These factors, we suggest, are more important than measures of the personal political beliefs and abstract programmatic commitments of lawyers, which are the focus of some studies in cause lawyering.

The following pages will develop this general argument. Before proceeding, however, we offer some caveats. First, the descriptions of our research findings offered in this paper are very general and impressionistic. More detailed documentation of our data is available in our other publications.[4] Second, our sketch of factors that explain variations among different movement lawyers are, at this stage, speculative. While confident about our empirical findings, we view our broader claims about contextual factors as preliminary hypotheses deserving further study. In short, our primary goal here is to open up questions about (rather than simply refute) the predominant critical stance toward social movement lawyers and to provide specific conceptual tools with which to proceed in this continuing exploration. Finally, it should be noted that our primary empirical studies and generalizations are specifically oriented to the United States context. Thus, our claims here are intended to be limited in geographical scope, although we hope to contribute to the development of more broadly comparative perspectives regarding legal activism in diverse cultural settings.

The Conventional Critical Picture

We begin by briefly outlining the general contours of existing critical arguments regarding movement lawyers. Such critical perspectives build upon two different but related assumptions. First, critics assume that cause lawyers are heavily inclined toward litigation as the preferred means to achieve reform goals. After all, the primary professional training, socialization, and experiences of lawyers all work to privilege formal legal advocacy. Moreover, critics contend that lawyers' backgrounds frequently cultivate an unduly optimistic, even naively romantic view of law's transformative potential. This general attraction to litigation often finds support in the self-interest and personal aspirations of lawyers. Like the Western hired gun, movement lawyers are said to be motivated by glory, status, and prestige to expand their reputations by engaging in legal duels from which they might emerge victorious. As a result, campaigns for justice become synonymous with triumphs in court for movement lawyers.[5]

Critics commonly maintain that lawyers overwhelm movements with this single-minded commitment to litigation as a tool for social change. Given the widespread acceptance of the "myth of rights" and deference to professional expertise in our society, movements often fall under the spell of legal professionals and their legalistic biases.[6] In Rosenberg's terms, entire movements thus routinely fall prey to the "lure of litigation" as legal tactics favored by lawyers function like "fly paper," attracting and trapping movement advocates with their alluring logic of transformation.[7]

Were litigation actually as successful as lawyers often think it is, the focus on lawsuits might not be terribly problematic. But critics further hold that the propensity to concentrate on judicial intervention has several problematic and costly implications. First, and most obvious, are the high tangible costs of litigation that result from significant expenditures of time, energy, and monetary resources. Second, such expenditures of resources are often inefficient because inherent institutional weaknesses and constraints impede the judiciary's ability to deliver on the promise of promoting reform.[8] Third, the legalistic propensities of lawyers tend to directly and indirectly inhibit alternative movement strategies by depleting scarce movement resources and by diverting concerns away from long-term projects such as grassroots mobilization, alliance building, or more radical tactics such as public protest.[9] Fourth, the inclination of lawyers to frame movement goals in terms of disputes among discrete parties can narrow the range of movement demands as well as undermine broad-based movement organization and alliance building. The result is a tendency to atomize struggles, dividing and separating rather than uniting those who desire social change.[10] Fifth, the limited ideological biases of legal professionals, which privilege individual controversies to the detriment of collective struggles and goals, unconsciously narrow lawyers' conceptions of movement ends.[11] Finally, problematic tensions between cause lawyers and their clients (i.e., between lawyers and other movement leaders on the one hand, and lawyers and general movement constituents on the other) often develop as lawyers come to dominate movement efforts.[12]

Overall, critics thus have identified numerous dangers and drawbacks associated with lawyers who distract and divert movement efforts. Lawyers, it is suggested, push social movements in narrow directions that are, at best, ineffective and, at worst, harmful. Lawyers, caught up in the myth of rights and in their own career and personal goals, tend to infuse movements with the misleading and mythical promise of legal justice. Even when lawyers sincerely identify with movement aims, therefore, their own biases and beliefs can crowd out alternative substantive agendas, organizational approaches, and tactical actions. Legal activists, along with their perspectives and methods, contribute to illusions of change without advancing real reform. In so doing, cause lawyers tend to reaffirm more than resist and challenge status quo hierarchies.

Cause Lawyers in Two Movements

The conventional critique of movement lawyers outlined above has informed our own studies of social reform activism. However, our research has suggested the need to reconsider these assumptions. Our own reconsideration leads us to put forth a more complex, context-specific, relational portrayal of legal activists. Before presenting this portrayal, we briefly describe our research.

The Research

The data for this paper derive from separate but related research on two recent social movements in the United States: the pay equity movement and the animal rights movement. Over the course of our respective studies, we engaged in a detailed and contextually oriented exploration of the strategies, designs, and activities of these movements. Our research emphasized in particular the deployment of legal strategies and examined the relationship between lawyer and nonlawyer activists as well as the relationship between legal and extralegal tactics and practices. In doing so, however, we attempted to balance an instrumental view of law with attention to law's "constitutive" power. As such, the "legal mobilization" approach we employed focused on how law at once shaped and was reshaped by the political struggles at stake; law thus was viewed as both a constraint and a resource for differently situated parties in complex, ever-changing ways. We also employed similar multidimensional research methodologies featuring analysis of official legal texts, news media coverage, internally oriented movement communications, externally directed movement publicity as well as participant observation and open-ended interviews with movement activists.[13] The findings presented here draw on all of these sources, although the interviews with activists will be invoked most prominently.

The *pay equity movement* was comprised of relatively decentralized campaigns that arose in dozens of states during the 1970s and 1980s to challenge the systematic undervaluation and underpayment of jobs primarily occupied by women and minorities. Its core organization has been rooted in groups of defiant working women in public sector unions along with allies in various women's, civil rights, religious, and other civic associations. The research into this pay equity activism (McCann 1994) entailed interviews with 140 activists from more than twenty sites of reform action around the nation. Of these, one hundred interviewees were administered a formal, semistructured survey addressing a variety of topics regarding political tactics, participants, and experiences. Thirteen of the surveyed movement activists were attorneys by training, although only nine had litigation experience in wage equity cases. Four of these nine litigators were union staff lawyers; four had served as special counsel for unions in wage cases; and one worked for an independent women's rights organization. Of the four nonlitigating attorneys, one had become a union field organizer; one was a union political consultant; one was an independent feminist political activist; and one was a director of a national pay equity rights organization. Two other union staff attorneys and two feminist attorneys were interviewed but not surveyed. Interview material from all of these sources contributed to our data; survey results comparing responses of the nine litigating attorneys to other activists will be cited specifically below.[14]

The contemporary animal rights movement in the United States has sought, through the extension of legal rights, to liberate animals from human-induced suffering. Unlike the more mainstream animal welfare movement, the animal rights movement has transformed the terms of the debate by calling not simply for humane treatment of animals but for animal rights and an end to exploitation. Investigation of this movement (Silverstein 1996) included in-depth, open-ended interviews with twenty-five activists located in several cities around the country.[15] Given the still rather limited pool of lawyers engaged specifically in animal issues, the number of animal rights lawyers interviewed was, not surprisingly, small. Six animal rights attorneys participated in lengthy interviews. Two of the six were staff attorneys for national animal rights organizations;[16] two more worked part-time for local organizations; one headed an organization specifically devoted to legal action for animals; and one was a law professor and activist who frequently litigated on behalf of several organizations. In addition to those interviewed, many articles in law journals, newspapers, magazines, and movement literature provided additional data into the practices and approaches of animal rights attorneys. Moreover, the twenty additional interviews with nonlawyer activists supplemented the data gathered from interviews with the attorneys.

Identifying Cause Lawyers

The above outline of our research identifies a particular conceptual problem for our analysis. In short, movement lawyers comprise a rather diverse group, at least with regard to their organizational affiliations. While this topic will be addressed at greater length in the last section of this essay, we have chosen to distinguish here among four categories of movement lawyers. Three categories are immediately apparent from the above discussion: *staff lawyers* who work (usually for a mix of salary and case fee) in established organizations such as unions or women's rights groups; *independent cause lawyers* who work for fee as special counsel on particular movement cases; and *nonpracticing lawyers* who have stepped out of professional roles to contribute in other ways to the cause. Interviews with pay equity activists further suggested the value of distinguishing two ideal types of staff lawyers—between what one equity movement advocate called *legal staff "technicians"* and *legal staff "activists."* The major difference between these two types was the degree to which they displayed independent initiative and leadership in pressing their organizations to support movement causes. Staff technicians, in this view, tend to restrict themselves to executing the more narrowly technical legal aspects (consultation, negotiation, litigation) of campaigns initiated by others. Staff activists, by contrast, distinguish themselves as leaders in formulating group demands, developing group strategies, waging broader political campaigns, and even challenging their own organizations on behalf of constituent interests or principles. We emphasize here that these diverse types of movement lawyers are not distinguished by personal political values or attitudes so much as by their political roles and institutional relationships within the movement.

The following pages will focus primarily on two of these groups, the legal staff activists and the independent cause lawyers. These actors are both most closely aligned with the particular policy campaigns at stake and potentially most influential as tactical leaders in the movement. If legalistic cooptation of reform efforts were to take place, one might expect them to be most responsible.

An Alternative Image of Cause Lawyers

General Findings

Our research has not confirmed the standard critical view of legal activists sketched above. Although cause lawyers in our study certainly did encourage the use of tactics associated with the judicial system, they tended to be highly circumspect, critical, and strategically sophisticated about the pitfalls of legal action, the "liberal" biases of legal norms, and the imperatives of effective political struggle. What is more, we found striking similarities between the understandings, goals, and tactical preferences of cause lawyers and nonlawyer activists in the two movements. The following section outlines these general findings in more specific terms.

Legal Advocacy as Political Strategy

The first and most general point is that *nearly all of the cause lawyers in our movement studies viewed law, litigation, and legal tactics in a skeptical, politically sophisticated manner.* In short, they were far more inclined toward what Scheingold calls a "politics of rights" than the "myth of rights" perspective.[17]

For one thing, most lawyers were extremely critical of the overwhelmingly "conservative," tradition-bound character of the courts that, they felt, betrayed claims to neutrality, consistency, and impartial justice. "Logic and legal analysis do not seem to be particularly relevant. . . . It is clear that the Supreme Court is taking away rights that were previously guaranteed," one wage equity lawyer complained about federal court rulings in the 1980s. Indeed, lawyers and nonlawyers alike in the equity movement repeatedly assailed the tendencies of, in one attorney's words, "rich white male elites" on the bench who cannot see past their own biases. Moreover, the lawyers we interviewed were equally aware that winning in court alone rarely generated substantial social change beyond specific, often inadequate remedies for particular clients. "You have to be pretty naive, politically, to think that winning a lawsuit, even a big test case, even a whole string of cases, by itself really makes a difference in the scheme of things," a feminist wage discrimination lawyer reported in typical fashion.

At the same time, however, lawyers whom we studied did believe that legal tactics can advance movement goals under certain conditions and when "used in the right ways." For most of our subjects, these "right" uses involved careful coordination of litigation and legal advocacy with other tactics and resources. Indeed, lawyers in both movements repeatedly talked about litigation as an ancillary tactic that was most effective in tandem with other movement efforts, as one dimension in a larger strategic approach to reform politics. As lawyer and nonlawyer activists for animal rights responded when asked to compare the effectiveness of litigation with other strategies, "It's all part of a menu," "It all goes hand in hand," and "It's part of a total campaign." This was also evidenced by the fact that over three-fifths of all activists and all of the lawyers interviewed in the equity movement agreed that litigation was "one of several most effective" tactics, while very few ranked it either as the "single most important" or as "ineffective."[18] Moreover, while the "direct" benefits of winning lawsuits for specific client groups was highly valued, it was the "indirect" benefits of litigation and legal tactics for the broader campaign that were most salient in the lawyers' reflections about their efforts. In particular, most of our lawyers discussed the ways in which litigation could be effectively used to bolster efforts for constituent education and mobilization, political lobbying, negotiation with management, and winning allied support.

Two dimensions of movement struggle were especially notable in pay equity struggles. The first tactical use of litigation that equity movement lawyers emphasized was in political organization and movement building. It is relevant here that half of all activist interviewees asserted that the single most important use of litigation was for "consciousness-raising" and movement organization; 95 percent agreed that this indirect effect was one of litigation's two most important contributions.[19] As the National Committee on Pay Equity (NCPE) director summarized, "I think litigation has played a very important educational role. . . . Litigation brings the media in a way that nothing else has so far."

One longtime civil rights and union attorney was most commonly recognized as the primary architect behind this tactical effort. His guiding logic was laid out during a well-known forum on pay equity strategies published in a 1976 issue of *Signs*. "The best kind of education is the kind that results . . . from making those

who break the law give restitution to discriminatees. The best way to do this . . .
is to enforce the law by filing charges and lawsuits," he argued.[20] In another context, he urged the use of lawsuits to "educate the public to the open defiance of
law by virtually every public and private employer." In his writings, speeches, and
interviews, he often referred specifically to the role of early court cases brought by
the National Association for the Advancement of Colored People in catalyzing the
civil rights movement as his working model of legal strategy.[21]

Wherever this attorney worked—as pay equity litigator with at least four
unions, for example, as well as advisor to the NCPE—litigation thus was carefully
coordinated with publicity campaigns to dramatize the wage discrimination issue,
to educate the public, and to activate potential advocates for the cause. In fact, he
left his job as general counsel at one union to work for a much larger union
precisely because the latter was more able and willing to expend considerable
resources publicizing pay equity legal battles. Not surprisingly, the union spent
significant amounts of money and time to ensure that "the AFSCME [American
Federation of State, County and Municipal Employees] case (against Washington
state) has become the best educational tool available."[22] As this attorney stated,
"When we won the district court decision, AFSCME had more people working on
this issue in its P.R. division than lawyers. Obviously they felt it was very useful.
They paid out very little in legal fees but the P.R. operation was very big."[23] Well-
publicized litigation, in his words, was the key for awakening the "sleeping giant"
of protest against sex- and race-based wage discrimination. Nearly every other
union attorney interviewed echoed this view of how to use litigation for the
movement-building effort. "I am a firm believer that you need to think very carefully before you legalize a conflict . . . and organizing is always the key to measure
what you are trying to do," one local nurses' association attorney stated in typical
terms.[24]

Litigation was similarly used by equity lawyers to increase leverage in collective bargaining and other modes of wage negotiation. For most union activists,
not surprisingly, "collective bargaining is the only answer" to wage inequities.[25]
Indeed, one local leader argued, "Being a union person I have a real aversion to
moving everything into the courts all the time. I would much rather that we dealt
with it at the bargaining table. . . . If it is only in the courts people forget about
it and it is something that is happening out there somewhere."[26] What was surprising was that nearly all attorneys agreed with this assessment. "Unions are
about bargaining for workers; litigation cannot, or should not, be used to replace
that process," noted one.[27] However, both attorneys and most other activists
agreed that legal tactics can provide crucial pressure forcing concessions from
employers in the bargaining process. As two leading attorneys put it, "[D]iscrimi-
nation will generally not be corrected at the bargaining table . . . without using
the law for support."[28] Their position was even more explicitly laid out in a movement newsletter: "Unions must see litigation as part of the collective bargaining

process . . . [as well as] helpful in their organizing drives."[29] Other movement lawyers echoed the same basic understanding. "Effective collective bargaining is when you get something out of it," a female legal counsel suggested. "I don't think you get something out of it without the threat of litigation. You have to show that you are willing to file the charges and the lawsuits to make them take you seriously at the bargaining table."[30] A California attorney agreed, noting that "what unions need is a lawyer who will push and litigate to create a favorable context for negotiation."[31] Again, nearly half of all activists interviewed agreed with lawyers in ranking this ancillary leveraging function of litigation as its most important contribution, while 90 percent ranked it as one of the two most important contributions.[32]

This strategic approach to litigation was similarly expressed by animal rights attorneys. Lawyer and nonlawyer activists alike noted the significant contribution litigation made to political education and publicity, and, in turn, to movement building. In addition, lawyers for the cause pointed to the pressure litigation can place on intractable institutions. Pressure generated by the threat of litigation was successfully used against the National Institutes of Health, the navy, universities, the U.S. Department of Agriculture, and other establishment foes to secure the right to protest, to stop the deployment of dolphins, to create alternatives to dissection, and to compel government enforcement of regulations. This leveraging component of litigation, some lawyers noted, was especially important for a movement, like the animal rights movement, that is often not taken seriously.

All in all, legal victories were hardly seen as ends in themselves by the lawyers we studied. Instead, legal tactics and norms were viewed with a critical eye and approached in a very politically sophisticated, long-term manner.

Litigation versus Other Tactics

The points outlined in the previous section are related to other more specific themes regarding the understandings and practices of cause lawyers in our case studies. Perhaps most obvious is that, *because lawyers did not view litigation as an exclusive end in itself, they were very committed to encouraging, enhancing, and supplementing rather than discouraging movement deployment of other political tactics.* Indeed, cause lawyers in our studies strongly urged, led, and coordinated multidimensional strategic campaigns in many cases. Exemplifying this approach, one animal rights attorney suggested that litigation activity always contains three parts: litigation, education, and legislation. When engaging in a lawsuit, "ideally, there should be a piece of legislation ready to go so that an angry public that has just read about it . . . can say 'now Mr. or Ms. Assemblyperson, vote for this.' " Wage equity lawyers repeatedly emphasized as well that litigation could not be separated from organizing, lobbying, public demonstrations, and other tactical activities.

It is relevant to emphasize here that most lawyers in both movements person-ally played a variety of roles not directly tied to litigation, negotiation, and other forms of official counsel work. As already documented, these lawyers spent much of their time actively generating movement publicity, rallying existing or potential movement supporters, coalition building, and political strategizing. "Preparing and arguing cases in the narrow sense takes up only about 10% of my time," one equity attorney reported. "The largest portion of time is spent out there talking to people, educating, mobilizing, organizing, proselytizing, ranting and raving if necessary" about issues of concern to workers.[34]

Not surprisingly, such endeavors generated among many cause lawyers whom we encountered a very complex view regarding legal effectiveness and impact, and especially regarding the value of winning cases in court. On the one hand, as we have already noted, most cause lawyers were skeptical about the transformative impacts of victorious lawsuits alone, in the absence of other well-coordinated po-litical actions. On the other hand, they were equally well aware of the power that could be derived from legal actions that did not necessarily depend on winning their primary claims. Where courts were relatively unsupportive of larger move-ment goals, for example, equity lawyers often focused on narrower legal claims that might at least fuel mobilizing efforts, focus attention on larger claims, or threaten employers refusing to negotiate wage issues. Moreover, equity lawyers formed a national committee in the late 1970s to coordinate and "control" litiga-tion efforts among different groups. The primary concern was that "small" gains were more valuable to catalyze the growing movement, while losses in "big risk" test cases could undermine organizing momentum. At the same time, careful screening work was undertaken to identify the most promising points where ad-vances in case law would recognize "radical" discrimination claims with the least risk of loss in court. And finally, lawyers recognized the value sometimes of press-ing litigation even in the face of several major losing causes in court. Specifically, even unsuccessful lawsuits in some circumstances could be useful for dramatizing worker claims and putting pressure on employers fearful of being branded as "dis-criminators."

Animal rights lawyers followed in much the same path. "You can lose in court and still win if you're doing sufficient public education by exposing the public to what you have assiduously prepared just in court papers," one lawyer observed.[35] Another attorney similarly noted the educational effects of litigation. "The way you educate people is to get the issue before them," and litigation is one way perform this task.[36] As these comments indicated, winning in court as a sole or primary goal was not valued by many lawyer or nonlawyer activists. Indeed, many legal activists appreciated the strategic gains to be derived from litigation that never gets to the trial stage. Pay equity activists, for instance, defined as most "successful" those legal actions that generated concessions without ever making it to trial. As one union attorney put it, "From the union's perspective, it does not matter if a remedy comes out of the settlement or the judgment. The goal is to get these people [employers] to change what they are doing, and we will use every method that is available."[37]

None of this meant that our cause lawyers used litigation purely as a mobilizing tool or as a leveraging "threat." Lawyers with whom we spoke noted the ethical code of conduct that must be adhered to in avoiding "frivolous" suits.[38] As one animal rights attorney noted, "I have a real responsibility not to just go out to get publicity. I have to believe that I have a good case that should win."[39] Moreover, while lawyers appreciated the indirect benefits of litigation, they were not unconcerned about potential losses in court. According to one animal rights attorney, there is little reason to invest resources in pursuit of a case that will certainly lose in court while there are so many other potentially successful issues to litigate.[40] On another note, one animal rights activist suggested that producing a contrary precedent through litigation would be bad "even though you have a couple of good public relations pieces."[41] In short, most lawyers we talked to considered a wide range of factors related to political "success" and "effectiveness" when considering whether and how to litigate. And this did not preclude advocacy of "lawless" action—such as illegal union strikes, public protests, minor property sabotage, and the like—to challenge legal policies that they thought were unjust. "If you have to break the law to make the law just, then so be it," added a union lawyer in reference to a local strike over unfair wage rates.[42]

Lawyers were no less sophisticated about the costs of litigation that might adversely affect deployment of other movement tactics. While it is true that litigation can entail many costs, our interviews suggested a number of factors that can lessen the severity of this problem. For one thing, lawyer and nonlawyer activists revealed a sober sensitivity to the issue of costs. There was considerable awareness of the time and monetary costs associated with litigation, and these costs were heavily weighed when deciding whether or not to proceed with litigation. Moreover, activists noted several ways to offset these costs. According to one nonattorney, litigation costs can be lowered by enlisting pro bono help, willing lawyers, and group coalitions to join as plaintiffs in legal action. This activist also noted that these types of assistance are increasingly becoming the norm.[43] Additionally, pay equity attorneys pointed out that judicial victories generally paid for most of their costs, including unsuccessful ventures. Indeed, the leading architect of wage discrimination cases boasted with only a little exaggeration that his legal actions "were fully self-supporting through attorneys' fees and never costed the union a penny."[44] In this sense, it thus is important to recognize that lawsuits can generate as well as consume operating revenue for movements.[45] Finally, pay equity lawyers pointed out that litigation more often expedited rather than protracted negotiations, especially in wage discrimination suits during the 1980s.

In sum, while litigation does involve costs and absorb resources, the conventional critique of cause lawyers proved far too simplistic for the movements that we have studied. Overall, the lawyers we observed neither privileged litigation as an end in itself nor allowed legal actions to undermine other movement tactics; quite the opposite: movement lawyers strategically used their legal skills in ways that complemented and augmented movement political action on multiple fronts. These efforts were not always successful, of course, but failure owed more to powerful opponents and systemic constraints than the lure of legalistic illusions.

Movement Atomization and Containment

These comments suggest a third component of our divergent picture. *When legal action is combined with other strategies, there is little reason to believe that cause lawyers contribute to the fragmentation of social movements.* Lawyers who approach legal action in a strategic and politically savvy fashion often can significantly reduce the atomizing character of formal legal action. Moreover, when lawyers come to view themselves more broadly as movement activists, this too can diminish the tendencies toward particularistic, internally divisive or disaggregating action.

Legal activity did not produce any significant amount of disaggregation or atomization in the two movements we studied. To the contrary, litigation seemed to help build connections among various groups allied with the causes. In the pay equity movement, legal activity connected local unions through networks of communication; it shaped parallel and interactive tactical action among union locals; and, perhaps most important, it helped to forge long absent bonds between working women in unions and independent feminist activists. The movement did remain highly decentralized for most of the 1970s and 1980s, it is true. But the primary reason for this was the concerted opposition mounted by federal officials during the Reagan administration. Litigation under federal civil rights laws sponsored by national union organizations enhanced tactical coordination for the movement and, in turn, provided one of the greatest sources of unity.

In the animal rights movement, litigation often brought groups and interests together to fight common battles as well. By joining together as plaintiffs in a lawsuit, litigation frequently facilitated interaction among different and sometimes competing advocacy groups. Furthermore, litigation in one part of the country, for a select organization or on a particular issue, often spurred activity in other parts, for other groups, and on other issues. Indeed, rather than fostering containment, litigation appeared in certain instances to facilitate broad and coordinated strategic attacks. For example, animal rights activism against hunting prompted hunter harassment laws prohibiting protests in designated hunting zones. In response to these laws, some animal rights groups engaged in "illegal" protests with the goal of initiating legal action to protect their First Amendment rights. Successful legal action in a few of these cases directly inspired similar challenges around the country. To further these challenges, activists working on behalf of specific organizations and causes connected with and assisted activists from other organizations around the country.[46] What some observers might see as a potentially containing and atomizing legal strategy thus became a means of connecting differing organizations, creating coalitions, and coordinating broad-based movement attacks.

Our studies of the animal rights and pay equity movements thus offer an alternative perspective on the atomizing quality of litigation. While we would not argue that litigation is never disaggregating for political struggles, we would say that the propensity to individualize disputes often can be overcome by legal actors well connected to the larger movement. Indeed, when initiated by politically sophisticated advocates, legal action has the potential to generate or enhance communication, alliances, and broad-based coordination.

The Movement's Substantive Agenda

Our research on lawyers suggests a fourth point. Not only were cause lawyers conscious and skeptical about the tactical limitations of formal legal actions, but they also were *conscious and often critical of the ideological and discursive frames associated with the prevailing legal system.* As such, the lawyers we encountered routinely encouraged manipulation of the prevailing framework in ways that at times challenged the dominant ideological biases of official law and advanced alternative constructions to them.

Evidence for this argument is well documented in our larger studies on this subject, and is too cumbersome to replicate here. However, some summary is relevant. For one thing, both cause lawyers and nonlawyer activists for the pay equity movement displayed a remarkably adroit capacity to engage in critical discussions of key categories—ideas of "market," "merit," "equality," and "justice," for example—in the antidiscrimination doctrines on which they relied to advance their substantive cause. These activists displayed capacities both to "unmask" familiar euphemisms for domination in prevailing legal rhetoric *and* to refashion them for various subversive and even potentially transformative purposes. Moreover, both lawyers and nonlawyers again displayed notably clear-sighted understandings about both the biases and promises of "rights talk" in general for movement campaigns. For example, lawyers variously embraced categories of the legal right to defend women's work as similar to men's work, as different but comparable to men, and as deserving because of women's basic needs as family members. "There is no reason that we can't have a multidefinitional approach" that mixes traditional and new types of rights understandings, one activist leader suggested. "It is still a rights issue, but different."[47]

Animal rights lawyers and activists displayed a similar critical approach to legal frames. Indeed, several interviewees echoed aspects of the conventional critique of law. Their attitudes toward rights discourse were especially illustrative. According to the comments of several advocates, rights discourse as used in Western liberal legal systems is inherently divisive. Rights language fosters conflict, competition, and individualism. According to one legal activist, rights are problematic "because they're dualistic, and they assume a competition-based type of arena for resolving the issues and for meting out justice. . . . [E]very right is considered conflicting with another right. A women's right not to be harassed on the street is conflicting with the man's right of freedom of speech and to harass women. It's one right against another. In that sense rights are very limiting and they're inadequate."[48]

While animal rights lawyers recognized the problematic ideological underpinnings of rights discourse, they also offered ways to overcome its limitations. For instance, some suggested that we should strive to move beyond the individualistic foundations of legal discourse toward a more collective understanding of rights. In doing so, these advocates put forth a community-oriented notion of rights that privileges responsibility and obligation to others. As a staff attorney for PETA (People for the Ethical Treatment of Animals) observed after discussing the limits of legal discourse, "[R]ights connote reciprocal duties. . . . Our realization that we have duties to animals . . . is so overdue that I prefer any analysis that imposes some duty on us."[49] Similarly, other lawyer and nonlawyer activists sought to advance rights discourse in ways that challenge competing constructions of opposing groups.

Overall, many of our interviewees approached legal discourse informed both by critical awareness of its ideological foundations and by a strategic commitment to challenging these foundations. Thus, our findings suggest that the conventional critique has exaggerated the constraining ideological effects of discursive legal frames and underestimated the ability of lawyers to manipulate or move beyond those frames.

Lawyers and Clients

Our final counterpoint pertains to lawyer/client relations generally, and specifically to the claim that lawyers dominate movements. Our findings from the two case studies suggest the opposite: *cause lawyers did not tend to dominate movements or clients, nor did they ignore rank and file movement members.* In contrast, the relationships between lawyers and other movement leaders on the one hand, and lawyers and movement constituents on the other, were characterized in large part by interdependence, interaction, and cooperation.

Several factors worked against lawyer domination in these movements. First, lawyers were often significantly more dependent on their clients than critics suggest. Lawyer independence was checked by clients' inherent suspicion of legal elites, by widespread activist reluctance to pour resources into litigation, by competing strategies available to clients, and by other organizational and resource constraints. The tactical and purposive preferences of clients who, after all, provided the monetary resources for legal activity worked especially to encourage this inter-dependence. In short, most lawyer activists did not act alone or independently develop their strategies of action. Rather, they were bound by both the influence of competing leadership groups and the goals of the larger organizations to which they were connected. This was especially true of union lawyers in the pay equity movement who were largely constrained by their union clients who paid the bills. Indeed, analysis of the pay equity movement demonstrated that unions ultimately called the shots for pay equity attorneys, or at least provided important checks on their independence. Likewise, animal rights lawyers were significantly guided and limited by the preferences and concerns of their clients.

A second factor that mediated the relationship between clients and lawyers was movement solidarity. Solidarity among lawyers, movement leaders, constit-uents, and individual plaintiffs typically worked to undermine lawyer domination and to bring lawyers and clients together in a common battle. Where strong inter-personal structures of solidarity existed, opportunities for lawyers to connect with grassroots constituencies and participate in local political activism were expanded. As a result, solidaristic bonds facilitated and enhanced communication and coop-eration between lawyers and clients. This, combined with the generally strong and assertive characters of movement leadership and plaintiffs, helped to inhibit the potential for lawyer domination.

Finally, and perhaps most important, lawyers' self conceptions and ap-proaches to activism influenced their relations with clients. Pay equity and animal rights lawyers who conceived of themselves as movement activists tended to iden-tify closely with the nonlawyer leadership as well as movement members. The cause lawyers who approached activism not simply as legal technicians but as movement activists understood the importance of developing mutual and ongoing relationships with the diverse movement constituencies. These lawyers, character-ized by their commitment to broad movement goals, recognized the need to con-nect with movement constituents both through and beyond litigation—through speeches, writing, lobbying, organizing, and educational campaigns. Moreover, these lawyers clearly testified to us that effective advancement of litigation required the support of movement leaders and constituents. For example, in the pay equity movement, the solidarity of unions behind lawyers was the most important factor in the effective deployment of litigation. In short, most of the lawyers we observed worked hard to build collegial, cooperative relations as movement teachers, boost-ers, and listeners.

None of this is meant to suggest that movement lawyers passively followed the organizational line at every point. Like independent feminists in the pay equity movement, lawyers have often sided with rank-and-file workers against more cau-tious or indifferent union leaders. For example, a team of three lawyers actively pushed resistant leaders in the International Union of Electrical, Radio, and Ma-chine Workers (IUE) to take a lead on the equity issue during the 1970s; the chief union counsel was released from a different prominent public sector union several years later in part because he pushed too hard. These cause lawyers thus identified themselves as what one called "policy leaders" rather than mere "technical servants" in their organizations. But even when relatively independent on policy goals, such lawyers tended to be bound by both organizational constraints that foster interdependence and their own commitments to viewing formal legal action in a visionary, tactically sophisticated manner. This meant above all that litigation must be assessed with regard to benefitting the overall organization—whether by helping organizing drives or pressuring employers—rather than as an end in itself, or even as the primary form of political advocacy. Contrary to many critics' expectations, there thus was little incentive or opportunity for either lawyers or litigation to "take over" either of the movements.[50]

The Alternative Image Summarized

Overall, when it came to deploying litigation, most of the legal activists we studied tended to be wary, tactically astute, and committed to long-term movement goals. Approaching litigation in this way was viewed as essential to reducing the costs and dangers associated with a legal strategy as well as maximizing legal effectiveness. On the whole, our research thus revealed what Susan Olson calls a "new style" of public interest litigation. With this new style, movement lawyers have "developed a notion of 'flexible lawyering' to encompass the variety of activities in which they are engaged."[51] According to Olson: "The greater participation of nonlawyers in decision making and the greater realization by lawyers of the limitations of judicial pronouncements alone to induce change have resulted in a melding of political and legal strategies. Some litigation has become so integrated with political activity outside the courts that its goal is as much to increase bargaining leverage externally as to secure victory in court."[52] Pay equity and animal rights lawyers, by and large, followed this model of "flexible lawyering," deploying litigation and other legal tactics in a manner that betrays few affinities with what Scheingold has called the "myth of rights."

Explaining the Differences:
Toward Some General Hypotheses

Although most lawyers in the movements we studied approached activism in a flexible manner, we are not arguing that all movement or cause lawyers share similar understandings or practice their politics in the same way. Indeed, as we noted earlier, not all attorneys in even these two movements fit this "new style" of legal activism to the same degree. And while we question the findings of some other scholars, we accept the relevance of their general critiques for many types of activist lawyers in other movements or for other causes. Hence the key questions:

What explains the varying approaches and characters of different legal activists? Why does our evidence diverge from the conventional critique? It is to these points that we now turn.

The first point for consideration is whether critics have overstated what they view as the problematic tendencies of cause lawyers. Scholarly critiques of cause lawyers draw on a key assumption made by critics of the average lawyer: legal socialization and professionalization foster biases that privilege narrow types of litigation activity. It is hardly surprising, critics argue, that lawyers have a predilection toward litigation and other conventional models of institutionalized legal action. "Lawyers are by training, socialization, and expertise inclined to exclusive use of litigation and negotiation. They tend to find politics somewhat distasteful and ordinarily try to steer away from militant confrontations," Scheingold has written.[53] According to critics, socialization through legal education and the profession leads most lawyers to emphasize litigation over politics, rights over needs, elite professional activity over grassroots activity, and winning cases over negotiation and changing relations. The ordinary lawyer, indoctrinated by legal education, influenced by the norms and practices of conventional legal players, and situated within the realm of official legal institutions, is thus likely to press for a court-oriented strategy.

We think that this critical contention that the ordinary lawyer and, in turn, the cause lawyer are conditioned to privilege litigation may be somewhat exaggerated. After all, most ordinary lawyers are less rights-oriented and litigious than critics often allege. There is ample evidence that most lawyers work to keep cases out of the courtroom, to push for negotiation, and to press for settlement.[54] Most lawyers tend to be cautious about formal legal proceedings, and use the prospect of a lawsuit to leverage bargaining and to resolve conflicts before they make their way into the courtroom.[55] Thus, the stereotype of the overly litigious lawyer may be just that: a stereotype.[56]

In these respects, then, our cause lawyers are similar to ordinary lawyers in that they are not overly inclined to resolve disputes or advance causes through courtroom battles. But this is not to say that professional socialization does not matter, nor that there are few differences between the actions of cause lawyers and other types of attorneys. Rather, we emphasize that diverse contexts of advocacy may help to explain the significant differences between ordinary lawyers and the cause lawyers. In terms of socialization pressures, professional interactions, and the lawyer-client relationship, the cause lawyer and the ordinary lawyer typically find themselves differently situated. For example, the ordinary lawyer, unlike the cause lawyer, is more likely to be situated conventionally with respect to legal education, other legal players, law firms, clients, and official legal institutions. The typical lawyer thus is a regular player, one who works inside of particular legal institutions,[57] and one who is connected to more establishment-oriented clients. In contrast, the cause lawyer, working within an alternative context, is likely to be less traditional and to work from the outside.[58] The cause lawyer is likely to have a greater personal commitment and connection to clients, to share those clients' systemic social critiques and commitments to long-term change, to be more willing to sustain rather than to settle struggles over moral principles and rights, and to resort more frequently to extralegal tactics to achieve certain goals. Hence, the associational affiliations of the cause lawyer often tend to generate a somewhat different mix of socializing influences, professional pressures, group relationships, and advocacy techniques.

The second point to consider is that many analysts either directly or indirectly focus their exploration of variable lawyer practice on matters of personal attitudes, political beliefs, or "ideology." We see some merit in such an approach. However we found little clear correlation between how well attorneys could "talk the talk" of radical or defiant political causes and how they practiced their political craft. In the pay equity study, for example, the attorney who could most compellingly marshall radical left—a mix of neo-Marxist, feminist, and postmodern—arguments and discourses in interviews was probably the most narrowly legalistic in practice. He castigated the "myth of rights" in the abstract but departed little from the behavior associated with it in practice.[59]

This last point underlines why our study focuses more on the particular relational contexts in which lawyers act to explain their various practical understandings and modes of action. This approach does not discount ideology but understands ideology more impersonally as modes of cultural knowledge developed through material activity in particular institutionalized settings. At bottom, the assumption is that abstract beliefs matter rather less for action than do the practical understandings derived through mobilizing particular cultural conventions in actual social interaction over time. This accumulated knowledge is manifest in what often is referred to by the term "consciousness." A person's legal consciousness, Ewick and Silbey write, is "part of a reciprocal process in which the meanings given by individuals to their world, and law and legal institutions as part of that world, become repeated, patterned and stabilized, and those institutionalized structures become part of the meaning systems employed by individuals."[60]

Our examination of the pay equity and animal rights movements leads us to believe that contextual factors contribute to differences in political consciousness among cause lawyers. In particular, we hypothesize that at least four context-specific factors may explain divergences among the lawyers within our sample and divergences between our overall findings and those of critical scholars. These factors include (1) the formal roles and relationships of cause lawyers in movement organizations; (2) the general organizational structures of the movements within which lawyers act; (3) the systemic opportunities for tactical legal success; and (4) the lawyers' own historically developed experiential knowledge and insights about political lawyering.[61]

Organizational Roles/Relationships of Cause Lawyers

We noted earlier that lawyers we encountered in our social movements could be categorized into four "ideal types." First is the *staff technician*. These attorneys are hired by movement organizations to work as a regular staff members. However, despite their organizational connections, staff technicians are by definition not highly active movement proponents. Although they may, and often do, sympathize and identify with broad movement goals, staff technicians are motivated less by the desire for social change than by fulfillment of technical functions. These attorneys typically do not work as movement leaders or organizers. Hence, they are more appropriately understood more as conventional professional lawyers serving clients in the strict sense and not as legal activists. The second ideal type is the *staff activist* lawyer. Like staff technicians, staff activists are ongoing (usually salaried) employees of formal movement organizations. Unlike staff technicians, however, these attorneys tend to function as movement leaders and organizers. Their focus rests not on litigation in the narrow sense, but on movement activism and political strategy more broadly construed.

The third type of lawyer is what equity movement activists often called the *hired guns*. These attorneys are not regular employees of movement organizations. Rather, they are hired to work on particular legal cases, conflicts, or campaigns. In unions and other organizations, these are identified by the label of "special" rather than "general" counsel. Hired-gun lawyers vary in terms of their ideological commitments. Some are politically very progressive in abstract commitments and are avid movement supporters, while others feel less of a connection to movement goals. Hired guns also vary with respect to activism and leadership. Some function like staff activists, viewing themselves and litigation in the broader social movement context. Others function more like staff technicians, as legal experts whose emphasis lies with litigation or narrow legal counsel. Finally, we encountered a variety of *nonpracticing lawyers*—that is, persons formally trained as attorneys but who now play roles not directly dependent on legal credentials. While these were very interesting contributors with interesting views about legal activity, we did not focus on them in this study.

The accuracy of these generalizations varies according to a number of factors. For one thing, these categories are "ideal" types and, as such, most attorneys do not "fit" perfectly into these classifications. For example, one staff technician may have little concern with anything aside from litigation while another may be somewhat active in extrajudicial realms, thus leaning more toward the staff activist type. Individual fit is also complicated by the fact that some attorneys work as part-time staff but may also be employed for specific cases as hired guns. Even if attorneys at specific moments do fit these ideal types, moreover, variation over time is likely to occur. For instance, staff technicians may with experience become more strategically oriented and connected to broad movement activism, thereby becoming more like a staff activist. As these examples illustrate, ideal types help to distinguish between lawyers, but they are by no means absolute and must be considered as idealizations.

Despite these caveats, our interviews suggested some important differences among the first three types of lawyers.[62] In general, staff technicians exhibited many of the characteristics expressed in the standard critique of lawyers. Staff technicians concentrated on formal counsel, negotiation, and litigation tasks assigned them by others rather than contributing individual political leadership or creative strategic initiatives to movement activities. Staff activists, on the other hand, generally were the most strategically oriented, the most wary about formal legal tactics, and the most connected to activities beyond the judicial realm. Although hired guns as a whole were inclined to view litigation more narrowly and to stress victories in court, the organizational contexts within which they worked contributed to variance among these attorneys. In particular, the hired gun closely situated within movement organizations over sustained periods of time tended to be a broader movement activist. In contrast, the more distantly and independently located hired gun was less likely to employ a multipronged strategy. Thus, the sophistication and practical participation of the hired gun in the "politics of rights" usually fell somewhere on the continuum between the staff technician and activist.

It is worth noting that these different roles are only in part self-chosen, and vary with the expectations of others in the organization. For example, a staff technician in a union characterized her role in this way: "I just do what they tell me. I offer counsel and pursue cases that I am instructed to pursue. My agenda is to follow those who pay my salary."[63] This raises a particularly important aspect of organizational connection, that of attorneys' compensation. As the quote suggests, staff technicians whom we encountered tended to identify themselves largely as employees; they were subordinate to movement "managers." Differences in how staff activists viewed their organizational roles, by contrast, were related to how they viewed and arranged their financial compensation. In the equity movement, these attorneys were usually salaried, but they took a greater hand in planning the financial aspects—both revenues generated and costs absorbed—of their activities. They saw themselves as more financially independent and more as self-employed—less as employees who must defer to management. Indeed, staff activists in the equity movement were often much more committed to movement constituents or organizational causes than to leader/managers, and were far more willing to jeopardize their job security in advancing political goals than were staff technicians. More tied to causes and constituents than to organizational structures per se, staff activists changed organizational affiliations and employers somewhat frequently within the larger movements.

On the other hand, hired guns in the equity movement were often committed to causes but had little ongoing, historical, personal relationship to particular constituencies. This less stable connection to a movement's grassroots seemed to discourage, or render less realistic, the close working relations with other movement activists that are necessary for long-term political coordination. Many hired guns were very sensitive to the need for multipronged political action but were not well situated to contribute effectively to such political activities. In short, the more legalistic activities of such lawyers derived less from acceptance of the "myth of rights" or their personal values than from their constrained organizational circumstances.

Staff technicians working in animal rights organizations exhibited tendencies comparable to pay equity staff technicians. However, unlike staff activists in the equity movement, those employed by animal rights groups were more directly connected to organizational leaders and structures than to broader movement constituents. This difference was likely related to the fact that grassroots constituents were more numerous, active, and organized in the pay equity movement than in the animal rights movement. Differences resulting from organizational relationships were also evident between hired guns affiliated with the pay equity and animal rights movements. Hired guns working on behalf of animal rights issues and organizations frequently developed long-lasting and personal relationships with movement activists. These enduring ties contributed to greater coordination between hired guns and organizational leadership. Hence, the similarly situated hired guns and staff activists in the animal rights movement displayed common tendencies.

Movement Resources and Solidarity

Organizational structures and relationships provide the foundational frames of understanding and tactical options from which lawyers act. Not surprisingly, therefore, the political resources and opportunities available to movement lawyers and other activists significantly affect their political propensities. In general, the amount and type of resources (money, expertise, constituents, political alliances, public support, etc.) available to a movement shape somewhat its political options.[64] A movement that develops strong alliances with key legislators is more likely to pursue a legislative lobbying strategy, for example. Movements with considerable potential for mobilizing support from broad general publics—like the civil rights movement—are more likely to direct energies to taking advantage of those resources. And the more that nonlegalistic tactics are realistic and actionable, the less likely is it that lawyers, litigation, or "legalism" will come to dominate a movement.

One less easily defined and more elusive resource deserves special attention in this regard. Our research suggests that when organizational structures of *solidarity* vary, so do lawyers' relationships with clients. For one thing, movements with strong grassroots solidarity and communication linkages have at their disposal significant resources and options—voting power, lobbying power, popular demonstrations, strikes or boycotts, and so on—that can lessen the exclusive focus on legal tactics. With such resources at hand, lawyers have reason and opportunity to view litigation in a more tactically sophisticated, flexible fashion. Moreover, when an organization has a highly solidaristic grassroots constituency, movement lawyers have many opportunities to become more closely tied to the membership. In the pay equity movement, lawyers often spent much time with local union members in educational campaigns, fact-finding projects, political strategizing, and the like. Although the linkages between lawyers and grassroots constituents in the animal rights movement may not have been as extensive as in pay equity, regular interactions did create important ties. In movements where constituents are mostly unorganized or highly divided, by contrast, lawyers are likely to work in a far more independent and insular fashion that privileges and leaves unchecked more "legalistic," litigation-oriented activities.

In this regard, it is worth noting that critics often overstate the centrality of lawyers and legal tactics in social movements. After all, most movements are complex, pluralistic coalitions of multiple, differently situated groups and actors. In such alliances, lawyers rarely play a central leadership role or command the authority to lure others toward an exclusive litigation strategy.[65] To be sure, some specific movement organizations—such as the NAACP, various legal defense fund groups, and national public interest groups—have been led by lawyers and have privileged litigation as a primary political tactic.[66] But many have not. More important, focus on these specific actors ignores their often (but not always) limited role and power in the broader movements for change with which they are allied. Legal tactics are but one of many resources, and lawyers are but one of many actors, in most political struggles. Both may prevail in some weakly organized movements, but this is a rare thing.

The Temptations of Legal "Success"

The opportunities for legal victory, that is, winning in court, also shape the perspectives and actions of cause lawyers. In general, the fewer the opportunities for viable litigation victories, the less powerful the temptations for lawyers and others to become captive to the myth of rights. Moreover, limited options encourage lawyers to mobilize law more selectively and creatively. If clear victories that bring the desired reform seem unlikely, then lawyers have reason both to downplay legalistic hopes and to structure legal actions in ways that maximize secondary benefits. Furthermore, constrained possibilities can lead lawyers to search creatively for openings within the legal system in order to broaden opportunities for success. According to one animal rights lawyer, activists must "be creative, and look for . . . areas in which there are holes in the legal system which you can get into, and ways in which you can manipulate the legal system to bring the issue that you want into focus without necessarily bringing that issue directly into focus."[67]

Attorneys for both pay equity and animal rights illustrated the significance of constrained opportunities. Pay equity lawyers, for example, never won a single case of comparable worth at the federal level that withstood review on appeal. They did win some key legal cases that provided openings for certain types of claims, and they then used those lawsuits very effectively for educating, organizing, and leveraging purposes. Yet, the fact that the early big defeats in the 1970s were costly and the courts backed off from the implications of some promising landmark cases after the 1980s cultivated considerable caution among cause lawyers and other activists. In short, broadside legal attack was never a viable option for the movement, and the lawyers were never central actors after their initial efforts to put the issue on the union and feminist agendas.

Animal rights attorneys have worked within an even more highly constrained legal context. Neither legislatures nor the courts have extended formal rights directly to animals. Moreover, only a limited number of laws can be easily accessed for litigation. As a result, legal activists have adjusted their practices in the face of these narrow opportunities to litigate. As one attorney put it, "Since I can't just go out and start lawsuits all the time, I do a lot of legislative [work] to try and change the law. Then you end up using your influence as a lawyer, what limited amount you might have, and call someone up and say I'm a lawyer and this has come to my attention. It seems to help push things along."[68] Several other attorneys suggested the strategy of broadening legal opportunities for partial or secondary gains in the face of constraints. For animal rights advocacy, this meant creatively using resources like free speech laws and open meetings laws to heighten awareness about hunting, dissection, and animal experimentation. One attorney expressed her attempts to be more creative in these ways:

> Usually a traditional lawyer's reaction is there is no method or existing procedures for us to go into court and undo this wrong, either because we're not the right people to do it under traditional guidelines or because the kind of wrongdoing we wish to undo is not covered by the law. That's my traditional reaction. But I'm learning to go way beyond that because usually I'm wrong when I say that. . . . In research, I'm beginning to identify areas of the law that will provide citizens, your average citizen and citizen organizations, with opportunities to redress grievances in court.[69]

Although both the animal rights and pay equity movements experienced constraints on legal activism, our analysis revealed an important difference in the constraints. For the pay equity movement, the narrow legal opportunities were no less a constraint on options than were the internal dynamics of intergroup movement politics. Within pay equity organizations and labor unions, conflict over varying goals and agendas contributed to competition among diverse strategies. As a result, litigative strategies competed with several alternative approaches; and it was often this internal competition, rather than external judicial limitations alone, that constrained the turn to more formal legal tactics. In the animal rights movement, internal group dynamics appeared less important in explaining the limited turn to litigation. Most significant for this movement were the various constraints that came externally from the courts and existing law.

Despite this difference, the narrow opportunities for success fostered a combination of creativity, flexibility, and skepticism among animal rights and pay equity lawyers alike. The irony associated with this point is apparent: with fewer short-term legal options provided by unsupportive courts, cause lawyers' contributions to "success" require subtle, politically astute, long-term perspectives. Given this situation, it would be surprising to find among movement lawyers and activists the widespread naive faith in the promises of legalistic action that scholarly critics often allege.

Historical Experience

Consistent with the points in the previous section, practical experience is a factor that significantly influences the understandings and tactical actions of cause lawyers. Our findings suggest that two levels of experience are important to consider in distinguishing among lawyers. First, the extent of lawyers' personal experiences within a particular social movement or for a cause appears to be significant. Second, lawyers' familiarity with experiences of other social movements or causes may be crucial for understanding differences between cause lawyers. While these points may seem obvious, they are important to highlight especially because they have generally been downplayed and overlooked in most analyses of legal activism.

It should not be surprising that lawyers' experiences within a social movement influence their approaches and perspectives on the law. Many who are drawn to becoming cause lawyers tend to be idealistic and hopeful at the outset. They often believe that they will be able to generate social change through the law. Over time, with experience and practice, this idealism may give way to a more realistic radicalism that envisions differently the role of legal tactics in political struggles. One animal rights proponent exemplified this initial idealism and the change that can come with experience. "I expected naively to become a lawyer and just sue. That's really not possible. It was disappointing, but it made me understand that this is a big movement, and it's going to take time. I had immature dreams of changing everything myself." This lawyer went on to express the broad and strategic approach that developed in light of her experiences.

> What I do is I try to take one little problem at a time and try to pursue it. I work with [a local animal advocacy group]; I'm on their board. I offer what I can to make the organization strong. I give a lot of legal advice, I update their bylaws, I

look out for them from a liability standpoint. On another level, I get calls a lot from people who call [the advocacy group] with animal problems. Sometimes they turn into lawsuits. Other times I'll just call the prosecutor and try to push something along, or call animal control and try to get something investigated. I try to network a lot, bring people together. I find that being a lawyer doesn't help in the way I thought it would, at least not yet.[70]

In the particular case of the animal rights movement, much of this pragmatism developed from experience with limited opportunities to pursue litigation. However, this wary, tactical orientation also often developed as lawyers reflected upon the various indirect effects of litigation. One animal rights attorney heavily involved in litigation related an example of learning, through experience, about the important secondary effects of lawsuits. Describing one piece of litigation, this attorney noted that she had put together a case that featured the state-of-the-art veterinary testimony on the leghold trap. After winning the suit, this attorney learned what she described as "a bitter lesson"—the lesson of failing to publicize the case and educate the public. "[W]e wanted to do more publicity but we didn't," she said. "I will never again do something of that magnitude where those affidavits go to waste."[71] With this "bitter lesson," the attorney drew upon her experience to take a broader and more tactically oriented approach to litigation.

The pay equity movement also illustrated that strategic and pragmatic orientations often grew with experience. Many pay equity lawyers were drawn to the movement as a result of abstract ideological motivations. Over time, this ideological motivation was refracted through practical action. Most legal activists played multiple roles in movement campaigns and organizations, taking part in protests, legislative battles, and administrative battles. Their experiences with these varied strategies made activists more sensitive and knowledgeable about a multipronged political strategy. In addition, these experiences made many lawyers more sophisticated about the ironies and intricacies of political struggle. For example, one leading union and civil rights lawyer related how he came to view legal "success" more complexly. In the 1970s, he led a high-visibility litigation effort to win employment benefits covering pregnancy leave (a "disability") for female employees. Although initially crushed by his loss before the Supreme Court, he was very gratified by the quick action the case catalyzed at both the federal and state level to legislate important policy changes on the pregnancy benefits issue. "That was the biggest victory, if I can call it that, that I ever lost in court. I learned a lot about how you can use lawsuits in political campaigns," he reported.[72]

In addition to personal experiences, familiarity with the track records of other social movements appears to be important in explaining differences among cause lawyers. In both the pay equity and animal rights movements, many lawyer and nonlawyer activists knew about and drew upon the history and experiences of other movements. The legacy of the civil rights movement and its legal tactics in particular were important for most lawyers we interviewed. What struck us was less any uniform understanding about that legacy than the several sophisticated, critical, but informed perspectives that clearly influenced our cause lawyers' understandings of their roles and actions in their respective movements. Pay equity activists in particular were aware of scholarship on the civil rights legacy and held strong opinions about what lessons were significant. Informed reflections on other political legacies of struggles—especially workers' and women's movements—likewise guided equity lawyers.

Interviews with animal rights activists also displayed familiarity with other movements. One attorney who suggested the strategic connection between litigation and legislation drew this lesson from other social movements. "Legislation is essential. If you take a look at it, frequently litigation has been used to soften up and inform so that an aroused electorate can get behind a piece of legislation to change it that way. It's happened with civil rights [and] with labor in a lot of ways."[73] Another attorney noted the specific reliance on the civil rights movement. "We've looked at that movement . . . and tried to learn from that, maybe pattern aspects of our movement [after it]."[74] A third attorney suggested a similar reliance in very strong terms:

> [W]e can learn a great deal from other social reform movements. . . . A book that influenced me was the *NAACP's Litigation Strategy from 1925 to 1950*. In the 1920s, the NAACP decided to use litigation as a primary tool to combat racism. They knew they had to overturn *Plessy v. Ferguson*. . . . Finally, in 1954, in *Brown v. Board of Education*, the court ruled that "separate but equal is inherently unequal." This decision followed sixty years of lawsuits that didn't get anywhere because society wasn't ready to listen to them.
>
> We have to develop animal rights litigation with a sense of this history. We're going to lose some of the cases, but we've got to keep bringing them and use them to educate both the judges and the public.[75]

Although political experience appears to be significant, its influence certainly varies in character and degree among the different types of lawyers. In particular, staff activists seemed to have more broadly based experiences within their own movement, and this contributed to their heightened strategic orientation. Staff activists were also more likely to be more familiar with the histories of other social movements than were staff technicians and, to a lesser extent, hired guns. However, the hired guns who were closely connected to movement organizations were for the most part knowledgeable about other social movements and likely to be more broadly involved in movement activism.

Conclusion

We have sought in this essay to challenge the conventional critique of cause lawyers. As noted at the outset, our desire to do so grew out of the fact that our studies of two social movements did not confirm conventional criticism of law generally and cause lawyers specifically. With particular regard to cause lawyers, we found skeptically and politically oriented movement "activists" who were conscious of the constraints of litigation and legal discourse, yet strategically sophisticated in their attempts to overcome those constraints. By and large, these lawyers did not succumb to the "myth of rights," nor did they foster a narrow approach to litigation. While it is true that the lawyers still turned to litigation with the hope (albeit tempered with some skepticism) of achieving reform, this turn was indicative of a "new style" of legal activism. The lawyers we studied deployed litigation and legal discourse resourcefully within the context of broad-based movement campaigns and with an eye toward tactical coordination. In addition, these cause lawyers did not simply accept as neutral prevailing ideological and discursive legal frameworks, but critically questioned and challenged the foundations of law. Thus, despite the fact that both pay equity and animal rights lawyers expressed some faith in the utility of litigation, they were hardly naive or narrow about law's promises for advancing their movements' causes. Nor did their legal perspectives foster an uncritical, singular, or even privileged reliance on a litigative strategy.

This reconsideration has led us to argue for a more nuanced and complex portrayal of cause lawyers generally. We have argued that several context-specific factors may help to account for general variations among lawyers. In the animal rights and pay equity movements, comparable conditions relating to movement resources, barriers to legal "success," and historical experiences may account for the similar perspectives of cause lawyers. Some differences in the organizational relationships may help explain variations among the lawyers we studied, especially among the different types of cause lawyers. In general, our position is that none of these organizational, structural, and experiential factors alone are determinative in shaping lawyers' actions within social movements. However, these factors offer at least a starting point for a richer, context-specific understanding of variations in cause-lawyering activity.

We have also suggested that these context-specific factors, taken together, may help to explain why our studies diverge from others. We should stress once again that our objective is not to endorse a simple rejection of the conventional critique. In contrast, our intent is to offer what we take to be a more discerning relational approach to the study of cause lawyers. By examining the contextual factors that differently influence cause lawyers, we hope to gain a better understanding of the conditions under which cause lawyers are likely to conform to or move beyond the model described by critics. Although we have only just begun the process of defining these conditions, we hope that this beginning will provide the foundations for future analyses of cause lawyers and their potential contributions to collective political action.

Notes

We would like to thank Austin Sarat, Stuart Scheingold, and other members of the cause-lawyering project for their insightful comments on an earlier version of this paper. Stephen Wasby also provided useful suggestions.

1. This skeptical and admonishing view comes from legal experts in law schools and from social scientists but has also been expressed by "radical lawyers" themselves. See Stuart A. Scheingold, *The Politics of Rights: Lawyers, Public Policy, and Political Change* (New Haven, Conn.: Yale University Press, 1974), 179. See generally: Gerald S. Rosenberg, *The Hollow Hope: Can Courts Bring about Social Change?* (Chicago: University of Chicago Press, 1991); Susan M. Olson, *Clients and Lawyers: Securing the Rights of Disabled Persons* (Westport, Conn.: Greenwood Press, 1984); Derrick Bell, "Serving Two Masters: Integration Ideals and Client Interests in School Desegregation Litigation," *Yale Law Journal* 85 (1976), 470–516; Michael W. McCann, *Taking Reform Seriously: Perspectives on Public Interest Liberalism* (Ithaca: Cornell University Press, 1986).

2. McCann, *Taking Reform Seriously*; Helena Silverstein and Bob Van Dyk, "Social Movements in the Courts: Power and the Problems of a Legal Strategy," paper presented at the annual meeting of the Law and Society Association, Madison, Wisconsin, June 8–11, 1989.

3. See Michael W. McCann, *Rights at Work: Pay Equity Reform and the Politics of Legal Mobilization* (Chicago: University of Chicago Press, 1994); Helena Silverstein, *Unleashing Rights: Law, Meaning, and the Animal Rights Movement* (Ann Arbor: University of Michigan Press, 1996). The data cited in the following pages were culled from research for these two books, and most interview quotations and survey material appear in these books. However, several quotations contained in this essay do not appear in these books. These quotations are drawn from the interviews we each conducted with movement activists. They are cited, along with the interview date, as such.

4. McCann, *Rights at Work*; Silverstein, *Unleashing Rights*.

5. See Joel F. Handler, *Social Movements and the Legal System: A Theory of Law Reform and Social Change* (New York: Academic Press, 1978); Jack Katz, *Poor People's Lawyers in Transition* (New Brunswick, N.J.: Rutgers University Press, 1982); Scheingold, *The Politics of Rights*; McCann, *Taking Reform Seriously*.

6. Handler, *Social Movements and the Legal System*; Scheingold, *The Politics of Rights*; McCann, *Taking Reform Seriously*. See also Timothy J. O'Neill, *Bakke and the Politics of Equality* (Middletown, Conn.: Wesleyan University Press, 1985); Derrick Bell, "Foreword: The Civil Rights Chronicles," *Harvard Law Review* 99 (1985), 4–83.

7. Rosenberg, *The Hollow Hope*, 341.

8. For one thing, judges are trained to respect the conservative terms of established precedent and prevailing legal conventions that discourage change. Moreover, courts, unlike legislatures, are reactive institutions: they cannot directly initiate policy action and must instead wait for cases to be brought to them. This is related, further, to the fact that lawsuits tend to be discrete, piecemeal, and limited to narrow disputes that cannot easily be extended to broader movement pursuits and systematic campaigns. And even if courts were inclined to advance systematic policy reform, critics argue, they lack the capacity and expertise to do so effectively. The primary reason is that courts lack the power to implement their rulings. Even significant courtroom victories that lawyers celebrate thus are usually rooted in a fundamentally "hollow hope." In sum, movement lawyers not only use up scarce resources in litigation, but those resources often produce little beyond empty symbolic gains for movements. The arguments are summarized well by Rosenberg, *The Hollow Hope*. See also Donald L. Horowitz, *The Courts and Social Policy* (Washington, D.C.: Brook-

ings Institution, 1977); Kristin Bumiller, *The Civil Rights Society: The Social Construction of Victims* (Baltimore, Md.: Johns Hopkins University Press, 1988); Peter Gabel and Duncan Kennedy, "Roll over Beethoven," *Stanford Law Review* 36 (1984), 1–55.

9. As Scheingold argues, lawyers are beset with "tunnel vision" and "natural inclinations to think of litigation apart from other political tactics rather than as part of a coordinated strategy." *The Politics of Rights*, 6. Indeed, many scholars have commented on the random, uncoordinated character of much reform litigation by movement lawyers. See McCann, *Taking Reform Seriously*; Mark Tushnet, "An Essay on Rights," *Texas Law Review* 62 (1984), 363–1403; Stephen Wasby, "How Planned is 'Planned Litigation'?," *American Bar Foundation Research Council* 83 (1984), 83–138. The success of lawyers in court thus can actually be costly in that it misleads movement constituents into thinking the overall battle has been won and alternative—and arguably more effective—political actions are unnecessary. See Rosenberg, *The Hollow Hope*.

10. See Scheingold, *Politics of Rights*; McCann, *Taking Reform Seriously*; Rita Bruun, "The Boldt Decision: Legal Victory, Political Defeat," *Law and Policy* 4 (1982), 271–298; Linda Medcalf, *Law and Identity* (Beverly Hills, Calif.: Sage Publications, 1978); Mark Tushnet, *The NAACP's Legal Strategy against Segregated Education, 1925–1952* (Chapel Hill: University of North Carolina Press, 1987).

11. At the heart of this problem for most critics is the distinctive bias of traditional liberalism that dominates professional legal training and the entire official legal system. The result is a tendency to "reify" individualistic, formalized legal norms in ways that obscure systematic inequalities and constraints on human liberation as well as alternative visions of democratic restructuring and communitarian transformation. See, along with scholarship cited earlier, Peter Gabel, "The Phenomonology of Rights Consciousness and the Pact of Withdrawn Selves," *Texas Law Review* 62 (1984), 1563–1599; Robert W. Gordon, "Critical Legal Histories," *Stanford Law Review* 36 (1984), 57–126; Alan Freeman, "Antidiscrimination Law: A Critical Review," in *The Politics of Law: A Progressive Critique*, ed. David Kairys (New York: Pantheon, 1982), 96–116; Michael W. McCann, "Equal Protection for Social Inequality: Race and Class in American Constitutional Ideology," in *Judging the Constitution*, ed. McCann and Gerald L. Houseman (Glenview, Ill.: Scott, Foresman/Little, Brown, 1989), 231–264. Many studies specifically blame movement lawyers for diverting or misleading collective campaigns for change in this way. See Medcalf, *Law and Identity*; Nikolas Rose, "Unreasonable Rights: Mental Illness and the Limits of Law," *Journal of Law and Society* 12 (1985), 199–218; Neal Milner, "The Dilemmas of Legal Mobilization: Ideologies and Strategies of Mental Patient Liberation," *Law and Policy* 8 (1986), 105–129; Janet Rikfin, "Toward a Theory of Law and Patriarchy," in *Marxism and Law*, ed. Piers Beirne and Richard Quinney (New York: Wiley, 1982), 295–302.

12. Susan Olson's study of rights advocacy for the disabled suggests that domination by lawyers can take place at two levels: (1) controlling the substance and management of litigation; and (2) creating dependence on lawyers. *Clients and Lawyers*, 28–31. Either way, Olson recognizes that dominating lawyers can become unresponsive, insular elites who lose touch with or defy their broader movement constituency. Others suggest that dominating lawyers pushing litigation tactics tend to impede important movement goals, including education, consciousness-raising, and mobilization. See O'Neill's examination of lawyers involved in the litigation over *Bakke* and Bell's discussion of the NAACP Legal Defense Fund, "Serving Two Masters."

13. For elaboration of this conceptual framework and methodology, see the core works cited in n. 3 and Michael W. McCann, "Causal versus Constitutive Explanations (Or on the Difficulty of Being So Positive . . .)," *Law & Social Inquiry* 21 (Spring 1996), 457–482.

14. See McCann, *Rights at Work*, 15–22, 44–47, 312–314.

15. The cities included New York City, Washington D.C., San Francisco, and Seattle.

16. One of these "national animal rights organizations" has traditionally been associated with animal welfare. However, in recent years the organization has moved into animal rights issues and thus may appropriately be referred to as an animal rights organization.

17. Scheingold, *Politics of Rights*.

18. McCann, *Rights at Work*, 75.

19. Ibid., 76, and chap. 3 generally.

20. Winn Newman, "Policy Issues," *Signs: Journal of Women and Culture* 1 (1976), 266.

21. On the significance of landmark judicial decisions for civil rights activists, see Doug McAdam, *Political Process and the Development of Black Insurgency, 1930–1970* (Chicago: University of Chicago Press, 1982); Aldon Morris, *The Origins of the Civil Rights Movement* (New York: Free Press, 1984). But also see Rosenberg, *The Hollow Hope*.

22. McCann, *Rights at Work*, 62.

23. Ibid.

24. Ibid., 62–63.

25. Ibid., 141–142.

26. Ibid., 142.

27. Interview conducted by McCann, August 1, 1989.

28. Winn Newman and Carole W. Wilson, "The Union Role in Affirmative Action," *Labor Law Journal* 32 (1981), 323–342.

29. McCann, *Rights at Work*, 142–143.

30. Ibid., 143.

31. Ibid.

32. Ibid., 76.

33. Silverstein, *Unleashing Rights*, 205.

34. Interview conducted by McCann, June 9, 1989.

35. Silverstein, *Unleashing Rights*, 198.

36. Ibid., 197.

37. McCann, *Rights at Work*, 149; see also Olson, *Clients and Lawyers*, 196.

38. The ethical code at issue here is contained in Rule 11, which states that lawyers may face sanctions for bringing frivolous lawsuits.

39. Silverstein, *Unleashing Rights*, 270.

40. Ibid., 213.

41. Ibid., 212.

42. Interview conducted by McCann, June 10, 1989.

43. Silverstein, *Unleashing Rights*, 271.

44. Interview conducted by McCann, September 3, 1988.

45. It should be noted that this tendency was much more common for litigation surrounding pay equity than animal rights.

46. To provide just one example, an activist for The Fund for Animals in Washington, D.C., was invited to meet with PAWS Action, a Seattle-based group. At this meeting, the activist spoke of her experiences in challenging hunter harassment laws and assisted the group in planning its own protest against hunters. The legal ramifications of the protest were prominently featured in her talk and in the planning. The next day this activist joined with members of PAWS Action in a hunting protest to challenge Washington State's hunter harassment law.

47. Interview conducted by McCann, October 29, 1989.

48. Silverstein, *Unleashing Rights*, 94.

49. Ibid., 106.

50. Nationally prominent lawyer activists in the 1970s expressed a concern that some early cases pressed by local lawyers should not have been litigated. Weak cases not only set bad precedents, but they also were less useful to movement building than victories, even small ones. One goal of a founding 1979 national conference, the National Committee on Pay Equity, and various specialized task forces that grew from these efforts was to try to reign in imprudent lawsuits and to coordinate litigation activity to maximize its contributions to the overall movement.

51. Olson, *Clients and Lawyers,* 9.

52. Ibid., 5. See also Stephen L. Wasby, *Race Relations Litigation in an Age of Complexity* (Charlottesville: University of Virginia Press, 1995).

53. Scheingold, *Politics of Rights,* 141. See also Medcalf, *Law and Identity*; McCann, *Taking Reform Seriously*; Rosenberg, *The Hollow Hope.*

54. According to Blumberg, this is certainly true of defense lawyers who, pressured by the organizational structures of the criminal court, become "agent-mediators." As Blumberg argues, "The lawyer has often been accused of stirring up unnecessary litigation, especially in the field of negligence. He is said to acquire a vested interest in a cause of action or claim which was initially his client's. . . . However, the criminal lawyer develops a vested interest of an entirely different nature in his client's case: to limit its scope and duration rather than do battle." Abraham S. Bumberg, "The Practice of Law as a Confidence Game," *Law and Society Review* 1 (1967), 15–43. Decades of law and society research tend to underline that most legal interaction takes place in the shadow of courts, not directly within their terrain.

55. Sarat and Felstiner likewise suggest that divorce lawyers are generally inclined toward negotiation and settlement. "While many clients think of the legal process as an arena for a full adversarial contest, most divorce disputes are not resolved in this manner. Although not all lawyers are equally dedicated to reaching negotiated agreements, most of those we observed advised their clients to try to settle the full range of issues in the case." Austin Sarat and William F. Felstiner, "Law and Strategy in the Divorce Lawyer's Office," *Law and Society Review* 20 (1986), 93–134.

56. Relatedly, it may also be the case that claims of a litigation explosion in the United States are overstated. See Marc Galanter, "Reading the Landscape of Disputes: What We Know and Don't Know (and Think We Know) About Our Allegedly Contentious and Litigious Society," *UCLA Law Review* 31 (1983), 4–71.

57. These lawyers are characteristic "repeat players." See Marc Galanter, "Why the 'Haves' Come Out Ahead: Speculations on the Limits of Legal Change," *Law and Society Review* 9 (1974), 95–160.

58. This is not to say that the cause lawyer is not a repeat player. The cause lawyer may well fit the definition of a repeat player and, as such, may well be connected to the insider world of the courthouse. However, the cause lawyer is more likely than the ordinary lawyer to bring an outsider view and systemic critique of law to the inner workings of the courtroom.

59. Our approach privileges pragmatic effectiveness in advancing movement causes over ideological purity or radical political correctness in beliefs. Some of those lawyers who rank highly on the tactical political sophistication scale ranked highly on the abstract beliefs scale, some did not, and many recognized that the two were only tenuously connected. We were struck in our particular studies that most "pragmatists" could link their particular endeavors well to long-term visions, while ideological purists often viewed their activities in a resigned, almost cynical fashion that found little justification in their abstract beliefs.

60. Patricia Ewick and Susan Silbey, "Conformity, Contestation, and Resistance: An Account of Legal Consciousness," *New England Law Review* 26 (1992), 731–749; Sally Engle Merry, *Getting Justice and Getting Even: Legal Consciousness among Working-Class Americans* (Chicago: University of Chicago Press, 1990); McCann, *Rights at Work.*

61. It should be stressed once again that the evidence pointing to these contextual variables is preliminary and speculative.

62. Most of the attorneys we interviewed fell into the categories of staff activist and hired gun. Of the nine pay equity attorneys (excluding nonpracticing attorneys), for example, six fit well our categories of "staff activist," two were hired guns (who split in tendencies, one more far more activist than the other), and one was very much a staff technicican. The distribution among animal rights attorneys was similar. While our case studies are limited (a very small *n*), we hope that our interviews suggest some hypotheses about the differences among these three types of lawyers.

63. Interview conducted by McCann, August 4, 1989.

64. McAdam, *Political Process.*

65. Alan Hunt, "Rights and Social Movements: Counter-Hegemonic Strategies," *Journal of Law and Society* 17 (1990), 309–328.

66. Tushnet, *NAACP*; Wasby, *Race Relations*; McCann, *Taking Reform Seriously.*

67. Silverstein, *Unleashing Rights,* 204.

68. Interview conducted by Silverstein, August 16, 1990.

69. Interview conducted by Silverstein, June 9, 1990.

70. Interview conducted by Silverstein, August 16, 1990.

71. Silverstein, *Unleashing Rights,* 198.

72. Interview conducted by McCann, September 3, 1988.

73. Interview conducted by Silverstein, June 11, 1990.

74. Interview conducted by Silverstein, August 16, 1990.

75. Ellen Bring, "Joyce Tischler: Legal Activist," *Animals' Agenda* (July/August 1991), 40–41.

CHAPTER 10

Caring about Individual Cases

Immigration Lawyering in Britain

SUSAN STERETT

Introduction: Working the Rules

If any political change through litigation is possible at all, it often seems to require some form of institutionalized rights, that is, binding statements of duties owed to individuals, along with an organization that has the power to enforce them despite what majoritarian institutions might say. In the United States, law and society scholars have pointed out the difficulty of institutionalizing rights. Because effective rights often require coordination among complex and multiple organizations that do not necessarily agree with the substance of enforceable rights, rights do not have the bite in fields as wide-ranging as employment discrimination and school desegregation that Americans might expect in a rights-based political system.[1] Still less would we expect ordinary statutory rights to matter in a system such as Britain's, which does not have institutionalized fundamental rights. Institutionalizing fundamental principles has become an international issue, despite all the difficulties of getting such rights enforced.[2] The European Convention on Human Rights and the European Court on Human Rights (ECHR) that applies the convention, together with the European Court of Justice, have provided important frameworks for the expansion of human rights discourse in Europe. In Britain those who are frustrated both with the dominance of the Conservative government since 1979 and, more broadly speaking, with the ability of any party in power to do what it wants, have argued that Britain needs a bill of rights. Formed in 1988, Charter 88 presses for constitutional reform; it has provided an organizational home for the arguments favoring a bill of rights. Their arguments and ideas draw on Europe and the European courts. Without entrenching rights similar to and expanded from those in the European Convention, to many it seems difficult or impossible to get rights-based critiques of British practices.

Even while the need for entrenched fundamental rights is debated in Britain, courts currently interpret ordinary legal rights as stated in statutes and rules. Rather than focus on advocacy of not-yet existent rights, those who study legal challenge can draw on analyses of the limited and pervasive ways that ordinary statutory rights make a difference. Courts in the United States make a difference at the margins and in conjunction with other institutions and forms of political activity;[3] in that they are no different from other political institutions. Statutory interpretation offers some of the same possibilities and works under the same constraints that apply to decisions under a bill of rights.[4] Therefore even within the British system, without a bill of rights but with statutes, litigation could make some difference in the application of rules to individuals.

British immigration law and practice provide a crucial place to analyze legal challenges relying on interpretations of existing rules. Immigration representatives have sometimes been able to win for individual clients, and their successes and losses are worth exploring for many reasons. First, immigration is a major political issue throughout Europe, and Britain is no exception. Successive British governments have used immigration law to address race relations issues, and immigration and racism have been deeply tied. According to the British state it is generally the responsibility of those whose families have moved to the British Isles over the years to assimilate to the dominant culture.[5] Second, if litigation in immigration matters in Britain, it is only indirectly through the ECHR. Britain is not a signatory to the protocol on immigration. Instead, when immigration is raised in the ECHR with regard to Britain, it is through a right to family life or the Convention's prohibition of sex discrimination or the ECHR requirement that state provide an adequate internal remedy for human rights complaints. Third, Britain is one of the most centralized and least rights-oriented states in Europe. Its political system is effective at choosing to incorporate or exclude nonproducer groups in consulting for policy making.[6] It has no established way of shaping majoritarian choice to account for any minority concerns. In addition, immigration is not the primary electoral concern of racialized minorities in Britain. Even if it were, there is no way they could get their concerns effectively represented at the national level because racialized minorities constitute only approximately 5 percent of the overall population.[7] Geographic concentration has meant that such groups sometimes have had substantial votes at the local level and have influenced political choices there.[8] However, although associational politics at the local level—that is, community organizations that sometimes bargain with state agencies—are often vibrant and well-organized, local governments have limited power.[9] Access to institutions to challenge immigration policy is, in sum, limited, and restricting immigration is popular with the majority of the population.

While I address immigration practice in Britain, I am asking questions about the possibilities of litigation that arise from American rather than British cultural concerns. In addressing the possibilities that litigation offers, I focus more on academic questions about what lawyering can accomplish in its attempts to effect some form of social change. I will not address questions that concern people in Britain now—whether they need an institutionalized system of rights or how it would be best to address immigration and racism. Instead, I address what the possibilities for litigation are in a system where the limits to liberal legalism are substantial.

The constraints on gaining positive rulings for clients in immigration are severe in Britain. They have become increasingly so as the British government has cut back on legal aid funding.[10] Proceduralism, with all its limits, is a significant element in British legal reasoning.[11] Lawyers believe that arguments based on claims that procedure is unfair are more successful than criticisms of the substantive interpretation of the rules.[11] The focus on procedures is consistent with the premises of much of liberal legalism. It is virtually impossible to argue that a court should overturn all the immigration rules. Even if someone were to argue that, the only legal basis would be that the rules, made under authority of a statute, were outside the bounds of the statute. It is also not possible to argue explicitly that a statute itself is wrong in any legal sense. Instead, lawyers must make arguments narrowly framed as interpretations of the existing rules. The European Court of Justice and the European Court of Human Rights hear more substantive claims, but they do not hear the majority of cases. Indeed, the lead time is long enough on cases brought to European courts that the government can more readily plan how to litigate and respond to them.[12] For most claimants, the British courts govern British immigration claims.

How, then, do practitioners find opportunity in British immigration law? The British courts have been generally and correctly understood to have an apolitical, unprincipled, and narrow approach to interpreting statutes. Indeed, within legal theory that is often taken to be their only justifiable position.[13] When critics debunk the idea that courts are "apolitical," they argue that the courts' approach is inherently conservative and provides little ground for criticizing administrative practices.[14] If the courts have narrow understandings of statutes, ones that favor government priorities, why should lawyers take on any cases? Once cases have been through legally trained adjudicators and administrative tribunals, any administrative decision that is wholly outside plausible statutory interpretation will have been excluded. And within such a conservative legal system, there is no point in challenging the principles of decisions. Courts in England will not aggressively challenge administrators. Despite these strictures, claimants in immigration do win sometimes in both administrative hearings and in the domestic courts. To explain this apparent paradox, an approach that focuses on judges would argue that the courts have become more active in recent years, which usually implies a change in judicial ideology toward making the "fair" decision.[15] Immigration cases, then, must be part of the courts' reemergent activism.[16] That seems implausible, however, for judges have argued that immigration cases do not belong in the general jurisdiction courts and would not be there if administrative adjudication were better.[17] Furthermore, judges do not control all of litigation. An alternative approach focuses not on judges but on how lawyers, other representatives, and claimants shape claims to accommodate the well-known limits of judges and rules. From the inaccessibility of the British central state it is not possible to conclude that the political system offers no strategic opening through law. Indeed, even highly repressive political systems offer opportunities to make claims within their existing frameworks.[18] Sometimes governing principles offer openings to make claims within the political system. The arguments for much substantial social change have initially been framed as claims within existing understandings, exploiting contradictions and tensions within them. In Britain statutes offer an opportunity to claim legal cultural expectations of fair treatment. Rules create spaces for claims—that the rules were inappropriately applied, that they should be interpreted in light of some other generally agreed-upon principle—and it would make sense to expect that such spaces would be used in Britain as they would be elsewhere. They have been.

To address questions about the possibilities of law on immigration in Britain, I interviewed lawyers in the spring of 1990 and 1991 and in the fall of 1995, both barristers and solicitors, who practiced largely in immigration. I also interviewed representatives who were not legally qualified. Most of the representatives identified themselves and were identified by others as being politically committed to fighting the restrictiveness of the immigration rules. I used a network sample approach, in which I asked practicing lawyers for the names of others significant in the practice of immigration law. I talked to many of the lawyers who were repeatedly named as very involved in immigration law in private practice. The sample did not include the lawyers whom those practitioners are concerned about—solicitors and barristers who only occasionally take cases. While the sample is neither representative of all who practice immigration law, nor complete with regard to experience in litigation, I can address what lawyers have seen as possible to gain from the legal system. I did not talk to clients, who are the most beleaguered of the participants in the immigration system.

I would expect that my being American colored our discussions. I am not sure how; some of the attorneys did want to contrast the American political system with the British. In particular some attorneys mentioned the aspiration toward rights in the United States, the significance of the courts, and the sense some of them shared that American activist lawyers were more highly organized than they were.

I also watched both administrative proceedings and judicial review applications and hearings, which allowed me to observe lawyers whom I had interviewed and lawyers I had not interviewed. I listened to a group discussion of immigration law issues, which incorporated ten more lawyers; it was a regular meeting of a British organization that educates and shares information, the Immigration Law Practitioners Association (ILPA). That group was more diverse by race and gender than my network sample of lawyers. Indeed, only one of the lawyers in my network sample appeared at the ILPA meeting, though lawyers in the network had been active in organizing the group. Finally, I sat in on a training session on administrative appeals and judicial review that ILPA sponsored.

My task in this essay is to explore the possibilities of change through litigation in a highly constrained system. I will first outline the political context and governance of immigration. Then I will discuss three different campaigns that immigration lawyers conducted in the mid- to late 1980s. These campaigns have shaped current political discussions and settlements: two were efforts to win changes in rule interpretation; a third was an effort to change the procedures used in interviewing refugees, which led to some more refugees being admitted to the country, a practice that changed dramatically when the government subsequently enacted the 1993 Asylum and Immigration Appeals Act.

Immigration Law and Politics in Britain

Allowing an increase in immigration has never been a popular electoral issue in Britain. One section of the Conservative Party has long been actively against immigration and sympathetic to the racism that underlies the English sense of being threatened by outsiders. The Labour Party has also been restrictive while sometimes taking the public strategy of avoiding the issue or criticizing government policies when the Conservatives are in power. Discussions in Parliament of each of the acts debated in 1988, 1993, and 1995 illustrate the Labour Party's caution with regard to the issue: while Labour has criticized the government continually, the government has tried to get Labour to publicly commit to more open immigration, which the Labour Party will not do.[19] Local Labour governments have sometimes been more sympathetic to immigrants with regard to schooling and rules regarding discrimination, though much of the most vibrant political organizing around race has been outside of any government, local or central.[20] Avoiding the issue of race has also extended to a leadership consensus to try to minimize the importance of racial categories in national politics.[21] When immigration has been raised as a political issue by the parties, it has usually been in support of a fear of too much immigration into Britain. Getting other perspectives on immigration into parliamentary discussion or other national debate is difficult, to say the least. Britain does, however, have an extensive state apparatus to address complaints within the rules.

People who want to visit from some countries or immigrate to Britain obtain a visa and entry clearance from street-level administrators.[22] Entry clearance officers sometimes deny entry based on their interpretation of the law; applicants sometimes then seek to appeal within the administrative system. Once in Britain, people are sometimes subject to deportation, which also brings them into contact with the legal system. Immigrants who lose their appeals at this level are to be informed of the availability of the government-funded Immigration Advisory Service, which before 1992 was the United Kingdom Immigration Advisory Service (UKIAS). Immigrants could either use it for advice and advocacy or go outside to a solicitor. UKIAS was badly underfunded and received repeated criticism as simply a front organization for the government; criticism led to its abolition and subsequent revamping and reincarnation.[23] When the Immigration Advisory Service was created, the government also created a separate organization to give advice to those claiming asylum, the Refugee Legal Centre. The staff of all these organizations include legally trained counselors; cases that are not won through representations to the Home Office or through arguments in administrative appeals are filtered through legally qualified advisers, who decide whether there is a good legal claim and refer cases to outside lawyers. UKIAS referred about half of the cases that lawyers handled.[24] The Joint Council for the Welfare of Immigrants, which is a political campaigning organization, also represents claimants and refers cases to solicitors.

Legal aid, which funds legal assistance for the poor by paying fees to private lawyers, does not fund representation before immigration appeals tribunals, which are the administrative hearing mechanism. That lack of funding has been credited with some of the difficulty immigrants have in succeeding before tribunals.[25] Since 1982 the government has left most of the funding to the financially strapped local governments.[26]

After representatives have made representations for clients to the Home Office, the government department that handles immigration, they can appeal unfavorable decisions to immigration adjudicators and then the Immigration Appeals Tribunal, an internal administrative appeal system. Ordinary appeals now go from there to the Court of Appeal, the intermediate general jurisdiction appellate court in Britain. Before 1993 the law did not provide for an in-country right of appeal. That is, people who were to be deported could not appeal that decision from England, Wales, Northern Ireland, or Scotland but had to go back to the country from which they emigrated to appeal. However, they could get decisions judicially reviewed from within the country. For that, they went to the High Court of Justice, the central trial general jurisdiction court in Britain.

Britain established judicial review as a discretionary procedure for reviewing administrative agency action in 1978.[27] Under judicial review the courts are supposed to judge whether an administrator acted outside the law; courts are not to substitute their judgment for that of an administrator. British legal commentators insist on the meaningfulness of this distinction.[28] In the mid-1980s immigration cases comprised 30 percent of the judicial review case load of the High Court.[29] Judicial review in Britain is a specific application to the court and a specific remedy, separate from ordinary appeals under statutes.

Solicitors decide whether to refer the cases to a barrister to take to the High Court or whether to work only on representations to the Home Office or members of Parliament. Among solicitors and barristers immigration practice is highly concentrated, although that concentration has decreased somewhat among solicitors in recent years.[30] Many cases end up in the hands of a few firms of solicitors, which often must turn cases away because they have too many to handle. In 1987 four firms of solicitors handled 43.6 percent of the cases; by 1989, when practice had diffused, the top four firms still handled 26 percent of cases.[31] Barristers represent clients both before the Immigration Appeals Tribunal and the High Court. Throughout, lawyers evaluate whether the case is good enough to pursue, dropping out cases for which they do not have time or that do not seem winnable.

Barristers and solicitors in Britain have organized an Immigration Law Practitioners Association, founded in 1984. Leading members have hoped that by controlling enough cases they could persuade the Home Office to listen to them. Caseloads provide a negotiating tool, as they have for some public interest lawyers in the United States.[32] While the hope has been that one can shape case law and negotiate through control, members readily acknowledge that anyone can bring an immigration case and that others might not share a concern to shape case law.

In addition to facilitating organization of claims about immigration, ILPA offers a place to exchange knowledge about Home Office practices. As one of the practitioners whom I interviewed said, "[O]n a thing like immigration much of the secret practices of the Home Office are not published, of course they're useful to know about. Then you can know what's going to attract them and what's not." Immigration lawyers who take on cases for business executives therefore join ILPA, as do those who take cases under the rules that severely limit the options for those from the Indian subcontinent and other less-favored nations. While some lawyers take both kinds of cases, many representatives practice primarily in one area or the other.

Immigration law does not get an enormous amount of respect from either judges or some barristers in other areas of law (one said it had the reputation of being "bad lawyers arguing badly for dishonest clients"). The idea floats around that clients are desperate and that some lawyers will take any case that comes up. Immigration barristers mentioned that problem as well, distinguishing between themselves and those who take cases simply for the fees with little concern for how good the case is. For at least some barristers and solicitors, there is a reason to filter cases to maintain their reputations as responsible practitioners, though lawyers insisted that the main problem is lack of resources rather than lack of good cases. A leading judge who is known for his sense of fairness, Lord Justice Woolf, has written that immigration cases are too fact-based to be in High Court; they require better administrative appeal procedures.[33] In arguing that some other less expensive institution should address these cases, Lord Justice Woolf was making an argument for informal justice that is most often made for low-status cases.[34]

In filtering cases practitioners sometimes decide that the Home Office has chosen to follow a policy that is particularly unjustifiable and that it might be possible to get favorable legal interpretations from the Immigration Appeals Tribunal and the courts. They decide to take claims because the cases challenge current practice under a conception of what rights people should have even under existing rules. In making those claims they draw on cultural understandings of what is right; in the United States one source for that has been the Bill of Rights. Much of immigration law for asylum seekers has focused on procedures; in Britain, arguments about what constitute fair procedures constitute the legal doctrine of "natural justice," or the procedures at the heart of liberal legalism.

A rough sense of substantive principles of fairness also provides a background to case-level decision making. In particular the race relations law in Britain has embodied a multicultural political settlement in which cultural differences are supposed to be respected.[35] That settlement at least nominally requires respect for different cultures, though it has seldom meant political power sharing.[36] Within the Conservative government even the multicultural settlement has been under assault. Furthermore, that settlement is contested within communities of color. Some have argued that more conservative and senior men have been chosen to represent a culture within the Community Relations Councils, local institutions that are to represent communities of color to the central state. Such selection practices have made it difficult to raise objections to sexism or fundamentalism within the culture.[37] Nevertheless, a sense of fairness within the multicultural framework has provided one way of thinking through challenges to immigration law in the courts. For example, as we will see later, the immigration practice of excluding immigrants who are part of an arranged marriage seems unconscionable to many practitioners. These practitioners needed therefore to find cases that they could use to persuade the courts that such exclusions *were* unconscionable.

Weberian legal rationality is hardly pursued in this field, for rules and their interpretation change frequently, and they are put together in response to circumstances and opportunities for closing out immigrants within a statute. But to the extent that rationality does prevail, it is highly dependent not on a universal articulation of abstract principle but on shared knowledge and a community of practice. Many of the cases, both cases in administrative appeals and in judicial review, are not reported. ILPA, however, can facilitate the diffusion of knowledge of cases. Furthermore, individual members sometimes talk to civil servants in the Home Office, making it more possible to know Home Office priorities and inform other members of them. ILPA also runs training sessions in immigration law. It has also provided a model for practitioners, who have established working groups in subfields of immigration law. Practitioners involved in Kurdish refugee claims in the late 1980s formed an ad hoc committee to address common concerns regarding Home Office practice; a working group on refugee law has continued since then.

Those critical of litigation for political change have argued in part that political activity and change of the rules is a collective good while litigation for the benefit of individual clients is a private good. In this view, if lawyers and representatives argue for individual clients, they are not challenging the rules. However, public and private goods are on a continuum rather than constituting a dichotomy. Some collective goods have benefits so largely concentrated on one participant that they resemble private goods in the incentives they establish.[38] Conversely, litigation can offer selective benefits to claimants and have spillover benefits for rule change. As we will see, the press of numbers of individual cases contributed to changes in the governance of marriage cases.

Furthermore, litigation in immigration, more likely to help individual claimants than change the rules, has political implications because immigration is so politicized in Britain. The context as much as the intent of individual litigators can create the cause. Individual claimants need not have any interest in changing the rules; they and the lawyers working for them may want more than anything else just to have an individual client stay in the country. But the restrictiveness of the rules and the highly politicized character of the issue means that like it or not, lawyering for immigrants becomes lawyering for a cause. Paying attention to meaning in context, rather than only to the intent of the practitioners, illuminates the cultural specificity of lawyering and political activity. As Ronen Shamir and Sara Chinski argue, the context of political struggle over rights of residence makes what would otherwise be ordinary land use cases into political causes in Israel.[39] Similarly, the political commitments of feminism in the United States mean that a lawyer's commitment to cause lawyering can entail a particular kind of treatment of clients, though the treatment of clients was once not politicized.[40]

Struggle over procedures in refugee law, substantive changes in the interpretation of the rules governing legal residence in Britain after a marriage, and gains in cases followed by setbacks illustrate the different configurations of wins and losses in immigration law. Victory for individual clients is possible and at times has also shaped political discussions of fairness. At the same time, these areas of legal change demonstrate the limits to change in an antirights parliamentary system. When the Home Office makes discretionary changes in procedures, it can rescind them. When victories in appeals seem wrong to the government, it can eliminate the appeals if officials believe the political fallout will not be too great.

Refugees: Changing the Procedures

Trouble in countries throughout the world has led to a rise in asylum seeking throughout Europe.[41] The established practice of immigration law has meant that there were people who could take the business as applications began to rise in the 1980s. According to data collected by the Home Office, the percentage of applicants accepted as refugees rose from 12 percent in 1986 to 32 percent in 1989, then dropped precipitously from 1991 onward.[42] Since 1993 the government has cut back substantially on the numbers of people granted either asylum or discretionary leave to remain. Britain has done an effective job of shutting down the settlement of refugees. During the mid- to late 1980s, when applications for asylum were first increasing, lawyers were able to expand the procedures used in deciding refugee status to provide a closer consideration of evidence than the Home Office initally gave.

In 1987 Britain had a wave of Tamil asylum seekers trying to enter the country; some sixty of them staged a demonstration at Heathrow Airport. The complaints occasioned discussion of the restrictiveness of the rules.[43] At that time the Home Office gave potential Tamil refugees a brief interview then refused refugee status if that interview did not prove to their satisfaction the claimant's refugee status. What is more, the Home Office would threaten to put claimants on an airplane in twelve hours. Lawyers described getting judges up in the middle of the night or going to their homes on weekends to get signatures on applications for leave to apply for judicial review; one barrister called it a time of "hand-to-hand combat" with the Home Office. With those applications they could then prevent the person from being deported immediately. ILPA asked the Home Office to agree upon a timetable, one that would stop the need for those efforts. When they did not obtain a more favorable timetable, they pressed cases. Applications for leave were granted, and the Home Office found itself waiting for hearings on the cases; as one plaintiff's lawyer put it, "[B]ack of the queue, wait nine months for it to come up."[44] When lawyers pressed these cases, the Home Office had some reason to listen to ILPA. If the court's timetable was allowing claimants to stay in the country for nine months, the Home Office was not winning the speedy exclusion it had wanted in the first place.

By pressing cases, the lawyers were able to obtain a second interview for their clients. If the immigrant raised a new point of law or new information relevant to the case, the immigration officer had to refer the case back. If the new information was true and could not have been found earlier, it had to be considered by immigration officers. This issue went through appeals tribunals, the High Court of Justice and the Court of Appeals.[45] Eventually, the cases were useful in gaining a change in administrative procedures.

Immigration officials had first denied a group of five Tamil people seeking asylum refugee status. After they were sent back to Sri Lanka, their solicitor continued to pursue the case. They won on reapplication with an adjudicator; the government lost its effort to get the decision overturned because a time limit for filing a claim had passed.[46] After that their solicitor urged the government to do its "moral and legal duty" and allow the applicants to stay.[47] The government granted exceptional leave to remain and the applicants reapplied for asylum. The case also occasioned debate in Parliament.[48] Thus, working for clients provided an opportunity for public debate of asylum and Britain's obligations to asylum seekers.

The European Court of Human Rights decided one set of Tamil cases in 1991. While reapplications for asylum were pending in Britain, the applicants sued, claiming that Britain did not provide an adequate internal remedy to protect human rights, including the right to asylum. The internal remedy at issue was judicial review.[49] Before that court the government argued that this remedy was very wide indeed; the government won on that ground.[50] In British law, commentators distinguish between appeal and judicial review; the latter is in fact a much narrower remedy than appeal. That the government argued that it was a broad remedy in the European Court of Human Rights so to avoid losing the case illustrates one of the more subtle effects the European Court of Human Rights can have.

When Kurdish claims came up in 1989, the Tamil cases provided a background for criticism of government practice. Solicitors applied for judicial review in June of 1989, claiming that Kurdish applicants were being denied the interviews they were entitled to. They won their application for review but the Kurds eventually were simply granted the interviews based in part on practices established in the Tamil cases.[51] One of the 1989 cases did come before the High Court; in questioning the procedural propriety of the Home Office's decision, it relied on *Thirukumar*, the earlier Tamil case. The Home Office had decided the Kurdish case after reinterviews, considering new information as the claimant presented it through an interpreter, in part because the court had concerns about translation. However, the Court found the Home Office procedures inadequate.[52] When the second batch of Kurdish refugee cases came in from early 1990 onward, practitioners were getting more favorable decisions from the Home Office without taking the cases to court.

Once the Home Office fixed its procedures so that it gave good reasons for decisions and offered interviews, there was nothing for the courts to review. The lawyers that I interviewed agreed that substantive critiques of decisions by immigration officials are difficult to bring in judicial review. The Home Office was likely to concede the best cases challenging procedure in its own preliminary review, though many lawyers claimed that concessions in such cases depended on who the lawyers were, not just the merits of the case. However, they also believed the reinterview often meant that the Home Office officials themselves might allow a claimant to stay. The change in Home Office policy, provoked by favorable court decisions and the time delay that litigation afforded, rippled through the litigation system. However, the change came not from especially "activist" or sympathetic courts, though lawyers did note that some judges have been more sympathetic than others. The process costs imposed by the courts on the administration, as well as the victories in procedural cases, helped to get practices to change.[53] Resistance to Home Office practice, based on the sense that it was simply ridiculous and unfair, and the possibility of playing one institution against another—the process costs of courts against the urgency of the Home Office—provided the basis for challenge in the courts. In order to make progress on this issue no one had to believe that the courts were terribly sympathetic to refugees. One needed only to be able to ask for further procedures.

Grants of permission to stay have often been discretionary; that is, the Home Office has not always granted refugee status but has allowed people claiming that status to stay outside any rules. At any rate, the number of people granted exceptional leave moved steadily downward from 70 percent of total decisions in 1986 to 55 percent in 1989 and 60 percent in 1990. While the percentages were down, the applications were up. The number of people granted exceptional leave to remain more than doubled between 1988 and 1989.[54]

The hoped-for result of arguing for better procedures, of course, is to change the substance of decisions. That indicates the similarity of British administrative legal ideology to that of America. While there have been important elaborations of administrative law in the courts, ones that have made substantive differences, they have largely been made in terms of procedure, not as substantive decisions based on a sense of what is right.[55] The greatest gains in welfare law in the United States, made at a time when lawyers had real optimism about the transformative possibilities of law, also centered on procedure.[56] The procedural claims rested on arguments and assessments about why the procedures were necessary: that is, the underlying substantive claim to property was important enough to deserve careful consideration. That sense of principle is evident in the British claims to reconsideration as well.

The importance of procedure is curious in the context of revived emphasis in political debate on holding administrators and states to the law, which many have argued the courts can now do in Britain. This implies that administrators can make substantively wrong decisions, ones that courts can overturn. Yet it is not considered a useful approach by immigration lawyers, at least not in judicial review. One lawyer put it this way: "It is a legal decision and you have got to have some sort of error of law: either failure to take into account relevant factors or taking into account irrelevant factors or some sort of procedural irregularity or breach of natural justice. And as I said, a manifestly unreasonable element is very, very rarely successful in refugee cases." Winning on procedures, in sum, provides opportunities to win for particular clients and to influence the immigration debate in Britain.

While lawyers were certainly trying to build favorable interpretations of the rules, at the same time they claimed that immigration is "hard law," not something that is shapeless and dependent entirely on the facts of cases. One woman mentioned this as a reason for why it had initially been difficult for women to get into immigration law practice; those who referred cases did not always see women as capable of practicing "hard law." Even the sympathy evident in refugee cases would not be enough to gain a victory in the courts, as one lawyer made clear: "So however strong your case is on its facts—and I've had a Tamil woman who had lost virtually the whole of her family—on the face of it, on the facts, you have an incredibly strong claim, but we couldn't find an error of law. The [immigration officials] had come to a decision neither of the courts was prepared to find was manifestly unreasonable. They just back away from that. You're stuck."

"Manifestly unreasonable" is a broad legal claim within British legal practice. It asks judges to use their own judgment to say that the officials really got the law wrong. That is exactly what legal scholars argue for in the literature when advocating an expanded judicial review, but it seldom accords with the choices judges usually see as available.[57] Procedural issues are the most attractive to take and a broad declaration of unreasonableness the most difficult to get.

Neither the Tamil nor the Kurdish cases were taken in isolation from any other political acitivity that would draw attention to the plight of asylum seekers. Asylum seekers who were subject to violence received news coverage; the Refugee Forum, a leading service and lobbying organization, worked with asylum seekers for rights broadly conceived, and antiracism community activists tied the concerns of asylum seekers to problems in international politics.[58] Taking cases was necessary to keep asylum seekers in the country, but few saw it as sufficient to address the wider concerns.

In 1992 the British government worked on enacting a new Asylum Bill that would restrict the numbers of refugees that Britain would admit. Efforts to restrict administrative appeals rights were so widely criticized that the government withdrew most of those provisions, including the complete exclusion of immigration claims from legal aid.[59] The government can change the law, but to do so in such a contentious area it must go through extensive debate, raising just the issues of principle that lawyers hope to address. The result was a new Asylum and Immigration Appeals Act, which was enacted in 1993 and took effect on July 26 of that year.[60] What the act did not do was limit judicial review. Because judicial review is a discretionary remedy, the courts control it. Parliament could eliminate judicial review but ideologically that would be difficult, given the importance in Conservative government rhetoric of abiding by the law. The Asylum Act provided for appeal for the first time to the Court of Appeal from the Immigration Appeals Tribunal. Before that there had been no in-country right of appeal. One reason for this provision, which Lord Justice Woolf had advocated, was to provide an alternative to judicial review.[61] While for the first time immigration cases could be appealed before a general jurisdiction court, the Court of Appeal is generally considered to be less sympathetic on immigration claims than some High Court judges are. Thus, although legal challenges provide the opportunity to gain ground for refugees, at the same time the central state retains substantial control over policy and can limit the meaning of case law challenges.[62]

In the next section I turn to the question of interpreting statutory standards and address how lawyers and claimants find room for substantive challenge without asking the courts to hold a decision manifestly unreasonable.

One Step Forward, Two Steps Back?: Compassionate Circumstances

As practitioners see it, it is difficult for the Home Office to change the rules all the time, especially if an interpretation from the courts looks sensible and humane. Even if the government does change rules in response to a victory for claimants, lawyers have won for their particular clients; Parliament does not change rules retroactively.

Representatives have argued for favorable rule interpretation for dependents joining family members in Britain and for people challenging deportation on the grounds of "compassionate circumstances." The immigration rules once only allowed parents of immigrant residents to live in Britain if they were dependent on their children and if their standard of living would not go up when they moved to Britain. One lawyer, citing a sympathetic decision by Justice Simon Brown, pointed out how strange that was: if the parent had been financially dependent on children when abroad, as required by the dependency rules, their standard of living had to go up once they moved to Britain.[63] However, in a case on judicial review, the court held that "emotional needs" could be considered in deciding whether a parent is dependent on a child.[64] It is this kind of issue that lawyers believe it is possible to change: one does not argue that the Home Office ought to consider everything as part of dependence, nor that the dependency rules are ridiculous. One argues points of law, narrowly construed in statutory or rule terms. While narrowly stated, such arguments are based on principled concerns such as the importance of family ties.

Just as lawyers could persuade judges to include emotional needs as part of the dependency rules, they persuaded judges to expand the grounds for arguments against deportation. Until 1988, immigration officials before deciding to deport had a duty under the statute to consider "compassionate circumstances." Litigation made specific what compassionate circumstances were. An important decision came out of the House of Lords in 1986, after the case had worked its way through the court system, holding that "compassionate circumstances" need not be personal. They could include community support as one of the relevant circumstances administrators should consider before deporting.[65]

The Immigration Act of 1988 eliminated compassionate circumstances as grounds for appeal for applicants who had been in the country fewer than seven years.[66] One could challenge the accuracy of the grounds for the decision to deport, but that was all. ILPA objected to that change, but it became part of the statute.

Lawyers limit their sense of political loss by focusing on professional responsibility. One barrister commented in these words on the 1988 statute and the compassionate circumstances campaign that preceded it: "One's duty as a lawyer is to one's client, not to the mass of other potential clients. So if there's a point you can get a result for your client on you have to pursue it. You can't say I won't take this point because it might be worse for other people unless the client wants to adopt altruistic self-sacrifice as part of his or her instructions to you. So the short answer is that if it's a point you can win on, even though the Home Office might reverse it, you have to take it." Even self-consciously political work in lawyering in Britain focuses on the responsibility to the individual client. As Stuart Scheingold has argued with regard to lawyering in Britain, "[R]adical lawyers are both resistant to, and influenced by . . . forces of conventional professionalism."[67] Those forces have been particularly strong in Britain. The inability to frame class action suits and the limits on standing[68] also mean that clients have to have something quite concrete at stake, keeping the lawyers closely tied to individual clients' concerns and only attending to longer-range political changes as a hoped-for additional benefit. The context in Britain means that lawyering first for a cause often means lawyering first for individual clients rather than focusing primarily on rule change.

The British barrister just quoted also noted that even serving individual clients could have indirect and broader political effects. He argued, "[T]he more things they have to reverse the more it clogs up parliamentary time; the more difficult it is, and depending on what the issue is, it may provoke a parliamentary debate. . . . [I]t took the Home Office five years to reverse the *Bakhtaur Singh* case." Debate is what Parliament does. Whether or not it leads to policy change, provoking a debate is a significant move within the official political system. Litigation is one strategy to bring that about. Furthermore, before the Home Office got *Bakhtaur Singh* reversed it had to follow the decision in its internal decisionmaking, and immigration adjudicators were to apply it in appeals. That meant for five years, applicants could raise the generous interpretation of compassionate circumstances.

The 1988 statute illustrates that Parliament can and does overturn judicial decisions. Litigation still has a point, as the barrister just quoted makes clear. Second, the fact that Parliament can and does sometimes overturn decisions distinguishes systems with a written constitution (particularly but not exclusively the American system) from systems without. However, in the United States, while it is more difficult to overturn a judicial decision, it has been done. Statutes have been altered in response to judicial interpretation.[69] In addition, it is hard to know what a constitution, almost no matter what its provisions, would do to stop these alterations in the rules and statutes. The ease with which ministers can get changes through Parliament means that any other strategy of political change is also difficult. The actual unpopularity of immigrants throughout the Western world suggests that any other political work is also unlikely to change the political meaning of immigration very quickly.

The importance of substantive marginal changes in the law through litigation has been evident to participants in what has repeatedly been one of the most contentious areas of immigration law: settlement in Britain as a part of marriage.

Elaborating the Rules: Primary Purpose

The 1983 immigration rules required that someone who claimed a right to settle in Britain because he had married someone who was legally settled in Britain had to show that the "primary purpose" of the marriage was not settlement. The rules discriminated against women trying to bring in husbands: only in those cases did the couple have to show that the primary purpose of the marriage was not settlement. Britain lost a sex discrimination case on this issue in 1985 in the European

Court of Human Rights.[70] In response the government changed the rules to make it equally difficult for men and women to bring in spouses.[71] The rules had three parts: a marriage could not have been entered into primarily to obtain admission to the United Kingdom, each of the parties had to intend to live together permanently, and the parties to the marriage had to have met.[72] Practitioners pointed to the problem of "proving a negative." The rule was also seen as inhumane: how could the Home Office exclude someone from the country on those grounds when the person had established a family life with someone settled in Britain? Because the Home Office sometimes tried to deport people some time after they had entered the country, or to exclude them after they had had children in another country, it was pursuing people with established lives together. From 1984 on both lawyers practicing in the area and UKIAS wanted to see if they could get the courts to limit the interpretation of the rules. Once again, the British context shaped the kind of claim that anyone could make. No one could claim that the rules violated any fundamental principle of fairness. Indeed it was important to argue almost the reverse: that the rules caused an injustice in a particular case.

From the point of view of lawyers practicing routinely in immigration, getting a favorable interpretation of the rules has depended on claiming it is just for a particular claimant. Judges' concerns about opening the floodgates to new cases require a limited form of argument. Rather than making sweeping statements of principle, it is important to make claims of simply interpreting the rules in this case. Then, as one lawyer said, one simply finds there are many cases like that particular one. But it has been important never to run an argument in general terms, not "at any stage." The conservative and limited sense of their power that the courts often have has not meant that it is impossible to challenge rules. Rather, it has channeled the types of challenges that were possible. As one practitioner observed,

> You've got to narrow it [a claim in a case] down to the facts of your case, rather than make it a big general submission that in every case things have got to be looked at again. I've succeeded on applications for leave just by doing that, by narrowing it down, looking at the facts for this case, and pointing to reasons why in this particular case the secretary of state had a duty of fairness which wasn't complied with. And then by doing that you are reassuring judges, because they are always susceptible to the floodgates argument, that if we let this one in we'll have to let them all in. So you are dealing with that, you are reassuring them that it is only on these particular facts. But then of course when you find another case the facts are fairly similar—and there are quite a lot—then you can say, ah, but, it was accepted in this other case.

Through those efforts, lawyers were able to pursue a change in the standards governing the primary purpose of marriages. While the Home Office can and does change the rules, it takes time, time in which individual clients can gain the right to stay in the country.

Lawyers used cases that made broader claims as lessons for what not to do.[73] *Bhatia*, a 1985 case, was bitterly cited by immigration lawyers as an example of a bad case to bring, one that dismantled previous work. The barrister in *Bhatia* argued that the burden of proof shifted to the Home Office once a genuine marriage had been proven, "which it doesn't and which you can't say, but because of that then the whole thing was set back for about a year because this case then got up to the Court of Appeal, with very bad submissions, which resulted in it being much more difficult," as a barrister critical of the decision said. Out of that case came a Court of Appeal decision reaffirming that the burden of proof lay with the defendant.

Challenges to the rules on the primary purpose of marriage started again through the immigration appeals system and the courts. The year after *Bhatia* UKIAS tried to refer more primary purpose cases out so to challenge the interpretation of the rules. Lawyers cited *Bhatia* as a reason for concentrating practice within an organized group of lawyers and as a reason for providing educational seminars through ILPA. *Bhatia* also highlights that what in the American context would be, if not small moves, at least not grand principled claims, look in the British context like claims far too sweeping to make before the courts. After all, no one in the case argued that the immigration rules were ultra vires or that the immigration officials had a manifestly unreasonable interpretation of the law. But in the United States, as well, interpretive struggles can focus on questions of burden of proof rather than appeals to what is fundamentally right or wrong. Employment opportunity, for example, has often focused on burden-of-proof questions.[74]

In July of 1986 the Court of Appeal issued an important decision revising *Bhatia* while claiming to be following it, *Kumar*. While the court insisted that there were three separate criteria, as listed previously, it held that "evidence of intervening devotion might make it easier to satisfy the officer that the parties' purpose at the time of the marriage was not primarily to obtain entry to the UK" and that "evidence bearing on one [question] would often cast a 'flood of light' on the other."[75]

Bhatia and *Kumar* have since provided touchstones for evaluating whether or not the primary purpose of a marriage was immigration at the time of marriage or subsequently.[76] The Immigration Appeals Tribunal has not always been generous in what it has counted as intervening devotion. The courts' job under judicial review is only to check whether a tribunal made a decision so unreasonable that it was outside the law. Judges do not see this as a standard inviting them to overturn administrative decisions, which means they do not always overturn what would seem to be an unhappy Immigration Appeals Tribunal decision. For example, in 1992 in *R. v. Immigration Appeal Tribunal ex p. Hussain* a judge rather unhappily concluded that he could not overturn the tribunal's conclusion that two children did not constitute enough intervening devotion. The judge could only point to the subsequent birth of a third child and ask the applicants to begin their case anew within the administrative system and hope that the administrative system would be more sympathetic.

Lawyers continued to try to wear away at the limits of the primary purpose rule. In 1992 the European Court of Justice, which only has jurisdiction over European Community member states, held that the primary purpose rules could not apply to citizens of a member state who had lived in another member state. By living in another member state a claimant obtained the rights that are guaranteed under the treaty creating the European community.[77] Before the decision was handed down the government revised its interpretation of the primary purpose rules without announcing the change; it decided that it would not object to settlement on the basis of marriage when the relationship had endured for five years or more or when there was a child with a right to settle in Britain as a result of the relationship. In explaining the change in policy the government cited the gains in case law that lawyers had achieved in the domestic courts, not the forthcoming decision from the European Court of Justice.[78]

The primary purpose rule has been widely criticized, though the more conservative press emphasizes the danger of recognizing fraudulent marriages. From a feminist perspective, the Southall Black Sisters have argued that the rules have been used to intimidate women in their homes by threatening them with deportation.[79] The concession from the government made a difference to people with children and those with long-standing relationships, and representatives have seen that as making a very real difference indeed. However, in contrast to the compassionate circumstances ground, for appeal, the government could not simply eliminate the primary purpose rule and avoid appeals and review. The compassionate circumstances grounds limited deportation while the primary purpose rule restricts settlement, and a restrictionist state therefore still finds it useful.

Gaining from Cases: What is There?

Litigation provides some victories for individual clients, and that can be reason enough to litigate. In a context in which immigration as an issue will receive little favorable attention from either major political party, litigation can be a way of gaining public time. Cases can be part of an effort to elevate an issue to the political agenda, occupying time in Parliament and the newspapers. Parliament, more than the American Congress, is organized around partisan debate. Judicial decisions provide material for that debate. Because of that, bringing a case sometimes make it possible to "jump the queue" and gain a debate in Parliament. Time in Parliament is a valuable and scarce resource. Civil servants would often prefer to change practices without using parliamentary time, in part because there is such competition for it. From outside government, strategies that get one into public partisan debate are useful because time is so difficult to get and it can win media attention. Some of the important cases, for example the Tamil suit, have been debated in Parliament. While the attention to the issue was not just about law but instead about the plight of refugees, the lawsuit did provide an occasion for comment. The lawsuit was *one part* of an effort to gain attention for the issue.

One barrister put the question of the public usefulness of legal claims this way:

> I think if politicians intrude too grossly upon perceived due process rights—that's a nebulous conception, what it should be—I think there is the beginnings of an emerging sense of impropriety and foul play. . . . I think politicians are creating trouble for themselves. A constitution is increasingly on the agenda because of the way they respond to judicial decisions. They're perfectly entitled to reverse a judicial decision. I'm not saying they're not entitled to. But if it impinges upon what would be seen as fundamental norms of procedural propriety—and I think that taking away a deportation appeal . . . to take away their right of appeal is . . . offensive to what a democratic and accountable government would be—it goes against a trend of devolvement of decision making where executive government ought to be prepared for their decisions to be reviewed by others.

While the Home Office does change practices and rules, practitioners know that it is not always easy to get it to do so. Using parliamentary time is valuable because of this and because it is difficult and embarrassing to revise judicial decisions too frequently (though that might be more true in areas other than immigration, and it is possible that lawyers in the field overestimate the government's embarrassment). That is in part because of the meaning that the High Court of Justice (and its judges) carry in British culture: that they articulate "the law," and that only those on the left would engage in debunking them.[80] Furthermore, it can just become not worth it to fight judicial decisions: the concession the government made in the primary purpose cases for long-standing relationships and those with children illustrates the possibility of very real victory, however grudgingly and quietly granted. Gaining public statements or debates in part through bringing cases means that participants sometimes see litigation as one more strategy within a political system that focuses on debate in Parliament.

Furthermore, the political debate regarding immigration has relied on anecdotes to highlight the different stories one could tell about immigration—whether about persecution or about people unfairly taking advantage of the riches of Britain. Lawyers have argued that anecdotes drawn from individual cases could make immigrants more acceptable. As one pointed out, "There is a difference between immigration as an issue and caring about individual cases. People do care about children and they do care about people being persecuted. They can relate to that. There's been a continuing high level of interest in the press on refugees, on, for example, primary purpose, which has provoked an endless stream of misery. And people care about those issues. You can tap that support. And that eventually gets to judges. As Lord Scarman said in the early proceedings in *Khawaja*, it is idle to pretend that judges don't read newspapers."

By raising questions through particular stories, litigation can appeal to the very particular human commitments we have, commitments not easily subsumed under general rules yet that make up the primary matter for our judgments.[81] Individuation is often understood to be a serious flaw of litigation as a political effort; it divides people from the collective context of an issue. The British Left has been especially concerned about this issue.[82] Yet the very individuation that is supposed to be a problem of litigation as a political strategy could in fact be a way to make the issue come alive. That is the hope of some of the solicitors and barristers concerned with immigration, and, indeed, individuating stories better fits public presentation of issues in the media. While the importance of individuating claims could be in part an artifact of the narrow British legal system, it is more than that. It addresses how we understand stories in Western postindustrial states. It is also a refuge when the collective issue is a losing one, as fighting for more generous immigration rules largely is in Britain.[83]

Immigration representatives do hope to help change perspectives on immigration in Britain, though they know how difficult and unlikely that is. No other strategy challenging immigration restrictions is guaranteed to work. It is not as though litigation has provided a false hope, distracting from some other, more effective strategy. Even after the five Tamil deportees had received sympathetic discussion in the national press, the news regarding immigration was dominated in 1988 and early 1989 by Viraj Mendis, who took refuge in a Manchester church to avoid deportation to Sri Lanka after having lost his asylum claim.[84] While people marched protesting his deportation and activists in Manchester found his case provoked alliances across some common divides, he was also criticized as manipulating the system. Yet even that case provoked commentary in the conservative *Times* on the shameful restrictiveness of British immigration rules, noting in particular the racial basis of that restrictiveness.[85] Breaking into official political debate in a political/administrative system known to be one of the most closed in the Western world is a real accomplishment.

As one lawyer said, "What else can be done?" Parliament was called a "desert" with respect to gaining relief for immigrants about to be deported. That remark involved no romanticism about the possibilities that courts offered. Rather, it spoke of comparative advantage. Critics of small victories or small resistances through law argue that they are an admission of failure, that the big issues have been lost. It is true that big victories, such as overturning all of the immigration law in Britain, are not possible. Legal representatives in Britain are acutely aware that they are taking cases in an extremely hostile climate. But in looking back at what have been generally understood to be the big victories in the United States—whether with regard to racism in schooling or rights in welfare—there never was any one place and any one time to overturn racism or expand the limits of the welfare state. In Britain, a political system in which it is difficult to raise political arguments that run counter to the parties' positions, litigation provides one way of sometimes winning for individual clients and of criticizing the practices of immigration officials. Working for individual clients, independent of a concern for long-term rule change, is crucial to the definition of lawyering for immigrants in a system in which it is difficult to change the rules through litigation. Yet even this extreme individuation, which is at the core of liberal legalism, draws attention to the broader politics of exclusion.

Notes

I am grateful to the lawyers and representatives in Britain who discussed with me the work they do; some also provided useful comments on earlier drafts of this article. I am also grateful for comments from Austin Sarat, Stuart Scheingold, and the participants in the cause-lawyering project. Some of the material in this essay appears in my book *Creating Constitutionalism?* (Ann Arbor: University of Michigan Press, 1997).

1. See, e.g., Lauren B. Edelman, and Stephen M. Petterson, "Symbols and Substance in Organizational Response to Civil Rights Law," unpublished manuscript, Department of Sociology, University of Wisconsin; Jennifer Hochschild, *The New American Dilemma* (New Haven, Conn.: Yale University Press, 1984).

2. Christopher McCrudden and Gerald Chambers, eds., *Individual Rights and the Law in Britain* (New York: Oxford University Press, 1994).

3. Michael McCann and Helena Silverstein, "Rethinking Law's 'Allurements': A Relational Analysis of Social Movement Lawyers in the United States," chap. 9 of this volume.

4. R. Shep Melnick, *Between the Lines* (Washington, D.C.: Brookings Institution, 1994).

5. Anthony Messina, *Race and Party Competition in Britain* (Oxford: Oxford University Press, 1989).

6. Colin Crouch and Ronald Dore, "Whatever Happened to Corporatism?," in *Corporatism and Accountability,* ed. Crouch and Dore (Oxford: Clarendon Press, 1990).

7. Muhammad Anwar, "The Context of Leadership," in *Black and Ethnic Leadership in Britain: The Cultural Dimensions of Political Action,* ed. Pnina Werbner and Muhammad Anwar (New York: Routledge, 1991).

8. Muhammad Anwar, "Ethnic Minorities' Representation: Voting and Electoral Politics in Britain, and the Role of Leaders," in *Black and Ethnic Leadership in Britain,* ed. Werbner and Anwar.

9. Pnina Werbner, "Black and Ethnic Leaderships in Britain: a Theoretical Overview," in *Black and Ethnic Leadership in Britain,* ed. Werbner and Anwar.

10. David Sugarman, "Cause Lawyers in a Postmodern World: The Case of England," Paper presented at cause lawyering conference, Amherst, Mass., August 1994.

11. P. S. Atiyah and Robert S. Summers, *Form and Substance in Anglo-American Law* (Oxford: Oxford University Press, 1987).

12. Maurice Sunkin and A. P. Le Sueur. "Can Government Control Judicial Review?," *Current Legal Problems 1991* (1991), 161–183. For a general discussion of the limits of litigation in liberal legalism, see Richard Abel's essay in this collection, "Speaking Law to Power: Occasions for Cause Lawyering."

13. Rupert Cross, *Statutory Interpretation* (Oxford: Clarendon Press, 1977).

14. J.A.G. Griffith, *The Politics of the Judiciary,* 4th ed. (London: Fontana Press, 1991).

15. Alan Paterson, *The Law Lords* (London: Macmillan, 1982).

16. On activism in the British courts, particularly in administrative law, see Robert Stevens, *The House of Lords as a Judicial Body, 1800–1976* (Chapel Hill: University of North Carolina Press), and Alan Paterson, *The Law Lords.*

17. Rt. Hon. Sir Harry Woolf, *Protection of the Public: a New Challenge* (London: Stevens and Sons, 1990); *R. v. Secretary of State for the Home Department ex p. Swati* [1986], All E.R. 717.

18. James C. Scott, *Domination and the Arts of Resistance* (New Haven, Conn.: Yale University Press, 1990).

19. The debate on the 1995 Immigration and Asylum Bill provides a recent illustration. *Times*, December 12, 1995, 10. See generally, Zig Layton-Henry, *The Politics of Immigration* (New York: Routledge, 1991).

20. A. Sivanandan, "All that Melts into Air Is Solid: the Hokum of New Times," *Race and Class* 31 (1989), 14–15, 24–27.

21. Messina, *Race and Party Competition in Britain.*

22. See generally Layton-Henry, *The Politics of Immigration,* chap. 7. On visitors' visas, see Joint Council for the Welfare of Immigrants, *Target: Caribbean* (London: JCWI, 1990). On street-level administrators, see Michael Lipsky, *Street-Level Bureaucracy* (New York: Russell Sage Foundation, 1980).

23. Carol Harlow and Richard Rawlings, *Law and Administration* (London: Weidenfeld & Nicolson, 1984); *Times*, July 9, 1992.

24. Ian Martin, "Combining Casework and Strategy: The Joint Council for the Welfare of Immigrants," in *Public Interest Law,* ed. Jeremy Cooper and Rajeev Dhavan (New York: Oxford University Press, 1986).

25. Legal Action Group, *A Strategy for Justice* (London: Legal Action Group, 1992).

26. Ibid., 9–10.

27. Susan Sterett, "Keeping the Law up to Date: The English Law Commission, Administrative Law, and the Idiom of Legalism," *Law and Social Inquiry* 15 (1990), 731–764.

28. Sir H.W.R. Wade, "The Rule of Law," *Times* (May 20, 1989), 11.

29. Maurice Sunkin, "What Is Happening to Applications for Judicial Review?," *Modern Law Review* 50 (1987), 432–467.

30. Rajeev Dhavan, "So Why Are There So Few Cases? Anti-Discrimination and Race Relations Law and Policy in the United Kingdom." Paper presented at the annual meeting of the Law and Society, Madison, Wisc., Association, June 1989; Maurice Sunkin, Lee Bridges, and George Meszaros, *Judicial Review in Perspective* (London: Public Law Project, 1993).

31. Sunkin, Bridges, and Meszaros, *Judicial Review in Perspective,* 35.

32. Mark Lazerson, "In the Halls of Justice, the Only Justice Is In the Halls," in *The Politics of Informal Justice,* vol. 2, ed. Richard L. Abel (New York: Academic Press, 1982).

33. Woolf, *Protection of the Public.*

34. Hazel Genn, "Tribunals and Informal Justice," *Modern Law Review* 56 (1993), 393–411.

35. Gita Sahgal and Nira Yuval-Davis, "Introduction," in *Refusing Holy Orders: Women and Fundamentalism in Britain,* ed. Gita Sahgal and Nira Yuval-Davis (London: Virago Press, 1992).

36. Ibid.; Ira Katznelson, *Black Men, White Cities* (New York: Oxford University Press, 1973).

37. Sahgal and Yuval-Davis, "Introduction"; Werbner, "Black and Ethnic Leaderships."

38. Russell Hardin, *Collective Action* (Baltimore, Md.: Johns Hopkins University Press, 1981).

39. Ronen Shamir and Sara Chinski, "Destruction of Houses and Construction of a Cause: Lawyers and Bedouins in the Israeli Courts," chap. 8 of this volume.

40. Louise Trubek and Elizabeth Kransberger, "Critical Lawyers: Social Justice and the

Structure of Private Practice," chap. 7 of this volume; Gerald Lopez, *Rebellious Lawyering* (Boulder, Colo.: Westview Press, 1992).

41. Aristide R. Zolberg, Astri Suhrke, and Sergio Aguayo, *Escape from Violence: Conflict and the Refugee Crisis in the Developing World* (New York: Oxford University Press, 1989).

42. Home Office Statistical Bulletin 17/94 (London: Government Statistical Service, 1994), table 1.2.

43. *Times*, March 4, 1987, p. 11; *Guardian*, February 28, 1987, p. 28.

44. In 1987, when the Tamil refugee cases first came through the system, 33.7 percent of all judicial review cases took between six months and one year from the time of application to the time of decision. I do not know what proportion of those cases was immigration. Forty-two percent of all judicial review cases took fewer than six months. In 1988 the proportion of cases that took between six months and a year went up to 49.6 percent. Sunkin, Bridges, and Meszaros, *Judicial Review in Perspective*, 58. The Rt. Hon. Lord Justice Woolf has expressed concern about the amount of time cases were taking (Woolf, *Protection of the Public*, 221–222). In 1993 judges complained about the amount of time cases were taking and urged the government to appoint more judges (*Times*, February 7, 1993, 22).

45. *R. v. Secretary of State for the Home Department ex p. Thirukumar and Others* [1989], Imm. A.R. 270, *Secretary of State for the Home Department v. Thirukumar and Others*, [1989], Imm. A.R. 402.

46. *R. v. Immigration Appeal Tribunal ex p. Secretary of State for the Home Department*, [1990], 3 ALL E.R. 652.

47. *Times*, July 28, 1989, 2.

48. July 4, 5, 28, 1989.

49. *Vilvarajah v. United Kingdom*, Eur. H.R. Rep. 248 (1991).

50. Officials and even legal commentators have not always argued the remedy was broad when they were arguing within the British courts. That they do when arguing in Europe points out the sometimes subtle effects that Europe has even on Britain, which has been most resistant to European integration. One barrister had a less kind comment. She said of the Home Office "they're so dirty" because they argue the remedy is wide when they are arguing before the ECHR and argue it is narrow when before the domestic courts.

51. *Times*, June 22, 1989; August 31, 1989.

52. *R. v. Secretary of State for Home Department ex p. Akdogan*, CO/2801/92, June 30, 1994.

53. While the Home Office attends to judicial review, it is common enough that they do not believe it is worth spending much time planning to avoid it. Maurice Sunkin and A. P. Le Sueur, "Can Government Control Judicial Review?," *Current Legal Problems 1991* (1991), 161–183.

54. Home Office Statistical Bulletin 17/94 (London: Government Statistical Service, 1994), table 1.2.

55. Richard Stewart, "The Reformation of American Administrative Law," *Harvard Law Review* 88 (1975), 1667–1813. However, Patrick Atiyah and Robert Summers have argued that an important contrast between the American and British legal systems is that the American relies on judgments of substance while the British rests on judgments about procedure. Atiyah and Summers, *Form and Substance*.

56. Martha Davis, *Brutal Need* (New Haven, Conn.: Yale University Press, 1993).

57. Jeffrey Jowell and Anthony Lester, "Beyond Wednesbury: Substantive Principles of Administrative Law," *Public Law 1989* (1989), 368–382.

58. Sivanandan, "All That Melts into Air Is Solid," 27–28.

59. *Times*, October 12, 1992, p. 10.

60. Asylum and Immigration Appeals Act 1993, ch. 23.

61. Zahir Chowdhury, "From Tribunal to the Court, part 1," *New Law Journal* 144 (1994): 207–208; Zahir Chowdhury, "From Tribunal to the Court, part 2," *The New Law Journal* 144 (1994): 240–241.

62. Abel, "Speaking Law to Power."

63. *R. v. Immigration Appeal Tribunal ex p. Begum* [1986], Imm. A.R. 385.

64. *R. v. Immigration Appeal Tribunal ex p. Khatun,* [1989], Imm. A.R. 482–501.

65. *Singh v. IAT* [1986], 2 ALL E.R. 721.

66. Immigration Act 1988 ch. 14, section 5.

67. Stuart Scheingold, "The Contradictions of Radical Law Practice," in *Lawyers' Work: Translation and Transgression,* ed. Maureen Cain and Christine Harrington (New York: New York University Press, 1993).

68. Carol Harlow, ed., *Public Law and Public Interest* (London: Butterworths, 1987).

69. R. Shep Melnick, *Regulation and the Courts* (Washington, D.C.: Brookings Institution, 1983).

70. *Case of Abdulaziz, Cabales and Balkandali* (1985), 7 Eur. H.R. Rep. 471.

71. WING [Women's Immigration and Nationality Group], *Worlds Apart* (London: Pluto Press, 1985).

72. H.C. 169, paragraph 41.

73. *Bhatia v. Immigration Appeal Tribunal* [1985], Imm. A.R. 50.

74. Vicky Schultz and Stephen Petterson, "Race, Gender, Work and Choice: An Empirical Study of the Lack of Interest Defense in Title VII Cases Challenging Job Segregation," *University of Chicago Law Review* 59 (1992), 1073–1181.

75. *R. v. Immigration Appeal Tribunal ex p. Kumar;* [1986], Imm. A.R. 446.

76. In another case the court explicitly tried to clarify the law, and thereby explicitly stated that evidence of intervening devotion did not require the conclusion that the primary purpose of a marriage was not immigration. *Immigration Appeal Tribunal v. Hoque and Singh* [1988], Imm. A.R. 216.

77. *R. v. Immigration Appeal Tribunal and Surinder Singh ex p. Secretary of State for the Home Department* (European Court of Justice), [1992], Imm. A.R. 565.

78. House of Commons, Parl. Debates, 6th series, vol. 30, col. 714 (June 1992).

79. *Observer,* October 18, 1992, 3.

80. Griffith, *The Politics of the Judiciary.*

81. Martha Nussbaum, "The Discernment of Perception: An Aristotelian Conception of Private and Public Rationality," in *Love's Knowledge,* (Oxford: Oxford University Press, 1991).

82. Valerie Kerruish, *Jurisprudence as Ideology* (New York: Routledge, 1991); Patrick McAuslan, "Administrative Law, Collective Consumption and Judicial Policy," *Modern Law Review* 46 (1983), 1–43; Allen Hutchinson, "The Rise and Ruse of Administrative Law and Scholarship," *Modern Law Review* 48 (1985), 293–322.

83. For a discussion of litigating a losing cause in the American context, see Austin Sarat, "Between (the Presence of) Violence and (the Possibility of) Justice: Lawyering against Capital Punishment," chap. 11 of this volume.

84. *Times,* June 18, 1988, p. 2; *R. v. Secretary of State for the Home Department ex p. Mendis; Times,* June 18, 1988, p. 23.

85. Ben Pimlott, "Britain Leads in Politics of Closed Door," *Sunday Times,* January 22, 1989, p. B3.

Between (the Presence of) Violence and (the Possibility of) Justice

Lawyering against Capital Punishment

AUSTIN SARAT

"Legal interpretation demands that we remember the future."
Drucilla Cornell, "From the Lighthouse: The Promise of
Redemption and the Possibility of Legal Interpretation"

"The ideality of the Good is an anticipatory ideal, but one in which anticipation
will prove itself to be a memory."
Judith Butler, "Deconstruction and the Possibility of Justice"

"[L]egal systems try to make the future by redesigning the past and their connection with it."
Robert Gordon, "Undoing Historical Injustice"

"[E]vil is the obliteration of personhood and hence the deprivation of all the
personal and political rights of one, few, some or many."
George Kateb, *The Inner Ocean: Individualism and Democratic Character*

"I had no evil intent when I taught the tricks of pleading, for I never meant them
to be used to get the innocent condemned but, if the occasion arose, to save the
lives of the guilty."

St. Augustine, *Confessions*

"I'd make my Supreme Court down in Texas,
and there wouldn't be no killers getting free.
If they were found guilty,
then they would hang quickly,
instead of writin' books and smiling on TV."
Hank Williams Jr., "If the South Would Have Won"

Justice, Violence, and "Cause Lawyers"

Justice, Drucilla Cornell argues, "is precisely what eludes our full knowledge." We cannot "grasp the Good but only follow it. The Good . . . is a star which beckons us to follow."[1] While Justice, or what Cornell calls the Good, is, on her account, always present *to* law, it is never completely realized *in* law.[2] "[T]he law posits an ideality . . . that it can never realize, and . . . this failure is constitutive of existing law."[3] Law exists both in the "as yet" failure to realize the Good and in the commitment to its realization. In this failure and this commitment law is two things at once: the social organization of violence through which state power is exercised in a partisan, biased, and sometimes cruel way,[4] and the arena to which citizens address themselves in the hope that law can, and will, redress the wrongs that are committed in its name.[5]

Perhaps no one had a deeper and more penetrating understanding of this duality than Robert Cover.[6] Cover compellingly called our attention to law's "jurisgenerative" and its "jurispathic" qualities.[7] "Law," he argued,

> may be viewed as a system of tension or a bridge linking a concept of reality to an imagined alternative. . . . Thus, one constitutive element of a *nomos* is the phenomenon George Steiner has labeled "alternity": the "other than the case", the counterfactual propositions, images, shapes of will and evasions with which we charge our mental being and by means of which we build the changing, largely fictive milieu for our somatic and our social existence. But the concept of a *nomos* is not exhausted by its "alternity"; it is neither utopia nor pure vision. A *nomos*, as a world of law, entails the application of human will to an extant state of affairs as well as toward our visions of alternative futures.[8]

Cover used the word *nomos*, "normative universe," to argue that law is crucially involved in helping persons "create and maintain a world of right and wrong, of lawful and unlawful, of valid and void."[9] The *nomos* that law helps to create, Cover believed, always contains within it visions of possibility not yet realized, images of a better world not yet built. But, he reminds us, law is not simply, or even primarily, a gentle, hermeneutic apparatus; it always exists in a state of tension between a world of meaning in which Justice is pursued, and a world of violence in which "legal interpretation takes place on a field of pain and death."[10]

Confronting this tension in law is the distinctive work of "cause lawyers" wherever they practice, and whatever cause they serve, including lawyers who devote themselves to opposing/ending capital punishment. Cause lawyers use their professional skills to move law away from the daily reality of violence and toward a particular vision of the Good.[11] For them, the Good is known in the causes for which they work even as its realization may be deferred. It is their work to give content to the "impossibility" of Justice. In so doing, they reject what David Luban calls the principle of professional "nonaccountability," namely the view that a lawyer is "responsible neither for the means used nor the ends achieved in legal representation."[12] Cause lawyers refuse to use their skills indiscriminately, to be the "hired guns" of anyone able to pay for their services.[13] They also reject the alternative role of "lawyer-statesman"[14] because it is elitist and disconnected from any conception of substantive justice. Instead, they self-consciously politicize their professional lives, and make lawyering a vocation of Justice rather than technique, of moral engagement rather than moral neutrality.[15]

Cause lawyers use the skills and knowledge that they possess to give life to law's ethical aspirations. As such it is crucial to their professional identity "that they are morally accountable for their representation, not to be sure for promoting their clients projects, but for advocating the political and legal principles they are trying to vindicate."[16] Studying cause lawyering is thus one way to understand how persons act in the face of legally imposed pain and death. In addition, it provides an opportunity for scholars interested in the way law is made meaningful in society to recapture the subject of Justice which, for too long, has been left to jurisprudence.[17]

Capital Punishment: The Contemporary Legal and Political Context

This essay takes up that opportunity by examining the work of lawyers whose cause is abolition of the death penalty, and the situation in the United States that those lawyers now confront. This group of lawyers specializes in representing death row inmates in appellate and postconviction procedures.[18] In their lawyering they give content to Justice by seeking to prevent the execution of their clients and, at the same time, to end capital punishment. In their practice they have daily contact with the violence of law, yet they continue to use legal processes in an effort to stop that violence. They confront the possibility that law may be little more than a killing machine, yet they pursue the Good through law.[19] Despite the importance of what they do, their work has been almost invisible to the scholarly community.[20]

In another era, say twenty-five years ago, these lawyers might have been called, or might have called themselves, the "abolitionist" bar,[21] but the mid-1990s in the United States are a very different time.[22] Twenty-five years ago, toward the end of the heyday of the Warren Court and the era of sustained civil rights activism, a favorable judicial response to the abolitionist movement seemed quite possible.[23] And, indeed, in 1972 in *Furman v. Georgia,* the Supreme Court provided such a response, holding that the death penalty as then *applied* was unconstitutional.[24] While the Court did not find that the death penalty was *per se* unconstitutional, there was a reasonable expectation that it might very well soon do so. As Philip Kurland wrote at the time, "[O]ne role of the Constitution is to help the nation to become 'more civilized.' A society with the aspirations that ours so often asserts can't, consistently with its goals, coldly and deliberately take the life of any human being no matter how reprehensible his past behavior. . . . [I]n the *Furman v.*

Georgia decision the inevitable came to pass."[25] Jack Greenberg of the National Association for the Advancement of Colored People Legal Defense Fund expressed a similar understanding of the significance of *Furman* when he said, "[T]here will no longer be any more capital punishment in the United States."[26]

Then something unexpected happened. Whereas in other Western nations the abolition of the death penalty was followed by a downturn in public interest and support for capital punishment,[27] in the wake of *Furman* a dramatic pro–capital punishment backlash occurred. "State legislatures . . . quickly responded to the Court's decision, but instead of conducting a thorough reevaluation of the subject, they enacted whatever statutory revisions they perceived as correcting the constitutional flaws contained in pre-*Furman* capital laws."[28] Public reaction followed a similar pattern, "with a hostile response all over the country."[29] Thus, four years after *Furman's* limited abolition of capital punishment, the Court, in *Gregg v. Georgia,* found that "it is now evident that a large proportion of American society continues to regard . . . [capital punishment] as an appropriate and necessary criminal sanction."[30] As a result, the Court held that "the punishment of death does not invariably violate the Constitution."[31]

Since the mid-1970s the political and legal climate for abolition of the death penalty has become more and more hostile.[32] The Supreme Court has moved rather methodically, if not in a linear fashion, to cut off all systemic, "wholesale" challenges to the constitutionality of capital punishment.[33] And public support for the death penalty has risen to unprecedented levels. Today most national polls show support in the 70–75 percent range.[34] The political and public appetite for legally imposed death seems almost insatiable;[35] where once an execution was the stuff of front-page, TV evening news coverage, today, except in unusual circumstances, execution has been routinized.[36] Politicians of every stripe do not want to be caught on the "wrong side" on the death penalty debate.[37] Abolition now has meager support, and the abolition movement has become virtually invisible.[38]

If that were not enough, the courts, including the Supreme Court, have grown impatient with the complex legal process that the Court itself constructed to ensure fairness in the administration of law's ultimate penalty.[39] They have thrown their weight behind law's violence and, in this area at least, not heard the beckoning call of Justice.[40] Thus, in recent years, in an apparent effort to limit the reach of the Eighth Amendment as a source of protection for capital defendants, the Supreme Court has gradually cut back on the availability of federal habeas corpus relief in death penalty cases.[41] Through decisions dealing with procedural default,[42] exhaustion,[43] and abuse of the writ through the filing of successive habeas petitions,[44] it has made it increasingly difficult for federal courts to reach the merits of a defendant's habeas claims.

Just a few years ago, in the most significant of these cutbacks, the Court declared that defendants must generally base their habeas petitions on asserted violations of the federal law as it existed at the time of the original state proceedings.[45] In a follow-up case, it held that if the federal law was unclear at that time, any reasonable, "good faith" interpretation of the federal law by the state courts immunizes the conviction and sentence from later habeas attack.[46] Even more recently, it extended the same principle to the method of application of the federal law to the facts of a particular case; if the state courts' method of application of the federal law was proper in view of the precedents that existed at that time, then federal habeas relief is unavailable (even if those precedents are later overruled or changed).[47]

These decisions have already made it much more difficult for a defendant who receives a death sentence to obtain federal habeas review of the merits of whatever decisions or rulings might have been made by the judge during his or her capital trial.[48] So hostile have the courts become to extended litigation in capital cases that in one case where there had been repeated last-minute requests for a stay of execution in several different courts, the Supreme Court, usurping the legal prerogatives of the lower courts, took the unprecedented step of ordering that no further stays be granted.[49] And, even new evidence of actual innocence has been found to be inadequate as the basis for challenging a death sentence.[50] For the current Supreme Court "finality is more important than hearing every meritorious legal claim; there simply comes a point when legal proceedings must end and punishment must be imposed."[51] As Bowers argues, "Now, 20 years after *Furman,* the current Court is adamant in its commitment" to maintaining capital punishment.[52] The result is that the population of death row, and the number of executions, have increased dramatically.[53]

In this hostile climate death penalty lawyers have not themselves escaped condemnation.[54] Rather than being respected as the guardians of important legal values rooted in the Fourteenth Amendment guarantee of due process of law, or the Eighth Amendment's prohibition of cruel and unusual punishment,[55] those lawyers are vilified as rogues who violate the canons of their profession by conducting an ideologically motivated guerilla war against capital punishment.[56] As the Supreme Court put it when it refused to grant a stay of execution to Robert Alton Harris,[57] "Harris seeks an equitable remedy. Equity must take into consideration the state's strong interest in proceeding with its judgment and Harris's obvious attempt at manipulation. This claim could have been brought more than a decade ago. There is no good reason for this abusive delay, which has been compounded by last-minute attempts to manipulate the judicial process."[58]

Death penalty lawyers, those who are indeed engaged in an ideologically motivated campaign against capital punishment, find themselves engaged in what increasingly looks like a losing cause.[59] While they have the advantage of being able to invoke the formal rights and protections of liberal legalism, the legal system seems ever more inhospitable to them and their work.[60] To oppose the death penalty through the legal process in the United States in the nineties is not unlike fighting against apartheid in the courts of South Africa in the 1970s, or litigating in behalf of Palestinian rights in the Occupied Territories in the 1980s.[61] In the face of a legal system intent on imposing violence and turning its back on the beckoning call of Justice, one might then ask why anti–death penalty lawyers do not abandon law as an arena of struggle? Or, how do they adapt their lawyering activities to the prevailing hostile legal climate? Answering these questions is the subject of this chapter.

Bearing Witness, Writing History

The usual answer to such questions is that legality, because it provides the legitimating ideology of the powerful, can be an important weapon in political struggle.[62] However, in the case of the death penalty in the contemporary United States this answer seems inapplicable. The legitimating promises of the law, found in the recognition that "death is different"[63] and the promise of "super due process" in death cases,[64] have been stripped away gradually but openly. There is now little room to hold law to its promises because so many of those promises seem to have been broken without embarrassment.

Another answer to the question of why (and/or how) law can be used by lawyers fighting for a losing cause might be found if we take seriously Drucilla Cornell's admonition in one of the epigraphs to this chapter: "Legal interpretation demands that we remember the future."[65] In that phrase, Cornell suggests that law fixes its gaze temporally, not on the possibilities (or impossibilities) of the present, but on a future promise of Justice. She reminds us that there are, in fact, two audiences for every legal act, the audience of the present (to which one might appeal for an end to law's violence), and the audience of the future (which stands as a figure of law's redeeming promise of Justice). In this sense, law, as Cover writes is "a bridge to alternity."[66]

In Cornell's and Cover's understanding, lawyering in a losing cause is a form of what Cover called "redemptive constitutionalism."[67] Through their activities, cause lawyers refuse to recognize the violence of the present moment as the defining totality of law, and they are the carriers of a vision of a future in which Justice prevails over that violence. For them, as Cover argues, "[r]edemption takes place within an eschatological schema that postulates: (1) the unredeemed character of reality as we know it, (2) the fundamentally different reality that should take its place, and (3) the replacement of one with the other."[68]

Cover uses the example of an abolitionist struggle of another era, namely antislavery activism in the mid-nineteenth century, to suggest that the work of "redemptive constitutionalism" reveals "a creative pulse that proliferates principle and precept, commentary and justification, even in the face of a state legal order less likely to hold slavery unconstitutional than to declare the imminent kingship of Jesus Christ on Earth."[69] In this view, the lawyer serving a losing cause speaks in a prophetic voice even as she supplies the argumentative and interpretive resources to bridge the gap between the violence of the present and the beckoning possibility of Justice.[70]

But there is perhaps a second way of understanding the work of lawyers who serve losing causes. In this second understanding Cover's image is reversed, and redemption gives way to Judgment. As redemption gives way to Judgment, the future is called on to remember the injustices of the present.[71] Given this imperative to remember, the lawyer for a losing cause serves as a witness testifying against those injustices. Such a lawyer provides

> the testimonial *bridge* which, mediating between narrative and history, guarantees their correspondence and adherence to each other. This bridging between narrative and history is possible since the narrator is both an *informed* and an *honest* witness. . . . All the witness has to do is to *efface himself*, and let the *literality of events* voice its own *self-evidence*. 'His business is only to say: this is *what happened*, when he knows that it actually did happen.'[72]

However, lawyers for a losing cause do more than give testimony. They write a history. They use legal processes to record a history of the present, and, in that history to preserve the present's pained voice. Because lawyers for a losing cause can, indeed, take advantage of one of the legitimating promises of law, namely its commitment to due process, the litigated case can be used to create a record, and the court can become the archive in which that record serves as the materialization of memory.[73] Due process guarantees an opportunity to be heard by, and an opportunity to speak to, the future. It is the guarantee that legal institutions can be turned into museums of unnecessary, unjust, undeserved pain and death.[74]

The legal hearing provides an opportunity to write and record history by creating narratives of present injustices.[75] By recording such history and constructing such narratives the lawyer for a losing cause calls on an imagined future to choose Justice over the jurispathic tendencies of the moment.[76] Constructing such narratives, cause lawyers ensure that, even when no one (including judges) seems willing to listen, the voices of the "oppressed" will not be silenced.

The movement from giving testimony to writing history is a movement from the immediacy of the eyewitness report to the mediation produced through narrativization.[77] In this movement lawyers for losing causes may, as Gordon indicates, frame the injustices they seek to record in one of three narrative styles. The first Gordon calls "legalist."[78] This narrative treats the injustices of the present as wrongs "done by specific perpetrators to specific victims."[79] It stays within the frame of liberal legalism and describes present injustice in terms of the remedies that law itself, should it be willing, could easily supply.

The second narrative also stays within the legalist mode though it involves what Gordon calls "broad agency."[80] In this narrative the history of injustice is a history of collective action taken by one *group* against another. The third narrative of the injustices of the present attributes injustice to "bad structures rather than bad agents. . . . This historical enterprise takes the form of a search for explanations rather than a search for villainous agents and attribution of blame."[81] In this third narrative, lawyers broaden the scope of inquiry by linking the particular injustices to which they are opposed with broader patterns of injustice and institutional practice.

The ability of cause lawyers to speak to the future and memorialize the present, to both give testimony and write history, has been ignored by those who have worried too much about the impact of cause lawyering on the political possibilities of the present.[82] For them, its value resides exclusively in its most immediate effects, and it poses dangers to the health of political movements. But, as Cornell reminds us, law is as much about the future as the present, and as much about the possibilities of memory as the current prospects of political success. Thus when cause lawyers insistently turn to law, they

> posit the very ideal . . . [they] purportedly find 'there' in the legal text, and as [they] posit the ideal or the ethical [they] promise to remain true to it. [Their] promise of fidelity to the ethical or to the ideal is precisely what breathes life into the dead letter of the law and provides a barrier against the violence of the word. . . . To heed the call to responsibility within law is to remind . . . [ourselves] of the disjuncture between law and the ideal and to affirm our responsibility to make the promise into the ideal, to aspire to counter the violence of our world in the name of universal justice.[83]

Lawyering in a losing cause is one way of "remembering the future" and of ensuring that the future remembers. It is both a kind of testimony and a way of recording a history of injustice. It seeks to put law's violence in a narrative context that juxtaposes it to the Good, and it preserves "the versions of legal meaning created by groups outside the mainstream of American law."[84] It turns courthouses into memorials to present injustice and uses the legal process to create memory in the face of an obliterating violence. Perhaps by paying attention to how such lawyering insures that the future will be remembered, and that the future itself remembers, we can gain a perspective on the way cause lawyers stand between present violence and the promise of Justice.

On the Evil of Capital Punishment: Lawyers' Views

In order to examine the ways cause lawyers stand between violence and Justice, I interviewed forty death penalty lawyers in ten states.[85] States were selected to represent the diversity of current experiences with capital punishment (e.g., the number of persons on death row, the number of persons executed), and lawyers were chosen to represent the range of settings in which death penalty practice takes place.[86] In each interview I began by inquiring about my respondent's views about capital punishment and the ways those views connect up with their broader moral and political commitments. Here diversity is the order of the day. Among the lawyers I interviewed, there was no singular view about the moral status of capital punishment and no one way in which that issue was fit into larger narratives about violence and justice.

There was, however, a widespread belief in the importance of political commitment and of linking death penalty work to such larger narratives. One older lawyer, who works in a private practice setting, exemplified this view even as he expressed anxiety about the extent of such commitment in the death penalty bar. "The people who were doing death penalty work in the 70s and 80s," he claimed,

> were doing it out of nothing but a sense of political commitment. They certainly were not making any money; they were just working their tails off for what they believed in. With the establishment of federally funded resource centers in the mid-80s that changed. Not great money, but suddenly you could make a living and support a family. But money doesn't insure that people will be there twenty-four hours a day, working, giving everything.

For him, the advent of resource centers was a mixed blessing. It brought people to the work of fighting capital punishment who might not otherwise be doing so, but it also diluted the "moral purity" of the community of lawyers doing such work.

The relationship of political commitment and the setting in which death penalty lawyers practice is, however, not as predictable as this lawyer's anxiety might make it seem. Thus a similar concern was expressed by a relative newcomer, who is himself employed in a resource center:

> I guess people could say "Well, I'm not an abolitionist and I think that there is someone out there who should get it" and still be driven by a certainty about their client's case. But I doubt it. Those people are not driven at the same level if they don't believe that this is more than just a job, and it is about more than just one client. They're going to avoid connecting with them as human beings because of a desire not to have it intrude on their lives. If there is a mob out there that wants to kill your guy, you are going to have to stop it singlehandedly and that means making some pretty serious exertions. At that point, you better not be thinking, "This is just a job." It better be a real important cause for you or you just won't do it.

Death penalty work is, on this account, "more than just a job," and it requires a commitment to "more than just one client." For this lawyer, political commitment can and should be expressed through client representation. But it needn't be a barrier to effective client advocacy. In fact, such commitment seems to be essential if a death penalty lawyer is going to "connect" with the person he represents. Connecting with the client at a human level, when everywhere he is regarded as subhuman because of what he has done, is, as we will see in a later section of this essay, a crucial component of the political work of death penalty lawyers.

Yet as the image of the death penalty lawyer standing up "singlehandedly" to the "mob" suggests, making such a connection is not, in itself, sufficient. This image is a vivid reminder of the dilemma of the lawyer for a losing cause, and of the political/moral commitment that sustains this work. Of course it is not surprising that for some of these lawyers the cause they see themselves as serving, the cause that motivates their "serious exertions," is traditional abolitionism, in which the death penalty is rejected as an immoral act. For them, Justice, though it may never be fully realized, is by no means unknowable. As they see it, the immorality of the death penalty is clear and beyond dispute; it is founded on a belief in the incompatibility of capital punishment on the one hand and the values of a civilized society on the other.[87] As a result, they seek to use their lawyering skills to stop at least this one aspect of law's violence.

One such abolitionist lawyer told me,

> I do this work because I'm opposed to the death penalty. I'm an abolitionist. I have responsibilities to individual clients, and those obviously override everything. But to me this is an ideological struggle. I do this work as an extension of my beliefs. We are going to take this person in and kill him. I think deciding to kill someone as a society is a decision that reveals society's corruption.

For this lawyer, the death penalty is a symptom of an unidentified social "corruption." Yet he himself seeks to avoid the corruption of his representational role that his reference to an "ideological struggle" might suggest. Thus as he explains his principled opposition to capital punishment, he notes a tension between his responsibilities to his client and his ideological motivation. In so doing he expresses a dilemma that faces all cause lawyers who use the representation of individual clients as a vehicle for political work.[88] Yet, despite his claim, it is, in fact, by no means any more "obvious" how those tensions are resolved in the context of lawyering against the death penalty than it is in any other area.[89]

For many death penalty lawyers, the "ideological struggle" is animated by a deep opposition to violence. This opposition is revealed in the comment of a young woman who has worked for several years in a resource center. "I oppose capital punishment," she explained,

> for a multitude of reasons, but mostly from a moral perspective. I don't think that the government should kill its citizens. It is a far more natural impulse to keep people alive than to kill them. And in my view government is a parent figure. The same reason I don't hit my daughter is why the government should not kill my clients. If the government responds in a violent way to the problem of violence it is, whatever its intention, sending the message that violence is okay.

Casting government as "parent" domesticates and familiarizes the debate about the death penalty.[90] It suggests that the question of the death penalty has to be seen not just in terms of the usual discussion of crime and retribution but in terms of its "radiating effects" in the larger society.

"The death penalty is wrong," another lawyer said, echoing this concern for its radiating effects, "because it denigrates humanness. The government shouldn't be in the killing business. It minimizes human life in the sense that you are saying the government is superior and more important than individual human lives."[91]

For others in the death penalty bar, however, opposition to the death penalty is not based on such traditional abolitionist sentiments. It is instead rooted in the belief that capital punishment cannot be administered in a manner compatible with due process of law. This "new abolitionism" describes the beckoning call of Justice as procedural rather than substantive, legal rather than moral. It was recently invoked by former Justice Harry Blackmun in a dissent from a denial of certiorari in a death case.[92] As Blackmun put it,

> There is little doubt now that *Furman's* essential holding was correct. Although most of the public seems to desire, and the Constitution appears to permit, the penalty of death, it surely is beyond dispute that if the death penalty cannot be administered fairly and rationally, it may not be administered at all. . . . Despite the efforts of the states and the courts to devise legal formulas and procedural rules to meet this daunting challenge, the death penalty remains fraught with arbitrariness, discrimination, caprice, and mistake.[93]

In this opinion, and in the new abolitionism that it embraces, opposition to the death penalty expresses itself as a form of legal conservatism. The death penalty is rejected, not because of its violent and dehumanizing qualities, or for what it says about the relationship of citizens to their government, but because of its corrupting and corrosive effects on the legal system and because it undermines the fundamental legal values of due process and equal treatment.

"I'm frustrated," one of the new abolitionists told me,

> because I'm not a great liberal. In fact, in many ways I'm pretty conservative. But I believe that if we are going to truly have a system of law, law has to operate in a way that insures fundamental fairness, and that is what we don't have in the death penalty. If they try to seek it against the wealthy, they don't get it because they get good lawyers who do the work and juries don't return it. But they can do what they want to minorities. In that situation, I have to use my skills to level the playing field. For me that is why I do it, to level the playing field. I can't do it in very many cases, but here I can do a bit to make it more level.

Or, as another explained,

> When I first thought about doing death penalty work I had very complicated views about the death penalty. I was agnostic on the underlying philosophical issues. I didn't, and don't, think of myself as an abolitionist. When I hear the Amnesty International People talk, I want to be distant from them because they speak in hyperbole. But when I started, I talked to people who said that you didn't have to be an abolitionist in the classic sense because the application of the system is so unfair that your interest should just be on fairness. I have come to think that it is inappropriate for the state to be executing individuals with very

few exceptions. I think that it's probably appropriate to execute people who commit crimes like high treason. However, my current view is that we should stop it. You can never get to the theoretical debate because the system we actually have is so far from perfect. If we had a perfect system, then we could think about the theoretical issue. But in fact we don't have anywhere near close to such a system. We are executing people just because they have crappy lawyers who do crappy jobs at trial. And the actual application of the death penalty is a travesty. So my views are primarily in opposition to the system that we have as well as any system I can imagine in the near future.

The new abolitionist position focuses attention on the daily realities of administering law's violence and refuses to engage with abstract, theoretical concerns. For some in the death penalty bar, this position is connected to a more far-reaching narrative of violence and justice in which race plays an especially pivotal role. For them, death penalty work is part of a broad-based political struggle for civil rights and political equality. The cause for which these lawyers are fighting is only incidentally to stop executions; the call of Justice that beckons is a call for a knowable, if not attainable, ideal, namely substantive equality and decent treatment for all persons. The narrative of injustice which they construct is "structural" and "systemic" rather than "legalistic,"[94] and the effort to stop executions is valuable insofar as it provides a strategic vehicle for addressing larger and more encompassing social issues. As one young lawyer, who is employed in a resource center, said,

> I think the litigation of death penalty issues in the criminal justice system in the 1990s is what civil rights litigation was in the 50s and 60s. You are dealing with a group of people who are in this situation not so much because of what they did, but because of who they are. And who they are has a lot to do with the color of their skin and their socioeconomic status.

Another lawyer described his death penalty work as "the civil rights work of our era." He noted that

> while there are established remedies for discrimination in other areas, whether education or employment, there is a way to remedy it that uses the courts. Whereas in our area, anyone who does this work knows that racism is one of the most important influences in deciding who gets the death penalty and who doesn't, who's prosecuted for capital murder and who's not. And yet a real remedy doesn't exist.

This lawyer went on to describe himself as "a political radical," who was "dedicated personally to the reconstruction of a lot of things in this society including the distribution of wealth." Like him, others are attracted to death penalty work because they see it as "a microcosm of everything that's wrong in society. There are poverty issues, race issues, classism, everything that's wrong in society at some point ends up in capital punishment."

Yet the prevalence of such a broad-based political critique among some death penalty lawyers should not be taken to suggest that radical political commitment is uniform in this community. As a woman in private practice explained, "I'm a mixed bag. I'm not like a knee-jerk liberal. I'm fiscally pretty conservative. I live out in the suburbs, a very conventional lifestyle. I have a little girl. I'm married. I guess I would say I'm a moderate." In this account, domesticity plays an important role in providing reassurance that even "normal" people can be death penalty lawyers.

"The Death Penalty Is Here to Stay"

For those less concerned to domesticate their identity, the notion that the death penalty is a microcosm for social evils endows their work with political meaning even as it raises the question of whether doing death work is the most strategically sound manner of addressing social justice issues.[95] This is an especially pressing question given what most death penalty lawyers acknowledge is the very hostile political and legal climate for their work. There is, in fact, a widely shared and rather acute recognition among lawyers who oppose capital punishment that they are lawyering in a losing cause, that the commitments that they bring to their work are not likely, in the near future, to be vindicated in either the legal or the political process. This sense that capital punishment is here to stay explains why, in spite of the fact that there has not been an opening of the floodgates of execution and that death penalty lawyers are often able on a case-by-case basis to win particular procedural victories, members of the death penalty bar see themselves as lawyering in a losing cause.

This recognition is captured by a lawyer who said, in a classic understatement, "We are not living in a very good climate for death cases. There might not ever be one, but today is certainly not a good one." Another lawyer, who currently works in a resource center, made the same point by highlighting a change from the days when she first started to represent people on death row to the present moment. "When I started," she said,

> there was still so much hope. Today the train is on the way down the track and everyone is jumping off, and we are here as the last hope. But now the cases are so miserable because of what the courts have done. The Supreme Court has continued to put up barriers in our way. And every time they point you down one road you go down that road and then they say, "We were just kidding. We don't allow you down here any more." So things have changed. It's an injustice what has happened, an absolute injustice.

This description of a movement from hope to an "absolute injustice" perpetrated by courts that are fully attentive and attuned to a belligerent, pro–death penalty political constituency, depends on what Gordon called an "agency"-based narrative.[96] A similar narrative was invoked by a veteran death penalty lawyer who claimed "We were beating them at every turn," one lawyer argued, "so long as they were taking due process seriously. Then they could never get past us. So they just changed the rules." Such a change occurred, he explained, because

> the pro–death penalty temperature is rising quite a bit. State legislators just foam at the mouth to see people executed. State courts are becoming much more angry and impatient with anything we say or do. Attorneys general are more organized in trying to prod and goad the courts into that kind of impatience. There is a real fight that we've been losing for the past seven or eight years about whether there is going to be even any pretense to real due process. The system is full of displaced aggression directed against us and the people we represent. And now there is a real capital punishment bureaucracy, maybe ten thousand people across the country. It's under pressure from people who are setting the budget to just move people along toward execution.

For this lawyer, the difficulty of successfully opposing capital punishment has been compounded by the creation of a death penalty bureaucracy with its own vested interests and desire for political survival.[97]

In an environment in which "the pro–death penalty temperature is rising quite a bit," courts, once sympathetic to the claims of opponents of the death penalty, now no longer even "listen." "You are continually working hard," one lawyer said, "to dig up new facts and identify good issues that will make them face the horrors of the death penalty, but the most frustrating thing is when you present it to a court that just doesn't care." In the words of one of her colleagues who practices in a public interest setting,

> I really do think that there is a deep sense in the community opposed to capital punishment that nobody listens. You can file something that's really long, but it doesn't matter because they (judges and legislators) aren't even going to read it. And if it is read, it is read with an eye to figuring out how to deny what you are saying.

The question for the death penalty bar, as one practitioner put it,

> is not figuring out a strategy for how you are going to win. If you do this work you quickly shed that illusion. The death penalty is here to stay, at least in our lifetimes. The question is almost always now "How do you want to lose?" and "Where do you want to lose?" not "How do you win?" Victory is minimizing the losses you take in certain places. You want to sneak by in the middle of the night, as it were, and be denied quietly without any sort of drawing undue attention to what may be your meritorious claims in the long, long run. It really is a question of knowing that you are going to lose. It's knowing what do you want to do in the act of losing. It's the last-word syndrome, "Right before you die, do you have any last words?"

Because proponents of capital punishment have such a strong hold on public opinion and are so firmly entrenched in the political process, death penalty lawyers generally accept that "the death penalty is here to stay" and that victory consists in "minimizing losses." For many, death penalty work has now become "like working with the terminally ill. You know that the cure rates are pretty low. So you cure the very few that you can and those many who you can't cure you make their lives comfortable and fight to keep them alive as long as possible." [98]

The perception that the courts no longer are listening to anti–death penalty arguments and that the best one can hope for is to keep one's clients alive "as long as possible" is further compounded by the sense that other kinds of political opposition to capital punishment are also futile.

> I'm a member of all the abolitionist groups, and we are clearly their major source of information. But the truth is that I think that they are so unrealistic. They are so far from where public opinion is these days. I guess it is not surprising that one of the things that I don't like about this job is how ineffectual we are so many times. I don't want to be next to the people who are holding the banners when there are six of them holding their little candles outside when someone inside is being executed, and the state is voting 85 percent for the death penalty. We get so hammered in public, by the press, and by the establishment that the bunker mentality is now really pretty pervasive. [99]

Lawyering in a Losing Cause

How do death penalty lawyers shape their professional identities, and adapt their strategies and tactics to the task of lawyering when "the death penalty is here to stay" and when they are getting "hammered"? How do they resist violence that seems so unstoppable and pursue Justice that seems so remote? In this section I identify three prominent responses among death penalty lawyers; I call these responses "redefining success," "pushing the ethical limits," and "remembering the future/making the future remember."

Redefining Success

In the heyday of anti–death penalty optimism between *Furman* and *Gregg*, and even in the period leading up to *McCleskey*, the abolition movement seemed alive and well, and the prospect of wholesale victories was, if not bright, then not beyond contemplation. In those days, the success of death penalty lawyering was measured in terms of the strides taken toward the political and/or legal abolition of capital punishment. [100] But with changing times have come new definitions of success among lawyers opposing capital punishment.

The sense that one is much more likely to be on the losing end of the contemporary politics of execution means, as one young, resource center lawyer put it, that

> [y]ou start looking at winning and losing in different ways. Even where a person is ultimately executed, if you get three votes from the Supreme Court, people act like that is a big win. Wins in terms of getting people off death row are very rare and getting new trials are very rare. So you set your sights on keeping your client alive from stay to stay, getting through an execution date, keeping your client alive.

Or, as a lawyer in a public interest setting said, "To the people I represent, they basically live their lives from stay to stay. They know that the death penalty is not going to go away so they live in thirty-day increments. And, you are successful every time you buy them an additional thirty days."

Keeping your client alive "for an additional thirty days" becomes the measure of political and personal accomplishment when the prospect of a frontal assault on the death penalty seems so remote.[101] In this sense, "the very hopelessness of the abolitionist cause ironically helps to suppress the typical conflict between clients and causes. In death penalty cases, there are neither great 'legal' victories to be won, nor much chance of altering the ultimate fate facing any individual client."[102] Anti–death penalty work becomes triage, a kind of hand-to-hand combat against the bureaucracy of law's violence, in which the good lawyer tries to save one life at a time. This "retail" approach, in which saving the client's life becomes the measure of success, is, in turn, complemented by another client-focused indicator of success. In this understanding, death penalty lawyers "succeed" when they invest those whose lives they cannot save with dignity.[103]

Such a dignitarian emphasis requires a recognition of the humanity of the death row inmate, even as it allows condemnation of his crime.[104] This response, death penalty lawyers believe, provides a model that law itself should embrace. One veteran lawyer explained his work to me in just these terms. "A lot of our clients," he said,

> have never had anybody in their whole lives who gave a shit about them. The first person they encounter in their lives who treats them with dignity and respect, who visits them regularly, who gives them Christmas presents, and who sacrifices for them is their lawyer. This turns people around. What we do is what the whole legal process should do with them.

Another lawyer made a similar point when she told me what happened when she met her first death row client:

> From that moment on I still remember it like it was yesterday. I remember sitting as close to him as I am to you and I thought I was going to faint. I remember the room closing in because I was so overwhelmed by the fact that this healthy,

living, breathing person sitting across from me, they were going to kill him. The state was putting so much effort into it. I started to hyperventilate. I liked him so much. He was gregarious, and he wanted me to like him. And I let him know that even though they were going to try to kill him, I liked him. You do feel like being a friend to someone who never had anyone care about him. His life matters both to him and to you. That feels really wonderful. We may not be able to end execution or to stop him from being executed. But what keeps us going is the connection we get from our clients just because we treat them like human beings.

Unlike cause lawyers who are sometimes criticized for being lawyers without clients,[105] this lawyer, and many others who litigate and work against the death penalty, has intense and important relations with her clients. For her, legal service and the political work to which she is committed require her to go beyond the conventionally defined boundaries of lawyer professionalism. She expresses her moral/political commitment in a deeply personal way. Success for her is found in the one-on-one dynamic of a particular lawyer-client relationship.

Pushing the Ethical Limits

A deep connection to their clients, combined with the perception that the legal systems is "corrupted by the death penalty," and that ethical values are threatened by law's embrace of the death penalty, fuels another response among some of the more politically radical anti–death penalty lawyers. This response takes the form of a principled refusal to honor the conventional constraints and limits imposed on the practice of law by the organized profession and the courts.[106] Recall that the Supreme Court in the *Harris* case castigated Harris and his lawyers for their conduct in the litigation.[107] What the Court characterized as "manipulation" and "abuse" of the legal process was, for some of the lawyers with whom I spoke, a form of "civil disobedience."

As one lawyer explained,

Where the death penalty is concerned the normal lines governing professional conduct do not exist. Because the death penalty is illegitimate, those lines are illegitimate. In South Africa they had their pass laws; here we have the death penalty. Just like you couldn't expect South Africans to fight apartheid on the terms laid down by the white South Africans, you can't expect those of us fighting the death penalty to follow the rules established by courts whose sole purpose is to facilitate execution.

For this lawyer the death penalty represents a form of "oppression" perpetrated under the cover of liberal legalism. As a result, it is a form of oppression that is hard to see and harder still to acknowledge. By comparing it to the situation in South Africa she seeks to make it visible and, in so doing, to prompt an acknowledgment of it. She also increases the stakes in her work and transforms the argument about how to fight an uphill struggle into an argument about the wisdom of playing by rules made by the enemy.

Another lawyer, who does his anti–death penalty work in private practice, explained his unwillingness to play by the rules in similar terms;

> Well, in all candor I think that what anti–death penalty people fear about those of us who do this work is that we'll do anything to stop an execution. We'll raise successive petitions and keep doing it. And, while I can't speak for anybody but me, for me that is absolutely true. I'll file last-minute petitions and keep doing it because I think the death penalty is wrong. The whole process is so skewed and so unfair that it is not going to deter me from doing whatever I need to do to stop the killing.

For this lawyer the call of Justice, the call to stop law's violence, is so strong that, with no trace of irony, he deploys the rhetoric of doing "anything."[108] Yet the "anything" he mentions, for example, filing repetitive, last-minute petitions, hardly seems to match the intensity of his claim.

Still another lawyer echoed a similar theme, albeit with a different rhetorical emphasis. She admitted, in reference to the norms of the profession and the procedural rules of the courts, "We break all those kinds of rules without thinking twice." By using the pronoun "we" she identifies her own acts of defiance with the struggles of a political movement. By saying that we do so "without thinking twice" she suggests that there is no profound moral issue at stake. In her view, while it was important for participants in the anti–death penalty movement to make sure that the end-justifies-the-means morality "doesn't get too far out of line," it is essential that lawyers opposed to the death penalty be willing to "break all the rules as to how lawyers should behave, at least as those rules are understood by conservative courts and white-gloved lawyers."

Some in the death penalty bar express their impatience with conventionally defined ethical limitations in terms of a struggle against the "bureaucracy of death." One lawyer said that he could provide a valuable service in the continuing movement against the death penalty because

> the ways you really keep people alive don't have anything to do with habeas. They have to do with the ability of institutions to process information and with addressing that capacity and finding the one link in the chain that has to be lined up and making sure that it can't be lined up. So a lot of things that are done don't have anything to do with the rules. In this environment I say "Anything goes." But I've never been sanctioned by a court. But goddammit, if they are going to play the way they play, I certainly am going to have no compunction about using their own faults against them. And one of their faults is that they are lazy bureaucrats. So the process doesn't move very fast, and, with a little help, things can get confused.

Another lawyer took up this same theme when he told me that his practice was like "throwing sand in the machine." For him, as for the others who respond to the hostile political and legal environment by stretching ethical limits, the contemporary political battle seems to have been lost, and the courts seem intent only on moving people forward toward execution. As a result, all that is left is strategic resistance. "While maybe we can't get the death penalty outlawed, he explained, "our job is to stop it in enough cases that we will have, in effect, stopped the death penalty. That's why I throw sand in the machine."

This posture of throwing "sand in the machine" by pushing the ethical limits is, however, deeply controversial in the death penalty bar. Many of the lawyers with whom I spoke regard such behavior as strategically unwise as well as politically dangerous. They speak of the necessity of "scrupulously playing by the rules" as a way of maintaining moral capital and moral leverage. As one young lawyer in a resource center in a southern state put it,

> It is very important for us never to get down to [the prosecution's] level. They break the rules all the time. Because they are under intense political presuure, they falsify evidence, or hide evidence from the defense, or conspire to keep relevant evidence from the jury. That's standard operating procedure. And if we hope to have any chance of saving our clients or stopping capital punishment it is by opposing the way it corrupts the legal process. We can't do that very well if we are doing the same things that our opponents are doing.

Or as a veteran death penalty lawyer said,

> I'm a lawyer, and law is all I've got to fight with. I want the courts to see what the death penalty is doing to law. We are the real protectors of the values that everyone says they care about. You know, you don't have to be any kind of radical to believe in not punishing the innocent, or in treating people equally regardless of their race. That's what this fight is about. That's what I'm doing with my work. And if I am going to have any credibility in making those claims I had better be purer than Caesar's wife. Anything else is just stupidity.

Remembering the Future and Making the Future Remember

But there is more to being a lawyer in a losing cause than forging close bonds with those whom one represents and "throwing sand in the machine." As I have already argued, such lawyers act as witnesses to present injustices and as historians recording the injustices they witness. While they provide eyewitness testimony about the redeeming human qualities of those they represent and the abuses that their clients suffer in the legal process, they also write history by creating narrative accounts linking their client's case to political and social conditions that give rise to the injustices of the present.[109] While the history that is written by these lawyers is mediated through the abstract, impersonal categories of law, the history itself is neither abstract nor impersonal. It is typically a story told as the biography of the person sentenced to die, a story made relevant by the law allowing the broadest range of evidence in mitigation.[110] It is also a story, told in vivid detail, of incompetent defense counsel, corrupt prosecutors, and/or inattentive judges.[111] By using their lawyering skills to narrate injustice, they help to keep alive the call of "alternity," of a Justice knowable as an unkept promise.

This component of the work of death penalty lawyers is referred to, within that community, as "making a record." By "making a record" death penalty lawyers do not just describe the legal work of building a case on appeal. In addition they refer to the broader work of witnessing and writing history. By making a record these lawyers surmount, if they cannot stop, the violence of law's present, and they keep alive the possibility of a more just future. They remember the future and insist that the future, if it is to be more just, must remember.

"Look, as a lawyer every single act or omission that I am doing is calculated to make a record," one experienced lawyer explained,

> but not just the record on appeal. It is bigger than that. I think you are making a record above and beyond the immediate case. You are making a record that even after you ultimately fail to save your client's life that he was a worthy human being, that there was an explanation for what he did which the legal system could not, or would not, hear. I know that because I know him in ways no one else does. And that there are other young men and women out there who can be helped if we learn from this case. You see what we do is we tell a story that would otherwise not be told, or remembered. There are lessons in the stories we tell, lessons about poverty, abuse, and injustice. Maybe they can't be heard just yet, but maybe they will be heard sometime.

This lawyer speaks first as a witness, whose work testifies to the humanity of those condemned to die. Here he speaks as someone who has first-hand knowledge. "I know that," he says, "because I know him in ways no one else does." But this lawyer also insists that his work is "bigger than that." "Making a record" involves recording the history of the present in which an instance of injustice to which he can testify is generalized and put into a narrative that ties his case to a larger picture of "poverty, abuse, and injustice." The process of generalization involves telling a story about "other young men and women out there." Such a story addresses the future, which may (and should) remember, but whose recollection can only be spoken about as the possibility of an indeterminant "sometime."

Without assurance that that sometime will ever arrive, a few death penalty lawyers seem more frustrated than hopeful. "Sometimes we talk like we are making a record for posterity," one longtime practitioner told me, "I hate that. I hate the idea that we are making a record for history. You know people say that all the time. But," she asked, "who the hell is going to read it? Who are we making a record for, God?"

Yet, in spite of such frustration, the belief in the importance of making a record remains pervasive. This belief is grounded in remembering the future and hearing its call to Justice. It is also the task of making the future remember that shapes the work of making a record. As one new resource center lawyer said,

> I think of what I do as sort of making a narrative. I'm telling a story with page after page of facts which are put together to show the richness and complexity of my client's life, of the crime, and of the injustices of his trial. I am trying to put it together in a way that people can understand, that pulls heartstrings by getting at what is really going on. This is the best way to win in court, and it is the best way to make sure that the story is not just pushed aside and forgotten. And if enough of these narratives get produced then maybe they won't be ignored when, say fifty years from now, people try to figure out why we were executing the people we were executing in the way we were doing it.

In his words, the work of trying to win in court and build a record that will compel the future to remember go hand in hand.[112] His imagination of the cumulation of such narrative accounts links lawyering for an individual client with the broader, political goal of ending capital punishment in an imagined future.

Other death penalty lawyers talk about their work in similar terms. "The story you are trying to construct," one lawyer told me,

> has a number of parts. As a narrative it could be told from any of several perspectives. There is the life story of the client. Where did he come from, who was he as a child, and that includes what are the influences on him. Then there is the story of the crime. And retelling the story of the crime is really important because once an inept defense lawyer and a malicious prosecutor are done, the story of the crime is always of a cold, calculating, deliberate person, delighting in people's suffering. While the truth is that the crime is a culmination of neglect and abuse which the client himself has suffered. And this is a story of social injustice. The third part of the story is what happened at trial. Did his lawyer even bother to interview any witnesses? Was the family contacted to find out about his background? Was the judge a racist who referred to all the black jurors as "coloreds"? And this is a story of legal injustice.

Such multiple-stranded narratives take on special significance because "they become part of the public record." Becoming part of the public record means that they have "staying power," they "won't go away." Making such a record, this lawyer explained,

> is our way of acting in the world, our way of struggling against the system. We create these papers that we write. They are not going anywhere. They will be in government document warehouses forever. And I think that someday somebody will look at this, maybe a hundred years from now, but someone will look and say "Oh my God, it was true that the death penalty was really just an engine of discrimination." Even if it seems fruitless now, it is worth doing because we are making a record of who is getting the death penalty, and it was just the people who were mentally ill and too poor for treatment who came from unhappy, bro-

ken families. And we did nothing to help these people, until they did something horrible so we could then get rid of them. We all, this is not just my perception, but I've talked with enough other people, to describe this work as a witnessing sort of function.

What seems "fruitless" now takes on meaning when viewed in the long term. A society now unwilling to see the linkages among poverty, neglect, and the death penalty, may, "a hundred years from now" be more receptive. Lawyering in a losing cause thus seems like trying to put a crucial piece of evidence in a time capsule. And, while the language of "witnessing" is explicit in this account, it is, nevertheless, as much an account of the recording of history as of giving of testimony. This lawyer just doesn't say what happened, he constructs an explanation that will focus the attention of the future on mental illness and poverty, on social neglect and the unforgivable desire to "get rid of" people with problems rather than trying to fix those problems. He, and others like him, does history by "claiming that they can give at least partial explanations of past events . . . that *in some sense* we may understand a particular event by locating it in narrative." [113]

Conclusion: A Democratic Optimism

As witnesses giving testimony and historians creating a narrative of the present, death penalty lawyers stand between the present reality of law's violence and the beckoning call of Justice. They give content to Justice even as they acknowledge that Justice is a beckoning call to an unattainable future. In so doing they thematize the knowability of the Good and impossibility of the Just. As witnesses and historians they remember the future and insist that the future remember. In so doing, they establish a political claim for their work even in an era when the odds of ending capital punishment are so heavily stacked against them.

Their political claim and their address to the future is based on what I would call a "democratic optimism," a belief that present support for the death penalty is rooted in ignorance rather than venality, misunderstanding rather than clear-headed commitment. [114] Here they embrace "false consciousness" as the explanation for present support for capital punishment, and they take instruction from the late Justice Thurgood Marshall, who, when confronted with evidence of widespread public endorsement of capital punishment, argued that "whether a punishment is cruel and unusual depends, not on whether its mere mention 'shocks the conscience and sense of justice of the people,' but on whether people who were fully informed as to the purposes of the penalty and its liabilities would find the penalty shocking, unjust, and unacceptable." [115] If they were given such information, Marshall believed, "the great mass of citizens would conclude . . . that the death penalty is immoral and therefore unconstitutional." [116]

Some death penalty lawyers argue, following Marshall, that the task of witnessing and writing the history of the present will indeed have such a predictable result. As one woman earnestly explained, "I do not think that the death penalty will exist X years from now. While I don't know what X is, I think at some point people are going to look back and think 'Holey, moley, look at what was going on back then.'" "Look at Blackmun," another lawyer said. "He is not so very different from the rest of the country. His evolution is very representative of what eventually this country will come to if we continue to do our work. We have to look a little longer down the road, beyond the present moment."

A third lawyer was even more explicit in his democratic optimism, his belief that witnessing and doing history will, in answering the beckoning call of Justice, pay off.

> I believe that the people of this state, and others, are good people. Their support for the death penalty is sustained through a set of interconnected beliefs none of which is true. They believe that the legal system is not racist. And if you could get them to see that the system picks out black people and sends them to the chair, they would say, 'That's not fair.' They believe that in some objective sense the worst offenders get the death penalty, that death row is full of Charles Mansons who killed more than one person and who are really super morally culpable. I think if they were told, like we are telling everyday, that there are a lot of young kids on the row who were stoned out of their minds or it isn't even clear if they pulled the trigger, it would matter. And they believe that everybody gets adequate representation. But if they knew how abysmally poor a lot of the legal representation is, they would be appalled. This is what we see and what we are trying to document. We are creating a database that is necessary for any political movement to build on. We are putting together the records through which people will one day learn the truth about capital punishment.

Such sentiments connect law to the future and establish a different understanding of the work of cause lawyers in general, and lawyers for losing causes in particular. They give law a life in and through time and describe the multiple audiences to which law speaks. They help explain the political dimensions of lawyering that appears, at first glance, to be entirely focused on the particularities of a single case, and they suggest that one of the tasks of lawyering in a losing cause is to resist the present reality of law's violence in the name of the redeeming possibility of Justice.

Notes

This paper was prepared for the conference on cause lawyering, Amherst College, August 1994. I am grateful for the helpful comments made by participants in that conference and by Roger Berkowitz, Martha Umphrey, and David Wilkins. A much-abbreviated version of the paper appeared under the title "Bearing Witness and Writing History in the Struggle against Capital Punishment" in *Yale Journal of Law and the Humanities* 8 (1996).

1. Drucilla Cornell, "From the Lighthouse: The Promise of Redemption and the Possibility of Legal Interpretation," *Cardozo Law Review* 11 (1990), 1697.

2. Drucilla Cornell, "Post-Structuralism, the Ethical Relation, and the Law," *Cardozo Law Review* 9 (1988), 1587.

3. Judith Butler, "Deconstruction and the Possibility of Justice: Comments on Bernasconi, Cornell, Miller, Weber," *Cardozo Law Review* 11 (1990), 1716. Butler argues that "this horizon of temporality is always to be projected and never fully achieved; this constitutes the double gesture as a persistent promise and withdrawal. . . . Cornell argues that it is necessary to repeat this gesture endlessly and thereby to constitute the posture of vigilance that establishes the openness of a future in which the thought of radical alternity is never completed."

4. See Alison Young and Austin Sarat, "Introduction to 'Beyond Criticism: Law, Power and Ethics,' " *Social and Legal Studies: An International Journal* 3(1994), 328. "[L]aw is simultaneously a denial of the ethical in the name of the political and a denial of the political in the name of the ethical."

5. See Sally Merry, *Getting Justice and Getting Even: Legal Consciousness among Working Class Americans* (Chicago: University of Chicago Press, 1990). Also Austin Sarat, " ' . . . The Law Is All Over': Power, Resistance and the Legal Consciousness of the Welfare Poor," *Yale Journal of Law and the Humanities* 2 (1990), 343.

6. For a collection of Cover's work, see Martha Minow, Michael Ryan, and Austin Sarat, eds., *Narrative Violence and the Law: The Essays of Robert Cover* (Ann Arbor: University of Michigan Press, 1993).

7. Robert Cover, "The Supreme Court, 1982 Term—Foreword: Nomos and Narrative," *Harvard Law Review* 97 (1983), 4.

8. Ibid., 9.

9. Ibid., 4.

10. Robert Cover, "Violence and the Word," *Yale Law Journal* 95 (1986), 1601.

11. As Lobel notes, "Law . . . arises from the clash between the state seeking to enforce its rules and . . . activist communities seeking to create, extend, or preserve an alternative vision of justice." Jules Lobel, "Losers, Fools and Prophets: Justice as Struggle," *Cornell Law Review* 80 (1995), 1333. And Anthony Alfieri suggests that for cause lawyers "[p]rofessing moral theory in practice is . . . [a] professional responsibility." Alfieri, "Mitigation, Mercy, and Delay: The Moral Politics of Death Penalty Abolitionists," *Harvard Civil Rights–Civil Liberties Law Review* 31 (1996), 352.

12. David Luban, *Lawyers and Justice: An Ethical Study* (Princeton: Princeton University Press, 1988), 160.

13. A more complete account of this position is provided by William Simon, "The Ideology of Advocacy: Procedural Justice and Professional Ethics," *Wisconsin Law Review* 1978 (1978), 29.

14. For a defense of this idea see Anthony Kronman, *The Lost Lawyer: Failing Ideals of the Legal Profession* (Cambridge, Mass.: Harvard University Press, 1993), chap. 1.

15. William Simon describes this kind of lawyering in "Visions of Practice in Legal Thought," *Stanford Law Review* 36 (1984), 469. Also Gary Bellow, "Steady Work: A Practitioner's Reflections on Political Lawyering," *Harvard Civil Rights-Civil Liberties Law Review* 31 (1996), 297.

16. Luban, *Lawyers and Justice*, 161.

17. See Marianne Constable, "Genealogy and Jurisprudence," *Law and Social Inquiry* 19 (1994), 551–590.

18. It is impossible to give a precise estimate of the number of people who comprise the "death penalty bar" in the United States. However, practitioners estimate that number to be about two hundred lawyers. Approximately that number regularly attend the annual

Airlie Capital Punishment Conference sponsored by the NAACP Legal Defense Fund. Those who do appellate and postconviction work practice in a variety of settings; some work for public interest organizations like the Southern Center for Human Rights, the Minnesota Advocates for Human Rights, the American Civil Liberties Union, or the NAACP Legal Defense Fund. Some are in private practice, and some are in agencies (e.g., so-called resource centers) funded by state or federal government for the purpose of providing representation to persons sentenced to death.

19. Alfieri, "Mitigation, Mercy, and Delay."

20. In outlining an agenda for future research in the area of capital punishment, Franklin Zimring recently described the significance of what he called "the capital punishment bar." Zimring suggested that "the litigation of death penalty issues has produced in some states a group of appeals lawyers who are a full-time capital punishment bar." He called on scholars to investigate how "attorneys in this sort of practice define their roles and . . . their attitudes toward the legitimacy of the criminal justice system. This study is the most immediately interesting, but not the only, research undertaking that would investigate the role of capital punishment as an influence on the legal profession." Zimring, "On the Liberating Virtues of Irrelevance," *Law and Society Review* 27 (1993), 15. But see Michael Meltsner, *Cruel and Unusual: The Supreme Court and Capital Punishment* (New York: Random House, 1973); "Note: The Legal Defense Fund's Capital Punishment Campaign: The Distorting Influence of Death," *Yale Law and Policy Review* 4 (1985), 158; Alfieri, "Mitigation, Mercy, and Delay"; Austin Sarat, "Narrative Strategy and Death Penalty Advocacy," *Harvard Civil Rights–Civil Liberties Law Review* 31 (1996), 353.

21. Meltsner, *Cruel and Unusual.*

22. See Welch White, *The Death Penalty in the Nineties* (Ann Arbor: University of Michigan Press, 1992).

23. Meltsner, *Cruel and Unusual.*

24. 408 U.S. 238 (1972).

25. Philip Kurland, "1971 Term: The Year of the Stewart-White Court," *Supreme Court Review* 1972 (1972), 296–297.

26. Quoted in Meltsner, *Cruel and Unusual,* 291.

27. Franklin Zimring and Gordon Hawkins, *Capital Punishment and the American Agenda* (Cambridge: Cambridge University Press, 1986), chaps. 1 and 2.

28. Ibid., 41.

29. Ibid., 42.

30. *Gregg v. Georgia,* 428 U.S. 153, 179 (1976).

31. Id., 169.

32. For a discussion of the implications of this hostile climate for the work of death penalty lawyers see Robert Weisberg, "Who Defends Capital Defendants?" *Santa Clara Law Review* 35 (1995), 535.

33. See Robert Weisberg, "Deregulating Death," *Supreme Court Review* 1983 (1983), 305. Also Anthony Amsterdam, "*In Favorem Mortis:* The Supreme Court and Capital Punishment," *Human Rights* 14 (1987), 14. Here perhaps the most important rebuff to the "wholesale" approach occurred in *McCleskey v. Kemp* in which the Court refused to invalidate the death penalty even in the face of statistical evidence of systemic racial disparities in the administration of capital punishment. See 481 U.S. 279 (1987). As William Bowers argues, "The Court's ruling in *McCleskey* meant that the kind of evidence that would suffice to save McCleskey's job could not save his life." See Bowers, "Capital Punishment and Contemporary Values: People's Misgivings and the Court's Misperceptions," *Law and Society Review* 27 (1993), 138.

34. For a discussion of the nature of public opinion about the death penalty see Austin Sarat and Neil Vidmar, "Public Opinion, the Death Penalty, and the Eighth Amendment: Testing the Marshall Hypothesis," *Wisconsin Law Review* 1976 (1976), 171, and Bowers, "Capital Punishment and Contemporary Values," 157.

35. Wendy Lesser argues that there is a "crucial connection between murder and theater—between death imposed on a human being by another human being, and dramatic spectacle." *Pictures at an Execution: An Inquiry into the Subject of Murder* (Cambridge, Mass.: Harvard University Press, 1993), 7.

36. Susan Blaustein, "Witness to Another Execution: In Texas Death Walks an Assembly Line," *Harper's* (May 1994), 53.

37. Marshall Frady, "Death in Arkansas," *New Yorker* (February 22, 1993), 105–118.

38. Michael Oreskes, "The Political Stampede on Execution," *New York Times,* April 4, 1990, A16.

39. Jack Greenberg, "The Capital Punishment System," *Yale Law Journal* 91 (1982), 908, and Franklin Zimring, "Inheriting the Wind: The Supreme Court and Capital Punishment in the 1990s," *Florida State University Law Review* 20 (1992), 7.

40. As Evan Caminker and Erwin Chemrinsky put it, "The tragedy . . . is that judges, sworn to uphold the law, disregard it to satisfy the State's desire to execute . . . according to schedule. Justice requires more than ensuring that the trains run on time." Caminker and Chemrinsky, "The Lawless Execution of Robert Alton Harris," *Yale Law Journal* 102 (1992), 253–254. See also Nancy Levit, "Expediting Death: Repressive Tolerance and Post-Conviction Due Process Jurisprudence in Capital Cases," *University of Missouri, Kansas City Law Review* 59 (1990), 55; also Nancy Levit, " 'The Door That Never Opens'? Capital Punishment and Postconviction Review of Death Sentences in the United States and Japan," *Brooklyn Journal of International Law* 19 (1993), 367.

41. The Court has long viewed itself as having the authority to alter the scope of federal habeas, even without new legislation; see *Wainwright v. Sykes,* 433 U.S. 72, 81 (1977) (referring to Court's "historic willingness to overturn or modify its earlier views of the scope of the writ, even where the statutory language authorizing judicial action has remained unchanged").

42. *Wainwright v. Sykes,* 433 U.S. 72 (1977).

43. *Rose v. Lundy,* 455 U.S. 509 (1982).

44. *McCleskey v. Zant,* 111 S. Ct. 1454 (1991).

45. See *Teague v. Lane,* 489 U.S. 288 (1989). The portion of Justice O'Connor's lead opinion in *Teague* referenced in the text garnered only three other votes, and thus is technically only a plurality opinion. However, in the subsequent case of *Penry v. Lynaugh,* 492 U.S. 302 (1989), Justice O'Connor picked up the additional vote of Justice White, who had refused to join the relevant portion of her opinion in *Teague.* Thus, the relevant portion of Justice O'Connor's opinion in *Teague* now represents the views of a majority of the Court.

46. *Butler v. McKellar,* 110 S. Ct. 1212 (1990).

47. See *Stringer v. Black,* 503 U.S. 222, (1992).

48. James Liebman, "More Than 'Slightly Retro': The Rehnquist Court's Rout of Habeas Corpus Jurisdiction in *Teague v. Lane,*" *New York University Review of Law and Social Change* 18 (1990–91), 537; Steven Goldstein, "Chipping Away at the Great Writ: Will Death Sentenced Federal Habeas Corpus Petitioners Be Able to Seek and Utilize Changes in the Law?" *New York University Review of Law and Social Change* 18 (1990–91), 357. The Supreme Court and Congress have recently considered whether to wipe out the last vestiges of vigorous, searching, nondeferential federal habeas review. In Congress, the effort succeeded to restrict habeas courts to reviewing only whether the state courts provided a "full and fair

opportunity" for adjudication of a federal constitutional claim. See generally Steven Goldstein, "Expediting the Federal Habeas Corpus Review Process in Capital Cases: An Examination of Recent Proposals," *Capital University Law Review* 19 (1990), 599 (discussing various legislative proposals to restrict federal habeas).

49. *Vasquez v. Harris,* 112 S. Ct. 1713 (1992). See also Stephen Reinhardt, "The Supreme Court, the Death Penalty, and the *Harris* Case," *Yale Law Journal* 102 (1992), 205.

50. *Herrera v. Collins,* 112 S. Ct. 2936 (1993). In response to *Herrera,* Justice Blackmun charged the Court with coming "perilously close to murder."

51. Caminker and Chemrinsky, "The Lawless Execution," 226. "[T]he Court's desire to expedite the process of death . . . has now accrued a life of its own." See p. 253. See Joseph Hoffmann, "Is Innocence Sufficient? An Essay on the United States Supreme Court's Continuing Problems with Federal Habeas Corpus and the Death Penalty," *Indiana Law Review* 68 (1993), 817.

52. Bowers, "Capital Punishment and Contemporary Values," 172.

53. As of July 1996 there were more than 3,000 people on death rows across the country, and more than 360 had been executed since *Gregg* reinstated capital punishment. For a different perspective on the rate of increase in executions see Samuel Gross, "The Romance of Revenge: Capital Punishment in America," *Studies in Law, Politics and Society* 13 (1993), 71.

54. This hostile climate does not just impacted death penalty lawyers and their work but affects generally the work of all progressive lawyers. See Martha Minow, "Political Lawyering: An Introduction," *Harvard Civil Rights-Civil Liberties Law Review* 31 (1996), 290.

55. This image is developed by Michael Mello, "Facing Death Alone: The Post-Conviction Attorney Crisis on Death Row," *American University Law Review* 37 (1988), 513. As Mello argues, "The post-conviction process has become an integral part of the system of capital punishment. The post-conviction component of the system is necessary because it exposes injustices. . . . It is necessary to the integrity of a legal system that strives to tame the death penalty within the rule of law. In turn, lawyers are essential to the integrity of the post-conviction process" (p. 606).

56. "Note: The Legal Defense Fund's." There is, of course, another side to this story. Death penalty lawyers still hold a place of relative honor in the bar. They are powerful reminders of the ideal of lawyer as champion of the downtrodden. I am grateful to David Wilkins for this argument.

57. Harris was the first person executed in California in the post-*Furman* era.

58. See *Gomez v. United States,* 112 S. Ct. 1652, 1653 (1992). For an important response see Charles Sevilla and Michael Laurence, "Thoughts on the Cause of the Present Discontents: The Death Penalty Case of Robert Alton Harris," *UCLA Law Review* 40 (1992), 345.

59. Louis Bilionis, "Litigating Death," *Michigan Law Review* 91 (1993), 1643. Also Levit, "Expediting Death" and Weisberg, "Who Defends," 539.

60. Weisberg, "Deregulating Death."

61. See Richard Abel, "Speaking Law to Power: Occasions for Cause Lawyering," chap. 3 of this volume. Also Ronen Shamir, "Litigation as Consummatory Action: The Instrumental Paradigm Reconsidered," *Studies in Law, Politics and Society* 11 (1991), 41. As Shamir argues, even in conditions of oppression, petitioners turn to courts because they "are able, for the first time, to express their grievances and to materialize their appeal for grace and abstract justice" (p. 61). Other comparisons are provided by Lobel, "Losers, Fools."

62. E. P. Thompson, *Whigs and Hunters: The Origins of the Black Act* (New York: Pantheon, 1975).

63. *Woodson v. North Carolina,* 428 U.S. 280, 305 (1976).

64. Margaret Radin, "Cruel Punishment and Respect for Persons: Super Due Process for Death," *Southern California Law Review* 53 (1980), 1143.

65. As Lobel puts it, "Even when prophetic litigation loses in court, it often functions . . . as an appeal to future generations." Lobel, "Losers, Prophets," 1347.

66. Cover, "The Supreme Court," 9.

67. Ibid., 34.

68. Ibid.

69. Ibid., 39.

70. Lobel explores the utility of the idea of prophecy to the work of lawyers who serve losing causes. See "Losers, Prophets," 1337.

71. See Jacques Le Goff, *History and Memory,* trans. Steven Randall and Elizabeth Clamon (New York: Columbia University Press, 1992).

72. Shoshana Felman and Dori Laub, *Testimony: Crises of Witnessing in Literature, Psychoanalysis, and History* (New York: Routledge, 1992), 101. Treating the lawyer for a losing cause as a witness giving testimony suggests that he addresses his work to the community of the future as much as the law of the present. "To testify—before a court of law or before the court of history and of the future," as Felman argues, "is more than simply to report a fact or an event or to relate what has been lived, recorded and remembered. Memory is conjured here essentially in order to address another, to impress upon a listener, to *appeal* to a community" (p. 204).

73. Pierre Nora, "Between Memory and History: *Les Lieux de Memoire,*" *Representations* 26 (1989), 7. As Nora argues, "Modern memory is, above all, archival. It relies entirely on the materiality of the trace, the immediacy of the recording, the visibility of the image" (p. 15).

74. As Martha Minow suggests, legal rights matter not just because they provide dignity to law's victims, or because they help to mobilize them to undertake political action, but because they provide an opportunity to tell a story that might not otherwise get to be told. "Interpreting Rights: An Essay for Robert Cover," *Yale Law Journal* 96 (1987), 1860.

75. The work of lawyers in a losing cause is to construct narratives since "history is . . . the establishment of the facts of the past through their narrativization." Felman and Laub, *Testimony,* 93. See also Hayden White, *The Content of the Form: Narrative Discourse and Historical Representation* (Baltimore, Md.: Johns Hopkins University Press, 1987).

76. See Cover, "The Supreme Court."

77. Feldman and Laub, *Testimony.*

78. Ibid.

79. Robert Gordon, "Undoing Historical Injustice," in *Justice and Injustice in Law and Legal Theory,* ed. Austin Sarat and Thomas Kearns (Ann Arbor: University of Michigan Press, 1996), 1.

80. Ibid., 2.

81. Ibid., 2–3.

82. See Michael McCann and Helena Silverstein, "Rethinking Law's 'Allurements': A Relational Analysis of Social Movement Lawyers in the United States," chap. 9 of this volume. Also Stuart Scheingold, *The Politics of Rights: Lawyers, Public Policy, and Political Change* (New Haven: Yale University Press, 1974). For an important exception see Lobel, "Losers, Prophets."

83. Cornell, "Post-Structuralism," 1628.

84. Lobel, "Losers, Prophets," 1337.

85. One of those states is in the East, three in the Midwest, four in the South or Southwest, and two are the far West.

86. Of these lawyers, twenty-five practice in government-funded agencies, ten are in private practice, five in public interest organizations, and one is an academic. In the remainder of this essay I use extensive quotations from these interviews. Given the small size of, and the public hostility toward, the death penalty bar, I mask the identities of my respondents by giving little detail about them and about those whose voices are included in the text.

87. See Hugo Adam Bedau, "The Eighth Amendment, Human Dignity, and the Death Penalty," in *The Constitution of Rights,* ed. Michael Meyer and William Parent (Ithaca: Cornell University Press, 1992).

88. See Derrick Bell, "Serving Two Masters: Integration Ideals and Client Interests in School Desegregation Litigation," *Yale Law Journal* 85 (1976), 470; Susan Olson, *Clients and Lawyers: Securing the Rights of Disabled Persons* (Westport, Conn.: Greenwood Press, 1984), and Deborah Rhode, "Class Conflicts in Class Actions," *Stanford Law Review* 34 (1982), 1183.

89. In fact, most of the lawyers with whom I spoke acknowledge such a tension, but do not see it as driving their work. Many develop unusually close relationships with their clients, and most believe that such relationships are both enormously rewarding personally and enormously important as an asset in their lawyering work.

90. The idea of government as "parent" is reminiscent of Justice Brandeis's belief that "[t]he Government is the potent, omnipresent teacher." *Olmstead v. U.S.,* 277 U.S. 438 (1928).

91. As Kateb argues, "[T]he institution of capital punishment strengthens the sentiment that the state owns the lives of the people. Many things can be said against capital punishment, but one of the most relevant . . . is that the state's power deliberately to destroy innocuous (though guilty) life is a manifestation of the hidden wish that the state be allowed to do anything it pleases with life." Kateb, *The Inner Ocean: Individualism and Democratic Culture* (Ithaca: Cornell University Press, 1992), 190–191.

92. *Callins v. Collins,* 114 S. Ct. 1127 (1994).

93. *Id.,* 1131 and 1129.

94. Gordon, "Undoing Historical Injustice."

95. See McCann and Silverstein, "Rethinking Law's Allurements."

96. Gordon, "Undoing Historical Injustice."

97. For an interesting study of one part of this bureaucracy see Robert Johnson, *Death Work: A Study of the Modern Execution Process* (Pacific Grove, Calif.: Brooks/Cole Publishing, 1990).

98. On the ways death penalty lawyers seek to keep clients alive through the strategic use of delay see Alfieri, "Mitigation, Mercy, and Delay," 334.

99. This sense of disconnection between the political and legal arms of the movement to end the death penalty was widespread among the lawyers with whom I spoke. As one put it, "I don't have the faintest idea what one could do from the point of view of a lay person trying to do political action on the death penalty at this point. If there is an abolitionist movement left in this country, it is largely composed of people like me doing legal work." Or, as another put it, "I think of the lawyers who do death penalty stuff as the foot soldiers of the movement. We are the activist arm because a group of people holding candles outside the governor's mansion are not going to end capital punishment." Still another expressed this same sentiment by saying, "It's hard for me to go to these meetings of do-gooders who are all beating their chests and upset about the death penalty. It is just a huge waste of time. It's nothing. I'd rather blow up the courthouse than sit around and whine about how bad things have gotten."

100. Meltsner, *Cruel and Unusual.*

101. Alfieri, "Mitigation, Mercy, and Delay," 334.

102. Letter to author from David Wilkins, September 29, 1994.

103. See Phyllis Goldfarb, "A Clinic Runs through It," *Clinical Law Review* 1 (1994), 65, 71. Goldfarb describes her own work in representing someone on death row as providing the opportunity for "empathetic connections even in situations where they seem most unlikely."

104. See Charles Ogletree, "Beyond Justification: Seeking Motivations to Sustain Public Defenders," *Harvard Law Review* 106 (1993), 1239.

105. For a discussion of this problem see Rhode, "Class Conflicts."

106. The way those constraints apply in this context is discussed in Luke DeGrand, "Representing the Condemned: Professional Responsibility and Death Row," *Illinois Bar Journal* 78 (1990), 30. Most of the lawyers with whom I spoke either refused to discuss this topic or talked about "bending" but never breaking the rules. This perspective is reflected in the article by Michael Mello, "Another Attorney for Life," in *Facing the Death Penalty: Essays on Cruel and Unusual Punishment,* ed. Michael Radelet (Philadelphia: Temple University Press, 1989), 87.

107. *Vasquez v. Harris,* 112 S. Ct. 1713 (1992).

108. For a critique of this position see Alfieri, "Mitigation, Mercy, and Delay."

109. See Felman and Laub, *Testimony.*

110. Many death penalty lawyers describe the crucial part of their work as coming after direct appeals have been exhausted in the process of relitigating the case in habeas review. They note that in making habeas claims under ineffective assistance claims they must reinvestigate the entire case to find what the trial counsel did not find and to show its material connection to the result at trial. For them, the process of making a convincing argument for habeas relief is not unlike trying a case, with its attention to the vivid details of lives lived and choices made.

111. Weisberg, "Who Defends," 539.

112. This point is developed outside the context of death penalty litigation by Lobel, "Losers, Prophets."

113. See Louis Mink, "The Autonomy of Historical Understanding," *History and Theory* 5 (1966), 24.

114. See Lobel, "Losers, Prophets," 1419.

115. See *Furman v. Georgia,* 408 U.S. 238, 361 (1972).

116. Id., 363.

PART IV

The Possibilities of Cause Lawyering beyond Liberal Legalism

CHAPTER 12

Cause Lawyering in the Third World

STEPHEN ELLMANN

This essay is a sketch of cause lawyering in the Third World. The picture I present is not meant to be definitive, and indeed it is hard to imagine how a definitive portrait could be drawn, for there may now be thousands of cause lawyers at work in the nations of the South. Instead, this essay grows out of interviews conducted in May, 1991 with representatives of twenty-two public interest law groups from eighteen countries in Africa, Asia, and Latin America.[1] The sample is not random, for all of these groups had been brought together at a conference on "Public Interest Law around the World," organized under the auspices of the NAACP Legal Defense Fund and with the funding assistance of the Ford Foundation.[2] Thus these are groups with contacts in the West, and with at least enough confidence in the legitimacy of an enterprise funded by the Ford Foundation to be prepared to participate in it.[3] As we will see, these may be important limitations on the representativeness of this sample.

If this sample is not random, however, I believe it is nevertheless illuminating, offering us as it does a set of organizations employing a considerable range of strategies toward a similarly diverse range of objectives. I will seek to make the study of this sample more illuminating, in any event, by setting the data on these particular groups in a larger context of developments around the world in the arena of human rights. To be sure, even my appraisal of these particular groups cannot rest on detailed study of the legal scene in most of the eighteen countries from which these groups came.[4] Such close-up study is needed and important, and several essays in this volume undertake it. But it is important as well to try to take the measure of cause lawyering on a broader scale.

In this essay I will use the terms "public interest law" and "cause lawyering" interchangeably. Both refer, following Sarat and Scheingold's formulation, to lawyers' work that is "directed at altering some aspect of the social, economic and political status quo."[5] This formulation, as Sarat and Scheingold emphasize, is by no means a rigid definition. I understand it to embrace the work of lawyers who affiliate with social movements, as well as the work of lawyers who struggle on in the service of a program of social change even when no movement exists. I also understand it to encompass both the work of poverty lawyers who simply handle the innumerable individual legal problems of poor clients in an effort to give their clients access to justice—who engage, that is, in the "traditional" legal aid to which I refer at times in this essay—and the more politically shaped work of lawyers who self-consciously aim to ally with political or community groups in a struggle for broad social change—among them, the practitioners of "alternative law" to whom I will also refer repeatedly in this essay. This formulation is also broad enough to encompass "lawyers' work" that consists of scholarly legal research, factual documentation and reporting of abuses, law teaching, paralegal training or community legal education, litigation of individual clients' claims, test case or class action litigation, lobbying, and other activities as well. I embrace this broad understanding of "lawyers' work" deliberately, for no other definition will allow us to see clearly the wide range of work actually being undertaken by lawyers seeking justice in Third World countries.[6]

This essay seeks to answer two broad questions about cause lawyering in the Third World. First, why has this work flowered so dramatically over the past two decades? To an important extent, this question calls for an effort to understand the personal, idiosyncratic, even accidental factors that shape the choices men and women make. Public interest practice in the Third World often requires not only legal ingenuity but also physical courage, and undoubtedly those who choose to undertake this work frequently draw their commitment from deep individual roots. Thus Silu Singh, the founder of the Women's Legal Services Project in Nepal, became a lawyer at her father's urging; he had been a freedom fighter and had been sentenced to life imprisonment.[7] Similarly Fazlul Huq, one of the founders of the Madaripur Legal Aid Association in Bangladesh, was inspired by his father, a lawyer and politician who did a lot of social service work.[8] For some, religious faith may play a role.[9] (For others, self-interest may be an important factor; cause lawyers must eat, and are not usually saints.)[10] In addition, an important part of the reason for the growth of cause lawyering in any particular country certainly will be the particular twists and turns of that country's history, events that may make cause lawyering attractive and feasible where it previously was fruitless or perilous. These may include not only reforms in the official order, but also changes of sentiment among its opponents.[11]

Without meaning to diminish the significance of either personal or national histories, however, I will focus here on two broader factors: the rise of an international human rights culture, and the utility and attractiveness of *legal* tools for change. I argue that the rise of cause lawyering is part and parcel of the tremendous expansion of human rights activism around the world in the past two decades, and I explore the fabric of this international human rights culture to demonstrate that, despite the great influence of Western nations in the growth of the world's human rights movement, cause lawyering in the Third World is the product of developments that Third World actors are shaping as well as being shaped by. I also contend that although legal institutions in the Third World are often decidedly less supportive of cause lawyering than the federal courts of the United States have sometimes been, nonetheless most Third World legal systems offer sufficient leverage for the advocates of change to make use of these systems attractive. Moreover, in some of these countries, as at some times in the United States, traditions of legal independence and professional commitment can provide valuable support for the enterprise of cause lawyering.

Second, this essay seeks to answer the question of whether cause lawyers in the Third World are actually speaking for the people and enabling the people to speak for themselves. It is hardly self-evident that lawyers would succeed in this enterprise, especially if cause lawyering has developed at least as much in response to worldwide movements and professional trends as to explicit popular demand. To assess cause lawyers' representativeness, we will need to understand what cause lawyers actually do, and this is a complex matter, since the thousands of cause lawyers in the Third World do a great many things. It is also a complex question because many of these lawyers understand their own work in terms that self-consciously distinguish their use of law from the use of law by class action lawyers or legal services lawyers in countries like the United States.

This essay can only suggest how these complexities are to be resolved. But I will urge that the nature of cause lawyering in the Third World does not provide it with any inevitable insulation against the pitfalls of lawyer domination that have plagued lawyering elsewhere. Third World cause lawyering, as I will try to demonstrate, is less distinctive than its exponents sometimes suggest, for actually there are substantial commonalities between "alternative" legal services in the Third World and relatively more traditional public interest law in the United States. Moreover, as its advocates themselves often recognize, cause lawyering in the Third World is as subject to the dangers of paternalism or insensitivity as lawyering anywhere else, and in a number of respects such groups frequently are not fully "representative."

But the final judgment this essay reaches is a positive rather than a negative one. For professionals to cross the barriers of class, culture, and privilege in order to listen to and aid disadvantaged clients is never simple. Yet the groups studied here appear to be pursuing this task with great dedication. Through a variety of techniques, ranging from test case litigation to community legal education to the provision of direct social services, cause lawyers in the Third World turn out to be engaged in consulting with, learning from, acting for, and supporting the work of their clients.

The International Human Rights Culture

Cause lawyering in the Third World today is not an isolated phenomenon. There have been legal aid efforts "in the Third World since the 19th century," and although these typically "only handled individual cases, focused almost exclusively on litigation, and were largely independent of community participation," still some of their work may well have qualified as a form of cause lawyering.[12] The 1994 Human Rights Internet *Masterlist,* a listing of "organizations worldwide concerned with issues of human rights and justice,"[13] names over two hundred Third World groups whose main focus is reported to be on "law (rule of), independence of lawyers and judges, administration of justice and legal aid." These groups are distributed among over fifty nations, including twenty-two in Africa (the great majority of these being Sub-Saharan states), twelve in Asia and twenty in the Americas.[14] Similarly, the International Human Rights Internship Program, a group "focused on enhancing the effectiveness of human rights organizations in countries of the South, East Central Europe and the former Soviet Republics,"[15] observes in a paper that "[o]ver most of the South, hundreds of groups are using law and law-related strategies to achieve social justice."[16]

Even this figure understates—perhaps dramatically understates—the number of cause-lawyering projects now under way in the Third World. An Indonesian legal aid lawyer reports that a survey found in that country alone "approximately 100 organizations active in the field of legal aid, some professional and others amateur"—and this survey included "only organizations which use signs"![17] Fernando Rojas reports the results of a survey of legal aid in Chile, Colombia, Ecuador, and Peru from 1983 to 1986 that found seventy-three traditional legal aid bodies in these four countries, and another seventy-five groups engaged in "new" and more political legal services.[18] And in 1991 Rojas and a colleague noted that the institution Rojas then led, the Latin American Institute of Alternative Legal Services (Instituto Latinoamericano de Servicios Legales Alternativos, or ILSA), "now has ongoing contact with approximately 1,500 of these groups [nongovernmental innovative legal services organizations] from Mexico to Southern Argentina. . . . These groups are composed of some 6,000 lawyers, paralegal workers, social workers and others who support and promote community development and human rights."[19] While other parts of the world have evidently not developed this new or "alternative" law practice as far as Latin America has,[20] it seems quite clear that "cause lawyering" is under way in many different parts of the Third World.[21]

Where have all these groups come from? One answer is that the rise of cause lawyering is only part of an even larger phenomenon, namely the rise of the human rights nongovernmental organization or NGO. Michael Posner and Candy Whittome of the Lawyers Committee for Human Rights have traced this larger development.[22] "The first phase," they observe, "was the creation and development of internationally focused NGOs."[23] Although one of these, Anti-Slavery International, began work in the nineteenth century,[24] as late as the mid-1970s the president of one of these groups named only six NGOs "with a full time commitment to international human rights."[25] Now, however, there are "several dozen other internationally focused human rights organizations, many of them based in Western Europe and North America."[26] Then, Posner and Whittome continue: "The second phase of the development of human rights NGOs has been the proliferation of national human rights monitoring and advocacy groups in all regions of the world. Fifteen years ago, there were only a small number of such groups outside of Europe and North America. Today, independent human rights groups exist in most countries of the world."[27]

The recognition that the rise of cause lawyering is a part of the rise of human rights NGOs naturally prompts the question of why human rights NGOs have expanded so dramatically.[28] No doubt the reasons for this development are multifaceted. The availability of some tools for human rights advocacy in the international system may have encouraged the growth of internationally focused NGOs that could employ these tools.[29] Widespread public disillusionment with the realpolitik of the Vietnam War and other features of Cold War big-power politics may have contributed to Western public support for more idealistic engagement with the world, a sentiment given force by President Jimmy Carter.[30] One participant-observer also emphasizes the "fairly dramatic shift in the position of the Church, both Catholic and Protestant," giving rise to such movements as liberation theology.[31] More prosaically, such developments as the perfection of mass mailing techniques may have enabled Western, or at least American, human rights advocates to find and organize their supporters more efficiently. With the departure of many dictators and the fading of the Cold War, political space opened up for the formation of such groups in many other countries as well. Over time, as a result of developments such as these, it seems fair to say that a human rights culture has developed that holds considerable sway in much of the world, and that in turn helps foster the rise of still more human rights effort.

My purpose here, however, is not primarily to explain the genesis of this international human rights culture but rather to examine the ways that international support for human rights has contributed to the rise of Third World cause lawyering. It is appropriate to begin this specific inquiry by putting to one side, for a moment, the question of the sources of idealism and asking instead about the sources of money.

Money is tight. In the Third World, resources for legal work are even scantier than they are in countries like the United States. Many Third World governments may be even less disposed to pay for lawyers to challenge them than the United States has been; what money Third World governments do make available may be spent on the least political, most traditional forms of legal aid.[32] The upshot is that very little of the funding for more innovative cause lawyering in Third World countries appears to come from Third World governments.[33] "[M]any Third World NGOs operate out of a member's house, consist of a few people, and rarely pay sustaining salaries. Membership dues amounting to a substantial percentage of an operating budget are unheard of."[34] For example, most of the budget for the Constitutional Rights Project in Nigeria "comes from the private law practice of CRP's founder and Executive Director. . . . Unfortunately, the more time Nwankwo spends on CRP activities, the less time he has to devote to his private practice, and the less money he therefore earns which he can contribute to CRP." [35]

As a result, it appears that many Third World cause-lawyering groups that achieve more substantial size—and perhaps especially those groups that seek to grow while directly challenging powerful domestic interests—do so largely with foreign money. Thus Rojas comments that "[g]iven the lack of domestic support from powerful groups, Latin American legal services committed to social change usually adopt a strategic combination of austerity, self-discipline, and a heroic type of attitude, on the one hand, and increased dependency on foreign funds and support in general, on the other." [36] Of the Third World groups at the 1991 symposium, only the Lawyers Collective in India reported a policy of not taking foreign funding. [37] The donors include Western governments, [38] wholly or partially government-funded foundations, [39] and fully private foundations such as the Ford Foundation. [40] In the eyes of Laurie Wiseberg, "[a]lmost all [human rights organizations] are heavily dependent on a very small number of foundations, development agencies, or churches." [41] Indeed, she writes, "the role of the Ford Foundation has been so central to human rights funding that a decision of Ford to pull out of the area, or substantially reduce its contribution, would be catastrophic." [42]

There is no denying that this funding reality means that foreign, First World donors have played an important part in shaping the contours of Third World cause lawyering as it exists today. If the donors did nothing more than enable groups to grow that would otherwise have remained small, their role would be significant. But of course the grantors must also have priorities and agendas, for they could not otherwise choose among potential recipients. Thus Gridley Hall, writing of the Ford Foundation's grant making in several countries of Latin America, notes that "our human rights program has given the highest priority to efforts to protect the integrity of the person," while also recognizing the significance of other human rights. [43] Later he describes Ford's "program strategy" in Uruguay of "identify[ing] a group with a broad, long-term approach to human rights problems that would permit it to play a useful 'watchdog' role after power was transferred back to civilian authorities," [44] and then mentions Ford's "difficulty identifying a national-level human rights organization with the impartiality necessary to address effectively the critical situation in Peru." [45] It can hardly be doubted that would-be recipients of these scarce and vital funds do their best to convince the grantors that funding *their* programs will achieve the grantors' goals. And while the grantors cannot foster growth in entirely infertile soil, they will often have some choice about what to nurture, or to plant. [46]

The influence of the West, moreover, goes well beyond the provision or withholding of money, significant as that is. Western "international nongovermental organizations" (INGOs) dominate access to the world's (largely Western) media, [47] and also have formal and probably informal access to United Nations human rights entities far superior to that enjoyed by Third World "national" NGOs.[48] The very idea of human rights, however firmly it can be linked to aspects of cultural traditions around the world, seems to have achieved most of its modern expression in the West, in the centuries since the Renaissance.[49] The INGOs, moreover, have not concerned themselves equally with all the rights now embodied in international instruments. Instead, groups like Amnesty International, Human Rights Watch and to a large extent the International Commission of Jurists have focused primarily on "first-generation" civil and political rights.[50] Third World NGOs perforce must operate in a world where these rights, and not economic or social rights or even broader societal rights such as the right to development, claim the greatest attention.[51]

In the legal field in particular, Western cause-lawyering styles likely have considerable appeal as models elsewhere. Lawyers concerned to achieve social justice in one country will look to other countries for tactics that have worked; they will look all the more quickly if they see few attractive exemplars in their own country's legal world. They will also do so if they themselves have a chance to study in these other nations; some Third World cause lawyers—though by no means all— have in fact pursued legal studies abroad.[52] A country's general cultural prominence (the result of complex considerations of power and fashion) may also influence the attention given to its legal institutions in particular.

In the United States, the pursuit of racial justice by the NAACP Legal Defense Fund (LDF) was probably the most dramatically successful, though not the first, systematic campaign for social change through law. It also appears to have been one of the first, or at least one of the first widely noticed, campaigns of this sort anywhere in the world. The American Civil Liberties Union has also emphasized court action as a means of protecting rights over many decades. This model of public interest law influenced the growth of other legal action groups in the United States[53] and elsewhere in the world as well.[54] In South Africa, for example, Jack Greenberg of the LDF played a role in the shaping of the Legal Resources Centre.[55] (American foundations, notably the Carnegie Corporation, also played a part in the original founding of this organization.)[56] Julius Chambers, who later succeeded Jack Greenberg as director-counsel at the LDF, played a central role in the creation of another South African group, the Black Lawyers Association.[57]

Other Westerners have also made personal contributions to the development of Third World cause lawyering. In Bangladesh, the idea for the Madaripur Legal Aid Association, a rural legal services organization, apparently came from a Canadian.[58] The Association for Civil Rights in Israel was founded by Israelis, but many of them had immigrated from English-speaking countries, and looked to groups like the ACLU as their inspiration.[59] In the Philippines, an American law professor helped inspire future cause lawyers.[60] ILSA, the Latin American alternative lawyering group, was first headquartered in Washington, D.C., and its executive director in its first years was an American.[61] One of the leading contributors to the work of the International Center for Law and Development, another group that has promoted conceptions of alternative lawyering, is Professor James Paul of Rutgers Law School. Asian, Latin American, and African networks of women legal activists have been organized in part as the result of efforts of the Women, Law and Development Program, a program directed by a North American woman from the United States; this program too has developed alternative law thinking.[62]

It might be thought, in light of all this, that Western funders, acting in tandem with Western NGO activists, have bent Third World activists to their will and shaped a cause-lawyering movement of their own devising. Claims like this are sometimes made, in particular by some Third World critics. One writer decries the secretiveness of Western funders and asks what hidden agenda they might be pursuing.[63] Another comments that

> Many of the new groups [human rights NGOs] were orchestrated, funded and supported or at the very least deeply influenced by individuals, human rights organizations, and foundations from the North. It is little wonder that most African human rights organizations echo AI, HRW and ICJ [Amnesty International, Human Rights Watch and the International Commission of Jurists] in mandate, structure and methods of work. . . . Many of them are miniature replicas of their more powerful counterparts in the North: they are funded by the same sources, they are organized similarly with almost identical mandates and use similar tactics and strategies of advocacy and work.[64]

Similarly, at the 1991 symposium, organized by the NAACP Legal Defense Fund and the Ford Foundation, a proposal for an international public interest law clearinghouse triggered sharp reactions from some Third World delegates, who saw this proposal, essentially, as another instance of what might be called human rights imperialism.[65]

But these concerns, serious as they are, understate the original and substantial contribution to the world's human rights culture being made by Third World cause lawyers. Even at the most exalted levels of INGO work and rights discourse, the dominance of the West has somewhat diminished. One of the leading INGOs, the International Commission of Jurists, has for many years given some emphasis to economic and social rights.[66] Recently, under the leadership of its new secretary-general, the Senegalese lawyer Adama Dieng, the ICJ has been increasingly sensitive to a variety of Third World concerns.[67] On an even wider stage, the "right to development" became part of the world's human rights discourse in the 1970s, in good part because of the advocacy of another Senegalese lawyer and judge, Keba Mbaye, who at one point was both president of the ICJ and chair of the United Nations Commission on Human Rights.[68]

Such concerns also seem to miss the degree to which Third World men and women have made the idea of human rights their own, and for good reason. In many countries in the Third World (and not only there), it is dangerous to be a human rights advocate.[69] People who risk their careers and lives probably do so because they have become convinced that the causes for which they sacrifice are vital, and anyone who holds human rights so dear is a much fuller participant in the human rights tradition than someone who merely inhabits one of the countries where that tradition has been prominent longest. Nor should it be assumed that those who embrace this tradition are somehow misled about its significance for their lives. People do not require the comforts of Western economies to decide that torture is abhorrent in *their* worlds.[70] They also need not succumb to the illusion that legal guarantees are the solution to their problems in order to value those guarantees as one tool in building a better life. On the contrary, it may be those who most need whatever tools they can acquire who best perceive the significance of legal rights, and who—by using these tools—actually make them more significant. Much of the tradition of public interest law in the United States is the product of the work of African American lawyers at the NAACP Legal Defense Fund.[71] And imperfect and incomplete as the civil rights revolution has been, a number of critical race scholars in the United States have been among those who are unwilling to abandon the field of rights argument.[72]

In addition, these concerns overlook the extent to which First World grantors and NGOs are actually working in tandem rather than in relationships of domination. Amnesty International, for example, has invested what one study calls "a very high proportion of its global resources (up to 10 percent of the budget) for its organisational development in the Third World."[73] As of 1993, the organization had "over a million . . . members, donors and subscribers in more than 150 countries in every region of the world," and declares its determination to "transcend its Western roots and continue to develop as a truly international, multicultural human rights movement."[74] Grantors and grantees often share philosophies, or at any rate have views that overlap enough for the two sides broadly to concur on what needs to be done. Thus Rojas writes that "[t]he group of [grantor] agencies supportive of new Latin American legal services is ordinarily staffed by highly committed people with definite ideas about social change and political development," and these ideas appear to be quite similar to those of their Latin American counterparts, though "more pragmatic and less theoretically oriented."[75] At the very least, it would seem, grantors and grantees are able to agree on vague general conceptions, such as "community development," which provide the two sides with a formula for their collaboration.[76]

Moreover, grantors *learn from* their grantees, and may come to applaud activities they might once have shied away from. In the United States, for example, the Ford Foundation was at one point quite hesitant to fund directly the work of the NAACP Legal Defense Fund;[77] today it funds cause lawyering around the world. Similarly, in the Philippines, a number of grantors and grantees alike evidently initially expected much cause lawyering to focus on test case litigation.[78] This strategy proved unworkable, and Stephen Golub—himself a former foundation staffer for the Philippines—reflected that what the grantors had really invested in was not the programs of litigation that fell through but the individuals who had the capacity to see the problems with this strategy and develop another one that would work better.[79] The donors, Golub says, "primarily view [the grantees] as respected colleagues."[80]

Meanwhile, a number of NGOs in the West have come to focus much of their work on support of Third World activists. A number of international NGOs are focusing much of their effort on the protection of Third World activists from persecution,[81] and this external attention may be as important to the survival or growth of human rights advocacy as any more material aid.[82] Some organizations have focused on building networks *among* Third World activists.[83] The Lawyers Committee for Human Rights has made it a priority to assist Third World groups with the kinds of inputs identified by those groups as needed.[84] Similarly, in the aftermath of the 1991 symposium, the International Human Rights Internship Program developed a program for training Third World activists that focuses on enabling activists to learn from colleagues elsewhere in the Third World rather than treating the United States as an inevitable model.[85] Another group, the London-based INTERIGHTS, "work[s] intensively with the human rights community in selected countries . . . to improve legal protection of human rights, by developing the capacity of lawyers to argue human rights cases, provision of materials or other activities."[86]

In the field of cause lawyering in particular, Third World activists have played a very important part in rethinking the ways that law should be used. To be sure, much of their work originally was, and may still be, focused on traditional, "first-generation" civil and political rights.[87] There continues to be an important role for work on this score; indeed, in some countries there is so little space for human rights work that even the stirrings of advocacy of civil and political rights are swiftly crushed. To a very important extent, what human rights activists do is determined not by grand theory but by opportunity.[88]

While this work continues, however, other efforts are also under way. In India, a remarkable period of judicial activism on behalf of the poor has surely captured the imagination of many lawyers around the world.[89] The Supreme Court of India decided that "any member of the public or a social action group acting bona fide" can file suit to redress injury to individuals or groups who by reason of poverty or disadvantage are unable to act themselves.[90] The court also decided that such cases could be initiated simply *by letter* (thereby invoking the court's "epistolary jurisdiction"), that the facts necessary for their adjudication could be gathered by court-appointed "socio-legal commissions of inquiry" rather than only by the litigants, and that "unorthodox and unconventional" remedial orders would also be available.[91] One observer has asserted that these changes generated "a virtual social revolution under law."[92] At roughly the same time, in southern Africa the example of South Africa's Legal Resources Centre appears to have become an independent source of inspiration to lawyers in such neighboring countries as Zimbabwe, now the site of the Legal Resources Foundation,[93] and Namibia, home of the Legal Assistance Centre.[94] Perhaps this model will now echo even more widely in Africa.

The most important intellectual development may have been the development and embrace by many Third World lawyers of a conception of "alternative lawyering." "Alternative lawyering" is a somewhat capacious term,[95] but in general it features an emphasis on working with and organizing community groups rather than simply taking a random set of individual cases; on deemphasizing litigation in favor of other legal avenues, including interventions with executive agencies and use of alternative dispute resolution techniques; on enhancing clients' understanding of, and ability to use, the law through such steps as "legal literacy" education and paralegal training, while diminishing lawyers' aura of dominance; and most broadly on consciously aiming lawyers' (and clients') efforts toward achieving sweeping social change rather than merely reforming particular laws or increasing "access" to an otherwise unchanged system.[96]

We should not overstate the uniqueness of the "alternative law" paradigm. On a theoretical level, the emphasis on working with client groups intersects with concerns stemming from such diverse sources as republicanism and feminism.[97] Similarly, the deemphasis on litigation may be seen in part as a strategic choice of forum, and it has been many years since even American lawyers reflexively assumed that the federal courts were the perfect forum for resolving rights issues. Alternative dispute resolution techniques have become widespread in the United States as well. And the desire to equalize the relationship between lawyer and client is apparent throughout American law schools' clinical teaching, which generally embraces the goal of "client-centeredness."[98] As a practical matter, moreover, it may be that what alternative lawyers actually *do* is often quite similar to conventional legal practice, however substantial the differences in theory.[99]

But if alternative law thinking intersects with many other, arguably more Western strands of thought, that does not mean that this perspective is insignificant. On the contrary, it certainly marks out a different path from the framework of "traditional" legal aid, focused on simply providing legal assistance to as many needy individual clients as possible, and different also from the once-reigning conception of public interest practice focused on sweeping test cases in the United States federal courts. Moreover, the combination of the various alternative law concerns into a single intellectual structure is greater than the sum of its parts; the "alternative law" perspective is a paradigm that organizes a number of discrete lawyering judgments and strategies into an overarching, and highly political, effort to achieve sweeping social reform. It is not the only paradigm of Third World cause lawyering today—such themes as human rights, women's rights, and indigenous people's rights provide other, sometimes overlapping, guides for lawyers' work—but it is an important one. Moreover, the sheer fact of its articulation seems to reflect an assertion of intellectual independence on the part of a widespread, if loose, network of Third World lawyers and legal workers.

My sense is that the articulation of this distinctive perspective has been primarily the work of Third World figures.[100] At the same time, even as a paradigm, alternative law thinking has analogs in the First World. Indeed, much of the "critical lawyering" literature of recent years offers comparably fundamental critiques of existing lawyering.[101] One reason for this intersection may be that some First World lawyers themselves contributed to the development of alternative law thinking *in the Third World.*[102] But another reason is that some First World lawyers have been learning from their counterparts in the Third World. For example, Lucie White's insightful article on the role of law in resistance to a forced removal in South Africa focuses in part on the relevance to lawyering of the educational perspectives of Paolo Freire.[103]

More broadly, the critical legal studies movement in the United States seems both to inform some alternative law thinking and to derive, in part, from American encounters with the Third World. No doubt the most important of these "critical" encounters was the Vietnam War, but on a more narrowly legal stage another important encounter may have been the "law and development" programs of the 1960s.[104] The law and development movement, whose funders included the Ford Foundation and the United States Agency for International Development,[105] was described by John Henry Merryman as "largely a parochial expression of the American legal style."[106] While it is important not to impute the errors of some participants in this movement to all, it appears that there *were* many errors. As Merryman summarizes it: "In its rawest and most unsophisticated form, law and development meant enacting American statutes, translated into the national language. But even in its more sensitive and informed manifestations it was a type of technical assistance, an effort to provide legal expertise to the developing society by persons who lacked both cultural familiarity and a respectable theory and who, as a result, could only project their own background."[107]

David Trubek and Marc Galanter, looking back ruefully on their own involvement in this movement, attribute its failings to the prevalence of a model of "liberal legalism," a model which they describe as embodying an idealized understanding of American law, and to the assumption that "legal development" in the Third World would bring similar results there.[108] Among the projects fostered by this movement was an effort to incorporate an instrumental approach to law in Third World legal curricula (a project whose inattention to the question of what goals law would be made instrumental *to* was vividly highlighted by the later use of legal realism to support dictators, notably in Argentina).[109] Another "law and development" effort was to increase access to the legal system through subsidized legal services for poor people (the very sort of "traditional" legal assistance against which alternative lawyers have reacted).[110]

Flawed as the law and development movement seems to have been, however, the Americans who participated in it were hardly blind to its problems. Trubek and Galanter write that American scholars not only came to realize that the model of liberal legalism missed crucial aspects of Third World reality but also came to doubt the truth of this model as a description of the United States as well. They emphasize that this disillusionment had many causes—not least of them the Vietnam War[111]—but they comment that "[m]any of the law and development scholars became sensitized to the limitations of the paradigm [of liberal legalism] through their efforts to apply it to the Third World."[112] They also comment that the "foreign scholars, including many from the Third World," with whom American law and development scholars worked, "produced ideas and studies that challenged the early law and development assumptions."[113] And they describe their own preferred response to the collapse of the liberal legalist paradigm, namely the development of the "critical perspective," in which the supposed achievements of Western law are no longer taken for granted at all, but the assumptions of liberal legalism are "retained . . . as guiding aspirations."[114]

What this account seems to suggest is that one reason that alternative law thinking intersects with critical legal studies viewpoints is that Third World scholars and Third World realities taught some Americans to be more critical. The flow of ideas, in short, has long been two-way. This mutual influence reflects that the world's human rights culture *is* a world, rather than just a Western, culture. That the West continues to play a very powerful role in this culture, perhaps even a dominant one, should not be denied. That non-Western men and women are equally owners of the human rights tradition, and that in a variety of ways—including, notably, in the field of cause lawyering—they are making their own voices heard is also clear.

The Roots of Public Interest Law in the Legal Cultures of the Countries in Which It Is Practiced

As important as the influence of the international human rights culture is, its existence does not by itself explain why so many countries have apparently provided sufficiently fertile soil for cause lawyering to take root. National developments, we should remember, are not only an effect but also a cause of the international trends. The international culture would surely not have the same vibrancy if human rights advocacy and cause lawyering in particular were not enjoying the measure of success they have achieved in so many nations. Certainly one central explanation, as we have already seen, is that cause lawyering grows out of the same conditions that prompt reformist or radical politics—out of the injustice of the existing order and the growing popular pressure for change.[115] But this explanation is incomplete, for it does not explain why those who seek such changes have chosen to pursue legal avenues to achieve them.

Two immediate answers can be offered that are pertinent but incomplete. The first is that law is what lawyers do, so those lawyers who out of commitment or self-interest wish to associate themselves with movements for social change will do so through law. But even the existence of massive social change does not, of course, necessarily mean that the practice of law will emerge as one of the vehicles by which change is pursued. Lawyers, and their fellow citizens, might all agree that other forms of action are far better suited to achieving their objectives. Even highly political lawyers might confine their political lawyering to the defense of political trials—certainly a form of cause lawyering but only one of the many forms this work can take—or might simply express their political commitments outside their law practices.[116] Over time, politically committed people who shared this assessment of the low value of legal work would choose other professions besides law, such as union or community organizing.[117] If this appraisal of the value of law is correct, and if lawyers and potential lawyers are not blinded by self-interest or social position from seeing it,[118] then ultimately law will *not* be what these men and women do to achieve their goals.

The second is that the idea of an entirely nonjuridical struggle for social change is fanciful. People struggling against acute injustice take risks when they forego any tactic that seems available to them. Nor are they likely to shy away from particular tactics because they are not perfectly effective or cost-free—there are no flawless tactics, and pragmatic leaders and oppressed citizens will tend to pick up the tools at hand. In some countries, moreover, many arguably more promising tactics, from democratic campaigning to civil disobedience to armed struggle, may simply be impossible to carry out. Even where other tactics are possible, those who ignore the law in situations where changes in the law may affect their future do so at their peril; the sheer fact of political movement may thus compel attention to its expression in the law.[119]

This second argument remedies the deficiency in the first, by offering a rationale for a conclusion by pragmatic, committed advocates of social change that law *is* worth employing in this effort. But this argument proves too much, for it implies that activists should have long since undertaken cause-lawyering efforts. Some have, whether in political trial work or in individual client service, but the flowering of organizations dedicated to the systematic use of law as a tool of social change is a new phenomenon everywhere, and even newer in the Third World than in the United States. Lawyers have had to learn that such work indeed is one of the "tools at hand." Even the impetus of developments in the international human rights culture might not have led them to this realization—if it were not well founded.

Moreover, the fact that no tactic is perfect does not mean that every imperfect tactic must be tried, let alone pursued intensely. The truth is that many of the world's legal systems hardly offer themselves as ready tools to be put to the service of social change. Leaving aside such egregious examples as North Korea, information about whose legal system was largely *classified*,[120] we can all too easily identify nations where law has functioned with little ambiguity as a tool of the powerful. In some states, independent judges may be sharply constrained by oppressive laws that they are obliged to enforce.[121] In others, judges are politically subservient, ideologically hostile, or simply corrupt.[122] In many, perhaps all, access to justice is slow and expensive and the judicial systems likely to seem profoundly alien to many of the people subject to them.[123] Henry Steiner, writing about the discussions of a group of human rights activists from around the world, observed that in the Third World the courts offer few genuine solutions, especially for those seeking to vindicate social and economic rights.[124]

As a result, many Third World people probably distrust their countries' legal systems profoundly.[125] Generalizing about the prevalence of such distrust is risky; my own research on South Africa suggests that legal systems may enjoy considerably more legitimacy among the oppressed than might be expected.[126] Certainly all countries' systems are not identical, and in some there seems to be more popular respect for the law than in others.[127] Even in countries where the law is much less admired, moreover, there are sometimes signs of some residual belief in the legal system. Stephen Golub notes the image of the fighting lawyer in the Philippines.[128] Clarence Dias emphasizes poor people's skepticism about the law, but also indicates that poor people, or their leaders, do (infrequently) attempt to "assert [legal] claims against oppression."[129] Francisco Díaz Rodríguez of El Salvador's CESPAD observed at the 1991 symposium that El Salvador has no culture of rights, yet the population refers to laws and respects lawyers—at the same time that the public, and disadvantaged communities, see law and lawyers as tools of the rich and of repression.[130] These nuances are significant, and help us understand how cause lawyers might persuade skeptical clients of their value, but the complexity of people's views of the law should not obscure the widespread centrality of their distrust for it.

Viewing their legal systems with such contempt, neither poor clients, nor their political allies, nor even their potential legal representatives might choose to invest scarce resources in playing so unfair a game. The likely results might easily have seemed scanty, while the diversion of scarce expertise and fragile popular mobilization into a blind and esoteric alley would hardly be good politics. Moreover, for political activists, if perhaps not for the oppressed people the activists sought to liberate, there also existed the gnawing concern that using the legal system would legitimate it. Thus we can understand why a cause lawyer from Mexico, for example, described his country as having a large and growing popular struggle that for a long time did not have legal assistance.[131] Similarly, a cause lawyer from El Salvador said in 1991 that in his nation there had been very extensive growth of human rights groups but very limited development in juridical contexts.[132] Two other observers comment that despite "the proliferation of new approaches to social change which emerged in the 1970s in Latin America . . . there seems to have been widespread consensus that law and legal practitioners had no significant role to play in change-oriented political programs."[133]

Undoubtedly the changes in such perceptions have been in part the result of profound social and political changes in the Third World and elsewhere.[134] Surely the simple accumulation of experience with the viability of legal tactics and the dissemination of this finding around the world have also opened lawyers' and clients' eyes to new possibilities. For many lawyers, moreover, the "alternative law" commitment to supporting popular struggles may have helped to ease the anxiety that their work within the legal system might inadvertently buttress the very oppression they opposed—even though it seems likely that making law meaningful to previously skeptical and mistrustful people *does*, in some measure, legitimate it.[135]

As I have already suggested, however, the accumulation of experience would probably not have fostered the use of legal tactics had it not been for the fact that legal tactics actually can be effective, even in deeply unjust nations. Two important factors help to give legal tactics their power. The first is the surprisingly widespread availability of potentially persuasive legal arguments on behalf of the victims of injustice. The second is the considerable support that cause lawyers can often obtain for their work from their fellow lawyers, and sometimes from the judiciary, and perhaps, even if grudgingly, from other parts of the society. These two factors together help make the practice of public interest law a potentially protected, yet meaningful, challenge to oppressive power.

The Tools for Legal Arguments

The fact is that in many Third World countries the law, as written, is actually quite receptive to the claims of oppressed people. Many of the cause lawyers interviewed at the 1991 symposium confirmed that their countries' law did provide at least some bases for argument in their clients' behalf.[136] Countries with profoundly discriminatory family law systems, for example, may have constitutional guarantees of equality that are potentially applicable to those discriminatory conditions.[137] India, a country plagued by caste discrimination, has special constitutional protections for "untouchables" or *harijans*, the most victimized caste.[138] So, too, the United States during the long decades of segregation still had the Fourteenth Amendment's Equal Protection Clause on its books, and this clause was not forgotten even if its meaning for African Americans was denied.[139]

It should not surprise us that such benign elements persist even in pernicious legal systems, for the truth is that it is very hard to write laws that altogether exclude the possibility of arguments on behalf of the victims of injustice. It is possible to try, but to succeed a lawmaker may have to abandon utterly the legitimizing mantles of due process, liberty, and fair governmental action. It is striking that many of the world's most egregious rulers have preferred not to dispense with law so totally. Indeed, Joan Fitzpatrick has observed that "[o]ne of the most disturbing and yet fascinating aspects of thoroughly oppressive states of emergency is the regime's typical effort to cloak repressive policies with the trappings of legality and officiality through the issuance of minutely detailed and prolix 'decree-laws.' "[140] Where governments are willing to cast these notions altogether aside, perhaps public interest law simply cannot be practiced; elsewhere, however, arguments *can* be made.

Law, moreover, is not a fixed quantity. International human rights law, embodied in treaty obligations or customary international law rules, may be invoked even where domestic law is unhelpful.[141] For example, one of the participants in the 1991 symposium, Femi Falana, had successfully urged a Nigerian court to invalidate Nigeria's death penalty for teenagers on the ground that it violated the African Charter on Human and Peoples' Rights, of which Nigeria is a signatory.[142] Domestic political changes can result in new constitutions, or new statutes, which present new avenues for legal action.[143] A number of cause lawyering groups are not waiting for other social forces to generate such changes, but are instead lobbying their legislatures themselves.[144]

Even without such constitutional or legislative reform, judges may, either on their own initiative or in response to the efforts of cause lawyers, open up legal doctrine in ways that very much enhance the courts' attractiveness as forums for challenges to injustice. The changes in standing rules in India and (perhaps to a lesser extent) in Israel have had this effect.[145] Admittedly, some legal systems may be much more amenable to such judicial innovation than others—common-law systems, in particular, may be more malleable than civil law regimes.[146] But Stephen Meili's account of legal innovation by Brazilian judges—some of whom appear to have shed their civil law bonds completely, while others are more deftly maneuvering for social change within the formal boundaries of conventional Brazilian argumentation—makes clear that here too the possibility of change exists.[147]

It is instructive to consider American experience on this score. The Warren Court's decisions in *Brown v. Board of Education*[148] and other cases influenced a generation of lawyers and activists to seek judicial remedies—too often, in the view of some critics. But it is a mistake to assume that American experience has no bearing on the strategic problems facing Third World lawyers, on the ground that American constitutional law and judicial institutions were always stronger than their counterparts in many Third World nations. Around 1930, when the NAACP was envisioning the long campaign that ultimately won the *Brown* case, the Fourteenth Amendment existed—but it had been authoritatively held to tolerate state-imposed racial segregation. A prominent human rights advocate, Roger Baldwin, "was convinced that the legal approach would misfire 'because the forces that keep the Negro under subjection will find some way of accomplishing their purposes, law or no law.' "[149] Beyond the law, lynching was widespread.[150] Decades later, when *Brown* was decided, "broad-fronted resistance to the Court's authority fueled and validated uglier efforts, such as violence and threats of vio-lence, bombings, and even murder. Ku Klux Klan activity and cross burnings erupted across the South."[151] It took decades of political and legal struggle to carve out the space for effective legal action against segregation in American law; that it may take decades in other countries as well does not mean that the legal efforts needed are misguided.

Rather, where inviting legal rules exist or can be advocated, the legal problems of the disadvantaged will often lie much more in profound barriers to enforce-ment of their rights than in the theoretical, or at least arguable, content of the rights they hold on paper. These enforcement problems can easily mean that in practice the law operates much more to oppress than to liberate—but if legal arguments are available to be made, then it makes considerable sense for cause lawyers to respond to the lack of enforcement by seeking to supply, through their efforts, the impetus that has been missing.

In doing so, admittedly, cause lawyers in some Third World countries may find the courts decidedly unhelpful, at least for now. But even if court victories will be rare, court action may be useful. In many countries, courts are likely to be open and under some obligation to hear these arguments when they are prof-fered—not because such procedural regularity is necessarily intrinsic to the very idea of courts but because it is so deeply and widely associated with the idea of courts that its abrogation carries a price. (There are, to be sure, times when such a price has been paid, for example during South Africa's state of emergency.)[152] There may well be symbolic, and important, victories to be won through court proceedings that end in legal defeat; bringing injustice to public attention is, in and of itself, a significant human rights strategy.[153] Lawyers may also be able to interfere with the smooth march of state power even where they cannot ultimately prevail on the legal merits—and enough interference may be a victory in itself.[154] Individual victories may be won, even where sweeping impact litigation cannot prevail, and these individual victories—for example, the successful defense of community leaders facing criminal prosecutions by the authorities they are chal-lenging—may be important to the viability of political struggles.[155] International pressure, moreover, may make domestic courts more attentive to human rights than they would otherwise have been.

Moreover, courts are not the only governmental forum with which lawyers can work. One of the significant elements of Third World cause lawyering seems to be the use of intervention with administrative agencies or local political author-ities.[156] In some countries, these institutions may well be more responsive than many courts. But there is nothing unusual about administrative advocacy or polit-ical lobbying as legal strategy.[157] Nor should we assume that what lawyers do when they enter these settings is nonlegal; it may be that legal arguments remain a major stock-in-trade in lawyers' extrajudicial interventions. Even where such strat-egies are in place, moreover, they do not appear to have replaced judicial action altogether. Even alternative lawyers go to court, and presumably they do so be-cause in one way or another they can get meaningful results—including, at least sometimes, legal victories. Despite the critique of Third World judiciaries, in fact, almost every group represented at this conference was engaged in litigation,[158] and a significant portion, in countries including India, Israel, Nigeria, Namibia, South Africa, and Zimbabwe, were engaged not simply in litigation but in "test case" litigation, the classic court-centered technique of law reform.[159]

Professional Support for Cause Lawyering

Not only are legal arguments likely to be available, but there is likely to be some social support for those who make them. In particular, cause lawyers may be able to obtain the support and protection of the larger legal profession by appealing to lawyers' attachment to the rule of law and to their traditions, however partial or even fictional these traditions sometimes are, of advocacy against injustice. Largely due to the exceptional standing of the advocate who spearheaded its formation, the Legal Resources Centre (LRC) in South Africa was able to quickly win the support of the organized legal profession, and to insulate itself from possible re-pression by recruiting a board of trustees made up of prominent members of the legal establishment, including certain judges.[160] In Namibia the nearby example of the LRC helped the Legal Assistance Centre to win support from the legal profes-sion—though more grudging than that accorded to the South African group—and the sympathy of the judiciary helped quench a government effort to shut down the fledgling Namibian group.[161]

In a variety of ways, many cause lawyers lay claim to professional recognition. This is not to say that cause lawyers always see themselves as members of a broad legal community of like-minded souls; there is much to be said in criticism of the legal professions of many nations,[162] and at least at the start of their careers or of their movements some cause lawyers may see themselves as fundamentally differ-ent from their professional peers.[163] Nonetheless, many cause lawyers bolster their claim to a professional mantle by making it a point to do high-quality professional work.[164] Doing so can win respect from judges, lawyers, and—not least im-portant—from clients.[165] Arthur Chaskalson, then the national director of South Africa's Legal Resources Centre, captured this point in his interview with the com-ment that "if we didn't need an adjective [in our legal papers], we didn't use it."[166] Many also reach out to the rest of the legal profession in various ways. A number publish journals;[167] Indira Jaising cites her organization's journal as a major accomplishment and an important link to the legal profession.[168] Some work with law students,[169] or directly with law schools,[170] or provide continuing legal education.[171] One, in Zimbabwe, has edited the country's law reports.[172]

How widespread, and how substantial, are the protective legal traditions that "professionalism" may invoke for cause lawyers? The practice of public interest law, in the sense of sustained, systematic use of law as an instrument of social reform, is quite new in the United States, and appears to be even newer in the Third World. Just how new is somewhat difficult to say, since traditions of individual lawyers' periodic and distinguished human rights work may date back half a century or much more, and at least one law reform effort, the challenge to slavery in the United States, took place in the first half of the nineteenth century. In general, however, sustained law reform campaigns and institutions are a more recent development. It seems reasonable to estimate that in most Third World countries this systematic practice of cause lawyering is not more than about two decades old.

But a number of countries do have considerably longer traditions of social action, or of lawyers involving themselves in politics, or of lawyers engaging in the vigorous defense of people charged with political crimes. Cause lawyers from Brazil, India, Indonesia, Peru, South Africa, and Zimbabwe have seen elements of such traditions in these countries.[173] I do not mean that in these countries *most* lawyers engage in public interest law, or even are strongly sympathetic to those who do. Nor am I saying that only lawyers have such aspirations; many other professionals have also tried to assist or empower their disadvantaged fellow citizens,[174] and in fact one of the important themes of alternative lawyering has been its interdisciplinary approach.[175] Nevertheless, in such states, cause lawyers can assert their fidelity to the "highest traditions of the bar," both to forestall opposition from other lawyers and to build political protection against the risk of having their operations closed down by the powerful state and private interests they offend.[176] Moreover, "traditions" can be built, and built quite quickly, as may be happening in Israel and the Philippines and, to some extent, in Nigeria.[177] This protection will be all the stronger to the extent that those who wield power in a country themselves respect, or at least acknowledge the prestige of, the law.[178] Finally, cause lawyering may also have some appeal among the victims of oppression, who paradoxically may well acknowledge a considerable measure of legitimacy for the idea of law even as they suffer at the hands of their nation's legal order.[179]

In some countries, however, cause lawyers cannot count on even this somewhat qualified support from professional tradition, or the particular traditions of lawyers as advocates may not carry much weight with other institutions in the society. Nepal, Silu Singh observes, has a long tradition of obedience to authority—although the Women's Legal Services Project in that country has won support from senior members of the nation's legal profession.[180] In Indonesia trial lawyers have for several decades spoken out for rule-of-law values;[181] the popular culture, however, reportedly frowns on claiming rights,[182] and the country's leaders have evidently given "rule-of-law" notions short shrift.[183] As for the Indonesian judiciary, it appears to be so much under the control of the state, as well as so often corrupt, that this sector of the legal profession is hardly a strong source of support for public interest practice.[184]

As the Indonesian example particularly vividly reflects, strong institutional protection is not a sine qua non for cause lawyering. Even physical safety is not a sine qua non, for cause lawyers in a range of countries have faced acute perils, physical, financial, and legal. Legal arguments are still available, and can still be made, if there are lawyers with the resources and the courage to make them—though it is important to remember that the degree of courage required may be very great.[185] The fact that public interest lawyering persists under such circumstances surely reflects the commitment and courage of the lawyers and clients in question; it may also reflect the support that international opinion and foreign funds provide for these efforts. Whatever the forces that can sustain cause lawyering in the absence of professional support, however, it is important to remember that professional support or at least tolerance are quite likely to be present—and that this support provides another reason why the strategy of legal activism is likely to be a productive one. But without such support it is also possible that the public interest practice that is carried on is more marginalized and less powerful than it would be if it were undertaken in a more congenial atmosphere.

Speaking for, and Speaking with, Clients

If public interest law owes its existence in part to an international human rights culture and in part to the characteristics of each country's law and legal profession, its ultimate impact and significance depend on the extent to which this form of practice actually articulates and defends the perspectives and interests of the people. The cases that a public interest group brings are a critical part of this process; the connections the group forges with the people and communities that it serves are also central to the character and effect of the group's work. Let us begin our examination of the representation provided by cause lawyers by looking first at the cases they handle, and then turn to the nature of their relationships with their clients.

The Cases

The work of Third World cause lawyers is extremely varied. Although the underlying conception of the 1991 symposium focused more on issues of poverty and discrimination than on "first-generation" civil and political rights,[186] some of the groups at this symposium focused primarily on civil liberties issues,[187] while others made such work part of their focus. In India, AWARE fought against bonded labor, a form of quasi-slavery.[188] ACRI, in Israel, took on free speech claims.[189] Nigerian groups challenged the Nigerian military government's rule by decree.[190]

Many others assisted people held in detention or put on trial for political reasons.[191]

As the symposium's conception suggests, however, most of the groups represented there were focusing primarily on a tremendous range of issues of equal treatment and economic justice.[192] Several were concerned particularly with the rights of women,[193] and some groups that were not working solely on these issues still gave them some attention.[194] Others worked on land claims, in particular claims by indigenous peoples,[195] on housing and homelessness,[196] on labor law,[197] on race discrimination,[198] and on other issues such as environmental law and consumer law.[199] A number of these organizations also undertook criminal cases, perhaps especially when doing so would challenge police conduct or defend community leaders who encountered criminal charges in the course of their efforts.[200]

The choice of different substantive areas of work reflects not only the particular legal problems present in one community or another but also the cause lawyers' varying conceptions of what service they should be rendering to the community. Thomas Hutchins and Jonathan Klaaren, in their report on the 1991 symposium, usefully distinguish between three types of work: efforts to increase poor people's "access to justice," campaigns for law reform, and programs of empowerment.[201] It is possible to see such broad differences in conception among the groups at this conference. Some worked primarily on access to justice;[202] some had a law reform or "test case" orientation;[203] and others focused on the alternative law touchstone of community empowerment.[204] Certain groups quite explicitly recognized the tensions between these different orientations and tried to respond to more than one kind of need.[205] Hutchins and Klaaren also rightly observe, however, that particular activities may fall in more than one of these categories and that the different forms of work can be reinforcing rather than mutually exclusive.[206] Representation of individual litigants, for example, can be the first step in identifying cases that will affect entire communities[207] or in developing a relationship with a community organization.[208]

Those who favor one perspective or another on the choice of the most valuable cause lawyering services might well maintain that some of these areas needed more attention, or less, than the cause lawyers in question were giving them. Debating what work is most valuable is important, but it is not my focus here. Rather, for our purposes what is most important is that it would be hard to deny that work on any of these problems addresses issues that are of tremendous importance to the clients and communities involved. A number of these groups further deepened their bonds with the clients they serve by working with them on nonlegal issues as well (or primarily)—for example, by providing development loans or health services.[209] Moreover, few of these groups, if any, are short of work. Characteristically, their lawyers reported in their interviews that lack of funds was a crucial obstacle to their work; with more funds, they would be able to do even more. If choice of cases is a measure of connection to community needs—and surely it is—then these groups have made powerful connections indeed.

The Clients

For a cause-lawyering group truly to represent its clients is much more difficult than it seems. It is not enough for the lawyers to identify important cases and pursue them zealously—essential as that basic lawyerly role is. Full representation, rather, entails the shaping of an organization in which the beneficiaries of the group's work are also participants in the work—as lawyers, as board members, or as paralegals. It entails the development of techniques of community legal education and paralegal training that will give clients the knowledge with which to formulate their own wishes in legal terms, and so to meaningfully guide their attorneys or to take their legal problems into their own hands. And it requires the organization's staff to engage with their clients—individual clients, and, even more importantly, community groups—in ways that provide the clients with the benefit of lawyers' expertise while also enabling the clients to articulate their own perspectives and shape their own lives. In this section we will look at each of these dimensions of representativeness. What we will find is that full and perfect representativeness is truly unattainable, but that cause lawyers in the Third World are working in many thoughtful ways to achieve the substantial degree of representativeness that they do attain.

THE DEMOGRAPHICS OF CAUSE LAWYERING

It would be easy to characterize cause lawyers as representative of their clients if the lawyers were themselves from the client communities. To some degree, they are. A women's rights group, for example, may be made up entirely of women;[210] a group located in a particular area may have staffers from an ethnic group that predominates there;[211] a group challenging racial discrimination may have substantial numbers of lawyers who have themselves been the victims of such discrimination.[212]

In most cases, however, cause lawyers are unlikely to be able to rest their connection with their client groups on being, themselves, entirely "representative" of those groups in terms of race, or gender, or other such criteria.[213] Access to law school is a privilege unequally distributed in any society, and disadvantaged groups generally "do not have the resources to generate lawyers within their ranks."[214] Graduation from law school is a basis of prestige and probably, even for some public interest lawyers, of income; both of these are likely to further separate even dedicated and caring lawyers from their clients' lives. To the extent that such patterns of class and prestige affect which public interest lawyers are able to make the most convincing case for funding, moreover, the pattern of funding may inadvertently echo a society's unrepresentative distribution of privilege. In short, lawyers, including cause lawyers, are likely to be from middle class or even more privileged backgrounds.[215] Though some cause lawyers may seek to overcome the impact of such gaps between themselves and their clients by adopting the lifestyle of their clients, I suspect that few can completely accomplish such a transformation—and I wonder how many of their clients would find it credible in any case.[216]

In some organizations, furthermore, cultural patterns around gender still seem to constrain the role of women. In one Latin American group, for example, only one woman had been employed as a lawyer, and this woman had found the job very stressful because it required her to spend so much time away from her home and children.[217] In an African country, a male cause lawyer commented that women tended not to become cause lawyers because human rights issues "seem[] like a male thing, it requires a lot of strength to be able to get involved in an activity that would pit you into some confrontation with the government, so, it is not really seen as a female thing."[218] An African woman lawyer, for her part, explained her group's entirely female staffing as the result of their recognition that men simply would not be sympathetic to women's perspective on such issues as wife-beating.[219]

While the allocation of legal knowledge and other factors make it almost inevitable that cause lawyers will come from different backgrounds than their clients, this form of nonrepresentation could be balanced by ensuring that the governing boards of the organizations are more demographically representative. In fact, however, even the boards do not generally seem to be representative in this sense. Nonrepresentativeness can result from the organization's decision to have a board that is self-perpetuating, in the sense that the board itself chooses new board members, and to select the board members with a view to lending prestige and protection to the organization's activities. Such a board can be extremely helpful to the program's survival, precisely because its elite members are in a position to fend off hostile pressures.[220] Yet obviously the more the board becomes an elite body, the more the organization sacrifices a potential site of representativeness.[221]

This problem is not easily escaped. Henry Steiner has commented that "[m]ost NGOs consist of a small group of policy makers and administrators without a broad membership. Some are effectively one-person organizations."[222] Similarly, another scholar, seemingly focusing primarily on Western bodies, bluntly writes that "[w]hether pursuing the public good or private advantage, domestic interest groups rarely govern themselves as participatory democracies."[223] Many of the cause lawyering groups at the 1991 symposium have chosen not to have self-perpetuating boards, and instead elect their directors at general meetings of the groups' members.[224] But this solution is likely to produce a board not much more representative than the group's own membership.[225] Steiner writes that "[i]n the

Third World, the small membership of NGOs consists mostly of intellectuals, professionals, and activists. . . . Most NGOs experience great difficulty in enlarging the number of active members."[226] A number of the groups at the 1991 symposium seem to reflect these patterns. In at least some of these groups, the members appear to be predominantly lawyers or other professionals. In some, the total number of members is very small.[227] In some circumstances, a membership organization of lawyers might actually be less representative of community aspirations than a group governed by a self-perpetuating board drawn from a wider range of concerned, albeit elite, sources.[228]

PARALEGALS AND COMMUNITY LEGAL EDUCATION

One of the central goals of cause lawyers in the Third World is to educate their potential clients about their legal rights. Most of the groups at the 1991 symposium were engaged in this work.[229] It is work that can take many forms. At the broadest level, community legal education may be directed at the entire public, and may rely on techniques such as booklets, newspaper columns, or radio programs.[230] Other programs rely on far more innovative methods of reaching people who may not be educated or even literate,[231] including street theater, role-plays, comic books, posters, and wall newspapers.[232] At least one group, India's AWARE, sometimes uses mass meetings.[233] Others rely on intensive, multiday workshops;[234] or on extended courses, for example in an "alternative law school" for NGO and community group members;[235] or, most remarkably, on a year-long, three-times-weekly course that seeks to build the participants' determination to assert their rights at the same time that it teaches them the methods of doing so.[236]

This work rests on the premise that knowledge is power. Experience with this work, however, has confirmed that that simple formulation is not always accurate. It is open to question, for example, just how much legal knowledge can be imparted in programs aimed at entire communities through the mass media. Certainly there is room for doubt that such programs, or even a single three-day workshop, will always convey enough legal knowledge to enable the participants to handle their own or their fellow community members' legal problems effectively.[237] To enable disadvantaged people to function effectively in these ways—in other words, to train them as paralegals—probably requires extended training and follow-up or supervision.[238] Some advocates argue, moreover, that what is needed is not simply "legal literacy" but "critical legal literacy," in which understanding of legal rules is set against an appreciation of the role the law plays in the larger society and fuels a commitment to changing the injustices of both society and law.[239]

When legal literacy is achieved, however, those empowered by their knowledge may well be more likely to protect their rights or to call on cause lawyers for help in doing so, for they will understand much better what their rights are and what help they can get. When organizations employ or work with paralegals, moreover, they can substantially enhance their connections with their client communities— and thus increase their representativeness.

In part paralegals' value can be called economic or logistic. They can dramatically expand the caseload the organization can handle, and presumably at relatively modest cost. In its campaign against bonded labor, for example, AWARE has been able to rely (in the words of a newsmagazine account) on "a squad of paralegal staff (trained in basic law) who fanned out into the villages identifying bonded labourers, educating them and helping them to break free."[240] Paralegals can also staff offices in outlying areas. In South Africa, for instance, the Legal Resources Centre at one point was working with well over one hundred independent "advice centers," most or all of which would have served poor, and sometimes inaccessible, communities.[241] Most of the groups represented at the 1991 symposium either employed paralegals or worked with paralegals in the communities they served.[242]

In addition, the paralegals can come from the affected communities. In the words of one lawyer, explaining his group's effort to place local people in rural projects, "[Y]ou must put into projects people who understand the way people live, because they can correctly interpret the things which should be given to these people."[243] Members of the client communities and perhaps former clients themselves, trained by the groups to provide service to their peers, such paralegals can connect lawyers and clients across the substantial gulfs of background that are likely to separate them. In addition, the paralegals may actually be selected by the community, or by activist groups within the community.[244] In Namibia, for example, the Legal Assistance Centre's paralegals "in fact have usually been chosen by the community to work in the office."[245] In Colombia and Mexico, client community groups have "juridical committees," whose members in effect work with cause lawyers as paralegals on their own cases.[246]

Moreover, community paralegals need not always work *with*, or *under*, lawyers; a central goal of training paralegals is often to enable people to act on their own, and their fellow citizens', behalf. In the Philippines, for example, SALAG operates an "alternative law school" for this purpose. Community groups or more formal NGOs designate people to attend the school, in order to become "more or less . . . legally self-reliant in their communities."[247] (The school agenda is also shaped with the aid of these groups.)[248] The participants are also "expected to re-echo the sessions with their own non-governmental organization, or with their own communities."[249]

All of these functions, and more, are summed up in the conviction of Perú Mujer that its contribution to addressing the legal problems of women in Peru should not be to take cases itself but rather to train women from Peru's various communities as paralegals or, in the Peruvian term, "promotoras legales." Perú Mujer's training program also echoes a theme evident in much alternative lawyering work, namely that an important part of empowering poor people is to foster their own personal sense of capacity. Elizabeth Dasso told the symposium that Perú Mujer's paralegal training—which meets three times a week for a year—begins with self-affirmation and consciousness raising. Then it turns to the law, which it teaches in part through comics—because many of the people in the program are illiterate—and through games—because many of the participants work long days before they come to class. As Dasso inspiringly said, "If we want to disseminate rights and to talk about how to respect our rights, we have to deal with [these kinds] of limits, and to make the legal education very understanding and very . . . [joyful]."[250] The result is not only that poor women, even those previously illiterate,[251] come to be able to handle a range of legal problems but also that these women experience a transformation in their sense of themselves—and that other women around them are inspired as well.[252]

Yet there is a representational difficulty latent in even this admirable work, for a critical legal education needs to be not only a statement of particular rules of law but also an assessment of the meaning of those legal details for the lives of the people studying them. That assessment is inevitably a value judgment, and perhaps a controversial one. Theoretically, both students and teachers could jointly participate in making this assessment through a process of joint discovery, and the outcome would then in a sense equally "represent" both clients' and lawyers' thinking.[253]

In practice, however, the training lawyers are likely to have messages that they want to convey. Thus a Philippine lawyer explained that his group sought "to make [their clients] realize that, while in order to alleviate or improve their situation, structural and legal reforms are necessary, they can nevertheless make use of existing laws to their advantage."[254] Similarly a Latin American lawyer told the symposium that his group, in working on ordinary daily problems that disadvantaged people encountered, sought to conscientize the people, to show them the reality of the structural violation of their rights, and thus to foster community organization and popular pressure.[255] Still other lawyers self-consciously hoped to foster a rights culture in their countries.[256] Lawyers have good reason to seek to deliver these important messages, but we must recognize that public legal education built around such messages is not simply a refinement of popular sentiments or a joint examination of the law but also an effort at persuasion, an effort with roots partly in the perspectives of relatively nonrepresentative lawyers.

The more fundamental the transformation, moreover, the more significant the kinds of professional guidance that may be required to nurture it. In Perú Mujer's program, for example, the training aimed to achieve a series of objectives, which began with "highlight[ing] the right of women to self-affirmation" and "the right to organize."[257] Then came training on law, rights, judicial procedures, and the techniques of operating a community legal office. After this instruction came the practicum, but "[n]ot all of the women who completed the [earlier] training sessions went on to the legal practicum; this depended on their motivation, their responsibilities in their organization, and the evaluation done by Perú Mujer's team of facilitators."[258] In the seven-month practicum, the women formed groups that planned and operated legal programs in their communities.[259] During the practicum,

> [e]ach group of paralegals received visits to their zones three times a week by a group advisor specializing in social psychology or social work, and from a legal supervisor/advisor (law students and lawyers). The group advisor helped the group deal with conflicts and problems that arose as the group developed, and with educational and organizational issues related to the work plan. The legal supervisor/advisor helped prepare comments, case follow-up, extralegal remedies, legal information, and analysis of experiences.[260]

As Dasso concludes, "Our experience affirmed the need for high-quality comprehensive and technical training to guarantee the transference to the community of self-sustaining and self-managing legal services."[261]

This accomplishment is remarkable, and uplifting. At the same time, it is fair to infer from Dasso's account that professional guidance, evaluation, and intervention, not only about legal matters but about personal or interpersonal issues, were an important part of the program. In saying this, I do not mean to criticize these aspects of the program, but only to make this point—that although Perú Mujer initiated this program by inviting communities to participate, the interaction between professionals and participants is in some measure a transformation of the participants by their teachers rather than merely a process through which the professionals supplied particular tools of representation to the people whom they trained. It seems likely that a similar transformative element is present, to greater or lesser degree, in most community and paralegal education efforts.

ENGAGING WITH CLIENTS

The impact of lawyers' advice. Just as lawyers influence the perceptions of those to whom they provide legal education or paralegal training, so they influence the judgments of those whom they represent and advise in actual cases. The advice lawyers give is often extremely influential for clients of every class, and in every country.[262] The advice of public interest lawyers is no exception. In Bangladesh,[263] in India,[264] in Indonesia,[265] in Namibia,[266] in the Philippines[267]—and no doubt elsewhere—lawyers' advice is powerful.[268] As the discussion of public legal education reflects, some—perhaps most—cause lawyers do have messages they want to convey about the law. Thus one lawyer spoke of his group's efforts "to get people to be committed to the kinds of things that you think are right then, and for them to embrace them as their issues."[269] Another described her group's efforts to overcome women's own reluctance to welcome the rights they should enjoy, and emphasized the value of legal education as the only way to "disabus[e] their minds from [these] beliefs."[270]

The impact of this advice may be especially great because clients accurately see that the conditions of their lives leave them with few options (and no alternative counsel). As Indira Jaising observed, "[L]egal groups have a lot of influence on community groups, because the legal resource is an important resource, and the kind of breathing space that these groups get in the legal framework is so important for their survival that it does happen that the legal group has a lot of influence on the decision-making process."[271] Moreover, the lawyers, themselves leading lives of considerable sacrifice or even risk, visibly deserve trust and may confirm it by the quality of the services they provide.[272] In addition, the lawyers' advantage over their clients in terms of social class and expert knowledge may be even greater in these contexts than it is in many Western attorney-client relationships. A number of cause lawyers commented on the warmth of their relationships with their clients,[273] and although these same lawyers may strongly desire *not* to supplant their clients' judgment,[274] this very warmth could easily reinforce the impact of the lawyers' advice.

Discussion of lawyers' role in advice giving also requires recognition of the significance of lawyers' role in picking cases (and thus selecting the clients to whom they will be giving advice). A number of cause-lawyering groups see part of their function as the handling of test cases,[275] and at least occasional groups are consciously looking for clients to enable them to bring such cases.[276] Other groups just as consciously are choosing cases based on the degree to which they contribute to the protection or mobilization of a community,[277] and may also be choosing *communities* based on whether the potential clients are already organized enough to benefit from an empowerment approach.[278] The client selection process may be especially significant in lawyering focused on empowerment because the lawyers may be contemplating a long, close involvement with each group they represent.[279] In a broad sense, finally, almost all of the groups studied here can be seen as owing their existence in good part to lawyers' or professionals' initiative, not necessarily in the selection of particular cases but in the creation of organizations that would make their services available to particular groups or on particular issues. Client or community initiative certainly may be present too,[280] but the lawyers' role is much more than just reactive.

That lawyers' influence on their clients is so substantial does not mean that lawyers are giving advice in a way that overrides clients' actual needs and desires. "Overriding" is surely rare; "influencing" surely less so. Moreover, the tension between effectively advising a client and fully supporting the client's own decision making is endemic to traditional Western law practice just as it may be to Third World cause lawyering. But it is important to recognize that these tensions become more acute the more the lawyer's role expands from merely representing clients to organizing the very communities that are to be represented. And the greater the transformation that the lawyer-as-organizer seeks, the greater the authorship that the lawyer is likely to acquire.

The lawyer as organizer. It is striking, therefore, that so much Third World cause lawyering is linked to community groups.[281] More than half the groups at the 1991 symposium were engaged, in one way or another, in such work.[282] To be sure, lawyering for groups can take many forms. Some cause lawyers expressly disavowed any "organizing" role, on the ground that this function was a task for the community groups' own leaders.[283] There is still a great deal that these lawyers can do for groups, including assisting them in establishing their own constitutions,[284] protecting them and their leaders against state harassment,[285] training them in meeting their own legal needs,[286] and advising them on the options they have available to them as they make important, perhaps even extralegal, policy decisions.[287] At least a few of the groups at the 1991 symposium, however, were themselves engaged in community organizing, in the sense that they were directly involved in building groups or institutions in the communities they served.[288] We have already looked at the impressive work of one such group, Perú Mujer. Let us now look at the efforts of another of the symposium groups, India's AWARE and at an account of organizing work by a Salvadoran group not represented at this symposium, in order to understand more fully the potentials, and the pitfalls, of this form of "representation."

(a) AWARE: It is hard to imagine a group more intensely engaged in community organization than India's AWARE. To call AWARE a "cause-lawyering" group may indeed be a misnomer, since most of its work appears to go beyond lawyering and is done by people who are not lawyers.[289] Law is a part of its effort, however, and the "alternative law" embrace of interdisciplinary professional engagement with disadvantaged communities counsels against excluding AWARE from our consideration simply because it is far from purely a law group. In principle, in any event, lawyers can be organizers, as Lucie White affirms in her study of a South African struggle in which two people, a lawyer and a community organizer, jointly "occupied the 'lawyer' role."[290] Indeed, in some very conventional settings lawyers routinely are organizers of human lives.[291] In any event, as we will see, AWARE vividly combines responsiveness to clients with almost paternalistic guidance to them.

AWARE—Action for Welfare and Awakening in Rural Environment—has a remarkable history. It was founded in 1975, and is still led, by P. K. S. Madhavan, an anthropologist and the grandson of an Indian king.[292] Working with India's tribal minorities and its untouchables, perhaps the most disadvantaged of all India's citizens, AWARE has reportedly produced remarkable results. It began work in three villages, by 1991 worked or had worked in four thousand, and hopes to reach ten thousand by the end of the century.[293] Its legal education programs reach a hundred thousand people each year.[294] Struggling against a legacy of submissiveness bred by a thousand years of colonialism, as well as against the many powerful "vested interests" of modern India,[295] AWARE has been able to affect the lives of 1.5 million of India's least fortunate people.[296]

Moreover, AWARE has remarkably combined an ability to mobilize people with a determination to listen to them. AWARE "chooses to stand behind and with the people, and never ahead of them."[297] Despite having a large staff, at the top levels including many former civil servants, it has worked to structure itself in decentralized, rather than top-heavy, fashion.[298] It aims to render itself redundant in any given village in approximately ten years by enabling the villagers themselves to take over the work and has actually left some villages because its work was done.[299]

And it responds to villagers' ideas. Its founder says that "AWARE aims to *awaken* the people, to make them identify their *own* problems and to prepare them to devise their *own* solutions and plan of action. The oppressed must not *only* recognize that they are oppressed but must also be aware of what they *can do* legally, peacefully and constructively to overcome their oppression."[300] It evidently aims at community development that "amounts to a *community developing itself in accordance with its own perceptions of its needs* and the *resources* at its command to fulfil those needs."[301] In practice, moreover, AWARE has modified not only its internal organization but also its entire approach to women in response to criticism from the people it sought to serve.[302]

The transformation of the organization's approach to women seems to have been especially dramatic. According to a profile in the Indian newsmagazine *The Week*, at an early stage of AWARE's work, when the organization was making progress but not such rapid progress as it now achieves, P. K. S. Madhavan (AWARE's founder and leader) went to a village meeting. There, "[o]ne Lambada woman got up and said in her rustic rude manner that AWARE was of no relevance to the women. 'Then woman after woman got up and started a tirade against us for being male chauvinistic,' recalled Madhavan who was spellbound for some time."[303] After this revelation, AWARE systematically began empowering and involving women. In 1987 twenty thousand women participated in an AWARE women's meeting,[304] and now 60 percent of the workers at the project level (though only 30 percent at the top level) are women.[305]

Yet it seems fair to say that AWARE's work is not just liberating but also, again, transformative, and that the methods AWARE uses to promote transformation entail not just encouragement but also certain forms of pressure. *The Week* describes Madhavan's initial inability to win the confidence of the communities he wished to help and comments that "[f]inally he went in for the good old missionary tactic—giving sweetmeats to the children and a few strips of aspirin and such common cures for common indispositions. Gradually he learned the local tongue and added a dash of mythological stories to his sermons."[306] Madhavan himself has become a charismatic figure; in the eyes of the people with whom AWARE works, according to a book published under AWARE's auspices, he "is the messiah who has given their life a new direction."[307]

AWARE seeks to make the oppressed aware of their own oppression and of the steps they can take to challenge it, but these ideals of empowerment also contain a substantial measure of paternalistic guidance, inducement, and direction. Madhavan told *The Week,* with respect to the problem of alcohol abuse in the villages, that "[w]e told [the villagers] that they came to be debtors to the landlords and moneylenders through drinking and gambling. We made them aware of the need to break away from such habits. After a continuous dialogue for a year or two, we could mould them into socially productive villagers."[308] One element of this process was a policy under which AWARE, which gives loans to assist villagers in economic development, "made it known that [it] would give loans only to non-alcoholics."[309] *The Week* describes AWARE's antialcohol policy as including "persuasive tactics, backed by friendly coercion"; the result has been "a kind of voluntary prohibition" in as many as 2,500 villages.[310] Another of AWARE's policies, meant to encourage bonded laborers to give up the thin security they enjoyed in that status of semienslavement, was to offer each laborer freeing himself from bondage a grant of five hundred rupees.[311]

In short, AWARE is a liberating force in the lives of a million people and more, who through AWARE are learning to press for their rights and to reshape their lives. AWARE fights for the rights of the oppressed through lawsuits and demonstrations, and it assists oppressed people to undertake their own economic transformations. Yet in some respects the organization seems to be led from above, and in its liberating work with oppressed people it also tempts them, pressures them, and perhaps proselytizes them. All of these steps may be truly essential to the liberation of people as stunningly and stultifyingly oppressed as India's untouchables and "tribals," and it is not my purpose to criticize them. Certainly these techniques are quite similar to methods that are familiar in other areas of human activity, from religious faiths to government conditional-spending programs.[312] But we should recognize nonetheless that this process of community organization entails profound influence by the organizer on the aspirations and achievements of the organized.

(b) "La Tierra es Nuestra": One response to the intense organizing pressure generated by AWARE, however, is to search for ways of engaging with disadvantaged people that (while perhaps infeasible in the context in which AWARE works) would enable organizers in other contexts to catalyze popular organization with less intrusive methods. Lucie White has thoughtfully described the contours of such a legal practice, in which professionals would more truly "learn and teach" with their clients, by engaging in a delicate, bottom-up, process of collective learning and struggle.[313] As White describes it, however, this process is certainly not one in which the professional effaces himself or herself. Rather, while trying "to engage the group to displace her as authority . . . [t]his does not mean that she withholds her own judgments. Rather, she tries to speak honestly, as a person with a different experience, and to demand that her views be taken seriously in the group's practice of understanding."[314]

This is an admirable model, and certainly easier to square with lawyerly presumptions of client control than more aggressive modes of community organizing. A number of cause-lawyering groups represented at the 1991 symposium would surely have endorsed its aspirations for a shared processs of reflection.[315] But its norm of "critical reflection" may sometimes mask a process of propaganda; White herself has reported an instance where members of a Los Angeles community group so perceived it.[316] Indeed, to the extent that this approach finds inspiration in Paolo Freire's *Pedagogy of the Oppressed,* it seems relevant to point out that this "pedagogy" had some distinctly directive features.[317]

Even when this model is applied with great delicacy, however, it does not remove the reality of organizer (or lawyer) influence. This is apparent from the thoughtful, first-hand account by Richard Klawiter of the work of a campesino organizer with other campesinos, members of a rural cooperative that Klawiter calls "Santa Maria," in El Salvador. As Klawiter recounts it, Antonio, the organizer, believes that "change must come from below and originate within the community. He places a premium on widespread participation among community members, and actively solicits the views of the community's more reserved and hesitant members."[318] Before a cooperative meeting, he invites any interested members to attend—but only members of two of the cooperative's established committees do.[319]

In the meeting itself, Antonio seeks to facilitate and not to direct, but the line between facilitation and direction is ambiguous. The participants raise the issue of their very real fear of government violence; Antonio encourages them to speak, then asks what "we" can do about this situation, and "encourages the participants to consider how the community might respond to the violence." Then "[o]ne man turns to Antonio, and asks 'What do you think we can do?' Suddenly, everyone's eyes are on Antonio. . . . One man anticipates Antonio's response: 'You know what he's going to tell us,' he says. 'He'll say that since we're the administrative council, we're the bosses. It's our responsibility to do something.' Antonio relaxes, and the discussion resumes." Yet after some further discussion, "Antonio interjects, 'Would it be possible to form a committee to study this problem? That way, other people will get involved and you won't have to do everything,'" and the group agrees on further study.[320]

Then another issue emerges, essentially the issue of the members' dependency on the organizer. Antonio meets the issue head on, and the members make progress, but it is apparent that the problem is a deep-rooted one, and that the process of dealing with it is very slow. The initial trigger is a discussion of the fact that a meeting scheduled to deal with a particular problem had not taken place. The group members "claim that their meetings are unsuccessful when Antonio does not attend. . . . Antonio detects that their excuses belie the real explanation for their failure to meet: Perhaps his own prodding more than their genuine commitment had been the only real impetus for the group meeting. . . . [H]e has succeeded at gaining the trust and confidence of the community. But his success is also his failure. For accustomed as they are to being passive objects, the campesinos ceded Antonio authority over the direction of their lives."

Impressively, Antonio "initiate[s] a dialogue" on this very point; it becomes clear that the campesinos are ashamed "that they have failed Antonio and, more importantly, that they have failed themselves." The group members spend an hour agreeing on a new time to meet without Antonio, and this is time well spent, for in the process the members "commit themselves to the larger group and [are] renewed in their faith that they can control their own destinies." Then the meeting ends, *seven hours* after it began.[321] The campesino members *are* building their control over their own lives, but only slowly, and only through participation, indeed immersion, in an extremely drawn-out process of interaction with their organizer. It is not surprising that most members of the cooperative do not attend such meetings! And surely it is clear that lawyers who embrace the role of organizer—and often those who do not organize but provide more traditional legal aid to groups organized by others—are inevitably part of a process in which the organizers' empathy, skill, and intelligence are not just assisting but also changing the people with whom they work.

(c) *Being, or Not Being, Political.* Just as the impulse to respond to the problems of disadvantaged communities by empowering those communities presses the lawyer beyond the model of representation as implementation of client wishes, so the impulse to respond to unjust political power by building political power can also take the lawyer beyond the ordinary realm of professional work. It is not hard to see why cause lawyers might take a political stance. Identification with the oppressed people the lawyer seeks to represent may seem to call for rejecting "the norm of 'professional distance' "[322] in favor of concurrence in the political as well as the more narrowly legal aspirations of those people. Adherents of one political position or another may press lawyers to lend their direct and explicit support, and lawyers may in fact share the views of those who ask them for such endorsements.[323] Moreover, rights talk, especially when extended to encompass the full panoply of claims now encompassed in such discourse—including social and economic rights and the right of "peoples" to self-determination—is obviously very much concerned with political issues. Protection of rights equally obviously often depends on challenging unjust political power, as Claude Welch emphasizes.[324]

At the same time, there are profound pitfalls on this course. Political polarization may make the notion of enhancing "representativeness" by identifying with one particular political party controversial.[325] In South Africa, conflicts between antiapartheid groups aligned with the ANC and those adhering more to black consciousness principles have sometimes been acute. The Legal Resources Centre scrupulously avoided taking sides in these conflicts (for example, it declined to affiliate with the United Democratic Front), and this position was honored by the various groups affected. The result was that the LRC was able to work with a variety of groups; in a sense, therefore, the LRC was able to be representative of a wide range of groups, but it achieved this result only by foregoing a closer identification with any one group's "representation" of the community.[326]

In addition, taking an explicitly political stance may undermine the lawyer's ability to appeal to others on behalf of his or her clients. The more the language of rights coincides with the language of politics, the easier it is for critics to maintain that the cause lawyer's "rights" agenda is not really about rights at all, but rather about one partisan view of the correct policies for society.[327] The more lawyers act politically, moreover, the harder it presumably is for them to claim the protective mantle of professionalism or to persuade authorities that their legal arguments have some objective claim to correctness. And the lawyer who takes an overtly political stance against the government risks encountering equally blunt political power in response.[328]

The groups represented at the 1991 symposium have often responded to these conflicting considerations by trying to split the difference. None was explicitly identified with any particular political party. Some describe themselves as nonpolitical.[329] Yet at least one was apparently engaged in such decidedly political activity as organizing mass demonstrations.[330] Several emphasized, moreover, that although they were not aligned with any political party they were certainly political, or described themselves as part of broad (and political) efforts such as the struggle for human rights and democracy.[331] This position—which has the advantage of reflecting the truth that there is substantial overlap between law and politics, while still affirming that the two are not the same—may enable lawyers to affirm their ties to their clients while not sacrificing the "professional" character of their work.

Sometimes, however, cause-lawyering groups go further. Some do associate with particular political parties,[332] and perhaps some urge votes for one party or another.[333] One, the Indonesian Legal Aid Foundation, "has become Indonesia's most prominent center of social-legal and political-legal criticism and reform activity."[334] Perhaps most dramatically, a few months after the 1991 symposium, two of the Nigerian groups that had participated in it took a vividly political step.[335] As Claude Welch recounts, in late 1991 the Civil Liberties Organisation and the National Association of Democratic Lawyers were among the founders of the Campaign for Democracy, a group that took the premise of human rights opposition to military rule to its ultimate conclusion by spearheading massive demonstrations that for a moment seemed capable of dislodging the military government from power.[336] The effort failed, but these lawyers were surely correct in believing that the protection of human rights in Nigeria required not just legal but political changes.[337] That is true in many countries around the world, and as long as this is so, cause lawyers will have to wrestle with the difficult questions involved in asserting, or avoiding, a political identity as part of their representation of poor and disadvantaged people.

Conclusion

This essay has explicitly traced the roots of cause lawyering in the Third World in part to such sources as an international human rights culture and domestic professional values. In part because such factors are among the sources of cause lawyering, the question of the representativeness of cause lawyering is an important and troubling one. Moreover, the preceding section's detailed examination of representational issues has confirmed that there are no easy solutions to the many dilemmas of representation. Yet it seems fair to say that the fear of overprofessionalism and cooptation can easily be overstated.

The reality of public interest law in the Third World seems quite different. Lawyers are acutely aware of immense injustice; they are eager to connect with others in their communities to oppose it; they are repeatedly, and gravely, hampered in their efforts by the resistance of the powerful and the limited funds available for their work. The cases they bring certainly respond to client needs—even if the lawyers themselves might argue over which sets of cases, in which forums, do this best. The efforts they make to educate the public and to train paralegals surely contribute to bringing law to the people and enabling the people to control the law—even if some modes of education are more successful than others, and even though the most empowering programs may also be those that move furthest along the spectrum from representation to transformation. The advice they give, the interactions with community groups they undertake, and the political positions they carefully stake out, all similarly betoken intense efforts to assist and sometimes to empower clients—even if, as is surely the case, vigorous efforts to empower clients are likely to entail lawyers' potent influence over their clients as well.

In short, the work of Third World cause lawyers seems, in general, far from a reincarnation of traditional elite power in public interest guise. Rather than being engaged in a unilateral imposition of priorities on client communities, these lawyers seem, instead, to be striving to employ not only their capacity to challenge existing authority, but also their ability to influence and transform their clients, on behalf of those very clients. What this study in the end suggests is that Third World cause lawyers are deeply and fruitfully engaged in the arduous, slow, important—and at times inescapably ambiguous—struggle to serve the people.

Notes

I thank the Ford Foundation, the NAACP Legal Defense Fund, and New York Law School for financial support of this work. I appreciate the helpful comments of Ann Blyberg,

Marguerite Garling, Paul Lebensohn, Mary McClymont, James Paul, Emma Playfair, Michael Posner, Austin Sarat, Stuart Scheingold, and Stephen Golub, and the valuable research assistance of Beth Levine, Yvonne Hernandez, Thomas Sipp, and Nicole Krug. I am also grateful to the librarians at Columbia and New York Law Schools for their help with my research. I also thank Elizabeth Benjamin, Catherina Celosse, Michelle Davila, Astrid Gloade, Kate Harrison, Thomas Hutchins, Jonathan Klaaren, Scott Mason, and Selena Mendy for carrying out almost all of the interviews done in connection with this study. I also thank all those who worked on the transcription of these interviews and of the conference sessions I refer to in this essay, and those who helped me to contact some of the interviewees years later. Finally, I am particularly indebted to Thomas Hutchins and Jonathan Klaaren, who also compiled a report on the conference around which this research was originally organized, a report whose descriptions of the various groups involved in the conference I have relied on repeatedly. Responsibility for any remaining errors and for all views expressed, however, is solely my own.

1. This conference, the "International Public Interest Law Symposium," took place at Columbia University in New York on May 20 and May 22–23, 1991. This draft reflects information concerning the following twenty-four groups that attended the conference (including two groups for which I do not have an interview transcript):

(1) *Africa:* in Kenya, Kituo Cha Sheria (Legal Advice Centre) (no interview transcript); in Namibia, the Legal Assistance Centre (LAC) (interview with David Smuts); in Nigeria, the Constitutional Rights Project (CRP) (interview with Clement Nwankwo), the Civil Liberties Organization (CLO) (no interview conducted), the National Association of Democratic Lawyers (NADL) (interview with Femi Falana), the Anambra State Family Law Centre Project of the International Federation of Women Lawyers (FIDA) in Enugu, Nigeria (interview with Obiageli Nwankwo), and the Nigerian Institute of Advanced Legal Studies (interview with Isabella Okagbue); in South Africa, the Legal Resources Centre (LRC) (interview with Arthur Chaskalson) and the Black Lawyers Association (BLA) (interviews with Justice Moloto and Godfrey Pitje), as well as an interview with a leading activist judge of South Africa, Justice John Didcott; in Zimbabwe, the Legal Resources Foundation of Zimbabwe (interview with Wilson Manase) and Women in Law and Development–Africa (WiLDAF), based in that country (interview with Florence Butegwa and Lisa VeneKlasen);

(2) *Asia (including the Middle East):* in Bangladesh, the Madaripur Legal Aid Association (interview with Fazlul Huq); in India, Action for Welfare and Awakening in Rural Environment (AWARE) (interview with P. K. S. Madhavan) and the Lawyers Collective (interview with Indira Jaising), as well as an interview with Justice P. N. Bhagwati, a former chief justice of the Supreme Court of India, who played a crucial role in the rise of Indian public interest law; in Indonesia, the Legal Aid Institute (interview with Artidjo Alcostar); in Israel, the Association for Civil Rights in Israel (ACRI) (interview with Neta Ziv); in Israel's Occupied Territories, Quaker Legal Aid and Information Services (interview with Maha Abu-Dayyeh Shamas); in Nepal, the SUSS Women's Legal Services Project (WLSP) (interview with Silu Singh); in the Philippines, Structural Alternative Legal Assistance for Grassroots (SALAG) (interview with Carlos Medina);

(3) *Latin America:* in Brazil, Geledes—Instituto da Mulher Negra (interview with Antonio Carlos Arruda da Silva); in Colombia, Fundación Comunidades Colombianas (FUNCOL) (interview with Adolfo Triana Antorveza); in El Salvador, Centro de Estudios para la Aplicación del Derecho (CESPAD) (interview with Francisco Díaz Rodríguez); in Mexico, Despecho de Orientación y Asesoria Legal (interview with Efrén Rodríguez González and Ernestina Godoy Ramos); in Peru, Asociación Perú Mujer (interview with Elizabeth Dasso).

Interviews with the representatives of the Colombian, Salvadorian, and Mexican groups were done in Spanish (I have relied mainly on my own, imperfect translations); the interview with the Brazilian lawyer Antonio Carlos Arruda da Silva was conducted in English and Portuguese, through an interpreter; and all other interviews were carried out in English. I have relied here primarily on the (somewhat imprecise) transcripts rather than the original tapes, though some tapes have unfortunately been hard to transcribe. I have also used the account of the 1991 conference, and the descriptions of the attending groups, in Thomas Hutchins and Jonathan Klaaren, reporters, *Public Interest Law around the World: An NAACP-LDF Symposium Report* (New York: Columbia Human Rights Law Review, 1992); in addition, from time to time I refer directly to transcribed portions of the conference proceedings themselves. All interview and conference transcripts cited in this essay are in the author's possession. All or almost all transcript citations in this essay have been compared with the original tapes, primarily by my research assistants, though quotations generally may not indicate language, such as interruptions or trivial errors of speech, omitted in the transcripts.

2. I refer to this conference hereafter as the "1991 symposium."

3. For a general account of the 1991 symposium, and descriptions of all of the groups whose representatives attended, see Hutchins and Klaaren, *Public Interest Law.* At least fourteen of the twenty-four groups listed in note 1 were also receiving, or about to receive, Ford Foundation funds for their ongoing program activities. See ibid., passim. Readers of the symposium report will note that a number of the participants in the symposium were from public interest groups in countries outside the Third World, including Australia, Britain, Japan, Poland, and the United States; the present essay, however, focuses only on public interest law in the Third World (including Israel and South Africa).

4. Two of the groups, however, are from South Africa, and a third, from Namibia, was founded when that country was still under South African control. I have written elsewhere about the South African legal system. See, e.g., Stephen Ellmann, *In a Time of Trouble: Law and Liberty in South Africa's State of Emergency* (Oxford: Clarendon Press, 1992). My study of these three groups naturally was informed by that work.

5. Austin Sarat and Stuart Scheingold, "Cause Lawyers and the Reproduction of Professional Authority: An Introduction," chap. 1 of this volume.

6. As stated, this conception of cause lawyering is also broad enough to encompass lawyering on behalf of either the powerless, who seek to claim legal protections they have been denied, or the powerful, who seek to buttress their privilege by invoking the law in their favor. Nevertheless, my focus here is on the efforts of lawyers for the (relatively) powerless.

7. Singh, interview, 1.

8. Huq, interview, 17.

9. Thus the Philippine organization SALAG was founded by a group of people just out of law school, who while in law school "were members of an organization which focused not only on spiritual activities but also on . . . socially oriented activities." Medina, interview, 2. Medina comments that "the thrust of [this school's] education is to form good Catholic lawyers, and some of us take the thrust seriously." Ibid., 12. Church groups have played important roles in sponsoring or protecting cause lawyers in other countries as well. See Henry J. Steiner, *Diverse Partners: Non-Governmental Organizations in the Human Rights Movement* (Cambridge, Mass.: Harvard Law School Human Rights Program; Ottawa, Ontario: Human Rights Internet, 1991), 75 (referring to NGOs associated with the Catholic Church in six countries); Fernando Rojas, "A Comparison of Change-Oriented Legal Services in Latin America with Legal Services in North America and Europe," *International Journal of the Sociology of Law* 16 (1988), 226–228.

10. George Bisharat suggests that self-interest has played a major part in forming the Palestinian cause lawyering community. George E. Bisharat, "Attorneys for the People, At-

torneys for the Land: The Emergence of Cause Lawyering in the Israeli-Occupied Territories," chap. 14 of this volume. Lawyers' self-interest and the interests of the broader groups whom they might represent in public interest law may coincide. Thus South Africa's Black Lawyers Association has devoted much of its effort to increasing the number of black lawyers in that country, a move certainly needed as part of the transformation of that nation. The BLA also owes its genesis in part to the solidarity developed among black lawyers in the late 1970s when they resisted a government effort to bring criminal charges against some of their number for maintaining offices near the courthouses, in what were then areas reserved for white occupancy. Hutchins and Klaaren, *Public Interest Law,* 152–153.

11. Rajeev Dhavan, for example, regards legal activism in India as valuable in part in light of the defeat of armed insurrection as a tactic. Rajeev Dhavan, "Managing Legal Activism: Reflections on India's Legal Aid Programme," *Anglo-American Law Review* 15 (1986), 304.

Stephen Golub sees the rise in cause lawyering around economic and social issues, rather than civil and political rights, in the Philippines as attributable to a number of causes, including the end of the Marcos dictatorship and "a series of murderous internal purges [that] tarnished the far left's 'Robin Hood' image" and so diminished the appeal of lawyering work on behalf of underground organizations. Stephen Golub, "Democratizing Justice: Philippine Developmental Legal Services and the Patrimonial State," paper presented at the annual meeting of the Association for Asian Studies, March 24–27, 1994, 29. Golub also notes that "the worldwide decline of communism led many to rethink their assumptions about radical change," surely an effect not confined to the Philippines. Ibid.

Fernando Rojas suggests that the growth of Latin American cause lawyering resulted in part from the "crisis of the left." This crisis, whose complex intellectual sources Rojas sketches, has meant among other things a condemnation of "ideological dogmatism, party sectarianism, and intellectual vanguardism . . . open[ing] the possibilities for professional non-doctrinaire work with low-income people." Moreover, Rojas writes, "[w]orkers and intellectuals try to find the seeds of social change within their daily struggles, not in externally imposed party ideologies." Rojas, "A Comparison of Change-Oriented Legal Services," 221; see ibid., 220–223. Perhaps reflecting these changes, Elizabeth Dasso describes her own involvement as "a sort of social compromise," a way of pursuing politics while not becoming linked to a political party. Dasso, interview, 11.

The growing prominence of new groups demanding human rights protection may also have contributed to the rise of cause lawyering, as older activist strategies lost at least some of their relevance. Thus two observers of Latin American cause lawyering suggest that the day of rural, campesino-based revolutions in South America is over and cite a variety of new social movements for which cause lawyering may be helpful. Edgar Ardila and Jeff Clark, "Notes on Alternative Legal Practice in Latin America," *Beyond Law* (March 1992), 109–110.

One of the most important of these, around the world, surely has been the women's movement; developments that have promoted this movement have likely promoted cause lawyering focused on it as well. Thus Elizabeth Dasso of Perú Mujer cites the Decade for Women as having helped lay the foundation for her organization's work. Dasso, interview, 18.

12. See Gridley Hall and Burton Fretz, "Legal Services in the Third World," *Clearinghouse Review* 24 (1990), 785.

13. Human Rights Internet, *Masterlist: A Listing of Organizations Concerned with Human Rights and Social Justice Worldwide* (Ottawa: Human Rights Internet, 1994) (supplement to vol. 15 of the *Human Rights Internet Reporter*), 2. Most but not all of these organizations are nongovernmental organizations (NGOs). Ibid.

14. Ibid., 229–233. Almost a third of these groups, however, were located in just two nations, the Philippines and South Africa. It should also be noted that some groups included in this section of the *Masterlist* probably are not, or at least not solely, "cause-lawyering" bodies. In the United States, for example, the American Society of Comparative Law is listed. Ibid., 230.

15. *International Human Rights Internship Program* (Washington, D.C.: International Human Rights Internship Program [1995 or 1996], 1.

16. International Human Rights Internship Program (IHRIP), "The Legal Resources Project and Its Understanding of Public Interest Law," (Washington, D.C.: IHRIP, 1996), 1 (copy on file with the author). This memorandum is "[b]ased in part on a Draft Working Paper written by Mario Gomez," a cause lawyer in Sri Lanka, and was "[e]dited and adapted for the Legal Resources Project by staff of the International Human Rights Internship Program." Ibid.

17. T. Mulya Lubis, "Legal Aid: Some Reflections," in *Access to Justice: Human Rights Struggles in South East Asia,* ed. Harry M. Scoble and Laurie S. Wiseberg (London: Zed Books, 1985), 40. Another Indonesian legal aid lawyer, writing in the same volume, observes that while "many legal aid activists *in practice* still adhere to a traditionalist approach," a "broader, more progressive"—and more politicized—"concept . . . has now been widely accepted." Buyung Nasution, "The Legal Aid Movement in Indonesia: Towards the Implementation of the Structural Legal Aid Concept," in *Access to Justice,* ed. Scoble and Wiseberg, 36.

18. Rojas, "A Comparison of Change-Oriented Legal Services," 210.

19. Fernando Rojas and Jeff Clark, "Editors' Introduction," *Beyond Law,* February 1991), 11. Stephen Meili reports an estimate of "ap[p]roximately 500 public interest lawyers in Brazil." Stephen Meili, "The Interaction between Lawyers and Grass Roots Movements in Brazil," *Beyond Law* (July 1993), 64 n.7.

20. See Golub, "Democratizing Justice," 5.

21. George Bisharat suggests that there may be hundreds of Palestinian cause lawyers at work in the military courts of the West Bank and Gaza, and mentions at least eleven organizations engaged in or connected with this work. Bisharat, "Attorneys for the People."

22. Michael H. Posner and Candy Whittome, "The Status of Human Rights NGOs," *Columbia Human Rights Law Review* 25 (1994), 269–272.

23. Ibid., 269.

24. Claude E. Welch Jr., *Protecting Human Rights in Africa: Roles and Strategies of Non-Governmental Organizations* (Philadelphia: University of Pennsylvania Press, 1995), 35 n.3.

25. Jerome J. Shestack, "Sisyphus Endures: The International Human Rights NGO," *New York Law School Law Review* 24 (1978), 91. Shestack was then the president of the International League for Human Rights, one of the six groups he mentions.

26. Posner and Whittome, "The Status of Human Rights NGOs," 270.

27. Ibid.

28. Moreover, the rise of human rights NGOs is itself part of an even broader development—the rise of NGOs of all sorts. Claude Welch Jr. cites an estimate that in 1939 "there were fewer than 800 worldwide." Now, he notes, "researchers estimate that between 18,000 and 20,000 NGOs . . . exist." Welch, *Human Rights in Africa,* 44–45.

29. See Posner and Whittome, "The Status of Human Rights NGOs," 269.

30. In the 1970s, "first the U.S. Congress and then President Jimmy Carter insisted that aid recipients respect human rights." Howard B. Tolley Jr., *The International Commission of Jurists: Global Advocates for Human Rights* (Philadelphia: University of Pennsylvania Press, 1994), 137. Laurie S. Wiseberg, the executive director of Human Rights Internet, calls "the role played by President Carter and U.S. foreign policy" a "very major factor" in the rise of

human rights NGOs. Wiseberg, "Human Rights NGO's," in Alex Geert Castermans, Lydia Schut, Frank Steketee, and Luc Verhey, eds., *The Role of Non-Governmental Organizations in the Promotion and Protection of Human Rights: Symposium Organized on the Occasion of the Award of the Praemium Erasmianum to the International Commission of Jurists* (Leiden: Stichting NJCM-Boekerij, [1991 or 1992]), 26.

31. Wiseberg, "Human Rights NGO's," 25.

32. Rojas comments that in Latin America "[d]omestic contributions pay for traditional legal services." Rojas, "A Comparison of Change-Oriented Legal Services," 232. See also, for a skeptical view of the attitude toward legal aid and public interest law of the Indian government, despite that government's assertions of commitment to the interests of the poor, Dhavan, "Managing Legal Activism," 293–294 and passim.

33. See Hall and Fretz, "Legal Services," 792 (public financing rare, at least for "law reform and impact representation").

34. Steiner, *Diverse Partners,* 77.

35. Hutchins and Klaaren, *Public Interest Law,* 123. Similarly, the annual budget of the Family Law Centre Project of the Federación Internacional de Abogadas (FIDA) in Enugu, Nigeria, based solely on membership dues and other local funds, was less than $8,000; a Ford Foundation grant was about to make it possible for the center to expand substantially. Ibid., 114–115.

36. Rojas, "A Comparison of Change-Oriented Legal Services," 232. See also Welch, *Protecting Human Rights in Africa,* 72 ("Almost all African human rights NGOs derive most of their budgets from external sources, notably from developed Western states."); Golub, "Democratizing Justice," 29 (stating that all of the alternative law groups in the Philippines "mainly or exclusively rely" on foreign funding). But Brandt appears to overstate the case when he says that legal service activities "are exclusively financed by international organizations." Hans-Jürgen Brandt, "Human Rights, Legal Services and Development: Theory and Practice," in *Law, Human Rights and Legal Services: A Neglected Field of Development Cooperation: Proceedings of an International Conference in Königswinter, Federal Republic of Germany, 30th June–4th July, 1986* (Augustin: COMDOK-Verlagsabteilung, 1988), 43.

37. Indira Jaising, the secretary of the Lawyers Collective, said that "[t]he main reason why we don't believe in accepting foreign funding is because we think groups which do that often end up developing a vested interest in being professionals rather than servicing the community, and they get very alienated from the community for whom they work." Jaising, interview, 18. Members of the Lawyers Collective, like some American cause lawyers described in this volume, have been able to subsidize work without fee in good part by taking fee-paying, but still politically meaningful, cases. Indira Jaising, speaking at 1991 symposium, plenary session on "Funding: Strategies and Sources, Part I" (May 23, 1991). (This session was not transcribed; I have relied on the tape of the proceedings, which I have on file.) Another Indian group at the 1991 symposium, AWARE, reported that a majority of its substantial budget ($5 million annually) came from domestic sources, though more than two-fifths came from foreign donors. Hutchins and Klaaren, *Public Interest Law,* 53. Steiner implies that some of the Third World NGOs at the 1989 conference he describes also did not take foreign funds. See Steiner, *Diverse Partners,* 78.

38. Among the donors to the groups at the 1991 symposium have been the United States, Canada, Australia, Britain, Sweden and Norway. See Hutchins and Klaaren, *Public Interest Law,* passim.

39. Particularly in Western Europe, apparently, governments often fund such institutions as church foundations or foundations linked to political parties. See Tolley, *International Commission of Jurists,* 16. Prominent examples of such institutions engaged in funding Third World cause lawyering include the Friedrich Naumann Foundation in Germany, de-

scribed by one of its officials as "an institution closely associated with Liberalism both at home and abroad," Stefan Melnik, "Introduction," in *Law, Human Rights and Legal Services: Proceedings,* 9–10; and the Netherlands Organization for International Development (NOVIB). See Tolley, *International Commission of Jurists,* 143. Friedrich Naumann funds helped support at least four of the groups at the 1991 symposium (the Indonesian Legal Aid Foundation; Namibia's Legal Assistance Centre, the Women's Legal Services Project in Nepal, and SALAG in the Philippines); NOVIB funds went to at least three (AWARE in India, the Indonesian Legal Aid Foundation, and the Legal Assistance Centre). Hutchins and Klaaren, *Public Interest Law,* 53, 65, 103, 109, 145.

40. The groups attending the 1991 symposium appear to have received funding from over thirty different foundations or other private bodies (though some of these may in turn have been utilizing government funds). See Hutchins and Klaaren, *Public Interest Law,* passim.

41. Wiseberg, "Human Rights NGO's," 43.

42. Ibid., 43 n.35. Hall and Fretz similarly observe that "[t]he Ford Foundation has been the largest single source of support and innovation [in 'new legal services'], contributing to more than 24 projects in Latin America, Africa, and Asia." Hall and Fretz, "Legal Services," 787. (Gridley Hall had himself been a Ford Foundation officer.) On the other hand, one NGO activist has pointed out to me that some groups may consider American funds especially suspect.

43. Gridley Hall, "Ford Foundation Support for Human Rights and Social Justice in the Andean Region and Southern Cone," in *Law, Human Rights and Legal Services: Proceedings,* 68.

44. Ibid., 71.

45. Ibid., 72.

46. Actual and perceived foundation priorities may have various effects on would-be grantees. Welch notes that grantors tend to fund specific projects rather than general budgets, and comments that "[o]rganizational diffuseness resulting from over-expansion to obtain earmarked funds thus is a danger." Welch, *Protecting Human Rights in Africa,* 294. Stephen Golub, a former foundation staffer, generally appears to feel that grantors support rather than distort the initiatives of Philippine cause lawyers; he observes, however, that those grant recipients who best meet the funders' documentation requirements get the most funding. Golub, "Democratizing Justice," 95. Whether documentation is a benefit (promoting accountability) or a curse (constraining flexibility) probably depends on the context. From the perspective of the Kenyan group Kituo Cha Sheria, "[d]onor organizations call for form-filling and large-scale project proposals with a lot of verbiage when a local NGO applies for financial support. Project directions may change midway due to increasing pressure of new and unforeseen demands on the local operating NGO, but donors find this difficult to accept as it does not meet with their funding criteria." Hutchins and Klaaren, *Public Interest Law,* 90. Kituo Cha Sheria also questions how well-informed foundation staff are, and contends that they are typically "intellectuals from the home country." Ibid.

In South Africa, the Black Lawyers Association felt that it had encountered repeated problems in raising funds because of foreign donors' inaccurate impression that only blacks could be members. Justice Moloto, interview, B12–13. Another group, Women in Law and Development in Africa, reported that potential grant recipients sometimes "operate in isolation in the mistaken belief that they are protecting their source of funds." This is an ironic result, since actually, according to WiLDAF, grantors welcome coordinated approaches. Hutchins and Klaaren, *Public Interest Law,* 172–173.

Occasionally such foreign priorities may even produce exceptions to the rule that money is always tight. Thus it is striking, but not entirely surprising, that the Legal Assistance Centre in Namibia, which opened its doors when Namibia was still under South African rule, was actually *not* short of funds at that time. In 1991, however, after the end of South African rule in Namibia, the LAC had to reckon with the possibility that funds might be cut, though as of then their funding remained "reasonably secure." Smuts, interview, 54–55. A similar prospect may await the Legal Resources Centre in South Africa, though as of 1991 many of its major donors continued to see its work as a priority. Chaskalson, interview, B29, C1–2.

47. See Welch, *Protecting Human Rights in Africa*, 219.

48. See Wiseberg, "Human Rights NGO's," 27–28; Posner and Whittome, "The Status of Human Rights NGOs," 286–287. Wiseberg notes that one organization, "[t]he International Service for Human Rights, was created in an attempt to assist NGO's to find their way around the UN system and to bring some measure of coordination into NGO UN work. The Service, however, operates with very limited resources; it is only a beginning and only a partial solution." Wiseberg, "Human Rights NGO's," 40 n.33.

49. Welch observes that the debates in Africa over the origin of rights thinking have faded, a development he welcomes as a sign of the growing embrace of rights by Africans themselves. Welch, *Protecting Human Rights in Africa*, 289. But an African reviewer maintains that the question of cultural imperialism remains very important. Makao wa Mutua, "The Politics of Human Rights: Beyond the Abolitionist Paradigm in Africa," *Michigan Journal of International Law* 17 (1996), 597. No doubt in part for reasons not of principle but of political advantage, some Asian states mounted an "assault on the universality of human rights" at the Second World Conference on Human Rights, held in Vienna in 1993. Tolley, *International Commission of Jurists*, 260.

50. Steiner observes that "most of the powerful international NGOs that investigate events primarily in the Third World" are "committed to traditional Western liberal values," focused on civil and political rights. Steiner, *Diverse Partners*, 19. He cites as examples Amnesty International, the Lawyers Committee for Human Rights, and Human Rights Watch. Ibid., 21. Similarly, Welch notes that "[f]ew human rights NGOs have dealt explicitly and easily with the right to development. To many, most notably certain international NGOs, the issue has been perceived as a distraction from seemingly more important tasks." Welch, *Protecting Human Rights in Africa*, 275. See also Tolley, *International Commission of Jurists*, 11–12; Wiseberg, "Human Rights NGO's," 36–37.

Amnesty International describes "[its] specific contribution to the global human rights movement" as "international activism against the violation of certain civil and political rights," principally focused on just four (crucial) issues: "freeing all prisoners of conscience [a category excluding those who have 'used or advocated violence'], ensuring fair and prompt trials for political prisoners, abolish[ing] the death penalty and other cruel treatment of prisoners, [and] end[ing] extrajudicial executions and 'disappearances.'" Amnesty International, *Amnesty International Report: 1994* (London: Amnesty International Publications, 1994), 16 and inside cover page.

Claude Welch Jr., a member of the Human Rights Watch/Africa board, observes that "[f]or most of [Human Rights Watch's] history, civil and political rights have received far greater attention than economic, social, and cultural rights. The specific mandate and 'institutional culture' of Human Rights Watch as a whole emphasize the former." Welch, *Protecting Human Rights in Africa*, 220.

Although the International Commission of Jurists has long given some attention to economic and social rights, a recent study concludes that even in the 1990s the ICJ's "core values remained procedural and Western—democratic elections, popular participation, and fair laws enforced by an independent judiciary." Tolley, *International Commission of Jurists,* 267–268.

The Lawyers Committee for Human Rights "above all seeks to build enduring legal systems and to hold all governments accountable to established human rights standards." Norman Dorsen, "Letter from the Chairman—*The Advisor:* Welcoming Your Participation," *Advisor* (Lawyers Committee for Human Rights) (July 1996), 2. It "see[s] advancing the rule of law as a critical part of [its] mission because it is laws and legal systems that have the capacity to protect human rights in the long term." Fund-raising letter from Michael Posner, executive director of the Lawyers Committee for Human Rights, to Stephen Ellmann, November 21, 1995, 2.

Similarly, another of the oldest international human rights NGOs, the International League for Human Rights, was described in the mid-1970s as "generally . . . Western/ 'liberal' in terms of ideology." Laurie S. Wiseberg and Harry M. Scoble, "The International League for Human Rights: The Strategy of a Human Rights NGO," *Georgia Journal of International and Comparative Law* 7 (1977), 299. The league was one of the parents of the Lawyers Committee for Human Rights, discussed in the preceding paragraph; the other was the Council of New York Law Associates, "a group of some 1,600 young 'public interest' lawyers of the New York City area." Ibid., 308.

51. Wiseberg comments that "a few international NGO's . . . carry enormous weight in determining which issues will be taken up and how they will be framed, which countries and which violations will get maximum exposure, what strategies will prevail, etc." Wiseberg, *Human Rights NGO's,* 41.

52. Many members of the Philippine group SALAG, for example, have learned from both degree programs and shorter conferences abroad. Medina, interview, 26. Justice John Didcott of South Africa commented that a "really quite small group" of South African advocates had had "a lot of exposure" to United States law, and agreed that this had contributed to the rise of public interest practice and adjudication in that country. Didcott, interview, 25. David Smuts, founder of the Legal Assistance Centre in Namibia, "came into close contact with American civil rights lawyers" while studying at Harvard Law School early in the 1980s. Welch, *Protecting Human Rights in Africa,* 185. On the other hand, Obiageli Nwankwo of the FIDA Family Centre Centre in Enugu, Nigeria, observed that the members of her group who had foreign degrees were not the ones who had been most active in their program. O. Nwankwo, interview, 17.

53. Jack Greenberg, former director-counsel of the NAACP Legal Defense Fund, describes his participation in the founding of the Mexican American Legal Defense Fund, the Puerto Rican Legal Defense Fund, and the Asian American Legal Defense Fund, as well as his early assistance to what became the Lambda Legal Defense Fund, in Jack Greenberg, *Crusaders in the Courts: How a Dedicated Band of Lawyers Fought for the Civil Rights Revolution* (New York: Basic Books, 1994), 487–489. Many lawyers with whom the Legal Defense Fund may have had no such direct organizational links, moreover, were undoubtedly inspired by its model. Cf. ibid., 522.

54. The International Human Rights Internship Program (IHRIP) observes, in a memorandum based in part on the work of Mario Gomez, a Sri Lankan alternative lawyer, that "[s]ome of the law-related activities in countries of the South have been influenced by the PIL [public interest law] movement in the U.S., which had a particularly productive period in the 1950s, 1960s and 1970s." IHRIP, "The Legal Resources Project," 2.

55. Greenberg, *Crusaders in the Courts,* 492–493.

56. Chaskalson, interview, A1–4.

57. Moloto, interview, B27.

58. Huq, interview, 16–17.

59. Ziv, interview, 1.

60. Golub, "Democratizing Justice," 28 (discussing the role of Owen Lynch, an American who taught on "indigenous law" at the University of the Philippines law school).

61. Telephone interview with Paul Lebensohn, July 1996. ILSA's new president is also an American (ibid.) and its board has included a limited number of North American members. Rojas and Clark, "Editors' Introduction," 14. ILSA received funding support from the Carter administration (Lebensohn, interview), and in the 1990s its funders have included the Canadian government, the Ford Foundation, the MacArthur Foundation and NOVIB. See *Beyond Law* (an ILSA publication) (title pages of issues 9–12, published 1994–1995).

62. Representatives of one of these networks, Women in Law and Development in Africa (WiLDAF), participated in the 1991 symposium. The others are the Asia Pacific Forum of Women in Law and Development, and the Latin American Committee for the Defense of Women's Rights. Moreover, these different networks apparently interact, as evidenced in the visits by Elizabeth Dasso of Perú Mujer to Africa. Dasso, interview, 16. All three of these groups grew out of a Third World Forum on Women, Law and Development, held in Nairobi in 1985; this forum was the culmination of the "first phase of the WLD [Women, Law, and Development] Program." Willie Campbell and Elise Smith, "Foreword," in *Empowerment and the Law: Strategies of Third World Women,* ed. Margaret Schuler (Washington: OEF International, 1986), xii. The WLD Program is a project of OEF International, a group started by, but now independent of, the League of Women Voters. Butegwa and VeneKlasen, interview, 1 (VeneKlasen). Dr. Margaret Schuler of the United States initiated the WLD Program in 1983. Margaret Schuler and Sakuntla Kadirgunar-Rajasingham, eds., *Legal Literacy: A Tool for Women's Empowerment* (New York: Women, Law and Development-OEF International, 1992), xi. Funding support has come from the Ford Foundation and other sources. Margaret Schuler, "Acknowledgements," in *Empowerment,* ed. Schuler, xiii.

For a brief indication of the links between this program and alternative law conceptions, see Margaret Schuler and Sakuntla Kadirgunar-Rajasingham, "Legal Literacy: A Tool for Women's Empowerment," in Schuler and Kadirgunar-Rajasingham, eds., *Legal Literacy,* 34–35, 65 n.5.

63. Yash Tandon, "Foreign Ngos, Uses and Abuses: An African Perspective," *IFDA Dossier* (April–June 1991), 68–78. Tandon stresses that Western donors are accountable first and foremost to their own societies and/or governments, and that all of these societies "have had a history of over 400 years of plunder of Africa." Ibid., 74.

64. Mutua, "The Politics of Human Rights," 607, quoting Makao wu Mutua, "Domestic Human Rights in Africa: Problems and Perspectives," *Issue* 22 (1994), 31. See also Arthur W. Blaser, "Human Rights in the Third World and Development of International Nongovernmental Organizations," in George W. Shepherd Jr. and Ved P. Nanda, eds., *Human Rights and Third World Development* (Westport, Conn.: Greenwood Press, 1985), 276–277.

65. For one expression of such criticisms, emerging out of the 1991 symposium, see the discussion of "[o]rganizational problems with funding and donor organizations" from the perspective of the Kenyan group Kituo Cha Sheria (Legal Advice Centre), in Hutchins and Klaaren, *Public Interest Law,* 90–91.

The tense discussion at the 1991 symposium may have influenced a carefully circumscribed form of international linkage that was initiated afterward. This linkage consists of a Legal Resources Project, under the auspices of the International Human Rights Internship Program, that is meant to enhance internship placement decisions and "to develop a clearinghouse of information on legal services, human rights [and] public interest law, and clinical legal education programs that will be accessible to other organizations." IHRIP, *Staff Development and Training Grants Available for 1994–95* (Washington, D.C.: International Human Rights Internship Program, [1993]). The IHRIP, of which this project is a part, places particular emphasis on arranging "South-South" training experiences, in which activists from one Third World, or southern, nation learn from their counterparts in another. IHRIP, *IHRIP Program*, 5.

66. Tolley comments that "[s]ince 1959 the ICJ had advocated a dynamic rule of law that included economic justice." Tolley, *International Commission of Jurists*, 144; see ibid., 71–72. He also notes, though, that the International Covenant on Economic, Social and Cultural Rights approved by the United Nations "went far beyond the ICJ's general call for economic justice." Ibid., 77. The ICJ's attention to economic rights gradually increased; "[i]n a major 1981 conference at The Hague, the ICJ connected development to the rule of law." Ibid., 144; see 145. Still, Tolley comments, "[p]rogressive American and European [ICJ] leaders advocated economic rights to a greater extent than did other NGOs but made minimal demands for enforceable standards." Ibid., 183.

67. "Within eighteen months of Dieng's appointment [in 1990]," Tolley writes, "a transformed [ICJ] Executive Committee had a new chairman and third world majority." Ibid., 248. The staff came to have "no leading Western professionals." Ibid., 266. (As in many NGOs, staff in the ICJ have substantial discretion, see ibid., 255, 268–269.) Although "[f]ew new Third World [affiliate] groups organized," ibid., 253, the ICJ continued its already established pattern of appointing substantial numbers of Third World jurists as members of the commission. See ibid., 251. Third World lawyers were also appointed to carry out a number of studies and missions for the commission; in one case, an Ecuadorian lawyer monitored a trial in the United States, something of a reversal of ordinary INGO patterns. Ibid., 265–266.

Moreover, economic, social, and cultural rights were identified as one of the ICJ's "three main issue areas," (ibid., 259), with particular attention given to land rights, government corruption, and the rights of indigenous peoples (ibid., 257–258). Dieng also took advocacy of development beyond abstraction by "criticizing Western banks and debt relations with the Third World." Ibid., 257. But while "[t]he ICJ's substantive rule of law doctrine was expanded to include land rights and more elements of democratic socialism . . . the core values," as noted earlier, "remained procedural and Western." Ibid., 267.

68. Welch, *Protecting Human Rights in Africa*, 164, 274. Welch calls Mbaye's analysis "highly influential," though he notes that it was not the first call for recognition of this right. Ibid., 281 n.18 (citing earlier, apparently Western sources).

69. See text and note at note 185. For this very reason, organizations such as Amnesty International, the International Commission of Jurists, and the Lawyers Committee for Human Rights have all made the protection of activists a special concern. See *Amnesty Report: 1994*, 1–9; Tolley, *International Commission of Jurists*, 218–240 (describing the work of the ICJ's Centre for the Independence of Judges and Lawyers); ibid., 224 (describing the Lawyers Committee's Lawyer to Lawyer Network, which organizes letters on behalf of victimized legal professionals through a mailing list of over five thousand lawyers, judges, professors, and others); Lawyers Committee for Human Rights, *Shackling the Defenders: Legal Restrictions on Independent Human Rights Advocacy Worldwide* (New York: Lawyers Committee for Human Rights, 1994) (compiling instances of suppression of human rights advocacy around the world).

70. For an analysis of both the limits and importance of rights as resources for the poor, by a leading exponent of an alternative or "legal resources approach" to legal practice,

see Clarence Dias, "Human Rights and Legal Resources for Development," in *Law, Human Rights and Legal Services: Proceedings,* 45–66.

71. LDF's work has surely influenced other lawyers' sense of the strategic potentials of law reform campaigns and, I suspect, has also fostered an emphasis on, and belief in the effectiveness of, highly "professional," technically adept legal work. In an astonishing passage, Jack Greenberg writes that "[w]hen Thurgood [Marshall] was in law school he once carried some legal papers to court for a black practitioner. They were messy. The clerk looked them over and commented, 'A nigger brief.' Thurgood vowed we [at the NAACP Legal Defense Fund] never would file 'nigger briefs.'" Greenberg, *Crusaders in the Courts,* 71.

72. See Patricia J. Williams, *The Alchemy of Race and Rights: Diary of a Law Professor* (Cambridge, Mass.: Harvard University Press, 1991), 146–165; Kimberlé Williams Crenshaw, "Race, Reform and Retrenchment: Transformation and Legitimation in Antidiscrimination Law," *Harvard Law Review* 101 (1988), 1356–1369, 1381–1387; Richard Delgado, "The Ethereal Scholar: Does Critical Legal Studies Have What Minorities Want?", *Harvard Civil Rights–Civil Liberties Law Review* 22 (1987), 303–312.

73. Jan Egeland and Thomas Kerbs, eds., *Third World Organisational Development: A Comparison of NGO Strategies,* HDI Series on Development no. 1 (Geneva: Henry Dunant Institute, 1987), 58.

74. *Amnesty Report: 1994,* 12, 13. According to the report, the 1993 biennial AI International Council Meeting (the organization's "supreme policy making body") "was the most internationally representative ever." Ibid., 16. It is not clear from the report, however, whether the growth in the organization's Third World structures has actually resulted in Third World members becoming a larger proportion of the total membership; as of the mid-1980s the rapid growth of First World membership meant that its Third World members "constitute[d] a small and decreasing portion of its total membership." Egeland and Kerbs, eds., *Third World Organisational Development,* 62. Commenting on a 1989 conference, Steiner characterizes Amnesty's "International Executive Committee [as] includ[ing] a cross-section of Third World members, while its staff has a First World character and the great percentage of its members live in the First World." Steiner, *Diverse Partners,* 61.

Human Rights Watch/Africa was wrestling with similar concerns. Welch describes the concern of Abdullahi An-Na'im, a scholar and the executive director of Human Rights Watch/Africa from 1993 to 1995, that his organization should "work cooperatively with African human rights NGOs to break what he calls a growing 'human rights dependency.'" Attention needed to be given, An-Na'im felt, "to the 'context and experience' of individual cultures. Human Rights Watch/Africa 'needs to collaborate with competent and credible local human rights NGOs in collecting information, verifying and corroborating allegations of violations, planning and implementation of advocacy strategies, and so forth.'" Welch observes that "[p]artnerships of this sort would represent a new direction, and to critics within HRW as a whole might undercut its civil and political rights emphasis, and its quality control through largely self-generated studies." Welch, *Protecting Human Rights in Africa,* 221–222.

75. Rojas, "A Comparison of Change-Oriented Legal Services," 229.

76. Rojas comments that new legal services groups have rapidly embraced the terminology of "community development," and suggests that "this is a 'compromise word', one of those vague and fancy development notions that one way or another are acceptable to most if not all political ideologies. As such, it satisfies the ideological and bureaucratic requirements of funding development agencies while still providing legal services groups with enough room to configure their own organizational purposes." Ibid., 253 n.6.

77. See Greenberg, *Crusaders in the Courts* 211, 371–372. Years later, an LDF alumna, Lynn Walker, became the head of Ford's Rights and Social Justice program, through which many of the groups at the 1991 symposium were probably funded. See ibid., 522; see also note 3 (on Ford support for groups at this symposium.)

78. Golub, "Democratizing Justice," 54.

79. Ibid., 111.

80. Ibid., 94.

81. See note 69.

82. Foreign support, however, can also open an NGO to damaging charges that it is a pawn of foreign interests. On both the benefits and costs of international links, see, e.g, Steiner, *Diverse Partners*, 69–70.

83. The work of the Women, Law and Development Program has been briefly described in text and note at note 62.

The Latin American Institute of Alternative Legal Services (ILSA), described in text and note at note 61, has not only worked to develop a Latin American and Caribbean network but also published an English-language journal meant to reach alternative lawyers around the world. See Rojas and Clark, "Editors' Introduction," 10, 12.

The International Commission of Jurists has also worked to develop regional networks. In Africa, according to Welch, a series of ICJ-sponsored workshops held in advance of sessions of the African Commission on Human and Peoples' Rights have not only enhanced activists' awareness of ACHPR processes but also "encourag[ed] NGOs' awareness of each other." Welch, *Protecting Human Rights in Africa*, 166. Welch calls this "[t]he most important recent ICJ contribution to human rights in Africa," and maintains that "[t]he ICJ thus took on an undisputed (though not tension-free) role as the leading international NGO focused on networking among African human rights NGOs." Ibid., 167. The ICJ "encouraged ASEAN (Association of Southeast Asian Nations) civil rights lawyers to create a Regional Council on Human Rights in Asia"; two of its twelve founders were ICJ members. Tolley, *International Commission of Jurists*, 151–152. It attempted to foster a Caribbean organization, and succeeded in starting the Andean Commission of Jurists. See ibid., 153.

The International Center for Law and Development sought to foster a three-tier approach to the legal needs of the Asian poor, in which "[t]he Hong Kong-based Asian Coalition of Human Rights Organizations was to operate on an international tier." Golub, "Democratizing Justice," 27. The ICLD's president, Clarence Dias, is also on the board of ILSA.

84. The flavor of the Lawyers Committee's approach is reflected in a fundraising appeal by its chairman, Michael Posner. He asks: "But how do we, a US-based organization, help develop protective legal frameworks and enforcement mechanisms in other countries? The answer is by collaborating with local partners, in this case, local human rights advocates and organizations—who are the ones in the position to challenge, prod and ultimately change their own legal systems. Local groups set the agenda for reform, and our job is to do whatever we can to support their efforts." He goes on to list forms of support including "legal strategies, research, communications equipment, entree to powerful international and multilateral bodies, access to the media, international pressure and/or validation, [and] links to other grassroots human rights groups." Fund-raising letter from Michael Posner to Stephen Ellmann, November 21, 1995, 2 (punctuation altered from original).

85. The International Human Rights Internship Program project is described in note 65. Human Rights Internet (HRI) has also played a valuable role in stimulating networking, both by compiling the information contained in the *Masterlist* (see text at note 13) and by direct efforts to bring groups together, for example in Asia in the early 1980s (see Scoble and Wiseberg, eds., *Access to Justice*, xi–xii). See also Steiner, *Diverse Partners* (reporting on

1989 meeting cosponsored by HRI). HURIDOCS (Human Rights Information and Documentation Systems International), chaired by a Ghanaian law professor, "seeks to establish the technical foundation on which systematic monitoring [of human rights abuses] will be possible," both by developing a standardized format for reporting information and by training people in documentation, for example in workshops in Africa. Welch, *Protecting Human Rights in Africa,* 225.

86. Emma Playfair, "INTERIGHTS—An International Human Rights Law Centre," *Public Law* 1994 (1994), 574. Playfair is the executive director of this organization.

87. Steiner writes that "[t]he large majority of today's human rights NGOs . . . start[ed] . . . as critics of governmental repression of political activitiy through intimidation or violence." Steiner, *Diverse Partners,* 9. Among these groups would be Tutela Legal of El Salvador, founded in 1982, which Steiner cites (ibid.) as an example of a group that has chosen not to expand its work to include economic rights. Another was FLAG, the Free Legal Assistance Group of the Philippines (founded in 1974), which "was principally concerned with preventing human rights abuses and defending Filipinos against politically motivated imprisonment and accusations of national security offenses by the Marcos regime and the military." Golub, "Democratizing Justice," 25. But even some of the older groups have had wider concerns. The Vicaría de la Solidaridad, which "officially began its work in 1976," was a response to Pinochet's ferocious repression in Chile, but it provided health and nutritional services and also sought to assist poor Chileans in developing economic self-help programs. Americas Watch, *The Vicaría de la Solidaridad in Chile: An Americas Watch Report* 8, 10–11, 27–29 (New York: Americas Watch, 1977). South Africa's Legal Resources Centre, which opened in 1979, appear to have focused much more on the injustices of apartheid than on the additional evils of that nation's internal security regime. See Hutchins and Klaaren, *Public Interest Law,* 159–161.

88. Michael Posner emphasized this point for me.

89. David Smuts mentions in his interview that, with the assistance of Arthur Chaskalson of South Africa, he "was instrumental . . . in getting Judge Bhagwati to come to Namibia, and it was very important to have him speak to our judges and people within the government, because I think that the Indian experience of their Constitution and their interpretation of it is very helpful." Smuts, interview, 31. Cf. Olisa Agbakoba, "The Role of Non-Governmental Organisations in the Development and Protection of Individual Rights," in *Individual Rights under the 1989 Constitution,* ed. M. A. Ajomo and Bolaji Owasanoye (Lagos: Nigerian Institute of Advanced Legal Studies, 1993), 148–150 (citing Bhagwati and expressing his hope that the Nigerian Supreme Court will "unequivocally and authoritatively endorse the attitude of the Indian and Canadian Supreme Courts on the question of *locus standi* within the context of Public Interest Disputes").

90. P. N. Bhagwati, "Judicial Activism and Public Interest Litigation," *Columbia Journal of Transnational Law* 23 (1985), 571.

91. Ibid., 571, 574, 575–576. For additional information on public interest litigation in India, see Jill Cottrell, "Courts and Accountability: Public Interest Litigation in the Indian High Courts," *Third World Legal Studies—1992* (1992), 199–213; Susan D. Susman, "Distant Voices in the Courts of India: Transformation of Standing in Public Interest Litigation," *Wisconsin International Law Journal* 13 (1994), 57–103. Justice Bhagwati himself was a principal architect of these changes. Ibid., 70 (citing the role of Bhagwati, Justice Krishna Iyer, and two other justices).

92. Dias, "Human Rights and Legal Resources," 61–62. There are commonalities between Indian developments and those in Indonesia and the Philippines, as Dias suggests (ibid., 63), but there also appear to be important differences between Indian public interest

law and the new conceptions of structural or alternative legal service in Indonesia and the Philippines. In both of these other countries, new directions in legal service appear to have been at least partly the result of the gross inadequacies of those nations' judiciaries. See Golub, "Democratizing Justice," 22–23, 54–56 (Philippines); Lawyers Committee for Human Rights, *Shackling the Defenders*, 45 (characterizing the Indonesian judiciary as "a minor player within the state bureaucracy and lack[ing] independence"); Mario Gomez, "Bogota and Beyond: The South's Search for Alternatives," *Beyond Law* (July 1992), 144 (mentioning Indonesia as a country in which political elites "usurped the legal system, to such an extent that the system lost all credibility with the bulk of its population"). By contrast, India's public interest litigation, is (at least in the view of Justice Bhagwati) "primarily judge-led and even to some extent judge-induced." Bhagwati, "Judicial Activism," 561.

Perhaps more important, while alternative lawyering theories often place great emphasis on responsiveness to clients (see text at note 96), the judicial relaxation of standing requirements in India means that clients need not exist at all. It appears, in fact, that some Indian public interest litigation—though certainly not all—may be conducted by lawyers who have no contact, or almost none, with those for whom they are allowed to speak. Cases can be brought by activists who invoke the court's epistolary jurisdiction after reading a newspaper article rather than after meeting with the people the article is about. Cf. Susman, "Distant Voices in the Courts of India," 58, 89 (citing such a case); Bhagwati, "Judicial Activism," 573 (observing that "the relationship between social action groups and the press has provided a fertile ground for the growth of public interest litigation"). In truth, it may be difficult or impossible for would-be advocates to have substantial contact with the people they want to assist. Susman reports an example of a case in which the lawyers met with the clients' community once, "but then assumed responsibility for pursuing the suit as they thought best. Further consultation was nearly impossible because the lawyers did not have time to return to the village with any frequency, nor were there any telephones in the village. . . . The lawyers (named petitioners) used their best judgment, both as to what the injured parties might have wanted as the case developed, and as to what the court would be likely to give, and therefore, how far they could push. . . . [They] cannot be faulted for doing only what was humanly possible." Susman, "Distant Voices in the Courts of India," 92–93.

93. Aside from a similar name, the Legal Resources Foundation appears to share at least one significant structural feature with the Legal Resources Centre: both are ultimately governed by boards of trustees composed, at least in part, of people of notable prestige in their respective countries. See Manase, interview, 8, 11; Chaskalson, interview, B14–B18.

94. Welch mentions the inspiration provided by the Legal Resources Centre, and also notes that Geoff Budlender, later the national director of the LRC, recommended establishing a similar organization in Namibia in a feasibility study for the Ford Foundation. Welch, *Protecting Human Rights in Africa*, 186–187. In his interview at the 1991 symposium, David Smuts commented that the reputation of the Legal Resources Centre was critically important to the successful establishment of the Legal Assistance Centre in Namibia. Smuts, interview, 9–10. At one point, Arthur Chaskalson, then the South African group's national director, successfully represented the Namibian group when it faced a government attempt to close it down, and Geoff Budlender as of 1991 was serving on the Namibian group's board. Ibid., 28–29; Chaskalson describes the court case in question in my interview with him, C8–10.

95. And it is not the only term in use. Stephen Golub chooses the term "developmental legal services" and comments that organizations of this sort are "described by a

plethora of labels (e.g., alternative law, legal resources, developmental legal aid, structural legal aid, strategic legal services, innovative legal services) and often distinguished from each other by their operations, priorities, country contexts and even philosophies, [but] they share an orientation of seeking to address underlying developmental issues by enhancing popular participation in formulating and implementing laws, policies and other government decisions." Golub, "Democratizing Justice," 5.

96. See Brandt, "Human Rights," 29–34; Dias, "Human Rights and Legal Resources," 63–65; Golub, "Democratizing Justice," 5–11; Gomez, "Bogota and Beyond," passim; Hall and Fretz, "Legal Services," 786; Nasution, "Legal Aid Movement in Indonesia," 35–37; Rojas, "A Comparison of Change-Oriented Legal Services," 208–209, 238–240.

97. See Stephen Ellmann, "Client-Centeredness Multiplied: Individual Autonomy and Collective Mobilization in Public Interest Lawyers' Representation of Groups," *Virginia Law Review* 78 (1992), 1103–1104 (and sources cited there).

98. The literature of client-centeredness is now extensive. One of the leading texts embodying this perspective is David A. Binder, Paul Bergman, and Susan C. Price, *Lawyers as Counselors: A Client-Centered Approach* (St. Paul, Minn.: West, 1991).

99. Rojas observes that "[t]he types of legal issues new legal services engage in are not particularly different from those assumed by other legal services in Latin America or elsewhere. As usual, legal advice is the most frequent service legal groups provide, followed by representation in courts, police or administrative agencies." Rojas, "A Comparison of Change-Oriented Legal Services," 245. Most programs in the survey Rojas reports apparently placed relatively little emphasis on mediation or alternative dispute resolution. See ibid. Despite the alternative law paradigm's critique of legalistic efforts at piecemeal law reform, Rojas reports that 63 percent of the alternative legal services groups surveyed "participate in law reform efforts." Ibid., 246. Similarly, despite the alternative law emphasis on the training of paralegals, the seventy-five programs in four countries that Rojas examines apparently were working with only a total of thirty-nine paralegals. Ibid., 242. This is not to say that change-oriented and traditional legal services were identical, for the new legal services groups placed greater emphasis on "popular education and paralegal training, sociolegal research and organization activities" than their traditional counterparts, and also handled cases dealing with different issues. Ibid., 245. But the differences in practice should not be exaggerated. See also Steiner, *Diverse Partners,* 29 (suggesting that Third World NGOs may analyze rights issues differently from their Western counterparts but often act similarly in response to the sheer exigency of gross human rights violations); Meili, "The Interaction between Lawyers and Grass Roots Movements," 66 n.12 (quoting a Brazilian cause lawyer who maintains that alternative law activities "represent practical ways of dealing with problems. 'And these practical ways of dealing with problems have existed since the first lawyer existed. So, there's nothing "alternative" in that.' ").

Even as a matter of theory, one leading exponent of alternative law has suggested that lawyers can provide valuable "legal resources" to the poor in decidedly conventional areas of law, which cause lawyers "have usually neglected, such as international trade law. Subsidies, dumping, countervailing duties, and non-tariff barriers become legal concepts of vital importance and relevance to communities of producers and consumers alike." Clarence Dias, "Challenging the Structures of Injustice in the South and in the North: Asian Legal Resource and Human Rights Organizations in the 'New' World Order," *Beyond Law* (July 1992), 127.

100. All of the following commentators maintain or imply that alternative law thinking is the work of people from one or more areas of the Third World: Brandt, "Human Rights," 29 ("During the past decade, above all in Latin America and Asia, new legal aid strategies

have been developed."); Dias, "Human Rights and Legal Resources," 59–66 (at one point [ibid., 66] referring to "uniquely Asian approaches"); Gomez, "Bogota and Beyond," 139 ("[t]he movement for alternative law originated in response to the failure of traditional political elites to effect any significant tranformation in the societies of the South"); Rojas, "A Comparison of Change-Oriented Legal Services," 204 (Latin American new legal services "are different from legal services in other regions of the world," and in particular from those of the West); ibid., 220 ("Latin American new legal services . . . are the meeting place of a variety of forces and social phenomena peculiar to the recent history of the subcontinent"). Hall and Fretz suggest a somewhat different view, arguing that the flawed efforts to export American legal perspectives in the "law and development movement," together with "successful efforts to promote legal services for the poor within the United States, created interest in legal services in the developing world during the 1980s." Hall and Fretz, "Legal Services," 785. As the preceding comments suggest, alternative law seems to have developed in more than one location, but apparently not equally in all. Golub observes that alternative law is "most prevalent in Latin America," whereas it seems to be much less widespread in Asia and to have only a "limited presence" in Africa. Golub, "Democratizing Justice," 5.

Third World activists and scholars who have contributed to the growth of alternative law thinking clearly include Fernando Rojas (Hurtado), who led ILSA for many years, and Clarence Dias, the president of the International Center for Law and Development. Dias also emphasizes the roles of José Diokno of the Philippines and T. Mulya Lubis and Buyung Nasution of Indonesia. See Dias, "Human Rights and Legal Resources," 59–61.

In addition, among the Third World practitioners of alternative law are a number of lawyers interviewed at the 1991 symposium. Such groups as the Indonesian Legal Aid Foundation, SALAG in the Philippines, Mexico's DOAL, Colombia's FUNCOL, Perú Mujer, and CESPAD in El Salvador all can probably be categorized as alternative law groups. A number of others, such as the Lawyers Collective in India, Kituo Cha Sheria in Kenya, the Legal Assistance Centre in Namibia, the Legal Resources Centre in South Africa, the Legal Resources Foundation in Zimbabwe, and Women in Law and Development in Africa would share at least some common philosophical ground with "alternative" law thinkers. Indeed, Hutchins and Klaaren report that at the 1991 symposium "[a]ll agreed that political empowerment [certainly a touchstone of alternative lawyering] was a valuable use of public interest law." Hutchins and Klaaren, *Public Interest Law*, 11.

It seems likely that the thinking of the Brazilian educator Paolo Freire has also played a significant role in shaping alternative law, and in particular its concern with the process of empowerment through popular legal education. In this regard Margaret Schuler and Sakuntala Kadirgamar-Rajasingham, who focus on "legal literacy" programs in the context of women's struggles, have observed that "[u]nderstanding the dynamic of transformative, liberative learning for women is essential to developing a framework for legal literacy. The work of Paolo Freire provides an important source for this understanding, concerned as it is with the processes by which the oppressed became liberated from the structural constraints that limit social, intellectual and political participation." Schuler and Kadirgamar-Rajasingham, "Legal Literacy," 41. See generally Paolo Freire, *Pedagogy of the Oppressed*, trans. Myra Bergman Ramos (New York: Continuum, 1972).

101. Rojas observes that "Latin American lawyers involved in new legal services seem to share some of the concerns and practices of critical lawyers and activist lawyers in the North, such as the Critical Legal Studies movement and the National Lawyers Guild in the U.S., or the law and state working group of the CSE in Great Britain." Rojas, "A Comparison of Change-Oriented Legal Services," 212.

Among works of scholarship in the United States that similarly seek to recast the relations between lawyers for poor and subordinated people and their clients are Anthony V. Alfieri, "Reconstructive Poverty Law Practice: Learning Lessons of Client Narrative," *Yale Law Journal* 100 (1991), 2107–2147; Gerald P. López, "Reconceiving Civil Rights Practice: Seven Weeks in the Life of a Rebellious Collaboration," *Georgetown Law Journal* 77 (1989), 1608–1717; William H. Simon, "Visions of Practice in Legal Thought," *Stanford Law Review* 36 (1984), 469–507; Stephen Wexler, "Practicing Law for Poor People," *Yale Law Journal* 79 (1970), 1049–1067; Lucie E. White, "To Learn and Teach: Lessons from Driefontein on Lawyering and Power," *Wisconsin Law Review* 1988 (1988), 699–769. Carrie Menkel-Meadow has been a leader of the related enterprise of reconceiving lawyer-client relations in light of feminist perspectives. See, e.g., Carrie Menkel-Meadow, "Portia in a Different Voice: Reflections on a Women's Lawyering Process," *Berkeley Women's Law Journal* 1 (1985), 39–63; Carrie Menkel-Meadow, "What's Gender Got to Do with It?: The Politics and Morality of an Ethic of Care," *New York University Review of Law and Social Change* 1996 (1996), 265–293. See also Stephen Ellmann, "The Ethic of Care as an Ethic for Lawyers," *Georgetown Law Journal* 81 (1993), 2665–2726, and sources cited ibid., 2678 n.35.

102. See text and notes at notes 60–62.

103. White, "To Learn and Teach," 760–765.

104. For reflections on this movement, see John Henry Merryman, "Comparative Law and Social Change: On the Origins, Style, Decline and Revival of the Law and Development Movement," *American Journal of Comparative Law* 25 (1997), 457–491; James C. N. Paul, "American Law Teachers and Africa: Some Historical Observations," *Journal of African Law* 31 (1988), 18–28; Robert B. Seidman, "The Lessons of Self-Estrangement: On the Methodology of Law and Development," *Research in Law and Sociology* 1 (1978), 1–29; David M. Trubek and Marc Galanter, "Scholars in Self-Estrangement: Some Reflections on the Crisis in Law and Development Studies in the United States," *Wisconsin Law Review* 1974 (1974), 1062–1102.

105. On "law and development" funding, see Merryman, "Comparative Law," 457–458; Trubek and Galanter, "Scholars in Self-Estrangement," 1066–1067.

106. Merryman, "Comparative Law," 479.

107. Ibid., 483.

108. Trubek and Galanter, "Scholars in Self-Estrangement," 1070–1074.

109. Ibid., 1075–1076. On the legal realism of the "legal apologists" for the Argentine junta, see Mark J. Osiel, "Dialogue with Dictators: Judicial Resistance in Argentina and Brazil," *Law and Social Inquiry* 20 (1995), 514–516; and for the more mixed impact of legal realism in Brazil, see ibid., 538–539. Speaking of the continent generally, Osiel comments that "[w]hile Latin America's most conscientious democrats and constitutionalists were deeply skeptical, those who supported the new authoritarian regimes in the region were keenly attracted to legal realism. . . . The legal realism from North America facilitated a rapprochement between the important segments of the legal profession and authoritarian rulers." Ibid., 539.

110. On this aspect of law and development, see Trubek and Galanter, "Scholars in Self-Estrangement," 1076–1078.

111. Ibid., 1092.

112. Ibid., 1091.

113. Ibid., 1092.

114. Ibid., 1099–1100.

115. See text and notes at notes 7–11, 28–31.

116. For an instance of political lawyers without a tradition of legal activism, see Bish-

arat, "Attorneys for the People" (this volume). At the 1991 symposium, David Smuts characterized Namibian lawyers as having no human rights tradition except in the defense of political crimes. Smuts, interview, B44. Indira Jaising, similarly, commented that the Indian legal profession had no public interest law tradition as such, but that there was a tradition of defense of political activists (and that many leading politicians had been lawyers). Jaising, interview, 8–9. (Another Indian observer, however, perceived a tradition of human rights work in the Indian legal profession, because of the inspiration of the independence movement. Madhavan, interview, 7.)

117. Ellmann, *In a Time of Trouble,* 252.

118. Lawyers, like other members of the middle classes, may also often be disposed to favor agendas of social change that emphasize peaceful and ordered social life rather than the chaos of revolutionary transformation. Daniel Lev, for example, suggests that in both Indonesia and Malaysia a number of social sectors, notably including various segments of the middle class, share an interest in the strengthening of the rule of law. Lev, "Lawyers' Causes in Indonesia and Malaysia," chap. 13 of this volume. Similarly, Claude Welch observes that "lawyers and professors took the lead in creating . . . [explicitly human rights oriented NGOs in Africa], drawing on their professional skills and interests. An urban, middle-class, civil and political rights orientation has been a natural consequence." Welch, *Human Rights in Africa,* 312–313.

119. Francisco Díaz Rodríguez, of El Salvador's Center for Studies on the Application of Law (CESPAD), criticized the tendency of progressives in El Salvador and Latin America to ignore the task of changing the law in favor of the job of changing the state, a decision which he said diminished the contribution that law could make. Díaz Rodríguez, speaking at 1991 symposium, plenary session on "Methods of Using Law to Effect Social Change (continued)—Alternative Uses of the Law and Participating Popular Education/Investigation" (May 20, 1991), 10. He also offered a striking instance of the need to keep the law in mind. The very cumbersome procedure available for amending El Salvador's constitution at one point became the focus of intense attention because it posed a potential obstacle to constitutional changes envisioned as part of the settlement of the civil war—and yet the traditional human rights groups of that country had nothing to say on this issue. Ibid., 13; Díaz Rodríguez, interview, 5.

120. Hiroshi Oda, "The Procuracy and the Regular Courts as Enforcers of the Constitutional Rule of Law: The Experience of East Asian States," *Tulane Law Review* 61 (1987), 1346.

121. Perhaps the most vivid modern example of a statutory order meant to constrain the theoretical, and sometimes very real, independence of judges was in South Africa under apartheid. See, e.g., Ellmann, *In a Time of Trouble,* 11–25.

122. See, e.g., Hutchins and Klaaren, *Public Interest Law,* 32 (reporting the Madaripur Legal Aid Association's "continual struggle of trying to find justice for its clients through a judicial system that is prohibitively expensive, exceedingly slow, and influenced by political pressures and corruption"); LCHR, *Shackling the Defenders,* 45 (Indonesian judiciary "a minor player within the state bureaucracy and lacks independence"); Agbakoba, "The Role of Non-Governmental Organisations," 157 (referring to Nigeria's "highly compromised and dependent judicial system"); Elizabeth Dasso, "Paralegals as Community Resources in Peru: Asociación Perú Mujer," in *Legal Literacy,* ed. Schuler and Kadirgamar-Rajasingham, 164–165 (Peruvian judges "generally apply a law conditioned by a dominant ideology that discriminates against, and undervalues persons who are not part of the group in power"); Madhavan, interview, 8–9, 12 (lower level judges in India tend to be in the local authorities' pockets); Meili, "The Interaction between Lawyers and Grass Roots Movements," 75 (char-

acterizing Brazilian judges as having been spineless and corrupt; but for a more positive appraisal of the Brazilian judiciary, see Osiel, "Dialogue with Dictators," 533–540).

123. For an analysis of the systemic inequities of American courts, see Marc Galanter, "Why the 'Haves' Come Out Ahead: Speculations on the Limits of Legal Change," *Law and Society Review* 9 (1974), 95–160. For examples from the Third World, see Hutchins and Klaaren, *Public Interest Law,* 54 (citing, from the perspective of the Indian group AWARE, the Indian courts' "backlog of 500,000 cases pending from as far back as 25 years ago," and other prohibitive barriers to poor people's effective access to justice); Dasso, "Paralegals," 170 (citing a Perú Mujer survey of disadvantaged communities in Lima that finds "that 40 percent of the population did not 'exist' from the standpoint of the law, which is to say they did not have a birth certificate, a requirement for exercising civil and political rights").

124. Steiner, *Diverse Partners,* 33, 44.

125. Bhagwati, interview, 20 ("[T]he poor and the disadvantaged [in India] have no faith in the capacity of the legal and judicial system to give them justice. They always find that they are on the wrong side of the law."); Dias, "Human Rights and Legal Resources," 57 ("[T]he rural poor tend to adopt an attitude of legal nihilism; the least they can have do with law the better!"); Clarence J. Dias and James C. N. Paul, "Lawyers, Legal Resources and Alternative Approaches to Development," in *Lawyers in the Third World: Comparative and Developmental Perspectives,* ed. C. J. Dias, R. Luckham, D. O. Lynch, and J. C. N. Paul (Uppsala: Scandinavian Institute of African Studies and New York: International Center for Law and Development, 1981), 372 (noting that in Third World rural communities "there is often a general ignorance of the content and nature of official legal structures, and aversion to them"); Golub, "Democratizing Justice," 54–55 (attributing limited use of test case litigation in the Philippines in part to client popular organizations' reportedly "tend[ing] to shy away from courts"); Meili, "The Interaction between Lawyers and Grass Roots Movements," 75 (observing that most lawyers and nonlawyers in Brazil do not see the courts as a path to redress for the poor); Schuler and Kadirgamar-Rajasingham, "Legal Literacy," 26–27 ("[I]t is probably safe to conclude that most women on the face of the earth do not think of themselves as having rights, much less as having any relationship with the official legal system."); Adolfo Triana Antorveza, speaking at 1991 symposium, plenary session on "Methods of Using Law to Effect Social Change (continued)—Traditional Uses of the Law in Non-Traditional Settings" (May 22, 1991), 17 (citing the delegitimation of law ["un gran desprestigio de la administración de justicia"] in Latin America and especially Colombia).

126. Stephen Ellmann, "Law and Legitimacy in South Africa," *Law and Social Inquiry* 20 (1995), 407–479. George Bisharat also observes that Palestinian lawyers in Israel's Occupied Territories "seemed to have begun with a nearly naive trust in the bona fides of Israeli legal institutions." Bisharat, "Courting Justice? Legitimation in Lawyering under Israeli Occupation," *Law and Social Inquiry* 20 (1995), 382. He concludes, however, that the courts' "largely unfulfilled promise of relief from arbitrary military government actions arguably has engendered greater cynicism among Palestinians toward Israeli rule than might have been true had military government policies been pursued by unmediated force." Ibid., 384.

127. See IHRIP, "Legal Resources Project," 2–3 (observing that the legal system has more credibility in some former British colonies than elsewhere and mentioning legal work in India, Pakistan, Sri Lanka, and Malaysia); Andrew Harding, "Public Interest Groups, Public Interest Law and Development in Malaysia," *Third World Legal Studies—1992* (1992), 234 (human rights–minded lawyers generally agreed "that whatever the performance of the [Malaysian] judges before 1988, they enjoyed an independence worth preserving"). More-

over, there are some countries, happily, in which cause lawyers are able to see the law as on their side. See, e.g., Manase, interview, 9 (Zimbabwe); Smuts, interview, 16–19 (post-independence Namibia).

128. Golub, "Democratizing Justice," 68.

129. Dias, "Human Rights and Legal Resources," 57.

130. Díaz Rodríguez, speaking at 1991 symposium, plenary session on "Methods of Using Law to Effect Social Change (continued)—Alternative Uses," 10–11 (commenting, in part, that "en El Salvador, puedo afirmar, no existe una cultura de derecho. Y sin embargo, y creo que es el caso de todos los países de América Latina, la población es legalista. La población hace referencia a las leyes y respeta al abogado.").

131. Efrén Rodríguez González, speaking at 1991 symposium, plenary session on "Methods of Using Law to Effect Social Change (continued)—Traditional Uses," 3–4 ("una lucha muy importante durante mucho tiempo sin accesoria jurídica").

132. Díaz Rodríguez, interview, 5; see also Richard F. Klawiter, note, "¡La Tierra Es Nuestra! The Campesino Struggle in El Salvador and a Vision of Community-Based Lawyering," *Stanford Law Review* 42 (1990), 1661 (referring to "use of the legal arena" as the "newest strategy adopted by campesino advocates," apparently only in 1989).

133. Ardila and Clark, "Notes on Alternative Legal Practice," 108.

134. See text and notes at notes 7–11, 28–31.

135. For exploration of legitimation issues in a number of Third World contexts, see the articles in the "Symposium: Lawyering in Repressive States," *Law and Social Inquiry* 20 (1995), 339–599. I outline the issues raised by these articles in my "Editor's Introduction: Struggle and Legitimation," *Law and Social Inquiry* 20 (1995), 339–348. See also Ellmann, *In a Time of Trouble*, 248–274. Important as these questions are, they are not my primary concern here; I will only sketch the kinds of arguments that may contribute to cause lawyers' willingness to pursue their work despite the risk of legitimation.

One alternative law response to the problem of legitimation has been articulated by Ardila and Clark, who argue that unlike labor law work, which "tend[s] to combine the legal and the legitimate," legal action on behalf of the new community movements of Latin America "seldom bring[s] results, leading to the need for and legitimacy of extra-legal action, which in turn undermines state authority". Ardila and Clark, "Notes on Alternative Legal Practice," 109–110. Lawyers who have struggled with these problems may also have become more adept at handling them, by choosing their tactics to avoid inadvertent legitimation. Thus Indira Jaising comments that "when you're working in a legal system where you're demanding those very rights which the system promises you, you are working in a consensual framework. But when you challenge the very fundamentals of the system, then you cannot hope to get any assistance from the law. So you have to know when to challenge it. It doesn't mean we don't challenge it. But it's always a delicate process, of using the system, and yet standing outside it." Jaising, interview, 31.

A related perspective emphasizes the need to help poor people acquire not just an abstract knowledge of their rights, but a "critical" legal literacy that understands the profound limits on what the law can deliver. Schuler and Kadirgamar-Rajasingham, "Legal Literacy," 22–23, 35–36, 47–51. Sharp attacks on the injustice of the existing order, even when framed in the language of the law, may contribute to such critical awareness and thus call into question the very system in which these arguments are made. See Klawiter, "La Tierra Es Nuestra," 1684.

Greater sensitivity to the immediate needs of poor clients may also contribute to diminished concern about the possibility of unsought legitimation. See Rojas, "A Comparison of Change-Oriented Legal Services," 221. So may the recognition that for the poor and disadvantaged, the discovery that they can invoke law on their behalf may help mobilize and legitimate their struggle for justice. See Bhagwati, interview, 5–6 (Public interest litigation "is not a solution for all problems. It is only a catalytic agent, something which sort of gives some support to the public interest groups."); Dias and Paul, "Lawyers, Legal Resources, and Alternative Approaches," 366–367; Jaising, interview, 14 (commenting that the liberalization of standing rules in Indian law has given "a lot of the groups of the oppressed . . . legitimacy, visibility, and a certain respectability that they did not have in the past. This is a major contribution to justice."); Schuler and Kadirgamar-Rajasingham, "Legal Literacy," 32–33 (citing Stuart Scheingold, *The Politics of Rights* [New Haven: Yale University Press, 1974], 136–137).

More broadly still, it may be that legal work on behalf of the poor legitimates the *idea* of the rule of law, and that this powerful idea then operates as a basis for critique of the existing society and as a guide to the building of a new one. So David Smuts suggested in the context of Namibia (Smuts, interview, 49), and the same may be true in South Africa (see Ellmann, "Law and Legitimacy in South Africa," 473–476), and perhaps in Israel's Occupied Territories (see Bisharat, "Courting Justice?" 403–404).

136. Representatives of a substantial range of cause lawyering groups offered such characterizations of their countries' legal systems. See Huq, interview, 18 ("[I]n every state, society, there are good laws and bad laws. And we [in Bangladesh] have got the same."); Jaising, interview, 12 ("[T]here is a tremendous pressure on the Indian political system and on the Indian legal system to respond to the needs of the poor. To that extent, the law is on your side. But there are great obstacles indeed, e.g., implementation of rights."); Madhavan, interview, 16 (citing rights guarantees of the Indian constitution) *(semble)*; Manase, interview, 9 (Zimbabwean law plays an important role in everything his organization does, "and we can always suggest changes to the law to reflect the real situations we live in."); Medina, interview, 16 (the Philippine constitution "provides for all civic, political, economic, social and cultural rights"); Rodríguez González and Godoy Ramos, interview, 8 ("El problema es que las leyes son muy buenas. Las leyes en nuestra constitución [son] muy buena[s], nuestra ley de reforma agraria, nuestro codigo civil. . . . El problema es que no se aplica.") (Rodríguez González) (Mexico); Ziv, interview, 21–22 (despite, or because of, Israel's lack of a bill of rights as such, "the judiciary . . . has leeway and space" to render decisions protecting human rights); cf. Bhagwati, interview, 21 (citing the "tremendous impact" of the Indian constitution's chapter on fundamental rights). See also note 137. Not all lawyers saw their legal systems even this positively, however. See, e.g., Smuts, interview, 16–17 (remarking that the law in pre-independence Namibia "was very much against us"); Shamas, interview, A24 (stating that the function of military law in the Israeli Occupied Territories is "to control the population" and as such it is "against the people").

137. Butegwa and VeneKlasen, interview, 4 (commenting that "in many cases the constitutions and the laws [other than customary laws] in many of these [African] countries are quite good" with respect to women's rights) (VeneKlasen); Florence Butegwa, "Challenges of Promoting Legal Literacy among Women in Uganda," in *Legal Literacy*, ed. Schuler and Kadirgamar-Rajasingham, 142 (citing activists' realization that "most of the practices that oppressed women [in Uganda] were illegal, and . . . women had a legal remedy in the courts of law"); Dasso, interview, at 12 ("[W]e can use [Peruvian law] . . . as an instrument of our struggle. But there is a big gap between the reality, the social reality and what is written in the constitutional law," in particular the constitutional prohibition on sex discrimination.); O. Nwankwo, interview, 8–9 (Nigerian constitutional prohibition on sex discrimination); Singh, interview, 16–17 (contrasting Nepalese constitutional prohibition against sex discrimination with the practical reality of unequal treatment).

138. For an overview of the rights provisions of the Indian constitution, see Susman, "Distant Voices," 61–63. Article 15 of the constitution not only forbids discrimination "on grounds only of religion, race, caste, sex, place of birth or any of them," India Constitution, art. 15(1), but also specifies that its mandate against discrimination does not "prevent the State from making any special provision for the advancement of any socially and education-ally backward classes of citizens or for the Scheduled Castes and the Scheduled Tribes." Ibid., art. 15(4).

139. See generally *Plessy v. Ferguson,* 163 U.S. 537 (1896).

140. Joan F. Hartman (Fitzpatrick), "Book Review," *Human Rights Quarterly* 6 (1984), 131 (reviewing International Commission of Jurists, *States of Emergency: Their Impact on Human Rights* [Geneva: International Commission of Jurists, 1983]). For examples see Thomas Friedman, *From Beirut to Jerusalem* (New York: Farrar Straus Giroux, 1989), 352–360 (Israel); Joseph Lelyveld, *Move Your Shadow: South Africa, Black and White* (New York: Times Books, 1985), 81 (South Africa); Osiel, "Dialogue with Dictators," 510–511, 529–530 (Brazil and, to some extent, Argentina); William D. Zabel, Diane Orentlicher, and David E. Nachman, "Human Rights and the Administration of Justice in Chile: Report of a Delega-tion of the Association of the Bar of the City of New York and of the International Bar Association," *Record of the Association of the Bar of the City of New York* 42 (1987), 436 (Chile).

141. One international human rights NGO, INTERIGHTS, has focused on assisting human rights advocates to invoke "[t]he growing body of international human rights case law" in the courts of their own countries. Playfair, "INTERIGHTS," 572. In conjunction with the Commonwealth Secretariat, INTERIGHTS has also "been instrumental in the de-velopment of a Commonwealth-wide network of senior judges endorsing the importance of international and comparative human rights law in domestic decisions." Ibid., 577.

142. Hutchins and Klaaren, *Public Interest Law,* 13, 119. In August 1996 Falana, who by then was imprisoned for his human rights work was one of three Nigerians to whom the American Bar Association's Section of Litigation gave its 1996 International Human Rights Award. Lawyers Committee for Human Rights, "Nigerian Attorneys to Receive Human Rights Award," *Lawyer to Lawyer Network* (Lawyers Committee for Human Rights, New York), August 1996.

143. Such changes have probably been widespread, as the wave of democratization has been felt in countries around the world. These welcome transformations ironically can also present cause lawyers with new strategic dilemmas, as the lawyers seek to fashion roles for themselves in relation to governments with which they may now be in deep sympathy. For a description of the role being played by one of the 1991 symposium participants, Namibia's Legal Assistance Centre, in post-independence Namibia, see Welch, *Human Rights in Africa,* 191–197.

144. Cause lawyers have engaged in at least some legislative advocacy in such countries as Colombia (Hutchins and Klaaren, *Public Interest Law,* 38 [legislative advocacy by FUN-COL]), El Salvador (Díaz Rodríguez, interview, 5), India (Hutchins and Klaaren, *Public Interest Law,* 59 [Lawyers Collective]), Indonesia (Alkastar, interview, 29), Israel (Ziv, inter-view, 8, 32–34), Namibia (Hutchins and Klaaren, *Public Interest Law,* 102 [Legal Assistance Centre's work on a "draft labor code"], Nigeria (Agbakoba, "The Role of Non-Governmental Organisations," 153 [Civil Liberties Organization's "empowerment pro-gramme for the state houses of parliament"], Okagbue, interview, 14 [drafting advice given by the Nigerian Institute of Advanced Legal Studies]), Peru (Hutchins and Klaaren, *Public Interest Law,* 138–139 [Perú Mujer's preparation of draft legislation], and the Philippines (Golub, "Democratizing Justice," 52–54; Medina, interview, 6, 10). Cause lawyers may also

seek to influence administrative lawmaking, at national or local levels. See Golub, "Democratizing Justice," 47–49 (Philippine cause lawyers' engagement with "executive agency policy formulation").

Not all cause lawyers choose to engage with their nations' legislatures. The Black Lawyers Association did not lobby the apartheid parliament in South Africa, for the BLA had adopted a policy of noncooperation with apartheid institutions. Moloto, interview, A25–26. Other groups may have seen such work as simply pointless. See Huq, interview, 9 (Bangladesh). No doubt Third World legislatures, like Third World courts, are often deeply flawed institutions. Nevertheless it appears that many cause lawyers have decided that, despite these flaws, both of these structures provide some opportunities for fruitful advocacy.

145. On India, see text and notes at notes 89–92. On the flexibility of Israeli standing requirements, enabling groups like the Association for Civil Rights in Israel to appear as plaintiffs in their own right, see Ziv, interview, 14–16. In the United States, Jack Greenberg reports, class action rules were rewritten by "Al Sachs, a Harvard law professor (later dean) who lectured often at our [the NAACP Legal Defense Fund's] lawyers' training conferences. He understood civil rights cases and, therefore, wrote the rules so that victims of discrimination would not face unreasonable obstacles in achieving their rights." Greenberg, *Crusaders in the Courts,* 415.

146. John Merryman, reflecting on the "law and development" movement, comments that in civil law thinking "[t]he conception of the lawyer as social engineer is not widely held. Old ideas about the separation of powers and a rather modest role for judges still exert great power. . . . There is some basis for the view that the cultural distance between the civil law and the common law is decreasing, but it is still substantial." Merryman, "Comparative Law," 478–479.

147. The first of these groups, the "well known (some might say notorious)" group known as "alternative judges," "do not feel bound by the positivist strictures of the Civil Code. Accordingly, they frequently decide cases based on what they perceive to be higher notions of justice and fundamental fairness, or simple common sense." Meili, "The Interaction between Lawyers and Grass Roots Movements," 67. In contrast, the president of another group of innovative judges, the Association of Judges for Democracy, maintains that "there is no need to rule on cases from such an 'alternative' perspective because all of the necessary principles for socially just decisions are contained in the Constitution and laws." Ibid., 67. In the words of a Brazilian law professor whom Meili quotes, the "alternative" judges "believe that justice is above the law; . . . [the members of the second group] believe that justice must be done, but it must be done on a strictly legal basis. The objectives are the same but the strategies are different." Ibid., 68.

148. *Brown v. Board of Education,* 347 U.S. 483 (1954).

149. Richard Kluger, *Simple Justice: The History of* Brown v. Board of Education *and Black America's Struggle for Equality* (New York: Vintage Books, 1975), 132.

150. "By 1940, there had been almost 3,500 lynchings in the country, mostly in the small towns and rural areas of the South. Between V-J day, the end of the war against Japan, and June 1947, less than two years later, there were twenty-six lynchings of blacks." Greenberg, *Crusaders in the Courts,* 17.

151. Ibid., 216.

152. See Ellmann, *In a Time of Trouble,* 98–113 (discussing a decision by the South African Appellate Division to give effect to a statutory provision ousting the courts' jurisdiction to review emergency regulations); cf. Agbakoba, "The Role of Non-Governmental Organisations," 150–152 (describing Nigerian courts' limitation of the effect of similar clauses in Nigerian military decrees).

153. See, e.g., Hutchins and Klaaren, *Public Interest Law*, 131 ("reporting nation-wide awareness and outcry" in reaction to multiple lawsuits brought on behalf of detainees by Nigeria's Civil Liberties Organization, and resulting release of many detainees).

154. See, e.g., ibid., 156 (on the impact of legal representation in South African pass law cases). In the United States, the capital punishment litigation spearheaded by the NAACP Legal Defense Fund never succeeded in making the death penalty unconstitutional per se, but it has tremendously slowed the process of executions.

155. See, e.g., Hall and Fretz, "Legal Services," 790 (community organizations see criminal defense work by Colombia's FUNCOL in cases resulting from land disputes as "an essential tactic in their struggle to regain their land and an important mechanism for deterring victimization of Indians by local authorities"); Hutchins and Klaaren, *Public Interest Law*, 95 (citing a "major accomplishment" of the Mexican group DOAL, namely that "[t]hrough its legal defense of grassroots leaders it has helped to create a social and political atmosphere in which such leaders cannot be persecuted with impunity by those opposed to their work").

156. At least thirteen of the cause lawyering groups at the 1991 symposium were engaged in administrative advocacy of some sort. See Hutchins and Klaaren, *Public Interest Law*, 35 (Brazil's Geledes); 38 (Colombia's FUNCOL); 43 (El Salvador's CESPAD); 52 (India's AWARE); 64 (Indonesian Legal Aid Foundation); 70 (Association for Civil Rights in Israel); 87 (Kenya's Kituo Cha Sheria); 93, 95 (Mexico's DOAL); 100 (Namibia's Legal Assistance Centre); 107 (Nepal's Women's Legal Services Project); 147 (Philippines' SALAG); 154 (South Africa's Black Lawyers Association); 160–161 (South Africa's Legal Resources Centre).

157. Burton Fretz of the National Senior Citizens Law Center discussed American techniques of administrative advocacy at the 1991 symposium. Hutchins and Klaaren, *Public Interest Law*, 8.

158. See Hutchins and Klaaren, passim. The only exceptions appear to be Nigeria's Family Law Centre Project, which was about to add attorneys who would handle cases but had been referring clients who needed to go to court to volunteer counsel (see ibid., 112, 115); the Nigerian Institute of Advanced Legal Studies, which is primarily a research and education institution (though it has also created a family law clinic) (see ibid., 125); Perú Mujer, which trains paralegals and provides them with assistance from a lawyer if needed (see ibid., 139); and WiLDAF, a training and networking organization, many of whose member groups pursue "law reform and legal literacy strategies" in their own countries (see ibid., 171–172). On the considerable similarities between the actual practices of alternative lawyers and their more traditional colleagues, see note 99.

159. See Hutchins and Klaaren, *Public Interest Law*, 100 (test cases brought by Namibia's Legal Assistance Center); ibid., 160 (test cases brought by South Africa's Legal Resources Centre); Jaising, interview, 4, 18 (Lawyers Collective in India); Manase, interview, 16 (Zimbabwe); C. Nwankwo, interview, 4 (Nigeria's Constitutional Rights Project); Shamas, interview, 12–15 (Quaker Legal Aid and Information Service, in Israel's Occupied Territories); Ziv, interview, 15–16, 25 (ACRI in Israel). Others were interested in developing a greater emphasis on test cases. See Butegwa and VeneKlasen, interview, 7 (WiLDAF exploring the possibility of "using, encouraging and helping groups to use test cases more and more") (VeneKlasen); Huq, interview, 28, 39 (expressing interest in developing more public interest litigation in light of the 1991 symposium).

160. Chaskalson, interview, B14–19, C7–8. This characterization of the role of this founding lawyer, Arthur Chaskalson, is my own; he would not be so immodest. A measure of the transformation of South African life is that Arthur Chaskalson in 1994 became the first president of South Africa's new Constitutional Court.

161. See note 94.

162. See Richard L. Abel, "The Underdevelopment of Legal Professions: A Review Article on Third World Lawyers," *American Bar Foundation Research Journal* 1982 (1982), 893 (Third World "[l]awyers enjoy extraordinary privileges of wealth, power, and status, accentuated by the enormous distance separating them from the vast mass of their fellow citizens. They use their security as professionals not to challenge state illegality but to protect and expand their privileges."); Dias, "Rights and Resources," 57 ("Lawyers and legal professions today tend to be very much a part of the problem."); Dias and Paul, "Lawyers, Legal Resources, and Alternative Approaches," 374 (surveying demographic, economic and professional obstacles to lawyers' developing the capacity to provide the sorts of legal resources needed by the poor).

163. In the Philippines, Stephen Golub reports, many alternative lawyers initially "viewed themselves as outside the [legal] mainstream," but more recently they have grown to feel "that they represent not just an alternative *to* traditional legal practice, but at least a partial alternative *for* traditional legal practice." As of 1994 "there seems to be a cautious consensus building around the desirability of influencing the legal profession and the students who constitute the profession's future." Golub, "Democratizing Justice," 70–71.

164. On the concern for professionalism of the NAACP Legal Defense Fund, see note 71. Neta Ziv emphasized the relationship that Israel's ACRI has with the government, in which "we're suing them again and again and again, and still they say, " 'You're credible, because you're professional.' " Ziv, interview, 41. Similarly, Maha Abu-Dayyeh Shamas of the Quaker Legal Aid and Information Service, which focuses on Palestinian issues, said that this organization chooses its staff lawyers "very carefully" and has "very strict standards that we try to uphold in terms of how we perform our service. And we feel like, we earn their [the judges'] respect. . . . That doesn't mean we win cases, but they treat our lawyers differently." Shamas, interview, A18. In Nigeria, Femi Falana observed that "basically, if you prepare your case very well, and your argument is all right, usually you are welcome in our court. We have not been met with institutionalized antagonism." Falana, interview, 4. In Nepal, Silu Singh commented that "being a professional organization . . . we [the Women's Legal Services Project] have very good relation[s] with other lawyers, also." Singh, interview, 14. And in India, Indira Jaising of India's Lawyers Collective noted that all of the collective's members not only do pro bono public interest law cases, but also "do fee-paid work in the mainstream of the legal profession," and therefore they "are not isolated . . . but . . . are seen as part of the mainsteam legal profession actively intervening in on-going legal issues." Other lawyers and judges "have the opportunity to observe our work not only as public interest lawyers, but also as members of the profession." Jaising, interview, 8.

Not every cause-lawyering group wishes to build warm relations with the established profession. In South Africa under apartheid, the Black Lawyers Association not only maintained a policy of noncollaboration with the government, but also applied this policy to the professional association of attorneys in South Africa, the Law Society. Moloto, interview, 34; Pitje, interview, 42. Though this policy was not applied in all possible respects, see Moloto, interview, 34–35, it surely limited the connections that would be established.

165. Efrén Rodríguez González of Mexico's DOAL pointed out that although DOAL people have experience as organizers, their client groups have their own leaders and organizers. What these groups need is good legal technicians and this has been DOAL's focus; moreover, doing effective legal work, including trial work, is the first step to DOAL's winning the clients' trust. Rodríguez González, speaking at 1991 symposium, plenary session on "Methods of Using Law to Effect Social Change (continued)—Traditional Uses," 4 ("[H]emos preferido desarrollar más nuestro trabajo profesional como técnicos jurídicos,

como abogados. . . . Y para podernos ganar la confianza primero requerimos ser buenos técnicos."). For a similar reflection on the role of American lawyers in working with community groups, see Richard D. Marsico, "Working for Social Change and Preserving Client Autonomy: Is There a Role for 'Facilitative' Lawyering?" *Clinical Law Review* 1 (1995), 639–663.

166. Chaskalson, interview, B20. As he explained, this careful work meant that those in the legal profession who were "very uneasy" about the LRC's work "could never find anything to say. They couldn't point to anything. They couldn't say 'look at that' or 'look at this.' Because they were getting properly written letters, well presented arguments, well presented documentation." Ibid.

167. Among the groups at the 1991 symposium, several are publishing journals, including the Civil Liberties Organization in Nigeria (Agbakoba, "The Role of Non-Governmental Organisations," 156); the Nigerian Institute of Advanced Legal Studies (Hutchins and Klaaren, *Public Interest Law,* 125); the Constitutional Rights Project, also in Nigeria (ibid., 121); the National Association of Democratic Lawyers, also in Nigeria (ibid., 118); the Black Lawyers Association in South Africa (ibid., 155); the Legal Resources Foundation in Zimbabwe (ibid., 166); and the Lawyers Collective in India (ibid., 58). The Indonesian Legal Aid Foundation publishes an English-language quarterly bulletin (ibid., 64). A number of groups also publish various materials directed to lay readers.

168. Jaising commented in 1991 that "it always amazes me that . . . it took a group like ours, a handful of people on the fringes of the profession, to start something like this [magazine] and keep it going. Well, it's reached a stage when the magazine has . . . become almost the voice of the underprivileged within the legal community. It's become one of the major forums through which these issues can be articulated and disseminated amongst the judiciary and the legal profession." Jaising, interview, 28.

169. Thus the Madaripur Legal Aid Association runs an internship program, for law students and others, whose goal is "the consciousness raising of potential lawyers on human rights and legal aid issues." Hutchins and Klaaren, *Public Interest Law,* 30. The Legal Resources Centre in South Africa maintains a fellowship program, targeted for black law graduates; as of 1991 approximately one hundred people had been fellows, and many are now "engaged directly or indirectly in public interest law." The program has also "made a significant contribution towards the training and placement of young black lawyers." Ibid., 161. Also in South Africa, the Black Lawyers Association carries on a number of different programs to increase the representation of blacks in the South African legal profession. Ibid., 155.

170. In some Third World countries, clinical programs at law schools—like their counterparts in the United States—are engaged in cause lawyering. See, e.g., Frank S. Bloch and Iqbal S. Ishar, "Legal Aid, Public Service and Clinical Legal Education: Future Directions from India and the United States," *Michigan Journal of International Law* 12 (1990), 92–120.

171. Three groups engaged in continuing legal education are the Black Lawyers Association in South Africa (Hutchins and Klaaren, *Public Interest Law,* 156); Zimbabwe's Legal Resources Foundation (ibid., 166), and the Nigerian Institute of Advanced Legal Studies (Okagbue, interview, 2, 9).

Perhaps a measure of the mutual trust between a cause-lawyering group and a government is the government's willingness to have the cause-lawyering group provide government staff with legal education; in Zimbabwe and in Israel cause lawyers are training the police! Hutchins and Klaaren, *Public Interest Law,* 166 (LRF in Zimbabwe); 69–70 (ACRI in Israel). In South Africa as apartheid ended, Arthur Chaskalson of the Legal Resources Centre was speaking to the police as well. Chaskalson, interview, C3.

172. According to Wilson Manase, these and similar resources are "things which the profession . . . valued and they buy this from us. And that has actually built some confidence between us over the years." Manase, interview, 7. Other groups have engaged in somewhat similar legal research, including the Women's Legal Services Project of Nepal, which has produced a compilation of Supreme Court decisions bearing on women's rights (Hutchins and Klaaren, *Public Interest Law*, 108) and El Salvador's CESPAD, whose Basic Support Program seeks to identify what El Salvador's laws actually are (ibid., 42).

173. See Arruda da Silva, interview, 5 (Brazil); Dasso, interview, 9 (Peru); T. Mulya Lubis et al., "The Indonesian Legal Aid Foundation: An Introduction," in *Law, Human Rights and Legal Services: Proceedings*, 201, 205 (describing the role of the Indonesian Bar Association, PERADIN, in the establishment of the Legal Aid Foundation); Manase, interview, 7 (Zimbabwe); Moloto, interview, B1–2 (South Africa; on the human rights tradition of the South African bar, see also Ellmann, *In a Time of Trouble*, 205–244). For somewhat contrasting views on India, see note 116; see also Bhagwati, interview, 6, 19 (maintaining that India had no prior tradition of public interest law, but that it did have a "long tradition of voluntary social action groups").

174. Thus Fernando Rojas situates the rise of alternative lawyering in Latin America in a broad reassessment by leftist intellectuals and professionals. Rojas, "A Comparison of Change-Oriented Legal Services," 220–221.

175. See Brandt, "Human Rights," 31–32; Gomez, "Bogota and Beyond," 138. Many of the groups represented at the 1991 symposium were offering some nonlegal services to the people with whom they worked, see text and note at note 209. Some had been founded by groups made up partly or wholly of nonlawyers, including Colombia's FUNCOL (Hutchins and Klaaren, *Public Interest Law*, 37); El Salvador's CESPAD (ibid., 41; Díaz Rodríguez, interview, 1); and Perú Mujer, established by four women, none of whom was a lawyer. (Dasso, interview, 1; Dasso, speaking at 1991 symposium, plenary session on "Methods of Using Law to Effect Social Change (continued)—Alternative Uses," 6).

176. More prosaically, the simple fact that lawyers may constitute a community may protect those members of the community who practice cause lawyering. David Smuts commented that in Namibia "although I have differed quite vehemently from a number of my colleagues [in the legal profession], I have maintained on a personal level reasonably cordial relationships with most of the colleagues, even those with whom I quite seriously differ. And I think the general climate, because we are so small a community and know each other, has also assisted in that way." Smuts, interview, 12.

177. Carlos Medina of the Philippines commented, "[W]hen I was in law school, all I thought was that, you become a lawyer, you join a law firm and go [into the] corporate world or do business. But little by little, you saw that there is another kind of career, which is alternative lawyering. I don't think it is a tradition at this point . . . but it is turning into one, so, it is . . . a growing tribe of lawyers who focus more and more into public interest." Medina, interview, 12. Neta Ziv, similarly, said that Israel's legal profession did not have a human rights or public interest tradition, but that a public interest tradition is now "gaining a lot of momentum." Ziv, interview, 14. In Nigeria, relations between the National Bar Association and at least one cause-lawyering group, the National Association of Democratic Lawyers (NADL), have had their ups and downs (see Falana, interview, 2), but Falana commented in 1991 that "[e]ven the Nigerian Bar Association is also forced *[semble]* to develop a tradition of human rights now." Ibid., 3.

178. Israel provides a striking variation on these themes. The Association for Civil Rights in Israel (ACRI) has "no relationship . . . at all" with the bar association, which is "very inactive in the whole area of public interest"—though the bar hasn't made any move

to enforce its minimum fee rules against ACRI, as theoretically it might. Ziv, interview, 11. But ACRI's relationship with the government is, as Neta Ziv said, "a unique relationship . . . something unheard of." Ibid., 13. The government's lawyers often sympathize with ACRI's positions, sometimes invite ACRI to sue when they (the state's lawyers) have been unable to press other government officials to adhere to a legal position that the lawyers accept, and have taken a generous view of standing in cases brought by ACRI. Ziv, interview, 11–13, 15. (It is worth mentioning that ACRI's relationship to the government seems much warmer than the relationship between the government and the Quaker Legal Aid and Information Service, a group focused on the problems of Palestinians on the West Bank— though this group too has apparently found it useful to practice in a distinctly professional style; see Shamas, interview, A18.)

179. See text and notes at notes 125–130.

180. Singh, interview, 14–15.

181. Lev, "Lawyers' Causes."

182. Alkastar, interview, 72.

183. Lev, "Lawyers' Causes."

184. Ibid.

185. As noted earlier (see note 142), one Nigerian lawyer interviewed for this study, Femi Falana, is now (as of 1996) in prison. Another participant in the 1991 symposium, Olisa Agbakoba, was detained at one point but "was out the following morning when news of it was carried by the BBC and VOA." Agbakoba, "The Role of Non-Governmental Organizations," 156. For illustration of government pressures against Indonesian cause lawyers, see Lev, "Lawyers' Causes." In India, P. K. S. Madhavan, founder of AWARE, has survived seven attempts on his life. Madhavan, interview, 23. See also note 69.

186. This emphasis is reflected in Hutchins and Klaaren, *Public Interest Law,* 16 (referring to the "common commitment to advancing social and economic justice through law"); see also ibid., 4.

187. Groups with this primary focus apparently included ACRI in Israel (see ibid., 68); the Quaker Legal Aid and Information Service, in Israel's Occupied Territories (see ibid., 75); and the Civil Liberties Organisation (see ibid., 130) and the Constitutional Rights Project in Nigeria (see ibid., 121–123).

188. Ibid., at 51.

189. Ibid., 68.

190. See ibid., 117 (NADL); 122 (CRP); 131 (CLO); Agbakoba, "Role," at 150–151.

191. See Hutchins and Klaaren, *Public Interest Law,* 57 (prisoners' rights work by India's Lawyers Collective); 63 (Indonesian Legal Aid Foundation, political trials); 69 (prisoners' rights work of ACRI in Israel); 75 (main focus of Quaker Legal Aid is on cases of Palestinian detainees); 85 (Kenya's Kituo Cha Sheria representing detained lawyers); 92–94 (Mexico's DOAL defending community leaders facing unjust prosecutions); 101–102 (challenges to security force activities by Namibia's Legal Assistance Centre); 117–118 (NADL in Nigeria working on prisoners' rights); 122 (Nigeria's Constitutional Rights Project); 125–126 (research on the administration of justice by the Nigerian Institute of Advanced Legal Studies); 131 (Nigeria's Civil Liberties Organisation); 154–155 (political defense work by Black Lawyers Association in South Africa); 160 (Legal Resources Centre in South Africa challenging abuses of power, such as unlawful arrests); Chaskalson, interview, A21.

192. Carlos Medina of SALAG (Philippines) explained that his group "decided to focus on the less controversial but equally important and equally urgent economic, social and cultural rights." Medina, interview, 4. "Alternative lawyering" in general appears to share this focus. See Golub, "Democratizing Justice," 5 (some Third World alternative law groups

concentrate on first-generation rights, but "many focus on social, economic and environmental problems"); Hall and Fretz, "Legal Services," 787; Rojas, "A Comparison of Change-Oriented Legal Services," 234 (citing survey findings that only 12 of 162 groups with which alternative law entities were working were "human rights groups").

193. These included Perú Mujer, Women in Law and Development in Africa (WiLDAF), the Women's Legal Services Project in Nepal, and the Family Law Centre Project of Anambra State of Nigeria, a project of the local chapter of the Federación Internacional de Abogadas. The particular issues these groups addressed ranged from problems of discriminatory customary law of the family in Africa to the difficulty many poor people in Peru face in obtaining identification cards, which are essential to their lawful existence.

194. Among groups making women's rights some part of their work are India's AWARE (see text at notes 303–305); the Madaripur Legal Aid Association in Bangladesh (see Hutchins and Klaaren, *Public Interest Law,* 28–29); the Lawyers Collective in India (see ibid., 57); ACRI in Israel (see ibid., 68); Kituo Cha Sheria in Kenya (see ibid., 85–86); the Legal Assistance Centre in Namibia (see ibid., 100–101); and SALAG in the Philippines (see ibid., 143).

195. See ibid., 28–29 (Madaripur Legal Aid Association); 37–40 (FUNCOL in Colombia); 52 (AWARE); 63 (Indonesian Legal Aid Foundation); 160 (Legal Resources Centre in South Africa). South Africa's Legal Resources Centre worked on behalf of African communities facing removal by the state and also found holes in the state's elaborate system of pass laws or "influx control," by which South Africa had dreamt of segregating an entire nation. The Black Lawyers Association of South Africa also contributed to the legal attack on influx control. See ibid., 153.

196. See ibid., 43 (CESPAD in El Salvador); 57 (Lawyers Collective in India); 71 (ACRI challenge to military sealing and demolition of Palestinian homes); 86–87 (Kituo Cha Sheria in Kenya); 94 (DOAL in Mexico); 130 (Civil Liberties Organisation in Nigeria). Stephen Meili has found that "[t]he area in which Brazilian cause lawyers are most actively involved with grass roots groups is property rights, in both urban and rural settings." Meili, "The Interaction of Lawyers and Grass Roots Movements," 72.

197. See Hutchins and Klaaren, *Public Interest Law,* 58 (Lawyers Collective in India); 86 (Kituo Cha Sheria in Kenya); 94 (DOAL in Mexico); 100 (Legal Assistance Centre of Namibia); 130 (Nigeria's Civil Liberties Organisation); 154 (Black Lawyers Association in South Africa); 160 (Legal Resources Centre in South Africa). See also Alkastar, interview, 13 (Indonesian Legal Aid Foundation).

198. Besides the South African groups, other cause lawyering bodies that have challenged racial or ethnic discrimination have included Geledes (Brazil), FUNCOL (Colombia), AWARE (India), and ACRI (Israel). See Hutchins and Klaaren, *Public Interest Law,* 33–36, 37–40, 49–50, 68.

199. Indonesia's Legal Aid Institute, for example, works on environmental issues. Ibid., 63. Nigeria's Civil Liberties Organization has also taken on environmental issues (ibid., 130), as has India's Lawyers Collective, notably in the Bhopal case (ibid., 57). SALAG (Philippines) conducts training in such topics as "agrarian laws" and "urban poor laws." Ibid., 143. Groups working on consumer issues affecting poor people include both the Black Lawyers Association and the Legal Resources Centre in South Africa. Ibid., 154, 161.

200. In addition to many, if not all, of the organizations cited in note 191, two other groups have engaged in at least some criminal defense work: FUNCOL in Colombia (see Hall and Fretz, "Legal Services," 790) and the Madaripur Legal Aid Association (see Hutchins and Klaaren, *Public Interest Law,* 27). See also Meili, "The Interaction of Lawyers and

Grass Roots Movements," 62–63 (on the role of alternative lawyers in Brazil in *prosecuting* perpetrators of violence against peasant activists).

201. Hutchins and Klaaren, *Public Interest Law,* 4.

202. Perhaps the groups most concerned with access to justice were the Women's Legal Services Project of Nepal, the FIDA Family Law Centre in Nigeria, and the Madaripur Legal Aid Association. Interestingly, one important device for access to justice is, as Hutchins and Klaaren note (ibid., 6), alternative dispute resolution, which provides access to justice by taking disputes out of the formal justice system. Alternative dispute resolution can also play a role in programs of community empowerment, to the extent that it enables people to resolve disputes through institutions they themselves have shaped. Many of the cause-lawyering groups at the 1991 symposium are making use of some form of alternative dispute resolution. See ibid. (citing endorsement of alternative dispute resolution, for varying reasons, by Fazlul Huq of the Madaripur Legal Aid Association, Florence Butegwa of Women in Law and Development in Africa, and Murtaza Jaffer of Kituo Cha Sheria); ibid., 38 (FUNCOL in Colombia); 43 (CESPAD in El Salvador); 52 (AWARE in India); 107 (Women's Legal Services Project of Nepal); 160 (Legal Resources Centre lawyers acting as mediators in South Africa). The FIDA Family Law Centre does family law mediation or counseling (see O. Nwankwo, interview, 22, 24–25). See also Bloch and Ishar, "Legal Aid," 114 (mentioning Indian "legal aid camp[s]," in which "[law] students, under faculty and legal aid board supervision, lend advice to the rural people for settling disputes among themselves without having to seek legal redress in courts" as well as student work in "*lok adalats,* which are projects aimed at facilitating conciliated settlement of large numbers of matters pending before the regular courts and tribunals").

203. Among the groups that appeared to have the strongest "test case" orientations were the Legal Resources Centre of South Africa, the Lawyers Collective in India, the Constitutional Rights Project in Nigeria, and the Association for Civil Rights in Israel. Other groups, however, were also engaged in test case litigation. See note 159.

204. See note 100 (identifying alternative law groups).

205. The Indonesian Legal Aid Foundation "offices try to maintain a balance between representing individuals with cases involving only those individuals' interests and representing groups whose cases could bring about structural change benefiting broad areas of society." Hutchins and Klaaren, *Public Interest Law,* 63. South Africa's Legal Resources Centre in principle "give[s] preference to cases which affect a lot of people over individual cases," but lawyers find it very difficult to turn away individual cases where no other legal aid will be available, and "[s]o quite a lot of work gets taken on which I think theoretically shouldn't be taken on." Chaskalson, interview, B4, B6.

206. Hutchins and Klaaren, *Public Interest Law,* 12–14.

207. Chaskalson, interview, B8.

208. Carlos Medina explained that when community groups ask SALAG for its assistance, SALAG goes beyond the particular assistance requested, and "at the same time offer[s] paralegal training sessions, invite[s] them to the alternative law school, give[s] seminars to the members of the organization, so, we try to maintain continuing relationship with these organizations." Medina, interview, 27–28. Similarly, Stephen Meili reports that "[l]ike 'alternative' lawyers in other Latin America[n] countries, most Brazilian cause lawyers avoid taking individual cases unless they will lead to work on behalf of a larger group or organization." Meili, "The Interaction between Lawyers and Grass Roots Movements," 72.

209. Groups providing such nonlegal services included the FIDA branch in Anambra State, Nigeria, which was educating young people about drugs. O. Nwankwo, interview, 4–

5; the Mardaripur Legal Aid Association in Bangladesh, which has a "welfare program for women," Hutchins and Klaaren, *Public Interest Law*, 29; Geledes of Brazil, which had a Women's Health Program, presumably addressing health issues (see ibid., 33); FUNCOL in Colombia, which provides medical assistance, (ibid., 37); India's AWARE, most of whose extensive programs are nonlegal (see ibid., 50–51); and Perú Mujer, which had programs on women and work, health, and family, in addition to the "women and law" program on which I focus in this essay (see ibid., 137). See also Americas Watch, *Vicaría*, 27–31 (describing a variety of nonlegal programs maintained by the Vicaría while it simultaneously challenged human rights violations in Pinochet's Chile). Rojas found that most new and traditional legal service programs in the countries he studied were "part of a major institution which provides other services for the poor." Rojas, "A Comparison of Change-Oriented Legal Services," 237.

210. The FIDA Family Law Centre in Enugu, Nigeria has only women members. O. Nwankwo, interview, 15. In Peru, Perú Mujer's "general assembly" consists of ten people, nine of them women. Dasso, interview, 13.

211. The FIDA Family Law Centre in Enugu, Nigeria insists that its staff be Ibospeaking. Not surprisingly, it also appears that each state branch of FIDA in Nigeria tends to be drawn from the particular ethnic group that dominates that state. See O. Nwankwo, interview, 15–16.

212. South Africa's Legal Resources Centre, "with about 45 percent of its professional staff being Black . . . is the largest employer of Black lawyers in the profession in South Africa." Hutchins and Klaaren, *Public Interest Law*, 161. Similarly, all board members and staffers—though not every member—of the Black Lawyers Association are black. Moloto, interview, 12, 24–25.

213. Many Third World countries pose even greater challenges to an organization wanting to have a representative staff than would often be the case in the United States, for such countries may be divided not only on lines of race and gender, but also by multiple distinctions of language, ethnicity, and geography. In the Legal Assistance Centre's office in Windhoek, Namibia, for example, five languages may be spoken on a single day (Smuts, interview, 28)—though there may be legal services offices in the United States where the same is true. Elsewhere in Namibia is one area for which "costs are very high to fly there, and then also the road is really so bad; it takes about two days to get there." Ibid., 27.

214. Jaising, interview, 18 (describing the situation of the groups represented by India's Lawyers Collective).

215. Fernando Rojas has observed that "a majority of [alternative lawyers in the countries he studied] seem to have graduated from élite, traditional schools." Rojas, "A Comparison of Change-Oriented Legal Services," 244. (Meili describes a somewhat different situation in Brazil, where he suggests that the dramatic expansion of Brazilian law schools in the past three decades has opened the profession to many people who are not from Brazil's elite—though they are still from the middle classes—and who are interested in alternative law. Meili, "The Interaction of Lawyers and Grass Roots Movements," 69.) So, too, in the Philippines many alternative lawyers "come from fairly affluent backgrounds. Most graduated from the country's top law schools." Golub, "Democratizing Justice," 33. In Indonesia, the Legal Aid Foundation lawyers are generally from middle-class, though not upper-class, families. Alkastar, interview, 63–64. In India, AWARE's lawyers are also middle-class people. Madhavan, interview, 8.

216. Cause lawyering in the Third World demands a great deal of its practitioners, in terms of dedication, courage, and sometimes financial sacrifice. Interestingly, however, some cause lawyers are reasonably well paid. See Golub, "Democratizing Justice," 75 (starting

Philippine cause lawyers are paid at rates comparable to private practitioners, though "a gap grows in ensuing years"); Rojas, "A Companion of Change-Oriented Legal Services," 241 (scattered data suggest that staff lawyers at externally financed groups are earning salaries equivalent to market rates, though more senior lawyers are not).

How readily, and for how long, these lawyers could add economic deprivation to the other demands of their work is uncertain, though it is clear that some cause lawyers have not shrunk from financial sacrifice. The founder of one group, the Madaripur Legal Aid Association, initially worked entirely without salary, and considers the potential for such self-sacrifice an important source of hope that the organization can survive potential funding cuts. Huq, interview, 38. Another lawyer, Clement Nwankwo, is supporting the group he founded largely from the proceeds of his part-time private practice. See text at note 35. In Mexico, DOAL's lawyers earn four times the minimum wage, but half the starting salary for lawyers in other forms of practice. Hutchins and Klaaren, *Public Interest Law,* 96.

AWARE is an example of an organization that has called upon its lawyers to bridge the gap between themselves and their clients. Cf. ibid., 11 (Adolfo Triana Antorveza of FUNCOL maintaining that "professionals [must] share the life and anguish of the communities they are seeking to serve if they are to help with any real self-mobilization"); Dias and Paul, "Lawyers, Legal Resources, and Alternative Approaches," 369 (suggesting that the alternative lawyer, "[i]f he is to help the group develop collective capacities . . . should probably be a part of its cadres"). Although AWARE's lawyers are apparently expected to live in the villages where they work, and to send their children to village schools, the lawyers themselves are middle-class and none has yet actually crossed the gulf of class to marry someone from the villages. See Madhavan, interview, 7–8. Rojas reports that some lawyers do accomplish what seems a more modest transition: "[T]hey communicate their rejection of the profession through minute symbols: informal dress, adoption of working class forms of speech, or casual (as opposed to formal) manners." Rojas, "A Comparison of Change-Oriented Legal Services," 245.

217. Triana Antorveza, interview, 6 ("Claro que el trabajo pues realmente es en el campo. Hay que hacer mucho trabajo en el campo. Una vez hubo una abogada, pero se cansó muy rápido, porque era casada entonces le dificultaba mucho en el trabajo separarse de su hogar para hacer trabajo en el campo. . . . [D]uraba ocho días, o quince días fuera de su casa sin sus hijos.").

218. C. Nwankwo, interview, 21. Isabella Okagbue of the Nigerian Institute for Advanced Legal Studies attributed her group's predominantly female permanent staff to the fact that in "most of the public service in Nigeria, there is a growing trend for there to be more women than men, because the salaries just aren't adequate" and also because "most women prefer to go to something that is more organized and more secure" than private practice. Okagbue, interview, 19–20.

219. Obiageli Nwankwo commented that "we can't have a man, we cannot employ [a] full-time male lawyer to handle cases that have to do with women . . . [b]ut a woman will understand and appreciate" a woman client's situation. O. Nwankwo, interview, 15. Paradoxically, gendered social stereotypes can sometimes heighten the role of women. In at least one country, women are overrepresented on the staff of a public interest law group, because they are less likely to be subject to interfering governmental restrictions than are men.

220. The NAACP Legal Defense Fund has a self-perpetuating board, see Greenberg, *Crusaders in the Courts,* 20. Perhaps the most striking example of the use of an elite board in the Third World is South Africa's Legal Resources Centre. Chaskalson, interview, B14–18. Other groups which appear to have adopted such systems, at least in part, include Nigeria's

Constitutional Rights Project (C. Nwankwo, interview, 1–2, 17); Namibia's Legal Assistance Centre (Smuts, interview, 20), and Zimbabwe's Legal Resources Foundation (see Manase, interview, 8, 11). Cf. Hutchins and Klaaren, *Public Interest Law*, 105 (Women's Legal Services Project in Nepal is part of a "non-profit philanthropic organization founded by prominent lawyers, judges, and law teachers").

Such elite support may not enhance, and in fact could undercut, a group's legitimacy with its non-elite clients. Both the Legal Resources Centre and the Legal Assistance Centre, operating in countries where liberation struggles were in full swing, consulted with, and received the approval of, community and/or liberation groups before they began operations. Chaskalson, interview, B22; Smuts, interview, 3–4.

221. Most members of the Legal Resources Centre's board, for example, have been white, although by far the majority of the LRC's clients and of South Africa's population are black. Chaskalson, interview, B14. Another instance of this problem is the low representation of women on the self-perpetuating board of trustees of the Black Lawyers Association's Legal Education Centre. Moloto, interview, B15–17, B25–26.

222. Steiner, *Diverse Partners*, 77.

223. Tolley, *International Commission of Jurists*, 19.

224. Groups with such elected boards include the Madaripur Legal Aid Association in Bangladesh, Geledes in Brazil, FUNCOL in Colombia, AWARE in India, the Lawyers Collective in India, ACRI in Israel, Kituo Cha Sheria in Kenya, the FIDA Family Law Centre in Enugu, Anambra State, Nigeria, Nigeria's National Association of Democratic Lawyers, Perú Mujer, and the Philippines' SALAG. As to these groups, see Hutchins and Klaaren, *Public Interest Law*, 32, 35, 38, 53, 59, 70, 86, 120, 139, 144; O. Nwankwo, interview, 12–15 (FIDA). DOAL in Mexico also is at least partially governed by a membership assembly. See Hutchins and Klaaren, *Public Interest Law*, 95. South Africa's Black Lawyers Association apparently also has an elected executive committee, though the BLA Legal Education Centre has a self-perpetuating board of trustees. Cf. ibid., 156 (referring to "General Meeting" of membership); Moloto, interview, B15–17. As of 1991, Women in Law and Development in Africa "has a 14–member Steering Committee which was elected in February 1990 at the conference which founded" this group. Hutchins and Klaaren, *Public Interest Law*, 172.

225. Elections may also produce a board that is somewhat *less* representative than the membership. AWARE's governing board is elected from a "general body" of 260 members, of whom a majority are members of tribal minorities or untouchables (Hutchins and Klaaren, *Public Interest Law*, 53), but the board itself has no tribal minority members. Madhavan, interview, 19–20. The "general body" itself meets twice a year. Neera K. Sohoni and Meera Singh, *People in Action* 84 (New Delhi: Har-Anand Publications, 1990) (published "[u]nder the auspices of AWARE"). However, board elections are held only once every five (perhaps four) years (see Hutchins and Klaaren, *Public Interest Law*, 53), and presumably the result is that the general body's formal power in the governance of the organization is somewhat less than it would be in a group with more frequent elections.

226. Steiner, *Diverse Partners*, 77–78. Claude Welch comments that African human rights NGOs face "[s]evere obstacles" to becoming "large membership organizations," Welch, *Human Rights in Africa*, 305, and also observes that "[m]ost African human rights NGOs have yet to make the crucial transition from leadership by the 'founding father' or 'founding mother' to selection of new heads and directions without organizational collapse. The first generation of chairs/presidents remains in control. To a substantial extent, the organizations are personalized." Ibid., 293.

227. I do not have complete data on all of the 1991 symposium groups, but it seems clear that of those that are membership organizations a number are quite small and that

much of the membership in these groups tends to be professional. El Salvador's CESPAD appears to have been founded, and still be governed, by a ten–person board, made up primarily of lawyers and other professionals, who have known each other "de mucho tiempo atrás, identificados con los problemas del interés público." The founders kept the board small for various reasons, including their desire to guarantee the institution's survival against potential political repression. Díaz Rodríguez, interview, 1. In India, the Lawyers Collective "[o]ver the years . . . has remained a small activist group of lawyers and non-lawyers." Hutchins and Klaaren, *Public Interest Law,* 55. "Membership in [Kenya's] Kituo Cha Sheria is open to all Kenyan lawyers and law students as well as non-lawyers committed to the promotion of the rule of law and justice," and as of 1991 totalled 100. Ibid., 87. In Nigeria, the Family Law Centre in Enugu, Anambra State appears to be governed by the local branch of FIDA (the International Federation of Women Lawyers), which has approximately 45 members. see O. Nwankwo, interview, 13. Nigeria's National Association of Democratic Lawyers is a lawyers' organization, "open to all lawyers who have a burning commitment to the realization of social justice." Hutchins and Klaaren, *Public Interest Law,* 120. Perú Mujer is governed by a membership assembly, but there are only ten members, and none of the paralegals the group has trained is among these ten. Ibid., 140; Dasso, interview, 13, 15–16. In the Philippines, SALAG was founded by lawyers; its membership was around 10 to 20 people, and has grown to 30, an increase Carlos Medina cites as an organizational achievement. Medina, interview, 1, 20, 32. Membership in Women in Law and Development in Africa is "flexible and open to individuals of any profession involved in women's rights initiatives" (and to NGOs) (Hutchins and Klaaren, *Public Interest Law,* 172), but a majority of members are lawyers and the rest apparently professionals of other sorts. Butegwa and VeneKlasen, interview, B5 (VeneKlasen). Fourteen national branches evidently are the result of the efforts of some 250 African women over a three-year period. Ibid., B12 (VeneKlasen).

The larger groups include India's AWARE, which has a governing "general body" of 260, a little over 40 precent of them professionals (and a vastly larger number of supporters) (see Madhavan, interview, 19), and ACRI in Israel, which has 1,500 members and can be joined by "[a]ny person who supports ACRI goals" (Hutchins and Klaaren, *Public Interest Law,* 71).

Even if the board is not entirely a professional body, of course, it may delegate important decisions, such as the choice of cases, to its lawyers. This allocation of case selection may be quite common. Namibia's Legal Assistance Centre, however, is a notable example of a group consciously trying to limit the internal distinctions in the roles of lawyers and paralegals, and to consult with communities about case choices as well. It is also an example of a group which, in an improving political climate, has been able to make its board of trustees much more representative. Smuts, interview, 23–24, 26.

228. Jack Greenberg describes the conflict in the NAACP Legal Defense Fund over whether to represent Angela Davis in her trial on major criminal charges arising out of the "Soledad Brothers" affair. Almost all of LDF's legal staff wanted to undertake the representation; Greenberg, backed by the board, refused. In the course of the dispute, the lawyers on the staff almost unanimously urged that they should be allowed to override the director-counsel's decisions about which cases the organization would take on. Greenberg sharply opposed this proposal, which the board ultimately rejected as well; the board also unanimously supported Greenberg's decision not to represent Davis. Greenberg comments that "[w]e had a charter, a tradition, a board that defined the role of LDF, and contributors who gave for that program. The staff now proposed that lawyers, most of whom had been at LDF only a few years and some not even that long, and who soon might move on, should be the ones to commit LDF funds and personnel to the litigation of suits. Such a

change in policy would place the resources of the LDF at the service of causes of the staff's choice, including violent and separatist ones." Greenberg, *Crusaders in the Courts*, 409. On a much milder level, Neta Ziv noted the tension between ACRI's branches and its central office, as the central office tries to ensure that all activity undertaken in ACRI's name is consistent with its professional reputation. Ziv, interview, 40–41; Hutchins and Klaaren, *Public Interest Law*, 72.

229. The great majority of the groups represented at the 1991 symposium were engaged in one form of lay legal education work or another, and over half were involved in paralegal training (or similar work) in some way. Those with some involvement in such training include the Madaripur Legal Aid Association in Bangladesh, FUNCOL in Colombia, India's AWARE (annually training about 8,000 people), the Lawyers Collective in India, the Indonesian Legal Aid Foundation (holding "annual one-month training sessions" for 40–50 law students), ACRI in Israel, Kituo Cha Sheria in Kenya, DOAL in Mexico, Namibia's Legal Assistance Centre, Nepal's Women's Legal Services Project, Perú Mujer (a central activity of this group), SALAG in the Philippines (in particular, through its "alternative law school"), the Black Lawyers Association in South Africa, the Legal Resources Centre in South Africa, and Zimbabwe's Legal Resources Foundation. See Hutchins and Klaaren, *Public Interest Law*, 30, 38, 52, 58, 64, 70 (see also Ziv, interview, 9 [characterizing ACRI work as training "paralegals"]), 87, 94, 100, 106, 138–139, 142–143, 160, 165; Moloto, interview, A12 (Black Lawyers Association). In addition, El Salvador's CESPAD was considering paralegal training. Hutchins and Klaaren, *Public Interest Law*, 42. The FIDA Family Law Centre in Enugu, Nigeria, planned to undertake such training with grant funds it was about to receive. O. Nwankwo, interview, 3. The Nigerian Institute for Advanced Legal Studies was also exploring this idea. Hutchins and Klaaren, *Public Interest Law*, 128. And Women in Law and Development in Africa is very much concerned with training others in "strategies for legal education." Ibid., 169.

230. See, e.g., Hutchins and Klaaren, *Public Interest Law*, 42 (CESPAD newspaper column); 70 (ACRI civil rights lecture course for Israel Defense Forces Radio); 106 (Women's Legal Services Program's use of simple training booklets, radio, and television in Nepal); cf. Bhagwati, interview, 9 (documentary films).

231. The Indonesian Legal Aid Foundation's training has reached "groups of laborers, fishermen, farmers, students and *hunter-gatherers,*" Hutchins and Klaaren, *Public Interest Law*, 63 (emphasis added).

232. See, e.g., ibid., 51–52 (posters, wall newspapers, and theatrical groups used by AWARE); 106–107 (comic-strip training materials used by Nepal's WLSP); 138 ("pamphlets, audio-visual sets, drawings, role playing, and games that build self-confidence, promote community development, and combine concern with women's rights with entertainment" employed by Perú Mujer).

233. See ibid., 52 (AWARE "reaches about 100,000 people a year with its legal campaigns and mass meetings to discuss legislation.").

234. Nepal's WLSP invites "[g]roups of approximately 100 women . . . to attend workshops organized in their villages. The workshops last two to three days. From among the 'graduates' of these short term on-the-spot classes, a smaller group of women are chosen and are given workshop training of longer duration and greater depth." Ibid., 106.

235. For a brief description of SALAG's "alternative law school," see text and notes at notes 247–249. For a description of the elaborate, perhaps more lawyerly, system of training and utilizing paralegals devised by the Legal Resources Foundation in Zimbabwe, see Wilson Tatenda Manase, "Legal Services in Rural Areas: The Zimbabwean Experience," *Third World Legal Studies—1992* (1992), 179–198.

236. For more information on this Perú Mujer program, see text and notes at notes 250–261.

237. Stephen Golub raises questions about the impact of "generalized human rights education" in Golub, "Democratizing Justice," 109–110. He suggests that "to the extent that any efforts along these lines . . . can focus on the aspects of the law most applicable to the audiences, those efforts would have a greater chance of being effective." An example of such generalized, but highly relevant, lay legal education could be the " 'civil rights card,' printed in Swahili by the Kituo Cha Sheria, informing citizens of their rights when arrested, or Kituo's leaflet telling women about steps to take after being raped," tools Claude Welch suggests may be extremely useful. Welch, *Human Rights in Africa*, 203. Welch also rightly reminds us of the potential accomplishments of public rights education over a long term, as in the campaign carried out by the Inter-African Committee on Traditional Practices Affecting the Health of Women and Children, against female genital circumcision. See ibid., 88–106.

238. For thoughtful comments on the elements of "successful paralegal development," see Golub, "Democratizing Justice," 104–109. Golub points, in particular, to the need for "paralegal development, not just training," including careful "initial screening and prepara-tion" of potential paralegals, and subsequent ongoing consultations or advice for the parale-gals from people with greater legal expertise.

In addition, Golub suggests that "at least some [Philippine paralegals] . . . tend to be better educated and slightly more affluent than their fellow PO ["people's organization"] members." Ibid., 108. Rather than "barefoot lawyers," as they are sometimes called, Golub suggests paralegals might better be thought of as "track shoe lawyers, reflecting what is often their slightly better incomes and security." Ibid., 109. These observations, ironically, point to another dilemma of representativity: if the most effective paralegals are slightly more privileged than their communities, then they may be tempted to distinguish their own interests from those of their fellows. Perhaps in part for this reason Golub also observes that paralegals may need the support (or supervision?) of a strong popular organization to make it "more likely that the paralegal will resist the temptation to adopt an attitude of superior-ity based on superior knowledge of the law." Ibid., 108. See also Dasso, "Paralegals," 180–181 (on tensions between Perú Mujer's paralegals-in-training and the community organiza-tions that had originally chosen them for training).

239. See, e.g., Butegwa, "Challenges of Promoting Legal Literacy," 150; Schuler and Kadirgamar-Rajasingham, "Legal Literacy," 23 and passim. Clarence Dias and James C. N. Paul have much the same objective in mind when they declare that "the rural poor will not be able to organize and press claims of immediate, direct concern unless legal resources are developed within communities—unless people themselves gain of functional knowledge of law and administration and learn how to use shared concepts of justice, customs and shared norms as part of the process of catalyzing participatory, self-reliant, collective action." Dias and Paul, "Lawyers, Legal Resources, and Alternative Approaches," 368.

240. G. S. Radha Krishna, "The Man from AWARE," *The Week*, December 31, 1989, 20.

241. Chaskalson, interview, A6. Zimbabwe's Legal Resources Foundation similarly su-pervises advice centers, staffed by LRF paralegals, and also takes referrals from "Advice Volunteers," "employees of the government or other NGO's . . . [who] use LRF's training to add another aspect to their work of grassroots education." Hutchins and Klaaren, *Public Interest Law*, 165; see Manase, "Legal Services," 185–91 (describing LRF's paralegal system in detail).

242. Groups employing one or more paralegals, or working with paralegals in the communities they serve, include Bangladesh's Madaripur Legal Aid Association, India's

AWARE, the Lawyer's Collective (also in India), the Indonesian Legal Aid Foundation, Mexico's DOAL, the Legal Assistance Centre in Namibia, Nepal's Women's Legal Services Project, Nigeria's Civil Liberties Organisation, Perú Mujer, the Black Lawyers Association in South Africa, the Legal Resources Centre (also in South Africa), and the Legal Resources Foundation in Zimbabwe. See Hutchins and Klaaren, *Public Interest Law*, 32, 51–53, 59, 65, 95, 102–103, 106, 109, 132, 136–140, 155, 161, 166–167.

In addition, Adolfo Triana Antorveza of FUNCOL emphasized the importance of paralegals to his organization's work, declaring that "[n]osotros sin paralegales no podemos trabajar." The paralegals with whom FUNCOL works, however, are evidently not on its staff; instead, they include a variety of people, from state functionaries to priests and, notably, the juridical committees ("comité[s] jurídico[s]") of the communities FUNCOL serves. Triana Antorveza, interview, 5. SALAG in the Philippines also does not have paralegals on its staff, but does have them in the communities, Medina, interview, 18–19, and works to train community paralegals through its "Alternative Law School." Hutchins and Klaaren, *Public Interest Law*, 142–143. In Mexico, DOAL has two paralegals on staff (see ibid., 95), but it too links up with the "comisiónes jurídicas" of the organizations it serves, and Efren Rodríguez González of DOAL commented that these groups have often had to go to court despite the difficulties of doing so and have acquired their own substantial legal experience. Rodríguez González, speaking at 1991 symposium, plenary session on "Methods of Using Law to Effect Social Change (continued)—Traditional Uses," 5.

243. Manase, interview, 18. Thus "in the rural areas where we provide the majority of our services, we have taken people who have lived there, people who know the kind of problems which are there." Ibid. There is a price to be paid for this form of representativeness, however, in representativeness of another sort—for the more important it is that paralegals be from the communities they serve, the less acceptable it will be to bring into the community paralegals from other backgrounds, including, for example, other ethnicities.

244. Here, too, however, a dilemma of representativeness can arise, for a paralegal chosen by a "community" will likely be one approved by that community's power structure, and sometimes—in particular, in the representation of women—cause lawyers may need to challenge that very power structure. To circumvent such problems, lawyers may need to look for potential paralegals in more distinct groups within the community, such as women's organizations—although even this step does not guarantee the absence of tension between the paralegal and the group of which she is a part (see note 238). Alternatively, advocates must find a way to enlist local power holders in their cause. In Uganda, for example, despite the continued force of the discriminatory heritage of customary law, a FIDA legal literacy effort targeted to women has received governmental support from the president, members of parliament, and local chiefs. Butegwa, "Challenges of Promoting Legal Literacy," 157.

245. Smuts, interview, 25. The paralegals may themselves be activists, as in Namibia (ibid., 15), and South Africa (see Ellmann, "Law and Legitimacy," 457 [establishment and staffing of South African advice centers largely the work of activists from community, church, and student groups]).

246. See note 242.

247. Medina, interview, 7–8.

248. Carlos Medina, speaking at 1991 symposium, plenary session on "Methods of Using Law to Effect Social Change (continued)—Traditional Uses," 7.

249. Ibid.

250. Elizabeth Dasso, speaking at 1991 symposium, plenary session on "Methods of Using Law to Effect Social Change (continued)—Alternative Uses," 6–7.

251. Dasso states that "[o]ne third of the women were illiterate and more than half

had little experience in reading and writing, a strong barrier to training." The challenge of reading and writing "was overcome by the women's interest in learning about their rights, since they needed to practice reading and writing to do so." Dasso, "Paralegals," 185.

252. Ibid., 177, 182–183.

253. This ideal, reminiscent of aspects of Paolo Freire's pedagogy, see note 317, is reflected in Francisco Díaz Rodríguez's description of the studies ("estudios") which his organization, the Centro de Estudios para la Aplicación del Derecho (CESPAD), undertakes. Díaz Rodríguez emphasized that CESPAD's studies are not academic but rather are a form of participative, popular education, in which the ordinary practice of the people is studied, but *with* the people rather than apart from them. ("[E]ntendemos la investigación participativa como un componente metodológico de una concepción de educación popular en la cual partimos de analizar la práctica ordinaria de la gente, pero lo hacemos con la gente no en nuestra oficina.") Díaz Rodríguez, speaking at 1991 symposium, plenary session on "Methods of Using Law to Effect Social Change (continued)—Alternative Uses," 11.

254. Medina, interview, 3. Medina also told the symposium that the discussions at SALAG's alternative law school "eventually lead to law reform advocacy and also to mobilization." Medina, speaking at 1991 symposium, plenary session on "Methods of Using Law to Effect Social Change (continued)—Traditional Uses," 7.

255. Thus Francisco Díaz Rodríguez explained that the participatory studies his group undertakes with the people (see note 253) generate popular recognition of the reality of violation of their rights ("[L]ogramos que la gente descubra que hay un sistema normativo en el país que por una parte establece cierto[s] derechos a su favor, que le estan haciendo sistemáticamente negados."). This theoretical perception in turn reverberates in action ("Con ese nivel de teorización . . . hay que volver a la práctica; a la práctica organizativa de la comunidad; a la práctica de la autogestión, y de la denuncia.") Díaz Rodríguez, speaking at 1991 symposium, plenary session on "Methods of Using Law to Effect Social Change (continued)—Alternative Uses," 11–12.

256. See Moloto, interview, A5 (South Africa); Smuts, interview, 49 (Namibia). Francisco Díaz Rodríguez of CESPAD expressly shared Smuts's view of "la necesidad de inculcar una cultura de derecho a la gente." Díaz Rodríguez, speaking at 1991 symposium, plenary session on "Methods of Using Law to Effect Social Change (continued)—Alternative Uses," 10.

257. Dasso, "Paralegals," 174.

258. Ibid., 171.

259. Ibid., 174.

260. Ibid., 171.

261. Ibid., 175.

262. See generally Stephen Ellmann, "Lawyers and Clients," *UCLA Law Review* 34 (1987), 717–779.

263. Huq, interview, 32.

264. See text at note 271.

265. Alkastar, interview, 70 (saying that community groups "[n]ever refuse" to follow the Indonesian Legal Aid Foundation's advice about the best course of action).

266. David Smuts pointed out that the influence of the Legal Assistance Centre varies, depending in part on the extent to which the decision in question turns on legal considerations, and also on the character of the relationship between the LAC and the client group. In addition, he emphasized that where the decision is a difficult one, the lawyer would try to explain both sides of the issue carefully. Nonetheless he concluded that "certainly I think that the role of our advice is quite significant in the outcome in the decision they'll take about their course of action." Smuts, interview, 42–43.

267. Like David Smuts (see note 266), Carlos Medina of SALAG emphasized that his group lays out the options for its clients and lets the clients decide, "because we don't actually want to impose our decisions on a community or push them to take a particular stand." Even so, he commented, "we do exercise a lot of influence on their decisions, so, normally, what we think is best for them, they usually follow, if they are prepared to face the consequences." Medina, interview, 29.

268. In Israel, the Association for Civil Rights in Israel will defer to a client decision not to take a case all the way to the High Court, but "if [the client] says, 'I don't want you to argue this argument,' we ask them to go to a private lawyer." Ziv, interview, 32. This division of authority resembles the standard American understanding of the spheres of client and lawyer decision, and perhaps would be echoed in other countries as well.

Writing from the perspective of "alternative law," Rojas comments that "[l]awyers cannot impose their own strategies or points of view. Neither are users allowed to completely deviate the project from its original goals. The required symbiosis of users and lawyers brings into existence potential frictions between the two." Rojas, "A Comparison of Change-Oriented Legal Services," 234.

269. Smuts, interview 38.

270. O. Nwankwo, interview, 20. Ms. Nwankwo also described a case in which a client sought the group's assistance to enable her to assert her right to participate in mourning rituals for her spouse, rituals the FIDA Clinic saw as degrading. "[W]e advised her that these rites were . . . one of the practices we are trying to eradicate in our laws and that since she was separated from her husband before he died, we didn't see why she should subject herself to such indignity. . . . So she said, " 'Oh, you're not talking like an Ibo lady.' " (In fact, the client did ultimately perform the mourning rituals.) O. Nwankwo, interview, 11.

271. Jaising, interview, 26.

272. In Bangladesh, Fazlul Huq said that "it is through our work they trust us, they believe in us." Huq, interview, 32. In Mexico, according to Efrén Rodríguez González, to win community groups' trust, DOAL's attorneys must first of all be skillful legal technicians, notably in the courts, the only place where they can challenge the legal resources of the rich. ("[P]ara podernos ganar la confianza primero requerimos ser buenos técnicos. . . . Y, solamente lo vamos a poder hacer si somos buenos abogados en los tribunales.") Rodríguez González, speaking at 1991 symposium, plenary session on "Methods of Using Law to Effect Social Change (continued)—Traditional Uses," 4.

273. In Namibia, David Smuts described his relationship with clients as not so strictly lawyer and client as "friends and co-partners in trying to achieve more social justice in our country." Smuts, interview, 58–59. Silu Singh, in Nepal, commented that clients could not tell their stories if they did not feel some friendship from their lawyer. Singh, interview, 36. In the Philippines, Carlos Medina thought that SALAG's client communities "appreciate what we do and like us for it. . . . We trust them because we find that they also trust us." He also observed that their relationships begin as lawyer-client ties, "and then, as the relationship grows, we become friends and then the relationship gets deeper." Medina, interview, 36–37.

274. Adolfo Triana Antorveza, for example, emphasized FUNCOL's desire for strong solidarity with community groups, but a solidarity entailing respect both for FUNCOL and for the community groups' independence ("Queremos manejar unas relaciónes de mucha solidaridad bilaterales, pero con el respeto mutuo en torno a nuestra organización y la independencia que ellos tienen que tener.") Triana Antorveza, interview, 7. Arthur Chaskalson observed that "in private practice lawyers are always telling people this is what we are going to do and this is a solution and the clients tend to hand over their cases to the

lawyers. And I think in this kind of [cause-lawyering] work the lawyers have got to be tremendously sensitive to what the community wants." Chaskalson, interview, A23. In similar vein, Francisco Díaz Rodríguez of CESPAD emphasized that his group would try to assist a community group to address a typical legal problem on its own, with more direct engagement only if the community's own efforts failed, because CESPAD's goal is not to substitute itself for the clients but to develop in them the ability to accomplish their ends ("[L]a idea nuestra no es substituir a las personas, sino desarrollar en ellos la capacidad de trabajo."). Díaz Rodríguez, interview, 4.

275. See text and note at note 159.

276. Ziv, interview, 29 (ACRI in Israel); Jaising, interview, 18 (Lawyers Collective in India). ACRI also often approaches the government on a policy question without having a specific client. Ziv, interview, 30. Probably much of the reporting and lobbying done by cause lawyers around the world is similarly done without the necessity of actually locating a client, and so reflects, again, the lawyers' ability to choose the causes on which they will focus. The opportunity for such initiative, in the Third World as well as in the United States, creates the possibility (though hardly the certainty) that cause lawyers will speak only for themselves while purporting to represent the public interest.

277. In the Philippines, for example, SALAG's case decisions depend in part on whether "the issue at stake . . . [is] one which affects a community, i.e. the client may either be an entire community belonging to a target sector or an individual faced with a problem the resolution of which will affect other persons similarly situated." Hutchins and Klaaren, *Public Interest Law*, 142. Stephen Meili comments that "[l]ike 'alternative' lawyers in other Latin America[n] countries, most Brazilian cause lawyers avoid taking individual cases unless they will lead to work on behalf of a larger group or organization." Meili, "The Interaction of Lawyers and Grass Roots Movements," 72. Cf. Dias, "Human Rights and Legal Resources," 50 (referring to the "cruel dilemmas" that can arise when activists working with the poor in Asia "[balance] the rights of collectivities and groups over those of individuals").

Political polarization may mean that a public interest group represents some communities, or parts of communities, and not others. The Legal Resources Centre in South Africa, for example, had an "adversary relationship" with the controversial Zulu organization Inkatha and went to court against it. Chaskalson, interview, A27–28. See also Smuts, interview, 40 ("[T]here are some people in the communities who we haven't traditionally worked with. Unfortunately, things are often a bit polarized politically . . . [b]ut they're not usually people who have consulted us."). Similarly, a women's rights group is unlikely to serve its clients well if it is prepared to let men's definitions of community concerns override women's needs. At the same time, however, groups seeking social change may need to pay close attention to the norms of the communities they seek to reform if they wish to make their proposed changes effective. In the words of Wilson Manase of Zimbabwe's Legal Resources Foundation, the LRF initially tried too much to "dictate what the people want. Now these days we have changed that condition, we actually take into account what the society wants and then we draft the materials based on that. So, it is a bottom-to-top approach, not a top-to-bottom approach." Manase, interview, 22. Diplomacy may be essential; cooptation is the attendant peril.

278. See Jaising, interview, 22–23 (because community groups are needed to make litigation victories effective, "in order to make the maximum use of scarce resources, it is better to take up litigation in areas where the communities are already well organized, and are able to service the members of the community"); Meili, "The Interaction of Lawyers and Social Movements," 72 (commenting that for cause lawyers involved in the most active

field of work, poor people's property rights, generally "a grass roots group must already exist; it would be anathema to the goal of de-emphasizing the hierarchical role of lawyers for them to create such an organization"); Rojas, "A Comparison of Change-Oriented Legal Services," 249 (mentioning that "some groups, particularly those more influenced by religious commitment, feel that disorganized communities or those with a low level of political development should not be excluded from new legal services projects"; presumably *other* groups disagree).

279. See Jaising, interview, 24 (stating that long-term relationships enable lawyers to build up the legal expertise of group members—and "many people from within those groups have gone on to . . . become lawyers and get on with handling their own problems without necessarily turning back to us"); Medina, interview, 28 (SALAG's effort to "maintain continuing relationship with these organizations"); Rojas, "A Comparison of Change-Oriented Legal Services," 233–234 (noting that alternative lawyers carefully select their "users" or "beneficiaries," since "a long-term relation is going to be built up between lawyers and grassroot groups or communities"). In the United States the NAACP Legal Defense Fund maintained a long-term relationship with Martin Luther King's Southern Christian Leadership Conference. Greenberg, *Crusaders in the Courts,* 347–348.

280. For example, the Legal Resources Centre in South Africa "never goes out and looks for a community." The initial contact might either result from the community leaders approaching the LRC themselves, or from a referral by a support group working with the community. Chaskalson, interview, A18. Somewhat similarly, Meili comments that in property rights work in Brazil, ordinarily "the group must approach the [cause] lawyer for assistance, rather than vice versa," but he adds that "[m]any cause lawyers render service to individual members of a group in order to convince their fellow group members to seek legal support on a group-wide basis." Meili, "The Interaction of Lawyers and Social Movements," 72 and n.22.

Community group initiative may go beyond seeking representation. Such groups may become directly involved in the operation of the cause-lawyering project. In Namibia, for instance, the Legal Assistance Centre operates one office for which a community organization functions as a kind of advisory board (Smuts, interview, 35), and in 1991 was planning to open another office but awaiting the presentation of plans for it from a community-formed committee. Ibid., 27.

281. Hall and Fretz emphasize "group representation" as one of the primary characteristics of "innovative legal services" in the Third World. Hall and Fretz, "Legal Services," 786. One reflection on the field, however, indicates that there is wide variation in the degree of actual work in partnership with groups, and that claims of such partnering can exceed reality. IHRIP, "Legal Resources Project," 3 and n.3.

282. These include certain organizations that are directly involved in community organizing, mentioned in note 288, and the following: Colombia's FUNCOL, El Salvador's CESPAD, the Lawyers Collective in India, DOAL in Mexico, the Indonesian Legal Aid Foundation, the Legal Assistance Centre in Namibia, Nepal's Women's Legal Services Project, SALAG in the Philippines, South Africa's Legal Resources Centre, and the Legal Resources Foundation in Zimbabwe. See Hutchins and Klaaren, *Public Interest Law,* 37–40, 43, 62–63, 93–95, 142–143, 160; Jaising, interview, 22–24 (Lawyers Collective); Smuts, interview, 8 (Legal Assistance Centre); Singh, interview, 12–13, 28 (Women's Legal Services Project); Manase, interview, 22–23 (Legal Resources Foundation). Women in Law and Development in Africa is a networking group that works with women's groups in many African countries (Hutchins and Klaaren, *Public Interest Law,* 168–173), and takes pride that it is, itself, "an African institution founded in Africa" (ibid., 171). At least some of the other groups at the 1991

symposium have links with NGOs, but not necessarily directly with the kinds of indigenous community groups that Stephen Golub calls POs or "popular organizations." Golub, "Democratizing Justice," 116.

283. Thus Arthur Chaskalson commented that "[t]he LRC has always seen itself as a supportive agency. It would never go out into a community and say we are going to organize this community. It would be quite contrary to what LRC believes lawyers should do. Quite contrary actually to the political etiquette in South Africa where communities take the lead themselves." Chaskalson, interview, A14–15. See also note 165 (views of DOAL in Mexico).

284. Chaskalson, interview, A15; Singh, interview, 28. Dias and Paul emphasize the importance of "internal 'constitutions,' " which they suggest can enhance resolution of disputes "in ways which emphasize the need for cohesiveness and, often, collective interests," and "may also serve as a check to prevent one group from exploiting or harassing another, to help people develop notions of law as a reflection of shared values and principles." Dias and Paul, "Lawyers, Legal Resources, and Alternative Approaches," 367.

285. Groups that have pursued this strategy include DOAL in Mexico (see Hutchins and Klaaren, *Public Interest Law,* 94–95); and the Legal Resources Centre in South Africa (Chaskalson, interview, A21).

286. See note 274 (describing the approach of CESPAD in El Salvador).

287. Stephen Meili reports that Brazilian cause lawyers give advice to client groups contemplating "occupation" of land. He notes that several lawyers "emphasized that the cause lawyers do not advise the groups to undertake an illegal occupation; they simply provide advice as to the legality and possible ramifications." Meili, "The Interaction of Lawyers and Grass Roots Movements," 73 and n.24.

288. India's AWARE was intensely engaged in community organizing, including but not limited to generating "a massive, 90–day demonstration" by Indian tribal minorities. Hutchins and Klaaren, *Public Interest Law,* 50–52. For further discussion of AWARE's work see text and notes at notes 289–312. Perú Mujer's comprehensive program for training "promotoras legales" created a new legal services institution for poor communities. See text at notes 250–261. A third group that appears to have been engaged in community organizing, at least in the sense of raising community consciousness, is Geledes in Brazil, Arruda da Silva, interview, 4–5. It deserves emphasis that many of the group-focused activities of other cause lawyers, such as community legal education and assistance with internal constitutions, might well be considered "community organizing," and so a number of other groups at the 1991 symposium might also fairly be said to be engaged in organizing work.

289. AWARE's legal department employs approximately 100 people, including 12 lawyers and 26 social investigators. Hutchins and Klaaren, *Public Interest Law,* 53. The organization's total staff numbers 700 full-time people, as well as some 1,245 part-time organizers and tens of thousands of volunteers. See ibid.

290. White, "To Learn and Teach," 760–767. Some observers, however, might be very skeptical about lawyers' ability to perform the organizer role properly. See Schuler and Kadirgamar-Rajasingham, "Legal Literacy," 57 ("Lawyer-initiated, law-based legal literacy tends to be content-focused, information-oriented and rooted in the fallacious view that information and knowledge of the law are sufficient inputs for people to exercise their rights.").

291. William Simon has observed that in the 1960s "the leaders of the [American] corporate bar were considered creators of organizations for investors and managers, [though] it was unheard of for a legal aid lawyer to get involved in, say, forming a tenants union or a welfare rights organization." Simon, "Visions of Practice," 478; see also William H. Simon, "The Dark Secret of Progressive Lawyering: A Comment on Poverty Law Schol-

arship in the Post-Modern, Post-Reagan Era," *University of Miami Law Review* 48, 1106–1111 (1994).

292. Madhavan, interview, 1, 23–24; Krishna, "Man from AWARE," 14–18; Hutchins and Klaaren, *Public Interest Law,* 49–54.

293. Madhavan, interview, 18.

294. Hutchins and Klaaren, *Public Interest Law,* 52.

295. See ibid., 54.

296. See ibid., 50.

297. Sohoni and Singh, *People in Action,* 98.

298. Krishna, "Man from AWARE," 28.

299. See Sohoni and Singh, *People in Action,* 99–100.

300. Ibid., 20 (quoting Madhavan) (typographical errors corrected; emphasis in original).

301. Ibid., at 33.

302. On AWARE's administrative reorganization, to prevent itself from becoming an unresponsive bureaucracy, see ibid., 83–84.

303. Krishna, "Man from AWARE," 22.

304. Ibid.

305. Madhavan, interview, 19.

306. Krishna, "Man from AWARE," 16.

307. Sononi and Singh, *People in Action,* 110; see ibid., 90 (describing Madhavan as providing "a totally committed and charismatic leadership").

308. Krishna, "Man from AWARE," 18–20.

309. Ibid., 30.

310. Ibid. Even children, organized in the "children's association" that AWARE encourages each village to establish (along with an adult association, a women's forum, and a youth group), "[o]ften . . . get coopted to act as the 'eyes and ears' of the village women in ensuring the success of community campaigns such as the banning of liquor." Sohoni and Singh, *People in Action,* 86–87.

311. Krishna, "Man from AWARE," 28.

312. Cf. Simon, "Dark Secret," at 1108–1111 (describing "two traditional approaches to organizing disadvantaged people," the first of which, the "cathartic" method, "structures a situation to induce a sense of common interest, hope, and potency among the people [the organizer] is trying to organize," and the second of which "involves the conditional provision of benefits" in exchange for membership).

313. White, "To Learn and Teach," 723–745, 760–768.

314. Ibid., 763.

315. The groups at the 1991 symposium that were engaged in educational efforts sharing such aspirations included CESPAD in El Salvador, SALAG in the Philippines, Perú Mujer, and Women in Law and Development in Africa—and very possibly others.

316. Lucie E. White, "Collaborative Lawyering in the Field? On Mapping the Paths from Rhetoric to Practice," *Clinical Law Review* 1 (1994), 167.

317. As emphatically, and admirably, as Freire emphasizes in the *Pedagogy of the Oppressed* that oppressed people must be the authors of their own transformation and that pedagogy must be truly dialogical, he also seems to see the process of self-discovery the oppressed would follow as having only one appropriate end. "This pedagogy makes oppression and its causes objects of reflection by the oppressed, and from that reflection will come their necessary engagement in the struggle for their liberation. And in the struggle this pedagogy will be made and remade." Freire, *Pedagogy of the Oppressed,* 33. To professionals

who participate in the Freirian process of "decoding concrete situations" and who maintain that they are being manipulated, Freire responds that "[t]he coordinator isn't trying to 'steer' them anywhere; it is just that in facing a concrete situation as a problem, the participants begin to realize that if their analysis of the situation goes any deeper they will either have to divest themselves of their myths, or reaffirm them." Ibid., 155.

318. Klawiter, "La Tierra Es Nuestra," 1674.

319. Ibid., 1673–1674.

320. Ibid., 1675.

321. Ibid., 1677. The several preceding excerpts from Klawiter's account of this meeting are all drawn from ibid., 1675–1677.

322. White, "To Learn and Teach," 763.

323. See Ellmann, "Client-Centeredness Multiplied," 1167–1169.

324. Welch, *Human Rights in Africa,* 240–241. Welch also illuminates the potential breadth of rights discourse, for example with respect to the right of self-determination and the right to development. Ibid., 107–111, 274–276.

325. Brandt considers entanglement with "a specific local political party" a dangerous course for an alternative law group. "In Latin America," he writes, "there are cases where left wing parties have regarded some legal services projects as a means of making political contact with grass-roots groups in society. Such a strategy oriented towards catching voters regularly leads in the long run to political squabbles within the grass-roots groups, and, as a result, to the failure of the orginal aims of the project." Brandt, "Human Rights," 43.

326. Chaskalson, interview, B21, B25–26; see also Moloto, interview, B14, B31–32, B34 (The Black Lawyers Association in South Africa also remained neutral with regard to competing antiapartheid political groups in the black community and was "always . . . able to work with all groups. . . . There has been a problem only when there's been interorganizational violence."). For another example of such a stance, see Medina, interview, 31 (SALAG is prepared to help anyone, regardless of ideology or affiliation, "as long as they are covered by our terms of reference."). For a striking instance of a cause-lawyering group that felt, for reasons both of principle and pragmatics, that it needed to avoid working with certain political groups, see Greenberg, *Crusaders in the Courts,* 102–106, 402–411 (NAACP Legal Defense Fund's bleak attitudes toward Communists and advocates of revolutionary violence).

327. See Steiner, *Diverse Partners,* 36–37.

328. Welch illustrates this and other risks of politicization with his account of the Nigerian government's response to the Campaign for Democracy. Welch, *Human Rights in Africa,* 251–255, 303, 307; see text and notes at notes 335–337.

329. DOAL, in Mexico, is "independent of all political parties, churches, or academic institutions." Hutchins and Klaaren, *Public Interest Law,* 92. In Israel, ACRI was established to be "a non-political, non-partisan civil rights organization." Ziv, interview, 1. The Quaker Legal Aid and Information Service "tr[ies] to stay away from political elements. . . . Because we don't want to be closed or threatened with closure, we don't want to be accused of being a political group." Shamas, interview, B7. In Namibia, the Legal Assistance Centre has "a very clear-cut policy which we repeatedly spell out, of being independent from any political party, and serving only the goals that we seem to . . . further." Smuts, interview, 47. Nepal's Women's Legal Services Program is "purely social" and has "nothing to do with the political parties." Singh, interview, 31. In Nigeria, Obiageli Nwankwo explained that FIDA is "non-political" and has no links to political parties or political movements. O. Nwankwo, interview, 21. Zimbabwe's Legal Resources Foundation has no links to any political party, and its executive director in 1991, Wilson Manase, said that as far as political affiliations, "[p]ersonally, I would say, I don't know what I am." Manase, interview, 23.

Of the groups at the 1991 symposium, the Nigerian Institute of Advanced Legal Studies was officially perhaps the least political, or at any rate the least oppositional in its politics. NIALS's regular budget is funded by the Nigerian government and its governing council is made up primarily of military government appointees. Nonetheless the institute has been able to contribute to human rights thinking in Nigeria and indeed evidently felt that its "most recent research project, on Human Rights and the Administration of Criminal Justice, was successfully carried out in part because of the co-operation of the various government institutions involved, such as the police, the prisons and the courts. NGOs in Nigeria find such co-operation extremely difficult to achieve." Hutchins and Klaaren, *Public Interest Law,* 126–127; Okagbue, interview, 25 (noting that this study was "very critical of all the institutions we examined").

A number of other groups at the 1991 symposium were also working with their governments in one way or another, for example in training security forces (see Hutchins and Klaaren, *Public Interest Law,* 70 [ACRI in Israel]; 166 [Zimbabwe's Legal Resources Foundation]), or in other projects. India's Lawyers Collective, for example, accepts Indian government funds, for a prisoners' rights project, but takes no foreign funds. Jaising, interview, 17–18. AWARE, too, appears to work both with the government and, when necessary, against it. Sohoni and Singh, *People in Action,* 106. Doing so may often be an effective tactic; in some countries, it may be the *only* tactic possible.

330. India's AWARE apparently organized a march of 250,000 people from tribal minorities to the house of a senior judge, as part of a protest against an attempt to repeal a statute protecting tribal people's land rights. Madhavan, interview, 14; see Hutchins and Klaaren, *Public Interest Law,* 52. Other cause lawyers, though not engaging in such efforts themselves, may have advised their community-group clients when those clients considered such tactics (though this advice would have been constrained where the applicable law made these tactics illegal). Cf. notes 287, 337.

331. Thus Fazlul Huq of the Madaripur Legal Aid Association in Bangladesh said that "we do not side with any political party, but one thing we do, we fight for human rights, and . . . democracy is one." Huq, interview, 33. In Brazil, Geledes is "apolitical. Now it's not apolitical, it's just not aligned to any party." Arruda da Silva, interview, 13 (as expressed by the translator in the interview). Jaising said that the Lawyers Collective of India "doesn't have any links with any political parties, but it does have close sympathies with generally the Left in the country." Jaising, interview, 27. Similarly, AWARE is "non-party, although we are political, we don't support any political organizations." Madhavan, interview, 18. In Israel, ACRI lobbies with all parties but "[w]e usually get more help from the left." Ziv, interview, 33. Nigeria's National Association of Democratic Lawyers listed as one of its activities that it "[s]upports [l]iberation [m]ovements." Hutchins and Klaaren, *Public Interest Law,* 119. Elizabeth Dasso said that for some members of Perú Mujer work with this group "is a sort of a social compromise. I am not a member of a political party, most of our members . . . are not involved in political parties, but we think that this kind of work is . . . a political option." Dasso, interview, 11. In the Philippines, SALAG is "nonpartisan and nonideological," but "[o]f course, what we do is ultimately political in nature." Medina, interview, 31, 38. In South Africa, Arthur Chaskalson said that the Legal Resources Centre "would clearly see ourselves as part of a struggle for rights." Chaskalson, interview, B26.

332. Adolfo Triana Antorveza of FUNCOL said that his organization has always had a great deal of difficulty with existing political groups, and said that they harbored the hope of someday forming a new party. Triana Antorveza, interview, 8 ("Tenemos la esperanza de que alguna vez podamos formar un partido en Colombia."). Rojas comments that "Latin American new legal services groups do not always find it easy to remain independent from political parties. Nor do their personnel always want to be independent of political parties.

Indeed, most legal services groups are subject to lobbying efforts and pres[s]ures from radical political parties wishing to channel their proselytism through NGOs." Rojas, "A Comparison of Change-Oriented Legal Services," 247. But he maintains that the "overall conceptual and strategic approach to development [of the new legal services groups] is alien to the idea of a patronizing government or a clientelist political party." Ibid., 216.

333. Though not focusing on lawyers' groups in particular, Steiner mentions that "[d]uring the Indian Emergency, many NGOs quietly urged citizens to vote against Indira Gandhi and helped to draft the new government's five-year plan. In the Philippines, many NGOs urged votes for Aquino." Steiner, *Diverse Partners*, 71.

334. Lev, "Lawyers' Causes."

335. See Welch, *Human Rights in Africa*, 251–255.

336. Ibid., 252. The role of the Civil Liberties Organisation is especially striking, for in 1992—after the founding of the Campaign for Democracy, but before the 1993 demonstrations that constituted the campaign's most dramatic challenge to the military—Olisa Agbakoba, the CLO's president, wrote in a paper presented to a judicial conference organized by the Nigerian Institute of Advanced Legal Studies that "a typical human rights NGO is essentially apolitical. Political affiliation strikes at the credibility . . . (and the very essence) of a human rights organisation." Agbakoba, "The Role of Non-Governmental Organisations," 143.

337. Similar reasoning can lead lawyers to believe that the boundaries the law places on the struggle for human rights are unjust and should be disobeyed. Ardila and Clark observe that in most Latin American states "the most common forms of struggle—community mobilization, protest marches, sit-ins and other pressure tactics—are actually prohibited by criminal codes and the police. Legal strategies at most complement these struggles by attempting to provide legitimacy to illegal action." Ardila and Clark, "Alternative Legal Practice," 110.

CHAPTER 13

Lawyers' Causes in Indonesia and Malaysia

DANIEL LEV

The principal cause at issue in this essay is one dear to private lawyers every-where—the rule of law itself.[1] In Indonesia and Malaysia the private legal professions have produced activists in about the same proportion, most likely, as most other countries. In trying circumstances they defend political detainees, represent issues of human rights, challenge unsympathetic governments, and organize persistent efforts on behalf of imperiled citizens. As they do so, an associated concern is often at play in which many other lawyers not much inclined to causework and a crowd of laymen have a stake. This other claim to effective legal process emerges from an amalgam of professional interest and ideological commitment—favorable working conditions for private lawyers but also a supportive concept of state, in pursuit of which committed advocates have fought hard against tough odds.

The odds differ, however, along with the settings that determine them. Institutional, political, and ideological environments establish why and how lawyer-activists do their work and under what sorts of constraints. It is their quite different surroundings that make for a useful comparison of Indonesian and Malaysian lawyers.

Although the two countries share a few ethnic and religious features, for the rest their social structures, political organization, and histories diverge hugely. Indonesia, with a population of about 190 million, of whom 88 percent are Muslims, was a Dutch colony, from which it inherited a Continental European civil law system. It gained independence by way of a revolution (1945–1950) that mobilized large segments of society around the archipelago and set off rapid, jolting changes of political regime thereafter. Malaysia, by contrast, is much smaller, with a population of about 17 million, of whom a bare majority are ethnic Malay (52 percent), all of whom are Islamic, with substantial ethnic Chinese (35 percent) and ethnic Indian (10 percent) minorities. Under English administration until 1957, when sovereignty was transferred peacefully, its common law–derived legal system, though strained in recent years, has worked more effectively than any other in Southeast Asia.

By way of a preliminary comment on our topic, not much attention has been paid lawyer-activists in new states, partly perhaps because of an old suspicion, rooted in equally worn cultural analyses, that law cannot mean much outside the "West." Doubts about law extend to lawyers, whose peculiar interest in rule of law or *rechtsstaat* notions has not been taken overly seriously by scholars. Nor is the wider significance of what lawyers do in and out of court all that obvious to anyone concentrating on grander issues of "development" and the like. Lawyers, by and large, are not understood to be political actors or ideological spokesmen. Yet in Indonesia and Malaysia, as in a few other countries undergoing economic and social transformations, over the last quarter century or more the salience of private lawyers has grown along with the appeal of the issues they have raised. Their influence should not be exaggerated, but neither should it be ignored.

In this essay, my concern is not with whether some form of law state is likely or not, for whatever reasons, anywhere at all, but rather with a struggle over the question in two countries. In Indonesia and Malaysia, small contingents of private lawyers, articulate proponents of rule of law values, have gone out of their way to defend them. Why they take the trouble requires some explanation.

Indonesia

No profession in Indonesia has undergone so uncertain an evolution as the advocacy. The first few Indonesian advocates who began to practice in the 1920s, despite the misgivings of colonial authorities, constituted an essentially new group that was both nationalist and progressive. Contemptuous of the local customary structures maintained by the colonial administration, they leaned to an independent state fully outfitted with the modern legal institutions and codes in which they had proved themselves. More than most, they understood clearly the alternative models of state implicitly maintained in the Netherlands East Indies. In the plural colonial legal system, organized around distinct courts and codes for the different ethnic communities of Europeans, native Indonesians, and "foreign Orientals" (ethnic Chinese, Arabs, and Indians), Indonesian advocates were in a position to explore the whole of its geography. On the European side of the colonial state political-legal authority resided in rigorous codes and judicial institutions staffed by highly trained and respected public and private lawyers. Their normative values assumed legal equality, certainty, and predictability. On the Indonesian side, authority was patrimonial more than legal, vested less in courts than in a bureaucracy oriented to social and political hierarchy, not equality, and to the privileges of officials, not the rights of citizens. The one side appreciated lawyers; the other did not. In the courts for Europeans, legal counsel was obligatory; in the courts for Indonesians, anyone at all or no one might act as counsel.

Advocates decidedly favored the European over the Indonesian side of colonial administration, a choice that implied an interest in refashioning Indonesian social and political organization to suit a state of basically liberal design. During and after the revolution, politically active private lawyers consistently favored institutional reforms toward procedural uniformity and legal equality. In positions of authority they opposed traditional local privileges, eliminated customary (*adat*) courts, sought to create a nationally unified judiciary, and tried to strengthen courts against executive aggression.

While more influential than their numbers suggest, the size of the profession was limiting.[2] Even among the small group of legally trained Indonesians (fewer than four hundred when the Japanese army invaded in early 1942), private lawyers or advocates numbered only about eighty. Most indigenous lawyers joined the colonial regime as *landraden* (superior courts for Indonesians) judges or as administrators or scholars whose experience on the Indonesian side of the colonial legal system promoted another ideological perspective.

Tension between the two political-legal orientations broke out openly late in the Japanese occupation, before the revolution (1945–1950) began against the Dutch effort to restore the colony. In July 1945, a month before the Japanese surrendered, when the first constitution of the independent state was drafted, a debate erupted between Mohammad Yamin and Raden Sumpomo, the former a West Sumatran who worked briefly as an advocate and the latter a Javanese scholar-official. Yamin proposed a constitutional bill of rights, a supreme court with powers of judicial review, and clearly separated legislative, judicial, and executive functions. Rejecting the institutional experience of the colony, his premises—a distinction between state and society, recognition of individual interests and rights, and the need for institutional controls over political authority—challenged all the constructs of political authority that underlay the administration of Indonesian society in the Netherlands East Indies.[4]

Supomo, closely associated with colonial policies intended to preserve local customary law regimes, was the most influential legal technician in the preparatory commissions for independence and largely responsible for drafting the short, executive-heavy constitution of 1945. If some nationalist leaders accepted the institutional heritage of the colony because they knew no other, Supomo consciously preferred it. Against Yamin's radical proposal he insisted that Indonesian jurists had no experience beyond Continental European civil law, which had already been adapted to Indonesian conditions and was known to those who would have to staff the independent state. Supomo's political agenda was more interesting. Committed to preserving not only the existing legal order but the authority of the aristocracy on which colonial administration had depended, in Java especially, his analysis flowed logically from the ideology of colonial-Javanese patrimonialism.[5] Liberal individualism was out of the question, according to Supomo, for the new state was to be conceived as a family, whose interests superseded those of individual members. The constitutional rights against state authority that Yamin wanted were unnecessary, for state and society were indivisible, led by an ascriptive elite responsible for ascertaining and defending the interests of state-society. The evident superiority of this elite, and the totality of its responsibility, rendered controls superfluous.[6]

Both positions have survived in a long debate in which Supomo's case has had most of the political advantages but Yamin's has stayed alive and picked up support in recent decades. Supomo's political ideas lost out for a time during the early parliamentary period of independence, but his legal predilections were consolidated early in the revolution, to the disappointment of professional advocates. The revolutionary republic sustained the Japanese occupation decision to unify the judiciary around the colonial courts for Indonesians, the Landraden (now Pengadilan Negeri), rather than the European courts (Raad van Justitie), and adopted the procedural code for Indonesians (Herziene Indonesisch Reglement. HIR) rather than the European codes of civil and criminal procedure preferred by advocates. Thereafter, in effect, the independent state was governed by the most repressive side of the colonial procedural regime.[7]

Even so, if the legal system needed work, the liberal constitution of 1950 and the parliamentary system it supported until 1959 satisfied advocates. The profession was thin just after independence, in part because so many advocates took up positions in the government, but its members were optimistic. Constitutionalism and the parliamentary *rechtsstaat*—a *negara hukum* (law state) in its Indonesian version—seemed promising to the kind of evolution advocates took for granted.

As it turned out, however, their confidence was misplaced; what loomed instead was an abyss. With remarkable ease, beginning in early 1957 the army and President Soekarno swept aside the parliamentary system. Its successor, Guided Democracy, quintessentially charismatic and patrimonial, razed all the supports professional advocates thought secure—liberal constitutionalism, autonomous and effective legal process, and a legitimate private economy. Soekarno dismissed liberal *negara hukum* ideas as an instrument of those who would surrender Indonesian originality to European political fashion, a distraction from his own compelling quest for an independent Indonesia shaped from its own culture and purpose. Jeering at assorted liberals, among them lawyers—with whom (he quoted the German socialist leader Karl Liebknecht) one could not make a revolution—Soekarno erased the principles of separation of powers and judicial independence.[8]

The Guided Democracy years elated few lawyers of any sort, but advocates suffered most professionally, politically, and ideologically. Judges and even a few prosecutors regretted their own loss of institutional autonomy, yet retained the rewards of official status at a time of rising bureaucratic authority. Private lawyers lost clients, professional stature, and more. Their own institutional base and spring of professional legitimacy in the judiciary became instead a source of pain and indignity. Nakedly unofficial, advocates stood apart from the collegial circle of civil servants in the judicial system. They and their clients paid heavily for it, and still do. Professional satisfaction evaporated. Paralyzed and stagnant, the advocacy, numbering in the early 1960s 250 to 300 nationwide, if that, drew scarcely any new recruits. In March 1963, in an effort to save their profession, a dozen or so senior advocates finally organized a national association, PERADIN.[9]

When Guided Democracy came to a brutal end following the coup of October 1965, senior advocates were quick to join the forces of reform in and out of the legal system. They helped to frame many of the key issues of New Order politics from 1966 on—restoration of legal process, institutional reform, constitutionalism, and human rights. Because of the experience of the Soekarno years, and because fundamental political features of Guided Democracy also informed the military-dominated New Order, the arguments that advocates brought to bear on the state drew support among a larger and more critically interested audience than ever before. Not formally or exclusively, but unmistakably, reform advocates spoke to and for this audience.

By the time remaining pockets of old-regime resistance were mopped up in the late 1960s, a new debate broke out over the shape of the political system and state-society relations, tracing back to the Supomo-Yamin confrontation of 1945 but enriched by two decades of experience. The protagonists were the army and state bureaucracy, on the one hand, and a small but expanding universe of self-consciously private groups, on the other. Resting on military force and jealous of political privilege, the government took for granted the priority of state interests. The other view, emphasizing controls that were predicated inter alia on autonomous judicial institutions, favored a better balance between state and private interests. Across the chasm, advocates and their allies insisted on legal predictability, protection of private interests, and constitutional limits on state power while New Order leaders stressed stability, fuller control over a diverse society, expansion of state power, and consolidation of the army's special claim to leadership.

It was barely a contest. By the time General Suharto assumed the presidency in 1967–1968, army leadership had no reason to submit to institutional controls over political and bureaucratic authority. From the regime's point of view, autonomous legal process was not an appropriate means of social and political management, for it could only diminish the responsibilities (and prerogatives) of political leadership. Despite occasional public assurances to the contrary, the legal system was understood to be subordinate to the prior claims of political authority.

Legal officials, with few exceptions, accepted their submerged role. Like the rest of the civil service, judges needed few explicit reminders that they were subject to the will of political leadership. Any other view violated the solidary bureaucratic ethos of the New Order administration and endangered their careers. State leaders spoke the language of constitutional authority but acted confidently with nearly unconstrained power. At their disposal was a security apparatus staffed by the military, whose extralegal procedures paralleled and, at will, superseded or subordinated conventional legal process.[10]

Concessions to demands for administrative and judicial probity were largely symbolic, unenforceable without useful institutional machinery or political recourse. The government deflected an effort, led by judges and advocates, to give the Supreme Court (Mahkamah Agung) powers of judicial review over legislative and executive acts.[11] Complaints against judicial corruption and prosecutorial abuse went largely unanswered. Governnment promises to control administrative corruption meant little. A new statute on judicial organization (Law 14/1970) provided for legal representation of accused persons from the time of arrest, but the implementing legistation it required was not forthcoming.[12] Each reform was intended to impose restrictions on bureaucratic privilege, discretion, and prerogative: diminutions of public authority conceded on paper but rejected as long as possible in practice.[13]

Reform interests in legal process belong to various segments of a growing professional, commercial, and intellectual middle class, a rigidly controlled working class, and religious and ethnic minorities, among others: whoever lacks useful influence in the regime. The New Order confirmed the lesson of Guided Democracy that without a share in state power, one needed defenses against it.

No one articulated these views more clearly than the professional advocacy, which itself was transformed by New Order economic growth. Until the late 1960s the profession consisted of a small group of specialists in litigation—essentially, barristers. As foreign and domestic investment grew after 1966, so did the profession of advocacy, gradually transforming itself in the process. Numbering perhaps 250 in 1965, about the same as in the last years of the colony (including both Dutch and Indonesian attorneys), by 1970 the profession had doubled or better. From 1971 through 1984 a total of 1,075 new advocates registered with the Ministry of Justice. As many more, perhaps, did not bother to register, which saved them trouble and money but had little other effect. An uncertain current estimate of the number of legally educated private practitioners, both registered and unregistered, is 5,000 or more. Sometime during this period of expansion the ratio of advocates to population surpassed that in the colony, about one per 350,000 at best, and now may be in the vicinity of one per 40,000.

At the same time, the average age of advocates declined as seniors retired and younger lawyers began to find the private sector more attractive than the civil service. For the first time, the profession attracted lateral recruits from the ranks of retired judges, prosecutors, other civil servants, and military lawyers. Moreover, the features of private lawyering were redefined by the emergence of a stratum of nonlitigators, "consulting lawyers," specializing in commercial legal counseling and negotiation. Rather like solicitors or office lawyers who are not notaries but do not fit the traditional mold of advocates, the most successful of them are organized in new multimember law firms with incomes unimaginable only a couple of decades ago.[14]

Such changes have affected the social and political outlook of the profession, now quite diverse. Successful consulting lawyers (and a few advocates proper) exist in a lucrative, comfortable commercial stratosphere, well insulated from the everyday miseries of the courts and of clients who have to deal with them. They may appreciate reformers but themselves tend to political quiescence. Among advocates, those who rely on official contacts do not risk critical activism of any sort, whatever their sympathies. In 1978, when the advocates' association, PERADIN, proclaimed itself to be a "struggle organization" dedicated to reform, a few members pulled out, founding their own organization.[15]

The newfound size, prosperity, and public salience of the advocacy, however, also supported the reform efforts of a respectable number of lawyer-activists. Their most influential creation was the Legal Aid Institute (Lembaga Bantuan Hukum, or LBH) of Jakarta, now a national foundation, which started a legal aid boom involving many lawyers around the country. Founded with PERADIN sponsorship in 1970, the LBH institutionalized the political vision of reform advocates. More than a provider of legal assistance to the poor, it has become Indonesia's most prominent center of social-legal and political-legal criticism and reform activity.[16]

On issues of reform, private lawyers divide sharply according to professional interests and experience. Litigating lawyers, who see the shortcomings of the regime in the conditions under which they represent their clients, have always been the most committed reformers. Court work is miserable, not only because of the corruption involved, in which some advocates have participated more or less equitably in the so-called judicial Mafia of collusive prosecutors, judges, and private lawyers. Rather, since the Guided Democracy years these are just about the only terms on which the role of advocacy in the judicial system is accorded recognition and some respect.

Civil litigation is invariably difficult—time consuming, expensive, with no assurance that judgments will be executed—so that advocates avoid it if they can, and some have withdrawn from it altogether in favor of office practice. But criminal process incurs the most serious hardships. For advocates, criminal defense is treacherous, filled with abusive police, corrupt and extortionate prosecutors, bureaucratically minded judges who favor prosecutors as colleagues and regard defense attorneys as interlopers. Advocates have raised a perpetual clamour over these problems on behalf of their clients and themselves, leading now and then to open conflict with judges.[17]

Beyond the courts, reform advocates have done somewhat better. Paid attention to by the press and by a pertinent but largely powerless parliamentary committee, they have had some influence in statutory reforms whose effect, however, has been limited.[18] Few legislative improvements have been accompanied by the political and institutional changes that might consolidate them.[19] The government did not abide by the spirit or even the letter of a new code of criminal procedure promulgated in 1980 on any issue of political import. Dissidence remained subject to the attentions of the security apparatus; and even common criminality was often dealt with as if the code did not exist.[20]

Even so, the government has not been able to ignore the outcry raised by activist advocates. Particularly outspoken and courageous lawyers—the late senior advocates Yap Thiam Hien and Suardi Tasrif, for example, the LBH founder, Adnan Buyung Nasution, and former LBH directors Mulya Lubis and Abdul Hakim G. Nusantara, among several others—have captured public attention, but so have less well-known younger advocates for their defense of political detainees and promotion of human rights. Eventually, the government was likely to confront the activist bar not much more subtly than it dealt with the critical press.

New Order leaders domesticated the legal system as they had the rest of the state bureaucracy, in part by imposing military direction, which served the interests of both political security and patronage for (usually) retired generals. The national police were incorporated into the armed forces. In 1966 General Sugih-Arto was appointed Chief Public Prosecutor (Jaksa Agung); his successors were also from the military. The Ministry of Justice and the Supreme Court (Mahkamah Agung) were left to civilians for a time, but in the mid-1970s the ministry went to Lt. Gen. Mudjono, and then in succession to Generals Ali Said and Ismail Saleh. Finally, the Mahkamah Agung, packed with several retired officers appointed after 1974, was given over to Mudjono in 1981 and on his death in 1984 to Ali Said.[21] By 1981 retired army officers were in command of the entire core of the official legal system.

Except for Islamic courts, not relevant here, and the politically passive notariate, the one significant legal institution not dominated by the military or subdued by political authority was the troublesome, self-governing advocacy. Its only bureaucratic connection was with the Ministry of Justice, which merely registered advocates, from whom a few extralegal fees were extracted in the process, but registration had relatively little effect. Most advocates favored limited government intervention: a law governing practice, for example, to fortify professional legitimacy, define professional rights and responsibilities, and restrict casual competition. PERADIN was interested in a national bar association, which would require government assistance. But hostility to advocates in the courts, prosecution, police, Ministry of Justice, and elsewhere in the administration meant that any official attention might take a bad turn. It did.

It was not legal malpractice that moved the government to do something about the advocacy. By the early 1980s, New Order leaders were less concerned to protect public interests than to contain public criticism and resistance. Since the 1970s a strong NGO (nongovernmental organization) movement had taken hold, spawning independent reform organizations with little respect for either public policy or officialdom. The original model was PERADIN's Legal Aid Institute, the

LBH, which had grown into a national network with a dozen active branches around the country.

In the legal system as elsewhere in the public bureaucracy, these challenges reinforced corporatist urges to assert official dominance. The antagonism between public and private lawyers added animus. Judges and prosecutors, who resented professional advocates their independence and constant charges of corruption, incompetence, and abuse of authority, were eager to silence critics and run a test of prerogatives in which their parent institutions, including the Ministry of Justice and the Supreme Court, had to back them. But there were other political reasons for confining the advocacy. In political trials since 1966 defense attorneys from PERADIN and the LBH had embarrassed the government at home and abroad by challenging the staged affairs, turning them into platforms of political criticism. Private lawyers were prominent among the human rights activists whom state leaders regarded as a threat to the regime, along with hidden Communists and assorted other evils.

Consequently, the government initiated a strategy designed to absorb PERADIN and smaller organizations into a single national association and to impose disciplinary control over the entire profession. In 1981 at PERADIN's congress in Bandung, the Supreme Court chairman Mudjono, minister of justice Ali Said, and chief public prosecutor Ismail Saleh each proposed that the advocacy required a unified organization (*wadah tunggal*). It was left to Ali Said, as minister of justice and later as Supreme Court chairman, to engineer the new IKADIN (Ikatan Advokat Indonesia, or Indonesian Advocates Bond).

Many advocates were initially receptive, optimistic that an officially sponsored professional association would improve their opportunities and relationships with the bureaucracy. Senior PERADIN leaders, however, were skeptical from the start, assuming that Ali Said was mainly intent upon eliminating PERADIN's influence. At his disposal were numerous retired military law graduates, now practicing, who could be mobilized to take over the new association.

PERADIN delayed but could not avoid IKADIN, which was inaugurated in November 1985, with Harjono Tjitrosubeno of PERADIN as chair.[22] Still, the lawyers treated IKADIN cautiously. PERADIN and smaller associations refused to disband, despite official pressure, until IKADIN proved viable and useful. Engaging the government in a tactical struggle for control of the organization, IKADIN leaders fought for organizational autonomy and self-governance, which the Ministry of Justice countered by tightening registration requirements, establishing quotas of advocates (like notaries) in major cities, and dividing private legal professionals organizationally.[23] Advocates held out; in IKADIN's first elections, in 1988, PERADIN's influence remained dominant.

Ismail Saleh and Ali Said meanwhile surrounded the profession with a fence of disciplinary requirements, which advocates contested fiercely. The lawyers argued their case from legal premises, but the norms at work were political, not legal, in which case most advantages belonged to the government. An opportunity to have at the advocacy, and a particularly irritating advocate, arose in 1986, when Adnan Buyung Nasution, founder of the LBH, committed a breach of etiquette in the trial of Lt. Gen. Dharsono (retired) for subversive complicity in riots at the Jakarta port area of Tanjung Priok in September 1984. Minister of Justice Ismail Saleh, oblivious to the least subtle legal issues, set about making an example of Nasution. Applying ex post facto a provision from a new law, he accused Nasution of contempt of court, which does not exist in Indonesian procedural law; and a first instance judge, without hearing Nasution, handed down an "administrative decision"—which he later called a "report," though he had granted Nasution a right to appeal from it, but to whom was never made clear—recommending that the minister of justice revoke the advocate's certification. Ignoring the law, protests from foreign bar associations, and IKADIN's effort to deal with the matter itself, the minister revoked Nasution's registration for a period of one year.[24]

Soon afterwards, in July 1987, the minister of justice and chairman of the Supreme Court promulgated a "joint decision" on procedures for supervising and regulating legal counsel.[25] They construed an article of a new law (art. 54 (4) of Law 2/1986, on the lower courts) to grant judges wide authority over private practitioners for the sake of "guiding and developing" the profession. The actual purpose of this authority appears in article 3 (c) of the joint decision, which provides that measures may be taken against legal counsel who "act, behave, bear themselves, speak, or issue statements that indicate lack of respect for the law, statutes, public authority, the courts, or their officials." Negating the profession's claim to autonomy, the thrust of the joint decision was to remove disciplinary powers from the advocates' association to the judiciary and the Ministry of Justice.

Outraged advocates protested frantically, challenging the joint decision as an unlawful attempt to destroy their independence and to silence them forever.[26] Despite criticism from other groups, including legal aid circles and the press, legal officials stood their ground. Sympathetic members of a parliamentary commission argued with Ismail Saleh, who conceded little. Promising that the joint decision would be administered impartially, he also made clear that the government intended to have its way. Advocates were later denied police permission to hold a retreat to discuss the issue.

One advantage of the profession was its own chaotic disunity. In an effort to consolidate its control of advocates, the Ministry of Justice two years later supported its own candidate for the IKADIN chair, setting off a battle in the organization that led, in early 1991, to an embarrassing brawl between members of the rival factions.[27] The government's attempt to unify the profession under its wing failed utterly, as IKADIN promptly split into at least two organizations, one more or less amenable to official bidding, but the other, largely the old PERADIN group, still defiant.

What is remarkable in this history is not how determined the government was to corral the profession, but how little influence it had on activist lawyers. Among advocates a relatively small proportion are willing to incur the costs involved in political cases, in speaking out against abuse of power, or even in defending the independence of their profession. Yet even now there is seldom, if ever, a shortage of lawyers who step forward to do so, and their ranks are constantly replenished by new young recruits. How explain their commitment, given the personal and professional risks involved? To anticipate my concluding argument, any explanation that omits ideology is, I think, likely to miss the central motives involved.

Malaysia

The Malaysian case is at once simpler and yet more subtle than the Indonesian. It is easier to follow, at least, because the private legal profession in Malaysia is incomparably better organized, its evolution more consistent, its patterns and norms more stable. The same is true of its setting in modern Malaysian political and social history. Yet, complexities appear in the form of ethnic cleavages in the makeup of the Malaysian profession, and in some undertones of the stability and security that it has enjoyed. What is striking, however, despite the unmistakable differences between Indonesian and Malaysian lawyers, their institutions, and their outlooks, is how similar their reasons are for rushing to the forum. If Indonesian lawyers wish fervently to establish a *negara hukum,* Malaysian lawyers have been just as committed to preserving one.

Unlike Indonesia, Malaysia suffered relatively few breaks in the historical line between colony and independent state: no revolution, nor even an especially vehement nationalist struggle for independence. The same is true of the legal profession. Private lawyers from old British Malaya, unlike advocates from the Netherlands Indies, would not be especially startled by the changes in legal practice over a few generations. More Malaysian women are now in the profession, which is also ethnically rather better balanced. But otherwise most law offices would be familiar, with lawyers still speaking English, file systems much the same despite computerization here and there, and the same Daumier caricatures of English legal prominents hanging tritely on the walls. Many lawyers are from the same inns of court in London as their predecessors, and remain attentively devoted to common law values, habits, precedents, and lore.

Malaysian lawyers came late to activism, in large part because there seemed little enough to be activist about. Activism, after all, requires a sense that something in the political order or social structure or legal system is wrong, unjust, in need of righting. Malaysia's share of injustice was greater than the sense of it among lawyers, whose own status and welfare were reasonably assured, but there were few social rumblings that anyone supposed the government lacked the ability to deal with. The judiciary worked quite well, with highly educated, prestigious, and autonomous judges, whose membership in the national political and social elites disinclined them either to challenge seriously the decisions of political leaders or to toe the line too respectfully on institutional issues. The first three prime ministers of the country were legally trained, and one of them, Hussein Onn, was a practicing attorney, which gave lawyers confidence in their leadership and respect for the legal needs of Malaysian society. In Malaysia, unlike Indonesia, it was the government, not the legal profession, that took the initiative to establish limited legal aid services.

The government, moreover, was sensitive to the ethnic structure of Malaysia, to which private lawyers also had good reason to be sensitive, as most were themselves from minorities. In the colony almost all of the few Malays given legal training in England joined the administration. Ethnic Indians first and then ethnic Chinese, who paid for their own educations, made up the local component of the colonial bar. In 1970, thirteen years after independence and on the eve of a period of state-driven economic growth that transformed Malaysia—and its professions— of about 705 Malaysian private lawyers, only 38 (5.39 percent) were ethnic Malay, 364 (51.70 percent) ethnic Chinese, 251 (35.65 percent) ethnic Indian, and 52 (7.26 percent) British. That the political system dampened ethnic tensions until the riots of 1969 may account in some measure for the quiescence of legal activism then.

The government's response to the May 13, 1969 racial riots, set off by the results of national elections, was a new economic policy (NEP) meant to redress economic balances between the ethnic communities, largely through direct government help and encouragement to Malays, while developing the economy overall. Although it has come in for much criticism, in some respects the NEP has been remarkably successful on both scores. One example is the legal profession itself. By 1984 the number of lawyers had more than doubled since 1970 to 1,658, of whom 48.5 percent were ethnic Chinese, 32.25 percent ethnic Indian, and 16.25 percent ethnic Malay, up from about 5 percent.[28] By 1992 the profession had more than doubled again to over 3,800, of whom 1,704 (44.67 percent) were ethnic Chinese, ethnic Malays 865 (22.67 percent), ethnic Indians and others about 32 percent.[29]

Such rapid change in the demography of the profession might have caused extraordinary turmoil. Why it did not helps to explain some advantages of the Malaysian bar. For one thing, the organization of the profession, its competent internal regulation, the expansion of the (executive) bar council to reflect change, and its socialization of new recruits kept its affairs and standards relatively steady. So did the integration of the legal system generally. Ethnic tensions were not entirely absent as Malays joined the profession, but neither were they much exacerbated by economic competition, for economic growth proved a huge boon for private lawyers generally. New construction of huge housing estates, for example, provided extraordinary profits from conveyancing work, to the extent, one might argue, that the modern Malaysian legal profession is a house that conveyancing built. There was much other legal work in an active private economy.

The same growth encouraged a measure of ethnic amalgamation in the profession, helped along partly by a heritage of colonial ethnic stereotyping. Law offices brought together ethnic Chinese, Malay, and Indian lawyers, in one combination or another, for the sake of maximizing advantages: Chinese commercial abilities, Malay political connections, Indian litigating skills. The link to reality may have been little more than a self-fulfilling prophecy, but the ethnic mixing helped to consolidate corporate and professional relationships and kept the bar whole.[30]

Economic growth from the 1970s onward also generated the social and political tensions that finally ignited some lawyerly fuses and set the stage for serious activism among any so inclined. State-led economic growth naturally strengthened the government, but it also inevitably nurtured those middle social sectors that fed on it. The result, as in Indonesia too, was more or less predictable: as political leadership and public agencies grew more assertive, so did various social groups that grew more conscious of their own "privateness" and more testy about official intervention. If most were uninterested in grand state-society issues, enough were—usually professionals and intellectuals of one sort or another—to produce a nascent NGO movement, as elsewhere in the region. Not the least sensitive were private lawyers, jealous of their own institutional prerogatives but also the interests of their clients.

Tempers began to fray in the mid-1970s, escalating thereafter as the Bar Council and government moved further apart. Most (by no means all) lawyers may have been sympathetic to activism but no more willing than the middle class generally to engage openly, for to do so was either professionally distracting or politically dangerous. But activist lawyers, who tended to be active too within the profession, often wound up on the Bar Council.

After independence a few lawyers had taken issue with the government on policy matters. One involved the Sedition and Internal Security (ISA) Acts—products of the colonial administration during the 1948–1960 Emergency, the Communist rebellion—which proved equally useful later against others whom government leaders found bothersome. During the 1970s, however, the ISA question arose more insistently, as the government resorted to it more often and Bar Council members became more incensed. Other issues accumulated, among them the government party's inclination to use its large parliamentary majority to amend the constitution frequently to enhance its own powers or to reduce those of opposition.

The Bar Council, which took for granted its right to comment and advise Parliament on pending legislation, did so vociferously on the constitutional amendments problem. The government lashed back in the Legal Profession Act of

1976, intended to rationalize scattered rules. On the assumption that younger law-yers were the problem, the act disqualified lawyers from membership on the Bar Council or any bar committee until they had practiced for a minimum of seven years.[31] It was not young lawyers particularly, however, but also their elders who took the constitution and parliamentary institutions rather seriously. Protests con-tinued, now over the restrictive provision in the Legal Profession Act as well. In an amendment to the act in 1983 the government went further, erasing the Bar Council's right to advise Parliament and extending the attorney general's authority over the profession.[32] It did not help much.

By the late 1970s and early 1980s the Bar Council and government were al-ready frequently at loggerheads when, in 1981, Mahathir Mohammed became prime minister and soon raised the stakes of conflict. A medical doctor, Mahathir was Malaysia's first nonlawyer prime minister, whose no-nonsense commitment to efficiency and the like many lawyers at first found promising.[33] It was their mis-take, for a strong prime minister determined to guide "development" was less likely to brook opposition, dissidence, or even criticism. Tensions rose precipi-tously as activist lawyers, increasingly politicized, widened their scope of responsi-bility.

How much they did so is evident in the Bar Council journal, *Insaf* (Aware), which began in the late 1960s with routine contributions on the profession, legal education, and case commentaries, but soon thereafter offered a steady fare of pieces on police behavior, legal aid, the ISA, the responsibilities of lawyers, issues of parliamentary government, human rights in and out of Malaysia, and much else in similar vein. The annual conferences sponsored by the Bar Council also broadened both their concerns and their participation beyond formal law and the legal profession. Moreover, the Bar Council itself evolved towards increased appreciation of activism, particularly with the election to chair of Param Cumaras-wamy, an articulately engaged Kuala Lumpur lawyer with a major law firm.[34] The one focus in the journal and the Bar Council that matched matters of political, social, and legal reform was the profession itself, with a good deal of questioning and rethinking of its role and environment in state and society both.

By the beginning of the 1980s Malaysian state and society had begun to recog-nize each other as separate entities, with state leaders proving rather unhappy about it. Increasingly edgy about the activities of three or four well-known organi-zations prone to criticize public policy, the government introduced a bill to amend the Societies Act, requiring all private organizations to register either as political or nonpolitical, defining "political" as any activity meant to influence the govern-ment in any way at all.[35] The threat, of course, was that the official registrar of societies might well refuse or scratch the registration of any organization disap-proved by the government. Unexpectedly, the bill mobilized many private organi-zations, for the first time, against its implications.

The Bar Council, reflecting attitudes shared by many lawyers, took a strong stand against the bill, raising a cry over freedoms of association and speech. It expressed special worries about provisions of the bill that eliminated judicial review of actions by the registrar of societies, suggesting a direct threat to judicial authority and separation of powers.[36] So involved in the issues were many lawyers that in April 1981 they did the extraordinary thing, for Malaysia, of mounting a demonstration at the Parliament building. About two hundred lawyers attended, passing out copies of their objections to the proposed legislation. A highlight in the history of the profession, one can still get a debate going over whether lawyers now would take the risk of doing anything like it. The government compromised slightly on the bill, but the debate over it helped set a tumultuous stage.

By the mid-1980s, political leaders and the Bar Council were barely on speaking terms, or rather what passed for speech was mainly invective. Ideologically the two sides had moved miles apart. One sought to make a strong state stronger by extending executive authority and privilege, justified by reference to economic development and ethnic justice. The other emphasized the need to protect citizens against executive power by making sure that judicial institutions retained their authority to exercise controls over it. In two illuminating issues that also arose during the mid-1980s, one over amendments to the Civil Law Act of 1956 and the other over amendments to the Official Secrets Act, the government set out to reduce judicial authority to interfere at all with executive discretion, while the Bar Council, supported discreetly by federal judges, stood in outspoken opposition.[37] The principle raised by the Official Secrets Act had to do with freedom of information, but the institutional issue of judicial powers was quite as important, certainly to lawyers, whose own significance and political imagination were inextricably linked to the courts. Inevitably, the judiciary itself became a prime focus of conflict.

Judicial authority had been at issue since at least 1978, when the government began to whittle the Federal (supreme) Court's review powers.[38] By the mid-1980s Prime Minister Mahathir was as determined to subjugate the courts as he was to weaken other institutional, political, or social impediments to his government's freedom of action.[39]

In October 1987 the government stunned the country with a lightning raid, unprecedented since the Emergency, in which more than a hundred assorted figures—NGO activists, a few members of parliament, journalists, and others—were detained on grounds that they threatened ethnic peace.[40] Most were soon released, but the effect was to cast a pall over Malaysian politics, as many, including some shaken lawyers, retired anxiously from public activity.

A frontal assault on judicial authority followed not long after, in 1988, as the prime minister sought successfully to remove the lord president of the Federal Court and to replace him with a judge likely to prove more compliant.[41] A blunt assertion of executive primacy over the judiciary, it was also a slap across the face of the Bar Council and a contemptuous rejection of the vision it shared with prominent NGOs and others of a properly run state. Most Malaysian lawyers were undoubtedly distressed but also cowed by then into quietude. Yet others were not, and the Bar Council made its outrage elaborately clear. A number of lawyers boycotted sessions of the court chaired by the new lord president. The journal *Insaf* devoted much space to the issue, as well as to human rights and such procedural questions as preventive detention that many lawyers understood to depend on autonomous judicial authority. Since 1992 the Bar Council has elected Malay lawyers to chair the organization, in the hope no doubt of additional leverage in a Malay-dominated state, but ethnic diplomacy has made little difference in the posture of the Bar Council, or activist lawyers generally, on critical issues.

The story has not ended because enough professional lawyers refuse to let it end. That many decided to withdraw from the struggle, devoting themselves to professional work narrowly defined, is hardly surprising. That others—how many is hard to know—carried on, is more interesting and less easy to account for.

Conclusion

Two states, their political structures, institutional patterns, legal systems, and private legal professions could hardly be more different than Indonesia and Malaysia are from each other. Yet in both countries activist lawyers have responded similarly to challenging crises. The chief difference is that while the cause of Indonesian lawyers has been to create a law state, complete with an autonomous and effective judiciary, that of Malaysian lawyers has been to defend one in place.[42] Not all, not even most Indonesian or Malaysian lawyers have joined the efforts. Those who have done so, however, have taken substantial risks, endangered their professional lives and incomes—more so in Indonesia than Malaysia—and undertaken crusades with no realistic hope of immediate returns or satisfaction.

Why do they do it? Three analytical lines—personal interest, professional interest, lawyerly ideology—seem promising. Personal motives, if limited to quests for either political or professional name recognition, do not provide much grip on the problem unless they can account for persistence. But they may also include, more broadly, the concerns or commitments of minority lawyers—ethnic Chinese in Indonesia, ethnic Chinese or Indians in Malaysia, Christians or other religious minorities in both countries—to support those political values most hospitable to minorities. There may be something to this argument, for activist lawyers from ethnic or religious minorities are at greater risk than others. This is particularly so in Indonesia, where ethnic Chinese, who comprise only 3 percent of the population, have fewer defenses than the 35 percent ethnic Chinese or 10 percent ethnic Indians in Malaysia. The minority explanation, however, while worth exploring, hardly covers the universe of activists.

Professional interest reaches further, and the evidence for it is more compelling. Like other professions, lawyers seek sympathetic environments, doing whatever they can to fashion for themselves favorable institutional conditions and supportive political and social norms. Strong courts, binding procedural codes that allow space and leverage to attorneys—litigators above all—the *rechtsstaat* itself and the public values that surround it, make for a lawyer's paradise. In both Indonesia and Malaysia, as elsewhere, lawyers, activist or not, devote some energy to promoting such professional accommodations. This analysis makes good sense in some respects, but does not go far enough to account for why some activist lawyers extend themselves, again at professional and personal risk, to issues—human rights, to rely on a shorthand icon—that others regard as peripheral or hardly worth the trouble.

As persuasive as self- or professional interest may be, especially in a skeptical, even cynical, age, it is inadequate to the problem. Interest alone is too confining to explain the complexities and reach of legal activism. Ideology, however, alone or in conjunction with professional interest, goes further. Activist lawyers in Indonesia and Malaysia share at least two characteristics. One is that almost all are litigators, who take seriously the importance of strong and reasonably autonomous courts—in Indonesia because they do not exist, in Malaysia because they do but are threatened. The other trait of the activists, more nuanced, is that they have generalized technical legal skills into legal values and thence into political ideology. It is not entirely surprising. Lawyers are, after all, specialists of a sort in state-society relations, whose proclivities may be to one side or the other or rest professionally neutral. Activists who lean to the society side are likely to take notions of justice seriously, but while they do not ignore substantive justice, it is largely procedural justice, fairness of institutional treatment, that dominates their imaginations. This focus on procedural justice obviously suits their professional skills, but it also implies a conception of the state in which rule of law or *rechtsstaat* values determine. Their attraction to human rights ideas, like the concept of general law, affirms the same urge to surround society with a defensive shield of transcendent values against state power.

If most lawyers in Indonesia and Malaysia regard their vocation as a living, activist lawyers tend to transmute it into yet a higher vocation, whose dangers are balanced, if not submerged, by compulsions best understood as ideological commitments that arise from their understanding of the ethical and political implications of legal order itself.

Notes

1. This essay draws substantially on earlier publications of mine on related questions. In the discussion of Indonesian lawyers particularly, I have borrowed shamelessly from my *Lawyers as Outsiders: Advocacy versus the State in Indonesia* (University of London, School

of Oriental and African Studies Law Department, Working Paper No. 2, 1992) and "Between State and Society: Professional Lawyers and Reform in Indonesia," in *Making Indonesia,* ed. Daniel S. Lev and Ruth McVey (Ithaca, N.Y.: Cornell SEAP, 1996), 144–164. See also my "Social Movements, Constitutionalism, and Human Rights: Comments from the Malaysian and Indonesian Experiences," in *Constitutionalism and Democracy: Transitions in the Contemporary World,* ed. Douglas Greenberg et al. (New York: Oxford University Press, 1993), 139–155. All translations from the Indonesian are mine.

2. When comparing Indonesia and Malaysia it should be held in mind that civil law systems tend to generate fewer private lawyers than do common law systems, and to divide them up between litigating and notarial specialists.

3. In 1940 there were 206 professional advocates in the colony, of whom 125 were Dutch and 81 were Indonesian. The latter were about evenly divided between ethnic Indonesians and ethnic Chinese, which is relevant here mainly in that Indonesian lawyers were far more likely to be politically active. Ideologically, however, they were then and remain now much alike. The data are from the colonial *Regeerings Almanac* 1941/II, 156–159. See also Lev, "Origins of the Indonesian Advocacy," *Indonesia* 21 (April 1976), 135–169.

4. Muh. Yamin, *Naskah-Persiapan Undang-Undang Dasar 1945,* [Preparatory Documents of the 1945 Constitution] (Jakarta: Prapantja, 1959), 330–337. At the time, Yamin's ideas may well have surprised even the advocates in his audience.

5. See Soemarsaid Moertono, *State and Statecraft in Old Java* (Ithaca, N.Y.: Cornell Modern Indonesia Project, 1968), and Heather Sutherland, *The Making of a Bureaucratic Elite* (Singapore: Heinemann, 1979).

6. Unlike the federal constitution of 1949 and the provisional constitution of 1950, the 1945 constitution provides few institutional controls over executive authority and no stipulated political rights. For Supomo's arguments see Yamin, *Naskah,* 337–342. An English translation of Supomo's comments on the state can be found in Herbert Feith and Lance Castles, *Indonesian Political Thinking 1945–1965* (Ithaca, N.Y.: Cornell University Press, 1970), 188–192. For the fullest and most sophisticated analysis of Supomo's ideas and influence during the constitutional discussions of mid–1945, see Marsillam Simandjuntak, *Pandangan Negara Integralistik: Sumber, Unsur, dan Riwayatnya dalam Persiapan UUD 1945* [The Integralistic State View: Sources, Elements, and Their History in the Preparation of the 1945 Constitution] (Jakarta: Grafiti, 1994).

7. See Lev, "Colonial Law and the Genesis of the Indonesian State," *Indonesia* 40 (October 1985), 57–74.

8. See Laws 19/1964 on judicial authority and 13/1965 on the organization of the civil judiciary.

9. *Per*satuan *Adv*okat *Ind*onesia (Indonesian Advocates Association).

10. To take the most common example, the Command for the Restoration of Security and Order (KOPKAMTIB) could arrest and detain people without trial or, alternatively, have the prosecution investigate accused persons under the Anti-Subversion Act of 1963 (1968), which made it easier to convict, with harsher sentences, than the HIR procedural code. See inter alia Eddy Damian, ed., *The Rule of Law dan Praktek Penahanan di Indonesia* [The Rule of Law and Detention Practices in Indonesia] (Bandung: Alumni, 1970) and Kons Kleden and Imam Walujo, *Percakapan tentang Undang-Undang Subversi dan Hak Asasi Manusia* [A Discussion of the Subversion Law and Human Rights] (Jakarta: LEPPENAS, 1981).

11. Lev, "Judicial Authority and the Struggle for an Indonesian Rechtsstaat," *Law and Society Review* 13, no. 4 (1978): 37–71. Advocates and judges had different purposes. Judges sought improved bureaucratic status, advocates an autonomous judiciary capable of impos-

ing legal controls over executive authority. The brief alliance did nothing to moderate the antagonism between judges and advocates.

12. The same law provided for administrative courts, which were finally established only twenty years later, in 1991. The government avoided them largely because they were intended, after all, to allow actions against the government itself. Such misgivings proved valid, for in 1995 the state administrative court (PTUN) of Jakarta stunned the country by actually ruling against the Ministry of Information's banning of *Tempo*, an influential weekly, a year earlier in June 1994. The ministry promptly fled to the appellate court of Jakarta, with further appeal to the Supreme Court, which ruled for the minister.

13. A few reform concessions have taken hold, however. Apart from the administrative courts, a national human rights commission (KOMNAS HAM) was also created in response to international and domestic pressure, particularly after a massacre of East Timorese by army troops in late 1991. The human rights commission has also proved worrisomely unpredictable from the government's point of view. Moreover, legislative reforms, while easily manipulated by the legal bureaucracy, nevertheless make promises that activists can put to critical use.

14. Consulting lawyers did not generally register with the Ministry of Justice until compelled to do so during the late 1980s, nor did they join PERADIN, many of whose members refused to recognize them as genuine advocates. By measures of income and status, however, they are the elite of the private legal profession.

15. On professional organizations among Indonesian lawyers, see S. H. Abdurrahman, *Aspek-Aspek Bantuan Hukum di Indonesia* [Aspects of Legal Assistance in Indonesia] (Jakarta: Cendana Press, 1980) p. 265–271.

16. On the LBH see Lev, *Legal Aid in Indonesia*, Working Paper no. 44. (Clayton, Victoria, Australia: Monash University, Southeast Asian Studies, 1987) and the sources cited there.

17. Protests have had little effect in penetrating the privileged positions of judges, prosecutors, and police, for the government is obliged politically to protect its bureaucratic base. Prosecutors and judges have been transferred or even dismissed, occasionally as the result of extraordinary efforts by private lawyers, but their institutions remain essentially unchanged. Reform advocates were frustrated at every turn. See Todung Mulya Lubis, *In Search of Human Rights: Legal-Political Dilemmas of Indonesia's New Order, 1966–1990* (Jakarta: Gramedia, 1993), and Hans Thoolen, ed., *Indonesia and the Rule of Law: Twenty Years of 'New Order' Government* (London: Frances Pinter, 1987).

18. Since 1966 two statutes, pressed assiduously by reform advocates, have generated especially optimistic though brief public enthusiasm: Law 14/1970 on judicial organization and the new code of criminal procedure of 1981. Advocates were discouraged by the first, because it did not grant the Supreme Court review powers and because articles favorable to accused persons were not implemented by the supplementary legislation required. The new code of criminal procedure (*Kitab Undang-undang Hukum Acara Pidana*, or KUHAP) met a few more demands for reform, though again implementation proved to be problematic. That criminal process was taken so seriously reflects the extent to which political issues, or state/society issues, have dominated public debate about legal change. See the sources cited in note 16.

19. The new code of criminal procedure punished the public prosecution by turning over responsibility for preliminary investigation to the police, who were made subject to suits for wrongful damages. It also established a new procedure of pretrial judicial review of arrest and detention, and implemented (within limits) the principle of legal representation of accused persons from the time of arrest. Not one of these innovations has worked

according to promise, largely because of the resistance of the institutions responsible for them. See Lubis, *In Search of Human Rights*, passim, and the annual reports on human rights by the Indonesian Legal Aid Institute, *Catatan Keadaan Hak-Hak Asasi Manusia di Indonesia* [Notes on the Human Rights Situation in Indonesia].

20. For one example, in the early 1980s military death squads were detailed to kill petty criminals and the like who were generally regarded as a serious social and political irritation. President Soeharto took credit for these *Petrus* (mysterious shootings) killings in his memoirs, *Otobiografi*, as related to G. Dwipayana and K. H. Ramadhan (Jakarta: Citra Lamtoro Gung Persada, 1988), 364–367.

21. In recent years the leadership of the Ministry of Justice, Chief Public Prosecution, and the Supreme Court has been restored to trusted civilians, in part perhaps for political reasons related to tension between President Soeharto and the army.

22. On IKADIN's history see "Laporan Satu Tahun Berdirinya IKADIN 10 Nopember 1985–10 Nopember 1986" [First-Year Report on the Establishment of IKADIN] in the first issue of IKADIN's journal, *ERA HUKUM* 1, no. 1 (November 1987): 212–214.

23. Not all advocates joined IKADIN, any more than they had PERADIN or other organizations. By the end of 1986, of 1,125 advocates registered in the Ministry of Justice and practicing, only 645 were enrolled as members of IKADIN. *ERA HUKUM* 1, no. 1 (November 1987), 240. The Ministry of Justice brought pressure to bear by requiring registration of all practicing lawyers and refusing it before registrants joined IKADIN. Although IKADIN was intended at first to incorporate practicing private lawyers of all sorts, except for notaries, tensions among them, as well as the views of the Ministry of Justice, eventually led to separate organizations for registered advocates, unregistered "practical attorneys" (*pengacara praktek*, including non-degree-holding bush lawyers), and consulting lawyers. See *Indonesia Reports*, no. 36 (November 1988), 27, citing the weekly *Editor*, July 23, 1988. The fragmentation of the profession, broadly conceived, inevitably reduced its political influence.

24. On the Nasution case see Lev, "Adnan Buyung Nasution, Indonesian Civil Rights Lawyer under Attack," in *Human Rights Internet Reporter* 11, no. 2 (June 1986), 4–5. Nasution sued the minister of justice, partly on grounds that law 2/1986 had been applied ex post facto, but the first instance court of south Jakarta predictably rejected his claim, ruling, interestingly, that the ex post facto rule did not apply to administrative law, where public interest is the governing consideration. The daily *Kompas*, July 22, 1988, excerpted in *Indonesia Reports* 36 (November 1988), 26–27.

25. KMA/005/SKB/VII/1987–M.03–PR.08.05 tahun 1987, and see also Supreme Court circular no. 8, 1987, dated November 25, 1987, elucidating the joint decision and issuing instructions for its implementation.

26. On July 12 IKADIN published a defense of professional independence: "The special character of the advocate and the profession of advocacy, recognized universally in various international conferences and declarations, lies in autonomy. . . . [I]n this joint decision no freedom is left to legal counsel, for every act, attitude, and expression is under the control and authority of the chairmen of the first instance courts, the chairmen of the appellate courts, the chairman of the Mahkamah Agung, and the minister of justice. . . . [T]he wide authority vested by this joint decision [in the courts and ministry] will cause legal counsel to lose moral courage to carry out their functions in and out of court in accord with the free and autonomous character of their profession. In turn legal counsel will always posture and proceed only according to the taste and whim of the judge, which will greatly damage legal development in general and particularly those who seek justice."

Dewan Pimpinan Pusat Ikatan Advokat Indonesia, *Pernyataan Pendirian IKADIN atas Keputusan Bersama Ketua Mahkmah Agung dan Menteri Kehakiman Republik Indonesia tentang Tata Cara Pengawasan, Penindakan dan Pembelaan Diri Penasihat Hukum* [Declaration of IKADIN's View of the Joint Decision of the Supreme Court Chair and Minister of Justice of the Republic of Indonesia Concerning Procedures of Supervision, Measures against, and Defense of Legal Counsel] (July 12, 1987).

27. See *Tempo,* August 4, 1990.

28. These figures are by my own count and may be slightly off because of mistaken classification of some names. See Malaysian Bar Council, *Legal Directory,* August 25, 1984.

29. Calculated from *Legal Directory,* July 20, 1992. As the counting was tedious, there may again be some errors. The number of ethnic Malay and ethnic Indian lawyers may be slightly overstated or understated because of the difficulty, at times, of distinguishing ethnic Malay from ethnic Indian Islamic names.

30. Not entirely, however. During the late 1980s a small Islamicly oriented law organization was formed around a few Malay lawyers, but it never drew many members or developed much influence.

31. Legal Profession Act of 1976 (Act 166), art. 46 A. Other disqualifications included membership in either house of the Malaysian Parliament or a state legislature, office in a trade union or any political party or "(iii) any other organisation, body or group of persons whatsoever, whether or not it is established under any law, whether it is in Malaysia or outside Malaysia, which has objectives or carries on activities which can be construed as being political in nature, character or effect, or which is declared by the Attorney-General by order published in the *Gazette,* to be an organisation, body or groups of persons which has such objectives or carries on such activities." Moreover, "(2) An order made by the Attorney-General under paragraph (c)(iii) of subsection (1) shall not be reviewed or called in question in any Court." Which makes quite clear the government's intentions.

32. See Legal Profession (Amendment) Act 1983, Act A567.

33. See the editorial, "The Mahathir Administration and the Malaysian Bar," in the Bar Council's journal *Insaf* (December 1981).

34. Again, the number of activist lawyers in Malaysia should not be exaggerated, any more than in Indonesia or, no doubt, elsewhere. Most lawyers, to repeat, were (and are) not engaged, and if many are quietly supportive short of public stands, many others think activism either dangerous to the profession or, more narrowly, a waste of time or even unprofessional.

35. One of the best accounts and most consistent analyses of the events and issues dealt with here and elsewhere in my discussion of Malaysia can be found in an unpublished paper by Clifford Bob, J. D., now completing a Ph.D. in political science at M.I.T., "State vs Society in Malaysia and the Judiciary Crisis of 1988," typescript (1993).

36. For a clear-headed discussion of the issues, see ibid., 25–31.

37. Ibid., passim, and just about any issue of *Insaf* through the 1980s.

38. See *Insaf* 1983/4 December, 1983, a long editorial entitled "Further Erosion of Fundamental Rights," and the letter to P. M. Mahathir from Ronnie Khoo Teng Swee, then vice president of the Bar Council, dated September 15, 1983, 9–13.

39. See Bob, "State vs Society in Malaysia," 37–40 for an illuminating discussion of the rulers' crisis in 1983 as a prelude to the battle over judicial authority. The rulers' issue involved a contest between the government and the sultans, who head the nine constituent states of Malaysia, over the extent of their authority, which the prime minister was determined to restrict. In this ongoing constitutional conflict, many lawyers and liberal reform-

ers have supported the sultans, not out of devout loyalty or appreciation by any means, but rather from a wish to prevent the prime minister from accumulating more power. See also Lev, "Social Movements, Constitutionalism, and Human Rights," 148–151.

40. See Bob, "State vs Society in Malaysia," 36, on Operation Lallang, the raid of October 1987. The precipitating issue had to do with the appointment of Chinese school officials who may not have had a command of Mandarin Chinese. Given how many of those arrested had nothing to do with ethnic conflict, or had always been critical of it, however, the issue may have been an excuse more than a reason.

41. The judicial crisis generated a small mountain of commentary. See especially Tun Salleh Abas (with K. Das), *May Day for Justice* (Kuala Lumpur: Magnus Books, 1989). Tun Salleh Abas was the lord president forced out by the prime minister. Also Bob, "State vs Society in Malaysia," 47–50; *Insaf*, all issues following the affair; *Aliran Monthly*, the journal of the reform organization, Aliran, whose chair, Chandra Muzaffar, was one of those arrested in 1987; and Lev, "Social Movements, Constitutionalism, and Human Rights." What set off the judicial crisis was a string of decisions that went against the government on political issues, culminating in a case that directly involved a split in the dominant Malay party, the United Malay National Organization (UMNO).

42. There may be another difference worth mentioning, though it cannot be taken up at length here. While Malaysian lawyers remain devoted to common law principles, Indonesian advocates have begun to drift away from civil law towards common law procedural notions. It is not simply that the common law lends private lawyers more status, leeway, and influence, though these advantages have much to do with it, but that as advocates have become increasingly critical they have recognized the extent to which civil law institutions, especially in criminal procedure, tend to favor the state.

CHAPTER 14

Attorneys for the People, Attorneys for the Land

The Emergence of Cause Lawyering in the Israeli-Occupied Territories

GEORGE BISHARAT

As the study of lawyering for social and political causes extends beyond the familiar contexts of the United States and Western Europe, one of the principal concerns of researchers must be to define the institutional, political, cultural, market, and other conditions that facilitate or inhibit cause lawyering. To the extent that cause lawyering in the non-Western world differs from its counterpart phenomenon in the West, one must also ask, in what degree do these same factors account for the specific complexion and trajectory that cause lawyering assumes in different Third World societies?

This essay grapples with the above questions through an examination of the role of indigenous lawyers in defending and advancing the "Palestinian cause"— at the broadest level, the struggle to achieve Palestinian national self-determination—in the Israeli-occupied West Bank and Gaza Strip.[1] As a practical matter, this has translated most commonly into efforts by lawyers to protect the tangible resources for the establishment of an independent state, chief among them land, from Israeli control, and the defense of Palestinian individuals from repression at the hands of Israeli military government.[2]

As will be seen, Palestinian cause lawyering is still in its infancy, notwithstanding the considerable duration of Israeli occupation—approaching thirty years— and, it would seem, both ample cause and opportunity for defending the interests of the Palestinian community. There are at least four major interconnected features of the context within which Palestinian cause lawyering has unfolded that have contributed to its stunted development.

First, Palestinian lawyers have faced, in the Israeli military government, a state apparatus that is, while highly legalistic, strongly repressive. Without recourse to any judicial authority meaningfully committed to limiting the occupation administration's extensive powers, Palestinian lawyers have been relegated to the ancillary function of damage control vis-à-vis the nationalist movement and have largely failed as professionals to assume the positions of leadership attained by lawyers in social movements in the West.

Second, the growth of Palestinian cause lawyering has been limited in significant part by the nature of the cause itself, as a contest for the political control of a land area against a foreign occupying power. While this broad political confrontation between Israeli authorities and the Palestinian populace produced a large potential client base for Palestinian cause lawyers, that client base was only loosely unified by its experience of repression at the hands of the Israeli military government. This placed limitations on the growth and tactical choices of the lawyers, particularly complicating actions that might have demanded sustained personal sacrifice of a group characterized by uneven political commitment.[3]

Third, with the exception of the initial years of Israeli occupation, and now after the conclusion of the Oslo peace agreement, Palestinian lawyers have operated within a market for legal services in which supply has greatly exceeded demand, and in which the scope for anything but cause lawyering has steadily, or even precipitously, diminished. Some, perhaps even many Palestinian practitioners have become "cause lawyers" not by ideological election but by the force of unfavorable market pressures. This has created a "cause-lawyering bar" of lesser ideological coherence than has been achieved elsewhere and has dimmed the luster the group might otherwise have earned within broader Palestinian society.

Finally, cause lawyering is essentially a foreign import, or at least a product of interaction with alien societies, and appears to run counter not only to local legal professional traditions but also, in some regards, to wider Palestinian Arab sensibilities and political culture. The notion that law might be deployed for the advancement of some social or political interest *other* than one defined and promoted by the state is not intrinsic to Palestinian society and may be only slightly better established within the local legal profession itself.

In combination, these four factors have contributed to the rise of a Palestinian cause-lawyering bar that deviates in significant respects from its stereotypical Western counterpart,[4] even to the point that questions might be raised as to the propriety of categorizing Palestinian practitioners as "cause lawyers." I shall argue that, despite their apparent differences from American cause lawyers, West Bank and Gaza advocates of the Palestinian nationalist cause should be similarly categorized, in fact, perhaps, as representatives of an alternative path for recruitment to politicized lawyering to that of the ideologically motivated individual who self-consciously chooses law or a particular area of practice as an arena to promote a political interest. In this alternative, cause lawyers are *products,* rather than producers, of the cause they serve, or conscripts, rather than appropriators of a legal struggle for political ends.

I shall touch on these four factors repeatedly through the ensuing account. The section following this introduction outlines the institutional framework within which cause lawyers have operated under Israeli occupation.[5] The next section considers the emergence of cause lawyering during the early years of Israeli occupation of the West Bank and Gaza Strip. This is followed by a section examining the social organization of cause lawyering in the Occupied Territories. The fourth section addresses the nature and content of Palestinian cause lawyering. In the conclusion I attempt to summarize the respects in which the above-mentioned four factors have constituted brakes on the development of Palestinian cause lawyering under circumstances that otherwise might have been ripe for its efflorescence.

The Institutional Framework for Cause Lawyering

The Advent of Israeli Occupation

Israel has ruled the West Bank and Gaza Strip since the June 1967 war through military area commanders,[6] who, with their deputies, enjoy wide extrajudicial powers to impose deportation, house arrest, press and other censorship, administrative detention, curfews, collective punishment, house sealings and demolitions, and a variety of other sanctions.[7] There is credible evidence as well that Israeli security personnel have received official authorization for, and engaged in, a limited number of extrajudicial killings of Palestinian activists in the Occupied Territories.[8] The military administration has also spearheaded the Israeli government's drive to gain control over land in the Occupied Territories and to promote Israeli civilian settlements there, justifying the seizure of an estimated two-thirds of the West Bank and one-third of the Gaza Strip from Palestinian occupants by reference to military or security needs.[9]

However, the Israeli military—an emanation of a political entity in which liberal democratic ideals and notions of the rule of the law, while not always realized, are certainly taken seriously—has never governed the Occupied Territories simply through unmediated, brute force. Instead it has consistently sought to operate with some reference to legal norms and principles, modified to fit the circumstances of military occupation.[10] This was reflected in, among other things, the style and form of the foundation of the military governments themselves, the establishment of a system of military tribunals of wide-ranging jurisdictions, the subjection of acts of the military officials in the Occupied Territories to review by the Israeli High Court, and the maintenance of preexisting civil court systems in the regions. The dualistic nature of the Israeli military government in the Occupied Territories—both legalistic and repressive—establishes both the possibility for, and many of the constraints upon, Palestinian cause lawyering. Let us therefore examine the institutional stage upon which Palestinian cause lawyers have been called to perform.

The Military Legal System

Among the first of the legislative acts of the area commanders following the establishment of Israeli control over the West Bank and Gaza Strip was the creation of a system of military courts. These courts tried residents of the Occupied Territories charged with violations of security laws, and along with a secondary set of military tribunals, eventually became the principle institutional sites for the emergence and development of Palestinian cause lawyering.

Military trial courts in the Occupied Territories are either single-judge courts, empowered to adjudicate offenses bearing punishments up to ten years imprisonment or petty fines; or three-judge courts, which try more serious offenses.[11] For the first twenty-two years of occupation there existed no formal avenue of judicial appeal from judgments of the military courts.[12] However, in 1989, a military court of appeals, serving both the Gaza Strip and the West Bank was established. Either the prosecutor or the defendant may petition the court of appeals for modification of judgment or sentence.[13]

Judges in all Israeli military courts are officers in the Israel defense forces (IDF), and are appointed by the area commander. The judges and military prosecutors both belong to the same IDF unit, that of the military advocate general. In practice, judges, who do not possess rights of tenure, are culled almost exclusively from the ranks of prosecutors.

A second system of military administrative tribunals was created early in the occupation to handle civil claims by Palestinians against the military, such as those for damages to private movable or real property caused by the IDF.[14] The jurisdiction of these "objections committees," also exclusively staffed by IDF officers, has expanded gradually over the years to include a broad range of issues. Undoubtedly the most important category of claims assigned to them, however, are disputes over land, especially Israeli military requisitions of private property, and its assertion of state ownership over land under Palestinian control.[15]

While the above-mentioned extrajudicial sanctions employed by the occupation administration may be imposed without formal charges and, for the most part, without resort to any judicial authority, over the years, Israel has implemented avenues of recourse of greater or lesser formality for individuals subjected to some of these sanctions. Administrative detentions, for example, must now be approved, and thereafter periodically reviewed, by a military judge.[16]

Israeli occupation met with almost instantaneous, and essentially unremitting Palestinian resistance, reaching its zenith during the Intifada, or uprising, of the late eighties and early nineties.[17] Since 1967, more than a quarter of a million Palestinians have been tried in the military courts established in the Occupied

Territories or have been subjected to administrative sanctions of one kind or another.[18] Thousands of Palestinian landowners have also faced expropriation orders issued by the military government. These circumstances provided Palestinian lawyers with a multitude of occasions, and a variety of legal forums, in which to provide services to the cause.

The Role of the Israeli High Court

As mentioned earlier, Israel has subjected the actions of military government officials to review by the Israeli High Court, against international legal standards as well as against those established in Israeli administrative law.[19] The court agreed to hear cases arising in the West Bank and Gaza Strip—never formally annexed, and therefore outside the territory of the State of Israel—on the theory that it exercised personal jurisdiction over Israeli military governors acting in their official capacities wherever they may be.[20] Two aspects of this jurisdiction should be noted for their effect on the rise of cause lawyering in the Occupied Territories.

First, as the character of jurisdiction exercised by the High Court over the military governors was personal rather than territorial, the arrangement implied no formal change in the relationship between Israel and the Occupied Territories. Instead it was conceptualized as simply the "normal" operation of an Israeli court, and, accordingly, normal Israeli court rules and procedures applied. Foremost among these, given our concern here, was the requirement that lawyers pleading before the court be members of the Israeli bar. Lawyers from the Occupied Territories were thus institutionally cut off from direct participation in litigation in the most authoritative forum, and the one with the broadest ranging powers, that operated in the region.

This was not an insurmountable barrier to their participation in High Court cases—a number of attorneys from the Occupied Territories eventually developed standing relationships with Israeli lawyers and would work jointly with these Israeli lawyers on the presentation of a case to the High Court. It did mean, however, that fees had to be shared, and that lawyers from the Occupied Territories were unable to conduct the most publicly visible aspects of their cases themselves.

Second, the nature of the High Court's jurisdiction was such that some Israeli government action was a predicate for the filing of a petition. This fact has several important ramifications. For example, Palestinians cannot file petitions in the High Court to contest actions of Israeli settlers in the Occupied Territories. These settlers, who now number some 140,000 in the West Bank alone, have been responsible for many acts of violence (some retaliatory, to be sure) against Palestinians, and have repeatedly seized and occupied Palestinian land and buildings. In short, under another institutional arrangement, they would be likely targets for legal suits.[21] Moreover, the predicate of some governmental action has inhibited the growth of proactive, innovative legal strategies that might have been devised and implemented in a less constrained institutional environment. Hence, cases brought by Palestinians have tended to be limited to defensive reactions to military government acts.

The Emergence of Cause Lawyering

Lawyers and Early Protest Activity

Operations of preexisting civil departments in both the West Bank and the Gaza Strip, including those of the civil courts, were suspended during the initial months of occupation. As part of a general policy to "normalize" life for the residents of the Occupied Territories to the extent possible, the Israeli military government soon sought to revive these civil departments, pressing their former personnel to resume their positions and functions.

In the West Bank, the court of appeals (formerly seated in Jerusalem, but upon annexation of that city moved to Ramallah) was vested by the military government with the jurisdiction of the Jordanian High Court. This entitled residents of the region to petition the court of appeals against unjust or illegal actions taken by local level government officials. However, military orders passed early in the occupations of both the West Bank and Gaza, rendered the Israeli occupation administration and all its employees immune from suit in local courts. So little administrative authority remained in the hands of indigenous officials that this theoretical jurisdiction of the West Bank court of appeals was virtually meaningless, and, as a consequence, seldom if ever exercised.[22]

Palestinian lawyers—of whom there were approximately fifty remaining in the West Bank and a mere four in the Gaza Strip following the 1967 war[23]—played a vanguard role in early organizing efforts against Israeli occupation. For example, renowned Jerusalem lawyers were among signatories to proclamations protesting Israel's annexation of their city three weeks after the cessation of hostilities in 1967.[24] Lawyers were prominent leaders in committees established to organize and coordinate community opposition to the occupation, and, for their diligence, earned the dubious distinction of being among the first to suffer exile at the hands of the military government.

As professionals, however, their activities were relatively muted. In the West Bank, this was primarily due to the lawyers' collective decision—somewhat fateful, it would seem in retrospect—to boycott not only the newly established Israeli military courts, but also the preexisting civil courts, whose structure, jurisdiction, and independence were perceived as subject to Israeli control.[25] The strike was intended by its adherents to serve as a model of noncooperation with the Israeli authorities to be emulated by other professional groups and sectors of Palestinian society.[26]

The response of the Israeli military authorities was to issue orders authorizing Israeli lawyers to appear in West Bank civil courts, and assigning the supervisorial responsibilities and licensing powers of the Jordanian Bar Association—of which West Bank lawyers were members—to a military officer designated the "officer in charge of the judiciary." In Gaza, a similar transfer of authorities occurred, although there because the critical mass of attorneys needed to maintain an organized bar had simply dissipated during the hostilities of 1967.

The Jewish Israeli Pioneers

As I have suggested, the circumstances of occupation and Palestinian resistance to it left no lack of opportunities for lawyers to provide services to the cause in professional terms. In the West Bank, however, lawyers generally persevered in the strike, limiting their activities to the types of nonlegal political protest described above.[27] In Gaza, meanwhile, lawyers resumed practice in the civil courts, and slowly began to represent Palestinians charged with "security" or "political" cases (the two terms used by the local community to refer to cases stemming from alleged violations of Israeli military orders and regulations) in the military courts operating there.

Yet the growth of their military court practices were limited by two interrelated factors: first, there was a widespread community perception that Palestinian lawyers could not possibly represent their clients effectively and zealously in Israeli military courts. This was not wholly unreasonable, as these courts applied Israeli rules of evidence and procedure, and while offering Hebrew-Arabic interpreters, were staffed by judges and prosecutors who rarely spoke Arabic. Thus any arguments presented to the court were filtered through interpreters (generally, Israeli soldiers of the Druze sect)[28] whose interests and sympathies were assumed to lie with the military authorities. As important was the strong belief among many Palestinians that local lawyers would be hesitant to forcefully contest Israeli authorities. As one attorney put it to me: "It is a slave mentality. People simply refuse to believe that they can be helped by another slave in a conflict with the master." It should be added that the notion of the constraint of political authority by law, essential to the ideology of the rule of law, is not indigenous to Palestinian society. Instead, people are accustomed to managing relations with government— whether gaining a benefit or dodging a detriment—through the exercise of "wasta," or intermediation, typically effected by some individual (kin, sectarian leader, etc.) enjoying social proximity to the holder of power.[29]

Thus there should be little surprise in the ascendance of several Jewish Israeli lawyers, who nearly monopolized practice in the military courts in the early years, notwithstanding the deep and persistent distrust of Israelis within the Occupied Territories. The most prominent of these were the leftist lawyers Felicia Langer and Leah Tsemel, whose office waiting rooms were, through the seventies and later, overflowing with Palestinian clients seeking their aid.[30] Both were tireless defenders of Palestinian rights and interests and also played important roles as mentors for a number of young Israeli Arab lawyers who served all or parts of their compulsory two-year *estage,* or apprenticeship, following graduation from law school under their direction. These lawyers also indirectly demonstrated the possibilities of cause lawyering for attorneys with origins in the West Bank and Gaza Strip.

THE ASCENDANCE OF ISRAELI ARAB LAWYERS

By the late seventies to early eighties, former Arab *estagiares* (apprentices) of these two Jewish Israeli advocates were beginning to establish solid reputations as independent practitioners throughout the Occupied Territories. Elias Khoury, for example, litigated the famed "Elon Moreh" case before the Israeli High Court in 1979, which resulted in the dismantling of an Israeli settlement in the West Bank (among the few victories gained by Palestinian petitioners to the High Court, it might be added).

As Palestinians raised in Israel, these young lawyers were fluent in Hebrew. Having been educated in Israeli law schools, they were equally conversant in Israeli law and legal culture, and, as citizens of Israel, enjoyed legal status and protections not held by residents of the Occupied Territories. They also spoke Arabic and were at home in the Palestinian culture of the West Bank and Gaza Strip. In sociological terms, then, they were ideally situated to operate in the breach between the Israeli military authorities and the Palestinian population in the Occupied Territories. By the early to mid-eighties, this second generation of cause lawyers had not quite eclipsed their mentors, but they had become nearly their equals in stature in the Occupied Territories and were handling a significant proportion of cases in the Israeli military courts and those that were brought before the Israeli High Court.

It seems highly probable that the Israeli Arab lawyers, by the combination of their identities as Palestinians and their substantial professional abilities, helped to erode popular conceptions concerning the inability of Arab lawyers to successfully challenge Israeli authority. In doing so, they also widened the aperture for the contemporaneous entry to cause lawyering by individuals from the Occupied Territories themselves.

The Growth of "Indigenous" Cause Lawyering

By 1971, a number of lawyers in the West Bank began to reassess the wisdom of the strike they had maintained for four years. Their example had not been followed by other professions, as had been initially anticipated. The court system had not been brought to a grinding halt, as Israeli lawyers simply had stepped into the vacuum left by the striking lawyers.[31] Most of the latter were subsisting on a stipend provided by the Jordanian Bar Association, while their professional skills withered.

A small, then growing number chose to abandon the strike through the mid-seventies, some resuming practice only in the civil court system still functioning in the region, others making the more daring decision to begin appearing in Israeli military courts. The strike breakers were stridently castigated by the striking contingent and expelled from the Jordanian Bar Association. Considering that the functions of the Bar Association had been assumed since 1967 by the Israeli officer in charge of the judiciary, this measure was of no practical effect in the Occupied Territories (other than depriving working lawyers of their strike stipend, of course). Still, it was of symbolic significance and had at least limited effect outside the Occupied Territories.[32] By the mid-eighties, approximately one-third of the lawyers in the West Bank had joined the working faction, while the remainder adhered to the strike.

While a few of the local Palestinian advocates who undertook work in the military courts were original adherents of the 1967 strike, most were contemporaries, both in age and in level of professional experience, of the second-generation cause lawyers, the Israeli Arabs. As with the latter and their Jewish mentors, the West Bank and Gaza attorneys who came to the fore by the mid-eighties did not supplant their colleagues but simply created a more diverse, and more competitive, market for cause lawyering services.

The Social Organization of Palestinian Cause Lawyering

Social Profiles of Cause Lawyers

Cause lawyers in the Occupied Territories have been drawn from virtually all ranks within the local legal professions, and therefore mirror, to a considerable extent, the social characteristics of their colleagues at large. Yet there is a noticeable tendency for the stratification of the group of cause lawyers into two somewhat distinct categories. A small upper stratum, numbering, perhaps, no more than ten in both the West Bank and Gaza Strip, consists of those who are members of the local professional elite. This elite is composed disproportionately of members of either wealthy landowning Muslim families or of the Palestinian Christian minority (which has a history of differential access to education, itself a function of the historical interest of foreign Christian powers in cultivating local ties in Palestine). A few of these elite lawyers have received Western legal educations, although the majority has been educated in the better law faculties of the surrounding Arab countries.

Elite cause lawyers choose to devote substantial energies to military court cases and handle other claims against the military authorities, but typically have flourishing general legal practices as well. They tend to express strong commitments to ideals of the rule of law, as well as to Palestinian nationalism, conceptualize their military court and noncommercial practice as service to that cause, and pursue their work with both missionary zeal, formidable professional skill, and sometimes proficiency in Hebrew, English, or both, in addition to their native Arabic.

The second, lower, and generally larger stratum of the cause-lawyering contingent consists of those for whom military court practice is quite clearly a strategy for professional and financial survival. These lawyers, typically from poor to middle-class, some of them refugee families,[33] have often received their legal educations through correspondence from Beirut Arab University.[34] Many bring the most meager of professional abilities to their practice yet still defend their work rhetorically as constituting a form of service to the national struggle.

The size of this group has grown slowly over time, largely in response to the economic conditions prevailing in the regions. The first five years of occupation was a period of economic boom in Israel and the Occupied Territories. Remittances from Palestinians working in the nearby Arab oil economies further stimulated local business activity, keeping a high proportion of the actively practicing West Bank lawyers and Gaza lawyers occupied either with out-of-court provision of legal advice and other services or with cases handled within the local civil court systems. During this time period—also the one during which local reluctance to entrust cases to Palestinian lawyers was the strongest—the lower stratum of cause lawyers was minute.

By 1973 the Israeli economy had slowed considerably, as had growth in the Occupied Territories. The impact of the slowdown was delayed and mitigated somewhat by the continued flow of remittances from West Bank and Gaza Palestinians working abroad. By the early eighties, however, even this source of revenue was slowing to a trickle, coincident with the downturns in the economies of the Arab oil states. A prolonged period of economic stagnation afflicted the Occupied Territories, nearly eliminating demand for legal services from the business sector. During roughly the same span, however, the local professions had grown apace, in the West Bank multiplying tenfold, from the immediate post-1967 fifty practitioners to approximately five hundred by 1984.[35]

Perhaps fifty to seventy non-elite West Bank and Gaza lawyers were practicing in the military courts in the mid-eighties. Most had gained their toeholds in the market for military court services by their willingness to accept cases for fees that were a fraction of those charged by elite cause lawyers.

The Intifada resulted in the explosion of the number and range of opportunities for cause lawyering by attorneys in the Occupied Territories. Most directly, the sheer volume of cases before the military courts stimulated demand for legal services. While West Bank and Gaza lawyers had slowly undermined the popular penchant for Israeli lawyers even before 1987, the Palestinian community's former fear of the occupying authorities seemingly evaporated during the Intifada.

With it came the further weakening of the "slave mentality," a determination to wean the community of its dependence on Israeli resources of all kinds, and a new willingness to entrust cases to native sons and daughters of the Occupied Territories.

At the same time, the civil court system essentially ceased operations. Thus at the precise moment that opportunities for work in the military court system were multiplying, those on the civil side shriveled. The result was that scores, perhaps even hundreds, of West Bank and Gaza lawyers of non-elite status were drawn into work in the military legal system who had never before appeared in them.[36]

Needless to say, a number of the West Bank and Gaza lawyers who worked in the military legal system did not conform precisely to either the elite or non-elite models. A number of lawyers who entered the profession without the advantages of elite standing were nonetheless able, through their individual talents and industry, to achieve considerable status in the community and to develop flourishing legal practices.

Thus while military court practice has been lucrative for almost no one, it has probably meant professional survival for at least some, and has provided an avenue for accomplishment that is publicly venerated. There is a certain "stardom" that has accrued to the most prominent Palestinian cause lawyers, bringing with it both local and international media attention, travel abroad for conferences and speaking tours, and other tangible and intangible perquisites.

There was even some evidence to suggest that military court practice functioned as a career building step for a few, who, after establishing reputations in the community, moved into more lucrative and professionally stimulating areas of civil practice.[37] It also seems likely that cause lawyering in the Occupied Territories has, as elsewhere[38] paved the way for future careers and positions in public life for some lawyers. Gaza lawyer Freih Abu Middain, for example, has become the minister of justice for the new Palestinian Authority in Gaza and the Jericho district.

Organizational Development

In the first decade and more of the occupation, such cause lawyering as had developed on behalf of Palestinians in the Occupied Territories was almost exclusively constituted in the efforts of individual solo practitioners. This generally reflects the fact that the Palestinian legal profession is almost wholly formed of solo practitioners, the rare exceptions being a few partnerships of two or three attorneys, sometimes joined by kinship ties. While forming loose networks, and occasionally ad hoc committees (for example, to support a particular prisoners' strike), these individuals generally operated without benefit of formal organizational support.

Others, of course, have recognized the importance of the existence of organizations and institutions in providing "structured career opportunities" for fledgling attorneys contemplating the plunge into legal practice.[39] Thus, the birth of organizations willing to support cause lawyering is an auspicious development. In the Occupied Territories, this development began with the foundation of the American Friends Service Committee East Jerusalem Legal Aid Center in 1974.[40]

For many years the Quakers Legal Aid Center acted primarily as a clearing-house, directing the families of needy Palestinians facing charges in the Israeli military courts in the Occupied Territories to a panel of qualified attorneys, and paying for most of the legal fees.[41] While the center did not provide regular employment, tutelage by more senior attorneys, support staff, and other benefits associated with institutionally backed cause lawyering in, for example, the United States, the material support the center distributed to individual attorneys gave cause lawyering in the Occupied Territories an important boost. Lawyers were able to gain reasonable remuneration for their work in the Israeli military courts and, for the few most successful among them, to specialize in that form of practice.

The same is true for the *amwaal as-sumud,* or "Steadfastness Funds," a coffer established in the Baghdad Conference of Arab countries in 1978 to support the *sumud* or "steadfastness" of the residents of the Occupied Territories against perceived pressures by the Israeli authorities to force Palestinians to leave the region. Pledges to the Steadfastness Funds dried up by the mid-eighties, as a consequence of the recession in the Arab oil economies. But for a period of five to six years, families of Palestinian detainees were able to be reimbursed for legal expenses from the Joint Committee (the committee established by the PLO and Jordanian government to direct disbursal of the Steadfastness Funds) sitting in Amman, Jordan. Lawyers received fees that, both in number and in amount, probably could not have been generated solely on the basis of local resources. Again, this tangible support for the defense of Palestinian rights was instrumental in making cause lawyering a viable field of practice.

Two very important organizations were founded in the Occupied Territories by local initiative. One was *Al-qanun min ajl al-insaan,* translated as "Law in the Service of Man" (LSM) (the prefix *Al-haqq,* "Truth" or "Right" was added later), established in 1979 by several lawyers and nonlawyers in the West Bank town of Ramallah. Its purposes were to protect human rights and to uphold the principles of the "rule of law" in the region. Eventually staffed by two or three administrators, and a larger number of nonlawyer field workers, and aided by a fairly steady stream of foreign student interns[42] and other volunteers from abroad, Al-haqq/LSM sought to monitor, document, and publicize violations of human rights in the West Bank. Its findings were published in a series of pamphlets and books focused on discrete topics (such as censorship of the press, torture, deportations, administrative detention, and so on) that evoked considerable interest both within and outside the Occupied Territories. On a smaller scale, the group tried to promote citizen awareness of legal issues and respect for the rule of law. One of its members, for example, published a regular column in a local press. The group also assembled and distributed a short manual on citizens' rights.

Al-haqq/LSM's relative success in gaining attention to human rights violations in the Occupied Territories was significantly aided by two things. First, it succeeded in being designated as the local affiliate of the International Commission of Jurists, based in Geneva. This tie afforded the group a measure of legitimacy internationally, and also an umbrella of protection from the military government locally, that it would not have otherwise gained. Second, its prominence abroad was boosted greatly by the writings in English, as well as numerous speaking tours to England and the United States, of two of its principals, Raja Shehadeh and Jonathan Kuttab. Their individual credibility and that of the institution they helped to found was further enhanced by the relatively scrupulous documentation and legalistic argumentation they practiced and their steadfast refusal to be drawn into "politics" as such.

Ironically, some of the traits that contributed to Al-haqq/LSM's eminence abroad caused the group's partial isolation from both the wider Palestinian legal profession and the politically active segment of the local nationalist movement. While, from the Israeli perspective, the organization's works were simply the most thinly veiled nationalist rhetoric,[43] the group's eschewal of overt political discourse aroused suspicions in the Palestinian community as to its "real," hidden agenda. Of course, this reflects the fact that in contemporary Palestinian political culture, to be involved in the nationalist cause is to be affiliated with some political faction—for most of the period of occupation, one of the constituent organizations of the PLO, or, currently, the Islamist movement as well. Virtually all other unions, professional associations, women's groups, municipal chambers of commerce, and the like, are either assumed within the Palestinian community to be affiliates of particular political factions, or, in their elections, provide arenas for the demonstration of those factions' relative power.[44]

In this context, Al-haqq/LSM's determination to remain above the fray of partisan politics was anomalous and set the conspiratorially inclined thinkers in the local community only scrabbling that much harder for a way to categorize them. Some noted that Shehadeh, in his private law practice, represented virtually all the American corporations doing business in the West Bank, and that Kuttab had been associated with a Palestinian-American promoting nonviolence to Israeli rule in a period when the canon of the nationalist movement was still armed struggle. No one ever went so far as to outwardly denounce the institution as a front for foreign interests or the CIA, but for some time there was clear unease in the activist community with the group's Western, and particularly American, orientation and connections.[45]

The second organization, founded in 1980, was the *Lajnat al-muhamiin al-arab*, or Committee of Arab Lawyers (CAL). Initially limited to Jerusalem, then later expanded to encompass the entire West Bank, this organization was founded to provide some of the functions of the Bar Association for those lawyers who had abandoned the strike and resumed practice.[46] The group eventually became the de facto voice of the working lawyers, protesting adverse professional conditions to the Israeli military government, organizing short-term strikes against particular military orders, and directing the social and professional isolation of individual lawyers who exploited such orders to advance the interests of particular clients at the expense of the general community.[47] Those active in the Committee of Arab Lawyers tended to be enterprising practitioners of non-elite origins.

Although the Gaza Bar Association, a voluntary organization founded in 1976, spared itself the internal dispute cleaving the West Bank legal profession, Gaza had no counterpart to Al-haqq/LSM until 1986. At that time the Gaza Center for Rights and Law was founded, initially with funding from the family wealth of its director, attorney Raji Sourani. This group's program and activities were similar to that of Al-haqq/LSM (and there is cooperation between the two organizations). However, the Gaza group has been slower to achieve the international stature of Al-haqq/LSM, although it, too, eventually established affiliation with the International Commission of Jurists, and Sourani gained international recognition for his group's work with the award of the Robert F. Kennedy Prize for Human Rights in 1991.[48]

The Intifada witnessed both the proliferation of new organizations providing some kind of support for cause lawyering, and expansions in the range of services and opportunities offered by preexisting organizations. In the first category were such Jerusalem-based organizations as the Mandela Institute (a prisoner rights organization), the Land and Water Establishment for Studies and Legal Services (resisting Israeli seizures of Palestinian land and water resources), Defence of the Children International (focusing on the occupation's impact on children), the Society of St. Ives (specializing in test cases before the Israeli High Court), the Palestine Human Rights Information Center (documenting and distributing information about human rights violations), and the Gaza-based Palestinian Lawyers for Human Rights and the House of Right and Law (both focusing on human rights violations in the Gaza Strip). A number of these organizations hired staff attorneys to carry out their missions.[49]

Meanwhile, the Quaker Legal Aid Center hired two staff attorneys who engaged both in legal services for defendants in the military courts (though focusing on cases that implicated broad issues, such as the legality of the military order authorizing the military courts to demand bail from parents of incarcerated minors) and in litigation in the Israeli High Court. The United Nations Relief and Works Agency (UNRWA), established in 1949 to provide emergency relief to Palestinian refugees, hired a number of staff lawyers to monitor demonstrations and other events, and to provide legal advice to the agency and to individuals. UNRWA also began to provide funding for persons charged in military courts to retain private attorneys, as did a new Human Rights Office established by Bir Zeit University to serve its students facing charges in military court.[50] Al-haqq/LSM hired two paralegals who, though unqualified to appear in court, intervened on behalf of Palestinian clients facing problems with Israeli administrative authorities (obtaining exit visas, for example, driving licenses, or other permits).

Notwithstanding the proliferation of organizations supporting cause lawyering during the Intifada, it is necessary to point out the significant absence for most of the period of occupation of institutions that have sometimes been pivotal in the development of cause lawyering in the United States—namely, law schools. A number of institutions of higher learning have been either founded or expanded during the period of Israeli occupation, and although individual professors in several teach law-related courses, there was no formally constituted law faculty or degree program offered in the West Bank or Gaza Strip until 1992.[51]

It is further important to note that this organizational explosion stimulated by the Intifada actually did not generate significant employment opportunities for lawyers for the Occupied Territories. Many of the staff positions of the organizations were for nonlegal support (an appreciable portion of whom were, in addition, foreigners). Institutions that hired staff attorneys, such as the Quaker Legal Aid Center and the Society of St. Ives, tended to hire Israeli lawyers, who were able, if necessary, to appear in Israeli courts, including, most importantly, the High Court.

Lawyering for the Cause

Military Court Practice

The military court system is the principal institutional site for service to the cause of Palestinian independence by lawyers in the Occupied Territories. The most typical form this service has taken is plea bargaining for the reduction of fines and sentences of Palestinians charged with violations of security regulations. Trials, and more so, acquittals, are exceedingly rare.

This is a reflection, lawyers active in the military courts charge, of both formal rules of procedure and informal practices that nearly preclude any viable defense. Israeli soldiers are permitted to arrest any person without a warrant upon suspicion of having committed a security offense. Given the laxity of this standard, challenges to the legality of arrests are virtually pointless. Until 1992, military authorities were permitted to hold a detainee *incommunicado* and without charge or judicial scrutiny for up to eighteen days; that period was reduced for juveniles and defendants accused of minor offenses to eight days. Judicial approval is required for detention beyond this period; if the prosecution seeks this through an "extension hearing," the court may order the suspect held for up to six months without charge.

Once charges are filed, the defendant may be further held until termination of trial proceedings. Bail in security cases is almost entirely a theoretical proposition. There is no statutory or other recognition of a defendant's right to a speedy trial. Attorneys are regularly barred from seeing clients, often in violation of standing regulations, in excess of twenty days from their arrests, and almost always until "investigation" in the case—meaning, in effect, interrogation of the defendant—has been completed.

Lawyers engaged in military court practice claim that the overwhelming majority of defendants are brought to court with formal charges only when their interrogation yields an inculpatory statement.[52] These statements are typically reduced to writing in Hebrew, a language neither spoken nor read by most Palestinians in the Occupied Territories, and signed by the defendant. For many years lawyers have claimed that their clients' confessions had been coerced by means of psychological and physical abuse, often including severe beatings both by IDF and General Security Services (GSS) personnel, against denials by the Israeli government.[53]

However, in 1987, the Israeli government established a "Commission of Inquiry into the Methods of Investigation of the General Security Service Regarding Hostile Terrorist Activity," headed by former Israeli Supreme Court justice Moshe Landau.[54] The "Landau Commission" found that for a period of sixteen years, GSS interrogators had regularly employed psychological and physical "pressures" against Palestinian detainees and then lied in closed hearings held in military courts, in the attempt to conceal these methods and to ensure convictions. The commission censured the GSS for its record of perjury but rationalized the use of "moderate physical pressures" as a necessity in the war against "terrorism." In an unpublished portion of its report, the commission issued guidelines for the application of force during interrogations.

Nonlethal physical abuse of Palestinian detainees by Israeli soldiers and police interrogators thus continues to be routine and systematic.[55] Cases of severe, even fatal physical abuse, while not nearly as common, have also been documented.[56] Procedural rules in the military courts require a "minitrial," or "trial within a trial," on the admissibility of a statement challenged as involuntary. Practitioners report that, in their experience, minitrials almost never result in a finding that a confession was involuntary. Facing daunting odds at trial, and the prospect of pretrial detention that, for most offenses, promises to exceed the length of sentence, the rational course for nearly all defendants is to seek a negotiated disposition minimizing penalty.

Appeals against administrative sanctions, whether to military judges or to objections committees, have most often been similarly futile. Challenges to administrative detentions are hampered by the military judges' reliance on "secret evidence"—evidence supplied to it ex parte by the prosecution and never revealed either to the defendant or to defense counsel. Objections committees, empowered by statute to adopt their own rules of procedure and evidence, operated until 1984 without promulgating any such rules, and a further two years elapsed before the rules were published.[57]

Lawyers maintain that the lack of procedural and evidentiary guidelines in the objections committees were exploited by the Israeli authorities to foil their clients' claims. This was particularly strongly felt in reference to the military government's assertion of control over lands claimed by Palestinians as their own. The objections committees, for example, have rejected property tax receipts proffered by Palestinians as proof of ownership. Needless to say, attorneys were deeply embittered by the willingness of the Israeli authorities to recognize ownership for purposes of tax collection but to contest it in upholding an expropriation decree.

Though the gains of legal struggle in the Israeli military legal system are, from the Palestinian perspective, rather modest, they are not altogether nonexistent. For example, lawyers are permitted to visit detainees before their families are able to and, so, often function as links between defendants and the outside world. It also seems probable that lawyers are able to secure more favorable dispositions in plea bargaining than would unrepresented defendants.[58] However, from the perspective of practitioners, military court practice is nearly devoid of any intellectual or professional challenge, more resembling social work than legal practice. In the words of prominent West Bank attorney Jonathan Kuttab: "Many top West Bank lawyers refuse to practice before the military courts. I hate myself and question my integrity as a lawyer when I appear in the military court. I tell myself that I am a social worker and not a lawyer, bringing cigarettes to my client."[59]

Cases before the Israeli High Court

As indicated, Palestinian lawyers are able to participate in cases brought before the Israeli High Court only by cooperating with Israeli lawyers, who must actually present the case in court. I also noted that the character of High Court jurisdiction in the Occupied Territories leaves comparatively narrow scope for proactive lawyering, requiring, as it does, some form of governmental action.

The substantive law applied by the Israeli High Court in the Occupied Territories has also provided Palestinians little purchase against the military government. The international law of belligerent occupation, especially the version of it considered justiciable by the Israeli High Court,[60] affords far greater latitude to an occupier than the typical municipal law does to the Western democracies in which most cause lawyers have operated. The High Court has also tended to be highly deferential to the military government's assertion that its actions are required in the interests of "security."[61] Thus, in the first twenty years of the occupation, only five of sixty-five petitions from the territories that reached adjudication were granted.[62] Although such figures probably do not adequately measure the efficacy of the High Court's oversight of the military government, they are nonetheless daunting and certainly give Palestinian lawyers and litigants pause in deciding whether to sink substantial time, money, and other resources into High Court litigation.[63]

Pleading to the "Court of Public Opinion"

Lawyers from the Occupied Territories have been perhaps at their most effective in bringing local, Israeli, and international public attention to problems afflicting their clients.[64] They have written numerous academic articles and books, granted countless interviews, offered print and electronic media commentary, held public demonstrations, organized press conferences, called short-term strikes against the military courts, convened conferences of legal scholars, and acted as conduits for information to journalists, consulates, nongovernmental organizations, and others. Hence, they have played a key role in exposing some of the hidden ways in which the military legal system operates to the detriment of the Palestinian community.

They have been particularly effective members of a campaign to end torture in Israeli interrogation centers; their efforts in this connection have resulted in some significant shifts in Israeli policy, generally leading to less severe physical abuse of Palestinian detainees.[65] They also succeeded in drawing public attention to the plight of Palestinian prisoners in Israeli jails, demonstrating in their black robes outside Israeli prisons, conducting numerous press conferences, and other such activities.

Local Conceptions of Cause Lawyering

There is little question that political circumstances of occupation have allowed the development of only a narrow local conception of the scope of cause lawyering. As should be eminently clear, that narrow, even exclusive focus is on problems arising from the confrontation between the Palestinian community and the Israeli occupying authorities. In fact, there is a tendency, both within the legal profession and in the wider community under occupation, to attribute virtually all problems facing the Palestinians—social, economic, political, educational, professional, and so on—to Israeli rule. Indeed, it is often hard to see them otherwise.

On the other hand, there are many inequities internal to West Bank and Gaza society—between landowners and tenant farmers or residents, business owners and employees, men and women, to mention just a few—that might be addressed by cause lawyers, but instead have been subordinated to the "national struggle." Few Palestinian cause lawyers seemed to make the progressive restructuring of West Bank and Gaza society an explicit goal for their advocacy.[66]

Palestinian cause lawyers were curiously unreflective about the connections between their professional lives and the political world, at least to one familiar with cause lawyering in the United States, where such connections are more commonly thought through in systematic fashion.[67] Some, while espousing principles of justice and equality on the national level, harbored highly elitist views with respect to the legal profession and society more generally. Their relationships to court workers, support staff, and others encountered in daily professional life enacted the hierarchies that typify Palestinian society. Attitudes toward clients tended to be paternalistic; not a few described their clientele as lacking *al-hadara al-qanuniya*, literally, "legal civilization."[68]

The political peculiarities of foreign occupation further promoted a fundamentally conservative approach to cause lawyering among Palestinians. For example, notwithstanding the already mentioned jurisdictional limitations on proactive litigation in the Israeli High Court, more imaginative strategies were not altogether impossible. In principle, at least, it would have been feasible to initiate litigation in a new area by making a demand on the military government, say, for some legislation, then appealing the refusal of that demand to the High Court. This was, in effect, what occurred when a group of West Bank working lawyers appealed the military government's denial of their request for licensure of a professional association to the High Court. Even though the results were less than satisfactory, the case might be seen as a model for defining a litigation strategy reflective of the Palestinian community's positive needs, rather than simply its reactions to military government's acts.

This model has not been pursued in any meaningful way, however. In particular, Palestinian lawyers have, in criticizing legislative changes adopted by the military government believed to promote Israeli interests, repeatedly invoked the international legal doctrine that occupying powers are obliged to uphold the law in force on the eve of occupation. They would have been hard pressed to defend appeals for legislative changes directed to the same military authorities whose legislative powers they had refused to acknowledge as legitimate. Even if this had not been the case, the symbolism of seeking aid from what is perceived as an enemy regime would render this theoretical possibility beyond contemplation, in Palestinian political cultural terms.

Most Palestinian cause lawyers enunciated what in the West might be described as classically liberal notions about the importance of the "rule of law." Virtually none appeared to conceptualize law as a possible instrument of oppression in circumstances other than military occupation. Nor did any articulate a developed or coherent theory rationalizing the use of law to effect social or political change. Instead, law tended to be viewed in highly abstract, reified terms, as an entity "above" society and, at least in a "natural" state of affairs (that is, in the absence of military occupation), one distinct from politics. As one attorney remarked to me, reflecting on the ease with which the military government could amend laws: "If ever we find a legal loophole to exploit, some way of doing something positive for our clients, the Israelis just change the law the next day. *We* [Palestinians] *just don't have this idea*—that you can change laws, just like that."

The Israeli military government was typically critiqued primarily in terms of its perceived deviations from fundaments of the rule of law—principles of the separation of powers, notice, and the like, or, as I have stated, of the international law of belligerent occupation.[69] As to what had preceded occupation, or might supersede it, there was little critical reflection or discussion virtually until the eve of the Oslo accords.

Another consistent theme that emerged in the statements of the cause lawyers was the protest against conditions that impeded the lawyers' fulfillment of their professional function. The short-term strikes during the Intifada, for example, were articulated only in part as protests against substantive injustices—as one might see the beatings, jailings, killings, home demolitions, deportations, and other measures through which the military government sought to repress the uprising. The strikes were equally sparked by problems such as the inability of lawyers to locate clients and consult with them in privacy, lack of notice of important court dates, repeated failures to appear by government witnesses, and other such logistical deficiencies in the function of the military courts.[70]

Surely this did not represent the lawyers' acceptance of Israeli repression of their fellow community members. It may, as well, have reflected a deliberate decision to spotlight professional gripes as the only form of complaint likely to meet with a positive response from Israeli authorities. On the other hand, the focus on conditions detrimental to the profession betrays an outlook among at least some West Bank and Gaza lawyers that, had the occupation administration been simply more scrupulous in its observance of legal niceties, the lawyers might have had nothing to say *as professionals* about any remaining substantive injustices. Indeed, there were members of the profession who objected to what they saw as the "politicization" of legal practice and the use of professional associations for overt political purposes.[71]

This prominence of professional concerns, from one angle, is a reflection of the way in which most Palestinian lawyers "came to the cause"—not, in the first place, as political activists, who consciously selected law as a field in which to advance a political goal. Instead, they were lawyers first, who had been conscripted into the cause by a variety of circumstances and pressures beyond their wills. The priority of their professional identities over their sense of themselves as servants to a political cause is also evident in the lawyers' deep dissatisfaction, bordering on revulsion, with the social work aspects of military court practice, expressed in the above-quoted statement from lawyer Jonathan Kuttab. One might expect, among individuals whose first priority was promotion of the cause, a lesser level of repugnance for services that, though not specifically legal in the narrow sense, were nonetheless of substantial value to the national movement.

Lawyers' Involvement in Politics

The full extent of lawyers' integration into the struggle against Israeli occupation of the West Bank and Gaza Strip, whether in favor of a secular Palestinian state or a Muslim one, is currently impossible to assess. Membership in, or service to, "hostile organizations"—any constituent part of the Palestine Liberation Organization, until the Oslo peace agreement, and since then any of the various groups, Islamist or secular nationalist, which have actively, and sometimes violently, opposed the agreement—has been punishable under Israeli security regulations with imprisonment.

Certainly, Israeli authorities have suspected a number of lawyers of sub rosa political activities, either charging them with security offenses in military court, or more commonly, placing them under administrative detention.[72] It is also the case that particular lawyers became "known" within the Palestinian community as "the lawyers" for particular factions of the PLO. Whether this reflected lawyers' sympathies with, or even membership in, such factions, or simply the passing of their names from faction member to faction member during incarceration, is impossible determine. Whatever the case, one result was that these lawyers were able to corner a segment of the market for legal services. On the other hand, threat of arrest by Israeli authorities prevented lawyers from advertising their political affiliations too openly; indeed, it appears that the main evidence for the arrest and later administrative detention of Raji Sourani by the military government in Gaza was the fact that he had consistently represented suspected members of the Popular Front for the Liberation of Palestine.[73]

During the Intifada, lawyers may have helped to staff popular tribunals called "justice committees," established to "try" cases of Palestinians who violated the edicts of the Unified Leadership of the Uprising (as the secret body directing the protests became known).[74] While this service was unremunerated, it served to integrate some lawyers into the popular movement in an unprecedented manner and degree. These advocates, however, have been a small minority within even the cause-lawyering bar.

With some exceptions, it appears that a coordinated policy between lawyers and political activists as to how to handle cases in the military courts was never elaborated. In one notable exception, a group of administrative detainees opted not to exploit review procedures utilizing "secret evidence" out of a determination not to lend legitimacy to the military legal system.[75] It also appears that Fateh, the dominant secular nationalist group within the PLO, may have directed some decisions of the Committee of Arab Lawyers, in one case ordering CAL not to call a contemplated strike against the military courts at a sensitive point in negotiations between the PLO and the Israeli government.[76] Finally, there was a brief period during the Intifada when military court defendants held in several Israeli prisons vowed not to plead guilty but instead to contest their charges no matter what the cost.[77] Apparently this collective decision was adopted in response to a call from the Intifada leadership. The practice was not, however, sustained beyond a period of several weeks.

This latter example raises several interesting questions. Might not a sustained, universal refusal by Palestinian defendants to enter into plea negotiations and to demand trials have imposed intolerable costs on the Israeli occupation administration, or at least forced it to abandon the facade of the military legal system and expose its perceivedly unjust practices to broader public scrutiny? On the contrary, did not the regular capitulation of individual defendants through their acceptance of negotiated dispositions confirm for Israeli authorities the willingness of Palestinians, when push came to shove, to pursue personal, rather than communal interests, and thus inspire confidence in the occupiers in their ability to fragment and control the Palestinian national movement?[78]

Of course, it is conceivable that the resort to plea bargaining represented, in fact, a conscious and rational choice by the political leadership of the national movement to expose its activists to the least punishment possible, so as to return them to participation within the struggle within the shortest time possible. It may also have been calculated that a strategy of noncapitulation would simply have swelled the populations of Israeli prisons.

In fact, however, it appears that the plea-bargaining strategy was adopted purely by default. While there is evidence that noncapitulation was contemplated, at least by lawyers, it was never enacted on a wide scale due to its presumed infeasibility. The suspicion articulated by some lawyers was that "others," both defendants and other lawyers, would break ranks, unraveling the collective commitment to the program and undermining its efficacy.[79] Thus, defendants in military court cases were simply left by lawyers and by the political leadership to their own devices, to maximize their personal, individual interests within the narrow limitations imposed on them by the realities of the military court system.

The suspicion voiced by these lawyers may not have been unfounded. In the first place, such a strategy would surely have demanded, at least in the short term, significant sacrifice, in the form of longer sentences for defendants. This, in turn, would have required rigorous discipline of those facing charges in military courts. While such a high level of discipline might have been achieved among political cadres, many Palestinians caught up in the sweep of Israeli repression were not hardened activists. This was especially true during the Intifada, when Palestinians of all ages and walks of life were involved in some form of protest or pronationalist activity.[80] The spontaneous enthusiasm that led many in the community into support of the Intifada may not have been sufficient to support a strategy of legal resistance leading to years of imprisonment.

Refusal to plea bargain, obviously, would also have required that lawyers try many more cases, surely demanding more of their time and energy than the strategy actually pursued. This in itself may have been enough to dissuade many attorneys from noncapitulation. Perhaps more importantly, however, lawyers would have been forced to accept either fewer cases or a slower rate of case turnover. Here it should be noted that most lawyers working in the military courts made their livings not by charging high fees for few cases but by handling a high volume of cases, for which generally modest fees are charged. It is not at all evident, given the low per capita incomes in the West Bank and Gaza Strip, that lawyers could have maintained their practices by charging higher fees for the fewer cases they would have been obligated to accept.[81] Lacking the insulation from market pressures afforded cause lawyers in other societies by salaried positions in institutions, Palestinian lawyers' implementation of a strategy of noncapitulation may have been tantamount to professional suicide.

Conclusions

I suggested in the introduction that the circumstances of occupation created both the conditions favorable to the birth of Palestinian cause lawyering and those that led to its somewhat arrested development. Let me conclude by reviewing some of the respects in which the repressiveness of Israeli military government, the nature of the Palestinian national cause, the market conditions under which lawyers operated, and the alien quality of cause lawyering to Palestinian society contributed to this result.

Of course, had Israel's approach to governance in the Occupied Territories not been legalistic to begin with, cause lawyering might not have taken root there at all. Yet however elaborate, the legal regime placed by Israel in the West Bank was ultimately not designed to produce justice for a loyal citizenry, but rather to control, and where necessary, to repress, a hostile foreign one. This was especially true of the military courts. In the words of Hebrew University law professor David Kretzmer: "Both [Israeli and Palestinian] sides regard military trials as part of the struggle, not part of an impartial judicial system."[82] From this perspective, the low probability of success that Palestinian defendants experienced in the military courts would seem perfectly predictable. The Israeli High Court, for its part, only seemed willing to curb the military government's most egregious excesses.

Palestinian cause lawyers have consequently played at best a secondary, ancillary role in the nationalist movement in the Occupied Territories. Their stance is fundamentally defensive, rather than creative and innovative. In essence, what they provide to the Palestinian community under occupation is damage control—minimal protection to individual political activists and to social institutions that might form the basis of an independent state, minimizing, to the extent possible, the hardships of military occupation on common citizens.

It is hard not to feel that the resultant inability of the lawyers to measurably advance community interests, and their relegation to what I have referred to as damage control, constitutes a brake on the development of cause lawyering in the region. While regular success in court litigation or in other endeavors may not be necessary to the growth of cause lawyering, the example of Palestinian cause lawyers suggests that regular defeat is quite debilitating.[83]

It also suggests that a condition for the feasibility of cause lawyering, generally assumed in discussions of cause lawyering in the United States, is a set of legal institutions that are of sufficient independence and authority to constrain both private and state power and that have the inclination to do so when circumstances demand. This condition was lacking in Israel's military government in the West Bank and Gaza Strip. As the study of cause lawyering expands to consider examples outside of the United States and Western Europe, the existence of such basic conditions as a relatively independent judiciary may not be as easily assumed.

The lawyers in the Occupied Territories were likewise hampered by the fact that the crux of the issue in dispute—namely, the right to political control over the West Bank and Gaza Strip and, from the perspective of the Palestinians, their right to national self-determination—was never to be realized in any Israeli court. The most basic and needed changes, it was believed, could only come from the political process, and it is in that process that the Palestinian community—quite wisely, it would seem—staked its primary hopes and resources. In short, the nature of the cause was such that it was, under the circumstances, legally unobtainable.

The character of the Palestinian cause as one side of a struggle between two nationalities over the same territory had further profound implications for the development of cause lawyering. Political control of the West Bank and Gaza Strip was never the sole objective of Israeli military administration; rather, it was their settlement by Israelis and their functional integration into Israel that was sought. Thus, while the brunt of repression was doubtless borne by the most politically active and committed sectors of the Palestinian population, quiescence never guaranteed even the politically uninvolved members of the community that their rights and interests would not be infringed. Landowners suffering expropriations, whether wealthy absentees with extensive holdings or small peasants, constituted one of the more obvious categories of often relatively unpoliticized groups deeply aggrieved by the occupation.

While, on the one hand, the breadth of impact of Israeli repression diversified the range of opportunities for cause lawyers, it similarly created a Palestinian clientele that was unified only by its suffering at the hands of military government and that remained diverse, if not divergent, in many of its other interests. As we have seen in the discussion of the unemployed strategy of noncapitulation in the military courts, certain potentially promising approaches could not be exploited by cause lawyers in part because of the inability to achieve sustained discipline among clients only loosely united in interests and commitments.

Another part of this picture, we have seen, is that Palestinian cause lawyers—those who actually represent Palestinian interests before Israeli tribunals of various kinds and rhetorically rationalize and defend their work as constituting a form of service to Palestinian nationalism—themselves vary in social background, material interests, and, undoubtedly, levels of commitment to the cause. In what is essentially an intersocietal struggle, some attorneys have been pressed into lawyering for the cause who would not, one suspects, under any other circumstances have been cause lawyers. Palestinian cause lawyers thus exhibit perhaps less ideological sophistication and clarity about the uses of law to effect social and political change than lawyers whose service to a cause expresses a relatively conscious and free choice among real professional alternatives.

This effect has been reinforced by a market for legal services in which virtually all alternatives to cause lawyering have contracted severely. Again, the result is that some individuals who, under more favorable market conditions, might have chosen to devote their professional energies elsewhere have been more or less forced to become cause lawyers for the sake of professional survival. The fact that some lawyers who publicly presented themselves as champions of the cause were something less than paragons of nationalist virtue was surely not lost on the local community and doubtless contributed to the dilution of any positive image that more sincerely committed lawyers might have hoped to gain for themselves.

The local community in which cause lawyers struggled to be established, it will be remembered, was one already inclined to skepticism, if not disbelief, in some notions core to the cause-lawyering enterprise. Law is seen as an instrument of governmental authority, to be dodged, deflected, or ignored—but never to be deployed for the advancement of some nongovernmental interest. It has to said, however, that if Palestinian lay persons truly lacked "legal civilization," as their lawyers sometimes claim, the situation they confront in the military occupation itself is not terribly "legally civilized," if for reasons other than those maintained in popular conception. The experience of the Palestinian community under occupation has done little or nothing to establish the possibility of the constraint of government by law and only confirms its traditional view of the authorities as something akin to the uncontrollable forces of nature.

The absence of a conception of law as an instrument for social change initiated from outside the government is quite probably shared by many within the legal profession itself, not only in the Occupied Territories but elsewhere in the Arab world as well. While there is a strong tradition of nationalist political involvement by some Palestinian and other Arab lawyers in their capacities as prominent individuals, and even of Arab bar associations as collectivities, there is no parallel local tradition of the political use of law as such.[84]

As I have demonstrated at several junctures, many Palestinian attorneys would not easily conform to the model (or perhaps, stereotype) of the cause lawyer who consciously selects law as a profession, or a particular area of practice, to advance a social or political agenda. Indeed, the question might be raised as to the propriety of labeling as cause lawyers individuals who, though actually and self-consciously serving social or political causes, are arguably impelled by "impure" motives or interests. It would be misguided, I believe, to exclude such individuals from the definition of cause lawyering, for several reasons.

In the first place, Palestinian lawyers all profess devotion to the nationalist movement and publicly present their work as service to the cause. In a functional sense, they serve the cause essentially equally. Can one, then, distinguish empirically between "authentic" cause lawyers, presumably motivated by sincere political commitment, and "inauthentic" ones, motivated by meaner values? As a simple practical matter, I think not.

More importantly, the dichotomy between "authentic" and "inauthentic" cause lawyers is almost surely a false one. It is very likely that Palestinian lawyers' testaments of political commitment are sincere, even though in varying degree. It is equally likely that were the interests of lawyers serving causes in other societies scrutinized closely, both altruism and self-interest would be apparent in the mix of motives leading to their political involvement.

Finally, it seems quite possible that Palestinian lawyers who may have entered, for example, military court practice out of initially pragmatic interest, may in the process have been sensitized to the political movement—that is to say, to have been themselves politicized—by their interactions with clients and their experiences with Israeli military authorities.[85] Thus they may represent a significant alternate to the familiar model, according to which cause lawyers act as vanguards, or even founders, of the cause. They are not, for example, exploiting litigation to crystallize a popular but inchoate awareness of an injustice or to promote the definition of a new identity of a community of aggrieved parties.[86] In contrast, cause lawyers here, rather than *producing* the social or political movement, are themselves, in a sense, *produced by it.*

Notes

I received the able assistance for this article of student researchers Nagy Morcos and Khaldoun Baghdadi. I am also grateful for the comments of Ronen Shamir, Linda Bevis, Lisa Hajjar, Stuart Scheingold, Ruthanne Cecil, and Austin Sarat on earlier drafts of this study.
    1. Much of the empirical data for the current study was gathered during fourteen months of field research in the West Bank during 1984–85, when I conducted approximately two hundred interviews of roughly seventy West Bank lawyers, and perhaps ten interviews of four Gaza lawyers. In addition, I spoke with fifteen Jewish and Arab members of the Israeli bar, and with judges, human rights workers, municipal officials, former defendants, and others, and observed both military court proceedings and other transactions between lawyers from the Occupied Territories and functionaries of the Israeli military government. References to informants' comments below, unless otherwise noted, date to this period. I reported some of the findings of my research in *Palestinian Lawyers and Israeli Rule: Law and Disorder in the West Bank* (Austin: University of Texas Press, 1989).
    Cause lawyering by Israeli attorneys, whose social backgrounds and outlooks, legal training and experience, market pressures, and structural relationships to Israeli authority

all differ markedly from those of Palestinian attorneys, appears to be a considerably different phenomenon, and is not directly treated here.

2. Thus the title of this essay, inspired by the memoirs of prominent Palestinian advocate Hanna Dib Naqqara, "Attorney for the Land and People." Naqqara was an Israeli Arab attorney from the Akka-Haifa region, who struggled in Israeli courts to defend the interests of those Palestinians who remained within the areas falling under Israeli control after the 1948 Arab-Israeli war. His memoirs, *Muhami al-Ard wa'sh-Sha'b*, were compiled by his son, Hanna Ibrahim, and published in 1985 (Acre, Israel: Dar al-Asawir Publications).

3. Such uneven political response of a host population may well be typical of foreign occupations, as the example of Nazi occupation of France would certainly underscore.

4. Of American cause lawyers, for example, Handler states: "[T]he best evidence is that law-reform lawyers are committed social reformers. As compared with the rest of the bar, they are young, have proportionately better law-school records, are further to the left politically, and are taking about a 40% cut in salary to practice public interest law. Moreover, their financial sacrifice appears to be permanent." Joel Handler, *Social Movements and the Legal System: A Theory of Law Reform and Social Change* (New York: Academic Press, 1978), 29.

5. Some passages in the sections on the institutional framework and on lawyering for the cause are drawn from, or summarize sections of, my earlier article "Courting Justice? Legitimation in Lawyering under Israeli Occupation," *Law and Social Inquiry* 20 (Spring 1995), 349–405. That article provides a much more detailed and heavily referenced account of Israel's legal treatment of the Occupied Territories.

6. Article 3(a); Proclamation No. 2: Proclamation on Law and Administration, June 7, 1967; English translation in *Military Government in the Territories Administered by Israel, 1967–1980*, ed. Meir Shamgar (Jerusalem: Magnes Press,1982), 450–451. This order pertains to the West Bank; an equivalent order was issued for the Gaza Strip.

7. These powers are authorized under a set of defense emergency regulations enacted during the British Mandate, which Israel claims were never repealed and thus remain part of local law. See David Yahav, ed., *Israel, the "Intifada", and the Rule of Law* (Jerusalem: Israeli Ministry of Defense Publications, 1993), 45–47. A refutation of this claim is offered by Martha Moffet, *Perpetual Emergency: A Legal Analysis of Israel's Use of the British Defense (Emergency) Regulations, 1945, in the Occupied Territories* (Geneva: International Commission of Jurists, 1989).

8. This phenomenon was first noticed during the Intifada, the uprising of Palestinian residents that swept the Occupied Territories from late 1987 to the early nineties. The Palestine Human Rights Information Center claimed that at least seventy-four Palestinians were killed by undercover Israeli units in the years 1988–1991. Constantine Zureik and Anita Vitullo, *"Extrajudicial Killings: Israel's Latest War on the Intifada"* (unpublished manuscript on file with author, 1992). In 1992 and 1993, the alleged numbers were twenty-seven and forty-five respectively. For some time, Israel acknowledged the existence of undercover units in the Occupied Territories but claimed that they operated within standard rules of engagement that bar shootings of nonresisting arrestees. In the aftermath of the bombing of a bus in Tel Aviv causing twenty-two Israeli deaths in October, 1994, the Israeli government announced a crackdown on the Islamic groups that claimed responsibility, in the process admitting that undercover units had long operated with "kill on sight" instructions for some activists.

9. Anthony Coon, *Town Planning under Military Occupations* (Ashgate: Brookfield, Vt., 1992), 160–167; "Jewish Settlement in the West Bank and Gaza Strip," in *Survey of Jewish Affairs*, ed. William Frankel (Oxford: Blackwell, 1990), 42–59.

10. See generally Yahav, ed., *Israel, the "Intifada", and the Rule of Law.*

11. The courts were authorized to sit anywhere in the Occupied Territories. For most of the period of occupation, there were two regularly sitting courts in each of the Gaza Strip (Gaza City and Khan Younis) and the West Bank (Ramallah and Nablus). Shamgar, ed., *Military Government in the Territories Administered by Israel, 1967–1980.* During the Intifada, additional courts were activated in Hebron, Jenin, and Tulkarm in the West Bank. Daphna Golan, *The Military Judicial System in the West Bank* (Jerusalem: B'Tselem, 1989). Since the Oslo accords, a single Israeli military court has been sitting in the Gaza Strip, at the Erez checkpoint on the border with Israel.

12. Defendants were permitted to apply to the area commander to vacate a conviction or reduce a sentence. In addition, while the Israeli High Court does not function as an appellate court for the military courts of the Occupied Territories, it may issue writs of certiorari against the judgments of those courts should they err grossly or exceed their powers. David Yahav, ed., *Israel, the "Intifada", and the Rule of Law*, 98.

13. The court, which sits in Ramallah, in the West Bank, and until recently, for one day a week in Gaza, hears appeals of right from decisions of three-judge courts; defendants convicted in one-judge courts must petition for review.

14. Shamgar, ed., *Military Government in the Territories Administered by Israel, 1967–1980*, 469–476.

15. A list of matters falling within the purview of the objections committees includes such matters as income or value-added tax assessments, pension rights of civil servants, customs duties, driving and business licenses, and others. Raja Shehadeh, *Occupiers Law*, 2nd. ed. (Washington, D.C.: Institute for Palestine Studies, 1988), 88–89.

16. The requirement of review by a military judge of administrative detentions was instituted in the Occupied Territories in 1980, generally tracking changes in Israeli legislation applicable to administrative detention within Israel itself. Similarly, as of 1989, house demolitions may proceed only upon notice to the owner, including admonition of the right to an administrative appeal to the military commander, and to petition the Israeli High Court. Dan Simon, "The Demolition of Homes in the Israeli Occupied Territories," *Yale Journal of International Law* 19, no. 1 (1994), 1–79.

17. The Intifada was sparked when Palestinians suspected an Israeli truck driver had intentionally rammed a vehicle carrying Palestinian laborers, killing several of them in December 1987. Within days both Gaza and the West Bank were in upheaval. For the next two and a half years, until the Persian Gulf War of 1990, Palestinian protest against Israeli occupation was both qualitatively and quantitatively different than in any previous period. For the first time, there was, alongside the amply publicized demonstrations and riots, a thoroughgoing effort to wean the Occupied Territories of their economic and institutional dependence on Israel. Israeli products were boycotted, as residents of the West Bank and Gaza Strip struggled to provide for as many community needs as their resources permitted. An unprecedented level of communal solidarity united all sectors of Palestinian society and swept nearly everyone into support activities of one kind or another. See Jamal Nassar and Roger Heacock, eds., *Intifada at the Crossroads* (Greenwood, Conn.: Greenwood Press, 1990).

18. According to Israeli military sources, 83,321 Palestinians were tried in the military courts from 1988 to 1993 alone. Human Rights Watch/Middle East, *Israel's Interrogation of Palestinians from the Occupied Territories* (New York: Human Rights Watch, 1994), 2. In the first two and a half years of the uprising, nine thousand administrative detention orders were issued. Golan, *The Military Judicial System in the West Bank*, 6. Over two thousand homes have been demolished or sealed in the Occupied Territories, affecting perhaps ten

times that number of occupants. Lynn Welchman, *A Thousand and One Homes: Israel's Demolition and Sealing of Houses in the Occupied Palestinian Territories* (Geneva: International Commission of Jurists, 1993).

19. David Farhy, "Current Legal Trends in the Area Administered by Israel," *Military Law Review* 12 (1986), 47–60. In the Israeli judicial system, the High Court enjoys original jurisdiction over petitions alleging unjust or illegal actions taken by Israeli government functionaries acting in their official capacities. Elie Nathan, "The Power of Supervision of the High Court of Justice over Military Government," in *Military Government in the Territories Administered by Israel, 1967–1980,* ed. Shamgar.

20. The mixture of moral and political considerations behind the Israeli government's adoption of this policy are discussed in Moshe Negbi, "The Israeli Supreme Court and the Occupied Territories," *Jerusalem Quarterly* 27 (1983), 33–47.

21. Suits against Israeli civilians in the local civil court systems remain a theoretical possibility. However, the military government enjoys the authority to remove any case, whether criminal or civil, from the jurisdiction of the civil court systems and to either close the case file or transfer it to an Israeli court. In part as a consequence of this, such suits have been rarely filed following the initial years of occupation. Raja Shehadeh and Jonathan Kuttab, *The West Bank and the Rule of Law* (Geneva: International Commission of Jurists, 1980).

22. And, I discovered, virtually unknown among West Bank lawyers. Particularly little power was left in local hands after 1982, when almost all municipal officials in the West Bank resigned in protest against the introduction of what the Israeli government billed as a "civil administration" in the area. They were replaced mostly by Israeli military officers.

23. Bisharat, *Palestinian Lawyers and Israeli Rule;* Lisa Hajjar, "Authority, Resistance, and the Law: The Israeli Military Courts in the Occupied Territories," (Ph.D. diss., American University, 1995.

24. Ibrahim Dakkak, "The Transformation of Jerusalem: Juridical Status and Physical Change," in *Occupation: Israel over Palestine,* ed. Naseer Aruri (Belmont, Mass.: Association of Arab-American University Graduates, 1993).

25. Bisharat, *Palestinian Lawyers and Israeli Rule.*

26. This hope was never realized, for reasons that I cannot fully reconstruct. One might conjecture, however, that other occupational groups lacked both the financial resources enjoyed by the lawyers and the backing of a powerful outside institution equivalent to the Jordanian Bar Association.

The pattern of Palestinian lawyers' prominence in political protest activities *outside* of the legal domain, and relative political inaction *within it* is consistent not only with the tradition of the legal profession in Palestine, but also with that of lawyers in other Arab countries. Bisharat, *Palestinian Lawyers and Israeli Rule*; Donald Reid, *Lawyers and Politics in the Arab World, 1860–1940* (Minneapolis, Minn.: Biblioteca Islamica, 1981).

27. No more than a handful, such as Nablus attorney Wasfi al-Masri, declined to observe the strike from the outset and made early appearances in military courts. A somewhat larger number continued to practice law in the Islamic and ecclesiastical courts, which have jurisdiction over matters of personal status, and provided legal counsel to municipalities, community organizations, and religious bodies, as the terms of the strike permitted.

28. The Druze sect is an offshoot of Islam. Its adherents are, for the most part, concentrated in the mountainous regions of southern Syria (including the Golan Heights), southern Lebanon, and northern Israel. They are recognized within Israel as a distinct "nation" or minority; unlike most Arabs, they are conscripted for service into the Israeli

military. David Kretzmer, *The Legal Status of the Arabs in Israel* (Boulder, Colo.: Westview Press, 1990).

29. On the cultural practice of "wasta," see Robert Cunningham and Yasin Sarayrah, *Wasta* (Westport, Conn.: Praeger, 1993).

30. Other Israeli lawyers, a number of them former military prosecutors, also entered military court practice in the Occupied Territories, playing upon expectations that their personal ties with judges and prosecutors would translate into positive results for their Palestinian clients.

31. It should be clarified, however, that obstructing the operations of the court system was not an explicit goal of the strike. In fact, the boycott was intended exclusively as a symbolic act, and was addressed primarily to local Palestinian and Jordanian audiences.

32. By expulsion from the Jordanian Bar Association, through which recognition and membership is gained in the regional Arab Lawyers Union, strike breakers were officially no longer considered lawyers in any part of the Arab world. This, too, was of primarily symbolic effect, as virtually all of the strike breakers' work was contained within the Occupied Territories.

33. There are approximately 250,000 Palestinians living in U.N.-administered refugee camps or in towns and villages of the West Bank and Gaza Strip who fled the areas that fell under the control of Israel in the 1948 war. See Ann Mosley Lesch, *Transition to Palestinian Self-Government: Practical Steps toward Israeli-Palestinian Peace* (Bloomington: Indiana University Press, 1992).

34. This university is chartered as a branch campus of the University of Alexandria in Egypt. It was founded in 1969 by Gamal Abdel Nasser as an expression of commitment to pan-Arabism. Its educational standards are regarded to be among the lowest in the region.

35. I do not have comparable figures for the same timespan in Gaza. In 1994, however, over four hundred lawyers had registered with the Gaza Bar Association, while in the West Bank, the numbers exceeded one thousand. Much of this growth has apparently occurred in response to the Oslo peace accords and the attendant resurgence of economic activity in the two regions; many newly registered lawyers were not recent law graduates, but had simply been unable to find work in the profession previously and had assumed different occupations. Hajjar, *"Authority, Resistance, and Law."*

36. Some one hundred lawyers were taking military court cases in Gaza during the height of the Intifada. Ibid. This group, and the one like it from the West Bank, is comprised of many who are younger in age and possess less professional experience than either the Israeli Arab lawyers or the lawyers from the Occupied Territories who began practice in the early to mid-eighties. Thus, they may be seen as constituting yet a third generation of cause lawyers in the regions.

It should also be mentioned that opportunities for newer lawyers broadened somewhat with the retirement of Felicia Langer, one of the two above-mentioned Israeli leftist lawyers in the military courts, in 1990, over her concern that further practice in the military courts amounted to complicity in the injustices she perceived them to mete out. "A Judicial System Where Even Kafka Would Be Lost: An Interview with Felicia Langer," *Journal of Palestine Studies* 77, no. 24 (1990), 24–36.

37. I only observed this phenomenon among a few of the Israeli Arab lawyers. Those from the Occupied Territories had not been active for long enough, nor had realistic alternatives, to enjoy this luxury. I also do not intend to suggest that military court practice was consciously entered as career-building strategy, but that, much in the manner of some public defenders in the United States (see Anthony Platt and Randi Pollock, "Channeling Lawyers: The Careers of Public Defenders," *Issues in Criminology* 9, no. 1 [1974], 1–31), these

lawyers became "burnt out" and cynical after initial periods of high idealism. One Israeli Arab attorney who had abandoned military court practice after about five years denounced the courts to me as "theaters."

38. Stuart Scheingold, "Radical Lawyers and Socialist Ideals," *Journal of Law and Society* 15 (1988), 122–138.

39. Joel Handler, Ellen J. Hollingsworth, and Howard Erlanger, *Lawyers and the Pursuit of Legal Rights* (San Francisco: Academic Press, 1978).

40. John Dugard, "Quaker East Jerusalem Legal Aid Center: Program Evaluation" (unpublished manuscript on file with author, 1992).

41. Indigents charged with serious offenses in the military courts are entitled to appointed counsel under military court regulations. This is an option seldom exercised by Palestinians, as appointed lawyers are seen as craven to the authorities that appoint and pay them (much in the way criminal defendants often perceive public defenders in the United States). There is, moreover, a suspicion that following conviction (nearly inevitable for most defendants), the authorities would attempt to recoup its expenses in the form of stiffer punishments, especially fines. Ibid.

42. Of which the current author was one, in the summer of 1982.

43. See, for example, Israel National Section of the International Commission of Jurists, *The Rule of Law in the Areas Administered by Israel* (Tel Aviv: Israel National Section of the International Commission of Jurists, 1981); and Yahav, ed., *Israel, the "Intifada", and the Rule of Law.*

44. Membership in a "hostile organization," including all of the factions of the PLO and of the Islamist movements, constitutes a violation of security regulations enforced by Israel in the Occupied Territories. The connections between individuals and these organizations are therefore mostly covert.

45. While there is much admiration in Palestinian society for the American people, most Palestinians view the United States government to be Israel's primary supporter, and regard it as indirectly responsible for much of their suffering and the denial of their national rights.

46. An attempt to gain recognition from the Jordanian Bar Association was rebuffed, as were requests for licensure to the Israeli military government. Ultimately a petition was lodged with the Israeli High Court, seeking to compel the military government to recognize CAL. The petition was actually upheld, but in such a manner as to make the victory hollow. The High Court directed the military governor of the West Bank to permit the formation of a professional association for lawyers in the region, but stated that lawyers from East Jerusalem—which, it will be recalled, had been annexed by Israel in 1967—could not be members. CAL was unwilling to accede to this condition, as it would have signified capitulation to Israeli annexation, and thus has continued to function without official recognition.

47. This was so of Military Order 1060 in the West Bank, which changed procedures for the adjudication of disputes over the registration of previously unregistered lands, and supplanted the jurisdiction of local courts over such disputes in favor of military tribunals. The order was adopted not long after the ban on land purchases by individual Israelis on the West Bank was lifted, in 1979, and was widely seen by Palestinians as a measure to shield illicit land transfers between Palestinian landowners and Israelis from public scrutiny and control.

48. Also unlike the model of Al-haqq/LSM, Sourani—and the center he directs—is widely regarded as being affiliated with the Popular Front for the Liberation of Palestine. Sourani himself has been arrested and administratively detained several times by the Israeli authorities and claimed to have been tortured on at least one of them. Michael Posner, *An*

Examination of the Detention of Human Rights Workers and Lawyers from the West Bank and Gaza and Conditions of Detention at Ketziot (New York: Lawyers Committee for Human Rights, 1988).

49. Dugard, "Quaker East Jerusalem Legal Aid Center."

50. Interview with Emma Naughten, former director, Bir Zeit Human Rights Office, December 1994. Several Israeli human and civil rights groups also initiated or intensified work directed to the situation in the Occupied Territories at this same time. The Association for Civil Rights in Israel, primarily concerned with the advancement of civil rights within Israel itself, devoted up to one third of the efforts of its nine staff attorneys to cases arising in the Occupied Territories. Dugard, "Quaker East Jerusalem Legal Aid Center." B'tselem, a human rights monitoring group, was founded shortly after the outbreak of the Intifada, as was the Public Committee against Torture in Israel, led by Hebrew University law professor Stanley Cohen.

51. The Palestinian School of Law began operation in East Jerusalem with a faculty of twelve, and offers a four-year degree program to some 160 enrolled students. The institution is, as of this writing, still unaccredited. Personal communication from Dean Ali Khashan, December 1994. Bir Zeit University established a law center in 1990 and inaugurated a graduate program in law in 1995–1996. Personal communication from the Law Center director Camille Mansour, February 1995.

52. According to a study by the Israeli human rights organization B'tselem, practitioners estimate that confessions are obtained in 80 percent or more of cases in the military courts. B'Tselem, *Violations of Human Rights in the Occupied Territories, 1990–1991* (Jerusalem: B'Tselem, 1991), 93. Reports I gathered in the field suggested that this estimate is conservative. In the words of the former chief military prosecutor in Gaza, "As someone who is very familiar with both sides of the story, as a prosecutor and a lawyer, I have difficulty remembering one person accused of terrorist activity who was acquitted. There are almost no such instances. Every person who is accused is found guilty. Sometimes on the basis of criteria which no Israeli court of law would accept. In 99% of the cases the accused come to court with a signed confession of guilt. That's suspicious." Quoted in Virginia Sherry, *Background Memorandum: Boycott of the Military Courts by West Bank and Israeli Lawyers* (New York: Lawyers Committee for Human Rights, 1989), 7.

53. The General Security Service, sometimes referred to by its Hebrew initials, "Shin Beit," is Israel's main domestic intelligence and security agency.

54. The move was precipitated by two major embarrassments to the government. In the "Nafsu" case, it came to light that a Circassian officer of the General Security Service had been convicted of espionage on the basis of a coerced confession and perjured testimony by several of his fellow officers. In the "Bus 300 incident," a Palestinian who participated in the hijacking of an Israeli civilian bus on the coastal highway was revealed to have been beaten to death after his apprehension at the direction of the head of the GSS, in the wake of government statements to the press that all the hijackers had perished in a gun battle.

55. According to the most recent detailed study of the issue by Human Rights Watch, "The overriding strategy of Israel's interrogation agencies in getting uncooperative detainees to talk is to subject them to a coordinated, rigid, and increasingly painful regime of physical constraints and psychological pressures over days and very often for three or four weeks. . . . The methods used in nearly all interrogations are prolonged sleep deprivation, prolonged sight deprivation using blindfolds or tight-fitting hoods; forced, prolonged maintenance of body positions that grow increasingly painful, and verbal threats and insults." Human Rights Watch/Middle East, *Israel's Interrogation of Palestinians from the Occupied Territories*, x.

56. Liat Collins, "GSS Agent involved in Death of Harizat transferred from post," *Jerusalem Post,* May 1, 1995, 1; Yuval Ginbar, *The Death of Mustafa Barakat in the Interrogation Wing of the Tulkarm Prison* (Jerusalem: B'Tselem, September, 1992); Stanley Cohen, "Talking about Torture in Israel," *Tikkun* 6 (1991), 23–26.

57. Eyal Benvenisti, *Legal Dualism: The Absorption of the Occupied Territories into Israel* (Boulder, Colo.: Westview Press, 1990), 45.

58. See Bisharat, "Courting Justice?"

59. Quoted in Virginia Sherry, *Background Memorandum,* 17.

60. The Israeli High Court has ruled that the occupations of the West Bank and Gaza Strip are governed by the customary laws of belligerent occupation, and in particular by the Hague Convention of 1907. However, according to the court, the Fourth Geneva Conventions (which offer greater protections to occupied civilian populations than the Hague Convention), though binding on Israel as one of its signatories, are not justiciable in Israeli courts in the absence of parliamentary enabling legislation. Mazen Qupty, "The Application of International Law in the Occupied Territories as Reflected in the Judgments of the High Court of Justice in Israel," in *International Law and the Administration of Occupied Territories,* ed. Emma Playfair (Oxford: Oxford University Press, 1992), 87–124.

61. Ibid.

62. Ronen Shamir, "Litigation as Consummatory Action: the Instrumental Paradigm Reconsidered," *Studies in Law, Politics, and Society* 11 (1991), 41–68.

63. Jonathan Kuttab, "Avenues Open for Defence of Human Rights in the Israeli Occupied Territories," in *International Law and the Administration of Occupied Territories,* ed. Playfair, 489–504.

64. Ibid.

65. Bisharat, "Courting Justice?"

66. Only with the Oslo peace accords and the prospect of some kind of Palestinian self-rule have cause lawyers begun to seriously examine injustices internal to Palestinian society. Al-haqq/LSM, for example, sponsored an international conference in Toronto on the legal status of Palestinian women in 1994. The Gaza-based Palestinian Lawyers for Human Rights was recently announced to have received joint funding with an Israeli group to study the establishment of a system of juvenile justice in the region. Both these groups and the Gaza Center for Rights and Law have responded vociferously against human and civil rights violations committed by the new Palestinian Authority. Ibid.

67. Louise Trubek and M. Elizabeth Kransberger, "Critical Lawyers: Social Justice and the Structures of Private Practice," chap. 7 of this volume.

68. Bisharat, *Palestinian Lawyers and Israeli Rule.*

69. Illustrative of this kind of critique is Shehadeh and Kuttab's *The West Bank and the Rule of Law.*

70. Mona Rishmawi, "The Lawyers' Strike in Gaza," *Centre for the Independence of Judges and Lawyers Bulletin* 21 (1988), 23–25; Sherry, *Background Memorandum.*

71. In 1994, just such a contingent voted the politically aligned leadership of the Committee of Arab Lawyers out of office and installed new representatives who pledged to reorient the organization to address narrow professional concerns. Bill Hutman, "Fatah Loses Votes for Two Professional Associations," *Jerusalem Post,* January 30, 1994, 2.

72. Posner, *An Examination of the Detention of Human Rights Workers and Lawyers.*

73. Ibid.

74. Adrien Wing, "Legal Decision Making during the Palestinian Intifada: Embryonic Self-Rule," *Yale Journal of International Law* 18, no. 1 (1993), 95–153.

75. Joost Hilterman, "Israel's Deportation Policy in the Occupied West Bank and Gaza," *Palestine Yearbook of International Law* 3 (1986), 154–183.

76. Hajjar, *"Authority, Resistance, and Law."*

77. Ibid.; Yahav, ed., *Israel, the "Intifada", and the Rule of Law.*

78. Of an analogous phenomenon in the pre–1948 war period, Kenneth Stein writes: "Whether it was avarice or need, self-preservation or greed, Palestinian Arab land sales breathed life into Jewish aspirations and advanced Zionist goals. Indeed, Jews purchased only a small percentage of the total area of Palestine under the Mandate. The critical variable for Zionist motivation was Arab readiness to part with a portion of their patrimony. Palestinian Arab land sales meant the absence of true commitment to Palestinian nationalism. At a time of feverish anti-Zionist and anti-British sentiment, Palestinian Arab land sales to Zionists showed that individual priorities were equal to or more important than an emerging national movement." Kenneth Stein, *The Land Question in Palestine, 1917–1939* (Chapel Hill: University of North Carolina Press, 1984), 70.

79. Hajjar, *"Authority, Resistance, and Law."*

80. Nassar and Heacock, eds., *Intifada.*

81. Lawyers' fees for military court cases in the mid-1980s ranged between approximately $500 and $1,700. Bisharat, *Palestinian Lawyers and Israeli Rule,* 100. Per capita incomes in the West Bank and Gaza were $1,800 and $590 respectively in 1992. *CIA World Fact Book* (Washington, D.C.: CIA, 1992).

82. Bruce S. Rosen, "West Bank Story," *American Lawyer* (June 1990), 78–89, at 83.

83. I concur with Sarat's point that there is a certain elasticity in the definition of legal success; my data suggest, however, that this elasticity has limits. Austin Sarat, "Between (the Presence of) Violence and (the Possibility of) Justice: Lawyering against Capital Punishment," chap. 11 of this volume.

84. One emergent, and fascinating exception to this pattern is the growing employment of Egyptian courts by Islamist lawyers to enforce purportedly Islamic norms of behavior on others via the legal principle of *hezba,* which grants Muslims the right to bring suit to defend the "rights of God." In one widely reported case, Muslim Brotherhood lawyers convinced a judge to divorce Cairo University professor Nasr Hamid Abu Zayd from his wife against his will, on the claim that his writings made him an apostate. Karim el-Gawhary, "Shari'a or Civil Code? Egypt's Parallel Legal Systems: an Interview with Ahmad Sayf al-Islam," *Middle East Report* 197 (November-December 1995), 25–27.

85. A similar process is described for Taiwan in Jane Kaufman Winn and Tang-chi Yeh, "Advocating Democracy: The Role of Lawyers in Taiwan's Political Transformation," *Law and Social Inquiry* 20 (Spring 1995), 561–599.

86. Michael McCann, "Legal Mobilization and Political Advocacy: Some Basic Premises," *Studies in Law, Politics, and Society* 11 (1991), 227–254.

CHAPTER 15

Cause Lawyers and Social Movements

A Comparative Perspective on Democratic Change in Argentina and Brazil

STEPHEN MEILI

"When you question the system to its roots, there is a blockade from every direction; sometimes even from your own people." [1]

Introduction and Methodology

This chapter explores the relationship between cause lawyers [2] and grassroots popular movements in Argentina and Brazil. I selected these two countries for such a comparative study for several reasons, aside from their obvious geographic proximity: first, each has endured a period of military rule during at least part of the last four decades (1964–85 in Brazil; 1976–82 in Argentina), which had serious implications—but also presented certain opportunities—for cause lawyers; second, each has undergone a transition from that military rule to democratic consolidation over the past two decades, which permitted an opening for cause lawyering; third, each has active grassroots social movements in both urban and rural sectors; and fourth, each has a long tradition of a nonindependent and bureaucratic judiciary, which has rendered traditional forms of lawyering of limited use to many cause lawyers.

The research for this chapter is based primarily on interviews I conducted with lawyers, judges, law professors, and nonlawyer social activists in Argentina (primarily Buenos Aires) and Brazil (primarily São Paulo and Rio de Janeiro) in 1992 and 1994. The first section provides an overview of cause lawyers who work with grassroots social movements: who they are, how they support themselves financially, and the kind of work they do. Section 2 discusses the factors motivating social movement cause lawyers that are common to both countries. Section 3 analyzes the differences between social movement cause lawyering in the two countries and speculates as to why it is more prevalent in Brazil than Argentina. The last section suggests some overarching factors that may affect the degree of cause lawyering (and in particular social movement cause lawyering) under any given political regime.

Description of Social Movement Cause Lawyers in Argentina and Brazil

Introduction

Cause lawyering in Argentina and Brazil—indeed, in most of Latin America—is significantly different from what most observers have come to view as cause lawyering in the United States. First, Latin American cause lawyers enjoy far less financial support than their counterparts in the United States (despite frequent claims of poverty by the latter group); as a result, there are far fewer of them per capita, and most can only afford to do their cause lawyering on a part-time basis. Organizations similar to those that employ large numbers of full-time cause lawyers in the United States (such as the American Civil Liberties Union, the National Association for the Advancement of Colored People, and the Natural Resources Defense Council) are virtually nonexistent. Second, because the problems of poverty, malnutrition, illiteracy, economic disparity, and state violence are so widespread in Latin America, it is difficult—and daunting—for cause lawyers in that region to devote themselves to case work on behalf of individuals; instead, they focus on broader social issues like human rights, land ownership, and police violence. They must contend with judicial systems that are widely viewed as slow, costly, tremendously bureaucratized, and controlled by the more powerful executive branch. And they receive comparatively less support—be it financial, intellectual, moral, or professional—from institutions like law schools, bar associations, and private foundations.

A small number of cause lawyers in Brazil and Argentina work with grassroots community groups in urban shantytowns (*favellas* in Brazil; *villas miserias* or *villas* in Argentina) and rural sectors. Most of these cause lawyers (I will refer to them as "social movement cause lawyers" for purposes of this chapter) have either consciously or unconsciously rejected traditional forms of legal advocacy as inefficient, ineffective, and/or counterproductive. Rather than represent an individual person in a lawsuit before a court or administrative agency, they prefer to work as legal consultants with an organized grassroots community group that approaches them for assistance. And rather than dictate what they personally consider to be the appropriate legal strategy in a given situation, they offer information and advice as to the legal rights, obligations, and likely ramifications of actions or strategies that the group has already adopted or is contemplating. They always insist (or at least strongly encourage) that members of the movement "do the talking" when they meet with adversaries (usually government officials or private property owners). They consider legal training of members of the community groups to be an important part of their jobs, so that those groups will be able to perform certain legal tasks on their own in the future. Overall, these lawyers seek to demystify the law and deemphasize the lawyer's role in defending the interests of the poor.

Many of these lawyers are part of a larger movement of nontraditional lawyers throughout Latin America known by one of several titles, including "alternative lawyering," "new lawyering," or "change-oriented lawyering." These terms are controversial and subject to multiple interpretations. According to Fernando Rojas, formerly of the Latin American Institute of Alternative Legal Services (ILSA), "new" legal services are those "aimed at promoting social, legal, economic, and political changes in Latin America. . . . As pursued by new legal services, social change means imposing a new concept of justice [which] usually means replacing all or part of the liberal legal system by a different one."[3] Maria Elba Martínez, a lawyer working with grassroots community groups in Córdoba, Argentina, says "For some people, alternative lawyering means bringing the law to the people. For others, it means creating a type of law that is more just, more balanced, using principles and norms that emanate from the people."[4]

More experienced cause lawyers seem a bit put off by all of the attention given to these "new" forms of lawyering, since it implicitly criticizes earlier cause lawyering as more traditional and status quo–oriented. According to Miguel Pressburger, coordinator of the Institute for Popular Legal Support (AJUP) in Rio de Janeiro, lawyers in the alternative law movement are doing nothing novel; instead, they are taking a practical approach to problems: "And these practical ways of dealing with problems have existed since the first lawyer existed. So, there is nothing 'alternative' in that."[5] Similarly, Octavio Carsen, director of the Center for Social Investigations and Popular Legal Assistance (CISALP) in Buenos Aires,[6] and a longtime human rights lawyer, asks the question "Is it really alternative law, or is it using the law to reach people who have been ignored? Is it really rebellious lawyering to use the legal system to try to help people? . . . The only person who can use the law alternatively is a judge, because he or she can break with tradition at any point. The lawyers and popular groups are stuck with the law."[7]

Examples of Social Movement Cause Lawyering

The following anecdotes exemplify social movement cause lawyering in Brazil and Argentina:

Alicia Curiel is the only attorney who works on a full-time basis for the Center for the Study of Law and Society (CELS), created in 1985 to defend the interests of the "disappeared" during Argentina's "Dirty War." She spends most of her time working with *villeros* (residents of *villas miserias*) in and around Buenos Aires.[8] In most *villas*, residents elect a civil association to represent them in matters before the government. In July 1994 I accompanied Curiel to a meeting with members of one such civil association to discuss land ownership issues prior to a meeting with local government officials the following day. This particular *villa*, known informally as *Villa Oculta* because of the wall built around it by the government to conceal it from surrounding middle-class neighborhoods, contains about 2,600 families, although it originally was intended for only 900. Adding to the problems of such overcrowding, different parcels of land within the *villa* are owned by different entities; that is, the local municipality, the federal government (Buenos Aires is a federal district, much like Washington, D.C.), and private, "absentee" owners. About twelve members of the civil association attended the meeting (there are about twenty members in all), which was held at the *villa*, about twenty kilometers from downtown Buenos Aires. Curiel responded to members' questions about acquiring ownership of individual land parcels but remained mostly silent during the ensuing debate. She offered her own advice about the next day's meeting: listen to what the officials have to say but make no commitments until the *villa* residents have been polled during a subsequent meeting. In the end, this became the consensus strategy of the association members. She stressed quite forcefully that the association, and not she, would do the talking during that meeting.

One of the most active grassroots movements in rural Brazil is the Landless Peasant Movement. Community groups within this movement occupy abandoned or unused private property, claiming it for their own. Prior to such an occupation, leaders of the landless group will frequently consult a lawyer about a host of issues, including the claim of title to the targeted property (which is often extremely convoluted),[9] whether or not the occupation is legal,[10] and the likely ramifications of such an occupation.[11] The lawyer presents a variety of options and strategies for the group to consider.[12] If the group decides to occupy the land, the lawyer will frequently remain with the group in order to continue providing legal information and advice, as well as to forestall violence from the police and/or the landowner.[13] The lawyer will also train group members to negotiate with the landowner.[14] Some of the landless groups have a very sophisticated division of labor: certain members of the group are in charge of deciding what part of the abandoned property is best suited for occupation; others organize internal tasks such as working the land, creating a collective kitchen, and taking care of children; others are responsible for outside political and media relations.[15] These groups will often request assistance from outside experts in addition to lawyers, such as architects and economists.[16]

Lawyers employed by CISALP in Buenos Aires work with a group of about forty families who live under an arched railroad bridge on the outskirts of the city. The group closed off the bridge's arches and made their homes within the enclosed structure. As long as the railroad was government-owned, the squatters were permitted to maintain that living space. But as soon as the railroad was privatized, the owner tried to evict them from the property, claiming that the arrangement was unsafe—not for the landless group, but for the trains riding on the bridge over their heads (there are businesses on either side of the railroad bridge that house explosive material. The railroad owners have made no attempt to relocate them).[17] At that point, leaders of the group contacted CISALP, about which they had heard through word of mouth. CISALP lawyers met with the group and together devised a two-part strategy: delay eviction for as long as possible, while simultaneously investigating alternate living sites. As a result of the ensuing negotiations between the group and the railroad company, the company allowed a grace period of several months and suggested another housing site on property owned by a different railroad company. The CISALP lawyers have also helped the "squatting" group to form a legal cooperative, which gives it more status and power in negotiating with both private and public entities.

According to Octavio Carsen, director of CISALP, the purpose of projects like these is to help the grassroots groups define their objectives and how they will go about achieving them: "This office doesn't lead the discussions. It waits for the people to initiate the discussions with authorities. This office goes with them and helps them with the discussion; but the people are the ones who speak."[18]

Maria Elba Martínez is a lawyer who works with Peace and Justice Service (SERPAJ) in Córdoba, a city of approximately 1.2 million in central Argentina. (SERPAJ is a nongovernmental human rights organization founded in 1974). One of Martínez's current projects concerns the documentation of immigrants. Although the government requires all immigrants to be registered, many of those in the *villas* where Martínez works have been reluctant to do so. As she tells it, they argue, "Why do we need to document everything? The only thing that we are going to accomplish is to be identified by the police." On the other hand, Martínez knows that without documentation the people cannot vote, get married, or purchase certain goods. They will also have more problems with the police ("auto-criminalizing themselves," as she puts it). Martínez, who recognizes both the benefits and pitfalls of such forced registration, meets regularly with *villeros* to discuss the ramifications of registering and not registering, and to offer information on the registration process to those who decide to undertake it.[19]

Martínez sees community legal education as one of her most important functions: "It is very important to get people interested in the law. After all, their dependency, their punishment, their marginalization, goes through the law."[20]

In Brazil's rural state of Goies, a community priest working on behalf of landless peasants was blinded by an unknown assailant who had attempted to murder him. Members of the community knew who committed the crime and put great pressure on local officials to prosecute him.[21] Once the decision was made to prosecute, members of the community, working with a human rights group active in the area, contacted attorney and Catholic nun Sister Michael Mary Nolan, who agreed to work with members of the community as assistant prosecutor on the case.[22] Together with Nolan, members of the community conducted a parallel investigation which included contacting potential witnesses, encouraging them to testify, and researching the backgrounds of potential jurors.[23] Most members of the community attended each of the preliminary hearings in the case and met with Nolan afterward to discuss future strategy. Community members also organized security for the trial and forced town officials to open a school so that people from neighboring communities who wished to see the trial had a place to store their belongings. In the end, both the attacker and the person who contracted the killing were convicted. The latter turned out to be one of the defense lawyers. Nolan observed that "the community had more responsibility for this conviction than we [the lawyers] did".[24]

These examples illustrate several aspects of social movement cause lawyering that are similar in Argentina and Brazil. First, many social movement cause lawyers are employed by—or at least affiliated with—established organizations. In many cases, especially in Argentina, these are human rights organizations that broadened their focus after the fall of the military to include a broad range of community-based issues, such as health care, housing, police violence, and immigration rights. While some of the lawyers who work for these groups do so on a full-time basis, most can only afford to work part-time. In Brazil, many of these lawyers are affiliated with religious organizations.

Second, while most social movement cause lawyers work outside the mainstream judicial system, they utilize that system when it suits the goals of the community. As Martínez points out, "we must use all the tools that the judicial system gives us."[25] The most common examples are the prosecution of government-sanctioned (usually police) violence and defenses to eviction. According to one Argentine cause lawyer, the notorious delays in the judicial system work to the advantage of the community in eviction cases.[26] In addition, the lawyers who work on individual cases usually have motives that go beyond winning or losing that particular battle: police violence cases can attract significant media attention, which—in theory—will reduce the likelihood of such incidents being repeated in the future. Fighting an individual eviction case offers the opportunity for community organizing and solidarity.[27] Moreover, even unsuccessful cases can be helpful in the long run, since they can shed media light on an underlying problem, as well as the judicial system's inability to deal with it effectively.[28] According to

Beverly Keene, one of the coordinators of Argentina's SERPAJ, trials over human rights abuses serve the purpose of "recognizing and attributing to the judicial system itself a much more important role in society, even if that has been established negatively through focusing on the lack of justice and the lack of access to justice."[29] And cause lawyers used the judicial system to expose state violence in Argentina after the Dirty War. According to Luis Moreno Ocampo, a human rights lawyer in Buenos Aires who prosecuted military officials after the dictatorship, "The most important thing about those times, and what we are trying to repeat now, is the power of the truth. The human rights groups made files about the situation; they used information in the newspapers. . . . In some cases we can use the judiciary for good things; for example the military trials, the trials after the military rebellions."[30]

Third, several cause lawyers and social activists discussed the importance of the media in their work. Ocampo, who is also the cofounder of the citizen advocacy group *Poder Ciudadano*,[31] notes that in most cases "the newspapers are more effective than the courts."[32] To emphasize his point, as well as the weakness of the legislative and judicial branches of government, Ocampo offered the following analogy: "Think about Watergate without Sirica, Cox, and the Senate Committee; only the *Washington Post*."[33]

Similarly, Alejandro Carrió, an Argentine lawyer who has established a human rights organization modeled after the American Civil Liberties Union, argues that even though he is unsure whether he can win court cases on behalf of disenfranchised groups, "I know we will be successful in that the issues will come into the open. We have contact with the media, who will take an interest in these issues."[34] And according to Keene of SERPAJ, using the media in police violence cases "establishes a transparency to the judicial proceedings that is not normally present."[35] Apparently, many members or the Argentine public also prefer the media to the justice system for the redress of grievances. According to Beatrice Kohen of *Poder Ciudadano*, "People have more confidence in the media and the church than in the justice system. If there is a conflict they would rather go to a TV program than into court."[36]

On the other hand, the media often make commitments it does not keep and treats the subjects of stories in a very stereotypical, condescending fashion. Curiel of CELS says that she avoids making promises about media coverage to members of *villa* civil associations because if no coverage results, it can reflect badly on CELS.[37] She is also uncomfortable with *villeros* serving as "guinea pigs" for the media.[38]

Just as the theoretical underpinnings and strategic norms of social movement cause lawyers in Argentina and Brazil are similar, so too are many of the factors which have influenced their decisions to pursue this type of work. The following section analyzes these factors.

Common Motivations for Social Movement Cause Lawyering

The Emergence of Grassroots Social Movements

The most self-evident motivating factor for social movement cause lawyers in Brazil and Argentina is the one that makes their work possible at all: the emergence in both countries—and indeed in all of Latin America—of numerous grassroots social movements over the past several decades. These movements range from neighborhood-based collective action for securing basic material needs such as food, housing, health care, and sanitation, to more political mobilizations for the rights of women and indigenous persons, environmental protection, and compensation for human rights violations. Although these movements are generally more organized and effective in Brazil than in Argentina (for reasons which will be discussed in the next section), their presence in both countries has enabled cause lawyers to work for social and democratic change outside the realm of individual client representation.[39]

The Failures of the Judiciary

The strongest jurisprudential influence on social movement cause lawyering in both Argentina and Brazil is the inefficiency and lack of independence of the judiciary. Both countries share a legacy of strong and centralized executive power (often in league with the military) that dominated the judiciary, rendering the latter unable to check abuses of power by the other branches of government.[40] The following observations of Joseph Thome about this historic legacy, based on the writings of Argentine scholar Julio Maier, are also applicable to Brazil:

> As it did with other institutions, the Spanish colonial regime imposed on its colonies a judicial system based on its own political model; namely a centralized, hierarchical system with highly developed control mechanisms over the lower courts. The judiciary was structured as a bureaucratic organization, where power was delegated from the top down to inferior officials, and where every judge and other judicial personnel was a functionary at the service of the State, not of the individual. The judicial system thus was not really conceived as an institution to resolve the conflicts of the population at large, but rather as a component of the administration of State power; that is, as an instrument of social control.[41]

Well after declaring its independence from Spain in 1816, Argentina was ruled by a series of powerful leaders. The provincial *caudillos* (primarily Juan Manuel de Rosas) who dominated the nation prior to the adoption of the 1853 Constitution, as well as the presidents elected thereafter, continually increased their power vis-à-vis the other branches of government. As Banks and Carrió note, "[A]mong all the divisions which became apparent in the first half of the nineteenth century, just about the only point upon which the competing dominant groups agreed was that strong leaders were good and necessary."[42] The constitution of 1853 codified the strength of the executive. Although based on the U.S. Constitution, with a more extensive list of individual liberties than the U.S. Bill of Rights, the Constitution of 1853 retained the Spanish emphasis on the centralization of powers.[43] The constitution enshrined the president as "supreme head of the Nation" for one six-year term, permitted him to appoint high-ranking officials without congressional approval, and granted him the authority to declare a "state of siege" and suspend constitutional rights when internal unrest endangered the constitution or the government.[44] The latter provision has enabled a succession of Argentine leaders to suspend the constitution and individual rights while pledging to obey the law. Thus, there have been five military coups since 1930, the Argentine Supreme Court has been completely or partially restructured seven times, and no civilian president before current president Carlos Menem has ever served out his entire term.[45] Neither the judiciary nor the legislature has ever been strong enough to assert itself against the executive.

The weakness of the judiciary was never better illustrated than during the Dirty War. As Mandler notes, "The junta immediately dismissed the national Supreme Court, the federal Attorney General and the supreme courts of the provinces. The new members of the judiciary were required to swear allegiance both to the Constitution and to the Process.[46] The military also required the president to automatically confirm its nominees to the vacant seats. While the Process retained the . . . guarantee of life tenure during good behavior for the new appointees, this manipulation of the judiciary severely curtailed its ability to act independently."[47]

Brazil's pre- and postcolonial history has also been marked by strong centralized power. Indeed, for sixty-seven years after it declared independence in 1822, Brazil was ruled by an emperor. And except for a forty-year period of decentralized federalism after the emperor was exiled in 1889 (the so-called First Republic), Brazil's history has been marked by ever-increasing federal power vis à vis the states.[48] Although the Brazilian Constitution (of which there have been seven since independence) created a tripartite system of government, neither the judiciary nor the legislature has traditionally exercised much of a check on executive power.[49]

The lack of independence of the Brazilian judiciary was, like its Argentine counterpart, at its zenith during the most recent military regime. In the Brazilian case, much of the executive's aggrandizement of power came through the 1967 and 1969 constitutions, which, as Rosenn notes, was designed to legitimize a *de facto* military regime: "One of [the 1969 constitution's] basic features was centralization of power. It transferred a considerable amount of power from the states and municipalities to the federal government, leaving Brazilian federalism a shadow of its former self. Although formally providing for a tripartite division of power among the executive, legislative, and judicial branches, a substantial amount of legislative power was transferred to the Executive. Moreover, both the Legislature and Judiciary were purged of elements whom the military deemed insufficiently sympathetic to the goals of the 1964 Revolution."[50]

The impotence of the judiciary was summed up by Nelson Hungria, a former judge of the Brazilian Supreme Federal Tribunal: "[A]gainst the historical fatalism of military uprising the Judicial Power is of no avail."[51]

As a result, in both countries, the judiciary is viewed by most cause lawyers as an extension—and/or facilitator—of executive and military power, rather than as a defender of individual rights and liberties. According to Brazilian political science professor Paulo Sergio Pinhiero: "The judiciary in Brazil was never perceived as an instrument of the rule of law. The rule of law was a disguise for domination. . . . In Brazil the law is not supposed to be an instrument for guaranteeing the rights of the majority of the population. The traditional role of the judiciary was to regulate exploitation, repression, oppression."[52]

Similarly, Luis Moreno Ocampo noted that "[in Argentina] we do not have an open and independent judiciary. In the United States people use the judiciary; here, it is closed, broken, a bureaucratic machine. . . . People don't believe in the judges. The judges work in a bureaucratic way. . . . [T]he law is a tool of the power against society." He then quoted a traditional Brazilian phrase: "To my friends, everything; to my enemies, the law."[53]

And Octavio Carsen of CISALP observed that the Argentine judiciary "is not independent; [it is] tied to the executive; they carry out whatever the executive wants them to do."[54]

Another similarity of the judicial systems in the two countries is the public's perception that they are inefficient, expensive, corrupt, and intended primarily to serve the interests of the wealthy. Sào Paulo lawyer and law professor Jose Eduardo Faria observed, "The Brazilian legal system is driven by the ideological perspective of protection of property. This means that the poor [which he estimates as 92 percent of the population] have been put out of the legal system and only have access to the legal system as criminals."[55] Another commentator has observed that "Brazil has been characterized as a defendant's jurisdiction, one in which being sued is generally not cause for major concern. There are no moral or punitive damages, . . . the loser is burdened with paying the court's award, plus all court costs and legal fees, including those of his or her opponent. Inflation has reduced the real value of court awards for those cases where monetary correction is not applied."[56]

Moreover, even though Brazil has laws on the books ostensibly designed to protect the interests of the poor, they are rarely enforced.[57] Brazilian judges are often accused of corruption, particularly in the rural northeastern states, which remain under the influence of wealthy landowners.[58]

Cause lawyers and activists in Argentina offer a similar assessment of the Argentine legal system. According to Alicia Curiel of CELS, "[T]here is . . . corruption in the judicial system, where no one has confidence in it. The judges are named as part of political pacts.[59] Judges can be easily removed here. This means that the poor have no access to the justice system—it is corrupt and expensive."[60]

According to Maria Elba Martínez of SERPAJ, "Let's say you file a lawsuit. What eats you up is all the procedural process. . . . [Y]ou never get any results, or the results are minimal, because you are trapped in some sort of procedure. . . . Justice turns into something slow, heavy, full of bureaucracy. It is like something that does not work. And I think this is rather perverse. This generates a disaster, a breakdown; it generates disbelief. [Moreover] justice in Argentina is extremely expensive. . . . You need about $4,000 to begin a trial. That is absurd. . . . [T]hat is a way of denying justice."[61]

Much of the inefficiency and confusion within the Argentine judicial system is due to its almost complete reliance on written advocacy. Only recently have oral arguments been permitted, and even then, only in criminal cases. According to lawyer Roberto de Michele of Poder Ciudadano, most lawyers did not favor this change, since now "they had to go to court and argue with the judge rather than play golf with him."[62] Civil litigation is still conducted exclusively in writing. According to CELS founder Emilio Mignone, this renders the entire system more bureaucratic.[63]

Octavio Carsen of CISALP observes that judges "ignore both the Argentine Constitution and international conventions" that it has signed, such as those on economic and social rights.[64] Carsen further noted that although the constitution contains a right to housing, the legislature has not passed the enabling legislation necessary to give that provision any impact, and judges favor the constitutional right to private property over the housing rights of squatters.[65] Similarly, Carlos Vásquez, who is active in issues affecting the Argentine indigenous population, noted that in conflicts between citizens and the federal government, the judicial system "gives preeminence to the interests of the government over the rights of the people."[66]

The Legal Codes and the Positivist Tradition

Another feature of the Argentine and Brazilian judicial systems that frustrates many cause lawyers and has caused them to reject that system is its reliance on a set of legal codes. Unlike common law countries, jurisprudence in these nations is not based on stare decisis, or case precedent. Rather, it is based on judicial interpretation of the legal codes (e.g. civil, penal, commercial, etc.), which were drafted in order to take into account all social interactions and potential conflicts. According to leading Brazilian jurist Orlando Gomez, the Civil code was prepared by middle-class men to provide the country with a system of private law defending the capitalist system of production.[67] And Wiarda and Kline observe that "the authoritarian, absolutist nature of the [legal] codes is also reflected by (and helps reinforce) an absolutist, frequently authoritarian political culture.")[68]

Most judges are reluctant to rely on any authority except the legal codes (and sometimes the constitution) when ruling on a case. And without stare decisis, legal opinions that do not strictly apply the legal codes have little precedential value.[69] Thus, the broad interpretation of statutes that led to early civil rights and other cause lawyering victories in the United States has been virtually nonexistent in Argentina and Brazil.[70]

The legal codes are consistent with—and indeed were inspired by—the positivist traditions in Argentine and Brazilian legal theory and practice. Influenced by positivist theorists, the jurisprudence in both countries views law in an isolated vacuum, separate and distinct from the political, economic, and social forces that shape the problems that present themselves to the legal system.[71] According to this view, positive law—as codified in legal codes—is the best means for achieving justice,[72] and the legal system best addresses social problems by applying codes rather than by analyzing the causes of those problems.[73]

The ramifications of positivism for cause lawyering in the two countries are clear. Judges who abide by it will reject legal arguments that rely on anything but the codified provisions of the law. Traditional legal strategies, such as litigation, which are designed to ameliorate the problems of the poor, have usually been unsuccessful since they rest on arguments that go beyond the confines of the codes. Thus, as CISALP's Octavio Carsen observes, the positivist tradition is a "serious obstacle" to public interest work in Argentina.[74]

The Failure of Legal Education

Lack of support for cause lawyering at law schools in Argentina and Brazil has also spurred many cause lawyers to seek alternative means of working for democratic change. Legal education in both countries is very traditional, emphasizing memorization of the legal codes, with little emphasis on legal theory, the role of law in society, or the interconnectedness of law, politics, and economics. Clinical programs, where law students receive school credit for working on actual cases (usually of the public interest variety), are rare.

According to Celso Campilongo, a professor at the University of São Paulo: "Law schools have been conservative and do not support the alternative law movement. This could be the remains of the aristocratic makeup of the legal population. The traditional educational training is very technical; the graduate should come out knowing how to manipulate the codes, etc. The more innovative practices of the law demand much more than this; they demand an understanding of social reality, of sociological aspects, etc. [Graduates] should be able to take the manipulation of the codes and fit it into the broader sociological aspects."[75]

Similarly, Martin Bohmer, a University of Buenos Aires law professor who is attempting to formulate a public interest–oriented exchange program with Yale Law School, observes that law school in Argentina is "pretty much professors speaking and students taking notes," without any discussion. "There is very little critical thinking about the law."[76] He says that there is simply no institutional support for public interest work at law schools, since they "are controlled by conservative professors and lawyers." Bohmer links the authoritarian nature of Argentina's law schools with the country's authoritarian public discourse, in which there is very little room for discussion or dissent: "There is very little critical thinking about the law; so there is a linkage between the way we teach law and public discourse."[77] Julio Garcia of CISALP believes that the reason for the lack of support for public interest work is that it is interpreted by the power structure as a criticism of the legal system.[78]

Maria Elba Martínez of SERPAJ observes that Argentine law schools "are interested in preparing law students to do a strict application of the legal rules. It does not matter how these rules were developed nor what they will actually do. The rest of the world is interested in discussing possibilities for new theories of the law; interested in attacking positivism. Here, the lawyer's education has been circumscribed to the application of the rules under the guise of pragmatism."[79]

To the extent that law schools offer nontraditional courses, they are dismissed by the mainstream faculty—and by many students—as inconsequential. Celso Campilongo teaches an innovative course on the sociology of law that, by his own admission, students refer to pejoratively as "judicial perfume."[80] Bohmer, who teaches a course on legal interpretation, notes that whenever he challenges more traditional law teachers on a point, they just say "That's legal philosophy," and dismiss it.[81] And Roberto Saba of Poder Ciudadano, who is working with Bohmer and others in an effort to develop a curriculum to address the relationship between law, public policy, and economics, says that these efforts have met with strong resistance at the University of Buenos Aires: "We are going against a big structure that is going in exactly the opposite direction."[82]

Legal Culture

Whether it is a cause or effect (or, more likely, both) of these common characteristics of the judicial systems in Argentina and Brazil, each nation possesses a legal culture that simply does not view the judiciary as a means of protecting the rights of most citizens or of redressing everyday grievances. For example, according to a recent poll, 89 percent of *porteños* (residents of Buenos Aires) think the Argentine justice system is poor.[83] The causes of such a cultural phenomenon are extremely complex and have their roots in long years of national experience, but there is no denying that such a view is reinforced by the continuing inability of the judiciary to act as an independent source of power and protection.[84]

The following comments during my interviews in the two countries sum up this phenomenon:

> [In Brazil] you have a social group [i.e., the poor] that has been incapable of getting access to the legal system. . . . The Brazilian legal system is driven by the ideological perspective of protection of property. This means that the poor have been put out of the legal system, and have access to it only as bandits and murderers. This is one of the reasons why the legal system is in crisis in Brazil. . . . The values that underlie the legal system are exclusively middle-class values, in a society in which the majority is poor.[85]

> [In Argentina] people do not believe in the legal system, and they possess a very healthy intuition which tells them that the law is outside of their lives. Because generally the legal system . . . does not help them. The law claims one thing but has a different result in its application. So these people are in total disbelief of the law, and of those who apply the law—including the lawyers.[86]

As a result, most people resort to other means to resolve disputes. According to Alejandro Carrió:

> [In Argentina] people don't trust the judiciary as a means to assert rights. . . . It's more important to be on good terms with a politician or public official. We have made a culture of *amiguismo*. Rather than litigating disputes, we try to find someone who can help us get around the problem. It could be a friendly contact or a sheer bribe; we have a history of both. There is no culture that courts are the proper forum for litigating problems, or to find solutions to the problems.[87]

Luis Moreno Ocampo makes a similar observation:

> The informal mechanisms are more effective than the formal ones. For example, I worked for five years as a prosecutor in cases of corruption. I tried to use the judiciary to control the executive, but finally what happened is that the executive [i.e., President Carlos Menem] approved a new law to change judges around; [the executive] appointed their friends as judges and prosecutors.[88]

Of course, most poor people have neither access to public officials nor the money with which to bribe them if they were so inclined. As a result, they often turn to community-based means for resolving disputes and obtaining necessary services. Indeed, many of the social movements that have emerged in both countries over the past three decades began as neighborhood-centered efforts to secure the basic necessities of life. And just as the judiciary's failures caused many citizens to look elsewhere for relief from the problems associated with poverty, they also motivated many cause lawyers to pursue non-traditional strategies. As a result, many cause lawyers began to work collaboratively with the grassroots community groups that sprang up in both countries—and indeed throughout Latin America—at the same time.

Personal Motivations

Since many social movement cause lawyers do not readily discuss their personal motivations for devoting their time to this type of work, one must glean them from offhand comments frequently made in other contexts. Moreover, as Menkel-Meadow notes, people, including cause lawyers, seldom act from a "unified, single purpose motivation."[89] Nevertheless, these motivations seem to fall into two discrete categories: a very personal and frequently moral desire to fight injustice, and a more public sense of their individual role in the transition to democracy; that is, a transition that includes adherence to the rule of law.

Argentine lawyer Maria Elba Martínez articulated the former motivation: "I decided to become a lawyer when I was nine. And all my life I was called an attorney. . . . What used to bother me was the injustice. When something came up, I would come out in its defense. So they called me the attorney for the poor, for the defenseless. I continue to see a lot of injustice in society. . . . I cannot be indifferent. It is not in my nature.[90]

The motivation for Octavio Carsen appears to stem from a desire to continue working on behalf of the victims of the Dirty War: "The best way to honor the disappeared isn't to put up a monument, but to do the work that the disappeared were trying to do: to defend the rights of the marginalized; to bring about equality in the society. The great majority of the disappeared are those who gave up their lives to work for marginalized groups. The Processo didn't get rid of the conflict in society; only some of the people. The causes of the conflict—socioeconomic disparity—are still there."[91]

On a more pragmatic level, many cause lawyers pursue grassroots community work because it provides the greatest opportunity for progressive social change. As Patrick Rice of the Movimiento Ecumenical in Buenos Aires notes, legal reform is easier to work on at the local level than on a systemic basis.[92]

Distinctions Between Argentine and Brazilian Social Movement Cause Lawyering

Despite similarities in the type of work social movement cause lawyers perform in Argentina and Brazil, as well as the circumstances compelling them to perform it, social movement cause lawyering (and, indeed, cause lawyering generally) is much more prevalent and organized in Brazil than in Argentina. This section discusses some of the reasons for this distinction.

Unity within Neighborhood-Based Social Movements

One of the most important reasons for the disparity in community-centered cause lawyering between Brazil and Argentina is that the neighborhood-based grassroots groups with whom such lawyers interact are more organized in Brazil. There are several factors contributing to this phenomenon. The Argentine *villas*, at least in Buenos Aires, are much more ethnically heterogenous than the Brazilian *favellas*. According to Alicia Curiel of CELS, only 40 percent of the residents in the Buenos Aires *villas* are Argentine; most of the rest are from Bolivia and Paraguay, with smaller numbers from Chile and Uruguay.[93] Most of these poor immigrants come to Argentina to find work. Brazil's *favellas*, by contrast, are ethnically homogenous, a result both of the obvious language barrier, as well as Brazil's more troubled economy. Argentina's ethnically diverse *villas* make community organizing more difficult and require cause lawyers to spend much time on immigration-related issues, which does not foster solidarity within the *villas* as a whole.

In addition, Argentina's *villas* are more tied to the vagaries and corruption of local politics than Brazil's *favellas*. Many *villas* were created during the administration of Juan Perón and the Peronist Party. Some of their leaders have historically been beholden to local politicians and thus sometimes act against the interests of the *villa* residents. This legacy was intensified in the early 1990s when Argentine president (and Peronist Party member) Carlos Menem put *villa* leaders on municipal payrolls, effectively making them government functionaries. As a result, services in *villas* (such as utilities, water, infrastructure supplies, etc.) have become much more politicized, dependent on the proclivities of (and favors rendered to) local politicians, rather than the organizing efforts of the community. And the high turnover rate among these paid functionaries only exacerbates existing barriers to effective community organizing.[94]

Impact of the Military Regimes

Much of the disparity in the amount of social movement cause lawyering in the two countries is related to the differences in their recent military dictatorships and transitions to democracy.

ARGENTINA

Argentina's dictatorship of 1976–82 began with the overthrow of the ineffective government of Maria Estela [Isabel] Martínez de Perón, who had succeeded her husband after his death in 1974.[95] One of the first acts of the military junta was to issue the Statute of the Process of National Reorganization ("Processo"), which dissolved the federal and provincial legislatures, fired principal government officials, prohibited political party and union activities, and declared that the constitution would remain in effect only to the extent that it did not conflict with the main objectives of the junta.[96] According to Guillermo O'Donnell, the Argentine dictatorship was "economically destructive and highly repressive."[97] Arbitrary abductions, torture, and "disappearances" were common. Estimates of the number of persons killed in the government's efforts to eradicate suspected subversives and their sympathizers range from nine thousand to thirty thousand.[98]

The pervasiveness of the junta's methods is reflected in the following two statements. General Ibérico Manuel Saint-Jean, former governor of Buenos Aires province, declared: "First, we are going to kill all of the subversives; then their collaborators; then their sympathizers; then the indifferent; and finally, the timid." The final two categories, according to the general, were "useful idiots . . . converted into automatons" because subversive ideology was "clouding their understanding and automatizing them like mechanical parts."[99]

Striking a similar note of terror, General Tomás Sánchez de Bustamenti summarized the attitude of the military toward traditional legal processes and individual rights: "There are legal norms which do not apply in this instance, for example, the writ of habeas corpus. In this type of struggle, the inherent secrecy with which our special operations must be conducted requires that we not divulge whom we have captured and whom we want to capture; everything has to be enveloped in a cloud of silence."[100]

Progressive lawyers were a frequent target of the military regime: by 1978, 23 lawyers were murdered, 109 were detained, and 41 disappeared.[101] According to Alicia Curiel of CELS, lawyers who were involved with grassroots social movements before the dictatorship "were disappeared during it."[102] As Carrió notes, the disappearance of so many lawyers had a significantly adverse impact on public interest law.[103] Similarly, judges suspected of being too lenient with suspected subversives were threatened with murder.[104]

Courts continued to function and, by not condemning the junta's tactics, gave them official imprimatur. As Fred Snyder has observed:

> Legal process . . . has been singularly important in the mobilization of state terror in that it has enabled the junta to address society not only through the amplifier at the rally, the proclamation in the newspaper, the rifle butt on the street, and the electrode in the torture chamber, but through a vocabulary of reason and right as well. . . . [C]ourts stay open for business . . . draw[ing] the junta into the enviable world of formal rationality where it shares the benefits that only an apparatus of justification can confer.[105]

The dictatorship ended abruptly, as a result of the military's disastrous decision to invade the Malvinas Islands, which was intended to divert public attention from the faltering economy.[106] Shortly after the military suffered a humiliating defeat by the British navy, the generals promised an election by 1983 and a return to civilian government by 1984.[107] Radical Party leader Raul Alfonsín was elected president in 1983. Although he had campaigned on a commitment to prosecute those responsible for persons killed, "disappeared", and tortured during the Dirty War, a series of amnesties and pardons over the ensuing years by both Alfonsín and his successor, Carlos Menem,[108] resulted in the conviction and imprisonment of only a few military officials.[109]

BRAZIL

Brazil's most recent military dictatorship began in 1964 with a coup against the democratically elected government of João Goulart.[110] The most repressive period of the twenty-year military regime was 1968–73, when the government instituted a systematic and ruthless eradication of numerous small guerilla movements that arose in the wake of political polarization and labor unrest.[111] Even during this period, however, the government's repressive measures were "less massive, less continuous, and less systematic" than in Argentina and affected "to a far lesser degree the sense of personal security of entrepreneurs and middle sectors."[112] Approximately 200 people were killed and 125 were "disappeared" during the dictatorship. Thousands were tortured.[113] The repression was much more focused on known opponents of the regime than on the population as a whole. On the other hand, its rhetoric could be just as chilling. In his 1967 book *Geopolitica do Brasil,* General Golbery do Couto e Silva, designer of the military's infamous national intelligence service (SNI), wrote: "There is thus a new dilemma, that of well-being versus security. This was pointed out by Goering in the past, in an imprecise but highly suggestive and well-known slogan: 'More guns, less butter.' And, in truth, there is no way to escape the need to sacrifice well-being for security, once the latter is truly threatened. The peoples who refuse to admit this learned the lesson they deserved in the dust of defeat."[114]

Another key distinction between the recent dictatorships in Argentina and Brazil is that the transition to democracy in Brazil was far more gradual. The eleven-year transition, or *apertura* ("opening"), which began after the guerilla movement was vanquished in 1973 and intensified as the military's economic policies continued to falter, allowed for a more gradual introduction of liberalization measures. It also allowed the military to arrange for its own amnesty as a condition for transferring power to civilians.[115]

The distinctions between the dictatorships and transitions to democracy outlined above provide several explanations for the disparity in social movement cause lawyering between the two countries. At perhaps the most fundamental level, as noted above, many Argentine cause lawyers were killed or "disappeared" during the Dirty War. Several interviewees mentioned that an entire generation of public interest–minded lawyers and law professors was wiped out during that period, leaving an old guard of conservative lawyers and a new guard of recent law school graduates just learning their way around the system.[116] In contrast, progressive lawyers were not singled out for repression during the Brazilian dictatorship.

Second, the Brazilian regime gave community-based social movements much more freedom to develop than did the Argentine junta. Neighborhood-based social movements sprang up throughout Brazil during the early days of the dictatorship. Because of the relative harshness of the regime at that time, most of these movements focused on material needs rather than political issues.[117] In response to the problems resulting from abject poverty and the lack of significant social policies to combat them, these movements formed food cooperatives, sought better housing, health care, and garbage pick-up, arranged group child care, and devised means of internal dispute resolution.[118] In the late 1970s, as government repression abated, the number of grassroots groups increased and their political activities intensified. The women's movement, the human rights movement, and the environmental movement, to name a few, all gained momentum and power during this period. These and other grassroots organizations formed, or merged with, squatters' rights groups in urban and rural areas, attempting to claim ownership to land and buildings that had been abandoned (or at least not used for productive purposes) by the owner. Residents of *favellas* staged sit-ins and other forms of public protest to press their demands in the areas of housing, health care, human rights, and government reform.[119] At all times during the dictatorship, however, these community-based social movements interacted with the government in order to meet the material needs of their members.[120] These groups had clearly become a potent force both locally and nationally.[121]

By contrast, the military regime in Argentina was much more consistently hostile toward community-based movements. In its zeal to root out all "subversives," the regime attempted to physically eliminate the *villas* prior to the World Cup in 1978, which was held in—and won by—Argentina. In Buenos Aires, for example, *villeros* were forcibly picked up at night or in the early morning, shepherded into waiting trucks with whatever possessions they could carry, and unceremoniously dumped on the edge of the city. Bulldozers then demolished what had been their homes.[122] Although this campaign was not completely successful, after four years municipal officials proudly declared that 76 percent of the Buenos Aires slum dwellers had been "removed."[123] As a result, the community organization and solidarity developed in previous years was seriously disrupted.[124] As Curiel commented, the community organizers had to start from scratch after the dictatorship.[125] Since most cause lawyers only work with grassroots groups *after* such groups have been organized and have some form of internal organization and structure, it has been much more difficult for cause lawyers to work with grassroots community groups in Argentina than in Brazil.

The arbitrariness of the repression in Argentina also created a more pervasive climate of fear and distrust among the people. As Martin Andersen has observed, "Fear was an essential weapon in the military's plan to seize, purge, and remold

Argentina. After the coup arrogant and aggressive soldiers armed to the teeth patrolled quiet neighborhoods for no apparent reason, checking documents and making random arrests. For those who lived through it, the climate had the same nerve-racking quality of a civil war." [126]

And one foreign observer who visited the country in 1977 reported that "[m]ore and more parents begin to fear for the safety of their adolescent children, as increasing numbers of ordinary citizens are rounded up, detained for 24 to 48 hours and abused while in detention." [127] Given this recent legacy, many citizens, including lawyers, remain nervous about engaging in any activity that might suggest dissent from authority. As Alicia Curiel notes, because of both the dictatorship and the deteriorating economic and social situation in the country, people in *villas,* as well as the rest of the country, "are into themselves now." [128] Roberto de Michele of Poder Ciudadano says that "Argentina isn't like the movies where good guys are always good and bad guys are always bad. Friends would sometimes inform on you." [129] De Michele's colleague, Beatrice Kohen, observes that Argentines "lost the participation habit because of the Processo." [130]

A less direct, yet very significant, impact of the two recent dictatorships on cause lawyering is the disparate influence they had on outside funding for cause-lawyering activities. The organizations that employ cause lawyers in both countries receive nearly all of their funding from abroad; that is, from foundations and individuals in Western Europe and the United States. Philanthropy from domestic sources is very rare. However, according to several of the people I interviewed, Brazilian organizations receive proportionally more of these financial contributions than their Argentine counterparts. Almost every Argentine interview subject noted that while Argentine human rights groups received substantial financial assistance from abroad during the Dirty War, such contributions slowed to a trickle once the dictatorship was ousted because the international conventional wisdom held that Argentina's problems could be solved through a democratically elected government and its judicial system. In addition, because of the magnitude of the repression, Argentine cause lawyers did little else but human rights work during the Dirty War, leaving them with an unspecified agenda—and not as much appeal to funding sources—thereafter. [131]

On the other hand, because of Brazil's less draconian—and less internationally publicized—dictatorship, financial support for Brazilian cause lawyering has not been as strongly linked to the existence (or fall) of the dictatorship. Rather, such support was—and is—intended to address long-term social issues related to poverty, which were not altered in any significant way after the dictatorship fell. Indeed, one influence on the relative levels of philanthropic support for cause lawyering in the two countries seems to be their relative poverty. As Octavio Carsen notes, Brazil receives more international philanthropy because inequality between the classes is much greater there. [132]

Support from Other Institutions

Brazilian social movement cause lawyers receive more nonfinancial support from legal institutions such as law schools, the bar association, and the judiciary than their Argentine counterparts.

LAW SCHOOLS

Although law schools in both countries generally impede rather than promote cause lawyering, this seems to be especially the case in Argentina. One of the reasons for this is the close interconnectedness among law schools, the judiciary, and the private bar. Because full-time law professors are paid very poorly (about one hundred dollars per month), there are very few of them. Instead, most law teachers are practicing members of the bar, making them reluctant to criticize sitting judges (before whom they may later appear in court), or to offer innovative legal theories that may come back to haunt them in their interaction with clients. Roberto de Michele puts it succinctly: "Few law professors will say that a judge is an idiot, since the lawyer will have to face that judge later on." [133] This dearth of full-time professors, insulated from the pressures and politics of legal practice, has contributed to a lack of intellectual and/or scholarly support for either cause lawyering or an alternative approach to the study of law. [134] One of the only academic voices supporting such work, Professor Carlos Nino of the University of Buenos Aires Law School, died in 1993.

In Brazil, on the other hand, a handful of law professors at the University of São Paulo have attempted to alter the curriculum to include courses that focus on the interdisciplinary relationship between law and social problems. As Professor Jose Eduardo Faria noted, "My plan with the group which I work with is to emphasize an alternative line of law school. . . . [O]ur goal is to give the students a very theoretical background so that they will understand the culture in which they live, so as to prepare themselves to understand the real meaning of the law in a concrete case." [135]

Moreover, student enthusiasm for alternative legal careers in Argentina seems to have diminished recently. According to Maria Elba Martínez: "The law schools graduate professionals who during the military dictatorship were interested in social issues. But not any more. These days having an interest in social issues carries a stigma, so that people are only interested in themselves. The attorney goes to his office and does not have to worry about political and social issues. Unless that person is politically ambitious." [136] Alicia Curiel agrees: since most law students are from the higher classes, they "come out of law school thinking only of making money; they have the peso sign on their foreheads." [137] Roberto Saba observes that "most students are not interested in public interest work. Ninety percent of the students only want to work for a law firm." [138]

While law remains a profession primarily for the elite in Brazil, a dramatic increase in the number of law schools during the dictatorship (ironically enough) opened the doors to middle-class law students, many of whom were more inclined to adopt an alternative vision of the law as attorneys and judges.[139]

BAR ASSOCIATIONS

Another legal institution that has offered dissimilar amounts of support for cause lawyering in the two countries is the bar association. The Argentine Bar Association has, according to Roberto Saba, always been run by a conservative group of lawyers, some of whom oppose *any* type of lawyers union or organization.[140] According to Alejandro Carrió, the Argentine Bar Association is "absolutely disorganized"; it has no committee devoted to public interest issues. "Nobody will give you a hand" with such work, he says.[141]

In Brazil, conversely, there seems to be substantially more support for cause lawyering within the professional bar. According to Celso Campilongo, there are sectors within the bar association who support the alternative law movement, as well as a greater focus on interdisciplinary pedagogy in law school.[142]

The Brazilian Bar Association was also much more active in condemning the excesses of the most recent military regime than its Argentine counterpart.[143] The national bar association protested before the Brazilian Congress in August 1974 against government torture and disappearances.[144] In October 1975 the association issued a statement charging the government with the torture of Vladimir Herzog, a prominent journalist and director of a widely respected noncommercial television channel, who died while in prison.[145] Such opposition to the regime had negative consequences: the bar association headquarters were bombed by right-wing terrorists in 1980 and 1981.[146] There is no evidence of any similar protests by—or conservative backlash against—the Argentine bar.

THE JUDICIARY

Although the judiciary in both countries is generally conservative and controlled by the executive, the Brazilian judiciary has a stronger reputation for independence than its Argentine counterpart.[147] Moreover, in Brazil there is a small but growing movement of judges who are receptive to the kinds of legal arguments—and tactics—used by cause lawyers. These judges fall into two main groups. The first, and more radical, group is a loose conglomeration of about sixty judges in the southern, industrial state of Rio Grande do Sul. These judges, who are simply known as "alternative judges,"[148] do not feel bound by the positivist confines of the legal codes. They frequently decide cases based on what they perceive to be higher notions of justice and fundamental fairness, or simple common sense.[149] Their decisions are influenced by the interrelationships among law, politics, economics, society, and culture.[150] They also refuse to base any decisions on laws passed during the military dictatorship.[151] These judges have received significant—and sometimes negative—publicity for a few incidents. For example, one judge refuses to wear a judicial robe, or even a coat and tie, so as not to intimidate lay people who appear before him in court. Another sawed off the legs of his judge's chair and table so that he would be at the same height as litigants in his courtroom.[152]

These alternative judges have been criticized by many, including ideologically sympathetic observers, who think that basing court rulings on some sense of "higher justice" is a dangerous precedent. Such a strategy, they contend, could just as easily be employed by right-wing judges who cannot find a basis in the codes or constitution for the result they seek in a given case. According to Antonio Villen, president of the more moderate Association of Judges for Democracy, there is no need to rule on cases from such an "alternative" perspective, because all of the necessary principles for socially just decisions are contained in the constitution and laws. Villen stated that "it is dangerous, especially in Brazil, to base judgments on other criteria." [153]

The second, and more moderate group of judges is exemplified by the São Paulo–based Association of Judges for Democracy, which claims approximately one hundred members, most of whom graduated from law school after 1980. While similar to the Rio Grande do Sul judges in that their interpretation of the legal codes is influenced by current social and political realities, they rarely look beyond the codes or the constitution to support their decisions. The difference in judicial philosophy was summarized by University of São Paulo professor Campilongo as follows: "The difference between the São Paulo and Rio Grande do Sul judges is that in Rio Grande do Sul they believe that justice is above the law; in São Paulo, they believe that justice must be done, but it must be done on a strictly legal basis. The objectives are the same but the strategies are different." [154]

Campilongo also observed that "[i]n the past there have always been isolated cases where the judge would make this type of decision [i.e., one based on an alternative view of the law]; what makes it different today is that the judges are making these decisions in an organized fashion as part of an organized movement." [155]

There is no such organized movement, radical or moderate, in Argentina. Most federal judges were appointed because of their allegiance to the executive. Many Argentine cause lawyers would probably agree with the assessment of Alejandro Carrió, who stated that while a few isolated judges may render an independent opinion from time to time, "I don't trust most of the judges." [156]

This distinction has a significant impact on the strategy of cause lawyers in the two countries. While all are *generally* reluctant to pursue traditional judicial remedies because of the tremendous limitations and barriers already described, the Brazilian lawyers expressed more of a willingness to occasionally test innovative legal theories in court in the hope that they might receive a sympathetic hearing on the bench.[157] Most Argentine cause lawyers would consider such efforts a complete waste of time and scarce resources.

LEGAL CLEARINGHOUSES

Another example of the difference in institutional support for cause lawyering in the two countries is the presence in Brazil of cause-lawyering clearinghouses, that is, organizations that provide technical and educational assistance to cause lawyers and link them with the individuals or grassroots organizations that are in need of their services. Two of the most prominent are the Institute for Popular Legal Support (AJUP) in Rio de Janeiro and the Legal Assistance Group for Popular Organizations (GAJOP) in Recife. AJUP maintains a data bank of cause lawyers throughout the country, so that grassroots groups in need of legal assistance can be connected with a lawyer who has expertise in a given field.[158] GAJOP works on issues relating to police violence against the urban poor. There are no such clearinghouses in Argentina. Indeed, according to Curiel, it is unclear whether there are any lawyers working on certain cause-lawyering issues in Argentina at all.[159]

These clearinghouses are no doubt largely responsible for the far greater number and influence of cause lawyers in rural areas of Brazil than similar sections of Argentina, even though the Brazilian rural regions are much more remote. For example, the Brazilian landless peasant movement has utilized AJUP on a number of occasions.[160]

THE CHURCH

The Catholic Church has also played a very different role with respect to cause lawyering, and social movement cause lawyering, in the two countries. From the late 1960s on, the Brazilian church was a frequent critic of the military regime.[161] Indeed, by 1973 (the end of the most repressive period of the dictatorship) "in the absence of viable voluntary associations and political parties, the Churches in general and the Catholic in particular had . . . become the single largest opposition force to military rule").[162] The Archdiocese of São Paulo, led by Cardinal Dom Paulo Evaristo Arns, was the focal point for church opposition to the regime.[163] Indeed, it was lawyers associated with the Catholic Church who compiled the legal documents from over seven hundred military trials (which described official acts of torture) that eventually led to the publication of *Brasil: Nunca Mais,* the most comprehensive report on human rights violations during the dictatorship.[164] And as Pressburger notes, most cause lawyers in Brazil are affiliated with church-connected human rights centers.[165]

At the same time that it was opposing the regime, the church was supporting grassroots community groups and social movements through its network of "peoples churches." The church assisted these movements by encouraging public participation, providing limited, yet essential resources, and legitimating the movements.[166] Thus, church employees have worked with and encouraged cause lawyers who work with the same communities and their movements.[167] Indeed, as in the case of Sister Nolan, some church employees *are* cause lawyers.

Such cooperation is—and was—simply not present in Argentina. Numerous interviewees described the Argentine church as extremely conservative.[168] Alejandro Carrió remarked that the church will help people in need but will not protest against government policies: "Every time someone from the church becomes active they are branded as Communist."[169] According to Alicia Curiel, the Argentine church is much more conservative than in Brazil and has no identification with the poor: "And when you do find a priest interested in the poor, he is stopped by superiors here . . . who say that it is not the place of the priest to be involved in political things, to be involved with the poor."[170]

This lack of support for community-based social movements, as well as the lawyers who work with them, is consistent with the church's consistent support for the Argentine military. Unlike its counterpart in Brazil, the hierarchy of the Argentine church supported the regime and its methods.[171] As Martin Andersen has observed, the church "offered the military both aid and comfort as they carried out their 'dirty war.' "[172]

Conclusion

The observations in this chapter suggest that the prevalence and effectiveness of social movement cause lawyers in newly emerging democracies depends far more on a series of external factors than on the professional or personal proclivities of the attorneys themselves. Unlike many cause lawyers in the United States who have been accused of "creating" lawsuits in order to further their own political or personal agenda, social movement cause lawyers in countries like Argentina and Brazil are much more constrained by the social and political realities of the present and the past.

Foremost among these external forces is the strength of the grassroots social movements with whom these lawyers work. As a general rule, when these movements are more established, organized, and unified—as in Brazil—it is easier for cause lawyers to work with them. The more these groups are beset by external hostility and internal dissension (over issues such as ethnic diversity and political cooptation), the less likely they will be able to foster a productive relationship with cause lawyers.

Second, cause lawyering is likely to be less widespread and organized where the authoritarian regime was more violent and arbitrary in its repression. In such situations (as in Argentina), community groups that were organized prior to the dictatorship are likely to be eradicated or displaced, and unable (or unwilling) to reorganize until well after the regime has been deposed. Moreover, many of the lawyers who might otherwise work with such groups are more likely to have been killed, "disappeared," exiled, or intimidated during such regimes. This depletes the number of social movement cause lawyers and disrupts their relationship with the movements.

In addition, cause lawyers in countries emerging from particularly repressive regimes are preoccupied with human rights work during (and often well after) the transition period. This work usually involves more traditional forms of lawyering (representing an individual victim or his/her family in habeas corpus actions or in assisting in the prosecution of perpetrators of state-sponsored violence). They have little time for (and sometimes expertise in) other types of cases, or for the more grassroots-oriented "alternative law" more prevalent in countries like Brazil and Colombia. Moreover, cause lawyers in such countries can become so identified with traditional human rights work that it is difficult for foreign funding sources to believe they are capable of (or interested in) performing any other type of lawyering once the most egregious human rights violations have ceased and the perpetrators have either been prosecuted or (as was the case with most of the Argentine military) pardoned.

A third factor influencing the extent of social movement cause lawyering in a country undergoing a transition to democracy is the amount of support it receives from institutional forces both within and outside the country. The disparate level of financial, intellectual, and professional support that Argentine and Brazilian cause lawyers have received from their respective bar associations, law school establishments, judges, and religious organizations, as well as international philanthropic sources, has played a crucial role in their prevalence and effectiveness.

Notes

Certain excerpts of this chapter dealing with Brazilian cause lawyers appeared in an article entitled "The Interaction between Lawyers and Grass Roots Social Movements in Brazil," which was published in *Beyond Law* 3, no. 7 (1993), 61–81; and Working Paper ILS 5-2 (Madison, Wisc.: Institute for Legal Studies, 1993).
I am extremely grateful to the following institutions and individuals for their assistance to this project: the Cyril Nave Fund, the University of Wisconsin, and the University of Wisconsin Law School for providing the funding for my field research; University of Wisconsin Law School professor Joseph Thome for providing conceptual and practical advice; University of Wisconsin law students Leticia Reyna Camacho and Tracey Conner for providing invaluable research and editorial assistance; Sandra Beuchert, Gabriela D'Angelo, and William Shelton for serving as translators during interviews; and George Rogers and Debbie Benchoam for helping to set up numerous interviews in Argentina.
    1. Maria Elba Martínez, interview by author, tape recording, Buenos Aires, August 8, 1994 (translated by Leticia Camacho).
    2. For purposes of this chapter, I consider "cause lawyering" to mean not-for-profit

legal work with and/or advocacy on behalf of individuals or groups who cannot afford to hire a lawyer, the ultimate aim of which is to achieve progressive social change.

3. Fernando Rojas, "A Comparison of Change-Oriented Legal Services in Latin America with Legal Services in North America and Europe," *International Journal of the Sociology of Law* 16 (1988), 203–256.

4. Martínez, interview.

5. Miguel Pressburger, interview by author, tape recording, Rio de Janeiro, August 12, 1992.

6. CISALP is comprised of lawyers and sociologists (about eight in all), most of whom were active in Argentina's human rights movement during the military dictatorship of 1976–82.

7. Octavio Carsen, interview by author, tape recording, Buenos Aires, July 1, 1994 (translated by Leigh Payne). For a detailed description of lawyers in the alternative law movement, see, e.g., Rojas, "A Comparison of Change-Oriented Legal Services"; Edward Ardilla and Jeff Clark, "Notes on Alternative Legal Practice in Latin America," *Beyond Law* 2, no. 4 (1992), 107. This movement also has adherents among legal practitioners and scholars in the United States, who stress a more client- and community-centered form of lawyering. See Tony Alfieri, "The Antinomies of Poverty Law and a Theory of Dialogic Empowerment," *New York University Review of Law and Social Change* 16 (1987–88), 659–712; Joel Handler, *Social Movements and the Legal System: A Theory of Law Reform and Social Change* (Madison: University of Wisconsin Press, 1978); Lucie White, "To Learn and to Teach: Lessons from Driefontein on Lawyering and Power," *Wisconsin Law Review 1988* (1988), 699–769; Gerald P. Lopez, *Rebellious Lawyering: One Chicano's Vision of a Progressive Law Practice* (Boulder, Colo.: Westview Press, 1992); Luke W. Cole, "Empowerment as the Key to Environmental Protection: The Need for Environmental Poverty Law," *Ecology Law Quarterly* 19 (1992), 619–683; Paul Tremblay, "Towards a Community Based Ethic for Legal Services Practice," *UCLA Law Review* 37 (1990), 1101–1156; Ruth Buchanan and Louise G. Trubek, "Resistances and Possibilities: A Critical and Practical Look at Public Interest Lawyering," *New York University Review of Law and Social Change* 19 (1992), 687–719; Christopher P. Gilkerson, "Poverty Law Narratives: The Critical Practice and Theory of Receiving and Translating Client Stories," *Hastings Law Journal* 43 (1992), 861–945; Jeffrey S. Lehman and Rochelle E. Lento, "Law School Support for Community Based Economic Development in Low-Income Urban Neighborhoods," *Journal of Urban and Contemporary Law* 42 (1992), 65–84.

8. CELS's work with *villeros* began after it intervened on their behalf to oppose a 1989 judicial order permitting the police to search homes at will. Alicia Curiel, interview by author, tape recording, Buenos Aires, July 15, 1994 (translated by Sandra Beuchert).

9. Based on his comprehensive study of Brazilian land ownership, Holston concludes that the early landed elites in Brazil, who had often obtained their vast tracts of property illegally, quite intentionally created an utterly incomprehensible paper trail of rights so as to frustrate any legitimate challenge to their ownership. Holston also notes that "Brazilian law regularly produces unresolvable procedural and substantive complexity in land conflicts. . . . [T]his jural-bureaucratic irresolution dependably initiates extrajudicial solutions. . . . [T]hese political impositions inevitably legalize usurpations of one sort or another." James Holston, "The Misrule of Law: Land and Usurpation in Brazil," *Comparative Studies in Society and History* 33, no. 4 (1991), 695. While the "extrajudicial solutions" to which Holston refers were historically initiated by the landowners for their own benefit (e.g., unilateral and often violent annexation of property), in recent years the landless groups have initiated some of their own (e.g., "squatting" on abandoned property).

10. Several lawyers I interviewed were careful to note that the cause lawyers of whom they spoke do not advise the landless groups to undertake an illegal occupation; they simply provide advice as to the legality and likely legal consequences of an occupation that the group is considering.

11. Pressburger, interview.

12. Celso Campilongo, interview by author, tape recording, São Paulo, August 14, 1992 (translated by William Shelton).

13. Pressburger, interview.

14. Sister Michael Mary Nolan, interview by author, tape recording, São Paulo, August 20, 1992.

15. Pressburger, interview.

16. Campilongo, interview.

17. Carsen, interview.

18. Ibid. This comment raises interesting questions such as, (1) Who really does the talking at these meetings? and (2) Even if the lawyers don't speak, does the adversary alter its behavior because it knows the lawyer are supporting the group? Of course, the presence of legal representatives influences the behavior of adversaries in traditional lawyer/client situations, as well.

19. Martínez, interview.

20. Ibid.

21. Not surprisingly, many officials in Brazil's rural states are loathe to prosecute those who commit crimes against people associated with the Landless Peasant Movement. Nolan, interview.

22. Brazilian and Argentine criminal law permit the family of a victim to hire a private attorney to assist the public prosecutor.

23. Each side in the case was permitted to disqualify three potential jurors. Nolan, interview.

24. Ibid.

25. Martínez, interview.

26. Victor Abromovitz, interview by author, tape recording, Buenos Aires, July 5, 1994 (translated by Gabriela D'Angelo). Abromovitz noted that eviction cases can take two years to complete: "You just complicate the case, and then work out a deal with the owner to buy the land or otherwise resolve the problem." Ibid. Of course, such delays can produce mixed results. In an eviction case in São Paulo on which attorney Nolan worked, the landlord had instituted eviction proceedings because the "intermediary," who collects rent from the tenant and (usually) delivers it to the landlord, had absconded with the rent. Although the tenants' organization ultimately prevailed in court, none of the original tenants lived in the building by the time the case ended. According to Nolan, since none of the tenants thought victory was possible, they succumbed to the landlord's pressuring tactics and moved out. Nolan, interview.

27. Nolan, interview.

28. McCann and Silverstein, and Sarat, have identified similar indirect benefits resulting from litigation pursued by cause lawyers in the United States (Michael McCann and Helena Silverstein, "Rethinking Law's 'Allurements': A Relational Analysis of Social Movement Lawyers in the United States," chap. 9 of this volume; and Austin Sarat, "Between (the Presence of) Violence and (the Possibility of) Justice: Lawyering against Capital Punishment," chap. 11 of this volume.

29. Beverly Keene, interview by author, tape recording, Buenos Aires, June 24, 1994.

30. Luis Moreno Ocampo, interview by author, tape recording, Buenos Aires, June 8, 1994.

31. Poder Ciudadano consists of about eight lawyers, sociologists and social workers who focus on corruption, government accountability, and reform of the judicial system. Roberto Saba, interview by the author, tape recording, Buenos Aires, June 1, 1994.

32. Ocampo, interview.

33. Ibid.

34. Alejandro Carrió, interview by author, tape recording, Buenos Aires, June 7, 1994.

35. Keene, interview.

36. Beatrice Kohen, interview by author, tape recording, Buenos Aires, August 10, 1994.

37. Curiel, interview.

38. Ibid.

39. For a detailed account of social movements in Brazil, Argentina, and the rest of Latin America, see Arturo Escobar and Sonia Alvarez, eds., *The Making of Social Movements in Latin America* (San Francisco: Westview Press, 1992); Alfred Stepan, ed., *Democratizing Brazil: Problems of Transition and Consolidation* (New York: Oxford University Press, 1989); David Slater, ed., *New Social Movements and the State in Latin America* (Amsterdam: CEDLA, 1985); Elizabeth Jelin, ed., *Women and Social Change in Latin America* (London: Zed Books, 1990); Paulo Freire, *Pedagogy of the Oppressed* (New York: Continuum, 1992); Joseph Page, *The Revolution That Never Was: Northeast Brazil, 1955–1964,* (New York: Grossman, 1972).

40. For detailed discussions of the historical dominance of the judiciary by the executive branch, see William C. Banks and Alejandro D. Carrió, "Presidential Systems in Stress: Emergency Powers in Argentina and the United States," *Michigan Journal of International Law* 15, no. 1 (1993), 1–76; Ivon d'Almeida Pires Filho, "Federative Republic of Brazil," in *Modern Legal Systems Cyclopedia* 10 (Buffalo, N.Y.: William S. Hein, 1991), 10.50.5–10.50.45; Irwin P. Stotzky, ed., *Transition to Democracy in Latin America: the Role of the Judiciary* (Boulder, Colo.: Westview Press, 1993); and Howard J. Wiarda and Harvey F. Kline, "The Latin American Tradition and the Process of Development," in *The Civil Law Tradition: Europe, Latin America, and East Asia,* ed. John Henry Merryman, David S. Clark, and John O. Haley (Charlottesville, Va.: Michie, 1990), 604–613.

41. Joseph R. Thome, "Administration of Justice in Latin America: A Survey of AID Funded Programs in Argentina and Uruguay" (Arlington, Va.: Development Associates, Inc., 1993), 34.

42. Banks and Carrió, "Presidential Systems in Stress," 9.

43. Ibid., 13.

44. Banks and Carrió, "Presidential Systems in Stress," 13, citing Articles 86(10), 86(1) and 23 of the constitution.

45. In addition, the constitution of 1853 was reformed in 1860, 1868, and 1898. The Peronists instituted their own constitution in 1949. The 1853 constitution was reinstated in 1957 and reformed once again in 1966. John P. Mandler, "Habeas Corpus and the Protection of Human Rights in Argentina," *Yale Journal of International Law,* 16, no. 1 (1991), 8. A constitutional convention in 1994, originally organized only to consider the repeal of the provision limiting the president to one term, resulted in additional reforms.

46. "The Process" or "Processo" is shorthand for the Statute for the Process of National Reorganization, instituted by the military in 1976.

47. Mandler, "Habeas Corpus and the Protection of Human Rights," 17.

48. During the New Republic power was concentrated in the tightly organized political machines that emerged in each of the states. Thomas E. Skidmore and Peter H. Smith, *Modern Latin America,* 3d ed. (New York: Oxford University Press, 1992), 161.

49. According to Wiarda and Kline, the framers of most Latin American constitutions never intended the judiciary or the legislature to be on equal footing with the executive, and condemn North American criticism of this imbalance as evidence of cultural ignorance and insensitivity: "Knee-jerk condemnation of a Latin American government that rules without giving equal status to the legislature or courts often reveals more about our own biases, ethnocentrism, and lack of understanding than it does about the realities of Latin America." Wiarda and Kline,"The Latin American Tradition and Process of Development," 605.

50. Keith S. Rosenn, "Brazil's New Constitution: An Exercise in Transient Constitutionalism for a Transitional Society," *American Journal of Comparative Law* 38 (1990), 774.

51. Martin Feinrider, "Judicial Review and the Protection of Human Rights under Military Governments in Brazil and Argentina," *Suffolk Transnational Law Journal* 5, no. 2 (1981), 197. Of course, this is not to suggest that the judiciary alone should take it upon itself to oppose a repressive regime. As Feinrider notes: "Judges cannot substitute judicial review for social justice, or judicial power for civilian control of government. For a short time, judges may be able to protect the rights of a few people, and courts may provide a useful stage for confronting the military and exposing the contradictions of military rule. In the end, however, bullets are more powerful than writs. The hope for opponents of military regimes is that ultimately a social consensus for a return to civilian government may be stronger than bullets." Ibid., 199.

52. Paulo Sergio Pinhiero, interview by author, tape recording, São Paulo, August 18, 1992.

53. Ocampo, interview.

54. Carsen, interview. One of the earliest, and most ominous, examples of the Argentine judiciary's abdication of power occurred in 1930, when the Supreme Court of Argentina recognized the new military regime as the "de facto" government despite the unconstitutionality of its origin. The court concluded that the new regime should be given legal sanction on the basis of "necessity" and "public policy" and for the purpose of "protecting the citizens, whose interests could be affected because it is not now possible for them to question the legality of those now in power." Decree of September 10, 1930, quoted in Banks and Carrió "Presidential Systems in Stress," 27–28).

55. José Eduardo Faria, interview by author, tape recording, São Paulo, August 19, 1992.

56. Filho, "Federative Republic of Brazil," 10.50.27.

57. James Holston, "The Misrule of Lowland Usurpation in Brazil," *Comparative Studies in Society and History* 33, no. 4 (1991), 695.

58. Campilongo, interview.

59. The most famous—or infamous—of these pacts is known as the Olivos Pact, in which Radical Party chief (and former president) Raul Alfonsín agreed to support a constitutional amendment permitting a second presidential term (which current president Carlos Menem seeks) in exchange for Menem (the Peronist Party leader) agreeing to unseat three Supreme Court judges and appoint replacements more amenable to the Radical Party.

60. Curiel, interview.

61. A graphic example of the delays in Argentine jurisprudence was provided by lawyer Victor Abromovitz, who works on labor law and worker safety issues. In a recent case, he represented a worker who was unlawfully terminated in 1992. Abromovitz filed a case on the worker's behalf in early 1993 and in May 1994 he received notice of a court hearing to be held in June, 1996. Abromovitz says that the average duration of a typical accident case is six to seven years. Abromovitz, interview.

62. Roberto de Michele, interview by author, tape recording, Buenos Aires, July 20, 1994.

63. Emilio F. Mignone, interview by author, Buenos Aires, July 29, 1994 (translated by Sandra Beuchert). Of course, there are some observers who contend that the inefficiencies of the countries' legal systems are no accident. As noted earlier, Holston concluded that, at least in the area of property ownership, the Brazilian system was intentionally constructed to defeat any claims to title by all social sectors save the elite. Holston, "The Misuse of Law," 695.

64. The constitutions of Argentina and Brazil, like those in many Latin American countries, contain several contradictory provisions. According to Wiarda and Kline, "Even though all the Latin American constitutions contain long lists of human and political rights, the same constitutions also give the executive the power to declare a state of siege or emergency, suspend human rights, and rule by decree. The same applies to privilege. While one section of a constitution may proclaim democratic and egalitarian principles, other parts give special privileges to the church, the army, or the landed elites. Although representative and republican precepts are enshrined in one quarter, authoritarian and elitist ones are legitimated in another." Wiarda and Kline, "The Latin American Tradition and Process of Development," 606.

65. Carsen, interview.

66. Dr. Carlos A. Vasquez Fuentes, interview by author, tape recording, Buenos Aires, July 8, 1994 (translated by Sandra Beuchert).

67. Filho, "Federative Republic of Brazil," 10.50.13.

68. Wiarda and Kline, "The Latin American Tradition and Process of Development," 607.

69. Filho, "Federative Republic of Brazil," 10.50.20.

70. As Michalowski notes in his study of cause lawyering in Cuba, another country with a civil code tradition, "[L]egal evolution depends much more on code revisions than on precedent-setting cases, as in the United States." Raymond J. Michalowski, "All or Nothing: An Inquiry into the (Im)Possibility of Cause Lawyering under Cuban Socialism," chap. 16 of this volume.

71. Faria, interview.

72. Filho, "Federative Republic of Brazil," 10.50.21.

73. Faria, interview.

74. Carsen, interview.

75. Campilongo, interview.

76. Martin Bohmer, interview by author, tape recording, Buenos Aires, June 6, 1994. Bohmer told the story of one law professor who, during a lecture, responded to a student who had raised his hand: "I am not here to answer questions." Ibid.

77. Bohmer, interview.

78. Julio Garcia, interview by author, tape recording, Buenos Aires, July 1, 1994 (translated by Leigh Payne).

79. Martínez, interview.

80. Campilongo, interview.

81. Bohmer, interview. Because of the marginalization of his interpretation course by the mainstream faculty, Bohmer has recently begun teaching corporate law and tries to inject it with critical legal analysis. Ibid.

82. Roberto Saba, interview by author, tape recording, Buenos Aires, June 1, 1994.

83. Kohen, interview.

84. Pinhiero, interview; de Michele, interview; Carrió, interview; Ocampo, interview.

85. Faria, interview.

86. Martínez, interview.

87. Carrió, interview. The dark side of "amiguismo," of course, is corruption. As Ocampo puts it, "[T]hat's why corruption is a big issue; we have different levels of rules: the formal rules and the secret, under the table rules—resolving the problem with money because you do not have a legal way of resolving the problem with the authority." Ocampo, interview. And as de Michele says, "There is an incentive not to comply with rules—who is going to take you to court?" de Michele, interview.

88. Ocampo, interview. Some of the most recent examples of events that contribute to the loss of public faith in the Argentine judiciary have occurred during the administration of President Carlos Menem. According to Alejandro Carrió, Menem has removed all of the "brave or independent" federal judges from sensitive political cases (such as the corruption trials of governmental officials) and replaced them with judges who were personal friends and/or sympathetic to his point of view. Carrió, interview; Ocampo, interview. In some cases, the appointees were not even lawyers; one such appointee, who never attended law school, was the son of Menem's fortune-teller. Ocampo, interview. In 1990, Menem increased the size of the Supreme Court from five justices to nine so as to be able to appoint political allies to the highest court (a proposal approved by the Congress after only seven minutes of debate). And he has made unprecedented use (with the approval of the newly packed Supreme Court) of executive decrees that were previously used only in emergency situations. (There were eight such decrees issued prior to Menem's presidency; he has issued about two hundred of them. De Michele, interview; Mignone, interview. This manipulation of the judiciary only exacerbated an Argentine phenomenon that Roberto Saba of Poder Ciudadano refers to as *inseguridad juridica* (legal uncertainty): "One cannot be sure if the law which exists today will disappear tomorrow because of a decree." Saba, interview.

89. Menkel-Meadow notes that the following factors interact to produce the motivation to work for or help others: biological and familial predispositions, social characteristics and personal traits, life experiences, personality attributes, social statuses, moral religious or ideological value systems, and situational opportunities or settings for expression of such values or attributes. Carrie Menkel-Meadow, "The Causes of Cause Lawyering: Toward an Understanding of the Motivation and Commitment of Social Justice Lawyers," chap. 2 of this volume.

90. Martínez, interview.

91. Carsen, interview.

92. Patrick Rice, interview by author, tape recording, Buenos Aires, June 9, 1994.

93. Curiel, interview.

94. Ibid.

95. Of course, military governments were nothing new to Argentina. Beginning in 1930, there have been six military coups: 1930, 1943, 1955, 1962, 1966, and 1976. Within that period, the Supreme Court was completely or partially restructured seven times. Banks and Carrió, "Presidential Systems in Stress," 25.

96. Ibid., 30.

97. Guillermo O'Donnell, "Transitions, Continuities, and Paradoxes," in *Issues in Democratic Consolidation: The New South American Democracies in Comparative Perspective*, ed. Scott Mainwaring, Guillermo O'Donnell, and Samuel Valenzuela (Notre Dame, Ind.: Notre Dame University Press, 1992), 24.

98. The exact number of the "disappeared" remains a topic of heated debate in some Argentine circles. CONADEP, the Argentine National Commission on the Disappeared, estimated the number at 8,960, but acknowledged that the exact count could be higher because many people were deterred from reporting disappearances. Estimates by the Argentina me-

dia range from 6,000 to 15,000. Many human rights groups place the number at 30,000. Mandler, "Habeas Corpus and the Protection of Human Rights," 3.

99. Frank Graziano, *Divine Violence: Spectacle, Psychosexuality, and Radical Christianity in the Argentine "Dirty War"* (Boulder, Colo.: Westview Press, 1992), 28.

100. Mandler, "Habeas Corpus and the Protection of Human Rights," 16.

101. Marguerite Guzman Bouvard, *Revolutionizing Motherhood: The Mothers of the Plaza de Mayo* (Wilmington, Dela.: Scholarly Resources, 1994), 38; Banks and Carrió, "Presidential Systems in Stress," 31.

102. Curiel, interview. The campaign against leftist lawyers actually began before the military officially took power in 1976. In July 1994 a bomb exploded at the headquarters of the Trade Association of Attorneys, which defended political prisoners. Several prominent leftist labor lawyers were executed on the street by death squads, and others had their homes and offices raided during the same period. Martin Edward Anderson, *Dossier Secreto: Argentina's Desaparecidos and the Myth of the "Dirty War"* (Boulder, Colo.: Westview Press, 1993), 114–115.

103. Carrió, interview.

104. Andersen, *Dossier Secreto*, 114–115.

105. Banks and Carrió, "Presidential Systems in Stress," 34.

106. Only days before the invasion on April 2, 1982, the public held the largest antigovernment demonstration since the military took control in 1976. *Modern Latin America*, Skidmore and Smith, 106.

107. Ibid., 107.

108. The election of Peronist Menem in 1989 was a significant event in Argentine politics for two reasons: it was the first time in sixty-three years that power was transferred between two constitutionally elected civilian presidents, and it was the first time ever that the Peronists came to power without either Peron himself or one of his spouses at the helm. Skidmore and Smith, *Modern Latin America*, 109; Mandler, "Habeas Corpus and the Protection of Human Rights," 6–7.

109. Military revolts staged in 1987, 1989, and 1990 to protest prosecutions and demand amnesty led to the pardons.

110. Like Argentina, Brazil has a history of a dominant military. Beginning with the Republican military coup in 1889 (which ended a sixty-seven-year postindependence period of empire) Brazil has experienced five military coups: 1889, 1930, 1937, 1945, and 1964. Bolivar Lamounier, "Brazil: Inequality against Democracy," in *Democracy in Developing Countries: Latin America*, ed. Larry Diamond, Juan J. Linz, and Seymour Martin Lipset (Boulder, Colo.: Lynne Reinner, 1989), 138–139. In many cases, the military assumed power, often at the request of the civilian regime, in order to suppress popular uprisings. Joan Dassin, ed., *Torture in Brazil: A Report by the Archdiocese of São Paulo* (New York: Vintage Books, 1989), 41–45.

111. Thomas E. Skidmore, "Brazil's Slow Road to Democratization: 1974–1985," in *Democratizing Brazil: Problems of Transition and Consolidation*, ed. Alfred Stepan (New York: Oxford University Press, 1989), 6.

112. O'Donnell, "Transitions, Continuities, and Paradoxes," 25–26.

113. *Torture in Brazil*, 205; Skidmore, "Brazil's Slow Road to Democratization," 22.

114. *Torture in Brazil*, 61.

115. The amnesty law of 1979 was a political trade-off: it pardoned all those who had been imprisoned or exiled for political crimes since September 2, 1961, including torturers. Skidmore, "Brazil's Slow Road to Democratization," 21–22.

116. Bohmer, interview; de Michele, interview; Saba, interview.

117. Scott Mainwaring, "Grassroots Popular Movements and the Struggle for Democ-

racy: Nova Iguaçu," in *Democratizing Brazil: Problems of Transition and Consolidation,* ed. Alfred Stepan (New York: Oxford University Press, 1989), 173.

118. Ibid.; Elizabeth Sussekind, "The Brazilian Woman during the 1980's: A View from Feminist Groups" (Madison, Wisc.: Institute for Legal Studies, 1992), 11–12; Miguel Pressburger, "Case Studies on the Transformative Potential of People's Legal Assistance Organizations: A View from Brazil," *Beyond Law* 1, no. 3 (1991), 35–42, 36.

119. Campilongo, interview; Sussekind, "The Brazilian Woman during the 1980's," 38–39; Pressburger, "Case Studies on the Transformative Potential of People's Legal Assistance Organizations," 36–37; Mainwaring, "Grassroots Popular Movements and the Struggle for Democracy," 174. A similar emergence of grassroots organizations occurred in Chile during the Pinochet regime of 1973–90, and has continued during the transition to democracy. Joseph R. Thome, "People versus the Authoritarians: Grass Root Organizations and Chile's Transition to Democracy," *Beyond Law* 1, no. 2 (1991).

120. Mainwaring, "Grassroots Popular Movements and the Struggle for Democracy," 177.

121. This is not to imply that grassroots social movements in Brazil were without problems. Many communities experienced internal disputes because of the different religious and racial backgrounds, status, and material needs of their members. In addition, broad-based mobilization was often difficult because many community members had little political interest or awareness. Mainwaring, "Grassroots Popular Movements and the Struggle for Democracy," 182.

122. Andersen, *Dossier Secreto,* 219.

123. Ibid. Guillermo Del Cioppo, former head of the Buenos Aires municipal housing commission, declared that "[o]ur only intention is that those who live in our city be culturally prepared for it. To live in Buenos Aires isn't just for everyone, but for him who deserves it. . . . We ought to have a better city for the best people." Ibid., 219.

124. During the Peronist period *villas* had a significant amount of local control over issues such as water and electricity, the building of schools and day care centers, and grocery stores. Ibid., 219.

125. Curiel, interview.

126. Andersen, *Dossier Secreto,* 214.

127. Ibid., 215.

128. Curiel, interview.

129. De Michele, interview.

130. Kohen, interview. It is difficult to gauge how much the Argentine avoidance of collective action is due to the repression of the most recent dictatorship and how much is attributable to a social phenomenon described to me as "individualismo." According to Attorney Roberto Saba of Poder Ciudadano, this cultural phenomenon is so well ingrained in the national psyche that it is unusual for Argentines to work cooperatively: "[T]he tradition is for people to be eternally divided." Saba, interview.

131. Organizations like CELS and SERPAJ, which focused almost exclusively on traditional human rights issues (i.e., defending the interests of the "disappeared") during the dictatorship, are now advocating a more holistic interpretation of "human rights"; i.e., one that incorporates issues involving economic, social, and cultural rights, such as adequate housing, health care, and sanitation. Curiel, interview; Keene, interview; Carsen, interview.

132. Carsen, interview. The 1994 estimate of per capita Gross National Product is $6,050 (US$) in Argentina and $2,770 in Brazil. In addition to being poorer, Brazil's population is more economically polarized: the wealthiest 20 percent of Brazilians (according to household income) control 68 percent of the nations wealth, whereas the poorest 20 percent control only 2 percent. In Argentina, the wealthiest 20 percent control 51 percent of the

wealth, while the lowest 20 percent control 5 percent. World Bank, *Social Indicators of Development: 1994* (Baltimore, Md.: Johns Hopkins University Press, 1994), 12, 13, 48, 49.

133. De Michele, interview.

134. Saba, interview; Bohmer, interview.

135. Faria, interview.

136. Martínez, interview. Martínez calls these recently graduated lawyers "judicial yuppies," since they apply "the rules without questioning the causes or effects." Ibid.

137. Curiel, interview.

138. Saba, interview.

139. Campilongo, interview. The increase in Brazilian law schools—from 35 in 1964 to 135 by 1972—was in response to student pressure over lack of available spaces. While allowing access to a more economically diverse range of students, the increase was criticized during my interviews as creating a series of "diploma factories" (Pinhiero, interview) and leading to a "brutal" decline in the quality of teaching, since all one needed to open a law school was a room, a chalkboard, and a professor, who is often a local judge (Campilongo, interview).

140. Saba, interview.

141. Carrió, interview.

142. Campilongo, interview.

143. Mignone, interview; Dassin, ed., *Torture in Brazil*, xi.

144. Albert P. Blaustein and Gisbert H. Flanz, eds., *Constitutions of the Countries of the World*, vol. 2, *Federative Republic of Brazil*, by Albert P. Blaustein (Dobbs Ferry, N.Y.: Oceana Publications, 1990) 1–51, 34.

145. Skidmore, "Brazil's Slow Road to Democratization," 11–12.

146. Dassin, ed., *Torture in Brazil*, xi.

147. Feinrider, "Judicial Review and the Protection of Human Rights," 176.

148. As I learned during my interviews, the use of the word "alternative" to describe these particular Rio Grande do Sul judges has made it a loaded term within the Brazilian legal community. Thus, I learned not to use the term "alternative law" when asking about lawyers who work with grassroots groups, since it has a very specific meaning in Brazil, one which can be quite negative (even among cause lawyers), depending on the interview subject's attitude toward the Rio Grande do Sul judges.

149. Campilongo, interview.

150. Faria, interview.

151. Campilongo, interview. Two specific cases illustrate the approach of these lawyers: in the first, the judge ruled in favor of a retiree who was demanding his pension, even though a recently enacted law clearly prohibited him from receiving it. The judge ruled that the law was an unconstitutional taking of property and also violated the retiree's pension rights, which had vested under the previous law. The judge then stated another basis for his ruling: Brazilian retirees should be accorded respect. In the second example, a judge acquitted a person accused of a minor crime on the grounds that the penitentiary system was not in satisfactory condition to receive him. The judge then led members of the press to the local prison in order to demonstrate his point. Ibid.

152. Ibid.

153. Antonio Carlos Villen, interview by author, tape recording, São Paulo, August 20, 1992 (translated by William Shelton).

154. Campilongo, interview. The members of the Association of Judges for Democracy do not wish to be confused with the "alternative judges" in Rio Grande do Sul. According to Campilongo, the alternative judges "got the reputation of being hippie judges, punk judges, irresponsible judges, inconsequential judges. So although the judges in São Paulo

think in a very similar manner, they make a point of emphasizing that they are not a part of the alternative law movement." Campilongo, interview.

155. Ibid.

156. Carrió, interview. Despite this negative view of the majority of the judiciary, Carrió has recently formed a nonprofit organization, using the ACLU as a model, that will file civil lawsuits to enforce rights-based statutes and constitutional provisions, such as disability rights laws. Ibid.

157. Nolan, interview.

158. Pressburger, interview; Pressburger, "Case Studies on the Transformative Potential of People's Legal Assistance Organizations," 35–42.

159. Curiel, interview.

160. Pressburger, interview.

161. Ralph Della Cava, "The 'People's Church,' the Vatican, and *Abertura*," in *Democratizing Brazil: Problems of Transition and Consolidation*, ed. Stepan, 143–167; Filho, "Federative Republic of Brazil," 10.50.10.

162. Della Cava, "The 'People's Church,' " 147.

163. Ibid., 147–48; Skidmore, "Brazil's Slow Road to Democratization," 8, 12, 21.

164. The only two people willing to assume public responsibility for *Nunca Mais* when it was first published in July 1985 (by the Catholic press *Vozes*) were Cardinal Arns and Dr. Jaime Wright, a Presbyterian minister, both of whom were longtime human rights activists. Dassin, ed., *Torture in Brazil*, x.

165. Pressburger, interview.

166. Mainwaring, "Grassroots Popular Movements and the Struggle for Democracy," 191.

167. Nolan, interview.

168. Carrió, interview; de Michele, interview; Carsen, interview; Abromovitz, interview.

169. Carrió, interview. Patrick Rice of the Movimiento Ecumenical was such a priest. A native of Ireland, he came to Buenos Aires in 1970 and began working in a neighborhood parish with *villeros*. Soon after the 1976 military coup he was arrested, imprisoned, and tortured for several weeks. Due to international pressure, he was released, but only on condition that he leave Argentina. He returned after the military fell, no longer a priest, and later married the layworker with whom he was abducted nearly twenty years before. Rice, interview.

170. Curiel, interview. For a more detailed description of the military's assault on the "People's Church" in Argentina, see Andersen, *Dossier Secreto*, 184–193.

171. Patrick Rice of the Movimiento Ecumenical noted that General Videla, one of the most infamous members of the military junta, was a daily communicant, which made it "difficult for the Catholic Church to have credibility within Argentine society." Rice, interview.

172. Andersen, *Dossier Secreto*, 271; Emilio Mignone, *Witness to the Truth: The Complicity of Church and Dictatorship in Argentina, 1976–1983* (Maryknoll, N.Y.: Orbis Books, 1988); Graziano, *Divine Violence*. A specific example of this support recently came to light through the public admission of Adolfo Francisco Scilingo, a former naval commander who dumped the bodies of still living torture victims from an airplane flying over the Atlantic Ocean during the Dirty War. According to Scilingo, he confessed his deeds at that time to a priest who absolved him on the grounds that such actions "had to be done to separate the wheat from the chaff" (*New York Times*, March 13, 1995, A5).

CHAPTER 16

All or Nothing

An Inquiry into the (Im)Possibility
of Cause Lawyering under
Cuban Socialism

RAYMOND MICHALOWSKI

This chapter examines whether or not possibilities for cause lawyering can exist within the context of Cuba's socialist legal system. In particular, it addresses whether cause lawyering is a unique characteristic of liberal-democratic states or if there exists a socialist analog to the more typical image of cause lawyering.

Most discussions of cause lawyering have focused on attorneys who pursue social change by making "a self-conscious choice to give priority to causes rather than to client service."[1] Studies of cause lawyering characteristically examine attorneys who represent social movements or activists targeted by the state for prosecution or harassment,[2] or who defend disadvantaged individuals against putative violations of their rights.[3] This understanding of cause lawyering presumes first a structural and ideological relationship between state and civil society that permits at least minimal development of independent social movements, and second a political and the legal construction of human rights that permits lawyers to contest the meaning, implementation, and/or inclusiveness of these rights. In short, the common image of cause lawyering assumes that these lawyers are operating within the structure and the ideals of at least a rudimentary liberal-democratic state.

The ideal-typical form of cause lawyering described above encompasses a number of characteristics that suggest there should be little room for cause lawyering in Cuba. First, typical cause lawyers—at least in the United States—most often pursue causes by using specific cases to obtain a general extension of some right.[4] Second, the rights to which these cause lawyers appeal are primarily accessible through a liberal democratic construction of citizen-state relations. Absent the ability to frame a case in terms of some liberal-democratic right, most cause lawyers would have little standing from which to enter legal contests on behalf of their cause. Third, cause lawyers are typically seen as pursuing progressive or left-leaning agendas designed to alter conservative social and legal formations. Fourth, ideal-typical cause lawyers work outside of, and usually against, government. Attorneys who work as state-managers or governmental officials, even if they entered these positions because they were devoted to a cause rather than to client service, are generally not considered to be cause lawyers.[5] Fifth, cause lawyering characteristically involves solidarity with, and is often supported by, nongovernmental social movements.

In sum, ideal-typical cause lawyering is a socially progressive practice that binds capitalism to democracy by deploying litigation—often on behalf of some social movement—to protect and/or extend the bourgeois rights that have come to play a critical role in establishing the legitimacy of the modern capitalist state.

In contrast to liberal-democratic cause lawyering, the relationships among law, lawyers, and social change in Cuba is configured quite differently. First, there is little scope in Cuba to use the claims of individual litigants as a strategy to achieve a general extension of some legal right. As a former Spanish colony, Cuba's juridical framework mirrors the more code-based civil legal systems of Europe rather than Anglo-American case law systems. All other factors aside, code-based systems limit the possibilities of promoting rights through case-based litigation.[6] Under these systems, legal evolution depends much more on code revision than on precedent-setting rights cases. Thus, the deployment of litigation, even if it were successful in a particular instance, would not have the same system-wide effect under Cuba's code-based legal system that it would in a more precedent-oriented context.

Second, Cuba's socialist construction of rights emphasizes the collective rather than the individual character of these rights. Human rights under Cuban socialism tend to be construed as *positive* rights to the enjoyment of some substantive benefit such as employment, housing, medical care, or education, rather than *negative* rights to be juridically free from private or governmental interference with the enjoyment of individual liberties. Under the Cuban constitution, key substantive rights have been constructed as benefits to be guaranteed by the state, rather than private juridical possession that individuals can deploy to protect themselves from unfair treatment by the state or within civil society.[7] Cuban employment law, for example, is based on the constitutional principle that the state will guarantee, through its socialist economy, that "every man or woman who is able to work will have the opportunity to have a job."[8] This differs notably from the right to compete on a level playing field for jobs that one might or might not obtain, as is the case with employment discrimination law in the United States. This emphasis on collective rights leads directly to the fourth limitation on ideal-typical cause lawyering in Cuba—the relative absence of private social movements.

There is little space in the Cuban political system for social movement organizations to operate independently of the government, or for cause lawyers to work outside of the formal organization of legal practice into law collectives known as *bufetes colectivos*. These limitations on independent social movements flow directly from the ideology of rights as prescriptive strategies to achieve collective rather than individual benefits, as noted above. Liberal democratic rights tend to be circumscribed in Cuba by the requirement that the exercise of these rights cannot interfere with the development of a socialist society. For example, the Cuban constitution provides that:

Artistic creativity is free as long as its content is not contrary to the Revolution.[9]

The socialist state recognizes and guarantees freedom of conscience and the right of everyone to profess any religious belief. . . . [However] [i]t is illegal and punishable by law to oppose one's faith or religious belief to the Revolution.[10]

Citizens have freedom of speech and of the press in keeping with the objectives of socialist society.[11]

This conditional framing of individual rights means that social movements that seek to promote individual rights against the wishes of the government would have little or no legal standing. In place of independent movements, the government has sought to direct social movement energy into officially sanctioned mass organizations such as the Cuban Federation of Women, the Association of Small Farmers, the Congress of Cuban Trade Unions, the Cuban Writers Union, and even the state-approved association of attorneys—the National Organization of Law Collectives (Organización Nacional de Bufetes Colectivos/ONBC). These official organizations enable the government to direct and discipline the impetus for social change in ways that are consistent with the overarching goal of crafting socialist responses to economic and social problems. This strategy also makes it easier for the Cuban leadership to declare that organizations promoting private interests or public solutions outside of officially sanctioned mass organizations are renegades from the revolution who have no legitimate voice in the nation's political discourse. The politics of mass organizations weakens the ability of lawyers to argue that social movement activities contrary to the approved goals of socialist development constitute legally protected behavior.

From one perspective Cuba's system of mass organizations can be seen as coopting and disciplining the energy of potentially independent activism. On the other hand, these mass organizations are influential in the development of Cuban law and the construction of Cuban socialism. The Cuban Family Code, for instance, which provides such things as paid maternity leave for working women and readily available day care and enshrines the equal division of domestic labor in law, resulted largely through the efforts of the Cuban Federation of Women. Lawyers, working with and on behalf of the interests of these mass organizations, in turn, have played a role in promoting social change in Cuba. Thus, while they may not fit the image of cause lawyers, there are definitely some Cuban attorneys who perform functions typically associated with cause lawyering.

Finally, the leftist nature of the Cuban state means that the typical image of cause lawyers engaged in struggles against a capitalist state raises several questions regarding lawyers in the Cuban context. Can those working *for* the Cuban government be viewed as cause lawyers on the basis of their left-oriented politics despite the fact that they are in harmony with the state? Can right-wing Cuban attorneys in the United States working for the downfall of the Castro government be viewed as cause lawyers despite the conservative nature of their agendas?

The apparent structural limitations on cause lawyering in Cuba are the starting point for the questions I want to pursue here. Specifically, do these limitations mean that lawyers play no role as social change agents under Cuban socialism? Are Cuban attorneys merely functionaries of a totalizing state, or are some proactive in maneuvering the state to live up to its promises in a manner similar to cause lawyers in liberal democracies? Finally, are there attorneys in Cuba who can be said to devote the bulk of their energy to a *cause?*

I will address these questions from the vantage point of my research in a *bufete colectivo* in Havana.[12] My central argument is that the formal organization of legal practice in Cuba generates contradictory tendencies regarding the potential for cause lawyering. On the one hand liberal-democratic forms of cause lawyering are virtually impossible under Cuban socialist legality because of the limitations on nongovernmental social movements and lawyering outside the *bufete colectivo* system. On the other hand, Cuba's system of socialist politics creates openings through which lawyers can and do affect social policy. My goal in examining the role of lawyers as social change agents in Cuba is to problematize the conception of cause lawyers as rebels operating in ideological and structural exile from the state. Instead, I will argue that the particular relationship between law, politics, and social change in Cuba has enabled its more activist lawyers to shape social change in a way that is analogous to what cause lawyers attempt to accomplish in the liberal-democratic societies. I suggest that the example offered by Cuban attorneys provides a useful model for expanding how we understand the role of activist lawyers and cause lawyering.

Socialist Legal Practice in Cuba

After a period of experimentation that lasted from the revolutionary victory in 1959 to around 1970, the Cuban government began a process of institutionalizing its new economic and political order.[13] Among other things, this meant replacing the prerevolutionary legal system with one that was better suited to the ideology and practice of an emerging socialist political economy. One component of this new legal system was the abolition of the private practice of law. After 1973 all attorneys providing direct services to the public were required to work in law collectives. These *bufetes colectivos* are self-financed and locally administered organizations in which attorneys are paid according to a fixed proportion of the client fees they generate. They do not, however, constitute private law firms in the free-market sense of the term "private." Instead, the individual *bufetes colectivos* are linked together under a single organizational umbrella and function according to rules and fees established by this organization in concordance with the Ministry of Justice.

In 1977 the National Assembly approved a new law of judicial organization that substantially revised the 1973 statute.[14] The promulgation of this new law had a number of significant consequences for *bufetes colectivos*. Most importantly, Article 146 of the 1977 law of judicial organization created an "autonomous national organization," in the form of the ONBC. The ONBC links the individual *bufetes colectivos* into a representative, national hierarchy with the authority to establish general rules for the conduct of lawyering. As parts of this autonomous organization the individual *bufetes colectivos* are independent with respect to the management of their day-to-day activities. They are subject, however, to the rules and regulations established by the ONBC and to oversight by the ONBC staff.

When Is Cause Lawyering?

The process that led to the establishment of the *bufetes colectivos* as the standard for the delivery of legal service delivery was not simply a top-down imposition of revolutionary ideology on the Cuban bar. The replacement of private legal practice with *bufetes colectivos* was, instead, the institutionalization of an informal process that had been under way for nearly a decade. As early as 1961 attorneys sympathetic to the egalitarian goals of the revolution began forming law collectives as a way of insuring public access to legal services[15] From their perspective, the goal of these revolutionary attorneys was to break the privileged access to legal services enjoyed by Cuba's traditional economic and political elites.[16] As late as 1990, those who led this movement were still seen as important figures in the struggle to create a socialist Cuba. One of the attorneys in the law collective where I have been a periodic participant observer since 1989 was held in particularly high esteem by a number of the other attorneys because he was one of the first in Havana to turn his private law practice into a *bufete colectivo* after the revolutionary victory of 1959.

The 1973 law of judicial organization that created Cuba's system of *bufetes colectivos* transformed what had been a social movement among Cuba's most radical attorneys for equality in legal services into the mandatory institutional arrangement for the provision of legal services. From one point of view, the success of the early *colectivistas* in transforming legal services from a market-based privilege into a public right, and lawyers from advocates for their clients to promoters of a broader social justice, could be viewed as an example of effective cause lawyering. That is, prorevolution lawyers committed to the cause of equal access to legal services set in motion a movement that eventually became the universal mechanism for providing legal services.

The idea that the creation of the *bufete colectivo* system might be an example of effective cause lawyering, however, raises the question of whether or not the concept of cause lawyering applies only to attorneys who advocate and litigate from a dissident position or on behalf of dissident groups. If cause lawyering is indeed limited to those who work against the political status quo from a position outside the state structure, then it would seem that lawyers who participate in political or revolutionary struggles can be considered cause lawyers only as long as these struggles *fail* to gain power. Are cause lawyers who continue to operate in support of revolutionary goals after revolutionary change ushers them into power still engaging in cause lawyering when they use their new positions to help build institutions consistent with their former dissident positions? Or do cause lawyers cease to be cause lawyers once they are representing, rather than opposing, state power? More specifically, can attorneys working with the government, such as those who brought about the *bufete colectivo* system in Cuba, be appropriately considered cause lawyers insofar as they were participants in a struggle to change some element of a status quo social order? I would argue that these attorneys were no less cause lawyers after the revolutionary victory than before. Struggles to change a social order continue long after the ascendancy of a new government in any politically transformative situation. The lawyers who created the early *bufetes colectivos* and struggled to have their model of service delivery established nationwide in order to guarantee what they believed was a more equitable system of legal representation were engaged in a form of cause lawyering through progressive social action, rather than through litigation. Their efforts differed from idealtypical cause lawyering through the deployment of litigation, yet they were equally aimed at bringing about social change and substantive extension of the right to legal counsel.

The particular case of lawyering for social change represented by the creation of the *bufete colectivo* system foregrounds the complexity of the relationships among lawyers, social change, and the state. The idea that lawyers can be proactive change agents in transformative political situations without invoking antigovernment litigation raises the question of how this can be done. It also raises questions regarding how long the transformative moment lasts before a new political economy is solidified into a status quo. I want to address these questions first by examining the contradictory tendencies arising from the political organization of lawyering in Cuba under the ONBC, and then considering how these contradictory tendencies articulate with the Cuban political process.

The ONBC: Limiting Legal Practice

Under the *bufete colectivo* system attorneys normally cannot represent individual citizens without working through a *bufete colectivo*, although there are a few exceptions to this rule.[17] This means that the vast majority of attorneys serving the public are subject to the rules and guidelines established within the system of *bufetes colectivos*, rules that in many ways do not favor cause lawyering.

As previously indicated, the individual *bufetes colectivos* are organized under the auspices of the ONBC. The ONBC operates as a combined corporate headquarters and bar association for the practice of law in Cuba. Like a corporate home office, the ONBC sets forth detailed administrative guidelines to ensure common procedures among the *bufete colectivos*, sets uniform fees for legal services (subject to review by the Ministry of Justice), and serves as the central clearinghouse for both income and expenditures of the individual *bufetes colectivos*. In the manner of a bar association, the ONBC also determines the standards and ethical principles governing the practice of law and promotes the interests of attorneys. Also like a bar association it can discipline attorneys who fail to conform to its standards, up to and including prohibiting an attorney from working in a law collective, the functional equivalent of disbarment.

The ONBC is organized on a democratic-centralist model that mirrors the Marxist-Leninist principles of Cuba's wider system of political organization. The supreme rule-making body of the ONBC is a general assembly, which, according to law, consists of elected delegates representing between 10 and 20 percent of the total number of attorneys working in the individual *bufetes colectivos*. The assembly meets annually to elect the national directorate for the ONBC, to evaluate and adopt reports submitted by the directorate, and to approve rules, regulations, and technical and economic plans governing the practice of law in Cuba.[18]

The ONBC serves as a representative mechanism through which attorneys working in *bufetes colectivos* can articulate and pursue goals and interests related to the provision of legal services to the public. The ONBC, however, is not designed to primarily promote the private interests of attorneys. The ONBC and the lawyers it represents are integrated into the broader socialist goals of the government through the supervision (*alta inspección*) of the Ministry of Justice (MINJUS). As it develops policies for the operation of the individual law collectives and for the conduct of attorneys, the ONBC must consider, not only the private interests of attorneys and/or their clients but also with how the *bufetes colectivos* can fulfill their "social mission" of implementing and advancing socialist legality.[19] In an address to the National Assembly of the ONBC in 1985, the then minister of justice, Dr. Juan Escalona Reguera, described this relationship between the practice of law in Cuba and advancing the socialist goals of the revolution in the following way: "In our society when we speak of a professional ethic [for attorneys], we are referring to an ethic freed from the deformed burden of individualistic motivation and corporate egoism. . . . It is not possible to separate the ethic of a profession from the general ethic of a socialist society."[20]

The idea that the proper practice of law includes a politicized commitment to the general ideal of perfecting a socialist society contradicts the liberal-democratic ideal that attorneys should be politically neutral providers of professional services to individual clients. Within the Cuban context, however, law is not viewed as a neutral framework for the resolution of disputes arising primarily from civil conflicts and interpersonal injuries. Rather, law is conceived as a proactive instrument for the development of socialism. Thus, lawyers are expected to behave not only in their own interests, or those of their clients, but in the interests of the greater good of a socialist Cuba.

The earliest formal expression of this ideal of socialist lawyering in Cuban law was contained in Article 143 of the 1977 Law of Judicial Organization. This article defined the function of attorneys as "properly defending the interests of those they represent," but added the proviso that in doing so the attorney must "avoid abusing the legal guarantees of defense in ways that would impede the social functions of justice." The idea that attorneys are answerable first to a socialist standard of justice and secondly to the interests of their clients, was further emphasized in Resolution no. 938—the Regulation of Law Collectives and Code of Ethics for Attorneys was passed the following year. Article 3.2 of the 1978 regulations stipulated that one of the goals of the *bufetes colectivos* is to

> direct the professional practice of law so that it develops as an aid to the performance of courts and other authorities in the realization of justice and socialist legality.

The 1978 Code of Ethics repeated this ideology, by including "acting in a way that impedes justice from fulfilling its social function" in the list of failings that could result in disciplinary action being taken against an attorney.

Under the *bufete colectivo* system attorneys are expected to define their role as contributing to development of a socialist society, as well as representing the interests of their clients. This emphasis on practicing law in ways that are consistent with the socialist goals of the Cuban revolution narrows the space for cause lawyering by creating a presumption that attorneys who behave in opposition to Cuba's socialist principles are operating out of morally or politically unacceptable motivations. In the extreme, lawyers who aligned themselves with antisocialist social movements could be deprived of their right to participate in the *bufete colectivo* system, which is to say, deprived their right to practice law. The only attorneys I know of who were removed from the practice of law, however, were dismissed for demonstrably poor performance not political or ideological leanings. Nevertheless, the possibility remains that overt antigovernment lawyering could result in disciplinary action by the leadership of the ONBC under Cuba's socialist conception of appropriate conduct for attorneys. This possibility, even if rarely actualized, could have chilling effect on overtly antigovernment forms of cause lawyering—although, as previously mentioned, the legal and structural construction of Cuban society substantially reduces the likelihood of the kinds of social movements that generate clients for cause lawyers in the first place.

Overall, the ONBC system would appear to significantly restrain cause lawyering in Cuba. This assessment, however, must be tempered by the recognition that one of the central tasks of the ONBC is to ensure that attorneys practice law with a view toward promoting the collective rights associated with Cuba's socialist political economy. That is, the ONBC seeks to ensure that lawyers practice law with a conscious commitment to "doing good" for the society, and as Menkel-Meadow notes, the goal of "doing good" is a key component of cause lawyering.[21]

Organizational Openings for Change

Both the practical and the legal meaning of lawyering in ways that promote the development of "socialist legality" in Cuba have changed since the 1977 and 1978 laws were drafted. They have moved in the direction of providing more client-centered autonomy for attorneys—and of interest here—they have done so as the result of the political efforts of attorneys, acting through the ONBC and the Union of Cuban Jurists.

In June 1984, the Cuban Council of State adopted Decree-Law 81, "Concerning the Practice of Law and the National Organization of Bufete Colectivos." This decree-law replaced those sections of the 1977 law of judicial organization concerning the *bufetes colectivos*. Six months later, in accordance with this decree-law, MINJUS promulgated a modified set of regulations governing the *bufetes colectivos* that had been developed by the ONBC. Decree-Law 81 and the subsequent 1984 Resolution no. 142, Regulations Concerning the Exercise of Legal Practice and the National Organization of Law Collectives, refined the definition of legal practice, emphasized the autonomy of attorneys, and placed greater emphasis on the professional quality of legal services. Article 143 of the 1977 Law of Judicial Organization, for instance, defined the function of attorneys simply as "defending the interests of their clients before the courts." In contrast, Article 1 of the 1984 Decree-Law 81 declares: "The practice of law consists in carrying out consultations, and advising, representing, and defending the rights of a natural or juridical person before courts of justice, bodies of arbitration and administrative agencies." By elaborating a broader range of legal representation, Decree-Law 81 recognized the expanded professional role of attorneys in both the Cuban system of noncourt dispute resolution, and in the growing economic and administrative systems. Article 2 of the same law emphasized the autonomy of legal practice. It begins with the claim that "[t]he practice of law is free" and specifies that in exercising this function "the attorney is free and must obey only the law."[22]

The 1998 regulations echoed this support of an independent legal profession and directed attention to the specific professional competence of attorneys: "In the practice of law attorneys enjoy the guarantees established in law, and in light of these no one can interfere with the decisions of a technical character made under their responsibility."[23]

The newer law and associated regulations retained some of the earlier sentiment that the role of the attorney is intimately linked with the broader attainment of socialist justice. In a number of places, however, in comparison to the earlier laws, this concern with the "social mission" of attorneys was muted in favor of an emphasis on professional skills and responsibilities to clients. For instance, Article 2c of Decree-Law 81 states that attorneys "contribute to the realization of justice by means of their observance and strengthening of socialist legality." This emphasis on attorney's positive contributions to justice differs from the more negative sentiments expressed in the 1977 and 1978 laws, which focused on the need for attorneys to avoid practices that would *interfere* with socialist justice. In the new laws attorneys are enjoined to "keep up to date on legislation in force and their modifications and to continually improve their knowledge of the law,"[24] to "continually advance the technical quality of their services to the population,"[25] and to "defend the interests of those they represent with the greatest diligence."[26] While the list of disciplinary actions set forth in the 1984 regulations covers a multitude of professional wrongs that can be committed by attorneys working in *bufetes colectivos,* such as violating lawyer-client privilege, receiving payments outside the officially promulgated pay scale, and suborning perjury,[27] it omits less specific forms of wrongdoing such as "acting in a way that impedes justice from fulfilling its social function," a stipulation found in earlier regulations.[28] Overall the legislation governing legal practice in Cuba lacks the paternalistic attitude toward clients that was characteristic of laws governing legal practice in Eastern bloc nations. There is little in Cuban law comparable to the requirement that attorneys "*admonish* citizens to fulfill their obligations towards the socialist state and society"[29] (emphasis added) typical of Eastern European law regarding legal practice.

At the level of everyday practice the question of exactly how attorneys should go about balancing the interests of their clients with the obligation to observe and strengthen socialist legality is open to divergent interpretations. For instance, in a 1985 interview with an attorney who worked in a *bufete colectivo* (but not the one I later came to study in depth) espoused his view of the relationship between serving the interests of the society and serving the interests of clients this way: "If I work to have a client I know is guilty, found innocent, then I would not be serving the interests of justice. Neither the society nor the individual would receive what they need. If a man is guilty of a crime it means he has a social problem. My job is to see that he gets the social services he needs, and to see that he does not suffer punishment he does not deserve." Many of the attorneys who worked in the *bufete* where I was a participant observer, however, did not share this particular interpretation of their role in criminal cases. Attorneys repeatedly told me that if the accused is guilty, but the case presented by the prosecutor's office is too weak to generate a conviction because of inadequate preparation or poor investigative work, it was not their responsibility to help ensure a conviction. As one attorney said, "I'm here to defend my clients, not to help the state convict them." This sentiment was shared by a number of attorneys in the *bufete*. Moreover, several attorneys suggested that a vigorous defense resulting in an acquittal would do more to promote the long range-goal of improving socialist legality by serving notice on prosecutors and police that they will have to improve the quality of their work if they hope to win convictions.

The claim that they actively contest criminal charges is more than mere rhetoric. The attorneys working in the *bufete* achieved a much higher rate of "not guilty" verdicts (*absuelto*) than has been reported for their counterparts in other (formerly) socialist countries. Peter Solomon for instance, reports an acquittal rate in Soviet courts of first instance of 1 percent, and Robert Rand quotes a similar figure for 1988.[30] Inga Markovitz suggests that the reason for this apparent inability of Soviet attorneys to achieve acquittals is that under socialist law there is "no forum and no formal structure that a lawyer could exploit to the clients advantage."[31] In sharp contrast to this characteristic of socialist legality in Europe, my review of the outcomes of criminal cases contracted in the *bufete* during the 1988–89 period, and for a similar sample of cases contracted in 1991, revealed an overall acquittal rate of 28 percent for the earlier period and 31.5 percent for the latter. For instance, in 1991 31.8 percent of those charged with crimes of violence, 28 percent of property offenders, and 22 percent of those charged with state security violations were acquitted at trial.

These comparatively higher acquittal rates are the results, in large part, of the ability of Cuban attorneys, operating through the ONBC, to shape both the laws and the ethic governing legal practice in ways which gave them greater scope to defend their clients than was the case in the Soviet Union and other Eastern European socialist states. It may be overextending the idea of cause lawyering to claim that creating the conditions through which attorneys can provide reasonably effective criminal defense is an example of successful cause lawyering in Cuba. However, it is also true that many cause lawyers in liberal-democratic states historically have struggled to create or protect legal systems in which defendants have a reasonable chance of proving their innocence against state accusations. The success of Cuban attorneys in improving the efficacy of criminal defense can be equally understood as a case of successful cause lawyering.

I noted earlier that there were contradictory tendencies in the organizational structure of lawyering in Cuba. The changes in the laws governing legal practices are a particularly good example of this. The ONBC operates in many ways to constrain the activities of attorneys by enforcing socialist standards of legal practice. The ONBC structure, at the same time, provided attorneys with inroads into the political system that enabled them to promote the establishment of rules that redefined and liberalized what it meant to practice law in an appropriately *socialist* manner. What differs substantially in the Cuban case, as compared to cause law-yering in liberal-democratic societies, is that change was brought about, not through lawyerly litigation, but by lawyerly politics. In order to understand how changes that liberalized the ethic of legal practice in Cuba came about without pressure from anti–status quo organizations outside the government, and without litigation, necessitates an examination of the way in which democratic centralism and the politics of mass participation interact within the Cuban political system to produce social change.

The ONBC and the Cuban Political Process

While the ONBC is what is known as an "autonomous" organization within Cu-ba's political system there is, as previously noted, a high degree of integration and coordination among the leadership of the ONBC and the leadership of MINJUS, the Office of the Attorney General (*Fiscal General*), and the councils of state and government. This coordination facilitates a system of legal practice consistent with the government's ideology of socialist legality. It also enabled the interests of attor-neys to be heard within the halls of power.

The Communist Party is one of the key vectors in this process of mutual influence. High-level officials and functionaries of the ONBC, the Ministry of Jus-tice, and the Office of the Attorney General are usually (although not always) members of the Communist Party. Consequently, representatives from the ONBC, MINJUS, and the Office of the Attorney General have frequent opportunities to interact, share ideas, and exert mutual influence within the party councils and committees charged with developing policy related to the advancement of socialist legality, including the socialist practice of law.

A good example of the degree of coordination that exists between the ONBC and other organs of government is the creation of the Regulations and Code of Ethics governing the practice of law in Cuba. The 1977 Law of Judicial Organiza-tion specified that the practice of law would be governed by a set of regulations and a code of ethics to be established by attorneys and approved by MINJUS. On December 13, 1978, in response to this mandate, drafts entitled "Regulations Re-garding Law Collectives" and "Code of Ethics for the Practice of Law," both of which had been developed by a commission of attorneys empaneled for that pur-pose, were presented to and adopted by the inaugural meeting of the National Assembly of the ONBC. These regulations and codes, in turn, were adopted as law two weeks later by MINJUS in the form of Resolution 938 (Regulation of Law Collectives).

The rapidity with which the regulations and code of ethics that had been ratified by the ONBC assembly were subsequently adopted as law by MINJUS reflects the fact that by the time the draft rules and regulations had been submitted to the ONBC assembly, the ONBC draft committee and MINJUS had *already* arrived at a general agreement about the nature of these rules and regulations. An attorney who had been an officer of the ONBC at the time the regulations and ethics codes were established explained the rapid adoption of the regulations and code of ethics to me by saying that "the [draft] committee worked many hours with the Ministry [of Justice] to be sure they had a proposal everyone could accept." After several years of experience under the 1977 regulations a number of leading attorneys became concerned that the laws governing legal practice did not adequately reflect the complexity of legal practice in the *bufetes colectivos,* and were promoting poor quality, pro forma, legal services.[32] Acting through both the Communist Party and their contacts with the leadership of the Ministry of Justice and the Office of the Attorney General, the leadership of the ONBC was able to obtain authorization to redraft the regulations and code of ethics for attorneys.

In order to explore the implications of this process for the ability of Cuban attorneys to shape social policy, I need to digress briefly into a consideration of the fundamental tension between centralization and mass participation that has characterized Cuban political ideology and political practice since the 1959 revolution.

The revolutionary leaders who seized state power in 1959, although they expressed support for the liberal-democratic Cuban constitution of 1940, had little trust in multiparty electoral politics. In their view, electoral politics in Cuba had served as the tool of a dependent democracy to ensure that a small local elite aligned with the interests of U.S. business remained in control of the government, despite the appearance of public political participation. In place of electoral democracy the revolutionary leadership pursued a strategy of what they viewed as direct democracy based on mass participation. In his May Day speech of 1960 Castro outlined this vision of democracy: "Democracy is where the majority governs. Democracy is that form of government in which the majority is taken into account. Democracy is that form of government in which the interests of the majority are defended."[33] The practical manifestation of this vision of direct democracy was the formation of a variety of mass organizations including the People's Militia, the Federation of Cuban Women, the Committees for the Defense of the Revolution, the Association of Small Farmers, and the Congress of Cuban Trade Unions, all of which were designed to provide a public forum for debate and participation in the political affairs of daily life.

While direct democracy through the influence of mass organizations was the underlying political ideal of the revolution, the emergence of Cuban Communism was also shaped by a belief in the need for both a vanguard party to direct the revolutionary impulses of the working class and a commitment to central planning as the route to a rationalized system of socialist production and distribution. Within the Cuban model of democratic centralism, however, neither vanguard leadership nor central planners were viewed as unilateral decision makers. Rather, the Cuban model, in theory, sought to blend popular input through mass organizations with rationalized decision making and planning by state and party leaders. Liberal democratic critics of Cuban politics tend to focus on the centralist tendencies of the Cuban government and the Communist Party, often concluding that Cuba is a dictatorial state wherein all social policy is determined by a small party elite with Castro at its head. Conversely, Cuban leaders and their supporters tend to draw attention to the power of the people through mass organizations, nationwide discussions of issues such as those that preceded the Fourth Party Congress, and Cuba's elected Assemblies of People's Power as evidence of popular democracy.

Dichotomizing the Cuban system as either top-down or bottom-up underestimates the complexity of politics in that country. Understanding the dynamics of Cuban political processes requires attention to the interplay between tendencies toward centralization and the tendencies toward mass participation. As Lutjens notes, "Although the power of the socialist state is generally attributed to the centralization of decision making and the vast scope of state administration, it is ultimately the extent and nature of participation rather than formal structures that reveal the dynamics of power and the possibilities of democratization."[34] While the state and the party exercise broad decision-making powers that affect nearly all aspects of Cuban life, the exercise of this power depends upon and is shaped by support and participation from some substantial proportion of the population operating through mass organizations. Cuba's revolutionary leaders staked their legitimacy and that of Cuba's socialist system on the promise of providing avenues for popular sentiment to shape public policy. Without some semblance of adherence to this ideal, the legitimacy of the party, the Cuban socialist state, and the institutional frameworks it represents would be seriously threatened.[35]

What does this all-too-brief inquiry into Cuban political processes mean for the potentiality of cause lawyering in Cuba? Although the ONBC emerged later than the early institutions of mass organizations and was more narrowly focused on a single profession, like broader mass organizations it enables attorneys to enter into the dialogue between mass and vanguard that is the core of the Cuban political process. I have detailed the way in which this dialogic process generated a liberalization of the laws governing legal practice itself, and how those changes improved the ability for individuals to receive criminal defense. A similar process of lawyerly influence contributed to the passage of a new, more liberal criminal code in 1988 and the development of a new law of penal procedure that extended the rights of the accused to counsel. In both cases, attorneys acting through the ONBC and the Union of Cuban Jurists played important roles in stimulating these changes. While instances such as these are not equivalent to ideal-typical cause lawyering in support of social movements, they do suggest that, despite the absence of the liberal democratic conditions for cause lawyering, some Cuban attorneys are able to bring their social policy interests to bear on the government, in this case, not through litigation, but rather by exploiting the channels for influence created by Cuba's systems of dialogic mass politics.

Who Are Cuba's Cause Lawyers?

Not all lawyers in Cuba can be characterized as being devoted to a "cause," or building a professional life around "doing good." Rather, like lawyers elsewhere, Cuban attorneys vary considerably in terms of skill, energy, motivations, and commitment to principle. I would characterize some of the Cuban attorneys I observed during my field work as cause lawyers, and many others that I would not. Based on my observations I would divide Cuban attorneys into four types: aging revolutionaries, technical competents, professional entrepreneurs, and socialist activists.

Aging Revolutionaries. This groups of attorneys is the smallest among those currently practicing law in Cuba. They are the ones who made willing transitions from private legal practices prior to the revolution to the *bufete colectivo* system after. In some cases these attorneys had *affirmatively* turned their own legal practices into *bufetes colectivos* as an expression of their own revolutionary commitment. They reminisced about their role in creating public access to legal services, and their other contributions to the revolutionary transformation of Cuba, particularly during the era of radical experimentation during the 1960s and early 1970s. The aging revolutionaries in the *bufete* where my fieldwork took place openly articulated a honest commitment to the *bufete colectivo* system, actively participated in the *bufete's* Communist Party nucleus, and frequently expressed frustration with what they saw as a younger generation of less politically committed attorneys. These aging revolutionaries, however, showed the wear and tear of life lived in a revolutionary regime in a Third World country. Years of political work, evening and weekend meetings, and hot, crowded bus trips to and from court have taken their toll. For these attorneys, most of their struggles were in the past, and many of them were looking forward to eventual retirement.

Technical Competents. This group of Cuban attorneys was the largest in the *bufete* where I conducted my fieldwork. They understood the law, kept appointments with their clients, completed and submitted appropriate forms to promote their clients' cases in court, and they worked cooperatively with their colleagues. The technical competents tended to view their role more as a professional job than as a career. Their primary goal was to trade their skill in handling clients' problems for an income. The technical competents performed well and were generally interested in their clients. They did not, however, evince any particular *polit-*

ical commitment to their occupation or to the ideology (as opposed to the formal procedures) of socialist legality. They were generally supportive of the status quo legal order, but in a way that was more passive and accepting than proactive.

Professional Entrepreneurs. The professional entrepreneurs in the law collective aggressively pursued the practice of law as a *career.* They were energetic in their efforts to win appellate cases, which were both more prestigious, and more lucrative, under Cuba's payment scale for legal services. The professional entrepreneurs actively sought to increase their income by increasing the number of cases they handled. They also appeared to be more energetic in developing advantageous networks through their clients. Cuba's highly centralized system for the distribution of consumer goods meant that black and gray market transactions were important avenues to obtain scarce goods. The professional entrepreneurs tended to have the most extensive connections in this arena. They were the ones who always seemed to be able to say "I know someone" or "I have a cousin" when it came to discussing how to acquire some scarce commodity whether it was a ham, soap, or a motorcycle. The professional entrepreneurs also tended to be better dressed and have prized but scarce goods such as watches, color televisions, air conditioners, videocassette players, and stereos produced in the capitalist West rather than in Soviet bloc nations. When it came to organizational activities within the *bufete* the professional entrepreneurs were relatively quick to participate in or organize professional seminars, and they also tended to be very active in the Union of Cuban Jurists, the nation's professional association for lawyers, judges, and legal advisors. Most professional entrepreneurs were members of the Communist Party of Cuba, but their discussions led me to feel that their participation was motivated as much by the professional benefit to be gained from party membership as it was by a commitment to ideals.

Socialist Activists. These attorneys, representing about 15 to 20 percent of the law collective staff, were closest to being the socialist equivalent of cause lawyers. Most of them had selected lawyering as a career because they saw it as a chance to "do good" and had not lost that focus even, in some cases, after years of practice. As one of the them said to me, "After the first few years of the revolution, I knew we would need a new legal system, and I wanted to be part of that." Beyond working for their clients these socialist cause lawyers acted on their commitment to Cuban socialism in a number of other ways. They participated in activities of the Communist Party both in the *bufete* and at higher levels of organization, they tended to be active in their local committee for the defense of the revolution (CDR), held positions in or worked on projects for the ONBC, and served on various law-drafting commissions for various organs, including the Ministry of Justice and the National Assembly of People's Power. It was this latter work, in particular, that gave the socialist activists the opportunity to pursue their political commitments toward the construction of socialism in Cuba. The socialist activists also tended to be the most scholarly of the attorneys. They periodically taught in the law school at the University of Havana, and some of them were active scholars, writing articles for legal journals.

The socialist activist group cut across age lines, including middle-aged and youthful attorneys, and they were as likely to be women as men. It was from this group that the leadership of the law collective was normally selected. Because Cuba's revolutionary project is based on a conscious ideology of "perfecting" socialist forms of organization, few individuals are selected for leadership positions unless they have demonstrated a commitment to socialist practice. Under this regime then, socialist activists lawyers constitute the logical pool from which to draw leaders for the collective.

This Cuban pattern of selecting activists as administrators in the law collectives runs quite counter to the experience of activist attorneys in the United States. To be an open activist in the United States is to risk being relegated to the political margins. Activists are perceived as guided by "ideology." Ideology, in turn, is viewed as antithetical to the pragmatic and positivist approaches to social life that constitute core elements of capitalist culture in the United States. Thus, it may be that the image of cause lawyers as those operating outside of and frequently in opposition to the government reflects the relative political marginalization of cause lawyers in the United States more than it does an inherent characteristic of lawyers who devote themselves to a cause. The socialist activist lawyers in Cuba have devoted themselves the cause of social justice as understood from the perspective of socialism. The harmony between their view and that of the government, however, may obscure the progressive nature of their project and make them appear to be collaborationist attorneys rather than cause lawyers. In light of this, I suggest that when we consider the meaning and nature of cause lawyering it may be valuable to incorporate the full range of how lawyers can devote themselves to social change, rather than privilege only those who litigate against governments.

Dealing with Dissidents

This essay has focused on the ways in which attorneys have influenced progressive legal developments in Cuba. It has not yet addressed the more typical question regarding the role of lawyers in defending those targeted by the state for political crimes. I would like to turn to this question briefly because it is so often central to discussions of cause lawyering.

For all the reasons discussed, Cuba has very little in the way of independent, antistate social movements. Thus, there are relatively few movement activists for attorneys to defend or to identify with politically. As part of my research in the *bufete colectivo* in Havana, I closely examined a one-third sample of all cases handled there between May 1, 1988 and April 30, 1989. Out of these 281 cases, 20 involved violations of state security laws. Seven of these were prosecutions of attempts to leave the country without having completed the formal procedures for immigration (*salida ilegal*). Each of these cases involved individuals who attempted to reach Florida via a small craft, raft, or lash-up of inner tubes. One case involved the failure of a government official to enforce a legal order (*desobediencia*). The remaining twelve cases were charges for the offenses of *atentado* and *desacato*. These offenses involve disrespect for or physical or verbal attacks on governmental authorities. Some critics of Cuba have suggested to me that these statutes are used primarily to prosecute individuals for public opposition to the government. The particular cases in my sample, however, appeared to involve more ordinary acts of resisting arrest. In several cases they occurred along with a charge of *riña tumultaria*—best described as the late-night Saturday party that ended in a brawl—more suggestive of someone slugging a cop than overt political activity. While there may be instances of *desacato* and *atentado* being used to punish those who criticize government officials, I could not verify this from the cases handled in the law collective where my research took place. Within the total universe of criminal cases contracted during the period studied, there were two cases that did not surface in my one-third sample that were more distinctly political. One involved the printing and distribution of antigovernment literature. The other concerned an individual who gave what the government charged was false and damaging information to a foreign journalist. In both cases the individuals were convicted, although the attorneys argued for, and obtained, sentences lower than requested by the prosecutor.

Attitudes toward political cases and political defendants varied in the *bufete*. Most of the attorneys, including those who expressed dissatisfaction with other aspects of the Cuban political system, agreed that prosecution of people for attempting illegal departures was an unfortunate, but necessary activity. The position of the Cuban government at the time, and one that most of the attorneys agreed with, is that the problem of immigration from Cuba is not caused by the Cuban government's refusal to allow people to leave but by U.S. government policy. Attorneys argued that the U.S. government promotes illegal departures by, on the one hand, issuing very few legal entry visas, and on the other, providing immediate political asylum and economic benefit to anyone who "fled" Cuba in a boat, a raft, or a stolen aircraft. Some attorneys went so far as to argue that this policy was a cynical attempt by the U.S. government to stimulate illegal departures because of their propaganda value in the United States, a policy pursued with callous disregard for the many Cubans who would lose their lives somewhere in the Straits of Florida on their way to the promised asylum. Without efforts to keep people from risking dangerous voyages in ill-suited craft, these attorneys argued, the number of Cubans who would die attempting to reach Florida would rise precipitously. The accuracy of this interpretation was powerfully demonstrated in 1994 by the dramatic rise in both illegal departures and Cubans lost at sea when the Cuba's government temporarily ceased enforcing the laws against *salida ilegal*.

In the late 1980s attempts at illegal departures, if they were not associated with other crimes such as the theft of small boats or inner tubes from earth-moving equipment, were handled by courts as relatively minor crimes, with many individuals receiving the equivalent of probation, or a short jail (rather than prison) sentence. The courts were not nearly so lenient with those whose attempted departure involved other criminal activities. Nevertheless, most of the crimes associated with illegal departures, in the past, tended to be nonviolent. In 1992, however, the killing of two police officers by three Cubans attempting to steal a boat shocked many Cubans and revealed the increasing desperation of some Cubans as the island's economy struggled to adjust to a post-Soviet world and an intensification of the U.S. embargo.

On the question of prosecutions for overtly political acts such as "enemy propaganda," illegal operation of a printing press, or illegal demonstrations, the opinion was less uniform—and in this case, the age of attorneys appeared to make a difference. While, several of the older attorneys said that defendants in such cases deserved a competent defense, they expressed little sympathy with the causes represented by these types of offenders. Their view was formed around the belief that open, antigovernment activities were either instigated by the United States, or if not, at least served as welcome opportunities for the United States to fish in troubled waters in its efforts to bring an end to Cuban socialism. Several recent university graduates, on the other hand, tended to view the prosecution of individuals for disseminating either antigovernment publications or expressing anti-government opinions to the foreign press as both violations of rights to free speech and as outmoded expressions of a fortress mentality on the part of the Cuban government. While, as far as I knew, these attorneys were not linked to or involved with any antigovernment movements, they indicated that they would be quite willing to defend someone charged with antigovernment propaganda. They told this to me, however, in separate conversations outside of the confines of the law collective and expressly asked that their opinions not be shared with the other attorneys. This suggests that they suspected that public support for antigovernment activists could have career ramifications, particularly since they were still on probationary status in the law collective.

Unfortunately, the limited number of overtly political cases passing through the law collective makes it difficult to draw definite conclusions about the relationship between attorneys and antigovernment social activists. What is interesting, however, is the relatively small proportion of all cases handled by the law collective that were political in nature. This suggests that the combination of a social organization designed to channel public concerns into mass movements and the lack of a liberal-democratic structure in which to contest rights has resulted in very limited social movement activity in Cuba. While there have been a number of small human rights organizations in Cuba, they have not figured prominently either as change agents or as irritants in Cuba's legal scene. Most of the Cuban attorneys I knew who worked in Havana, arguably the center of political activity on the island, were generally unaware of, or assigned little significance to, these movements despite the considerable attention they have received in the United States. This lack of interest in independent political movements may be a reflection of the limited role such movements can play within Cuba's socialist, civil law system. To the extent that there are few avenues for independent social movements to deploy law and litigation to promote their goals, they did not appear, at least in the early 1990s, to capture the attention or imagination of Cuban attorneys.

Conclusion

Cause lawyering, as it is normally understood, takes place outside of the state when attorneys deploy litigation in support of social movements seeking to pressure the state to grant some rights claim. This form of lawyering is nearly impossible in Cuba for several reasons.

First, Cuban law is organized according to a code-based civil legal system heavily influenced by its Spanish heritage. Secondly, the Cuban system of political organization has worked to institutionalize all social movement impetus within the state and the revolution through the participation of officially sanctioned mass organizations. Third, the focus on *positive* rights rather than negative juridical ones does not provide the abstract framework for rights litigation. Fourth, the conditional nature of individual rights in Cuba and the channeling of social movement energy into officially endorsed mass organizations means there are few, if any, independent social movements with which cause lawyers can align themselves. Lastly, the rules and ethics governing legal practice require attorneys to be sensitive to the "social mission" of promoting socialist legality, thereby placing active identification with antisocialist activists outside the realm of appropriate lawyerly activity.

The current organization of politics in Cuba limits the opportunities for lawyers to engage in causes outside of the formal structure of political participation. Cuba's particular blend of vanguard politics, democratic centralism, and direct democracy through mass organizations, provides little space for independent social movements with which lawyers can affiliate. Activist lawyers—loosely defined as those with an interest in promoting some type of legal or social change—are, however, not without any opportunities for participation. The creation of the *bufetes colectivos* was the product of activist lawyers. In more recent years the development of legislation governing both legal practice and various elements of procedural law have been influenced by proactive attorneys. In particular, lawyers acting through the ONBC and the Union of Cuban Jurists played important roles in promoting a revised criminal code that lowered penalties overall and eliminated a number of offenses against the state, and in developing new laws of criminal procedure that permitted earlier participation by defense attorneys in criminal cases.

The question remains whether these activities should be considered cause lawyering. The view that cause lawyering occurs through litigation would preclude identifying the changes stimulated by Cuban attorneys as true cause lawyering. Alternatively, I would suggest there are multiple avenues through which attorneys by virtue of their privileged positions vis-à-vis law-making institutions can serve as proactive agents of legal and social change. Thus, it may be useful to distinguish between cause lawyering as a broad category of attorney activism and *cause litigating* as a specific activist strategy. This would permit us to view lawyerly activism with a broader lens, and to examine the relationship between this activism and the specific conditions that promote or retard the use of specific strategies for social change.

Examining the multiplicity of ways in which lawyers can serve as proactive agents of social change, other than as antigovernment litigators, may have particular value for analyzing the political-economic transformations under way in the formerly socialist states of Eastern Europe and in the newly emergent states of the former Soviet Union. It is likely that some lawyers who played activist, antigovernment roles under the now defunct socialist governments will be in positions to influence government policies under new regimes. Like the left-leaning attorneys under Batista who became influential under Castro, these attorneys may constitute progovernment contributors to a transformative political-economic process, not through litigation, but through other political uses of the lawyerly role.

In the final analysis, the case of Cuban attorneys suggests there are alternative routes to the goals typically associated with cause lawyering. It also suggests a need to conceptualize forms of lawyerly activism outside of the liberal-democratic image of the progressive litigant in exile from political power.

Notes

1. Austin Sarat and Stuart Scheingold, letter, July 25, 1992.
2. For examples, see in this volume Austin Sarat, "Between (the Presence of) Violence and (the Possibility of) Justice: Lawyering against Capital Punishment," chap. 11; Aaron Porter, "Norris, Schmidt, Green, Harris, Higginbotham & Associates: The Sociolegal Impact of Philadelphia Cause Lawyers," chap. 5; Stephen Meili, "Cause Lawyers and Social Movements: A Comparative Perspective on Democratic Change in Argentina and Brazil," chap. 15.
3. For examples, in this volume see Steve Ellman, "Cause Lawyering in the Third World," chap. 12; Ronen Shamir and Sara Chinski, "Destruction of Houses and Construction of a Cause: Lawyers and Bedouins in the Israeli Courts," chap. 8; Susan Sterret, "Caring about Individual Cases: Immigration Lawyering in Britain," chap. 10. See also Daniel S. Lev, "Lawyers' Causes in Indonesia and Malaysia," chap. 13.
4. See Robert M. Hayden, "Cultural Context and the Impact of Traffic Safety Legislation: The Reception of Mandatory Seatbelt Laws in Yugoslavia and Illinois," *Law and Society Review* 23, no. 2 (1989), 283–294 for a discussion of the comparison between bourgeois and socialist rights deployment strategies.

5. Both Menkel-Meadow and Sterret in this volume raise the possibility that certain types of government attorneys in the United States (e.g., environmental lawyers) and Britain (e.g., immigration lawyers) may also be considered as cause lawyers. Their comments, however, also suggest that these forms of cause lawyering do not fit the typical model of the cause lawyer.

6. Erica Fairchild, *Comparative Criminal Justice Systems* (Belmont, Calif.: Wadsworth, 1993).

7. Raymond Michalowski, "Erocentrism vs. Logocentrism in Human Rights: A Comparison of Cuba and the United States," *Humanity and Society* 17, no. 3 (1993), 251–271.

8. Constitution of the Republic of Cuba, art. 8b.

9. Ibid., art. 38e.

10. Ibid., art. 55.

11. Ibid., art. 57.

12. I began researching Cuban legal processes in 1985. In 1989 I undertook participant observation in a law collective in Havana. I then returned for follow-up periods in the law collective in 1990, 1991, 1992, and 1993.

13. For more detailed discussions of the development of Cuba's socialist legal system see Max Azicri, "Crime, Penal Law, and the Cuban Revolutionary Process, *Crime and Social Justice,* no. 23 (1987), 51–79; Michael Bogdan, "Thirty Years of Cuban Revolutionary Law," *Review of Socialist Law,* no. 4 (1989), 319–332; James Brady, "The Transformation of Law under Socialism," *Insurgent Sociologist,* 10, no. 4 (Summer–Fall 1981), 5–24; Robert Cantor, "New Laws for a New Society," *Crime and Social Justice,* no. 2 (1974), 12–23; Debra Evenson, "The Changing Role of Law in Revolutionary Cuba," in S. Halebsky and J. Kirk, eds., *Transformation and Struggle: Cuba Faces the 1990s* (New York: Praeger, 1991), 53–65; Raúl Gómez Treto, "Thirty Years of Cuban Revolutionary Cuban Penal Law," paper presented at the conference entitled "Thirty Years of Cuban Revolution," Halifax, Nova Scotia, June 1989; Luis Salas, *Social Control and Deviance in Cuba* (New York: Praeger, 1979); Luis Salas, "Emergence and Decline of Cuban Popular Tribunals," *Law and Society Review* 17 (1983), 588–612; Adele van der Plass, *Revolution and Criminal Justice: The Cuban Experiment, 1959–1983* (The Hague: FORIS, 1987).

14. Ley no. 4 (1977), *Ley de Organización del Sistema Judicial.*

15. Evenson, "The Changing Role of Law in Revolutionary Cuba," 8.

16. Dr. Ana Belkis Pupo was the director of the *bufete* when I began my field work there in 1989. She remained in that position until 1991 when she assumed the leadership of a new law collective. I conducted a number of formal taped interviews with her, as well as sharing numerous informal conversations. This particular comment is from an interview conducted on June 17, 1990.

17. In addition to the *abogados* who represent individual citizens, there is another category of lawyers in Cuba known as *asesores.* Lawyers serve as *asesores* when they work as legal counsel for various economic entities, or governmental agencies. These attorneys can appear in court to represent their organizations without belonging to a *bufete colectivo.* The majority of disputes involving formal organizations or agencies, however, are handled in nonjudicial formats. Consequently, *asesores* are not regular actors in the typical courtroom work group.

18. *Resolución* no. 142 (1984), Reglamento sobre el Ejercicio de la Abogacia y la Organización de Bufetes Colectivos, art. 13.

19. Juan Escalona Reguera, "*Palabras de Apertura de la Asamblea,*" ONBC, Havana, (1985) 9.

20. Ibid., 10.

21. Menkel-Meadow, "The Causes of Cause Lawyering."

22. *Decreto-Ley* no. 81 (1984), Sobre el Ejercicio de la Abogacía y la Organización Nacional de Bufetes Colectivos, *capítulo* 1, art. 2a.

23. *Resolución* no. 142 (1984), Reglamento sobre el Ejercicio de la Abogacía y la Organización de Bufetes Colectivos, *capítulo* 1, art. 2.

24. *Decreto-Ley* no. 81, art. 2.

25. *Resolución* no. 142, art. 5e.

26. Ibid., art. 34b.

27. Ibid., art. 59-1a, 59-3c, 59-3d.

28. ONBC *Resolución, Código de Ética* (1978), art. 2-10.

29. Inga Markovitz, "Law and Glasnost: Some Thoughts about the Future of Judicial Review under Socialism," *Law and Society Review* 23, no. 3 (1989), 399–438.

30. Robert Rand, *Comrade Lawyer* (Boulder, Colo.: Westview Press, 1991); Peter Solomon, "The Case of the Vanishing Acquittal: Informal Norms and the Practice of Soviet Criminal Justice," *Soviet Studies* 39, no. 4 (1987), 531–555.

31. Markovitz, "Law and Glasnost," 401.

32. Victor Kautzman, interview, April 20, 1989.

33. Fidel Castro, "This Is Democracy," speech, May 1, 1960. In *Fidel Castro: Speeches,* vol. 3, *Building Socialism* (New York: Pathfinder Press, 1983), 32.

34. Sheryl Lutjens, "Democracy in Socialist Cuba," in Halebsky and Kirk, eds., *Transformation and Struggle,* 67.

35. The economic crisis that ensued after Cuba lost its socialist trading partners and the government's difficulty in responding to popular demands for a solution could eventually lead to just such an erosion of legitimacy of the Cuba's socialist state.

Select Bibliography

Abbott, Andrew. *The System of Professions*. Chicago: University of Chicago Press, 1988.

Abel, Richard. "Lawyers." In *Law and the Social Sciences*, ed. Leon Lipson and Stanton Wheeler. New York: Russell Sage, 1987.

———. "Lawyers and the Decline of Professionalism." *Modern Law Review* 49 (1986), 1–41.

———. *Politics by Other Means: Law in the Struggle against Apartheid, 1980–1994*. New York: Routledge, 1995.

———. "Socializing the Legal Profession: Can Redistributing Lawyers' Services Achieve Social Justice?" *Law and Policy Quarterly* 1 (1979), 5–167.

———. "The Transformation of the American Legal Profession," *Law and Society Review* 20 (1986), 7–17.

———. "Why Does the American Bar Association Promulgate Ethical Rules?" *Texas Law Review* 59 (1981), 639–688.

———, ed. "Lawyers and the Power to Change." *Law and Policy* 7 (special issue) (1985), 5–18.

Abrams, Kathryn. "Lawyers and Social Change Lawbreaking: Confronting a Plural Bar." *University of Pittsburgh Law Review* 52 (1991), 753–783.

Alfieri, Anthony. "Disabled Clients, Disabling Lawyers." *Hasting Law Journal* 43 (1992), 769–851.

———. "Mitigation, Mercy, and Delay: The Moral Politics of Death Penalty Abolitionists." *Harvard Civil Rights–Civil Liberties Law Review* 31 (1996), 325–351.

———. "Reconstructive Poverty Law Practice: Learning Lessons of Client Narrative." *Yale Law Journal* 100 (1991), 2107–2147.

Allen, Francis A. *The Crime of Politics: Political Dimensions of Criminal Justice*. Cambridge, Mass.: Harvard University Press, 1974.

American Bar Association Commission on Professionalism. *"In the Spirit of Public Service": A Blueprint for the Rekindling of Lawyer Professionalism*. Chicago: ABA Commission, 1986.

Ankar, Aharon. "Public Interest Litigation and the Professional Ethics of Lawyers." *Ha'-Praklit* 34 (1982), 403–412 (in Hebrew).

Arbogast, Rebecca, et al. "Revitalizing Public Interest Lawyering in the 1990's: The Story of One Effort to Address the Problem of Homelessness." *Howard Law Journal* 34 (1991), 91–113.

Arriola, Anita P., and Sidney M. Wolinsky. "Public Interest Practice in Practice: The Law and Reality." *Hastings Law Journal* 34 (1983), 1207–1224.

Auerbach, Jerold S. *Unequal Justice: Lawyers and Social Change in Modern America*. New York: Oxford Univrsity Press, 1976.

Bachmann, Steve. "Lawyers, Law, and Social Change." *New York University Review of Law and Social Change* 13 (1984–85), 1–50.

Balbus, Isaac. *The Dialectics of Legal Repression: Black Rebels before American Courts*. New York: Russell Sage, 1973.

Barkan, Steven E. *Protesters on Trial: Criminal Justice in the Southern Civil Rights and Vietnam Antiwar Movements*. New Brunswick, N.J.: Rutgers University Press, 1985.

Becker, Theodore L., ed. *Political Trials*. New York: Bobbs-Merrill, 1971.

Belknap, Michael R., ed. *American Political Trials*. Rev. and expanded ed. Westport, Conn.: Greenwood Press, 1994.

Bell, Derrick. "Serving Two Masters: Integration Ideals and Client Interests in School Desegregation Litigation." *Yale Law Journal* 85 (1976), 470–516.

Bisharat, George. *Palestinian Lawyers and Israeli Rule: Law and Disorder in the West Bank*. Austin: University of Texas Press, 1989.

Blaser, Arthur W. "Human Rights in the Third World and Development of International Nongovernmental Organizations." In *Human Rights and Third World Development*, ed. George W. Shepherd Jr. and Ved P. I. Nanda. Westport, Conn.: Greenwood Press, 1985.

Bogart, William A. *Courts and Country: The Limits of Litigation and Social and Political Life of Canada*. New York: Oxford University Press, 1994.

Brandeis, Louis. "The Opportunity in Law." In *Business—A Profession*. Boston: Hale, Cushman and Flint, 1933.

Bumiller, Kristin. *The Civil Rights Society: The Social Construction of Victims*. Baltimore, Md.: Johns Hopkins University Press, 1988.

Cahn, Edgar S. and Jean C. Cahn. "The War on Poverty: A Civilian Perspective." *Yale Law Journal* 73 (1964), 1317–1352.

Cain, Maureen, and Christine Harrington, eds. *Lawyers in a Postmodern World*. Birmingham, United Kingdom: Open University Press, 1994.

Carlin, Jerome E., Jan Howard and Sheldon L. Messinger. *Civil Justice and the Poor: Issues for Sociological Research*. New York: Russell Sage Foundation, 1967.

Casper, Jonathan D. *Lawyers before the Warren Court: Civil Liberties and Civil Rights, 1957–1966*. Urbana: University of Illinois Press, 1972.

Coles, Robert. *The Call of Service: A Witness to Idealism*. Boston: Houghton Mifflin, 1993.

Cooper, Jeremy, and Rajeev Dhavan, eds. *Public Interest Law*. Oxford: Basil Blackwell, 1986.

Davis, Dennis. "Violence and the Law: The Use of the Censure in Political Trials in South Africa." In *Political Violence and the Struggle in South Africa*, ed. N. Chabani Manganyi and Andre du Toit. London: Macmillan, 1990.

Delgado, Richard, and Jean Stefancic. *Failed Revolutions: Social Reform and the Limits of Legal Imagination*. Boulder, Colo.: Westview Press, 1994.

Edelman, Murray. *The Symbolic Uses of Politics*. Urbana: University of Illinois Press, 1964.

Ellmann, Stephen. *In a Time of Trouble: Law and Liberty in South Africa's State of Emergency*. Oxford: Clarendon Press, 1992.

Erlanger, Howard S. "Young Lawyers and Work in the Public Interest," *American Bar Foundation Research Journal* 1978 (1978), 83–104.

Escobar, Arturo, and Sonia E. Alvarez, eds. *The Making of Social Movements in Latin America: Identity, Strategy, and Democracy*. Boulder, Colo.: Westview Press, 1992.

Evenson, Debra. *Revolution in the Balance: Law and Society in Contemporary Cuba*. Boulder, Colo.: Westview Press, 1994.

Feinrider, Martin. "Judicial Review and the Protection of Human Rights under Military Governments in Brazil and Argentina." *Suffolk Transnational Law Journal* 5, no. 2 (1981) 171–199.

Finkielkraut, Alain. *Remembering in Vain: The Klaus Barbie Trial and Crimes against Humanity*. New York: Columbia University Press, 1992.

Fitzpatrick, Peter. "Law as Resistance." In *The Critical Lawyers' Handbook*, ed. Ian Grigg-Spall and Paddy Ireland. London: Pluto Press, 1992.

Freire, Paolo. *Pedagogy of the Oppressed.* Trans. Myra Bergman Ramos. New York: Continuum, 1972.

Gabel, Peter, and Paul Harris. "Building Power and Breaking Images: Critical Legal Theory and the Practice of Law." *New York University Review of Law and Social Change* 11 (1983), 369–411.

Galanter, Marc. "Why the 'Haves' Come Out Ahead: Speculations on the Limits of Legal Change." *Law and Society Review* 9 (1974), 95–160.

Gordon, Robert. "The Ideal and the Actual." In *The New High Priests: Lawyers in Post-Civil War America,* ed. G. Gawalt. Westport, Conn.: Greenwood Prss, 1984.

———. "The Independence of Lawyers." *Boston University Law Review* 68 (1988), 1–83.

———. "Legal Thought and Legal Practice in the Age of the American Enterprise, 1870–1920." In *Professions and Professional Ideologies in America,* ed. G. Geison. Chapel Hill: University of North Carolina Press, 1983.

Gordon, Robert, and Simon, William. "The Redemption of Professionalism." In *Lawyers' Ideals/Lawyers' Practices.* ed. Robert L. Nelson, David M. Trubek, and Raymond L. Solomon. Ithaca, N.Y.: Cornell University Press, 1992.

Greenberg, Jack. *Crusaders in the Courts: How a Dedicated Band of Lawyers Fought for the Civil Rights Revolution.* New York: Basic Books, 1994.

Hain, Peter. *Political Trials in Britain.* London: Allen Lane, 1984.

Hajjar, Lisa. "Authority, Resistance, and Law: The Israeli Military Courts in the Occupied Territories." Ph.D Diss., American University, 1995.

Handler, Joel F. "Postmodernism, Protest and the New Social Movements," *Law and Society Review* 26 (1993), 697–732.

———. *Social Movements and the Legal System.* New York: Academic Press, 1978.

Handler, Joel F., Ellen Jane Hollingsworth, and Howard S. Erlanger. *Lawyers and the Pursuit of Legal Rights.* New York: Academic Press, 1978.

Hicks, Neil. *Lawyers and the Military Justice System of the Israeli Occupied Territories.* New York: Lawyers Committee for Human Rights, 1992.

Hunt, Alan. "Rights and Social Movements: Counter-Hegemonic Strategies." *Journal of Law and Society* 17 (1990), 309–328.

Hutchinson, Allan, and Patrick Monahan. *The Rule of Law: Ideal or Ideology.* Toronto: Carswell, 1987.

Illich, Ivan. *Disabling Professions.* London: Marion Boyers, 1977.

Jack, Rand, and Dana C. Jack. *Moral Vision and Professional Decisions: The Changing Values of Women and Men Lawyers.* New York: Cambridge University Press, 1989.

Katz, Jack. *Poor People's Lawyers in Transition.* New Brunswick, N.J.: Rutgers University Press, 1982.

Kelly, Michael J. *Lives of Lawyers.* Ann Arbor: University of Michigan Press, 1994.

Kinoy, Arthur. *Rights on Trial: The Odyssey of a People's Lawyer.* Cambridge, Mass.: Harvard University Press, 1983.

Kirchheimer, Otto. *Political Justice: The Use of Legal Procedure for Political Ends.* Princeton, N.J.: Princeton University Press, 1961.

Kluger, Richard. *Simple Justice: The History of* Brown v. Board of Education *and Black America's Struggle for Equality.* New York: Vintage, 1975.

Kronman, Anthony T. *The Lost Lawyer: Failing Ideals of the Legal Profession.* Cambridge: Belknap Press of Harvard University Press, 1993.

Larson, Magali. *The Rise of Professionalism.* Berkeley: University of California Press, 1977.

Lawrence, Susan E. *The Poor in Court: The Legal Services Program and Supreme Court Decision Making.* Princeton, N.J.: Princeton University Press, 1990.

Lawyers Committee for Human Rights. *Shackling the Defenders: Legal Restrictions on Independent Human Rights Advocacy Worldwide.* New York: Lawyers Committee for Human Rights, 1994.

Lev, Daniel S. "Social Movements, Constitutionalism, and Human Rights: Comments from the Malaysian and Indonesian Experiences." In *Constitutionalism and Democracy: Transitions in the Contemporary World,* ed. Douglas Greenberg, et al. New York: Oxford University Press, 1993.

Lippman, Matthew, "They Shoot Lawyers, Don't They?: Law in the Third Reich and the Global Threat to the Independence of the Judiciary." *California Western International Law Journal* 23 (1993), 257–318.

Lopez, Gerald. *Rebellious Lawyering: One Chicano's Vision of Progressive Law Practice.* Boulder, Colo.: Westview Press, 1992.

Luban, David. *Lawyers and Justice: An Ethical Study.* Princeton, N.J.: Princeton University Press, 1988.

McCann, Michael W. *Rights at Work: Pay Equity Reform and the Politics of Legal Mobilization.* Chicago: University of Chicago Press, 1994.

Margulies, Peter. "Progressive Lawyering and Lost Traditions," *Texas Law Review* 73 (1995), 1139–1183.

Meili, Stephen. "The Interaction between Lawyers and Grass Roots Movements in Brazil." *Beyond Law* (July 1993), 61.

Meltsner, Michael. *Cruel and Unusual: The Supreme Court and Capital Punishment.* New York, Random House, 1973.

Milner, Neal. "The Dilemmas of Legal Mobilization: Ideologies and Strategies of Mental Patient Liberation." *Law and Policy* 8 (1986), 105–129.

Minow, Martha. "Breaking the Law: Lawyers and Clients in Struggles for Social Change." *University of Pittsburgh Law Review* 52 (1991), 723–751.

———. "Political Lawyering: An Introduction." *Harvard Civil Rights–Civil Liberties Law Review* 31 (1996), 287–296.

Neier, Aryeh. *Only Judgment: The Limits of Litigation in Social Change.* Middletown, Conn.: Wesleyan University Press, 1982.

Ogletree, Charles. "Beyond Justification: Seeking Motivations to Sustain Public Defenders." *Harvard Law Review* 106 (1993), 1239–1294.

Olson, Susan. *Clients and Lawyers: Securing the Rights of Disabled Persons,* Westport, Conn.: Greenwood Press, 1984.

Osiel, Mark J. "Dialogue with Dictators: Judicial Resistance in Argentina and Brazil." *Law and Social Inquiry* 20 (1995), 481–560.

Rabin, Robert L. "Lawyers for Social Change: Perspectives on Public Interest Law." *Stanford Law Review* 28 (1976), 207–261.

Rhode, Deborah. "Class Conflicts in Class Actions." *Stanford Law Review* 34 (1982), 1183–1262.

Rosenberg, Gerald. *The Hollow Hope: Can Courts Bring about Social Change?* Chicago: Chicago University Press, 1991.

Sarat, Austin. " '. . . The Law Is All Over': Power, Resistance and the Legal Consciousness of the Welfare Poor." *Yale Journal of Law and the Humanities* 2 (1990), 343–379.

———. "Narrative Strategy and Death Penalty Advocacy." *Harvard Civil Rights–Civil Liberties Law Review* 31 (1996), 353–382.

Scheingold, Stuart. *The Politics of Rights: Lawyers, Public Policy, and Political Change.* New Haven, Conn.: Yale University Press, 1974.

———. "Radical Lawyers and Socialist Ideals." *Journal of Law and Society* 15 (1988), 122–138.

Shamir, Ronen. "Litigation as Consummatory Action: The Instrumental Paradigm Reconsidered." *Studies in Law, Politics and Society* 11 (1991), 41–68.

Shklar, Judith. *Legalism.* Cambridge, Mass.: Harvard University Press, 1964.

Simon, William. "The Ideology of Advocacy," *Wisconsin Law Review,* 1978 (1978), 30–144.

———. "Visions of Practice in Legal Thought," *Stanford Law Review* 36 (1984), 469–507.

Sparer, Ed. "Fundamental Human Rights, Legal Entitlements and the Social Struggle: A Friendly Critique of the Critical Legal Studies Movement." *Stanford Law Review* 36 (1984), 509–574.

Spillenger, Clyde. "Elusive Advocate: Reconsidering Brandeis as People's Lawyer." *Yale Law Journal* 105 (1996), 1445–1535.

Stover, Robert V. *Making It and Breaking It: The Fate of Public Interest Commitment during Law School.* Urbana: University of Illinois Press, 1989.

Thompson, E. P. *Whigs and Hunters: The Origins of the Black Act.* New York: Pantheon, 1975.

Tremblay, Paul R. "Rebellious Lawyering, Regnant Lawyering, and Street-Level Bureaucracy." *Hasting Law Journal* 43 (1992), 947–970.

Tushnet, Mark V. *The NAACP's Legal Strategy against Segregated Education.* Chapel Hill: University of North Carolina Press, 1987.

Unger, Roberto. *Politics* vol. I, *False Necessity.* New York: Cambridge University Press, 1987.

Wexler, Stephen. "Practicing Law for Poor People." *Yale Law Journal* 79 (1970), 1049–1067.

White, Lucie. "Subordination, Rhetorical Survival Skills, and Sunday Shoes: Notes on the Hearing of Mrs. G." *Buffalo Law Review* 38 (1990), 1–58.

Wizner, Stephen. "Homelessness: Advocacy and Social Policy." *University of Miami Law Review* 45 (1990–91), 387–405.

Index

Abas, Irad, 247–48, 252, 254
Abel, Richard, 155
ACLU. *See* American Civil Liberties Union
ACRI (Association for Civil Rights; Israel),
    411–12n. 178
Act Up, 136
advice, 376–78
African American lawyers, 151–68, 171–76,
    357
    and contemporary race relations, 168–71
African Americans, 158–59, 164, 169–70, 174,
    175, 210, 364
Alfonsín, Raul, 503–4, 516n. 59
Al-haqq/LSM, 464–67
Allen, Macon B., 156
Allport, Gordon, 172
alternative dispute resolution, 414n. 202
alternative lawyering, 350, 359–61, 364, 404n.
    135
altruism, 37–42, 45, 59n. 56, 61n. 85
ameliorative activities, 8
American Bar Association, 42
American Civil Liberties Union, 43, 133, 140,
    143, 355
American Lawyers (Abel), 155
Amnesty International, 357, 391n. 50
animal rights movement, 264–65, 269–75,
    278, 281, 283, 285
An-Na'im, Abdullahi, 395n. 74
apartheid, 72, 382
Argentina, 487–504, 507–22
Arns, Cardinal Dom Paulo Evaristo, 510
attorneys. *See* legal profession
authoritarian regimes, 6
AWARE (Action for Welfare and Awakening
    in Rural Environment; India), 378–
    80, 416n. 216
Ayash, Jamia Salah Abu, 232–33

Bach, Justice, 253
Badhwar, Neera Kapur, 41

Bakhtaur Singh case, 307
Balancing the Scales of Justice, 202
Balchin, Olive, 85
Baldwin, Roger, 365
Bangladesh, 355
bar associations, 217–18, 508
Beckwith, Byron de la, 90
Bedouins, 34, 227–57
Bell, Derrick, 170
Bentley, Derek, 81
Bhatia case, 309
Birmingham Six, 82, 84, 85, 91, 92
Blackmun, Harry, 327, 339
blacks. *See* African Americans
Blakelock, Keith, 84
Bohmer, Martin, 499
Bolden v. Pennsylvania State Police, 167
Bousquet, René, 100–101
Brandeis, Louis, 43, 202
Brazil, 365, 415n. 215, 487–502, 504–22
Britain. *See* Great Britain
Brogden, Henry, 161
Brown, Homer, 161
Brown, William H. III, 152, 166, 167–68
Brown v. Board of Education, 365
Buchanan, Ruth, 204
bufetes colectivos, 527–33, 537

"cab rank" rule, 79, 96
Callow, Keith, 88
Campilongo, Celso, 498, 499, 508, 509
capital punishment, 317–46
    bearing witness and writing history, 322–
        24
    contemporary legal and political context,
        319–22
    democratic optimism, 338–39
    evil of, 324–29
    as here to stay, 329–31
    lawyering in losing cause, 331–38
    in Nigeria, 365

capital punishment (*continued*)
  pushing ethical limits, 333–35
  redefining success, 331–33
Carey, Susan, 214
Carrió, Alejandro, 493, 503, 508, 509
Carsen, Octavio, 489, 496, 497, 498, 501, 506
Carter, Jimmy, 353
Catholic Church, 510–11
cause, concept of, 231
cause lawyering, 157–58
  in Argentina and Brazil, 487–522
  causes, 31–68, 231
  commitment to, 48–51
  in Cuba, 523–45
  definition of, 33–37, 51–53
  and democratic project, 8–10
  demographics of, 371–73
  for disadvantaged, 175, 181–200
  and executive power, 86
  in Indonesia and Malaysia, 431–52
  in Israeli-occupied territories, 453–86
  and judiciary, 95
  left-activist, 118–48
  and legislatures, 77
  makings of cause lawyer, 31–33, 173
  motivations, 37–51, 191–94, 501
  parameters, 5–8
  poverty, 196–98
  professional support for, 367–69
  and reproduction of professional
      authority, 3–25
  social movement, 9, 261–92, 487–522
  Third World, 349–430
  through institutional analysis, 174
  See also critical lawyering; public interest
      law
CESPAD (El Salvadoran organization),
      422n. 253, 424n. 274
Chambers, Julius, 355
Chapin, Stuart, 154
Chaskalson, Arthur, 367
China, 92
Christie, John, 81
churches, 164–65, 510–11
CISALP (Argentinian organization), 491
civil disobedience, 138
civil law systems, 6, 35
civil rights, 159, 164
Civil Rights Act of 1965, 72

civil rights movement, 43, 169
Clarke, Eugene, 160
class action suits, 184, 189
clearinghouses, 510
client(s)
  empowerment at microsites, 9–10
  impact of lawyers' advice, 376–78
  individual, 183–84, 188
  lawyer collaboration, 211–13
  lawyer relationship, 274–76
  needy, 97
  Third World, 369–84
client voice lawyering, 186, 191
Coles, Robert, 43
collective action, 210–11
collective bargaining, 268–69
collectivities, 195
Colombia, 374
commitment, 38, 48–51
Committee of Arab Lawyers, 465–66
common law systems, 6, 35
Commonwealth vs. Local 542, 166
Communist regimes, 80
community action, 210–11
community legal education, 373–76
community organizing, 378–84, 426n. 288
Conlon, Gerald, 84
constitutions, Latin American, 517n. 64
Cornell, Drucilla, 318, 322, 324
courts. *See* judiciary
Couto e Silva, Golbery do, 504
Cover, Robert, 318, 322–23
critical lawyering, 9, 201–2, 203–5, 220–26
  private practice, 205–7
  social concerns, 207–11
  transformative aspects, 207–16
  viability of practices, 216–20
criticism, 236
Cuba, 34, 92, 523–45
Curiel, Alicia, 489–90, 493, 497, 502, 503,
      505, 506, 507, 510, 511

Dalyell, Tom, 93
Davis, Angela, 418n. 228
Dayan, Moshe, 227
death penalty. *See* capital punishment
Declining Significance of Race, The (Wilson),
      170
de Klerk, F. W., 83

delaying tactics, 240
democracy, 72
Democracy in America (Tocqueville), 156
democratic project, 8–10
demographics, of cause lawyering, 371–73
Denning, Lord, 92
Dharsono, Lt. Gen., 440
Díaz Rodríguez, Francisco, 363, 402n. 119, 422n. 253, 422n. 255
Dieng, Adama, 356
Diplock Courts, 87, 90
disadvantaged groups, 48, 49
    cause lawyering for in Pittsburgh, 181–200
    See also Third World cause lawyering
discrimination
    against African Americans, 168–70, 178n. 35, 178–79n. 46
    against Bedouins, 244–45
    in India, 364
districting, 72
divorce, 291n. 55
DOAL (Mexican organization), 409n. 165, 423n. 272
domestic violence, 49
domination, lawyer, 274, 289n. 12
Du Bois, W. E. B., 161
due process, 48

Earth First!, 136
ECHR. *See* European Court on Human Rights
education. *See* community legal education; law school
EEOC. *See* Equal Employment Opportunity Commission
El Centro (law firm), 205, 207, 208, 209, 210, 215, 218, 220
electoral process, 71–74
Elon Moreh case, 460
El Salvador, 363, 381, 402n. 119
    See also CESPAD
El-Sanaa case, 241–42
eminent domain, 166
empathy, 37–42, 60n. 66, 60n. 69, 61n. 80, 64n. 119
Equal Employment Opportunity Commission, 168, 169
equality, 9

European Convention on Human Rights, 293
European Court on Human Rights, 293, 294, 295, 302–3
Evans, Timothy, 81
evil, 31, 32
executive, 77–95

Falana, Femi, 365
family law, 208, 216
Faria, Jose Eduardo, 496, 507
Feagin, Joe, 170–71
fee structures, 209
finances
    funding of firms, 218–19
    lawyers' personal income, 129–30, 219, 415–16n. 216
    in private practice, 138
    Third World cause lawyering, 353–54
Fitzpatrick, Peter, 124
Fogelman, Eve, 38–39, 40
Ford Foundation, 349, 354, 357
France, 100–101
France, Anatole, 69
Freire, Paolo, 360, 382, 400n. 100, 427–28n. 317
Friedman, Milton, 77
Furman v. Georgia, 319–20

Galston, William, 41
Garcia, Julio, 499
Garvey, Marcus, 163, 172
Gaza Strip, 453–86
gender, 64n. 119
Genie, Jean Paul, 101
Genovese, Kitty, 38, 51, 65n. 131
gerrymandering, 72
Ginsburg, Ruth Bader, 44
Goies (Brazil), 492
Gomez, Orlando, 497
good, 31, 32, 35, 39
Gordon, Milton M., 169
Goulart, João, 504
Great Britain
    immigration lawyering in, 293–316
    judiciary, 87, 91
    legislature, 74, 75, 76
    media, 93
    police, 82, 84–85

Great Britain (*continued*)
  prosecutorial function, 79, 81
  See also Northern Ireland
Green, Clifford Scott, 151, 161, 164–65, 166,
    167, 174
Greenberg, Jack, 320, 355, 418n. 228
Greenfield, Albert M., 163
Gregg v. Georgia, 320
group representation, 425n. 280, 425n. 281
Guided Democracy (Indonesia), 434–35
Guildford Four, 84, 91–92
Guinier, Lani, 72, 74, 171

Hale, William, 152
Hall, William F., Jr., 151
Harris, Doris Mae, 151, 161, 166, 168
Harris, Robert Alton, 321, 333
Hastie, William Henry, 161
Henry, Ed, 161
Herzog, Vladimir, 508
Hien, Yap Thiam, 438
Higginbotham, A. Leon, Jr., 151, 161, 162, 163,
    164, 165, 166–67, 168, 174
Hill, Anita, 49
hired guns, 279, 280–81
Hobhouse, L., 154
Holocaust, 31, 32, 39, 40, 51
Houston, Charles Hamilton, 158–59
Hughes, Langston, 171
human rights
  activism, 350
  generalized education, 420n. 237
  international culture, 351–61
  international law, 365
  See also Third World cause lawyering;
    specific countries
Human Rights Internet, 396n. 85
Human Rights Watch/Africa, 395n. 74
Hungria, Nelson, 496
Huq, Fazlul, 350
Hurd, Douglas, 91
Hutton, Herbert, 151

ideology, 278
IKADIN (Inodonesian organization), 439–
    40, 450n. 23, 450n. 26
ILPA. *See* Immigration Law Practitioners
    Association

ILSA. *See* Latin American Institute of
    Alternative Legal Services
Immigration Law Practitioners Association,
    296–97, 299, 300, 302
immigration lawyering, in Great Britain,
    293–316
impact lawyering, 184, 188–90
income. *See* finances
incumbency, 73
independent cause lawyers, 265
India, 358, 364, 365, 398n. 92
  See also AWARE
individual client lawyering, 183–84, 188
Indonesia, 352, 368–69, 383, 431–41, 446–52
inequality
  of class, 170
  of power, 69
  See also discrimination
INGOs. *See* international nongovernmental
    organizations
initiative process, 75
institutional reform, 36
institutions, 153–54
INTERIGHTS, 358, 406n. 141
International Center for Law and
    Development, 356
International Commission of Jurists, 356,
    396n. 83
International Human Rights Internship
    Program, 352, 358, 393n. 65
International League for Human Rights,
    392n. 50
international nongovernmental
    organizations (INGOs), 354–55, 356,
    358
Intifada, 466, 473, 479n. 8, 480n. 17
Israel, 227–57, 355, 365
  Association for Civil Rights, 411–12n. 178
  cause lawyering in occupied territories,
    453–86

Jaising, Indira, 367, 377, 389n. 37, 404n. 135
Johnson, Charles W., 88
judges, 88–89, 90
  African American, 151, 161, 166
  "alternative" in Brazil, 365, 407n. 147,
    508–9, 521n. 148
  in Israeli military courts, 456
"Judicare" model, 202

judicial review, 77
judiciary, 87–95
  in Argentina and Brazil, 494–97, 500,
    508–10, 518n. 88
  in Israeli-occupied territories, 456–58,
    484n. 52
  Third World, 366–67
juries, 89–90, 167

Keene, Beverly, 493
Kituo Cha Sheria, 390n. 46
Kohen, Beatrice, 493, 506
Kretzmer, David, 475
Kumar case, 309
Kurdish refugees, 303, 305
Kuttab, Jonathan, 469, 472

Landau, Moshe, 468
Landau Commission, 468
Landless Peasant Movement (Brazil), 490
Langer, Felicia, 459
Larson, Magali, 155
Latin America, 352, 354, 357, 363, 488
Latin American Institute of Alternative
    Legal Services, 352, 355
law, 8
  as check on power, 69–117
  human rights, 365
  and politics during regime changes, 99–
    102
  social change through, 355
  Third World, 364–65
Law, Sylvia, 44
law offices
  environment, 213–15
  location of, 209
law school, 192, 371
  in Argentina and Brazil, 498–99, 507–8,
    521n. 139
Lawyer's Code of Professional
    Responsibility, 212
Lawyers Committee for Human Rights, 358,
    392n. 50
left-activist lawyering, 118–44, 144n. 3
  coping with political adversity, 133–36
  generational variation, 121–24, 145n. 7
  optimal, 124–31
  political disarray, 131–33

professional diversity and generation
    divergence, 136–41
  prospects for, 141–44
  under siege, 120
legal aid. *See* public interest law
Legal Aid Institute of Jakarta, 437
legal clearinghouses, 510
legal codes, 497–98
legal culture, 361–69, 499–501
legal institutions, 49
legal profession, 95–99
  African Americans in, 151–68, 171–76
  lawyering styles, 183–86
  social movement lawyers, 9, 261–92
  struggle to politicize, 118–48
  women in, 44–45, 47, 213–14, 217, 372
  workload, 138
  See also cause lawyering; critical
    lawyering; public interest law
Legal Resources Centre (South Africa), 367,
    374, 382–83, 398n. 94, 410n. 169,
    425n. 280
legislature, 74–77
Lev, Ron, 233–39, 241, 242
Levy, Guy, 246, 247, 254
Liacouras Committee Report, 167
liberalism, 69, 73
liberal legalism, 69, 360–61
liberal regimes, 5–6, 8
litigation, 291n. 54
  costs, 271
  model, 35
  political change through, 293–316
  social movement, 267–69, 272, 276, 277,
    288n. 8
  versus other tactics, 269–72
localism, 71
Luban, David, 35, 54n. 7
Lubis, Mulya, 438

Madhavan, P.K.S., 378, 379–80
Maguire Seven, 91
Maier, Julio, 494
Malaysia, 431–32, 441–52
Maller, Dov, 235
Maller, Meir, 249–51
Malvinas Islands, 503
Marcos, Ferdinand, 89, 126
Marshall, Thurgood, 156, 158, 338

Martínez, Maria Elba, 489, 491, 492, 497, 501, 507
Mbaye, Keba, 356
Mendis, Viraj, 312
Menem, Carlos, 88, 502, 516n. 59, 518n. 88
Mexico, 73, 363, 374
    See also DOAL
Michele, Roberto de, 497, 506
minority business development, 208
mixed motives, 37–42, 63n. 102
mobilization lawyering, 185–86, 191
Mohammed, Mahathir, 444, 445
money. *See* finances
Moore, Cecil B., 164
Moore, Louis Tanner, 161
moral activism, 3
morality, 31, 32
Moren, Motti, 254
Morris, Aldon, 172
motives, mixed, 37–42, 63n. 102
Mudjono, Lt. Gen., 438, 439
Mueller, Carol, 172

NAACP Legal Defense Fund, 349, 355, 357, 418n. 228
Namibia, 359, 367, 374
Nasution, Adnan Buyung, 438, 440
National Lawyers Guild, 119, 120, 122–23, 129, 130–31, 132, 139–41, 143, 195
Native Americans, 246–47
Nazi Germany, 87, 88, 89, 92, 95–97
Nepal, 368
Netherlands East Indies, 432, 433
New Deal, 42
NGOs. *See* nongovernmental organizations
Nichols, Edward, 161, 166
Nigeria, 353–54, 365, 383, 428–29n. 329
Nino, Carlos, 507
Nix, Robert N. C., Sr., 161
Nolan, Sister Michael Mary, 492, 511, 514n. 26
nongovernmental organizations, 352–53, 355, 356, 357, 358, 372–73, 391–92n. 50, 438
    See also international nongovernmental organizations
nonpracticing lawyers, 265, 279
Norris, Austin, 152–53, 159, 162–64, 165, 166, 167, 168, 172, 174

Norris, Schmidt, Green, Harris, Higginbotham & Associates, 151–53, 154, 159, 162–66, 168–69, 171–76
Northern Ireland, 79, 81, 87, 91
Northwest Immigrants Rights Project, 133, 143
Northwest Women's Law Center, 133, 143
Norton, Eleanor Holmes, 167
Nusantara, Abdul Hakim G., 438

Ocampo, Luis Moreno, 493, 496, 500
O'Connor, Sandra Day, 44
Ogletree, Charles, 46, 56n. 26
Oliner, Samuel and Pearl, 39, 40, 51, 61n. 80
Olivos Pact, 516n. 59
ONBC (Cuban organization), 525, 529–31, 533–37
Onn, Hussein, 442
organizing role, of lawyers, 378–84
Orr, Wendy, 83

Palestinian cause lawyering, 453–86
    cases before Israeli High Court, 469–70
    emergence of, 458–59
    indigenous, 460–61
    institutional framework for, 455–57
    involvement in politics, 473–75
    local conceptions of, 470–72
    military court practice, 467–69
    organizational development, 463–67
    pleading to court of public opinion, 470
    role of Israeli High Court, 457–58
    social organization of, 461–67
paralegals, 214, 373–76, 420n. 238, 420–21n. 242, 421n. 244
Parsons, Talcott, 169
Paul, James, 356
pay equity movement, 264–65, 268–69, 272, 273, 275, 278, 283, 285
Pedagogy of the Oppressed (Freire), 381, 427n. 317
Pennsylvania, 160, 167
PERADIN (Indonesian organization), 437, 438–39
Perón, Juan, 502
Perón, Maria Estela, 502
Peru, 354, 374
Perú Mujer, 374–76
Philadelphia (Pa.), 159, 160, 173, 174

Philadelphia American, 163
Philadelphia Independent, 163
philanthropy, 98, 506
Philippines, 355, 357, 363, 374, 409n. 163
Pinhiero, Paulo Sergio, 496
Pittsburgh (Pa.), 181–200
police, 81, 82–85, 167
political parties, 75
politics, 7, 8, 35, 36
   and immigration law in Great Britain,
     297–310
   and law during regime changes, 99–102
   of lawyers, 194
   and legal advocacy, 266–69
   and Palestinian cause lawyers, 473–75
   Third World, 382–84, 424n. 277
   trial strategies for, 80
   See also left-activist lawyering
Ponting, Clive, 93
Porter, Alan, 170–71
positivist tradition, 497–98
Posner, Michael, 352–53, 396n. 84
poststructural theories, 9
poverty law, 45–46, 185, 190, 196–98
power
   electoral, 71–74
   law as check on, 69–117
   legislative, 74–77
   spatial organization of, 70–71
   state, 69–71
Pressburger, Miguel, 489
primary purpose rule, 307–10
pro bono lawyering, 5, 7, 56n. 25, 186–87,
   194, 196
procedures, 295, 304
professional associations, 98–99
professionalism, 4, 10–12
   elasticity of, 11
   ideologies of, 11
   and poverty cause lawyering, 196–98
professionalism project, 202–3
prosecutorial function, 79–81
prosocial behavior, 38, 61n. 89, 65n. 131
public interest law, 7, 42, 137
   career in, 48, 50
   professionalism project, 202–3
   strategies, 36
   in Third World legal cultures, 361–69
public policy, 8

Quakers Legal Aid Center, 464, 466

Race Matters (West), 171
racism, 168, 170, 179n. 46, 179n. 47, 180n. 56
Ray, Ilana, 247–49, 251, 254
Reed, Thomas, 160
refugees, 301–5
regime changes, 99–102
Reguera, Juan Escalona, 529
representation, 231–32, 233–34
rescuer behavior, 38–42, 51, 59n. 64, 60n. 76,
   61n. 77, 61n. 80, 61n. 85, 62n. 93
Rice, Patrick, 501, 522n. 169
Roberts, Marcelle, 205, 207, 208, 209, 210,
   212, 218, 220
Rojas, Fernando, 352, 354, 357, 387n. 11, 399n.
   99, 489
Roskill, Lord, 91
Rowland, Walter, 85
Russia, 100

Said, Ali, 438, 439
Saint-Jean, Ibérico Manuel, 503
salaried practice, 130, 137
Saleh, Ismail, 438, 439, 440
Sánchez de Bustamenti, Tomás, 503
Schmidt, Harvey N., 151, 152, 160–62, 165, 174
Scilingo, Adolfo Francisco, 522n. 172
Scott v. J.P. Campbell College, 165
Scutnik, Leonard, 38
Seattle left-activists, 119, 121–28, 131–34, 146n.
   31
self-affirmation, 41
self-incrimination, 91
self-interest, 37–42, 62n. 92, 63n. 102
service-impact dichotomy, 204
sexual harassment, 49
Sharpeville Six, 91
Shatil (organization), 247, 248, 254, 257n. 21
Simpson, Nicole, 49
Singh, Silu, 350, 368
Sirjamaki, John, 154
Smith, Reginald Heber, 42
Smith & Associates, 205, 206, 208, 210, 214,
   218
Snir, Saul, 242–44, 246, 251
social change, 49, 355, 357, 362
social justice, 43, 220–21
social movement lawyers, 9, 261–92

alternative image, 266–69
in Argentina and Brazil, 487–522
conventional critical picture, 262–64
experience, 284–86
identifying, 265–66
and movement atomization and
    containment, 272–73
resources and solidarity, 281–82
temptations of "success", 282–84
Soekarno, President, 434
solidarity, social movement, 275, 281–82
Sourani, Raji, 473
South Africa, 355, 382
electoral process in, 72
executive, 78
judiciary, 88, 90, 91, 93
legislature, 74, 76, 77
police, 82, 83, 85
See also Legal Resources Center
Spencer, Herbert, 77, 153–54
staff activists, 266, 279, 280
staff lawyers, 265–66
staff technicians, 266, 279, 280, 281
state power, 69–71
Steadfastness Funds, 464
Strickland & Caldwell, 205–6, 208, 210–12,
    214, 215, 216–17, 218, 219, 220
Sturm, Susan, 36
Sugih-Arto, General, 438
Suharto, President, 435
Sumner, William, 154
Sumpomo, Raden, 433–34
Supreme Court
    and death penalty, 320, 321, 333
    justices, 88
Swing, Joseph, 130
sympathy, 60n. 69

Tamil refugees, 302–3, 305
Tangentopoli affair, 73, 81
Tasrif, Suardi, 438
Taylor, Howard, 160–61
Third World cause lawyering, 349–430
    international human rights culture, 351–
        61
    in legal cultures, 361–69
    See also specific countries
Thomas, Clarence, 49
Thomson, Alan, 124

Till, Emmett, 90
Tisdall, Sarah, 93
Tocqueville, Alexis de, 47, 156
tort litigation, 48, 138
Tottenham Three, 84
Touvier, Paul, 101
Trial Lawyers for Public Justice, 134–35
Trubek, Louise, 204
Tsemel, Leah, 460

union activism, 268–69
United Kingdom. *See* Great Britain
United Kingdom Immigration Advisory
    Service, 298
Urban Legal Advocates, 205, 206, 209, 211,
    212, 213, 214, 215, 218, 219
Uruguay, 354
U.S. Commission on Civil Rights, 169

Vásquez, Carlos, 497
Vichy France, 100–101
Vietnam war, 193
Villen, Antonio, 509
voting. *See* electoral process

Wald, Patricia, 48
Ward, Judith, 85
Ware, David, 85
Warren, Earl, 166
Washington, Booker T., 162
Wells, Ira, 167
West, Cornel, 171
West Bank, 453–86
Whittome, Candy, 352–53
Wilson, William J., 170, 175
women
    in AWARE, 379
    causes, 44, 45, 47
    lawyers, 44–45, 47, 213–14, 217, 372
    in public interest law, 64n. 119
Woolf, Lord Justice, 299
work environment, 49

Yamin, Mohammad, 433–34
Yaron, Amir, 242, 245–46, 248, 250, 254, 255

Zimbabwe, 359
Zionism, 486n. 78